Ethics: A Feminist Reader

Ethics: A Feminist Reader

Edited by

Elizabeth Frazer, Jennifer Hornsby and Sabina Lovibond

BLACKWELL
Oxford UK & Cambridge USA

First published 1992

Blackwell Publishers
108 Cowley Road, Oxford, OX4 1JF, UK

Three Cambridge Center
Cambridge, Massachusetts 02142, USA

Library of Congress Cataloging in Publication Data

Ethics: a feminist reader/edited by Elizabeth Frazer, Jennifer
Hornsby, and Sabina Lovibond.
    p.   cm.
Includes bibliographical references and index.
ISBN 0–631–17829–5   ISBN 0–631–17831–7 (pbk)
    1. Feminism—Moral and ethical aspects.   2. Social ethics.
I. Frazer, Elizabeth. II. Hornsby, Jennifer. III. Lovibond,
Sabina.
HQ1221.E84 1992
305.42—dc20   91–21227
                                       CIP

British Library Cataloguing in Publication Data

A CIP catalogue record for this book is available from the British Library.

Typeset in 11 on 13 pt Plantin
by Best-set Typesetter Ltd., Hong Kong
Printed in Great Britain by
Billing & Sons Ltd, Worcester

This book is printed on acid-free paper.

Contents

Preface

Stephan Chambers suggested to us the project of compiling a reader; we thank him and others at Blackwell – Annita Christie and Pam Shaheen – for assistance. At an early stage there were four editors: Diemut Bubeck had to pull out when she left Oxford in the summer of 1989; the contribution she made when the book was first taking shape was invaluable.

Peter Wiggins (b.1980) joined us when we paused to eat during our many Wednesday evening editorial sessions. He deserves praise for his patience in letting us get on with it.

E. J. F.
J. H.
S. M. L.

Acknowledgements

The editors and publisher are grateful to the following for permission to use the extracts, articles and chapters in this volume:

Grafton Books for permission to reproduce Rosalind Coward's 'Naughty but Nice: Food Pornography' from her book *Female Desire*, 1984, and Nickie Roberts's 'Sex, Class and Morality' from her book *The Front Line*, 1986.

The Women's Press for permission to reproduce Andrea Dworkin's 'The Politics of Intelligence' from *Right Wing Women*, London, 1983, and Sheila Jeffreys's 'Creating the Sexual Future' and 'Pornography' from her book *Anticlimax*, London, 1990.

W W Norton & Co Inc. for permission to reproduce Betty Friedan's 'The Sexual Sell' from her book *The Feminine Mystique*, 1983, 1974, 1973, 1963.

Curtis Brown Ltd for permission to reproduce extracts from chapters 4, 5, 7 and 9 of Cicely Hamilton's *Marriage as a Trade*, 1981.

Seyla Benhabib for permission to reproduce 'The Generalized and the Concrete Other: The Kohlberg-Gilligan Controversy and Feminist Theory' by Seyla Benhabib from *Feminism as Critique* edited by S. Benhabib and D. Cornell, 1987.

Virago Press Ltd for UK rights, and the author for US rights, to reproduce June Jordan's 'Report from the Bahamas' from her book *Moving Towards Home*, 1989 and Kate Soper's 'Contemplating a Nuclear Future', chapter 16 of *Over Our Dead Bodies: Women Against the Bomb*, edited by Dorothy Thompson, 1983.

Crossing Press and Audre Lorde for permission to reproduce 'Age, Race, Class and Sex: Women Redefining Difference' from *Sister Outsider*, The Crossing Press, Freedom, California, 1984.

Beacon Press, Boston, USA and Women's Press, UK for permission to reproduce Sara Ruddick's 'Maternal Violence: A Truth in the Making' from her book *Maternal Thinking*, 1989.

Marion Boyars Publishers, London, New York for permission to reproduce Judith Williamson's 'Nuclear Family? No Thanks' from her book *Consuming Passions*, 1986.

Allison and Busby Ltd for permission to reproduce Alexandra Kollontai's 'Sexual Relations and the Class Struggle' from *Selected Writings* translated by Alix Holt, 1977.

Harvard University Press, Cambridge, Massachusetts for permission to reproduce Catharine A. MacKinnon's 'Privacy v. Equality: Beyond Roe v. Wade', no. 8 from her book *Feminism Unmodified*, 1987.

The Radical Philosophy editorial collective for permission to reproduce Susan F. Parsons's 'Feminism and the Logic of Morality' from *Radical Philosophy*, 47, Autumn, 1987.

Verso for permission to reproduce Rosalind Pollack Petchesky's 'Toward a Feminist-Humanist Concept of Personhood' from her book *Abortion and Woman's Choice*, 1988.

W W Norton & Company Inc. and Virago Press Ltd for permission to reproduce Adrienne Rich's 'Women and Honor: Some Notes on Lying' from her book *On Lies, Secrets and Silence, Selected Prose 1966–1978*, 1979.

Radius Publishers for permission to reproduce Elizabeth Wilson's 'Utopian Identities', no. 21 in her book *Hallucinations: Life in a Postmodern City*, 1988.

Jaqueline Rose and *Feminist Review* for permission to reproduce 'Femininity and its Discontents' first published in *Feminist Review*, 1983.

Jonathan Cape for permission to reproduce Simone de Beauvoir's *The Second Sex*, translated by J. Parshley, 1953.

The Executors of the Estate of Virginia Woolf and Harcourt Brace Jovanovich for permission to reproduce extracts from Virginia Woolf's *Three Guineas*, 1938, Penguin, 1977.

Christine Delphy, Sheila Allen and Diana Barker, and Tavistock Publications for permission to reproduce Christine Delphy's 'Continuities and Discontinuities in Marriage and Divorce', from *Sexual Divisions and Society*, edited by Sheila Allen and Diana Barker, 1984.

Nickie Roberts and Grafton Books for permission to reproduce 'Sex, Class and Morality' from her book *The Front Line*.

Introduction

Our choice of title for this book expresses an intention to concern ourselves, as feminists, with the whole field of ethical theory. It may therefore be as well to begin by explaining why we announce the book as a *feminist reader on ethics* rather than as a *reader on feminist ethics*.

The general conception of 'ethics', or moral philosophy, which has guided our work as editors has been the classical one: ethics is the theory of the good life (both for individuals and for societies), and it involves the study of value – not just the empirical question of what people *actually* value, though no moral philosopher can be indifferent to this, but the normative question of what it is *right* or *appropriate* to value. We have also accepted as inevitable the tendency of ethical enquiry to give rise to questions in branches of philosophy which go by other names – not only social and political theory but also metaphysics, epistemology, aesthetics and philosophical anthropology (the theory of human nature).

Philosophical theories, and therefore ethical theories, always issue from the experience of a particular human community. With the passage of time, suitably placed individuals or groups develop a synoptic view of aspects of their own way of life – of what it means by their rights to participate in, say, mathematical or scientific enquiry, or in citizenship, or in the attempt to live well as an individual. Thus the collective experience, however strangely refracted through the medium of exceptional personalities, is raised to explicit consciousness in the form of a discourse.

Everyone who has studied philosophy knows that it is a subject in which nothing is sacred: a philosophical theory is open to revision not only in detail but also in respect of its fundamental assumptions. The more fundamental the assumption, however, the more likely it is to escape critical attention: for example, European thought trundled along for centuries without any sense that Aristotle's credentials as a political thinker were impugned by his view that in every department of life there are natural relations of dominance and subordination.[1] Yet radical, as opposed to piecemeal, changes do occur in philosophy in response to changes in the moral and intellectual experience of the communities from which it issues. In particular, the limitations or blind spots of existing theory become apparent as new social constituencies, new kinds of contributor, enter the conversation. Thus Aristotle's hierarchical model of the universe could not remain credible after the breakdown of feudalism and the inception of the modern period in Europe.

Philosophers such as Descartes, Hobbes and Locke, whose work helped to discredit what was left of the medieval neo-Aristotelian world-view, did not regard their own intellectual path as just one of several that lay open to them. They saw themselves as engaged in the emancipation of thought from a certain kind of error. The same can be said of the Marxist project, two or three centuries later, of emancipating thought from bourgeois ideology: Marxism *qua* theory was not – is not – supposed to be merely an intellectual *option* (to be taken up by those who find the literature appealing), but a *necessary* corrective to the mystification engendered by class society.

Socialism as it has been known in the West, namely as a movement centred on the industrial working class, is a phenomenon of the period since 1789 – an element in the political drama which has been unfolding since the French Revolution. But during the same period, social and political life in the industrialized world (and not only there) have been transformed by the appearance of a variety of other new movements with priorities different from those of the white, male worker. Among these has been the movement which underpins this book – that of women contending against their specifically sexual subordination. This movement, and not just its spectacular resurgence since the events of 1968, is what we shall mean by 'feminism'.

Feminism is first and foremost a politics, but like any other politics it comprises moments of reflection as well as of action. Feminist theory is the discourse which expresses the reflective side of the movement; it draws such unity as it possesses from a shared desire to understand the social reality of gender relations and to rid our thinking of the particular kind of flaws induced by our adaptation to a patriarchal (i.e. male-dominated) culture. Since feminists regard the ending of sexual oppression and injustice not as a pastime but as a moral imperative, it is logical for them also to regard the elimination of patriarchal habits of thought not as a specialist exercise but as a general imperative of the intellect. It is this attitude that accounts for the interdisciplinary impact of feminism on the academic world. For the project of enquiring into sexual power structures, and into their effects on individual existence, cannot be contained within any one traditional branch of learning.

In the light of these remarks about 'ethics' and 'feminism' respectively, it should be clear that the term 'feminist ethics' (as used, for instance, in the title of our final section) has a different logic from that of, say, 'legal ethics' or 'medical ethics'. To study ethics without paying particular attention to the special issues that arise within law or medicine is not automatically to be handicapped (except in the sense that ignorance of something worth knowing is always a handicap). But to study ethics without paying attention to feminism is to be disadvantaged from the outset. For it is to assume that we are all equally well equipped to understand ourselves in terms of theories which draw most of their vitality from the experience, not of human beings at large, but of *male* human beings. In contesting this assumption, 'feminist ethics' undertakes to be more than just another specialism in an increasingly fragmented academic world: where 'medical' or 'legal' modify 'ethics', *feminism*, we think, transforms *ethics*.

II

We proceed now to review our subject-matter in a less abstract way. What features of traditional moral theory and practice have feminists singled out for criticism, and what new themes have they introduced?

Let us begin with first-order thinking, and consider what feminist

writers have had to say about the values of the societies in which they
have found themselves – their contribution to substantive ethics.
Here the starting-point has naturally been women's anger at the facts
of sexual inequality, and at the exclusion of women *en masse* from
those areas of life and activity to which men have attached the
highest value. Feminists have found much to say about the evils of
life under a regime of male domination – about social institutions
and structures that patently benefit men at the expense of women.
Patriarchal marriage with all its consequences in terms of female
dependence and poverty; male violence, prostitution, pornography,
the symbolic equation of women with sexuality; education devoid of
the seriousness that might make women a threat to their future
husbands: these issues, which lie at the heart of sexual politics, are
moral issues *par excellence*.

It is appropriate then, in thinking about them, to turn to moral
philosophy for some conceptual resources over and above those
of common sense. But this is where feminism over the years has
encountered a curious blankness. The attitude of university philosophy departments until recently – and this is only now beginning
to change – was that ethical and political theory were already conceptually competent to deal with all the *interesting* questions about
virtue, rights, justice, equality and freedom; or at any rate that
if feminists had difficulty in articulating their distinctive concerns
in the dominant theoretical language, this must be due either to
women's legendary incapacity for abstraction, or to the inherent
triviality of the questions they were raising (as though, say, the
marriage relationship fell below some implicit threshold of scholarly
discussability).

Perhaps the greatest philosophical achievement of feminism over
the last twenty years (though this achievement rests, of course, on
earlier work) has been to demonstrate in practice – in the practice of
moral and political philosophy – that the long absence of women's
generic interests from the agenda of these subjects could not be so
innocently explained. Liberal political theory and its counterpart in
ethics perceived themselves as gender-neutral; feminism has exposed
the inaccuracy of this self-image. The standard texts spoke of an
inauguration of society (historical or hypothetical) through the
voluntary entry of pre-social individuals into a 'social contract'.
They spoke of citizens with a two-fold identity, on one hand as

participants in public political action, on the other as heads of discrete private households. They spoke of causally unconstrained moral legislation or 'commitment', the supposed expression of our rational nature, and of choices aiming at the maximum satisfaction of the chooser's own preferences within a given deliberative situation. Feminists pointed out that although there was no reason of abstract principle why these models should not be applied to both sexes indifferently, the fact remained that they were all sublimated portrayals of a distinctively male mode of being. It is *typical* of male life-histories that one makes, or anyway dreams of making, one's way in the world in accordance with one's own choice of career; that one develops an autonomous capacity for business and politics; that one founds one's own dynasty, however humble and suburban; that one regards the outlay of money and work as an investment on which a return is to be expected.

Of course, any or all of these experiences can feature in female life-histories too. But they are not *typical* of such life-histories – not the stuff on which a 'normal' (i.e. traditionally feminine) woman draws in constructing a sense of her own identity. Consequently, an account of human nature and agency which takes them as central must either be admitted to be radically incomplete, or it must be understood as implying that what it leaves out is unworthy of inclusion – that if we have difficulty in recognizing our own subjectivity in the dominant theoretical models, this is evidence that we are something other than fully fledged human subjects. Western philosophy down to our own century has in effect taken the latter course, playing an interminable series of variations on the Aristotelian theme that to be female is 'a kind of deformity, albeit one that occurs in the ordinary course of nature'.[2] It has pictured female identity in the same way that biological science has pictured female embodiment – that is, as an imperfect or incompletely achieved version of the real (male) thing.[3] Feminism by contrast, rejecting *a priori* the premiss of male superiority, has argued that if women perceive the normative structures of ethical theory as inadequately grounded in their own experience, then the fault lies with the theory and not with women.

What features of 'normal' female experience are in question here? Central to the phenomenon of gender difference (i.e. sexual difference as mediated by culture) is the contrasting relation of women and men to the fact of embodiment. To learn femininity, within the

European tradition, has been to learn that one *is* one's body in a sense in which males have not traditionally been taught this. As (future) women, we are encouraged in a lively sense of our own vulnerability and that of other sentient creatures; we find out that approval will not be withheld if we show timidity, and will be given (though perhaps in a disturbingly ambivalent way) if we are seen as physically pleasing; we gather, if only implicitly, that all this has something to do with the *function* of women – the biological function of bearing and rearing children. And later we find that if we allow the form of our lives to be determined by factors other than our own decisions, or if we invest our energy in work which brings no personal profit, this too will be seen as graceful and 'normal'. It is in this context that 'morality' for women becomes a matter of sexual respectability and modesty (see Mary Wollstonecraft, reading 1, and Andrea Dworkin, reading 6).

For present purposes, the important point about this distinctively 'feminine' character-structure is its incompatibility with the image of the untrammelled, self-determining subject so familiar from moral and political philosophy. What the feminist critique of ethics has helped us to see is that if the salient features of your social experience are seeking to please, fitting in with others, being the one whom others count on . . . , then it is no cause for surprise if you regard that familiar image either as irrelevant or as a cue for feelings of inadequacy. (And of course the case can be stated more concretely: a political discourse whose concern is with the 'individual' *qua* husband, or head of a household, will be at best problematic in relation to the 'individual' *qua* wife.)

The proposition that moral autonomy is more difficult for women than for men, or that women cannot be full moral subjects, may strike most of us as self-evidently absurd. Women are obviously as capable as men of taking up the subjective viewpoint, of making moral judgements, acting purposefully, exercising will and controlling desire. Indeed, we might share the view of several of our authors (Margaret Sanger, reading 3, Catharine MacKinnon, reading 21, Rosalind Petchesky, reading 24) that adult women of all people must be competent to make life and death decisions – for example about conception, birth, abortion, the care of the dying. Yet there is a massive contrast between male and female subjectivity in respect of the empirical conditions under which each is constructed. Male subjectivity enjoys the support of a panoply of social institutions, from the pub and the football ground to the learned society and the executive dining room, which generate a sense of selfhood and personal importance and which do so – in part at least – by positioning women as the excluded 'other'.[4] By contrast, men's absence from women's (traditional) groupings tends to be experienced, precisely, as an *absence* – perhaps a pleasant respite from taking orders, perhaps a state of suspended animation, but in any case a variant on the conditions under which life is lived with full intensity. (The different meaning of all-female gatherings with a self-consciously feminist motive no doubt explains the acute male hostility such gatherings often encounter.)

It might of course be objected that male selfhood is not really the idyllic affair just outlined. Men too, after all – actual men as opposed to the cardboard cut-outs of theory – have to bow to contingency, to choose and act within a complex social context not of their own making. Why then should the conceptual shortcomings of bourgeois 'ethics' give rise to any sexually specific criticism?

We can gladly concede the descriptive inadequacy of the dominant models in relation to men. In fact, this is something on which feminists have insisted. Moral and political theory misunderstand their subject-matter by exaggerating and naturalizing not only *women's difference from men*, but also – and no less damagingly – *men's difference from women*. The thought that men too are embodied and vulnerable; that for them too emotional and sexual life is a source of insecurity and disruption; that they too can think and choose only on the basis of what they have learned from a finite initiation into the 'ways of the world'; and that they are caught up, as women are, in social structures which they do not know how to alter – all these truisms are capable of serving as powerful *feminist* insights. (They also go some way towards explaining the attraction for feminists of the holistic tradition of social theory deriving from the Romantic movement; though as any reader of Rousseau or Hegel will know, this tradition is no rose-garden either when it comes to sexual politics.)

It would be a mistake, however, to underrate the influence exerted by abstract conceptions of agency – conceptions which treat the particularity or 'situatedness' of the agent as irrelevant to the main concerns of ethics. To label any component of lived experience theoretically uninteresting is to make a strong value-judgement. And when this label is attached to those aspects of life which differentiate real people most sharply from the ideal type of the free, rational deliberator, women – to the extent that we move within our gender-specific world of selflessness and 'coping' – receive a signal that our lives are not what the theorist had in mind.

The perception that standard models of moral subjectivity do not apply to us as women – or that they apply only in a problematic way – has brought a dawning recognition that what is *distinctive* in women's social experience is worthy of exploration in its own right. As the present book may illustrate, this has been one of the most important developments in recent ethical and social theory. It has opened up for discussion a wealth of issues which have often been seen (in the modern, if not in the ancient world) as peripheral to the subject-matter of ethics – issues of sexuality, the bodily self, moral connectedness, friendship, the emotions, psychological fluidity and finitude. But discussion of these issues takes place against the background of an awareness that women's generic qualities and concerns are, as a matter of socio-cultural fact, the qualities and concerns of a *subordinate* group. Feminist thinking about ethics, then, has to perform a delicate balancing-act. We need to be able to acknowledge without self-contempt the social reality of femininity (which, for women, is to a greater or lesser degree the form of our own social being); yet at the same time we must avoid any naïve celebration of 'feminine' characteristics which would be more accurately regarded as effects of oppression.

Which ingredients of our feminine selves should be seen under the aspect of weakness or damage, and which under the aspect of strength? To this question, there can be no *a priori* answer. To shed light on it through detailed moral reflection is, we believe, among the central tasks of feminism with respect to ethical theory; and so, indirectly, with respect to political practice. For whatever the substantive results of this kind of enquiry, feminist theory is decisively set apart from traditional practical philosophy by its attention to the realities of *male power* – social, economic, psychological and physical. Whereas philosophy has continually appealed to the supposedly *natural* facts of sexual difference to account for women's different (and inferior) status, feminism must chart the *social* facts of power difference and trace the way they have been encoded in philosophical discourse – whether by way of unspoken assumptions, silences, repressions, unintentionally revealing metaphors, or any of the other textual symptoms that such discourse may display. Feminism, in short, must construct an ethics which no longer relies on the concealment of power-relations but works actively to expose them.

III

It would have been impossible to set about compiling a book like the present one without some general preconceptions about the nature of ethics, feminism and the encounter between them, and in the foregoing part of this introduction we have tried to give an account of what these preconceptions were in our own case. But the actual work of selection raised a new set of questions.

The decision to include only writings by women was made without difficulty (though publications by men sympathetic to feminism do of course exist). Since men as such have a massive vested interest in the *status quo* with respect to sexual power relations, while women as such will be overwhelmingly the gainers by their egalitarian transformation, it seems right to view feminism as in principle a movement of women – a movement which owes its main creative energies to those on the receiving end of sexual oppression. And for the time being at least, it seems right to reserve for women whatever platforms become available under the banner of feminism: until the closure of that phase of history (or prehistory) in which women have been the silent sex, female speech will continue to deserve all the encouragement we can give it.

But was there already an established canon of 'great' feminist literature to which we could turn for material? There were of course some famous names; but the academic world has not been hospitable to feminism, and in many institutions in the UK (certainly in our own) students can count themselves lucky even to be supplied with a relevant reading-list. As editors, we did not have the sense of being directed in our choice by any firm consensus of opinion within a feminist tradition. Nor did we feel any constraints of chronology, apart from the decision to limit ourselves to the period since 1789. As it has turned out, seven of our authors might be regarded as 'historical' rather than 'contemporary' (and of these, six wrote in the first half of the present century). Seeing no difficulty in setting their writings alongside more recent ones, we were confirmed in our view that even in the absence of an established feminist 'republic of letters', there has been a continuing feminist movement in the world of moral and political thought.

We also had to consider how to fit our conception of 'ethics' to the vast and heterogeneous range of writings that suggested themselves. Should we apply strict formal criteria that would rule out anything not qualified, in point of style, for publication in a mainstream philosophy journal? Although many of the writers represented in this book are in fact university or polytechnic teachers, we did not in the end draw heavily on the output of academic philosophers, and we decided not to make academic diction and presentation an absolute requirement but to use our own judgement as to the terms of reference of ethical discourse.

We have included nothing that is not in our own eyes an example of lucid and orderly thinking (whatever detailed criticisms we might want to make of some of our selections). But we have resisted an over-professionalized view of what constitutes such thinking. Some of our contributors are deliberately intervening in current 'philosophical' debates; others are presenting arguments which have an obvious bearing on such debates, whether by way of critique or by way of imaginative enrichment; others again offer powerful analyses of moral phenomena which we hardly know at present how to relate to the existing philosophical agenda, so full are they of the rawness of (often painful) experience. The result is a collection which may strike some professional philosophers as a bewildering mixture of sociology, cultural criticism, psychoanalysis and outright polemic. We make no apology for this, because our main criterion of selection has been not a descriptive but a normative one – not whether a particular text is capable of slipping discreetly into place in existing bibliographies, but whether it is such as to promote a more thoughtful approach to the subject-matter of ethics.

We make no apology, either, for the fact that this collection breaks one of the ground-rules of analytical philosophy – the rule which prescribes neutrality with respect to substantive political questions. So much was to be expected, given the conception of ethics with which we began. For in associating this book with the project of enquiry into the nature of the 'good life', we deliberately dissociate it from the assumption (dominant in the English-speaking world for most of the last half-century) that moral philosophy ought to confine itself to studying the formal characteristics of (rational) moral thinking, leaving it to individual practitioners to fill in the content, as it were, in private. We assume the correctness of the standard, and by now familiar, critique of this liberal aspiration to 'value-freedom': that is, we regard as mythical the idea of a liberal society as a mere framework within which individuals can make their own choice of life, unconstrained by any brute facts about the political order. Western liberalism, in our view, is one scheme of values among others which have emerged in the course of human history: not by any means a contemptible one (for the formal freedoms it affirms deserve at least our qualified loyalty), but equally, not the occupant of a privileged position outside history from which to hurl accusations of irregularity at any ethical or political discourse informed by ideals that are at variance with its own.

Feminist theory is one such discourse. But it does not stand to liberal theory in a relation of mere difference; instead, it draws attention to certain defects of vision in liberalism which result from its masculine bias (for example, in connection with the 'social contract' account of political authority[5]). One element in the feminist theoretical programme, then, is to call into question the illusion of the liberal that while others can speak only from their various special perspectives (and so in a partial or partisan way), his own contribution is naturally entitled to hold the centre of the intellectual stage since *he* is a thinker pure and simple, unhampered by any 'perspective' of his own. In challenging this illusion wherever its influence can be detected in the male philosophical corpus, feminism gains definition as a theoretical stance in its own right.

IV

We move on now to explain in more detail how this book is constructed.

We have provided a short introduction to each reading, in which we focus on matters of specifically philosophical interest and draw attention to points of contact and of conflict between the different arguments; where necessary, we also situate the pieces historically and socially. Although the book represents a wide range of views within feminism, it does not attempt to give a comprehensive survey of feminist opinion. Even if we had tried to do this, we should probably not have succeeded, since we are conscious of a considerable measure of agreement (and hence lack of diversity of opinion) among the three of us.

Our bibliographies look further afield than the readings, and attempt to be more inclusive with respect to feminist thinking. The separate bibliography of male writing contains some works which are supportive of an improvement in women's social status. Most entries here, though, can only be described as misogynist in content; we have taken some pains to collect this canonical material because we believe that a credible feminist ethics must be based in a historically informed view of conceptions of gender.

We have tried to make the range of topics touched on in the readings themselves reasonably wide. But the overall organization of the book is not topic-based: if someone chose a particular issue such as education, pornography or abortion, she would be about as likely to find it treated in any one of our three sections as in any other. The division we have arrived at between sections springs from our idea of a 'feminist ethics' as being not so much something already available for inspection, but rather something currently in the process of emerging from the critical understanding of female subordination.

Our first section, 'Women's Condition', brings together writings which illustrate from different points of view the mismatch between gender-neutral conceptions of moral 'personhood' and the realities of female lives. A recurrent theme is the problematic character, in relation to women, of the ideal of autonomous subjectivity. What is the meaning of this ideal for a group whose generic self-image is so profoundly influenced by the knowledge that they are continually being pictured and appraised in the capacity not of *subjects* but of *objects* or *functionaries* – sexual partners (whether 'legitimate' or otherwise), personal helpmates, receptacles and carers for the next generation? Again, how do the facts of gender affect the meaning for women of central ethical concepts such as rights, justice, duty, virtue, pleasure, guilt, shame? And is it possible to sustain a 'normal' sense of female identity while trying to conceive of one's own relation to other persons in the terms suggested by modern (liberal-democratic or Marxist) political theory?

Our second section, 'Ethics and Gender Difference', explores the moral significance of women's 'otherness' *vis-à-vis* patriarchal culture. We have already seen that this 'otherness' has been full of ambiguity for feminism. On one hand, there has been a drive towards emancipation – a refusal to accept any longer the status of *second* sex, or to be a foil for male self-expression and achievement. On the other hand, there have been voices raised in warning against the uncritical acceptance by women of hitherto 'masculine' values. Would it not be ironic if feminism were to turn into one more thorn in our flesh, one more corpus of unfulfillable existential demands? Should we not savour to the full (with Virginia Woolf, reading 10) our sense of the ludicrous and sinister aspects of masculinity, our scepticism about the 'successful' man as role model? Feminists who have posed these questions have been unimpressed by the fact (in so far as it *is* a fact) of women's formal equality in modern societies. In the first place, they have pointed out how much more would have to change (for instance, with regard to the significance of parenthood) before it could be claimed that sexual difference entailed no difference in social status. But beyond this, they have thrown down a challenge to the very idea of equality which prevails in the intellectual world of liberalism (including liberal feminism). Why regard women's 'difference' or 'otherness' as a *problem*, they have asked? Why shouldn't a 'different voice' formulate different truths and values, no less compelling than those of the dominant culture?

But the affirmation of difference has in turn proved controversial for feminism. To begin with, there is the risk that we may end up congratulating ourselves on the very same sorts of qualities (whether docile and unthreatening or sexy and dangerous) which male conservatives have long been happy to attribute to us. And then there are objections, both theoretical and political, to any idea of a universal 'femininity' which would automatically generate sympathy and solidarity between women. Gender difference is central to our social experience, but it is only one of many systems of difference around which that experience is organized, and a common position in the system of gender may well be outweighed for practical purposes by opposed positions with respect to one of the other systems such as capitalist class, sexual orientation, age or 'race' (that is, relation to the historical structures of imperialism and colonialism). These systems interact with one another in such a way that the specific disempowerment of someone who is, say, both black and female is not a simple sum of what she shares with black men and white women. Perhaps the most hopeful outcome of these difficult debates would be an appreciation that 'otherness' extends beyond the phenomenon of gender, and a more generous conception (at least on the part of 'metropolitan' feminism) of the ideal of *unity in difference*.

Our final section, 'Towards a Feminist Ethics', contains writings whose purpose is either to make a distinctively feminist contribution to first-order ethics – to clarify what would be of moral importance in a post-patriarchal world – or to suggest how existing moral and political theory need to change if they are to serve as our guides in constructing such a world. This part of the book indicates some of the paths moral reflection might take when fuelled by an injection of avowedly female experience. It speaks, for example, of non-contractual relations like that between parent and child; of future-directed effort that is not an 'investment'; of the possibility of committed but non-possessive emotional experience; of women's moments of unreserved presence to each other, either as friends or as lovers, without male mediation; of reproductive freedom for women and of all that still has to be done to banish coercion from this area of our lives; and of the elusiveness of the sense of self, to which in recent times the destabilizing impact of feminism has made its own contribution. All these are themes on which women have, in one way or another, a strong claim to be heard; but they are not 'women's issues', if this implies a contrast with universal human issues. It is no more implausible that women, from the moral perspective of their own gender position, should succeed in 'moving some universal principle of the human frame' than that men should do so from theirs.

V

In III above we noted, and tried to disarm, certain traditionalist objections which might be directed at this book: firstly that our principles of selection were insufficiently academic, and secondly that our guiding interest is not in ethics (properly so called) but in political advocacy. Overall, however, it is probably true to say that we have devoted more thought to the possibility of a different kind of critical reaction – this time from readers who may feel that the political impulse represented here is, for one reason or another, *passé*. 'Post-feminist woman' may be an all-too-obvious figment of the journalistic imagination,[6] but the idea that the historical moment of feminism has passed and that, in that sense, we are living in 'post-feminist' times requires more serious attention.

There is, first of all, the optimistic view that (at any rate in 'advanced', democratic societies) women have already won the important prizes for which the feminist movement has struggled: not only such fundamental rights as the vote, entry to the professions and equal pay, but – more recently – a qualitatively new level of acceptance in the 'male' worlds of business and government. In these changed circumstances, the argument runs, old-fashioned feminist rage is no longer appropriate; instead, women and men are at last in a position to celebrate the possibilities and pleasures of gender difference, and the rigours of confrontation can give way to a milder, more playful sexual climate.

We question this view, to begin with, because we think it severely underestimates the continuing direct oppression of women by men – the state of affairs to which the contents of our first section, in their different ways, bear witness. More theoretically, though, we believe it relies on an insufficiently dialectical conception of gender. In other words, we believe the facts of sexual difference are misunderstood if rights, powers, citizenship and subjecthood are pictured as things that women merely *happen* to have been deprived of in the past. The real target of feminist critique has never been simply the empirical fact that various sorts of goods have been unequally distributed between the sexes. Rather, it has been the very existence of the social system denoted by the word 'gender': that system by which male and female individuals are assigned from birth to distinct classes whose identity is determined by their *relation to one another* (a relation of dominance in the case of 'men', and of subordination in the case of 'women').

Granted the existence of such a system, it follows that 'femininity' as we know it is *by definition* a subordinate status and 'masculinity' *by definition* a dominant one: not in the sense that sexed beings are timelessly destined to fall into these hierarchical relations, but in the sense that the gendered identities made available to us within the present social order are identities that situate us in a certain hierarchy of power. This hierarchy cuts to the depths of our social being and discredits any suggestion that it is 'just a matter of time' before women's formal equality as citizens is converted into an actual equality of representation in all walks of life. For this reason we would argue that gender difference – while it exists at all – must remain an object of suspicion, so that until it ceases to exist feminism cannot become redundant. And conversely, to the extent that we embrace our femininity uncritically we acquiesce in a system of meanings which is both hostile to us and beyond our individual control.

We must also be prepared to face a second, more sophisticated critique, focusing in this case on a supposedly conservative assumption of our own making – the assumption that 'feminism' is still, in the 1990s, a term with a more or less determinate meaning and with the power to direct women's energies into a common political effort.

The assumption of determinate meaning seems to be implicit in our project from the outset, for if feminism does not exist as an objective political formation, how can the production of a 'feminist reader' amount to more than an arrogant bid by the editors to force the term into an unhealthy union with their own local and generational concerns? Yet if we aspire to capture something that transcends these particular concerns – to make this book responsible to a specific historical movement with a long-term past and future – we must be prepared to face the predictable 'postmodernist' charge of moral nostalgia: are we not clinging for security to one of those 'meta-narratives of emancipation'[7] associated with an outmoded philosophy of history (human experience as a meaningful and goal-directed totality, as the dawning of 'Enlightenment')? And at a more practical level, are we not giving encouragement to a potentially oppressive myth of unity? Feminism, we shall be told, no longer has any essential identity; what now goes under this name is something irreducibly plural and decentred. And this is due not only to the diminished authority of the white, predominantly middle-class élite which played a hegemonic role in the women's movement of the late sixties and early seventies, but also to the declining credibility of the *moral critique of ordinary life* which passed during that period as characteristically 'feminist'. The 1980s have seen, on one hand, a dramatic diversification of women's autonomous political activity; on the other, an assertion of the validity of subjective experience – of women's *actual*, unscripted pleasures and sexual preferences, over against the imperatives of a politics which has presumed to dictate what, as a good feminist, one *ought* to feel. (Such an assertion clearly has something in common with the 'now-we-can-relax' tendency considered previously – but see Elizabeth Wilson, reading 22, for a more complex critique of feminist moralism.) Both these developments cast doubt on the legitimacy of continuing to use 'feminism' as a singular term. Are we entitled, then, to speak as we do?

With regard to the *totalizing* implications of our usage, we would return to a suggestion made in the previous section and point out that this usage is meant to convey not a dogma, but a hope. The hope is that by trial and error, through dialogue and experiment, women may find ways of co-operating politically across social divisions such as those of class, race and generation – that is, of pooling our capacities for resistance to the specifically sexual forms of oppression which we suffer in common, while at the same time acknowledging and confronting the power differentials which exist within the social class of 'women'. There is no *a priori* guarantee that a self-styled 'feminist movement' will avoid reproducing within itself the structures of domination (other than that of gender) which exist in the wider society around it, and it is indeed important, as Audre Lorde (reading 12) reminds us, that women whose personal experience of subordination is limited to the fact of femininity should recognize how much learning they still have to do. On the other hand, however, there is no *a priori* reason why the will to understand one another better should be doomed to frustration, or why the project of non-hierarchical political construction should necessarily fail. To suppose that it must do so – that whereas the forces of political and economic control are today reaching new heights of international co-ordination and efficiency, the forces of opposition cannot properly aim for anything but a fragmentary and radically particular perspective on social conditions – this is itself the dogmatic expression of a fashionable pessimism, natural enough perhaps after a decade of disappointment for radical movements in the capitalist world, yet none the less liable on that account to warm conservative (including anti-feminist) hearts.[8] In the present collection, June Jordan (reading 13) and Seyla Benhabib (reading 16) among others help to show what would be involved in resisting this pessimistic reflex.

With regard to the *normative* implications of our understanding of feminism, we had better confess without delay that despite the groundswell of protest in recent years against the perceived 'puritanism' of the movement,[9] we remain convinced of the political value of a sceptical attitude towards what is experienced, pre-theoretically, as *pleasure*. It is true of course that, in this as in any other matter, the only place critical thinking can start from is where you happen to be at the moment, so that in one sense the only way to avoid the charge of being 'against pleasure' is to accord a hearing to the inner murmur of sensation and fantasy rather than try to censor it. But to admit this is not yet to retreat an inch from the conviction that feminism can *call our pleasures into question* by revealing them to us in a new light – specifically, by bringing them into connection with the larger social fact of gender.

Again, it is right to point out that there is no algorithm which can tell us how to give practical expression to any bit of feminist insight we may gain into our own subjectivity; analysis may convince us of a link between the gender system and, for instance, the particular set of clothes we own, but this does not relieve us of the need to exercise our own judgement in deciding what to wear in future. Yet it does not follow from this undoubted truth that *any* way of negotiating social reality, *any* way of interpreting our own sexual identity, can in principle count as 'feminist'. Some patterns of self-interpretation, we would argue, are objectively inconsistent – taking present social reality as given – with the defence of women's collective interests; inconsistent, in particular, with the obligation to try to avoid behaviour which is expressive of consent to sexual abuse (or which affirms the values of 'heterosexuality', in Sheila Jeffreys's special sense of the word: see reading 26).

To say this is not to suggest that it is obvious what 'regimes of pleasure', what aesthetic options, are morally possible for feminism. We certainly do not claim any authority over the rest of the world in deciding questions of this kind; they are questions about which everyone has to think for herself. It is simply by doing this – not as 'experts', but as enquirers – that we have arrived at a selection of readings that excludes, for example, any statement of the case in favour of pornography or sado-masochism as potentially helpful to a politics of sexual equality. In this respect our choice is – deliberately – unrepresentative of the full range of views canvassed during the 1980s by women who profess a commitment to feminist goals.

NOTES

1 Cf. *Politics* I, 5, §§1–7; 13, §6.
2 Cf. *On the Generation of Animals* 775a15.
3 Genevieve Lloyd has traced the history of this way of thinking through successive changes in value-terminology, culminating in the 'transcendence/immanence' language of existentialism: *The Man of Reason: 'Male' and 'Female' in Western Philosophy* (London: Methuen, 1984).
4 This state of affairs illustrates in a homely way the thesis of French feminist philosopher Luce Irigaray that 'Sexual difference does not yet exist in the social imaginary of the West.' Cf. Margaret Whitford, 'Luce Irigaray's Critique of Rationality' in Morwenna Griffiths and Margaret Whitford (eds), *Feminist Perspectives in Philosophy* (Basingstoke, Hampshire: Macmillan, 1988), p. 122.
5 Cf. Carole Pateman, *The Sexual Contract* (Oxford: Polity, 1988).
6 Cf. Angela Neustatter, *Hyenas in Petticoats: A Look at Twenty Years of Feminism* (Harmondsworth: Penguin, 1990), pp. 232–3.
7 Cf. Jean-François Lyotard, *The Postmodern Condition: A Report on Knowledge*, trans. Geoff Bennington and Brian Massumi (Manchester: Manchester University Press, 1984), pp. 31–41.
8 Cf. David Harvey, *The Condition of Postmodernity* (Oxford: Blackwell, 1989), pp. 116–7.
9 Cf. for example Shelagh Young, 'Feminism and the Politics of Power' in Lorraine Gamman and Margaret Marshment (eds), *The Female Gaze: Women as Viewers of Popular Culture* (London: The Women's Press, 1988), especially pp. 178–9, 185.

I

Women's Condition

1

Mary Wollstonecraft
1759–1797

'MORALITY UNDERMINED BY SEXUAL NOTIONS OF
THE IMPORTANCE OF A GOOD REPUTATION' from
A VINDICATION OF THE RIGHTS OF WOMAN (1792)

Mary Wollstonecraft was famous in her own time for A Vindication of
the Rights of Man *(a response to Edmund Burke's reactionary attack on
the French Revolution) and* A Vindication of the Rights of Woman,
*published two years later in 1792. Her experiences as a woman earning
her own living, first as a governess, later as a translator, reviewer and
writer for journals, were a central ingredient in her social and political
thought, and were rehearsed again and again in her novels.*

In the Vindication of the Rights of Woman *we have a classic
expression of the liberal longing for (and belief in the possibility of) a
just social order in which individuals would be freed from the shackles
of superstition and false authority, and in which they would exercise
autonomous and objective reason. For Wollstonecraft the moral and intellectual capacities essential to such a society are already, to an imperfect
degree, present in humanity; or, to speak more accurately, in* men.
*Women, because of the rigid social distinctions between 'masculine' and
'feminine', and between standards of morality for the two sexes, are
unable to exercise genuine judgement or to attain genuine virtue.*

*In the chapter reproduced here Wollstonecraft shows how the women of
her time must inevitably be preoccupied with their 'sexual' reputation to
the detriment of their real moral character. In a social order which teaches
them to regard 'morality', 'honour' and 'virtue' as entirely* sexual *matters,*

women are positively encouraged to lie and dissemble; for the woman who has 'lost her honour', as common parlance would have it, is indeed forced into systematic vice. That is, the ever-present fear of incurring any suspicion of unchastity, and so of losing one's value in the marriage market, encourages women to behave in ways that attract the contempt of men. These servile habits and characteristics are then said to be 'natural', and to justify women's subordination.

Wollstonecraft (like Simone de Beauvoir, reading 11) argues for social and educational changes which would enable women to become fully human and fully autonomous subjects and citizens, as she assumes men already to be. This last assumption is one about which feminist readers today are likely to have reservations. Wollstonecraft, we may feel, offers us a powerful critique of the social construction of femininity while leaving masculinity unchallenged. But as an exposition of the way the double standard entraps women in a double bind her analysis is unrivalled.

It has long since occurred to me that advice respecting behaviour, and all the various modes of preserving a good reputation, which have been so strenuously inculcated on the female world, were specious poisons, that encrusting morality eat away the substance. And, that this measuring of shadows produced a false calculation, because their length depends so much on the height of the sun, and other adventitious circumstances.

Whence arises the easy fallacious behaviour of a courtier? From his situation, undoubtedly: for standing in need of dependents, he is obliged to learn the art of denying without giving offence, and, of evasively feeding hope with the chameleon's food: thus does politeness sport with truth, and eating away the sincerity and humanity native to man, produce the fine gentleman.

Women likewise acquire, from a supposed necessity, an equally artificial mode of behaviour. Yet truth is not with impunity to be sported with, for the practised dissembler, at last become the dupe of his own arts, loses that sagacity, which has been justly termed common-sense; namely a quick perception of common truths: which are constantly received as such by the unsophisticated mind, though it might not have had sufficient energy to discover themselves, when obscured by local prejudices. The greater number of people take their opinions on trust to avoid the trouble of exercising their own minds, and these indolent beings naturally adhere to the letter, rather than the spirit of a law, divine or human. 'Women', says some author, I cannot recollect who, 'mind not what only Heaven sees.' Why, indeed, should they? it is the eye of man that they have been taught to dread – and if they can lull their Argus to sleep, they seldom think of Heaven or themselves, because their reputation is safe; and it is reputation, not chastity and all its fair train, that they are employed to keep free from spot, not as a virtue, but to preserve their station in the world.

To prove the truth of this remark, I need not advert to the intrigues of married women, particularly in high life, and in countries where women are suitably married, according to their respective ranks, by their parents. If an innocent girl become a prey to love, she is degraded for ever, though her mind was not polluted by the arts which married women, under the convenient cloak of marriage, practise; nor has she violated any duty – but the duty of respecting herself. The married woman, on the contrary, breaks a most sacred engagement, and becomes a cruel mother when she is a false and faithless wife. If her husband have still an affection for her, the arts which she must practise to deceive him will render her the most contemptible of human beings; and, at any rate, the contrivances necessary to preserve appearances will keep her mind in that childish, or vicious, tumult, which destroys all its energy. Besides, in time, like those people who habitually take cordials to raise their spirits, she will want an intrigue to give life to her thoughts, having lost all relish for pleasures that are not highly seasoned by hope or fear.

Sometimes married women act still more audaciously. I will mention an instance.

A woman of quality, notorious for her gallantries, though as she still lived with her husband, nobody chose to place her in the class where she ought to have been placed, made a point of treating with the most insulting contempt a poor timid creature, abashed by a sense of her former weakness, whom a neighbouring gentleman had seduced and afterwards married. The woman had actually confounded virtue with reputation; and, I do believe, valued herself on the propriety of her behaviour before marriage, though when once settled to the satisfaction of her family, she and her lord were equally faithless, so that the half-alive heir to an immense estate came from Heaven knows where!

To view this subject in another light.

I have known a number of women who, if they did not love their husbands, loved nobody else, give themselves entirely up to vanity and dissipation, neglecting every domestic duty; nay even squandering away all the money which should have been saved for their helpless younger children, yet have plumed themselves on their unsullied reputation, as if the whole compass of their duty as wives and mothers was only to preserve it. Whilst other indolent women, neglecting every personal duty, have thought that they deserved their husbands' affection, because, forsooth, they acted in this respect with propriety.

Weak minds are always fond of resting in the ceremonials of duty, but morality offers much simpler motives; and it were to be wished that superficial moralists had said less respecting behaviour, and outward observances, for unless virtue, of any kind, be built on knowledge, it will only produce a kind of insipid decency. Respect for the opinion of the world, has, however, been termed the principal duty of woman in the most express words, for Rousseau declares, 'that reputation is no less indispensable than chastity'. 'A man,' adds he, 'secure in his own good conduct depends only on himself, and may brave the public opinion; but a woman, in behaving well, performs but half her duty; as what is thought of her, is as important to her as what she really is. It follows hence, that the system of a woman's education should, in this respect, be directly contrary to that of ours. Opinion is the grave of virtue among the men; but its throne among women.' It is strictly logical to infer that the virtue that rests on opinion is merely worldly, and that it is the virtue of a being to whom reason has been denied. But, even with respect to the opinion of the world, I am convinced that this class of reasoners are mistaken.

This regard for reputation, independent of its being one of the natural rewards of virtue, however, took its rise from a cause that I have already deplored as the grand source of female depravity, the impossibility of regaining respectability by a return to virtue, though men preserve theirs during the indulgence of vice. It was natural for women then to endeavour to preserve what once lost was lost for ever, till this care swallowing up every other care, reputation for chastity became the one thing needful to the sex. But vain is the scrupulosity of ignorance, for neither religion nor virtue, when they reside in the heart, require such a puerile attention to mere ceremonies, because the behaviour must, upon the whole, be proper, when the motive is pure.

To support my opinion I can produce very respectable authority; and the authority of a cool reasoner ought to have weight to enforce consideration, though not to establish a sentiment. Speaking of the general laws of morality, Dr Smith observes:

> That by some very extraordinary and unlucky circumstance, a good man may come to be suspected of a crime of which he was altogether incapable, and upon that account be most unjustly exposed for the remaining part of his life to the horror and aversion of mankind. By an accident of this kind he may be said to lose his all, notwithstanding his integrity and justice, in the same manner as a cautious man, notwithstanding his utmost circumspection, may be ruined by an earthquake or an inundation. Accidents of the first kind, however, are perhaps still more rare, and still more contrary to the common course of things than those of the second; and it still remains true that the practice of truth, justice and humanity is a certain and almost infallible method of acquiring what those virtues chiefly aim at, the confidence and love of those we live with. A person may be easily misrepresented with regard to a particular action; but it is scarce possible that he should be so with regard to the general tenor of his conduct. An innocent man may be believed to have done wrong: this, however, will rarely happen. On the contrary, the established opinion of the innocence of his manners will often lead us to absolve him where he has really been in the fault, notwithstanding very strong presumptions.

I perfectly coincide in opinion with this writer, for I verily believe that few of either sex were ever despised for certain vices without deserving to be despised. I speak not of the calumny of the moment, which hovers over a character, like one of the dense morning fogs of November over this metropolis, till it gradually subsides before the common light of day, I only contend that the daily conduct of the majority prevails to stamp their character with the impression of truth. Quietly does the clear light, shining day after day, refute the ignorant surmise, or malicious tale, which has thrown dirt on a pure character. A false light distorted, for a short time, its shadow. – reputation; but it seldom fails to become just when the cloud is dispersed that produced the mistake in vision.

Many people, undoubtedly, in several respects obtain a better reputation than, strictly speaking, they deserve; for unremitting industry will mostly reach its goal in all races. They who only strive for this paltry prize, like the Pharisees, who prayed at the corners of streets, to be seen of men, verily obtain the reward they seek; for the heart of man cannot be read by man! Still the fair fame that is naturally reflected by good actions, when the man is only employed to direct his steps aright, regardless of the lookers-on, is, in general, not only more true, but more sure.

There are, it is true, trials when the good man must appeal to God from the injustice of man; and amidst the whining candour or hissings of envy, erect a pavilion in his own mind to retire to till the rumour be overpast; nay, the darts of undeserved censure may pierce an innocent tender bosom through with many sorrows; but these are all exceptions to general rules. And it is according to common laws that human behaviour ought to be regulated. The eccentric orbit of the comet never influences astronomical calculations respecting the invariable order established in the motion of the principal bodies of the solar system.

I will then venture to affirm, that after a man is arrived at maturity, the general outline of his character in the world is just, allowing for the before-mentioned exceptions to the rule. I do not say that a prudent, worldly-wise man, with only negative virtues and qualities, may not sometimes obtain a smoother reputation than a wiser or a better man. So far from it, that I am apt to conclude from experience, that where the virtue of two people is nearly equal, the most negative character will be liked best by the world at large, whilst the other may have more friends in private life. But the hills and dales, clouds and sunshine, conspicuous in the virtues of great men, set off each other; and though they afford envious weakness a fairer mark to shoot at, the real character will still work its way to light, though bespattered by weak affection, or ingenious malice.[1]

With respect to that anxiety to preserve a reputation hardly earned, which leads sagacious people to analyse it, I shall not make the obvious comment; but I am afraid that morality is very insidiously undermined, in the female world, by the attention being turned to the show instead of the substance. A simple thing is thus made strangely complicated; nay, sometimes virtue and its shadow are set at variance. We should never, perhaps, have heard of Lucretia, had she died to preserve her chastity instead of her reputation. If we really deserve our own good opinion we shall commonly be respected in the world; but if we pant after higher improvement and higher attainments, it is not sufficient to view ourselves as we suppose that we are viewed by others, though this has been ingeniously argued, as the foundation of our moral sentiments. Because each bystander may have his own prejudices, beside the prejudices of his age or country. We should rather endeavour to view ourselves as we suppose that Being views us who seeth each thought ripen into action, and whose judgement never swerves from the eternal rule of right. Righteous are all His judgements – just as merciful!

The humble mind that seeketh to find favour in His sight, and calmly examines its conduct when only His presence is felt, will seldom form a very erroneous opinion of its own virtues. During the still hour of self-collection the angry brow of offended justice will be fearfully deprecated, or the tie which draws man to the Deity will be recognized in the pure sentiment of reverential adoration, that swells the heart without exciting any tumultuous emotions. In these solemn moments man discovers the germ of those vices, which, like the Java tree, shed a pestiferous vapour around – death is in the shade! and he perceives them without abhorrence, because he feels himself drawn by some cord of love to all his fellow-creatures, for whose follies he is anxious to find every extenuation in their nature – in himself. If I, he may thus argue, who exercise my own mind, and have been refined by tribulation, find the serpent's egg in some fold of my heart, and crush it with difficulty, shall I not pity those who have stamped with less vigour, or who have heedlessly nurtured the insidious reptile till it poisoned the vital stream it sucked? Can I, conscious of my secret sins, throw off my fellow-creatures, and calmly see them drop into the chasm of perdition, that yawns to receive them. No, no! The agonized heart will cry with suffocating impatience – I, too, am a man! and have vices, hid perhaps, from human eye, that bend me to the dust before God, and loudly tell me, when all is mute, that we are formed of the same earth, and breathe the same element. Humanity thus rises naturally out of humility, and twists the cords of love that in various convolutions entangle the heart.

This sympathy extends still further, till a man well pleased observes force in arguments that do not carry conviction to his own bosom, and he gladly places in the fairest light, to himself, the shows of reason that have led others astray, rejoiced to find some reason in all the errors of man; though before convinced that He who rules the day, makes His sun to shine on all. Yet, shaking hands thus as it were with corruption, one foot on earth, the other with bold stride mounts to Heaven, and claims kindred with superior natures. Virtues, unobserved by man, drop their balmy fragrance at this cool hour, and the thirsty land, refreshed by the pure streams of comfort that suddenly gush out, is crowned with smiling verdure; this is the living green on which that eye may look with complacency that is too pure to behold iniquity!

But my spirits flag; and I must silently indulge the reverie these reflections lead to, unable to describe the sentiments that have calmed my soul when, watching the rising sun, a soft shower drizzling through the leaves of neighbouring trees seemed to fall on my languid, yet tranquil spirits, to cool the heart that had been heated by the passions which reason laboured to tame.

The leading principles which run through all my disquisitions would render it unnecessary to enlarge on this subject, if a constant attention to keep the varnish of the character fresh, and in good condition, were not often inculcated as the sum total of female duty; if rules to regulate the behaviour, and to preserve the reputation, did not too frequently supersede moral obligations. But, with respect to reputation, the attention is confined to a single virtue – chastity. If the honour of a woman, as it is absurdly called, be safe, she may neglect every social duty; nay, ruin her family by gaming and extra-vagance; yet still present a shameless front – for truly she is an honourable woman!

Mrs Macaulay has justly observed that 'there is but one fault which a woman of honour may not commit with impunity.' She then justly and humanely adds –

This has given rise to the trite and foolish observation, that the first fault against chastity in woman has a radical power to deprave the character. But no such frail beings come out of the hands of Nature. The human mind is built of nobler materials than to be easily corrupted; and with all their disadvantages of situation and education, women seldom become entirely

abandoned till they are thrown into a state of desperation, by
the venomous rancour of their own sex.

But, in proportion as this regard for the reputation of chastity is
prized by women, it is despised by men: and the two extremes are
equally destructive to morality.

Men are certainly more under the influence of their appetites
than women; and their appetites are more depraved by unbridled
indulgence and the fastidious contrivances of satiety. Luxury has
introduced a refinement in eating that destroys the constitution;
and a degree of gluttony which is so beastly that a perception of
seemliness of behaviour must be worn out before one being could eat
immoderately in the presence of another, and afterwards complain
of the oppression that his intemperance naturally produced. Some
women, particularly French women, have also lost a sense of decency
in this respect; for they will talk very calmly of an indigestion. It
were to be wished that idleness was not allowed to generate, on the
rank soil of wealth, those swarms of summer insects that feed on
putrefaction; we should not then be disgusted by the sight of such
brutal excesses.

There is one rule relative to behaviour that, I think, ought to
regulate every other; and it is simply to cherish such an habitual
respect for mankind as may prevent us from disgusting a fellow-
creature for the sake of a present indulgence. The shameful indolence of many married women and others a little advanced in life,
frequently leads them to sin against delicacy. For, though convinced that the person is the band of union between the sexes, yet,
how often do they from sheer indolence, or, to enjoy some trifling
indulgence, disgust?

The depravity of the appetite which brings the sexes together has
had a still more fatal effect. Nature must ever be the standard of
taste, the gauge of appetite – yet how grossly is nature insulted by
the voluptuary. Leaving the refinements of love out of the question;
nature, by making the gratification of an appetite, in this respect, as
well as every other, a natural and imperious law to preserve the
species, exalts the appetite, and mixes a little mind and affection
with a sensual gust. The feelings of a parent, mingling with an
instinct merely animal, give it dignity; and the man and woman often
meeting on account of the child, a mutual interest and affection is

excited by the exercise of a common sympathy. Women then having some necessary duty to fulfil, more noble than to adorn their persons, would not contentedly be the slaves of casual lust; which is now the situation of a very considerable number who are, literally speaking, standing dishes to which every glutton may have access.

I may be told that great as this enormity is it only affects a devoted part of the sex – devoted for the salvation of the rest. But, false as every assertion might easily be proved, that recommends the sanctioning a small evil to produce a greater good; the mischief does not stop here, for the moral character, and peace of mind, of the chaster part of the sex is undermined by the conduct of the very women to whom they allow no refuge from guilt: whom they inexorably consign to the exercise of arts that lure their husbands from them, debauch their sons, and force them, let not modest women start, to assume, in some degree, the same character themselves. For I will venture to assert that all the causes of female weakness, as well as depravity, which I have already enlarged on, branch out of one grand cause – want of chastity in men.

This intemperance, so prevalent, depraves the appetite to such a degree that a wanton stimulus is necessary to rouse it; but the parental design of Nature is forgotten, and the mere person, and that for a moment, alone engrosses the thoughts. So voluptuous, indeed, often grows the lustful prowler, that he refines on female softness. Something more soft than women is then sought for; till, in Italy and Portugal, men attend the levees of equivocal beings, to sigh for more than female languor.

To satisfy this genus of men, women are made systematically voluptuous, and though they may not all carry their libertinism to the same height, yet this heartless intercourse with the sex, which they allow themselves, depraves both sexes, because the taste of men is vitiated; and women, of all classes, naturally square their behaviour to gratify the taste by which they obtain pleasure and power. Women becoming, consequently, weaker, in mind and body, than they ought to be, were one of the grand ends of their being taken into the account, that of bearing and nursing children, have not sufficient strength to discharge the first duty of a mother; and sacrificing to lasciviousness the parental affection that ennobles instinct, either destroy the embryo in the womb, or cast it off when born. Nature in everything demands respect, and those who violate her laws seldom violate them with impunity. The weak enervated women who particularly catch the attention of libertines are unfit to be mothers, though they may conceive; so that the rich sensualist, who has rioted among women, spreading depravity and misery, when he wishes to perpetuate his name, receives from his wife only an half-formed being that inherits both its father's and mother's weakness.

Contrasting the humanity of the present age with the barbarism of antiquity, great stress has been laid on the savage custom of exposing the children whom their parents could not maintain; whilst the man of sensibility, who thus, perhaps, complains, by his promiscuous amours produces a most destructive barrenness and contagious flagitiousness of manners. Surely nature never intended that women, by satisfying an appetite, should frustrate the very purpose for which it was implanted?

I have before observed that men ought to maintain the women whom they have seduced; this would be one means of reforming female manners, and stopping an abuse that has an equally fatal effect on population and morals. Another, no less obvious, would be to turn the attention of woman to the real virtue of chastity; for to little respect has that woman a claim, on the score of modesty, though her reputation may be white as the driven snow, who smiles on the libertine whilst she spurns the victims of his lawless appetites and their own folly.

Besides, she has a taint of the same folly, pure as she esteems herself, when she studiously adorns her person only to be seen by men, to excite respectful sighs, and all the idle homage of what is called innocent gallantry. Did women really respect virtue for its own sake, they would not seek for a compensation in vanity, for the self-denial which they are obliged to practise to preserve their reputation, nor would they associate with men who set reputation at defiance.

The two sexes mutually corrupt and improve each other. This I believe to be an indisputable truth, extending it to every virtue. Chastity, modesty, public spirit and all the noble train of virtues, on which social virtue and happiness are built, should be understood and cultivated by all mankind, or they will be cultivated to little effect. And, instead of furnishing the vicious or idle with a pretext for violating some sacred duty, by terming it a sexual one, it would be wiser to show that Nature has not made any difference, for that the unchaste man doubly defeats the purpose of Nature, by rendering women barren, and destroying his own constitution, though he avoids the shame that pursues the crime in the other sex. These are the physical consequences, the moral are still more alarming; for virtue is only a nominal distinction when the duties of citizens, husbands, wives, fathers, mothers and directors of families become merely the selfish ties of convenience.

Why then do philosophers look for public spirit? Public spirit must be nurtured by private virtue, or it will resemble the factitious sentiment which makes women careful to preserve their reputation, and men their honour. A sentiment that often exists unsupported by virtue, unsupported by that sublime morality which makes the habitual breach of one duty a breach of the whole moral law.

NOTES

1 I allude to various biographical writings, but particularly to Boswell's *Life of Johnson*.

2

Cicely Hamilton
1872–1952

Extracts from *MARRIAGE AS A TRADE* (1909)

Cicely Hamilton's life was the struggle of an unmarried woman for economic independence. She was a teacher and translator, and an actress for ten years, before she devoted herself to writing – Marriage as a Trade, *novels, plays, travel books and an autobiography. She was one of the founders of the Women Writers' Suffrage League, and a prominent suffragist. But, as she explains in the autobiography, she worked for women's enfranchisement not because she 'hoped great things from counting female noses at general elections, but because the agitation for women's enfranchisement must inevitably shake and weaken the tradition of the "normal woman"'.**

Hamilton's irreverence, and her disloyalty to contemporary social and moral values, place her in a militant tradition of writing that many people today will have encountered only in more recent work than Hamilton's. Although her detailed observations are historically and socially quite specific, they are founded in an enduring assumption: subjected classes must see things in their own way 'with an eye to their own interests, spiritual or material'. When women see marriage as the exchange of their persons for the means of their existence, they will see, for example, that their 'livelihood' is a subsistence wage, that the concentration of their energy on personal adornment is largely the outcome of a sound business instinct, that 'what it is natural for them to do' is what men do not care to do, that men's 'protection' is their dependence, that men's 'chivalry' is

*their being condescended to, and that childbearing is the involuntary
consequence of a compulsory trade.*

*Hamilton's analysis of marriage rests on an economic foundation (so
that, despite her very different political temperament, Hamilton's approach has clear affinities with that of Delphy, reading 5). But the
analysis is extended to familiar 'ethical' domains in its explanation of
gendered personalities. When Hamilton claims that a woman's character
is more artificial than a man's, she uses a model of character development
that helps itself to the idea of an underlying non-gendered human personality, capable of natural development; in women's case, where 'natural
lines' of development are thwarted, an artificial superstructure is added
socially. Nowadays most feminists would reject this model with its assumption of a pre-social personality which will develop 'naturally' if
allowed to do so. But Hamilton's use of the model does not prevent her
from giving a determinedly social analysis. She thinks that we understand
women's subordination only when we see women as trained for what a
dominant* class *has made inevitable for them – the married state.*

*The extracts reprinted below are taken from four chapters in which
Hamilton uses her account of marriage to explain various features of the
feminine personality. In later chapters, the artificial pressures on women's
development are used to explain women's standing in the labour market,
the sexual division of labour, and the failure of women to excel in the
arts. Hamilton's analysis is remarkable for its breadth: it accounts for
gendered power relationships at both the domestic and social levels in
terms of men's interest in preserving the* status quo. *Men are both
individual beneficiaries of existing arrangements and participants in a
collective project to sustain the power that these arrangements accord to
them.*

Marriage being to them not only a trade, but a necessity, it must
follow as the night the day that the acquirement of certain characteristics – the characteristics required by an average man in an
average wife – had been rendered inevitable for women in general.[1]
There have, of course, always been certain exceptional men who
have admired and desired certain exceptional and eccentric qualities
in their wives; but in estimating a girl's chances of pleasing – on
which depended her chances of success or a comfortable livelihood –
these exceptions, naturally, were taken into but small account, and
no specialization in their tastes and desires was allowed for in her

training. The aim and object of that training was to make her approximate to the standard of womanhood set up by the largest number of men; since the more widely she was admired the better were her chances of striking a satisfactory bargain. The taste and requirements of the average man of her class having been definitely ascertained, her training and education was carried on on the principle of cultivating those qualities which he was likely to admire, and repressing with an iron hand those qualities to which he was likely to take objection; in short, she was fitted for her trade by the discouragement of individuality and eccentricity and the persistent moulding of her whole nature into the form which the ordinary husband would desire it to take. Her education, unlike her brothers', was not directed towards self-development and the bringing out of natural capabilities, but towards pleasing someone else – was not for her own benefit, but for that of another person.

No one has better expressed the essential difference between the education of men and women than Mr John Burns in a speech delivered to the 'Children of the State' at the North Surrey District School on 13 February 1909. Addressing the boys the President of the Local Government Board said, 'I want you to be happy craftsmen, because you are trained to be healthy men.' Addressing the girls he is reported to have used the following words – 'To keep house, cook, nurse and delight in making others happy is your mission, duty and livelihood.'

The boys are to be happy themselves; the girls are to make others happy. No doubt Mr Burns spoke sincerely; but is he not one of the 'others'? And it is well to note that the 'making of others happy' is not put before the girls as an ideal, but as a duty and means of livelihood. They are to be self-sacrificing as a matter of business – a commercial necessity. It is because man realizes that self-sacrifice in woman is not a matter of free-will, but of necessity, that he gives her so little thanks for it. Her duty and means of livelihood is to make others happy – in other words, to please him.

. . .

There must be many attributes and characteristics of the general run of women which are not really the attributes and characteristics of their sex, but of their class – a class persistently set apart for the duties of sexual attraction, house-ordering and the bearing of children. And the particular qualities that, in the eyes of man, fitted them for the fulfilment of these particular duties, generation after generation of women, whatever their natural temperament and inclination, have sought to acquire – or if not the actual qualities themselves, at least an outward semblance of them. Without some semblance of those qualities life would be barred to them.

There are very few women in whom one cannot, now and again, trace the line of cleavage between real and acquired, natural and class, characteristics. The same thing, of course, holds good of men, but in a far less degree since, many vocations being open to them, they tend naturally and on the whole to fall into the class for which temperament and inclinations fit them. A man with a taste for an open-air life does not as a rule become a chartered accountant, a student does not take up deep-sea fishing as a suitable profession. But with women the endeavour to approximate to a single type has always been compulsory. It is ridiculous to suppose that nature, who never makes two blades of grass alike, desired to turn out indefinite millions of women all cut to the regulation pattern of wifehood: that is to say, all home-loving, charming, submissive, industrious, unintelligent, tidy, possessed with a desire to please, well-dressed, jealous of their own sex, self-sacrificing, cowardly, filled with a burning desire for maternity, endowed with a talent for cooking, narrowly uninterested in the world outside their own gates, and capable of sinking their own identity and interests in the interests and identity of a husband. I imagine that very few women naturally unite in their single persons these characteristics of the class wife; but, having been relegated from birth upwards to the class wife, they had to set to work, with or against the grain, to acquire some semblance of those that they knew were lacking.

There being no question of a line of least resistance for woman, it is fairly obvious that the necessity (in many instances) of making a silk purse out of a sow's ear and instilling the qualities of tidiness, love of home, cowardice, unintelligence, etc., etc., into persons who were born with quite other capacities and defects must have resulted in a pitiable waste of good material, sacrificed upon the altar of a domesticity arranged in the interests of the husband. But infinitely worse in its effect upon womanhood in general was the insincerity which, in many cases, was the prime lesson and result of a girl's education and upbringing. I do not mean, of course, that the generality of girls were consciously, of set purpose, and in so many words taught to be insincere; but it seems fairly certain to me that generations of mothers have tacitly instructed their daughters to assume virtues (or the reverse) which they had not.

It could not be otherwise. Success in the marriage-market demanded certain qualifications; and, as a matter of economic and social necessity, if those qualifications were lacking, their counterfeit presentment was assumed. When helplessness and fragility were the fashion amongst wives, the girl child who was naturally as plucky as her brothers was schooled into an affected and false timidity. Men were understood to admire and reverence the maternal instinct in women; so the girl who had no especial interest in children affected a mechanical delight in, petted, fondled and made much of them. (I myself have seen this done on more than one occasion; of course in the presence of men.) And – worst and most treacherous insincerity of all – since men were understood to dislike clever women, the girl who had brains, capacity, intellect, sought to conceal, denied possession of them, so that her future husband might enjoy, unchallenged, the pleasurable conviction of her mental inferiority to himself.

Of all the wrongs that have been inflicted upon woman there has been none like unto this – the enforced arrest of her mental growth – and none which bears more bitter and eloquent testimony to the complete and essential servility of her position. For her the eleventh commandment was an insult – 'Thou shalt not think'; and the most iniquitous condition of her marriage bargain this – that her husband, from the height of his self-satisfaction, should be permitted to esteem her a fool.

. . .

The insistent and deliberate stunting of woman's intellectual growth is . . . the best proof of her essentially servile position in the household; and that being the case, it is not to be wondered at that her code of honour and morals is essentially a servile code. That is to say, its origin and guiding motive is the well-being, moral and material, of someone else. Like her stupidity, woman's morality has been imposed on her, and to a great extent is not morality at all, in the proper sense of the word, but a code of manners formulated in the interests of her master.

I wish to make it clear that when I speak of morality in this connection I am not using the word in the narrow sense in which it is sometimes employed. By a standard of morality I mean a rule of life which we adopt as a guide to our conduct, and endeavour, more or less successfully, to apply to every action – to our dealings with others as well as to our dealings with our own hearts.

I cannot better explain what I mean by the essential servility of woman's code of morals than by quoting Milton's well-known line – 'He for God only, she for God in him.' That one brief verse condenses into a nutshell the difference in the moral position of the two sexes – expresses boldly, simply, straightforwardly, the man's belief that he had the right to divert and distort the moral impulse and growth in woman to serve his own convenience. No priesthood has ever made a claim more arrogant than this claim of man to stand between woman and her God, and divert the spiritual forces of her nature into the channel that served him best. The real superiority of man consists in this: that he is free to obey his conscience and to serve his God – if it be in him so to do. Woman is not. She can serve Him only at second hand – can obey His commands not directly but only by obeying the will of the man who stands between her and the Highest, and who has arrogated to himself not merely the material control of her person and her property, but the spiritual control of her conscience.

This is no fanciful piece of imagery. There are laws still in existence – laws of an earlier age – which prove how complete has been this moral control which we are only now shaking off, since they presume a man's entire responsibility for the actions of his wife, be those actions good or ill. That a woman at her husband's bidding should bend her conscience to his will as a reed bends; that, because he desired it of her, she should break and defy every commandment of God and man; this seemed to our forefathers a natural thing, and a course of action befitting her station and place in life. So far from blaming, they condoned it in her and have expressed that view of the matter in their law – sometimes with awkward and annoying results for a later generation. Woman, until she began to feel in herself the stirrings of independence – woman, when she was just the wife-and-mother-and-nothing-else, the domestic animal – seems to me to have been a creature whom you could not have described as being either moral or immoral. She was just unmoral. Whether she did good or evil was not, as far as her own individuality went, of very much account since the standard set up for her was not of her own setting up; it had been erected for the comfort and well-being of her master. Her virtues were second-hand virtues, instilled into her for the convenience of another; and she did what was right in his eyes, not in her own, after the manner of a child. Therefore she was neither moral nor immoral, but servile. The motive which guided and impelled her from childhood was a low one – the desire (disinterestedly or for her own advantage) of pleasing someone else. (To make others happy, as Mr Burns expresses it.) The desire to please being the motive power of her existence, her code of honour and ethics was founded not on thought, conviction or even natural impulse, but on observation of the likes and dislikes of those she had to please. Hence its extraordinary and inconsistent character, its obvious artificiality and the manifest traces it bears of having been imposed upon her from without. For instance, no natural ethical code emanating from within could have summed up woman's virtue in *a* virtue – physical purity. That confusion of one virtue with virtue in general was certainly of masculine origin, arising from the masculine habit of thinking of woman only in connection with her relations to himself. To other aspects of her life and character man was indifferent – they hardly existed for him. And of masculine origin, too, was that extraordinary article of the code by which it was laid down that a woman's 'honour' was, to all intents and purposes, a matter of chance – a thing which she only possessed because no unkind fate had thrown her in the way of a man sufficiently brutal to deprive her of it by force. Her honour, in short, was not a moral but a physical quality.

One sees, of course, the advantage from the male point of view of this peculiar provision of the code. In a world where the pickpocket class had the upper hand a somewhat similar regulation would, no doubt, be in force; and it would be enacted, by a custom stronger than law, that to have one's pocket picked was in itself a disgrace which must on no account be cried aloud upon the housetops or communicated to the police. To reveal and publish the fact that your purse had been snatched from you by force would be to make yourself a mark for scorn and for hissing, to bring upon yourself an obloquy far greater than that accorded to the active partner in the transaction, whose doings would be greeted with a shrug of the shoulders and the explanation that pickpockets are pickpockets, and will never be anything but what nature has made them; and, after all, you must have dangled the purse temptingly before his eyes. Under these circumstances, with the thief at liberty to ply his trade, the fact that you had money in your pocket would be, strictly speaking, an accident; and, to make the parallel complete, the lack of your money – the fact that it had been taken from you even against your will – would have to be accounted a black disgrace, leaving a lasting smear upon your whole life. That, it seems to me, is the exact position with regard to what is commonly termed a woman's 'honour'. I should prefer to put it that a woman has no honour; only an accident.

. . .

One peculiarity of the trade at which so many women earn their livelihood I have, as yet, hardly touched upon. It is this: that however arduous and exacting the labour that trade entails – and the rough manual work of most households is done by women – it is not paid except by a wage of subsistence. There may be exceptions, of course, but, as a general rule, the work done by the wife and mother in the home is paid for merely by supplying her with the necessaries of existence – food, lodging and clothing. She is fed and lodged on the same principle as a horse is fed and lodged – so that she may do her work, her cooking, her cleaning, her sewing and the tending and rearing of her children. She may do it very well or she may do it very badly; but beyond food, lodging and a certain amount of clothing, she can claim no wage for it. In short, her work in the home is not recognized either by the state or by the individual citizen (except in occasional instances) as work which has any commercial value.

There must, of course, be some reason why such intrinsically important work as the rearing of children and ministering to the comfort of the community should be held in such poor esteem that it is paid for at the lowest possible rate – subsistence rate. (Which means, of course, that wages in that particular branch of work have been forced just as low as they can go, since human beings cannot continue to exist without the means of supporting life.) And the principal reason for this state of things I take to be the compulsory nature of the trade. Given a sufficiently large number of persons destined and educated from birth for one particular calling, with no choice at all in the matter, and with every other calling and means of livelihood sternly barred to them, and you have all the conditions necessary for the forcing down of wages to the lowest possible point to which they will go – subsistence point. In that calling labour will be as cheap as the heart of the employer could desire; and incidentally it will tend to become what ill-paid labour always tends to become – inefficient. Exactly the same condition of affairs would prevail in any other trade – mining or boiler-making, for instance – if immense numbers of boys were brought up to be miners or boiler-makers, and informed that whatever their needs or desires, or whatever the state of the labour market in these particular callings, they could not turn their abilities into any other direction. Under those circumstances miners and boiler-makers would probably work for their keep and nothing more, as the ordinary wife has to do.

I shall be told, of course, that the position of a husband is not that of an ordinary employer of labour, and that the financial relations of a man and his wife are complicated by considerations of affection and mutual interest which make it quite impossible to estimate the exact wage-earning value of the wife's services in the household, or the price which she receives for them in other things than money. Even if, for the sake of argument, this be admitted as a general rule, it does not invalidate my point, which is that the compulsory nature of woman's principal trade is quite sufficient, in itself, to account for the fact that the workers in that trade are not deemed worthy of anything more than a wage of subsistence. Considerations of sentiment and affection may help to keep her direct monetary remuneration down; but to bring it down in the first instance nothing more was needed than compulsory overcrowding of the 'domestic service' market.

That the wage of subsistence – the board, lodging and clothing – dealt out to a married woman is often board, lodging and clothing on a very liberal and comfortable scale, does not alter the fact that it is essentially a wage of subsistence, regulated by the idea of what is necessary for subsistence in the particular class to which she may happen to belong. The plutocrat who wishes his wife to entertain cannot habitually feed her on fish and chips from round the corner, or renew her wardrobe in an old-clothes shop. But she does not get twelve-course dinners and dresses from the Rue de la Paix because she has earned them by extra attention to her duties as a wife and mother, but because they are necessary qualifications for the place in his household which her husband wishes her to take – because, without them, she could not fulfil the duties that he requires of her. The monetary reward of wifehood and motherhood depends entirely on the life, the good luck and the good nature of another person; the strictest attention to duty on the part of a wife and mother is of no avail without that. The really hard labour of housework and rearing children is done in those households where the wage of subsistence is lowest; and the women who receive most money from their husbands are precisely those who pass on the typical duties of a wife and mother to other persons – housekeepers, cooks, nurses and governesses. Excellence in the trade is no guarantee of reward, which is purely a matter of luck; work, however hard, will not bring about that measure of independence, more or less comparative, which is attained by successful work in other trades. Dependence, in short, is the essence of wifehood as generally understood by the masculine mind.

Under normal and favourable conditions, then, a married woman without private means of her own obtains a wage of subsistence for the fulfilment of the duties required of her in her husband's household. Under unfavourable (but not very abnormal) conditions she does not even obtain that. In the case of the large army of married women who support idle or invalid husbands by paid labour outside the home, the additional work inside the home is carried on gratis, and without a suggestion of payment of any kind.

I am inclined to believe that the principle that payment should be made for domestic service rendered does not really enter into the question of a wife's wages; that those wages (of subsistence) are paid simply for the possession of her person, and that the other arts and accomplishments she may possess are not supposed to have any exchange value. At any rate, a mistress, from whom the domestic arts are not expected, is often just as expensively kept as a wife – which seems to point to my conclusion. What Mr John Burns has called a woman's 'duty and livelihood' is, in the strict sense of the term, not her livelihood at all. Her livelihood, as an ordinary wife, is a precarious dependence upon another person's life; should that other person die, she could not support herself and her children by remaining in 'woman's sphere' – cooking, tending the house, and looking after her young family. That sort of work having no commercial value, she and her young family would very shortly starve. The profession of the prostitute is a livelihood; the profession of the wife and mother is not. A woman can support her children by prostitution; she cannot do so by performing the duties ordinarily associated with motherhood.

. . .

There is one element in the relations between man and wife to which, as yet, I have hardly referred. I mean that element which is known as the exercise of protection by the stronger over the weaker – by the man over the woman. In considering the rewards of wifehood, great or small, it cannot, of course, be passed over without examination, since it seems to be assumed that a man pays his wife for services unpaid in other ways by defending her against perils, physical or otherwise.

Now there can be no doubt that in former ages and all over the world – as in certain regions of the world today – this physical protection of the weaker by the stronger, of the woman by the man, was a thing that really counted in marriage. The women of a savage tribe which was constantly at war with surrounding savage tribes would have to rely on the strength and skill in warfare of their men to deliver them from capture or death. In such a primitive state of affairs every man might be called upon at any moment to exercise in his own person duties of defence and protection which the average man now delegates to the paid soldier and the paid policeman. In the beginning of things the head of every family possessed the right of private war and private justice, and it was on his success in both these fields of activity that the lives and the welfare of his womenfolk and children would very largely depend. It was only by virtue of his strength that he could maintain possession of his property in goods or in human flesh. It was by virtue of his superior strength that he reduced woman to subjection, and in return, and as a form of payment for her toil, defended her from the attacks of others. So arose and originated the idea of the physical protection necessarily meted out by husband to wife; an idea real enough in the beginning.

Circumstances alter cases; but they often take a long time to alter ideas, and this particular one continues to flourish luxuriantly in places where the order of things that gave it birth has passed into the forgotten. One still hears people talk as if a clerk or a greengrocer's assistant, married in a suburban chapel and going to Cliftonville for his honeymoon, undertook thereby to shelter his better half from heaven knows what of vague and mysterious peril. From other times and other manners, beginning with the days when a stone axe formed a necessary part of a bridegroom's wedding garment, into places where moral force has fought the worst of its bitter battle with physical force, into days when private war is called murder and the streets are policed, there has come down the superstition that the ordinary civilized man performs doughty feats of protection for the benefit of the ordinary civilized wife. And it seems to be accepted that the element of protection is a natural and unavoidable element in the relations of married man and woman – even of married man and woman living in a suburban flat.

. . .

I have not the least intention of casting any reflection upon the courage of the average civilized husband or inferring that he is not willing to offer up his life in defence of his better half if called upon to do so; I merely state the obvious fact that he is not very often called upon to make the sacrifice. Even in those countries where universal military service is established, the duty of defending the national (not the individual) hearth and home falls last upon men who are married and have a family to support; it is the young, unmarried men who are called upon to form the first line of defence and defiance. And in ordinary everyday life it is the strong arm of the law and not the strong arm of the individual husband which secures a woman from hurt and molestation. If it were not so the unprotected spinster would be in a truly piteous plight. As a matter of fact, she usually finds that the ordinary constable is quite adequate for all her requirements in the protective line.

Closely allied to this idea of individual masculine protection is that other, and still more vaguely nebulous, idea of chivalry or preferential treatment of women in general by men in general. Which necessitates an inquiry into what the average modern man really means when he talks of chivalry in this connection.

Frankly, it does not seem to me that he means very much. My own experience leads me to define chivalry – not the real thing, but the term as it is commonly used, say, in the public press – to define chivalry as a form, not of respect for an equal, but of condescension to an inferior; a condescension which expresses itself in certain rules of behaviour where non-essentials are involved. In very few really essential matters between man and woman is the chivalric principle allowed to get so much as a hearing; in practically all such matters it is, as I have already pointed out, an understood thing that woman gets the worst of the bargain, does the unpleasant work in the common division of labour, and, when blame is in question, sits down under the lion's share of it. In return for this attitude on her part – which, if voluntary, would be really chivalrous, but being involuntary is merely servile – man undertakes to regulate his conduct towards her by certain particular forms of outward deference. His attitude, so far as one can gather, is something like this: as long as you refrain from coming into competition with us, as long as you will allow us to look down upon you, as long as you are content to regard yourselves not only as our dependents, but as persons sent into the world to minister to our comforts and our pleasures, so long shall our outward behaviour towards you be framed in a particular code of manners which secures you preferential treatment in unimportant matters. But, in order to secure this preferential treatment in unimportant matters, you must put no strain upon our courtesy, and you must defer to our wishes in more important things; you must not trespass upon the domain that we have reserved for our own use, you must not infringe the rules which have been laid down for your guidance and whose aim is to secure our own comfort.

In other words, what is commonly known as 'chivalry' is not a spontaneous virtue or impulse on the part of modern man, but the form in which he pays his debt for value received from woman. Directly she fails to fulfil her own important share of the bargain, he considers himself at liberty to refuse payment; at least, one must conclude so from the frequency with which the 'independent' woman of today is threatened with the extinction of chivalry if she continues to assert herself in a manner which may be consistent with her own desires, but which is not consistent with the desires of average male humanity. Looked at in that light, the preferential code of manners, which is all that is usually understood by chivalry, bears distinct resemblance to the sugar that attempts to veil the flavour of a pill or the jam that does its best to conceal the noxiousness of a lurking powder. By a simple process of exchange and barter outward deference on the one side is given in payment for real deference and subjection on the other; and, that being the case, it is quite open to woman to look into the terms of her bargain, reconsider them, and ask herself whether she is not paying too high a price for value received. For, with every respect for courtesy, the opening of a door and the lifting of a hat, however reverential, are among the small things of life.

It will no doubt be objected that chivalry is something infinitely greater than what I have called outward forms of deference. I agree that that is not the true meaning of the word; but I maintain that, in general practice, the virtue of chivalry, in so far as it enters into the daily lives of most women, amounts to outward forms of deference and little more. As soon as we come to essentials, we realize that the counteracting principle will inevitably be brought into play – the principle that the woman must always be sacrificed to the interests of the man.

There are, of course, exceptions to that rule – and noble ones. It is written that in common danger of death the stronger must think first, not of his own life, but of the lives of those weaker and dependent upon him; and whatever other laws a man might break with impudence and impunity, he would very certainly be ashamed to confess to a breach of this particular commandment. One respects such habitual obedience as fine and finely disciplined; but it is not decrying it to point out that not every man is called upon to exercise it and that the form of chivalry cultivated by most is necessarily of a less strenuous type. And into chivalry of the less strenuous type the idea of self-sacrifice in essentials does not as a rule enter, since it is, as I have already shown, in the nature of a reward or payment for self-sacrifice in others.

I am quite aware that there are a great many women of the upper and middle classes – women, for the most part, who lead a leisured and comfortable existence – who attach an inordinately high value to outward forms of deference from the men with whom they come in contact. Considering their training and education, and the trend of their whole lives, it is perhaps only natural that they should. The aim of that training and education has been, as I have shown, not to develop their individuality and capacities, but to make themselves and their actions pleasing to the men with whom they may happen to come in contact; and, that being so, approval from the men with whom they may happen to come in contact is naturally a thing of the utmost importance to them. To lack it is to lack the whole reward of a well-spent life. By women with this narrow outlook on the world superficial courtesies and superficial deference are interpreted to mean approval and, therefore, success in pleasing – almost the only form of success open to them. Further, the lives of such women are usually sheltered, and thus they do not have very much opportunity of realizing that the meed of ceremony to which they are accustomed is largely a tribute paid, not to themselves or to their womanhood, but to the particular leisured class to which they happen to belong.

Whatever the reason, it is certain that many women of the 'comfortable' class do cling desperately and rather pathetically to the idea of their little privileges in this respect; I have over and over again heard such women oppose efforts to better their own position and that of others simply on the ground that 'men would not treat us in the same way – there would be no chivalry; they would not be polite to us any longer.' Apparently the good souls are under the impression that no man is ever polite to a person he does not despise; and this sort of argument shows how completely those who use it have learned to substitute the shadow for the reality and dissociate what is commonly called chivalry from respect. To them masculine courtesy is an expression not of reverence for women, but of more or less kindly contempt for them – and they are quite content that it should be so. Personally, this attitude – an attitude of voluntary abasement assumed in order that man may know the pleasure of condescension – is the only thing that ever makes me ashamed of being a woman; since it is the outward and visible expression of an inward servility that has eaten and destroyed a soul.

NOTES

* Cicely Hamilton, *Life Errant* (London: J. M. Dent & Sons Ltd, 1935), p. 65.
1 Copyright © 1981, Curtis Brown Ltd, London.

3

Margaret Sanger
1884–1966

'WOMAN'S ERROR AND HER DEBT' and
'BIRTH CONTROL – A PARENTS' PROBLEM OR WOMAN'S?'
from *THE NEW MOTHERHOOD* (1922)

Margaret Sanger lived in the second decade of the twentieth century in New York, where she associated with many notable activists of the United States' left and labour movements. Emma Goldman (readings 9 and 18) was a significant mentor. Sanger's work as a visiting nurse gave rise to her interest in contraception (for which she later coined the term 'birth control'). This interest was enhanced by several strands in current radical thought. Freud's psychoanalytic theory of human sexuality and sociality was gaining influence, and sexual relations ranked high on the progressive political agenda. Radicals were also impressed by the argument that moral codes must give way to individual self-determination and rational ethical choice. (In this connection the philosophy of Nietzsche was construed as an attack on bourgeois morality.)

In 1914 Sanger launched a feminist journal, Woman Rebel, *whose motto was 'No Gods, No Masters'. She published numerous books, pamphlets and articles, and spoke and campaigned tirelessly. She was prominent in the battle against the Comstock Act of 1873 which outlawed the advertisement or publication of any information on abortion or birth control as 'obscene'; and she founded birth control clinics in the United States and Britain.**

In the chapters reprinted here Margaret Sanger exhorts women individually and collectively to take responsibility, and challenge the existing

man-made order. They must educate themselves and raise their conscious-
ness so that they can, in Sanger's words, 'pay the debt' that they have
incurred – albeit involuntarily till now – in mothering too many children.
In short, they are to become ethical and political subjects.

Like Emma Goldman, Sanger is critical of the achievements of the
women's movement to date, for without sexual and reproductive freedom
women cannot fully enter into their role of citizen. Further, in Sanger's
view women's economic and political oppression, and the oppressed situa-
tion of the working classes generally, is caused in part by over-population.
She thought and debated about Malthusianism,** a doctrine which was
hailed by progressive thinkers like John Stuart Mill and Robert Owen,
but rejected by Marx (as inimical to the interests of the working class).
She came to agree with Havelock Ellis that eugenics offers the possibility
of enhancing sexual pleasure and freedom, while controlling their human
consequences with the aid of social science.

The eugenicism of Sanger's writing will lack intellectual credibility
for anyone who reads it in the light of the Nazi holocaust and, more
topically, of abuses like forced sterilization programmes in the so-called
'third world'. Nevertheless, Sanger's exhortation to women not to leave
their reproductive welfare in the hands of men still deserves a hearing
today.

WOMAN'S ERROR AND HER DEBT

The most far-reaching social development of modern times is the
revolt of woman against sex servitude. The most important force in
the remaking of the world is a free motherhood. Beside this force,
the elaborate international programmes of modern statesmen are
weak and superficial. Diplomats may formulate leagues of nations
and nations may pledge their utmost strength to maintain them;
statesmen may dream of reconstructing the world out of alliances,
hegemonies and spheres of influence, but woman, continuing to
produce explosive populations, will convert these pledges into the
proverbial scraps of paper; or she may, by controlling birth, lift
motherhood to the plane of a voluntary, intelligent function, and
remake the world. When the world is thus remade, it will exceed the
dream of statesman, reformer and revolutionist.

Only in recent years has woman's position as the gentler and weaker half of the human family been emphatically and generally questioned. Men assumed that this was woman's place; woman herself accepted it. It seldom occurred to anyone to ask whether she would go on occupying it for ever.

Upon the mere surface of woman's organized protests there were no indications that she was desirous of achieving a fundamental change in her position. She claimed the right of suffrage and legislative regulation of her working hours, and asked that her property rights be equal to those of the man. None of these demands, however, affected directly the most vital factors of her existence. Whether she won her point or failed to win it, she remained a dominated weakling in a society controlled by men.

Woman's acceptance of her inferior status was the more real because it was unconscious. She had chained herself to her place in society and the family through the maternal functions of her nature, and only chains thus strong could have bound her to her lot as a brood animal for the masculine civilizations of the world. In accepting her role as the 'weaker and gentler half', she accepted that function. In turn, the acceptance of that function fixed the more firmly her rank as an inferior.

Caught in this 'vicious circle', woman has, through her reproductive ability, founded and perpetuated the tyrannies of the earth. Whether it was the tyranny of a monarchy, an oligarchy or a republic, the one indispensable factor of its existence was, as it is now, hordes of human beings – human beings so plentiful as to be cheap, and so cheap that ignorance was their natural lot. Upon the rock of an unenlightened, submissive maternity have these been founded; upon the product of such a maternity have they flourished.

No despot ever flung forth his legions to die in foreign conquest, no privilege-ruled nation ever erupted across its borders, to lock in death embrace with another, but behind them loomed the driving-power of a population too large for its boundaries and its natural resources.

No period of low wages or of idleness with their want among the workers, no peonage or sweatshop, no child-labour factory, ever came into being, save from the same source. Nor have famine and plague been as much 'acts of God' as acts of too prolific mothers. They, also, as all students know, have their basic causes in over-population.

The creators of over-population are the women, who, while wringing their hands over each fresh horror, submit anew to their task of producing the multitudes who will bring about the *next* tragedy of civilization.

While unknowingly laying the foundations of tyrannies and providing the human tinder for racial conflagrations, woman was also unknowingly creating slums, filling asylums with insane, and institutions with other defectives. She was replenishing the ranks of the prostitutes, furnishing grist for the criminal courts and inmates for the prisons. Had she planned deliberately to achieve this tragic total of human waste and misery, she could hardly have done it more effectively.

Woman's passivity under the burden of her disastrous task was almost altogether that of ignorant resignation. She knew virtually nothing about her reproductive nature and less about the consequences of her excessive childbearing. It is true that, obeying the inner urge of their natures, *some* women revolted. They went even to the extreme of infanticide and abortion. Usually their revolts were not general enough. They fought as individuals, not as a mass. In the mass they sank back into blind and hopeless subjection. They went on breeding with staggering rapidity those numberless, undesired children who become the clogs and the destroyers of civilizations.

Today, however, woman is rising in fundamental revolt. Even her efforts at mere reform are, as we shall see later, steps in that direction. Underneath each of them is the feminine urge to complete freedom. Millions of women are asserting their right to voluntary motherhood. They are determined to decide for themselves whether they shall become mothers, under what conditions and when. This is the fundamental revolt referred to. It is for woman the key to the temple of liberty.

Even as birth control is the means by which woman attains basic freedom, so it is the means by which she must and will uproot the evil she has wrought through her submission. As she has unconsciously and ignorantly brought about social disaster, so must and will she consciously and intelligently *undo* that disaster and create a new and a better order.

The task is hers. It cannot be avoided by excuses. It is not enough for woman to point to the self-evident domination of man. Nor does it avail to plead the guilt of rulers and the exploiters of labour. It makes no difference that she does not formulate industrial systems nor that she is an instinctive believer in social justice. In her submission lies her error and her guilt. By her failure to withhold the multitudes of children who have made inevitable the most flagrant of our social evils, she incurred a debt to society. Regardless of her own wrongs, regardless of all other considerations, *she* must pay that debt.

She must not think to pay this debt in any superficial way. She cannot pay it with palliatives – with child-labour laws, prohibition, regulation of prostitution and agitation against war. Political nostrums and social panaceas are but incidentally and superficially useful. These are temporary measures of relief which anaesthetize, but do not cure. They do not touch the source of the social disease.

War, famine, poverty and oppression of the workers will continue while woman makes life cheap. They will cease only when she limits her reproductivity and human life is no longer a thing to be wasted.

Two chief obstacles hinder the discharge of this tremendous obligation. The first and the lesser is the prejudice of officialdom.

Those elected to guide humanity in its course through the channels of the Church, welfare work, and politics, would still deny to woman the knowledge of her own reproductive nature.

They would hold from her the right to decide how many children she should bring into the world. In many countries even today, prejudiced and short-sighted officials have put bans upon this right. When the state has not exercised its power to hold woman to her career as a breeder, the Church has taken into its hands that most unworthy task.

The second and more serious barrier is her own ignorance of the extent and effect of her submission. Until she knows the evil her subjection has wrought to herself, to her progeny and to the world at large, she cannot wipe out that evil.

To get rid of these obstacles is to invite attack from the forces of reaction which are so strongly entrenched in our present-day society. It means warfare in every phase of her life. Nevertheless, at whatever cost, she must emerge from her ignorance and assume her responsibility.

She can do this only when she has awakened to a knowledge of herself and the consequences of her ignorance. The first step is birth control. Through birth control she will attain to voluntary motherhood. Having attained this, the basic freedom of her sex, she will cease to enslave herself and the mass of humanity. Then, through the understanding of the intuitive forward urge within her, she will not stop at patching up the world; she will remake it.

BIRTH CONTROL – A PARENTS' PROBLEM OR WOMAN'S?

The problem of birth control has arisen directly from the effort of the feminine spirit to free itself from bondage. Woman herself has wrought that bondage through her reproductive powers and while enslaving herself has enslaved the world. The physical suffering to be relieved is chiefly woman's. Hers, too, is the love life that dies first under the blight of too prolific breeding. Within her is wrapped up the future of the race – it is hers to make or mar. All of these considerations point unmistakably to one fact – it is woman's duty as well as her privilege to lay hold of the means of freedom. Whatever men may do, she cannot escape the responsibility. For ages she has been deprived of the opportunity to meet this obligation. She is now emerging from her helplessness. Even as no one can share the suffering of the overburdened mother, so no one can do this work for her. Others may help, but she and she alone can free herself.

The basic freedom of the world is woman's freedom. A free race cannot be born of slave mothers. A woman enchained cannot choose but give a measure of that bondage to her sons and daughters. No woman can call herself free who does not own and control her body. No woman can call herself free until she can choose consciously whether she will or will not be a mother.

It does not greatly alter the case that some women call themselves free because they earn their own livings, while others profess freedom because they defy the conventions of sex relationship. She who earns her own living gains a sort of freedom that is not to be undervalued, but in quality and in quantity it is of little account beside the untrammeled choice of mating or not mating, of being a mother or not being a mother. She gains food and clothing and shelter, at least, without submitting to the charity of her companion, but the earning of her own living does not give her the development of her inner sex urge, far deeper and more powerful in its outworkings than any of these externals. In order to have that development, she must still meet and solve the problem of motherhood.

With the so-called 'free' woman, who chooses a mate in defiance of convention, freedom is largely a question of character and audacity. If she does attain to an unrestricted choice of a mate, she is still in a position to be enslaved through her reproductive powers. Indeed, the pressure of law and custom upon the woman not legally married is likely to make her more of a slave than the woman fortunate enough to marry the man of her choice.

Look at it from any standpoint you will, suggest any solution you will, conventional or unconventional, sanctioned by law or in defiance of law, woman is in the same position, fundamentally, until she is able to determine for herself whether she will be a mother and to fix the number of her offspring. This unavoidable situation is alone enough to make birth control, first of all, a woman's problem. On the very face of the matter, voluntary motherhood is chiefly the concern of the woman.

It is persistently urged, however, that since sex expression is the act of two, the responsibility of controlling the results should not be placed upon woman alone. Is it fair, it is asked, to give her, instead of the man, the task of protecting herself when she is, perhaps, less rugged in physique than her mate, and has, at all events, the normal, periodic inconveniences of her sex?

We must examine this phase of her problem in two lights – that of the ideal, and of the conditions working toward the ideal. In an ideal society, no doubt, birth control would become the concern of the man as well as the woman. The hard, inescapable fact which we encounter today is that man has not only refused any such responsibility, but has individually and collectively sought to prevent woman from obtaining knowledge by which she could assume this responsibility for herself. She is still in the position of a dependent today because her mate has refused to consider her as an individual apart from his needs. She is still bound because she has in the past left the solution of the problem to him. Having left it to him, she finds that instead of rights, she has only such privileges as she has gained by petitioning, coaxing and cozening. Having left it to him, she is exploited, driven and enslaved to his desires.

While it is true that he suffers many evils as the consequence of this situation, she suffers vastly more. While it is true that he should be awakened to the cause of these evils, we know that they come home to her with crushing force every day. It is she who has the long burden of carrying, bearing and rearing the unwanted children ... It is her heart that the sight of the deformed, the subnormal, the undernourished, the overworked child smites first and oftenest and hardest. It is *her* love life that dies first in the fear of undesired pregnancy. It is her opportunity for self-expression that perishes first and most hopelessly because of it.

Conditions, rather than theories, facts, rather than dreams, govern the problem. They place it squarely upon the shoulders of woman. She has learned that whatever the moral responsibility of the man in this direction may be, he does not discharge it. She has learned that, lovable and considerate as the individual husband may be, she has nothing to expect from men in the mass, when they make laws and decree customs. She knows that regardless of what ought to be, the brutal, unavoidable fact is that she will never receive her freedom until she takes it for herself.

Having learned this much, she has yet something more to learn. Women are too much inclined to follow in the footsteps of men, to try to think as men think, to try to solve the general problems of life as men solve them. If after attaining their freedom, women accept conditions in the spheres of government, industry, art, morals and religion as they find them, they will be but taking a leaf out of man's book. The woman is not needed to do man's work. She is not needed to think man's thoughts. She need not fear that the masculine mind, almost universally dominant, will fail to take care of its own. Her mission is not to enhance the masculine spirit, but to express the feminine; hers is not to preserve a man-made world, but to create a human world by the infusion of the feminine element into all of its activities.

Woman must not accept; she must challenge. She must not be awed by that which has been built up around her; she must reverence that within her which struggles for expression. Her eyes must be less upon what is and more clearly upon what should be. She must listen only with a frankly questioning attitude to the dogmatized opinions of man-made society. When she chooses her new, free course of action, it must be in the light of her own opinion – of her own intuition. Only so can she give play to the feminine spirit. Only thus can she free her mate from the bondage which he wrought for himself when he wrought hers. Only thus can she restore to him that of which he robbed himself in restricting her. Only thus can she remake the world . . .

Woman must have her freedom – the fundamental freedom of choosing whether or not she shall be a mother and how many children she will have. Regardless of what man's attitude may be, that problem is hers – and before it can be his, it is hers alone.

She goes through the vale of death alone, each time a babe is born. As it is the right neither of man nor the state to coerce her into this ordeal, so it is her right to decide whether she will endure it. That right to decide imposes upon her the duty of clearing the way to knowledge by which she may make and carry out the decision.

Birth control is woman's problem. The quicker she accepts it as hers and hers alone, the quicker will society respect motherhood. The quicker, too, will the world be made a fit place for her children to live.

NOTES

* David M. Kennedy, *Birth Control in America: The Career of Margaret Sanger* (Yale University Press: New Haven and London 1970).

** Thomas Robert Malthus (1966–1834) advocated moral restraint on the size of families because while population has a natural growth rate described by a geometric progression, the natural resources necessary to support the population grow at a rate similar to an arithmetic progression.

4

Betty Friedan
b.1921

'THE SEXUAL SELL' from
THE FEMININE MYSTIQUE (1963)

The 1950s saw the entrenchment of Cold War between the superpowers. In the US, a climate of conservative reaction prevailed, affecting the politics of gender no less than the contest of labour and capital. Betty Friedan's The Feminine Mystique *offered the first sustained critique of the flight from sexual equality in post-war America. Its subject is the drive to discredit and reverse any progress made in the first half of the century towards women's emancipation, and to reaffirm the suburban nuclear family as the moral norm.*

This chapter studies the reinvention through consumer advertising of an objectively obsolete role for women as full-time 'homemakers'. Like the book as a whole, it is motivated not by hostility towards the 'American way of life' as such but by liberal-humanist outrage at the exclusion of women from genuine moral dignity. For Friedan this dignity flows, in somewhat Victorian style, from commitment to an intellectual discipline or to ideals of public service; at any rate, to purposes which transcend mere personal interest. It is from these larger purposes that both sexes, but especially women, are becoming estranged by the progressive privatization of the (middle-class) American lifestyle.

The Feminine Mystique *has worn badly in some respects. Few readers today are likely to relish Friedan's strictures on moral 'immaturity', let alone her vision of 'homosexuality . . . spreading like a murky smog over the American scene'.* The chapter reprinted here, however, has lost none of its power to shock. Drawing extensively on sources internal to the* *advertising industry, Friedan lets us in on the deliberations of men who appreciate to the full the absurdity of the life they are trying to induce women to lead, but who depend for their own bread and butter on their skill in manipulating the nameless yearnings of frustrated housewives. Her discussion reveals just how far contemporary economic reality diverges from the Kantian principle supposedly enshrined in liberal democracies: rational nature must be treated as an end in itself, never merely as a means!*

By this 'morality that goes beyond the dollar', Friedan finds the manipulators guilty of a conspiracy to suppress the 'complex needs which home-and-family, love-and-children, cannot fill'. Her discussion will remain relevant as long as the advertising industry remains an institution serving the interests of the powerful, and as long as there continues to be something distinctively feminine in the habit of going shopping to compensate for feelings of futility and emptiness.

Some months ago, as I began to fit together the puzzle of women's retreat to home, I had the feeling I was missing something.[1] If, despite the nameless desperation of so many American housewives, despite the opportunities open to all women now, so few have any purpose in life other than to be a wife and mother, somebody, something pretty powerful must be at work.

There are certain facts of life so obvious and mundane that one never talks about them. Only the child blurts out: 'Why do people in books never go to the toilet?' Why is it never said that the really crucial function, the really important role that women serve as housewives is *to buy more things for the house*? In all the talk of femininity and woman's role, one forgets that the real business of America is business. But the perpetuation of housewifery, the growth of the feminine mystique, makes sense (and dollars) when one realizes that women are the chief customers of American business. Somehow, somewhere, someone must have figured out that women will buy more things if they are kept in the underused, nameless-yearning, energy-to-get-rid-of state of being housewives.

It was not an economic conspiracy directed against women. It was a byproduct of our general confusion lately of means with ends; just something that happened to women when the business of producing and selling and investing in business for profit – which is merely the way our economy is organized to serve man's needs efficiently –

began to be confused with the purpose of our nation, the end of life itself. No more surprising, the subversion of women's lives in America to the ends of business, than the subversion of the sciences of human behaviour to the business of deluding women about their real needs. It would take a clever economist to figure out what would keep our affluent economy going if the housewife market began to fall off, just as an economist would have to figure out what to do if there were no threat of war.

It is easy to see why it happened. I learned *how* it happened when I went to see a man who is paid approximately a million dollars a year for his professional services in manipulating the emotions of American women to serve the needs of business. This particular man got in on the ground floor of the hidden-persuasion business in 1945, and kept going. The headquarters of his institute for motivational manipulation is a baronial mansion in upper Westchester. The walls of a ballroom two storeys high are filled with steel shelves holding a thousand-odd studies for business and industry, 300,000 individual 'depth interviews', mostly with American housewives.[2]

He let me see what I wanted, said I could use anything that was not confidential to a specific company. Nothing there for anyone to hide, to feel guilty about – only, in page after page of those depth studies, a shrewd cheerful awareness of the empty, purposeless, uncreative, even sexually joyless lives that most American house-wives lead. In his own unabashed terms, this most helpful of hidden persuaders showed me the function served by keeping American women housewives – the reservoir that their lack of identity, lack of purpose, creates, to be manipulated into dollars at the point of purchase.

Properly manipulated ('if you are not afraid of that word,' he said), American housewives can be given the sense of identity, pur-pose, creativity, the self-realization, even the sexual joy they lack – by the buying of things. I suddenly realized the significance of the boast that women wield 75 per cent of the purchasing power in America. I suddenly saw American women as *victims* of that ghastly gift, that power at the point of purchase. The insights he shared with me so liberally revealed many things . . .

The dilemma of business was spelled out in a survey made in 1945 for the publisher of a leading women's magazine on the attitudes of women towards electrical appliances. The message was considered of interest to all the companies that, with the war about to end, were going to have to make consumer sales take the place of war contracts. It was a study of 'the psychology of housekeeping'; 'a woman's attitude towards housekeeping appliances cannot be separated from her attitude towards homemaking in general,' it warned.

On the basis of a national sample of 4,500 wives (middle-class, high-school or college-educated), American women were divided into three categories: 'The True Housewife Type', 'The Career Woman' and 'The Balanced Homemaker'. While 51 per cent of the women then fitted 'The True Housewife Type' ('From the psychological point of view, housekeeping is this woman's dominating interest. She takes the utmost pride and satisfaction in maintaining a comfortable and well-run home for her family. Consciously or subconsciously, she feels that she is indispensable and that no one else can take over her job. She has little, if any, desire for a position outside the home, and if she has one it is through force of circumstances or necessity'), it was apparent that this group was diminishing, and probably would continue to do so as new fields, interests, education were now open to women.

The largest market for appliances, however, was this 'True Housewife' – though she had a certain 'reluctance' to accept new devices that had to be recognized and overcome. ('She may even fear that they [appliances] will render unnecessary the old-fashioned way of doing things that has always suited her.') After all, housework was the justification for her whole existence. ('I don't think there is any way to make housework easier for myself,' one True Housewife said, 'because I don't believe that a machine can take the place of hard work.')

The second type – 'The Career Woman' or Would-Be Career Woman – was a minority, but an extremely 'unhealthy' one from the sellers' standpoint; advertisers were warned that it would be to their advantage not to let this group get any larger. For such women, though not necessarily job-holders, 'do not believe that a woman's place is primarily in the home'. ('Many in this group have never actually worked, but their attitude is: "I think housekeeping is a horrible waste of time. If my youngsters were old enough and I were free to leave the house, I would use my time to better advantage. If my family's meals and laundry could be taken care of, I would be delighted to go out and get a job."') The point to bear in mind regarding career women, the study said, is that, while they buy modern appliances, they are not the ideal type of customer. *They are too critical.*

The third type – 'The Balanced Homemaker' – is 'from the market standpoint, the ideal type'. She has some outside interests, or has held a job before turning exclusively to homemaking; she 'readily accepts' the help mechanical appliances can give – but 'does not expect them to do the impossible' because she needs to use her own executive ability 'in managing a well-run household'.

The moral of the study was explicit:

> Since the Balanced Homemaker represents the market with the greatest future potential, it would be to the advantage of the appliance manufacturer to make more and more women aware of the desirability of belonging to this group. Educate them through advertising that it is possible to have outside interests and become alert to wider intellectual influences (without becoming a Career Woman). The art of good homemaking should be the goal of every normal woman.

The problem – which, if recognized at that time by one hidden persuader for the home-appliance industry, was surely recognized by others with products for the home – was that 'a whole new generation of women is being educated to do work outside the home. Furthermore, an increased desire for emancipation is evident.' The solution, quite simply, was to encourage them to be 'modern' housewives. The Career or Would-Be Career Woman who frankly dislikes cleaning, dusting, ironing, washing clothes, is less interested in a new wax, a new soap powder. Unlike 'The True Housewife' and the 'Balanced Homemaker' who prefer to have sufficient appliances and do the housework themselves, the Career Woman would 'prefer servants – housework takes too much time and energy'. She buys appliances, however, whether or not she has servants, but she is 'more likely to complain about the service they give', and to be 'harder to sell'.

It was too late – impossible – to turn these modern could-or-would-be career women back into True Housewives, but the study pointed out, in 1945, the potential for Balanced Housewifery – the home career. Let them 'want to have their cake and eat it too . . . save time, have more comfort, avoid dirt and disorder, have mechanized supervision, yet not want to give up the feeling of personal achievement and pride in a well-run household, which comes from "doing it yourself". As one young housewife said: "It's nice to be modern – it's like running a factory in which you have all the latest machinery." '

But it was not an easy job, either for business or advertisers. New gadgets that were able to do almost all the housework crowded the market; increased ingenuity was needed to give American women that 'feeling of achievement', and yet keep housework their main purpose in life. Education, independence, growing individuality, everything that made them ready for other purposes had constantly to be countered, channelled back to the home.

The manipulator's services became increasingly valuable. In later surveys, he no longer interviewed professional women; they were not at home during the day. The women in his samples were deliberately True or Balanced Housewives, the new suburban housewives. Household and consumer products are, after all, geared to women; 75 per cent of all consumer advertising budgets is spent to appeal to women; that is, to housewives, the women who are available during the day to be interviewed, the women with the time for shopping. Naturally, his depth interviews, projective tests, 'living laboratories', were designed to impress his clients, but more often than not they contained the shrewd insights of a skilled social scientist, insights that could be used with profit.

He wrote in one report, for example:

> Every effort must be made to sell X Mix, as a base upon which the woman's creative effort is used.
>
> The appeal should emphasize the fact that X Mix aids the woman in expressing her creativity because it takes the drudgery away. At the same time, stress should be laid upon the cooking manipulations, the fun that goes with them, permitting you to feel that X Mix baking is real baking.

But the dilemma again: how to make her spend money on the mix that takes some of the drudgery out of baking by telling her 'she can utilize her energy where it really counts' – and yet keep her from being 'too busy to bake'? ('I don't use the mix because I don't do any baking at all. It's too much trouble. I live in a sprawled-out apartment and what with keeping it clean and looking after my child and my part-time job, I don't have time for baking.') What to do about their 'feeling of disappointment' when the biscuits come out of the oven, and they're really only bread and there is no feeling of creative achievement? ('Why should I bake my own biscuits when there are so many good things on the market that just need to be heated up? It just doesn't make any sense at all to go through all the trouble of mixing your own and then greasing the tin and baking them.') What to do when the woman doesn't get the feeling her mother got, when the cake *had* to be made from scratch? ('The way my mother made them, you had to sift the flour yourself and add the eggs and the butter and you knew you'd really made something you could be proud of.')

The problem can be handled, the report assured:

> By using X Mix the woman can prove herself as a wife and mother, not only by baking, but by spending more time with her family. . . . Of course, it must also be made clear that homebaked foods are in every way preferable to bakery-shop foods . . .

Above all, give X Mix 'a therapeutic value' by downplaying the easy recipes, emphasizing instead 'the stimulating effort of baking'. From an advertising viewpoint, this means stressing that 'with X Mix in the home, you will be a different woman . . . a happier woman.'

Further, the client was told that a phrase in his ad, 'and you make that cake the easiest, laziest way there is,' evoked a 'negative response' in American housewives – it hit too close to their 'underlying guilt'. ('Since they never feel that they are really exerting sufficient effort, it is certainly wrong to tell them that baking with X Mix is the lazy way.') Supposing, he suggested, that this devoted wife and mother behind the kitchen stove, anxiously preparing a cake or pie for her husband or children 'is simply indulging her own hunger for sweets'. The very fact that baking is work for the housewife helps her dispel any doubts that she might have about her real motivations.

But there are even ways to manipulate the housewives' guilt, the report said:

> It might be possible to suggest through advertising that not to take advantage of all 12 uses of X Mix is to limit your efforts to give pleasure to your family. A transfer of guilt might be achieved. Rather than feeling guilty about using X Mix for dessert food, the woman would be made to feel guilty if she doesn't take advantage of this opportunity to give her family 12 different and delicious treats. 'Don't waste your skill; don't limit yourself.'

By the mid-fifties, the surveys reported with pleasure that the Career Woman ('the woman who clamoured for equality – almost for identity in every sphere of life, the woman who reacted to "domestic slavery" with indignation and vehemence') was gone, replaced by the 'less worldly, less sophisticated' woman whose activity in PTA gives her 'broad contacts with the world outside her home', but who 'finds in housework a medium of expression for her femininity and individuality'. She's not like the old-fashioned self-sacrificing house-wife; she considers herself the equal of man. But she still feels 'lazy, neglectful, haunted by guilt feelings' because she doesn't have enough work to do.

> After an initial resistance, she now tends to accept instant coffee, frozen foods, precooked foods, and labour-saving items as part of her routine. But she needs a justification and she finds it in the thought that 'by using frozen foods I'm freeing myself to accomplish other important tasks as a modern mother and wife.'
>
> Creativeness is the modern woman's dialectical answer to the problem of her changed position in the household. Thesis: I'm a housewife. Antithesis: I hate drudgery. Synthesis: I'm creative!
>
> This means essentially that even though the housewife may buy canned food, for instance, and thus save time and effort, she doesn't let it go at that. She has a great need for 'doctoring up' the can and thus prove her personal participation and her concern with giving satisfaction to her family.

The feeling of creativeness also serves another purpose: it is an outlet for the liberated talents, the better taste, the freer imagination, the greater initiative of the modern woman. It permits her to use at home *all the faculties that she would display in an outside career.*

The yearning for creative opportunities and moments is a major aspect of buying motivations.

The only trouble, the surveys warned, is that she 'tries to use her own mind and her own judgement. She is fast getting away from judging by collective or majority standards. She is developing independent standards.' ('Never mind the neighbours. I don't want to "live up" to them or compare myself to them at every turn.') She can't always be reached now with 'keep up with the Joneses' – the advertiser must appeal to her *own* need to live.

Appeal to this thirst. . . . Tell her that you are adding more zest, more enjoyment to her life, that it is within her reach now to taste new experiences and that she is entitled to taste these experiences. Even more positively, you should convey that you are giving her 'lessons in living'.

'House cleaning should be fun,' the manufacturer of a certain cleaning device was advised. Even though his product was, perhaps, less efficient than the vacuum cleaner, it let the housewife use more of her own energy in the work. Further, it let the housewife have the illusion that she has become 'a professional, an expert in determining which cleaning tools to use for specific jobs'.

This professionalization is a psychological defence of the housewife against being a general 'cleaner-upper' and menial servant for her family in a day and age of general work emancipation.

The role of expert serves a two-fold emotional function: (1) it helps the housewife achieve status, and (2) she moves beyond the orbit of her home, into the world of modern science, in her search for new and better ways of doing things.

As a result, there has never been a more favourable psychological climate for household appliances and products. The modern housewife . . . is actually aggressive in her efforts to find those household products which, in her expert opinion, really meet her need. This trend accounts for the popularity of different waxes and polishes for different materials in the home, for the growing use of floor polishers, and for the variety of mops and cleaning implements for floors and walls.

The difficulty is to give her the 'sense of achievement', of 'ego enhancement', she has been persuaded to seek in the housewife 'profession', when, in actuality, 'her time-consuming task, house-keeping, is not only endless, it is a task for which society hires the lowliest, least-trained, most trod-upon individuals and groups. . . . Anyone with a strong enough back (and a small enough brain) can do these menial chores.' But even this difficulty can be manipulated to sell her more things:

One of the ways that the housewife raises her own prestige as a cleaner of her home is through the use of specialized products for specialized tasks. . . .

When she uses one product for washing clothes, a second for dishes, a third for walls, a fourth for floors, a fifth for venetian blinds, etc., rather than an all-purpose cleaner, she feels less like an unskilled labourer, more like an engineer, an expert.

A second way of raising her own stature is to 'do things my way' – to establish an expert's role for herself by creating her own 'tricks of the trade'. For example, she may 'always put a bit of bleach in all my washing – even coloured, to make them *really* clean'!

Help her to 'justify her menial task by building up her role as the protector of her family – the killer of millions of microbes and germs', this report advised. 'Emphasize her kingpin role in the family . . . help her be an expert rather than a menial worker . . . make housework a matter of knowledge and skill, rather than a matter of brawn and dull, unremitting effort.' An effective way of doing this is to bring out a *new* product. For, it seems, there's a growing wave of housewives 'who look forward to new products which not only decrease their daily work load, but actually engage their emotional and intellectual interest in the world of scientific development outside the home'.

The question of letting the woman use her mind and even participate in science through housework is, however, not without its drawbacks. Science should not relieve housewives of too much drudgery; it must concentrate instead on creating the *illusion* of that sense of achievement that housewives seem to need.

To prove this point, 250 housewives were given a depth test: they were asked to choose among four imaginary methods of cleaning. The first was a completely automatic dust-and-dirt-removal system which operated continuously like a home-heating system. The second, the housewife had to press a button to start. The third was portable; she had to carry it around and point it at an area to remove the dirt. The fourth was a brand new, modern object with which she could sweep the dirt away herself. The housewives spoke up in favour of this last appliance. If it 'appears new, modern' she would rather have the one that lets her work herself, this report said. 'One compelling reason is her desire to be a participant, not just a button-pusher.' As one housewife remarked, 'As for some magical push-button cleaning system, well, what would happen to my exercise, my feeling of accomplishment, and what would I do with my mornings?'

This fascinating study incidentally revealed that a certain electronic cleaning appliance – long considered one of our great labour-savers – actually made 'housekeeping more difficult than it need be'. From the response of 80 per cent of those housewives, it seemed that once a woman got this appliance going, she 'felt compelled to do cleaning that wasn't really necessary'. The electronic appliance actually dictated the extent and type of cleaning to be done.

Should the housewife then be encouraged to go back to that simple cheap sweeper that let her clean only as much as she felt necessary? No, said the report, of course not. Simply give that old-fashioned sweeper the 'status' of the electronic appliance as a 'labour-saving necessity' for the modern housewife 'and then indicate that the modern homemaker would, naturally, own both'.

No one, not even the depth researchers, denied that housework was endless, and its boring repetition just did not give that much satisfaction, did not require that much vaunted expert knowledge. But the endlessness of it all was an advantage from the seller's point of view. The problem was to keep at bay the underlying realization which was lurking dangerously in 'thousands of depth interviews which we have conducted for dozens of different kinds of house-cleaning products' – the realization that, as one housewife said, 'It stinks! I have to do it, so I do it. It's a necessary evil, that's all.' What to do? For one thing, put out more and more products, make the directions more complicated, make it really necessary for the housewife to 'be an expert'. (Washing clothes, the report advised, must become more than a matter of throwing clothes into a machine and pouring in soap. Garments must be carefully sorted, one load given treatment A, a second load treatment B, some washed by hand. The housewife can then 'take great pride in knowing just which of the arsenal of products to use on each occasion'.)

Capitalize, the report continued, on housewives' 'guilt over the hidden dirt' so she will rip her house to shreds in a 'deep cleaning' operation, which will give her a 'sense of completeness' for a few weeks. ('The times of thorough cleaning are the points at which she is most willing to try new products and "deep clean" advertising holds out the promise of completion.')

The seller must also stress the joys of completing each separate task, remembering that 'nearly all housekeepers, even those who thoroughly detest their job, paradoxically find escape from their endless fate by accepting it – by "throwing myself into it," as she says.'

> Losing herself in her work – surrounded by all the implements, creams, powders, soaps, she forgets for a time how soon she will have to re-do the task. . . . she seizes the moment of completion of a task as a moment of pleasure as pure as if she had just finished a masterpiece of art which would stand as a monument to her credit forever.

This is the kind of creative experience the seller of things can give the housewife. In one housewife's own words:

> I don't like housework at all. I'm a lousy houseworker. But once in a while I get pepped up and I'll really go to town. . . . When I have some new kind of cleaning material – like when Glass Wax first came out or those silicone furniture polishes – I got a real kick out of it, and I went through the house shining everything. I like to see the things shine. I feel so good when I see the bathroom just glistening.

And so the manipulator advised:

> Identify your product with the physical and spiritual rewards
> she derives from the almost religious feeling of basic security
> provided by her home. Talk about her 'light, happy, peaceful
> feelings'; her 'deep sense of achievement'. . . . But remember
> she doesn't really want praise for the sake of praise . . . also
> remember that her mood is not simply 'gay'. She is tired and a
> bit solemn. Superficially cheerful adjectives or colours will not
> reflect her feelings. She will react much more favourably to
> simple, warm and sincere messages.

In the fifties came the revolutionary discovery of the teenage
market. Teenagers and young marrieds began to figure prominently
in the surveys. It was discovered that young wives, who had only
been to high school and had never worked, were more 'insecure', less
independent, easier to sell. These young people could be told that,
by buying the right things, they could achieve middle-class status,
without work or study. The keep-up-with-the-Joneses sell would
work again; the individuality and independence which American
women had been getting from education and work outside the home
was not such a problem with the teenage brides. In fact, the surveys
said, if the pattern of 'happiness through things' could be established
when these women were young enough, they could be safely
encouraged to go out and get a part-time job to help their husbands
pay for all the things they buy. The main point now was to convince
the teenagers that 'happiness through things' is no longer the
prerogative of the rich or the talented; it can be enjoyed by all, if
they learn 'the right way', the way the others do it, if they learn the
embarrassment of being different.

In the words of one of these reports:

> 49 per cent of the new brides were teenagers, and more girls
> marry at the age of 18 than at any other age. This early family
> formation yields a larger number of young people who are on
> the threshold of their own responsibilities and decision-making
> in purchases. . . .
> But the most important fact is of a psychological nature:
> marriage today is not only the culmination of a romantic

attachment; more consciously and more clear-headedly than in the past, it is also a decision to create a partnership in establishing a comfortable home, equipped with a great number of desirable products.

In talking to scores of young couples and brides-to-be, we found that, as a rule, their conversations and dreams centred to a very large degree around their future homes and their furnishings, around shopping 'to get an idea', around discussing the advantages and disadvantages of various products. . . .

The modern bride is deeply convinced of the unique value of married love, of the possibilities of finding real happiness in marriage and of fulfilling her personal destiny in it and through it.

But the engagement period today is a romantic, dreamy and heady period only to a limited extent. It is probably safe to say that the period of engagement tends to be a rehearsal of the material duties and responsibilities of marriage. While waiting for the nuptials, couples work hard, put aside money for definite purchases, or even begin buying on an instalment plan.

What is the deeper meaning of this new combination of an almost religious belief in the importance and beauty of married life on the one hand, and the product-centred outlook, on the other? . . .

The modern bride seeks as a conscious goal that which in many cases her grandmother saw as a blind fate and her mother as slavery: to belong to a man, to have a home and children of her own, to choose among all possible careers the career of wife-mother-homemaker.

All these meanings she seeks in her marriage, even her fear that she will be 'left behind' can be channelled into the purchase of products. For example, a manufacturer of sterling silver, a product that is very difficult to sell, was told:

Reassure her that only with sterling can she be fully secure in her new role . . . it symbolizes her success as a modern woman. Above all, dramatize the fun and pride that derive from the job of cleaning silver. Stimulate the pride of achievement. 'How much pride you get from the brief task that's so much fun . . .'

Concentrate on the very young teenage girls, this report further advised. The young ones will want what 'the others' want, even if their mothers don't. ('As one of our teenagers said: "All the gang has started their own sets of sterling. We're real keen about it – compare patterns and go through the ads together. My own family never had any sterling and they think I'm showing off when I spend my money on it – they think plated's just as good. But the kids think they're way off base."') Get them in schools, churches, sororities, social clubs; get them through home-economics teachers, group leaders, teenage TV programmes, and teenage advertising. 'This is the big market of the future and word-of-mouth advertising, along with group pressure, is not only the most potent influence but, in the absence of tradition, a most necessary one.'

As for the more independent older wife, that unfortunate tendency to use materials that require little care – stainless steel, plastic dishes, paper napkins – can be met by making her feel guilty about the effects on the children. ('As one young wife told us: "I'm out of the house all day long, so I can't prepare and serve meals the way I want to. I don't like it that way – my husband and the children deserve a better break. Sometimes I think it'd be better if we tried to get along on one salary and have a real home life but there are always so many things we need."') Such guilt, the report maintained, can be used to make her see the product, silver, as a means of holding the family together; it gives 'added psychological value'. What's more, the product can even fill the housewife's need for identity: 'Suggest that it becomes truly a part of *you*, reflecting *you*. Do not be afraid to suggest mystically that sterling will adapt itself to any house and any person.'

The fur industry is in trouble, another survey reported, because young high school and college girls equate fur coats with 'uselessness' and 'a kept woman'. Again the advice was to get to the very young before these unfortunate connotations have formed. ('By introducing youngsters to positive fur experiences, the probabilities of easing their way into garment purchasing in their teens is enhanced.') Point out that 'the wearing of a fur garment actually establishes femininity and sexuality for a woman.' ('It's the kind of thing a girl looks forward to. It means something. It's feminine.' 'I'm bringing my daughter up right. She always wants to put on "mommy's coat". She'll want them. She's a real girl.') But keep in mind that 'Mink has contributed a negative feminine symbolism to the whole fur market.' Unfortunately, two out of three women felt mink-wearers were 'predatory . . . exploitative . . . dependent . . . socially non-productive . . . '

And so fur's 'ego-orientation' must be reduced and replaced with the new femininity of the housewife, for whom ego-orientation must be translated into togetherness, family-orientation.

> Begin to create the feeling that fur is a necessity – a delightful necessity . . . thus providing the consumer with moral permission to purchase something she now feels is ego-oriented. . . . Give fur femininity a broader character, developing some of the following status and prestige symbols . . . an emotionally happy woman . . . wife and mother who wins the affection and respect of her husband and her children because of the kind of person she is, and the kind of role she performs. . . .
>
> Place furs in a family setting; show the pleasure and admiration of a fur garment derived by family members, husband and children; their pride in their mother's appearance, in her ownership of a fur garment. Develop fur garments as 'family' gifts – enable the whole family to enjoy that garment at Christmas, etc., thus reducing its ego-orientation for the owner and eliminating her guilt over her alleged self-indulgence.

Thus, the only way that the young housewife was supposed to express herself, and not feel guilty about it, was in buying products for the home and family. Any creative urges she may have should also be home-and-family oriented, as still another survey reported to the home-sewing industry.

> Such activities as sewing achieve a new meaning and a new status. Sewing is no longer associated with absolute need. . . . Moreover, with the moral elevation of home-oriented activities, sewing, along with cooking, gardening, and home decorating – is recognized as a means of expressing creativity and individuality and also as a means of achieving the 'quality' which a new taste level dictates.

The women who sew, this survey discovered, are the active, energetic, intelligent modern housewives, the new home-oriented modern American women, who have a great unfulfilled need to create, and achieve, and realize their own individuality – which must be filled by some home activity. The big problem for the home-sewing industry was that the 'image' of sewing was too 'dull'; somehow it didn't achieve the feeling of creating something important. In selling their products, the industry must emphasize the 'lasting creativeness' of sewing.

But even sewing can't be too creative, too individual, according to the advice offered to one pattern manufacturer. His patterns required some intelligence to follow, left quite a lot of room for individual expression, and the manufacturer was in trouble for that very reason; his patterns implied that a woman 'would know what she likes and would probably have definite ideas'. He was advised to widen this 'far too limited fashion personality' and get one with 'fashion conformity' – appeal to the 'fashion-insecure woman', 'the conformist element in fashion', who feels 'it is not smart to be dressed too differently'.

Time and time again, the surveys shrewdly analysed the needs, and even the secret frustrations of the American housewife; and each time, if these needs were properly manipulated, she could be induced to buy more 'things'. In 1957, a survey told the department stores that their role in this new world was not only to 'sell' the housewife but to satisfy her need for 'education'.

Most women have not only a material need, but a psychological compulsion to visit department stores. They live in comparative isolation. Their vista and experiences are limited. They know that there is a vaster life beyond their horizon and they fear that life will pass them by.

Department stores break down that isolation. The woman entering a department store suddenly has the feeling she knows what is going on in the world. Department stores, more than magazines, TV, or any other medium of mass communication, are most women's main source of information about the various aspects of life. . . .

There are many needs that the department store must fill, this report continued. For one, the housewife's 'need to learn and to advance in life'.

We symbolize our social position by the objects with which we surround ourselves. A woman whose husband was making $6,000 a few years ago and is making $10,000 now needs to learn a whole new set of symbols. Department stores are her best teachers of this subject.

For another, there is the need for achievement, which for the new modern housewife is primarily filled by a 'bargain'.

We have found that in our economy of abundance, preoccupation with prices is not so much a financial as a psychological need for the majority of women. . . . Increasingly a 'bargain' means not that 'I can now buy something which I could not afford at a higher price'; it mainly means 'I'm doing a good job as a housewife; I'm contributing to the welfare of the family just as my husband does when he works and brings home the pay cheque.'

The price itself hardly matters, the report said:

Since buying is only the climax of a complicated relationship, based to a large extent on the woman's yearning to know how to be a more attractive woman, a better housewife, a superior mother, etc., use this motivation in all your promotion and advertising. Take every opportunity to explain how your store will help her fulfil her most cherished roles in life. . . .
  If the stores are women's school of life, ads are the textbooks. They have an inexhaustible avidity for these ads which give them the illusion that they are in contact with what is going on in the world of inanimate objects, objects through which they express so much of so many of their drives. . . .

Again, in 1957, a survey very correctly reported that despite the 'many positive aspects' of the 'new home-centred era', unfortunately too many needs were now centred on the home – that home was not able to fill. A cause for alarm? No indeed; even these needs are grist for manipulation.

The family is not always the psychological pot of gold at the end of the rainbow of promise of modern life as it has sometimes been represented. In fact, psychological demands are being made upon the family today which it cannot fulfil. . . .

Fortunately for the producers and advertisers of America (and also for the family and the psychological well-being of our citizens) much of this gap may be filled, and is being filled, by the acquisition of consumer goods.

Hundreds of products fulfil a whole set of psychological functions that producers and advertisers should know of and use in the development of more effective sales approaches. Just as producing once served as an outlet for social tension, now consumption serves the same purpose.

'The frustrated need for privacy in the family life', in this era of 'togetherness', was another secret wish uncovered in a depth survey. This need, however, might be used to sell a second car. . . .

In addition to the car the whole family enjoys together, the car for the husband and wife separately – 'Alone in the car, one may get the breathing spell one needs so badly and may come to consider the car as one's castle, or the instrument of one's reconquered privacy.' Or 'individual' 'personal' toothpaste, soap, shampoo.

Another survey reported that there was a puzzling 'desexualization of married life' despite the great emphasis on marriage and family and sex. The problem: what can supply what the report diagnosed as a 'missing sexual spark'? The solution: the report advised sellers to 'put the libido back into advertising'. Despite the feeling that our manufacturers are trying to sell everything through sex, sex as found on TV commercials and ads in national magazines is too tame, the report said, too narrow. 'Consumerism' is desexing the American libido because it 'has failed to reflect the powerful life forces in every individual which range far beyond the relationship between the sexes'.

Most modern advertising reflects and grossly exaggerates our present national tendency to downgrade, simplify and water down the passionate, turbulent and electrifying aspects of the life urges of mankind. . . . No one suggests that advertising can or should become obscene or salacious. The trouble lies with the fact that through its timidity and lack of imagination, it faces the danger of becoming libido-poor and consequently unreal, inhuman and tedious.

How to put the libido back, restore the lost spontaneity, drive, love of life, the individuality, that sex in America seems to lack? In an absent-minded moment, the report concludes that 'love of life, as of the other sex, should remain unsoiled by exterior motives . . . let the wife be more than a housewife . . . a woman . . .'

One day, having immersed myself in the varied insights these reports have been giving American advertisers for the last fifteen years, I was invited to have lunch with the man who runs this motivational research operation. He had been so helpful in showing me the commercial forces behind the feminine mystique, perhaps I could be helpful to him. Naïvely I asked why, since he found it so difficult to give women a true feeling of creativeness and achievement in housework, and tried to assuage their guilt and disillusion and frustrations by getting them to buy more 'things' – why didn't he encourage them to buy things for all they were worth, so they would have time to get out of the home and pursue truly creative goals in the outside world?

'But we have helped her rediscover the home as the expression of her creativeness,' he said. 'We help her think of the modern home as the artist's studio, the scientist's laboratory. Besides,' he shrugged, 'most of the manufacturers we deal with are producing things which have to do with homemaking.'

'In a free enterprise economy,' he went on, 'we have to develop the need for new products. And to do that we have to liberate women to desire these new products. We help them rediscover that homemaking is more creative than to compete with men. This can be manipulated. We sell them what they ought to want, speed up the unconscious, move it along. The big problem is to liberate the woman not to be afraid of what is going to happen to her, if she doesn't have to spend so much time cooking, cleaning.'

'That's what I mean,' I said. 'Why doesn't the pie-mix ad tell the woman she could use the time saved to be an astronomer?'

'It wouldn't be too difficult,' he replied. 'A few images – the astronomer gets her man, the astronomer as the heroine, make it glamorous for a woman to be an astronomer . . . but no,' he shrugged again. 'The client would be too frightened. He wants to sell pie mix. The woman has to want to stay in the kitchen. The manufacturer wants to intrigue her back into the kitchen – and we show him how to do it the right way. If he tells her that all she can be is a wife and mother, she will spit in his face.'

The motivational researchers must be given credit for their insights into the reality of the housewife's life and needs – a reality that often escaped their colleagues in academic sociology and therapeutic psychology, who saw women through the Freudian-functional veil. To their own profit, and that of their clients, the manipulators discovered that millions of supposedly happy American housewives have complex needs which home-and-family, love-and-children, cannot fill. But by a morality that goes beyond the dollar, the manipulators are guilty of using their insights to sell women things which, no matter how ingenious, will never satisfy those increasingly desperate needs. They are guilty of persuading housewives to stay at home, mesmerized in front of a television set, their nonsexual human needs unnamed, unsatisfied, drained by the sexual sell into the buying of things.

The manipulators and their clients in American business can hardly be accused of creating the feminine mystique. But they are the most powerful of its perpetuators; it is their millions which blanket the land with persuasive images, flattering the American housewife, diverting her guilt and disguising her growing sense of emptiness. They have done this so successfully, employing the techniques and concepts of modern social science, and transposing them into those deceptively simple, clever, outrageous ads and commercials, that an observer of the American scene today accepts as fact that the great majority of American women have no ambition other than to be housewives. If they are not solely responsible for sending women home, they are surely responsible for keeping them there.

> Love is said in many ways. It's giving and accepting. It's protecting and selecting . . . knowing what's safest for those you love. Their bathroom tissue is Scott tissue always. . . . Now in four colours and white.

How skilfully they divert her need for achievement into sexual fantasies which promise her eternal youth, dulling her sense of passing time:

Does she . . . or doesn't she? She's as full of fun as her kids –
and just as fresh looking! Her naturalness, the way her hair
sparkles and catches the light – as though she's found the secret
of making time stand still. And in a way she has. . . .

With increasing skill, the ads glorify her 'role' as an American
housewife – knowing that her very lack of identity in that role will
make her fall for whatever they are selling.

Who is she? She gets as excited as her six-year-old about the
opening of school. She reckons her days in trains met, lunches
packed, fingers bandaged, and 1,001 details. She could be you,
needing a special kind of clothes for your busy, rewarding life.

Are you this woman? Giving your kids the fun and advantages
you want for them? Taking them places and helping them do
things? Taking the part that's expected of you in church and
community affairs . . . developing your talents so you'll be more
interesting? You can be the woman you yearn to be with a
Plymouth all your own. . . . Go where you want, when you want
in a beautiful Plymouth that's yours and nobody else's . . .

But a softer toilet paper does not make a woman a better wife or
mother, even if she thinks that's what she needs to be. Dyeing her
hair cannot stop time; buying a Plymouth will not give her a new
identity; smoking a Marlboro will not get her an invitation to bed,
even if that's what she thinks she wants. But those unfulfilled promises can keep her endlessly hungry for things, keep her from ever
knowing what she really needs or wants.

A full-page ad in the *New York Times*, 10 June 1962, was
'Dedicated to the woman who spends a lifetime living up to her
potential!' Under the picture of a beautiful woman, adorned by
evening dress and jewels and two handsome children, it said: 'The
only totally integrated programme of nutrient make-up and skin
care – designed to lift a woman's good looks to their absolute peak.
The woman who uses "Ultima" feels a deep sense of fulfilment.
A new kind of pride. For this luxurious Cosmetic Collection is the
ultimate . . . beyond it there is nothing.'

It all seems so ludicrous when you understand what they are up to. Perhaps the housewife has no one but herself to blame if she lets the manipulators flatter or threaten her into buying things that neither fill her family's needs nor her own. But if the ads and commercials are a clear case of *caveat emptor*, the same sexual sell disguised in the editorial content of a magazine or a television programme is both less ridiculous and more insidious. Here the housewife is often an unaware victim. I have written for some of the magazines in which the sexual sell is inextricably linked with the editorial content. Consciously or unconsciously, the editors know what the advertiser wants.

> The heart of X magazine is service – complete service to the whole woman who is the American homemaker; service in all the areas of greatest interest to advertisers, who are also businessmen. It delivers to the advertiser a strong concentration of serious, conscientious, dedicated homemakers. Women more interested in the home and products for the home. Women more willing and able to pay . . .

A memo need never be written, a sentence need never be spoken at an editorial conference; the men and women who make the editorial decisions often compromise their own very high standards in the interests of the advertising dollar. Often, as a former editor of *McCall's* recently revealed,[3] the advertiser's influence is less than subtle. The kind of home pictured in the 'service' pages is dictated in no uncertain terms by the boys over in advertising.

The real crime, no matter how profitable for the American economy, is the callous and growing acceptance of the manipulator's advice 'to get them young' – the television commercials that children sing or recite even before they learn to read, the big beautiful ads almost as easy as 'Look, Sally, Look', the magazines deliberately designed to turn teenage girls into housewife buyers of things before they grow up to be women:

> She reads X Magazine from beginning to end. . . . She learns how to market, to cook and to sew and everything else a young woman should know. She plans her wardrobe round X Magazine's clothes, heeds X Magazine's counsel on beauty and beaux . . . consults X Magazine for the latest teen fads . . .

and oh, how she buys from those X Magazine ads! Buying habits start in X Magazine. It's easier to START a habit than to STOP one! (Learn how X Magazine's unique publication, X Magazine-at-school, carries your advertising into high-school home-economics classrooms).

Like a primitive culture which sacrificed little girls to its tribal gods, we sacrifice our girls to the feminine mystique, grooming them ever more efficiently through the sexual sell to become consumers of the things to whose profitable sale our nation is dedicated. Two ads recently appeared in a national news magazine, geared not to teenage girls but to executives who produce and sell things. One of them showed the picture of a boy:

I am *so* going to the moon . . . and you can't go, 'cause you're a girl! Children are growing faster today, their interests can cover such a wide range – from roller skates to rockets. X company too has grown, with a broad spectrum of electronic products for world-wide governmental, industrial and space application.

The other showed the face of a girl:

Should a gifted child grow up to be a housewife? Educational experts estimate that the gift of high intelligence is bestowed upon only one out of every 50 children in our nation. When that gifted child is a girl, one question is inevitably asked: 'Will this rare gift be wasted if she becomes a housewife?' Let these gifted girls answer that question themselves. Over 90 per cent of them marry, and the majority find the job of being a house-wife challenging and rewarding enough to make full use of all their intelligence, time and energy. . . . In her daily roles of nurse, educator, economist and just plain housewife, she is constantly seeking ways to improve her family's life. . . . Millions of women – shopping for half the families in America – do so by saving X Stamps.

If that gifted girl-child grows up to be a housewife, can even the manipulator make supermarket stamps use all of her human intelligence, her human energy, in the century she may live while that boy goes to the moon?

Never underestimate the power of a woman, says another ad. But that power was and is underestimated in America. Or rather, it is only estimated in terms that can be manipulated at the point of purchase. Woman's human intelligence and energy do not really figure in. And yet, they exist, to be used for some higher purpose than housework and thing-buying – or wasted. Perhaps it is only a sick society, unwilling to face its own problems and unable to conceive of goals and purposes equal to the ability and knowledge of its members, that chooses to ignore the strength of women.

NOTES

* *The Feminine Mystique* (Harmondsworth: Penguin, 1963), p. 240.
1 Copyright © 1983, 1974, 1973, 1963 by Betty Friedan and Victor Gollancz Ltd.
2 The studies upon which this chapter is based were done by the Staff of the Institute for Motivational Research, directed by Dr Ernest Dichter. They were made available to me through the courtesy of Dr Dichter and his colleagues, and are on file at the Institute, in Croton-on-Hudson, New York.
3 Harrison Kinney, *Has Anybody Seen My Father?* (New York, 1960).

5

Christine Delphy
b.1944

'CONTINUITIES AND DISCONTINUITIES IN MARRIAGE AND DIVORCE' (1976) from *CLOSE TO HOME*

It is now relatively uncontroversial that housework is work. It wasn't in 1970 when Christine Delphy, a French sociologist, first published. But it is the postulate of a distinctive mode of production *in which housework is located which is the particular innovation of Delphy's analysis of women's oppression in contemporary industrial societies. The analysis is materialist, not only requiring that women's oppression be explained in terms of social organization, but also invoking the Marxist principle that social organization is determined by the relations involved in production.*

Delphy has argued that to conceive of all oppression as deriving from capitalist relations, and to conceive of the household only as a sphere of consumption, is to ignore the principal site of women's economic exploitation. She draws her examples from French rural life. It is quite arbitrary to count, say, the growing of wheat as production, and to exclude what happens when wheat products are prepared for consumption in the home. Household cooking is one of those forms of social activity that must be thought of as constituting the domestic mode of production. *The distinguishing mark of this mode is the appropriation by the (male) head of a household of the labour of other household members in exchange not for pay but for maintenance. And it is this mode which forms the basis of the present gender system and defines the two classes of participants, of men and women. (When we speak of men and women, we must remember that, by the terms of this analysis, they are not biological sexual categories* *that have been separated: the separation is constructed from biological sexual difference –* female *children are selected for the position of womanhood –* but the products of the separation are genuine [social] classes.)*

Many of Delphy's arguments are designed to uncover the mechanisms by which women's subordination is sustained by its economic base. Marriage is the key institution, because it is through marriage that the head of a family contracts domestic work. 'The appropriation and exploitation of their labour within marriage constitutes the oppression common to all women.' In explaining how the institution operates, Delphy demonstrates why we should think of the relations defined by wifehood as constituting the class of women. She shows, for instance, that the labour market, in which women do not participate as wives, plays a role in the exploitation of domestic work. And she shows, in the paper reprinted below, how woman who are not now, but were, wives still belong to the class of women-wives, and continue to suffer the exploitation which the domestic mode of production provides for.

Some of the paper is exploratory in tone, and is revealing of the process by which feminist theory provides new interpretations. 'The bits into which a phenomenon is broken down are not those of immediate perception.'* Thus in default of a feminist analysis, we see production as the process whose products are destined for the market, and we forget, for instance, household cooking. In default of a feminist analysis, we see divorce as simply the end of marriage; but when we have an account of the social relations that are constituted by the institution of marriage, this will enable us to see divorce, like marriage, as an institution for the extortion of unpaid work.

The process of providing new interpretations is visible on a small scale when Delphy makes two alternative suggestions. According to the first of these, the legal dissolution of a marriage contract does not affect an ex-husband's power to appropriate his ex-wife's labour, so that divorce is the continuation of the very same exploitative relations that marriage itself constitutes. According to the second, some features of the divorced woman's disadvantaged position derive directly from her responsibility for children. If this second suggestion is right, then the institutionalized obligation of women to provide childcare assumes centre-stage theoretically: it must be seen now as prior to the obligations imposed by the marriage contract itself, being what makes the appropriation of wives' labour possible. It is an important question whether this is the correct point of view (whether the phenomena become intelligible if we take it). But the difference of point of view between the two alternative suggestions is small compared with the shift that is introduced when we move from the established disciplines of social science and ethics to Delphy's materialist perspective.

For someone who is as thorough-going a materialist as Delphy is, ethics begins with the unmasking of ideology: the prevailing negative image of women cannot be destroyed until its supposed 'justification' has been uncovered in society's structures.

Studies devoted to divorce in the past have presented it as the sum of individual divorce situations, they have not defined it.[1,2] This is doubtless because the definition of divorce and its sociological significance are taken for granted; divorce means the breakdown and failure of marriage. These are the words used by the individuals concerned and sociologists have implicitly approached the problem from the same point of view. Even if they have apparently (but not always) refrained from direct value judgements and emotionally laden terms such as 'failure', they have still considered that the definition of divorce as the end of marriage, its revocation, or as the opposite of marriage, was a satisfactory one.

By contrast, a great deal of attention has been paid to the individual causes of divorce, and here it is evident that sociologists have not limited themselves to the reasons advanced by the protagonists, nor to their psychological 'motivations', but have included in their studies more objective data: for instance, social characteristics such as class origin and educational level. They have, however, always directed their attention to the 'couple' or the individual union. This method may have enabled them to pinpoint the differences (if indeed there are any) between couples and/or individuals who are divorced and those who are not, but it cannot teach us about the institution of divorce, for this is not just a multitude of individual accidents.

Were a similar method of analysis to be applied to marriage as has been with divorce (and indeed this has unfortunately often been the way sociologists have approached marriage, unlike anthropologists) we would look for – and would in all probability find – differences between married and non-married individuals. But marriage is an institution and merely to look at those who enter or leave it cannot shed light on the institution or why it exists. Similarly with divorce. Divorce is an institution which follows certain rules; it is codified and subject to control, ranging from implicit but unformulated social control to penal control.

Furthermore divorce is organically related to the institution of marriage. In an old American film the heroine asks what the grounds for divorce are in the state where she lives, and the lawyer replies, 'being married'. But I would go further and argue that not only is marriage the necessary condition for divorce, but also that divorce is not inconsistent with marriage. For while a divorce signifies the end of *a* marriage (marriage meaning here a particular union), it by no means implies the end of *marriage* as an institution. Divorce was not invented to destroy marriage since divorce is only necessary if marriage continues to exist. Indeed, it is often argued that the increase in the incidence of divorce can be interpreted as proof, not that the institution of marriage is sick, but on the contrary that it is thriving.

Further, divorce reveals and throws into relief certain institutional aspects of marriage, and it makes clear what is otherwise latent. Conversely marriage sheds light on divorce. Not only do certain aspects of marriage make the institution of divorce more intelligible; what is more noteworthy is that they are carried over and perpetuated in divorce.

The institution of marriage is, of course, complex and it is imperative to specify which aspect and which function is being studied. This paper will focus attention exclusively on the economic aspect of marriage, and to make clear what this means, I will first summarize briefly the approach that is used.

A Theory of Marriage

My proposition is that marriage is the institution by which unpaid work is extorted from a particular category of the population, women-wives.[3] This work is unpaid for it does not give rise to a wage but simply to upkeep. These very peculiar relations of production in a society that is defined by the sale of work (wage-labour) and products, are not determined by the type of work accomplished. Indeed they are not even limited to the production of household work and the raising of children, but extend to include *all* the things women (and also children) produce within the home, and in small-scale manufacturing, shopkeeping or farming, if the husband is a craftsman, tradesman or farmer, or various professional services if the husband is a doctor or lawyer, etc. The fact that domestic work is unpaid is not inherent to the particular type of work done, since when the same tasks are done *outside the family* they are paid for. The work acquires value – is remunerated – as long as the woman furnishes it to people to whom she *is not related or married*.

The valuelessness of domestic work performed by married women derives institutionally from the marriage contract, which is in fact a work contract. To be more precise, it is a contract by which the head of the family – the husband – appropriates all the work done in the family by his children, his younger siblings and especially by his wife, since he can sell it on the market as his own if he is, for example, a craftsman or farmer or doctor. Conversely, the wife's labour has no value because it cannot be put on the market, and it cannot be put on the market because of the contract by which her labour power is appropriated by her husband. Since the production intended for exchange – on the market – is accomplished outside the family in the wage-earning system, and since a married man sells his work and not a product in this system, the unpaid work of women cannot be incorporated in the production intended for exchange. It has therefore become limited to producing things which are intended for the family's internal use: domestic services and the raising of children.

Of course, with the increase of industrial production (and hence the number of wage-earners) and the decrease in family production, many women-wives now work for money, largely outside the home. They are none the less expected to do the household work. It would appear that their labour power is not totally appropriated since they divert a part of it into their paid work. Yet since they earn wages they provide their own upkeep. While one could, with a touch of bad faith, consider the marriage contract as an *exchange* contract when women work only within the household, with married women providing domestic work in exchange for upkeep, when married women earn their own living that illusion disappears altogether. It is clear then that their domestic work is given for nothing and the feature of appropriation is even more conspicuous.

However, the modes of appropriation differ depending on whether the woman has a paid job or not. When she does not, her total work power is appropriated, and this thus determines the type of work she will do – if her husband is a doctor she will make appointments for the patients; if he has a garage she will type the bills, etc. It also determines the nature of the relations of production under which she operates – her economic dependency and the non-value of her work – for while she may accomplish exactly the same tasks as her well-to-do neighbour, the upkeep she receives will be different if her husband's financial status is not as good. When she has a job, however, she recuperates part of her labour power in exchange for the accomplishment of a precise and specific type of work: housework. Legally any woman can now choose the second solution, although in France the law requiring a husband's authorization for his wife to work outside the home was abolished only some ten years ago. In point of fact, however, it seems reasonable to suggest that the only women who work outside the home are those whose husbands give their consent if they consider that they do not need all their wife's time. Equally, in France, the obligation to do housework is not written in any law; all that is said in the *Code Civil* is that the wife's contribution to the 'household charges' can be in kind if she has no dowry or independent income. But this obligation is inscribed negatively, so to speak, in the sense that failure to assume it is sanctioned.

Some of the possible sanctions are social worker intervention or divorce.[4] When social control agents intervene, whether it be in the person of the children's judge, the social worker or the court, and if a divorce ensues or the family budget comes under the control of the social workers, the obligations of marriage are officially expressed and in particular the differential duties of the husband and the wife. This precision and differentiation contrasts markedly with the vague legal formulation of marriage contracts, which suggest an apparent reciprocity in the respective duties of the partners (notably the wife's contribution in kind and the husband's in money are represented as having the same value and producing a similar status for both partners).

Conclusions Following from this Theory of Marriage

It is clear that the position of women on the labour maket and the discrimination that they suffer, are the result (and not the cause as certain authors would have us believe) of the marriage contract as we have described it.[5]

If we accept that marriage gives rise to the exploitation of women, then it would be logical to suppose that pressure is brought to bear on women to persuade them to marry. Of course there are various sorts of pressure – cultural, emotional-relational, and material-economic – and one could argue that the last is not the most important, or that it is not perceived as a pressure at the time of marriage, or that it is not operational at this time. However, if we compare the standard of living to which a woman can aspire if she remains single and the standard which she can reasonably expect from being married, it seems certain that relative economic deprivation will be experienced by single women as time goes on. We are confronted with a paradox: on the one hand marriage is the (institutional) situation where women are exploited; and on the other hand, precisely because of this, the potential market situation for women's labour (which is that of all women, not just those who are actually married[6]) is such that marriage still offers them the best career, economically speaking. If the initial or potential situation is bad, it will simply be aggravated by the married state, which becomes even more necessary than ever. The economic pressure, in other words, the difference between the potential 'single' standard of living and the actual 'married' standard of living, simply increases as time goes on.

Marriage as a Self-perpetuating State

When women marry or have a child they often stop working or indeed studying; or even occasionally among the middle class – the American model is becoming general in France[7] – they stop studying in order to put their husband through college, by means of a job that has no future, and they stop working as soon as their husband has obtained his degree. If they continue working, they do so at the cost of enormous sacrifices of time and energy, and even then they are still not as free to devote themselves to their work. As a result they cannot aspire to the promotion which they might have had if they had not had to look after a husband and children materially as well as themselves. Ten years after the wedding day, marriage is even more necessary than before because of the dual process whereby women lose ground or at best remain at the same place in the labour market, while married men make great progress in their work as they are not hampered by household obligations. Of course, individual husbands are not responsible for this situation, but all men benefit from a situation that is taken to be normal. A 'normal' day's work is that of a person who does not have to do his own domestic work. But even though this is the norm, it is none the less made possible only by the fact that the household tasks are assumed by others, almost exclusively by women. It is evident that the career of a married man must not be compared for our purposes with that of other men, but with the life he would have led if he had remained single, or if he had had to share the household tasks including the raising of children. This dual process is particularly evident in the case where the wife gives up her own studies in order to finance her husband's. Here, even though both begin in more or less the same position (not taking discrimination into account), marriage results in the wife moving down the economic ladder and the husband moving up, and these changes combine to create an important gap between the economic possibilities of the two partners.

Thus it can be said that, from the woman's standpoint, marriage creates the conditions for its own continuation and encourages entry into a second marriage if a particular union comes to an end.

In this respect statistics are ambiguous, or, more precisely, are difficult to interpret. There are generally more divorced women at work than married women (annual statistics from the Ministère de la Justice 1973). This could be taken as confirmation that their economic situation, notably the absence of an independent income, discourages full-time housewives from getting divorced. But on the other hand many women begin to work just because they face a divorce – they start the moment they decide to get a divorce, long before the decree is issued. This explains why they are registered as 'working' at that particular time. Having a job enables some women to envisage divorce, while others in the same situation but lacking a job have to 'make a go' of their marriage. A large number of women who are divorced or about to be divorced come on the labour market in the worst possible conditions (as do widows), with no qualifications, no experience, and no seniority. They find themselves relegated to the most poorly-paid jobs. This situation is often in contrast with the level of their education and the careers they envisaged, or could have envisaged, before their marriage, the social rank of their parents, and not only the initial social rank of their husband but, more pertinently, the rank he has attained when they divorce, some five, ten, or twenty years after the beginning of their marriage. In addition, those with dependent children have to look after them financially, and this new responsibility is added to the domestic work which they were already providing before divorce. For the majority of women, the contrast between the standard of living that they enjoy while married and that which they can expect after divorce simply redoubles the pressures in favour of marriage or remarriage depending on the circumstances.

The State of Divorce as a Continuation of the State of Marriage

The fact that the material responsibility for children is assumed by the woman after divorce confirms the hypothesis concerning the appropriation by the husband of his wife's work, but it suggests as well that the appropriation which is a characteristic of marriage persists even after the marriage has been dissolved. This leads me to contend that divorce is not the opposite of marriage, nor even its end, but simply a change or a transformation of marriage.

At the beginning of a marriage this appropriation is legally masked; it is a matter of custom in the sense that the legal framework which underlines it is vague and unused and even useless. It only begins to operate – by means of the intervention of the judicial system – when the marriage comes to an end. Even then its apparent purpose is not to burden the wife with the entire responsibility for the children nor to exempt the husband totally. It *permits* such an outcome, but by omission rather than by a positive action. There *is* positive action, however, in the official guideline of considering 'the child's interest'.

Unofficially custody of the children is considered to be a privilege and even a compensation for the woman who may be left badly off in other respects. A real battle is staged to make the two spouses turn against each other and to keep them uncertain as to the outcome of the conflict for as long as possible. The custody of the children[8] becomes the main issue, and at the end of the battle the spouse who obtains this custody considers that he or she has won the war. But in fact when the children are young they are almost always entrusted to their mother. Officially both parents share the responsibility for the cost of looking after the children, but the woman's income after divorce is always very much lower than that of her former husband, and the allowance for the children decided by the courts is always ridiculously low.[9] The woman's financial contribution is thus of necessity greater in absolute value than her husband's, even though her income is lower. As a result her participation and her sacrifices are relatively much greater. Furthermore, 80 per cent of all allowances are never paid.[10] Even if the offical directives are respected and the allowance is paid, the amount agreed never takes into account the woman's time and work in the material upkeep of the children.[11]

Thus the courts ratify the exclusive responsibility of women both by positive actions, granting custody to the mother and assigning a low allowance for the children; and by negative action, failing to ensure the payment of the allowance. The 'child's interest' makes it imperative for him or her to be entrusted to his or her mother, be she poor, 'immoral' or sick, as long as he or she requires considerable material care: as long as there are nappies to wash, feeds to prepare and special clothes, toys, medicaments, lessons, etc. to pay for. As soon as the child reaches the age of 15 the courts usually regard the father more favourably than the mother:[12] she is thought to be unable to provide the child with as many advantages as the father, who is better off (for very good reasons). A child who has been entrusted to his or her mother can then be handed back to his or her father, again in the 'child's interest'. And yet, curiously enough, this aspect of the child's interest – the parent's wealth – did not come into play when the child was younger. Objectively the child's interest[13] has served to make his or her mother poorer and his or her father richer, creating thereby the conditions in which it will be 'in his/her interest' later on to return to the father.

Two conclusions can be drawn: in divorce, as in marriage, the work involved in raising children is carried out by the woman, unpaid, and the husband is exempted from this charge as part of the normal process. Furthermore, the financial care of the childen, which was shared by the couple or assumed by the husband alone in the marriage, is thereafter assumed predominantly or exclusively by the woman.

In compensation the woman no longer has to carry domestic responsibility for her husband. This casts a special light on the marriage contract. Indeed, when the married state is compared with the official as well as the real divorced state, it becomes clear that the material responsibility for the children is the woman's 'privilege' in both cases; while in marriage, in contrast to divorce, the wife provides for her husband's material upkeep in exchange for his contribution towards the financial upkeep of the children.

Marriage and Responsibility for Children: a Question of Theoretical Antecedence

An overriding concern in this paper so far has been to rethink the economic aspects of the institution of marriage and to give them the definition that they have lacked. Comparing marriage to divorce, it seems that the material upkeep of the husband by the wife is related to the participation of the husband in the financial upkeep of children. This provides grounds for viewing marriage differently. This approach is consistent with the contention that whereas marriage sheds light on divorce, the reverse is also true. So far this has meant only that divorce reveals the nature of the marriage contract, but it can also be taken to mean that divorce can shed light on what made this contract possible in the first place.

I contend that these conclusions allow us to see childcare (from the analytical not the empirical point of view) as separate from the rest of domestic work. The obligation of childcare may have to be viewed as not so much perpetuating the husband's appropriation of his wife's labour, as making it possible in the first place. Or, to put it slightly differently, these conclusions compel us to consider the possibility that the continuation of the obligation of childcare is a continuation of the marriage contract, *in so far as* the appropriation of the wife's labour includes the obligation of childcare; but that this obligation, while *carried out* in marriage, does not necessarily *stem* from it; that it might be antecedent to it, and might even be one of the factors that makes the appropriation of wives' labour – the free giving by them of the rest of housework – possible.

If marriage is considered as giving rise to the appropriation of the women-wives' work, the position of married women who work outside of the home suggests that this total appropriation can be transformed into a partial appropriation, bearing no longer on their time or work power as a whole but on a specific task, the household work, that can eventually be replaced by an equivalent sum of money.[14] This evolution of the system of appropriation of wives' labour may at first sight call to mind the evolution of the appropriation of the labour of slaves between the Roman Empire and the late Middle Ages. The appropriation by the seigneur of the slave's total work power became a partial appropriation, approximately half of his time, three days work per week,[15] when the slave became a 'serf' and was 'settled'. He then worked part-time for his own profit on a piece of land which he rented from the seigneur. The time debt to the siegneur was later itself transformed into the obligation to accomplish a specific task, the *corvée*, which later on could be commuted into a money payment.

However, this way of formulating the problem is perhaps false because the partial appropriation of the married woman's labour on this analogy should be counterbalanced by the woman partially recuperating her work power, when in fact she pays for the freedom to work outside, and to have an independent income, with a double day's work. It cannot be said that she recuperates either a period of time or a value. On the other hand she does partially escape from a relationship of production characterized by dependency.

Furthermore, if marriage as a state is characterized and differentiated from divorce by the 'contract' of appropriation, marriage and divorce can be considered as two ways of obtaining a similar result: the collective attribution to women of the care of children and the collective exemption of men from the same responsibility.

Seen from this angle, not only the married and the divorced states but also the state of concubinage, in short all the situations in which children exist and are cared for, have similar characteristics and are different forms of one and the same institution, which could be called X. The situation of the unmarried mother can be taken to be its extreme form, and at the same time its most typical form, since the basic dyad is the mother and child. Marriage could be seen as being one of the possible forms of X, in which the basic couple is joined by a man who temporarily participates in the financial upkeep of the child and in return appropriates the woman's labour power.

This view is similar to that of those anthropologists[16] who criticize Murdock[17] and say that the family defined as a trio proceeding from the husband and wife couple (taken to be the fundamental dyad) is not a universal type, whereas the mother–child association is. This point of view may become a new element in the study of Western societies, where it has generally been taken for granted that the family is patrifocal. This element may be new, but it is not contradictory; for if the family, considered as *the place where children are produced*, can be viewed as matrifocal, even in our own societies, it remains none the less true that as an *economic production unit* (for exchange or for its own use) it is defined, as during the Roman era,[18] as the group of relatives and servants who give work to the head of the family: the father.

Going a step further, the state of marriage-with-children appears as the meeting place for two institutions: on the one hand the institution relating to women's exclusive responsibility for childcare, on the other hand the institution relating to the appropriation by the husband of his wife's labour power.

Indeed if one considers marriage alone, it appears that the care of children, their upkeep, which is no different from the material upkeep of the husband by the wife and which is carried out in the same manner – the execution of work in exchange for maintenance (financial upkeep) – partakes of and flows from the appropriation of the wife's labour power by her husband. As long as there are two parents it can be postulated that the children, in accordance with the legal terms, are their common property, possession and responsibility. In this case, in the marriage situation half the work involved in the upkeep of the children is appropriated by the husband-father, and continues to be so after the divorce. But children do not always have two owners. In the absence of the father, their upkeep by the mother, or even half of this upkeep, is obviously of no benefit to any particular man. Besides, even in marriage or divorce it is doubtful whether the parents are the only ones, excluding society as a whole, to benefit from the children, and consequently it is not at all certain that the husband-father should be considered as the only one to benefit from his half of the work involved in looking after the children, or as the only one to appropriate his wife's work, since he does not carry it out with her. If this is accepted, then the raising of the children will have to be considered apart from the woman's family work (household or other) and the exclusive responsibility of women concerning the children will have to be treated as a relatively autonomous institution with respect to marriage.

If the relationship between marriage and divorce is viewed in this way, it appears slightly differently from what was suggested at the beginning of this paper. The husband's appropriation of his wife's work then ceases, in part or completely, as soon as the marriage comes to an end (depending on whether or not the husband is considered as continuing to benefit from the children, and from their upkeep, either partly or not at all). In this view divorce is not the continuation of marriage. However, the situation after divorce, in which the responsibility for the children is an important aspect, constitutes a strong economic incentive to remarriage for women.

When there are children, the responsibility for their care continues to be borne exclusively by the woman after divorce, and this burden is increased by the financial cost. However, rather than considering that this illustrates a continuation of the husband's appropriation of his wife's work, it would now seem more exact to say that it illustrates a new form of women's responsibility for children, which exists before the marriage, is carried on in the marriage, and continues afterwards. This responsibility can be defined as the collective exploitation of women by men, and correlated with this, the collective exemption of men from the cost of reproduction. The individual appropriation of a particular wife's labour by her husband comes over and above this collective appropriation. It is derived from, or at least made possible by, the collective appropriation which acts in favour of marriage, since if the husband appropriates his wife's work power, in return he contributes to her financial upkeep and the children's, and in this way he 'lightens' her burden by partially assuming a responsibility from which society exempts him. In other words, the institutional exemption from which he benefits allows him to claim his wife's total labour power in exchange for his contribution to the children's financial upkeep.

NOTES

* 'Introduction to the Collection', *Close to Home: A Materialist Analysis of Women's Oppression*, trans. and ed. Diana Leonard (London: Hutchinson, 1984), p. 22.

1 Copyright © 1976, Christine Delphy and permission granted by Tavistock Publications. First published in D. Leonard Barker and S. Allen (eds), *Sexual Divisions and Society: Process and Change* (London: Tavistock, 1976).

2 For example, W. J. Goode, *Women in Divorce* (New York: Free Press, 1956); G. A. Kooy, *Echtscheidingstendenties in 20ste eeuws Nederland*

inzonderheid ten plattelande [Divorce Trends in the rural areas of the Netherlands in the twentieth century] (Assen: Van Gorcum, 1959); R. Chester, 'Divorce and the Family Life Cycle in Great Britain', paper presented to the 13th Annual Seminar of the Committee on Family Research of the ISA, Paris.

3   I use the expression woman-wife to stress that the one is a person and the other a role. This ontological distinction is blurred by the fact that the social role is so widely associated with a biological category that they have become equivalent.

4   See Y. Dezalay in Barker and Allen, *Sexual Divisions and Society*.

5   The thesis of R. O. Blood and D. M. Wolfe, *Husbands and Wives: The Dynamics of Married Living* (Glencoe: Free Press, 1960), for example, is that no model exists, let alone a patriarchal one. If more married women do the housework than married men, it is because they have more time to do it and their husbands less since they work outside(!). And if married women are of less weight in making decisions, it is owing to the fact that since they do not work outside (this being compensated by the extra time they have to do the housework) so their contribution to the domestic economy is less important.

6   See R. Barron and G. Norris, 'Sexual Divisions and the Dual Labour Market', in Barker and Allen, *Sexual Divisions and Society*.

7   See, for example, couples where the husbands are at business school: J. Marceau, 'Marriage, Role Division and Social Cohesion: the Case of some French Middle-Class Families', in D. Leonard Barker and S. Allen (eds), *Dependence and Exploitation in Work and Marriage*, (London: Longman, 1976).

8   This is a legal notion which officially denotes official responsibility and, unofficially, the right to dispose of and enjoy as one may dispose of and enjoy any possession.

9   In a study I was involved in, we found in one provincial court that the ex-wife was awarded a *mean* of £10 per month per child. In general, courts in France will never instruct the ex-husband to pay more than one-third of his income to his ex-wife and children.

10   A. Boigeol, J. Commaille and L. Roussel, 'Enquête sur 1000 divorces', *Population* (1975).

11   I distinguish the financial and material upkeep of a family. The first is the part of the consumption that is bought. The second consists of services, or labour applied to goods bought by the wage.

12   This is based on statistics from the Ministère de la Justice (1973) and oral communications from a lawyer.

13   That this is a mere legal fiction is clear if we consider the result to which it leads, and that from the very beginning it is the judges and

not the children who talk of their 'interest'.

14 When for example the woman buys off her obligation by paying for a nurse or a public nursery, etc. out of her salary.

15 M. Bloch, *Les caractères originales de l'histoire rurale française* (Paris: Armand Colin, 1964).

16 R. N. Adams, 'The Nature of the Family', in J. Goody (ed.), *Kinship* (Harmondsworth: Penguin, 1971); M. Zelditch, 'Family, Marriage and Kinship', in R. E. L. Faris (ed.), *Handbook of Modern Society* (Chicago: Rand McNally, 1964).

17 G. B. Murdock, *Social Structure* (New York: Macmillan, 1949).

18 F. Engels, *The Origin of the Family, Private Property and the State* [1884], edited and with an introduction by E. B. Leacock (London: Lawrence and Wishart, 1972).

6

Andrea Dworkin
b.1946

'THE POLITICS OF INTELLIGENCE' from
RIGHT WING WOMEN (1983)

In Right Wing Women *Andrea Dworkin continues the assault on misogyny and patriarchy begun in her earlier work on contemporary pornography.* Here she turns her attention to a group which seems to share feminist outrage about pornography, but for different reasons and with completely different aims. The 'Moral Majority' and a cluster of similar conservative groups have been a significant political force in the United States in the 1970s and 1980s. Their manifestos comprise a chilling litany of hates – their* bêtes noires *include Jews, Catholics, homosexuals and communists, as well as feminists.*

Dworkin, as a press representative, attended the US National Women's Conference in Houston, Texas, in November 1977. Here, delegates from all the states gathered to consider the central business of the mooted Equal Rights Amendment, which would have enshrined civic equality for women in the US Constitution. The amendment was not, in the end, adopted. Several states' delegations were formed from the extreme right, even including individuals connected with the Ku-Klux-Klan. Dworkin, trying to interview the women who were voting and campaigning against the Amendment at the conference, faced frightening aggression, directed both at her Jewishness and at her feminism.

The conundrum of some women's willing and committed acceptance of policies and practices which condemn them to a restricted and inferior status is a central issue that feminism must face. Dworkin discovered that *the right-wing woman's understanding of sexuality and of gender relations is surprisingly consonant with the feminist's. As things are, masculinity is predatory and aggressive; social institutions like the sexual division of labour, the judiciary, education, pornography and a host of others consistently reinforce this state of affairs. Right-wing women know, as do feminists, that women who enter what is called the 'public' sphere can expect to have a difficult and unpleasant time there. A woman who strives for autonomy, inside the family or outside, is typically discontented, thwarted and stressed. When welded with anti-communism and other conservative obsessions, this analysis takes us far from the feminist project of altering and reconstructing social, erotic and economic relations, and reconstructing the definitions of public and private. The right-wing answer rests on the assumption that masculinity as we know it is natural, even God-given. Each woman must surrender totally to her husband, as she must to Jesus; she must devote herself to keeping her husband constant by catering to his special needs and tastes whether 'in salad, sex, or sport'.***

The chapter we reprint here is an excellent example of Dworkin's impassioned prose. Dworkin makes claims which are likely to strike many readers as shocking (for example, 'Men hate intelligence in women'). Even more shocking, though, are the passages she quotes from central figures of twentieth-century culture, such as Norman Mailer, D. H. Lawrence and Jean-Paul Sartre: these articulations of misogyny make Dworkin's own 'outrageousness' pale into insignificance.

Dworkin's construction of men and women as two separate classes, whose sexual destinies are relentlessly lived out in man to woman sadism, contempt and exploitation, has attracted much criticism. Her analysis tends to ignore the existence of any effective opposition to misogyny, as well as the differences between women and among men. Plurality and fragmentation unsettle any one account of social reality. The claim that 'men hate intelligence in women', no matter how compelling after reading the tradition which includes Mailer and friends, does not have universal validity. (However, to see how far it is valid, compare it with the converse claim, 'Women hate intelligence in men.' Consider which of the two claims more plausibly represents contemporary social reality.) We must expose the detailed workings of misogyny in our culture; but at the same time we need to be more optimistic than Dworkin is about social change. But we should not assume, as many feminists have done, that autonomy will follow from women's entry into the non-domestic workforce, for 'Women are paid too little. And right-wing women know it.'*** Only *through an end to the present 'woman-hating social system' will female sexuality, and with it female intelligence, begin to achieve adequate expression.*

In this chapter Dworkin argues that the means to develop literacy, intellect and creative intelligence have been kept from women, as have the means to discover and develop their sexuality. These various strengths are not natural or biological characteristics, but social attributes, the development of which is crucial for ethical life. In particular, the suppression of active sexual personality effectively destroys those qualities of perceptiveness and critical judgement which are essential for the development of the human virtue traditionally known as 'practical wisdom'.

> Why is life so tragic; so like a little strip of pavement over an abyss. I look down; I feel giddy; I wonder how I am ever to walk to the end. . . . It's a feeling of impotence: of cutting no ice.
>
> Virginia Woolf, her diary, October 25, 1920

Men hate intelligence in women.[1] It cannot flame; it cannot burn; it cannot burn out and end up in ashes, having been consumed in adventure. It cannot be cold, rational, ice; no warm womb would tolerate a cold, icy, splendid mind. It cannot be ebullient and it cannot be morbid; it cannot be anything that does not end in reproduction or whoring. It cannot be what intelligence is: a vitality of mind that acts directly in and on the world, without mediation. 'Indeed,' wrote Norman Mailer, 'I doubt if there will be a really exciting woman writer until the first whore becomes a call girl and tells her tale.'[2] And Mailer was being generous, because he endowed the whore with a capacity to know, if not to tell: she knows something firsthand, something worth knowing. 'Genius', wrote Edith Wharton more realistically, 'is of small use to a woman who does not know how to do her hair.'[3]

Intelligence is a form of energy, a force that pushes out into the world. It makes its mark, not once but continuously. It is curious, penetrating. Without the light of public life, discourse and action, it dies. It must have a field of action beyond embroidery or scrubbing toilets or wearing fine clothes. It needs response, challenge, consequences that matter. Intelligence cannot be passive and private through a lifetime. Kept secret, kept inside, it withers and dies. The outside can be brought to it; it can live on bread and water locked up in a cell – but barely. Florence Nightingale, in her feminist tract *Cassandra*, said that intellect died last in women; desire, dreams, activity and love all died before it. Intelligence does hang on, because it can live on almost nothing: fragments of the world brought to it by husbands or sons or strangers or, in our time, television or the occasional film. Imprisoned, intelligence turns into self-haunting and dread. Isolated, intelligence becomes a burden and a curse. Under-nourished, intelligence becomes like the bloated belly of a starving child: swollen, filled with nothing the body can use. It swells, like the starved stomach, as the skeleton shrivels and the bones collapse; it will pick up anything to fill the hunger, stick anything in, chew anything, swallow anything. 'José Carlos came home with a bag of crackers he found in the garbage,' wrote Carolina Maria de Jesus, a woman of the Brazilian underclass, in her diary. 'When I saw him eating things out of the trash I thought: and if it's been poisoned? Children can't stand hunger. The crackers were delicious. I ate them thinking of that proverb: He who enters the dance must dance. And as I also was hungry, I ate.'[4] The intelligence of women is tradition-ally starved, isolated, imprisoned.

Traditionally and practically, the world is brought to women by men; they are the outside on which female intelligence must feed. The food is poor, orphan's gruel. This is because men bring home half-truths, ego-laden lies, and use them to demand solace or sex or housekeeping. The intelligence of women is not out in the world, acting on its own behalf; it is kept small, inside the home, acting on behalf of another. This is true even when the woman works outside the home, because she is segregated into women's work, and her intelligence does not have the same importance as the lay of her ass.

Men are the world and women use intelligence to survive men: their tricks, desires, demands, moods, hatreds, disappointments, rages, greed, lust, authority, power, weaknesses. The ideas that come to women come through men, in a field of cultural values controlled by men, in a political and social system controlled by men, in a sexual system in which women are used as things. (As Catharine A. MacKinnon wrote in the one sentence that every woman should risk her life to understand: 'Man fucks woman; subject verb object.'[5]) Men are the field of action in which female intelligence moves. But the world, the real world, is more than men, certainly more than what men show of themselves and the world to women; and women are deprived of that real world. The male always intervenes between her and it.

Some will grant that women might have a particular kind of intelligence – essentially small, picky, good with details, bad with ideas. Some will grant – in fact insist – that women know more of 'the Good', that women are more cognizant of decency or kindness: this keeps intelligence small and tamed. Some will grant that there have been women of genius: after the woman of genius is dead. The greatest writers in the English language have been women: George Eliot, Jane Austen, Virginia Woolf. They were sublime; and they were, all of them, shadows of what they might have been. But the fact that they existed does not change the categorical perception that women are basically stupid: not capable of intelligence without the exercise of which the world as a whole is impoverished. Women are stupid and men are smart; men have a right to the world and women do not. A lost man is a lost intelligence; a lost woman is a lost (name the function) mother, housekeeper, sexual thing. Classes of men have been lost, have been thrown away; there have always been mourners and fighters who refused to accept the loss. There is no mourning for the lost intelligence of women because there is no conviction that such intelligence was real and was destroyed. Intelligence is, in fact, seen as a function of masculinity, and women are despised when they refuse to be lost.

Women have stupid ideas that do not deserve to be called ideas. Marabel Morgan writes an awful, silly, terrible book in which she claims that women must exist for their husbands, do sex and be sex for their husbands.[6] D. H. Lawrence writes vile and stupid essays in which he says the same thing basically with many references to the divine phallus;[7] but D. H. Lawrence is smart. Anita Bryant says that cocksucking is a form of human cannibalism; she decries the loss of the child who is the sperm.[8] Norman Mailer believes that lost ejaculations are lost sons and on that basis disparages male homosexuality, masturbation and contraception.[9] But Anita Bryant is stupid and Norman Mailer is smart. Is the difference in the style with which these same ideas are delivered or in the penis? Mailer says that a great writer writes with his balls; novelist Cynthia Ozick asks Mailer in which colour ink he dips his balls. Who is smart and who is stupid?

If an idea is stupid, presumably it is stupid whether the one who articulates it is male or female. But that is not the case. Women, undereducated as a class, do not have to read Aeschylus to know that a man plants the sperm, the child, the son; women are the soil; she brings forth the human he created; he is the originator, the father of life. Women can have their own provincial, moralistic sources for this knowledge: clergy, movies, gym teachers. The knowledge is common knowledge: respected in the male writers because the male writers are respected; stupid in women because women are stupid as a condition of birth. Women articulate received knowledge and are laughed at for doing so. But male writers with the same received ideas are acclaimed as new, brilliant, interesting, even rebellious, brave, facing the world of sin and sex forthrightly. Women have ignorant, moralistic prejudices; men have ideas. To call this a double standard is to indulge in cruel euphemism. This gender system of evaluating ideas is a sledgehammer that bangs female intelligence to a pulp, annihilating it. Mailer and Lawrence have taken on the world always; they knew they had a right to it; their prose takes that right for granted; it is the gravitational field in which they move. Marabel Morgan and Anita Bryant come to the world as middle-aged women and try to act in it; of course they are juvenile and imprecise in style, ridiculous even. Both Mailer and Lawrence have written volumes that are as ridiculous, juvenile, despite what they can take for granted as men, despite their sometimes mastery of the language, despite their genuine accomplishments, despite the beauty of a story or novel. But they are not called stupid even when they are ridiculous. When the ideas of Lawrence cannot be distinguished from the ideas of Morgan, either both are smart or both are stupid; and similarly with Mailer and Bryant. Only the women, however, deserve and get our contempt. Are Anita Bryant's ideas pernicious? Then so are Norman Mailer's. Are Marabel Morgan's ideas side-slappingly funny? Then so are D. H. Lawrence's.

A woman must keep her intelligence small and timid to survive. Or she must hide it altogether or hide it through style. Or she must go mad like clockwork to pay for it. She will try to find the nice way to exercise intelligence. But intelligence is not ladylike. Intelligence is full of excesses. Rigorous intelligence abhors sentimentality, and women must be sentimental to value the dreadful silliness of the men around them. Morbid intelligence abhors the cheery sunlight of positive thinking and eternal sweetness; and women must be sunlight and cheery and sweet, or the woman could not bribe her way with smiles through a day. Wild intelligence abhors any narrow world; and the world of women must stay narrow, or the woman is an outlaw. No woman could be Nietzsche or Rimbaud without ending up in a whorehouse or lobotomized. Any vital intelligence has passionate questions, aggressive answers: but women cannot be explorers; there can be no Lewis and Clark of the female mind. Even restrained intelligence is restrained not because it is timid, as women must be, but because it is cautiously weighing impressions and facts that come to it from an outside that the timid dare not face. A woman must please, and restrained intelligence does not seek to please; it seeks to know through discernment. Intelligence is also ambitious: it always wants more: not more being fucked, not more pregnancy; but more of a bigger world. A woman cannot be ambitious in her own right without also being damned.

We take girls and send them to schools. It is good of us, because girls are not supposed to know anything much, and in many other societies girls are not sent to school or taught to read and write. In our society, such a generous one to women, girls are taught some facts, but not inquiry or the passion of knowing. Girls are taught in order to make them compliant: intellectual adventurousness is drained, punished, ridiculed out of girls. We use schools first to narrow the girl's scope, her curiosity, then to teach her certain skills, necessary to the abstract husband. Girls are taught to be passive in relation to facts. Girls are not seen as the potential originators of ideas or the potential searchers into the human condition. Good behaviour is the intellectual goal of a girl. A girl with intellectual drive is a girl who has to be cut down to size. An intelligent girl is supposed to use that intelligence to find a smarter husband. Simone de Beauvoir settled on Sartre when she determined that he was smarter than she was. In a film made when both were old, toward the end of his life, Sartre asks de Beauvoir, the woman with whom he has shared an astonishing life of intellectual action and accomplishment: how does it feel, to have been a literary lady?

Carolina Maria de Jesus wrote in her diary: 'Everyone has an ideal in life. Mine is to be able to read.'[10] She is ambitious, but it is a strange ambition for a woman. She wants learning. She wants the pleasure of reading and writing. Men ask her to marry but she suspects that they will interfere with her reading and writing. They will resent the time she takes alone. They will resent the focus of her attention elsewhere. They will resent her concentration and they will resent her self-respect. They will resent her pride in herself and her pride in her unmediated relationship to a larger world of ideas, descriptions, facts. Her neighbours see her poring over books, or with pen and paper in hand, amidst the garbage and hunger of the *favela*. Her ideal makes her a pariah: her desire to read makes her more an outcast than if she sat in the street putting fistfuls of nails into her mouth. Where did she get her ideal? No one offered it to her. Two-thirds of the world's illiterates are women. To be fucked, to birth children, one need not know how to read. Women are for sex and reproduction, not for literature. But women have stories to tell. Women want to know. Women have questions, ideas, arguments, answers. Women have dreams of being in the world, not merely passing blood and heaving wet infants out of labouring wombs. 'Women dream', Florence Nightingale wrote in *Cassandra*, 'till they have no longer the strength to dream; those dreams against which they so struggle, so honestly, vigorously, and conscientiously, and so in vain, yet which are their life, without which they could not have lived, those dreams go at last. . . . Later in life, they neither desire nor dream, neither of activity, nor of love, nor of intellect.'[11]

Virginia Woolf, the most splendid modern writer, told us over and over how awful it was to be a woman of creative intelligence. She told us when she loaded a large stone into her pocket and walked into the river; and she told us each time a book was published and she went mad – don't hurt me for what I have done, I will hurt myself first, I will be incapacitated and I will suffer and I will be punished and then perhaps you need not destroy me, perhaps you will pity me, there is such contempt in pity and I am so proud, won't that be enough? She told us over and over in her prose too: in her fiction she showed us, ever so delicately so that we would not take offense; and in her essays she piled on the charm, being polite to keep us polite. But she did write it straight out too, though it was not published in her lifetime, and she was right:

A certain attitude is required – what I call the pouring-out-tea attitude – the clubwoman, Sunday afternoon attitude. I don't know. I think that the angle is almost as important as the thing.

What I value is the naked contact of a mind. Often one cannot say anything valuable about a writer – except what one thinks. Now I found my angle incessantly obscured, quite unconsciously no doubt, by the desire of the editor and of the public that a woman should see things from the chary feminine angle. My article, written from that oblique point of view, always went down.[12]

To value 'the naked contact of a mind' is to have a virile intelligence, one not shrouded in dresses and pretty gestures. Her work did always go down, with the weight of what being female demanded. She became a master of exquisite indirection. She hid her meanings and her messages in a feminine style. She laboured under that style and hid behind that mask: and she was less than she could have been. She died not only from what she did dare, but also from what she did not dare.

These three things are indissolubly linked: literacy, intellect and creative intelligence. They distinguish, as the cliché goes, man from the animals. He who is denied these three is denied a fully human life and has been robbed of a right to human dignity. Now change the gender. Literacy, intellect and creative intelligence distinguish woman from the animals: no. Woman is not distinguishable from the animals because she has been condemned by virtue of her sex class to a life of animal functions: being fucked, reproducing. For her, the animal functions are her meaning, her so-called humanity, as human as she gets, the highest human capacities in her because she is female. To the orthodox of male culture, she is animal, the antithesis of soul; to the liberals of male culture, she is nature. In discussing the so-called biological origins of male dominance, the boys can afford to compare themselves to baboons and insects: they are writing books or teaching in universities when they do it. A Harvard professor does not refuse tenure because a baboon has never been granted it. The biology of power is a game boys play. It is the male way of saying: she is more like the female baboon than she is like me; she cannot be an *éminence grise* at Harvard because she bleeds, we fuck her, she bears our young, we beat her up, we rape her; she is an animal, her function is to breed. I want to see the baboon, the ant, the wasp, the goose, the cichlid, that has written *War and Peace*. Even more I want to see the animal or insect or fish or fowl that has written *Middlemarch*.

Literacy is a tool, like fire. It is a more advanced tool than fire, and it has done as much or more to change the complexion of the natural and social worlds. Literacy, like fire, is a tool that must be used by intelligence. Literacy is also a capacity: the capacity to be literate is a human capacity; the capacity exists and it can be used or it can be denied, refuted, made to atrophy. In persons socially despised, it is denied. But denial is not enough, because people insist on meaning. Humankind finds meaning in experiences, events, objects, communications, relationships, feelings. Literacy functions as part of the search for meaning; it helps to make that search possible. Men can deny that women have the capacity to learn ancient Greek, but some women will learn it nevertheless. Men can deny that poor women or working-class women or prostituted women have the capacity to read or write their own language, but some of those women will read or write their own language anyway; they will risk everything to learn it. In the slave-holding South in the United States, it was forbidden by law to teach slaves to read or write; but some slaveowners taught, some slaves learned, some slaves taught themselves, and some slaves taught other slaves. In Jewish law, it is forbidden to teach women Talmud, but some women learned Talmud anyway. People know that literacy brings dignity and a wider world. People are strongly motivated to experience the world they live in through language: spoken, sung, chanted and written. One must punish people terribly to stop them from wanting to know what reading and writing bring, because people are curious and driven toward both experience and the conceptualization of it. The denial of literacy to any class or category of people is a denial of fundamental humanity. Humans viewed as animal, not human, are classically denied literacy: slaves in slave-owning societies; women in woman-owning societies; racially degraded groups in racist societies. The male slave it treated as a beast of burden; he cannot be allowed to read or write. The woman is treated as a beast of breeding; she must not read or write. When women as a class are denied the right to read and write, those who learn are shamed by their knowledge: they are masculine, deviant; they have denied their wombs, their cunts; in their literacy they repudiate the definition of their kind.

Certain classes of women have been granted some privileges of literacy – not rights, privileges. The courtesans of ancient Greece were educated when other women were kept ignorant, but they were not philosophers, they were whores. Only by accepting their function as whores could they exercise the privilege of literacy. Upper-class women are traditionally taught some skills of literacy (distinctly more circumscribed than the skills taught the males of their mating class): they can exercise the privilege of literacy if they accept their decorative function. After all, the man does not want the breeding, bleeding bitch at the dinner table or the open cunt in the parlour while he reads his newspaper or smokes his cigar. Language is refinement: proof that he is human, not she.

The increase in illiteracy among the urban poor in the United States is consonant with a new rise in overt racism and contempt for the poor. The illiteracy is programmed into the system: an intelligent child can go to school and not be taught how to read or write. When the educational system abandons reading and writing for particular subgroups, it abandons human dignity for those groups: it becomes strictly custodial, keeping the animals penned in; it does not bring human life to human beings.

Cross-culturally, girls and women are the illiterates, with two-thirds of the world's illiterates women and the rate rising steadily. Girls need husbands, not books. Girls need houses or shacks to keep clean, or street corners to stand on, not the wide world in which to roam. Refusal to give the tool of literacy is refusal to give access to the world. If she can make her own fire, read a book herself, write a letter or a record of her thoughts or an essay or a story, it will be harder to get her to tolerate the unwanted fuck, to bear the unwanted children, to see him as life and life through him. She might get ideas. But even worse, she might know the value of the ideas she gets. She must not know that ideas have value, only that being fucked and reproducing are her value.

It has been hard, in the United States, to get women educated: there are still many kinds of education off-limits to women. In England, it was hard for Virginia Woolf to use a university library. Simple literacy is the first step, and, as Abby Kelley told a women's rights convention in 1850, 'Sisters, bloody feet have worn smooth the path by which you came here.'[13] Access to the whole language has been denied women; we are only supposed to use the ladylike parts of it. Alice James noted in her diary that '[i]t is an immense loss to have all robust and sustaining expletives refined away from one!'[14]

But it is in the actual exercise of literacy as a tool and as a capacity that women face punishment, ostracization, exile, recrimination, the most virulent contempt. To read and be feminine simultaneously she reads Gothic romances, not medical textbooks; cookbooks, not case law; mystery stories, not molecular biology. The language of mathematics is not a feminine language. She may learn astrology, not astronomy. She may teach grammar, not invent style or originate ideas. She is permitted to write a little book about neurotic women, fiction or nonfiction, if the little book is trite and sentimental enough; she had better keep clear of philosophy altogether. In fiction, she had better be careful not to overstep the severe limits imposed by femininity. 'This then,' wrote Virginia Woolf, 'is another incident, and quite a common incident in the career of a woman novelist. She has to say I will wait. I will wait until men have become so civilized that they are not shocked when a woman speaks the truth about her body. The future of fiction depends very much upon what extent men can be educated to stand free speech in women.'[15] The constraint is annihilation: language that must avoid one's own body is language that has no place in the world. But speaking the truth about a woman's body is not the simple explication of body parts – it is instead the place of that particular body in this particular world, its value, its use, its place in power, its political and economic life, its capacities both potentially realized and habitually abused.

In a sense intellect is the combination of literacy and intelligence: literacy disciplines intelligence and intelligence expands the uses of literacy; there is a body of knowledge that changes and increases and also a skill in acquiring knowledge; there is a memory filled with ideas, a storehouse of what has gone before in the world. Intellect is mastery of ideas, of culture, of the products and processes of other intellects. Intellect is the capacity to learn language disciplined into learning. Intellect must be cultivated: even in men, even in the smartest. Left alone in a private world of isolation, intellect does not develop unless it has a private cultivator: a teacher, a father of intellect, for instance. But the intellect in the female must not exceed that of the teacher – or the female will be rebuked and denied. Walt Whitman wrote that a student necessarily disowns and overthrows a teacher; but the female student must always stay smaller than the teacher, always meeker; her intelligence is never supposed to become mastery. Intellect in a woman is always a sign of privilege: she has been raised up above her kind, usually because of the beneficence of a man who has seen fit to educate her. The insults to females of intellect are legion: so-called blue-stockings are a laughing-stock; women of intellect are ugly or they would not bother to have ideas; the pleasure of cultivating the mind is sexual perversion in the female; the works of literate men are strewn with vicious remarks against intellectual women. Intellect in a woman is malignant. She is not ennobled by a fine mind; she is deformed by it.

The creative mind is intelligence in action in the world. The world need not be defined as rivers, mountains and plains. The world is anywhere that thought has consequences. In the most abstract philosophy thought has consequences; philosophy is part of the world, sometimes its own self-contained world. Thinking is action; so are writing, composing, painting; creative intelligence can be used in the material world to make products of itself. But there is more to creative intelligence than what it produces. Creative intelligence is searching intelligence: it demands to know the world, demands its right to consequence. It is not contemplative: creative intelligence is too ambitious for that; it almost always announces itself. It may commit itself to the pure search for knowledge or truth, but almost always it wants recognition, influence or power; it is an accomplishing intelligence. It is not satisfied by recognition of the personality that carries it; it wants respect in its own right, respect for itself. Sometimes this respect can be shown toward its product. Sometimes, when this intelligence exercises itself in the more ephemeral realm of pure talk or mundane action, respect for creative intelligence must be shown through respect for the person manifesting it. Women are consistently and systematically denied the respect creative intelligence requires to be sustained: painfully denied it, cruelly denied it, sadistically denied it. Women are not supposed to have creative intelligence, but when they do they are supposed to renounce it. If they want the love of men, without which they are not really women, they had better not hold on to an intelligence that searches and that is action in the world; thought that has consequences is inimical to fettered femininity. Creative intelligence is not animal: being fucked and reproducing will not satisfy it, ever; and creative intelligence is not decorative – it is never merely ornamental as, for instance, upper-class women however well educated must be. To stay a woman in the male-supremacist meaning of that word, women must renounce creative intelligence: not just verbally renounce it, though women do that all the time, but snuff it out in themselves at worst, keep it timid and restrained at best. The price for exercising creative intelligence for those born female is unspeakable suffering. 'All things on earth have their price,' wrote Olive Schreiner, 'and for truth we pay the dearest. We barter it for love and sympathy. The road to honour is paved with thorns; but on the path to truth, at every step you set your foot down on your heart.'[16] Truth is the goal of creative intelligence, whatever its kind and path; tangling with the world is tangling with the problem of truth. One confronts the muck of the world, but one's search is for the truth. The particular truth or the ultimate character of the truth one finds is not the issue. The intrusion of an intelligent, creative self into the world to find the truth is the issue. There is nothing here for women, except intimidation and contempt. In isolation, in private, a woman may have pleasure from the exercise of creative intelligence, however restrained she is in the exercise of it; but that intelligence will have to be turned against herself because there is no further, complex, human world in which it can be used and developed. Whatever of it leaks out will entitle all and sundry to criticize her womanhood, which is the sole identity available to her; her womanhood is deficient, because her intelligence is virile.

'Why have women passion, intellect, moral activity . . .' Florence Nightingale asked in 1852, 'and a place in society where no one of these three can be exercised?'[17] When she referred to moral activity, she did not mean moralism; she meant moral intelligence. Moralism is the set of rules learned by rote that keeps women locked in, so that intelligence can never meet the world head on. Moralism is a defense against experiencing the world. Moralism is the moral sphere designated to women, who are supposed to learn the rules of their own proper, circumscribed behaviour by rote. Moral intelligence is active; it can only be developed and refined by being used in the realm of real and direct experience. Moral activity is the use of that intelligence, the exercise of moral discernment. Moralism is passive: it accepts the version of the world it has been taught and shudders at the threat of direct experience. Moral intelligence is characterized by activity, movement through ideas and history: it takes on the world and insists on participating in the great and terrifying issues of right and wrong, tenderness and cruelty. Moral intelligence constructs values; and because those values are exercised in the real world, they have consequences. There is no moral intelligence that does not have real consequences in a real world, or that is simply and passively received, or that can live in a vacuum in which there is no action. Moral intelligence cannot be expressed only through love or only through sex or only through domesticity or only through ornamentation or only through obedience; moral intelligence cannot be expressed only through being fucked or reproducing. Moral intelligence must act in a public world, not a private, refined, rarefied relationship with one other person to the exclusion of the rest of the world. Moral intelligence demands a nearly endless exercise of the ability to make decisions: significant decisions; decisions inside history, not peripheral to it; decisions about the meaning of life; decisions that arise from an acute awareness of one's own mortality; decisions on which one can honestly and willfully stake one's life. Moral intelligence is not the stuff of which cunts are made. Moralism is the cunt's effort to find some basis for self-respect, a pitiful gesture toward being human at which men laugh and for which women pity other women.

There is also, possibly, sexual intelligence, a human capacity for discerning, manifesting and constructing sexual integrity. Sexual intelligence could not be measured in numbers of orgasms, erections or partners; nor could it show itself by posing painted clitoral lips in front of a camera; nor could one measure it by the number of children born; nor would it manifest as addiction. Sexual intelligence, like any other kind of intelligence, would be active and dynamic; it would need the real world, the direct experience of it; it would pose not buttocks but questions, answers, theories, ideas – in the form of desire or act or art or articulation. It would be in the body, but it could never be in an imprisoned, isolated body, a body denied access to the world. It would not be mechanical; nor could it stand to be viewed as inert and stupid; nor could it be exploited by another without diminishing in vigour; and being sold on the marketplace as a commodity would necessarily be anathema to it, a direct affront to its intrinsic need to confront the world in self-defined and self-determining terms. Sexual intelligence would probably be more like moral intelligence than like anything else: a point that women for centuries have been trying to make. But since no intelligence in a woman is respected, and since she is condemned to moralism because she is defined as being incapable of moral intelligence, and since she is defined as a sexual thing to be used, the meaning of women in likening moral and sexual intelligence is not understood. Sexual intelligence asserts itself through sexual integrity, a dimension of values and action forbidden to women. Sexual intelligence would have to be rooted first and foremost in the honest possession of one's own body, and women exist to be possessed by others, namely men. The possession of one's own body would have to be absolute and entirely realized for the intelligence to thrive in the world of action. Sexual intelligence, like moral intelligence, would have to confront the great issues of cruelty and tenderness; but where moral intelligence must tangle with questions of right and wrong, sexual intelligence would have to tangle with questions of dominance and submission. One preordained to be fucked has no need to exercise sexual intelligence, no opportunity to exercise it, no argument that justifies exercising it. To keep the woman sexually acquiescent, the capacity for sexual intelligence must be prohibited to her; and it is. Her clitoris is denied; her capacity for pleasure is distorted and defamed; her erotic values are slandered and insulted; her desire to value her body as her own is paralyzed and maimed. She is turned into an occasion for male pleasure, an object of male desire, a thing to be used; and any willful expression of her sexuality in the world unmediated by men or male values is punished. She is used as a slut or as a lady; but sexual intelligence cannot manifest in a human being whose predestined purpose is to be exploited through sex, by sex, in sex, as sex. Sexual intelligence constructs its own use: it begins with a whole body, not one that has already been cut into parts and fetishized; it begins with a self-respecting body, not one that is characterized by class as dirty, wanton and slavish; it acts in the world, a world it enters on its own, with freedom as well as with passion. Sexual intelligence cannot live behind locked doors, any more than any other kind of intelligence can. Sexual intelligence cannot exist defensively, keeping out rape. Sexual intelligence cannot be decorative or pretty or coy or timid, nor can it live on a diet of contempt and abuse and hatred of its human form. Sexual intelligence is not animal, it is human; it has values; it sets limits that are meaningful to the whole person and personality, which must live in history and in the world. Women have found the development and exercise of sexual intelligence more difficult than any other kind: women have learned to read; women have acquired intellect; women have had so much creative intelligence that even despisal and isolation and punishment have not been able to squeeze it out of them; women have struggled for a moral intelligence that by its very existence repudiates moralism; but sexual intelligence is cut off at its roots, because the woman's body is not her own. The incestuous use of a girl murders it. The sexual intimidation or violation of a girl murders it. The enforced chastity of a girl murders it. The separation of girl from girl murders it. The turning over of a girl to a man as wife murders it. The selling of a girl into prostitution murders it. The use of a woman as a wife murders it. The use of a woman as a sexual thing murders it. The selling of a woman as a sexual commodity, not just on the street but in media, murders it. The economic value given to a woman's body, whether high or low, murders it. The keeping of a woman as a toy or ornament or domesticated cunt murders it. The need to be a mother so that one is not perceived as a whore murders it. The requirement that one bear babies murders it. The fact that the sexuality of the female is predetermined and that she is forced to be what men say she is murders sexual intelligence: there is nothing for her to discern or to construct; there is nothing for her to find out except what men will do to her and what she will have to pay if she resists or gives in. She lives in a private world – even a street corner is a private world of sexual usage, not a public world of honest confrontation; and her private world of sexual usage has narrow boundaries and a host of givens. No intelligence can function in a world that consists fundamentally of two rules that by their very nature prohibit the invention of values, identity, will, desire: be fucked, reproduce. Men have constructed female sexuality and in so doing have annihilated the chance for sexual intelligence in women. Sexual intelligence cannot live in the shallow, predestined sexuality men have counterfeited for women.

> I respect and honour the needy woman who, to procure food for herself and child, sells her body to some stranger for the necessary money; but for that legal virtue which sells itself for a lifetime for a home, with an abhorrence of the purchaser, and which at the same time says to the former, 'I am holier than thou,' I have only the supremest contempt.
>
> Victoria Woodhull, 1874

The argument between wives and whores is an old one; each one thinking that whatever she is, at least she is not the other. And there is no doubt that the wife envies the whore – or Marabel Morgan's ladies would not be wrapping themselves in Saran Wrap or wearing black boots with lacy neon nighties – and that the whore envies the domesticity of the wife – especially her physical sheltering and her relative sexual privacy. Both categories of women – specious as the categories finally turn out to be – need what men have to give: they need the material solicitude of men, not their cocks but their money. The cock is the inevitable precondition; without it there is no man, no money, no shelter, no protection. With it there may not be much, but women prefer men to silence, exile, to being pariahs, to being lone refugees, to being outcasts: defenceless. Victoria Woodhull – the first woman stockbroker on Wall Street, the first woman to run for president of the United States (1870), the publisher of the first translation of the *Communist Manifesto* in the United States (1871), the first person ever arrested under the notoriously repressive Comstock Law (1872)[18] – crusaded against the material dependency of women on men because she knew that anyone who bartered her body bartered her human dignity. She hated the hypocrisy of married women; she hated the condition of prostitution, which degraded both wives and whores; and especially she hated the men who profited sexually and economically from marriage:

It's a sharp trick played by men upon women, by which they acquire the legal right to debauch them without cost, and to make it unnecessary for them to visit professional prostitutes, whose sexual services can only be obtained for money. Now, isn't this true? Men know it is.[19]

Woodhull did not romanticize prostitution; she did not advocate it as freedom from marriage or freedom in itself or sexual freedom. Prostitution, she made clear, was for money, not for fun; it was survival, not pleasure. Woodhull's passion was sexual freedom, and she knew that the prostitution and rape of women were antithetical to it. She was a mass organizer, and the masses of women were married, sexually subordinated to men in marriage. At a time when feminists did not analyze sex directly or articulate ideas explicitly antagonistic to sex as practised, Woodhull exposed marital rape and compulsory intercourse as the purpose, meaning and method of marriage:

Of all the horrid brutalities of this age, I know of none so horrid as those that are sanctioned and defended by marriage. Night after night there are thousands of rapes committed, under cover of this accursed licence; and millions – yes, I say it boldly, knowing whereof I speak – millions of poor, heart-broken, suffering wives are compelled to minister to the lechery of insatiable husbands, when every instinct of body and senti-ment of soul revolts in loathing and disgust. All married persons know this is truth, although they may feign to shut their eyes and ears to the horrid thing, and pretend to believe it is not. The world has got to be startled from this pretence into real-izing that there is nothing else now existing among pretendedly enlightened nations, except marriage, that invests men with the right to debauch women, sexually, against their wills. Yet marriage is held to be synonymous with morality! I say, eternal damnation sink such morality![20]

Wives were the majority, whores the minority, prostitution the condition of each, rape the underbelly of prostitution. Woodhull's aggressive repudiation of the good woman/bad woman syndrome (with which women, then as now, were so very comfortable), her relentless attacks on the hypocrisy of the 'good woman', and her rude refusal to call the sufferance of rape 'virtue' had one purpose: to unite women in a common perception of their common condition. Selling themselves was women's desperate, necessary, unforgivable crime; not acknowledging the sale divided women and obscured how and why women were used sexually by men; marriage, women's only refuge, was the place of mass rape. Woodhull proclaimed herself a 'Free Lover', by which she meant that she could not be bought, not in marriage, not in prostitution as commonly understood. In telling married women that they had indeed sold their sex for money, she was telling them that they had bartered away more than the prostitute ever could: all privacy, all economic independence, all legal indi-viduality, every shred of control over their bodies in sex and in reproduction both.

Woodhull herself was widely regarded as a whore because she proclaimed herself sexually self-determining, sexually active; she spat in the face of the sexual double standard. Called a prostitute by a man at a public meeting, Woodhull responded: 'A man questioning my virtue! Have I any right as a woman to answer him? I hurl the intention back in your face, sir, and stand boldly before you and this convention, and declare that I never had sexual intercourse with any man of whom I am ashamed to stand side by side before the world with the act. I am not ashamed of any act of my life. At the time it was the best I knew. Nor am I ashamed of any desire that has been gratified, nor of any passion alluded to. Every one of them are a part of my own soul's life, for which, thank God, I am not accountable to you.'[21] Few feminists appreciated her (Elizabeth Cady Stanton was an exception, as usual) because she confronted women with her own sexual vitality, the political meaning of sex, the sexual and economic appropriation of women's bodies by men, the usurpation of female desire by men for the purposes of their own illegitimate power. She was direct and impassioned and she made women remember: that they had been raped. In focusing on the apparent and actual sexual worth of wives and whores, she made the basic claim of radical feminism: all freedom, including sexual freedom, begins with an absolute right to one's own body – physical self-possession. She knew too, in practical as well as political terms, that forced sex in marriage led to forced pregnancy in marriage: 'I protest against this form of slavery, I *protest* against the custom which compels women to give the control of their maternal functions over to anybody.'[22]

Victoria Woodhull exercised sexual intelligence in public discourse, ideas and activism. She is one of the few women to have done so. This effort required all the other kinds of intelligence that distinguish humans from animals: literacy, intellect, creative intelligence, moral intelligence. Some consequences of sexual intelligence become clear in Woodhull's exercise of it: she made the women she addressed in person and in print face the sexual and economic system built on their bodies. She was one of the great philosophers of and agitators for sexual freedom – but not as men understand it, because she abhorred rape and prostitution, knew them when she saw them inside marriage or outside it, would not accept or condone the violence against women implicit in them.

'I make the claim boldly,' she dared to say, 'that from the very moment woman is emancipated from the necessity of yielding the control of her sexual organs to man to insure a home, food and clothing, the doom of sexual demoralization will be sealed.'[23] Since women experienced sexual demoralization most abjectly in sexual intercourse, Woodhull did not shy away from the inevitable conclusion: 'From that moment there will be no intercourse except such as is desired by women. It will be a complete revolution in sexual matters . . .'[24] Intercourse not willed and initiated by the woman was rape, in Woodhull's analysis. She anticipated current feminist critiques of intercourse – modest and rare as they are – by a century. As if to celebrate the centennial of Woodhull's repudiation of male-supremacist sexual intercourse, Robin Morgan in 1974 transformed Woodhull's insight into a firm principle: '*I claim that rape exists any time sexual intercourse occurs when it has not been initiated by the woman, out of her own genuine affection and desire.*'[25] This shocks, bewilders – who can imagine it, what can it mean? Now as then, there is one woman speaking, not a movement.[26]

Woodhull was not taken seriously as a thinker, writer, publisher, journalist, activist, pioneer, by those who followed her – not by the historians, teachers, intellectuals, revolutionaries, reformers; not by the lovers or rapists; not by the women. Had she been part of the cultural dialogue on sexual issues, the whole subsequent development of movements for sexual freedom would have been different in character: because she hated rape and prostitution and understood them as violations of sexual freedom, which male liberationists did not. But then, this was why she was excluded: the men wanted the rape and prostitution. She threatened not only those sacred institutions but the male hallucinations that prettify those institutions: those happy visions of happy women, caged, domesticated or wanton, numb to rape, numb to being bought and sold. Her sexual intelligence was despised, then ignored, because of what it revealed: he who hates the truth hates the intelligence that brings it.

Sexual intelligence in women, that rarest intelligence in a male-supremacist world, is necessarily a revolutionary intelligence, the opposite of the pornographic (which simply reiterates the world as it is for women), the opposite of the will to be used, the opposite of masochism and self-hatred, the opposite of 'good woman' and 'bad woman' both. It is not in being a whore that a woman becomes an outlaw in this man's world; it is in the possession of herself, the ownership and effective control of her own body, her separateness and distinctness, the integrity of her body as hers, not his. Prostitution may be against the written law, but no prostitute has defied the prerogatives or power of men as a class through prostitution. No prostitute provides any model for freedom or action in a world of freedom that can be used with intelligence and integrity by a woman; the model exists to entice counterfeit female sexual revolutionaries, gullible liberated girls, and to serve the men who enjoy them. The prostitute is no honest woman. She manipulates as the wife manipulates. So too no honest woman can live in marriage: no woman honest in her will to be free. Marriage delivers her body to another to sue: and there is no basis for self-respect in this carnal arrangement, however sanctified it may be by church and state.

Wife or whore: she is defined by what men want; sexual intelligence is stopped dead. Wife or whore: to paraphrase Thackeray, her heart is dead ('Her heart was dead long before her body. She had sold it to become Sir Pitt Crawley's wife. Mothers and daughters are making the same bargain every day in Vanity Fair'[27]). Wife or whore: both are fucked, bear children, resent, suffer, grow numb, want more. Wife or whore: both are denied a human life, forced to live a female one. Wife or whore: intelligence denied, annihilated, ridiculed, obliterated, primes her to surrender – to her female fate. Wife or whore: the two kinds of women whom men recognize, whom men let live. Wife or whore: battered, raped, prostituted; men desire her. Wife or whore: the whore comes in from the cold to become the wife if she can; the wife thrown out into the cold becomes the whore if she must. Is there a way out of the home that does not lead, inevitably and horribly, to the street corner? This is the question right-wing women face. This is the question all women face, but right-wing women know it. And in the transit – home to street, street to home – is there any place, reason or chance for female intelligence that is not simply looking for the best buyer?

So ladies, ye who prefer labour to prostitution, who pass days and nights in providing for the wants of your family, it is understood of course that you *are degraded*; a woman ought not to do anything; respect and honour belong to idleness.

You, Victoria of England, Isabella of Spain – you command, therefore you *are radically degraded*.

Jenny P. D'Hericourt, *A Woman's Philosophy of Woman; or Woman Affranchised*, 1864

The sex labour of women for the most part is private – in the bedroom – or secret – prostitutes may be seen, but how the johns use them may not. Ideally women do nothing; women simply are women. In truth women get used up in private or in secret being women. In the ideal conception of womanhood, women do not do work that can be seen: women only do hidden sex labour. In the real world, women who work for wages outside of sex are dangerously outside the female sphere; and women are denigrated for not being ideal – apparently idle, untouched by visible labour.

Behind the smoke screen of ideal idleness, there is always women's work. Women's work, first, is marriage. 'In the morning I'm always nervous,' Carolina de Jesus wrote. 'I'm afraid of not getting money to buy food to eat. . . . Senhor Manuel showed up saying he wanted to marry me. But I don't want to . . . a man isn't going to like a woman who can't stop reading and gets out of bed to write and sleeps with paper and pencil under her pillow. That's why I prefer to live alone, for my ideals.'[28]

The woman in marriage is often in marriage because her ideal is eating, not writing.

Women's work, second, is prostitution: sexual service outside of marriage for money. 'I'd like so much to have the illusion that I had some freedom of choice,' said J. in Kate Millett's *The Prostitution Papers*. 'Maybe it's just an illusion, but I need to think I had some freedom. Yet then I realize how much was determined in the way I got into prostitution, how determined my life had been, how fucked over I was . . . So I believed I'd chosen it. What's most terrifying is to look back, to realize what I went through and that I endured it.'[29]

The woman in prostitution learns, as Linda Lovelace said in *Ordeal*, 'to settle for the smallest imaginable triumphs, the absence of pain or the momentary lessening of terror'.[30] The woman in prostitution is often in prostitution because her ideal is physical survival – surviving the pimp, surviving poverty, having nowhere to go.

Women's social condition is built on a simple premise: women can be fucked and bear babies, therefore women must be fucked and bear babies. Sometimes, especially among the sophisticated, 'penetrated' is substituted for 'fucked': women can be penetrated, therefore women must be penetrated. This logic does not apply to men, whichever word is used: men can be fucked, therefore men must be fucked; men can be penetrated, therefore men must be penetrated. This logic applies only to women and sex. One does not say, for instance, women have delicate hands, therefore women must be surgeons. Or women have legs, therefore women must run, jump, climb. Or women have minds, therefore women must use them. One does learn, however, that women have sex organs that must be used by men, or the women are not women: they are somehow less or more, either of which is bad and thoroughly discouraged. Women are defined, valued, judged, in one way only: as women – that is, with sex organs that must be used. Other parts of the body do not signify, unless used in sex or as an indicator of sexual availability or desirability. Intelligence does not count. It has nothing to do with what a woman *is*.

Women are born into the labour pool specific to women: the labour is sex. Intelligence does not modify, reform or revolutionize this basic fact of life for women.

Women are marked for marriage and prostitution by a wound between the legs, acknowledged as such when men show their strange terror of women. Intelligence neither creates nor destroys this wound; nor does it change the uses of the wound, the woman, the sex.

Women's work is done below the waist; intelligence is higher. Women are lower; men are higher. It is a simple, dull scheme; but women's sex organs in and of themselves are apparently appalling enough to justify the scheme, make it self-evidently true.

The natural intelligence of women, however expanded by what women manage to learn despite their low status, manifests in surviving: enduring, marking time, bearing pain, becoming numb, absorbing loss – especially loss of self. Women survive men's use of them – marriage, prostitution, rape; women's intelligence expresses itself in finding ways to endure and find meaning in the unendurable, to endure being used because of one's sex. 'Sex with men, how can I say, lacks the personal,'[31] wrote Maryse Holder in *Give Sorrow Words*.

Some women want to work: not sex labour; real work; work that men, those real humans, do for a living wage. They want an honest wage for honest work. One of the prostitutes Kate Millett interviewed made $800 a week in her prime. 'With a Ph.D. and after ten years' experience in teaching,' Millet wrote, 'I was permitted to make only $60 a week.'[32]

Women's work that is not marriage or prostitution is mostly segregated, always underpaid, stagnant, sex-stereotyped. In the United States in 1981 women earned 56 to 59 per cent of what men earned. Women are paid significantly less than men for doing comparable work. It is not easy to find comparable work. The consequences of this inequity – however the percentages read in any given year, in any given country – are not new for women. Unable to sell sex-neutral labour for a living wage, women must sell sex. 'To subordinate woman in a social order in which she must *work in order to live*', Jenny D'Hericourt wrote French socialist Joseph Proudhon in the mid-1800s, 'is to *desire prostitution*; for disdain of the producer extends to the value of the product; . . . The woman who cannot live by working, can only do so by prostituting herself; the equal of man or a courtesan, such is the alternative.'[33] Proudhon's egalitarian vision could not be stretched to include women. He wrote D'Hericourt:

> . . . I do not admit that, whatever reparation may be due to woman, of joint thirds with her husband (or father) and her children, the most rigorous justice can ever make her the EQUAL of man; . . . neither do I admit that this inferiority of the female sex constitutes for it either servitude, or humiliation, or a diminution of dignity, liberty or happiness. I maintain that the contrary is true.[34]

D'Hericourt's argument constructs the world of women: women must work for fair wages in nonsexual labour or they must sell themselves to men; the disdain of men for women makes the work of women worth less simply because women do it; the devaluation of women's work is predetermined by the devaluation of women as a sex class; women end up having to sell themselves because men will not buy labour from them that is not sex labour at wages that will enable women to divest themselves of sex as a form of labour.

Proudhon's answer constructs the world of men: in the best of all possible worlds – acknowledging that some economic discrimination against women has taken place – no justice on earth can make women equal to men because women are inferior to men: this inferiority does not humiliate or degrade women; women find happiness, dignity and liberty in this inequality precisely because they are women – that is the nature of women; women are being treated justly and are free when they are treated as women – that is, as the natural inferiors of men.

The brave new world Proudhon wanted was, for women, the same old world women already knew.

D'Hericourt recognized what Victoria Woodhull would not: 'disdain of the producer extends to the value of the product'. Work for wages outside sex labour would not effectively free women from the stigma of being female because the stigma precedes the woman and predetermines the undervaluing of her work.

This means that right-wing women are correct when they say that they are worth more in the home than outside it. In the home their value is recognized and in the workplace it is not. In marriage, sex labour is rewarded: the woman is generally 'given' more than she herself could earn at a job. In the marketplace, women are exploited as cheap labour. The argument that work outside the home makes women sexually and economically independent of men is simply untrue. Women are paid too little. And right-wing women know it.

Feminists know that if women are paid equal wages for equal work, women will gain sexual as well as economic independence. But feminists have refused to face the fact that in a woman-hating social system, women will never be paid equal wages. Men in all their institutions of power are sustained by the sex labour and sexual subordination of women. The sex labour of women must be maintained; and systematic low wages for sex-neutral work effectively force women to sell sex to survive. The economic system that pays women lower wages than it pays men actually punishes women for working outside marriage or prostitution, since women work hard for low wages and still must sell sex. The economic system that punishes women for working outside the bedroom by paying low wages contributes significantly to women's perception that the sexual serving of men is a necessary part of any women's life: or how else could she live? Feminists appear to think that equal pay for equal work is a simple reform, whereas it is no reform at all; it is revolution. Feminists have refused to face the fact that equal pay for equal work is impossible as long as men rule women, and right-wing women have refused to forget it. Devaluation of women's labour outside the home pushes women back into the home and encourages women to support a system in which, as she sees it, he is paid for both of them – her share of his wage being more than she could earn herself.

In the workplace, sexual harassment fixes the low status of women irreversibly. Women are sex; even filing or typing, women are sex. The debilitating, insidious violence of sexual harassment is pervasive in the workplace. It is part of nearly every working environment. Women shuffle; women placate; women submit; women leave; the rare, brave women fight and are tied up in the courts, often without jobs, for years. There is also rape in the workplace.

Where is the place for intelligence – for literacy, intellect, creativity, moral discernment? Where in this world in which women live, circumscribed by the uses to which men put women's sexual organs, is the cultivation of skills, the cultivation of gifts, the cultivation of dreams, the cultivation of ambition? Of what use is human intelligence to a woman?

'Of course,' wrote Virginia Woolf, 'the learned women were very ugly; but then they were very poor. She would like to feed Chuffy for a term on Lucy's rations and see what he said then about Henry the Eighth.'[35]

'No, it would not do the slightest good if he read my manuscript . . .', wrote Ellen Glasgow in her memoir. ' "The best advice I can give you", he said, with charming candour, "is to stop writing, and go back to the South and have some babies." And I think, though I may have heard this ripe wisdom from other men, probably from many, that he added: "The greatest woman is not the woman who has written the finest book, but the woman who has had the finest babies." That might be true. I did not stay to dispute it. However, it was true also that I wanted to write books, and not ever had I felt the faintest wish to have babies.'[36]

Woodhull thought that freedom from sexual coercion would come with work in the marketplace. She was wrong; the marketplace became, as men would have it, another place for sexual intimidation, another arena of danger to women burdened already with too many such arenas. Woolf put her faith in education and art. She too was wrong. Men erase; misogyny distorts; the intelligence of women is still both punished and despised.

Right-wing women have surveyed the world: they find it a dangerous place. They see that work subjects them to more danger from more men; it increases the risk of sexual exploitation. They see that creativity and originality in their kind are ridiculed; they see women thrown out of the circle of male civilization for having ideas, plans, visions, ambitions. They see that traditional marriage means selling to one man, not hundreds: the better deal. They see that the streets are cold, and that the women on them are tired, sick and bruised. They see that the money they can earn will not make them independent of men and that they will still have to play the sex games of their kind: at home and at work too. They see no way to make their bodies authentically their own and to survive in the world of men. They know too that the Left has nothing better to offer: leftist men also want wives and whores; leftist men value whores too much and wives too little. Right-wing women are not wrong. They fear that the Left, in stressing impersonal sex and promiscuity as values, will make them more vulnerable to male sexual aggression, and that they will be despised for not liking it. They are not wrong. Right-wing women see that within the system in which they live they cannot make their bodies their own, but they can agree to privatized male ownership: keep it one-on-one, as it were. They know that they are valued for their sex – their sex organs and their reproductive capacity – and so they try to up their value: through co-operation, manipulation, conformity; through displays of affection or attempts at friendship; through submission and obedience; and especially through the use of euphemism – 'femininity', 'total woman', 'good', 'maternal instinct', 'motherly love'. Their desperation is quiet; they hide their bruises of body and heart; they dress carefully and have good manners; they suffer, they love God, they follow the rules. They see that intelligence displayed in a woman is a flaw, that intelligence realized in a woman is a crime. They see the world they live in and they are not wrong. They use sex and babies to stay valuable because they need a home, food, clothing. They use the traditional intelligence of the female – animal, not human: they do what they have to to survive.

NOTES

* *Pornography: Men Possessing Women* (London: Women's Press, 1981).
** *Right Wing Women: The Politics of Domesticated Females* (London: Women's Press, 1983), p. 25.
*** *Right Wing Women*, p. 66.
1 Andrea Dworkin's 'The Politics of Intelligence' from *Right Wing Women* is reproduced by permission of the Women's Press, London, © 1983.

2   Norman Mailer, *Advertisements for Myself* (New York: G. P. Putnam's Sons, Perigee Books, 1981), p. 433.

3   Edith Wharton, 'The Touchstone', in *Madame de Treymes and Others* (New York: Charles Scribner's Sons, 1970), p. 12.

4   Carolina Maria de Jesus, *Child of the Dark: The Diary of Carolina Maria de Jesus*, trans. David St Clair (New York: New American Library, 1962), p. 47.

5   Catharine A. MacKinnon, 'Feminism, Marxism, Method and the State: An Agenda for Theory', *Signs: A Journal of Women in Culture and Society*, Vol. 7, No. 3, Spring 1982.

6   See *The Total Woman* (New York: Pocket Books, 1975); 'In the beginning, sex started in the garden. The first man was all alone. The days were long, the nights were longer. He had no cook, no nurse, no lover. God saw that man was lonely and in need of a partner, so He gave him a woman, the best present any man could receive' (p. 129). 'Spiritually, for sexual intercourse to be the ultimate satisfaction, both partners need a personal relationship with their God. When this is so their union is sacred and beautiful, and mysteriously the two blend perfectly into one' (p. 128).

7   For instance: 'Christianity brought marriage into the world: marriage as we know it. . . . Man and wife, a king and queen with one or two subjects, and a few square yards of territory of their own: this, really, is marriage. It is true freedom because it is a true fulfillment for man, woman, and children' (*Sex, Literature and Censorship* (New York: The Viking Press, 1959), p. 98). 'It is the tragedy of modern woman. . . . She is cocksure, but she is a hen all the time. Frightened of her own henny self, she rushes to mad lengths about votes, or welfare, or sports, or business: she is marvellous, out-manning the man. . . . Suddenly it all falls out of relation to her basic henny self, and she realizes she has lost her life. The lovely henny surety, the hensureness which is the real bliss of every female, has been denied her: she never had it. . . . Nothingness!' (*Sex, Literature and Censorship*, pp. 49–50). '. . . marriage is no marriage that is not basically and permanently phallic, and that is not linked up with the sun and the earth, the moon and the fixed stars and the planets, in the rhythm of days, in the rhythm of months, in the rhythm of quarters, of years, of decades, of centuries. Marriage is no marriage that is not a correspondence of blood. . . . The phallus is a column of blood that fills the valley of blood of a woman' (*Sex, Literature, and Censorship*, p. 101). 'Into the womb of the primary darkness enters the ray of ultimate light, and time is begotten, conceived, there is the beginning of the end. We are the beginning of the end. And there, within the womb,

we ripen upon the beginning, till we become aware of the end'
(*Reflections on the Death of a Porcupine* (Bloomington: Indiana University Press, 1963), p. 7).

8 For instance: 'Why do you think the homosexuals are called fruits?
It's because they eat the forbidden fruit of life. . . . That's why homosexuality is an abomination of God, because life is so precious to God and it is such a sacred thing when man and woman come together in one flesh and the seed is fertilized – that's the sealing of life, that's the beginning of life. To interfere with that in any way – especially the eating of the forbidden fruit, the eating of the sperm – that's why it's such an abomination. . . . it makes the sin of homosexuality all the more hideous because it's antilife, degenerative' (*Playboy*, May 1978).

9 For instance: '. . . but if you're not ready to make a baby with that marvellous sex, then you may also be putting something down the drain forever, which is the ability that you had to make a baby; the most marvellous thing that was in you may have been shot into a diaphragm or wasted on a pill. One might be losing one's future' (*The Presidential Papers* (New York: Bantam Books, 1964), p. 142). 'Of the million spermatozoa, there may be only two or three with any real chance of reaching the ovum . . . [The others] go out with no sense at all of being real spermatozoa. They may appear to be real spermatozoa under the microscope, but after all, a man from Mars who's looking at us through a telescope might think that Communist bureaucrats and FBI men look exactly the same. . . . Even the electron microscope can't measure the striation of passion in a spermatozoon. Or the force of its will' (*The Presidential Papers*, p. 143). 'I hate contraception. . . . There's nothing I abhor more than planned parenthood. Planned parenthood is an abomination. I'd rather have those fucking Communists over here' (*The Presidential Papers*, p. 131). 'I think one of the reasons that homosexuals go through such agony when they're around 40 or 50 is that their lives have nothing to do with procreation. They realize with great horror that all that wonderful sex they had in the past is gone – where is it now? They've used up their being' (*The Presidential Papers*, p. 144). 'It's better to commit rape than masturbate' (*The Presidential Papers*, p. 140). 'what if the seed be already a being? So desperate that it / claws, bites, cuts and lies, / burns, and betrays / desperate to capture the oven . . .' ('I Got Two Kids and Another in the Oven', (*Advertisements for Myself*, p. 397).

10 De Jesus, *Child of the Dark*, p. 29.

11 Florence Nightingale, *Cassandra* (Old Westbury, NY: The Feminist Press, 1979), p. 49.

12 Virginia Woolf, *The Pargiters: The Novel-Essay Portion of 'The Years'*,

ed. Mitchell A. Leaska (New York: The New York Public Library & Readex Books, 1977), pp. 164–5.

13   Abby Kelley, in a speech, cited by Blanche Glassman Hersh in *The Slavery of Sex* (Urbana, IL: University of Illinois Press, 1978), p. 33.

14   Alice James, *The Diary of Alice James*, ed. Leon Edel (New York: Dodd, Mead & Company, 1964), p. 66.

15   Woolf, *Pargiters*, pp. xxxix–xxxx [sic] (speech given 21 January, 1931).

16   Olive Schreiner, *The Story of an African Farm* (New York: Penguin Books, 1979), p. 148.

17   Nightingale, *Cassandra*, p. 25.

18   Woodhull wrote an exposé of Henry Ward Beecher's adulterous affair with Elizabeth Tilton, the wife of his best friend. Beecher was an eminent minister. His hypocrisy was the main issue for Woodhull. The exposé was published by Woodhull in her own paper, *Woodhull and Clafin's Weekly*. She was arrested, as was her sister and co-publisher, Tennessee Clafin, for sending obscene literature through the mails. She was imprisoned for four weeks without trial.

19   Victoria Woodhull, 'Tried As By Fire; or, The True and The False, Socially', 1874, *The Victoria Woodhull Reader*, ed. Madeleine B. Stern (Weston, MA: M & S Press, 1974), p. 19.

20   Ibid., p. 8.

21   Victoria Woodhull, cited by Johanna Johnston, *Mrs Satan* (New York: G. P. Putnam's Sons, 1967), p. 205.

22   Woodhull, 'The Principles of Social Freedom', 1871, *Victoria Woodhull Reader*, p. 36.

23   Woodhull, 'Tried As By Fire . . .', *Victoria Woodhull Reader*, p. 39.

24   Ibid.

25   Robin Morgan, 'Theory and Practice: Pornography and Rape', 1974, *Going Too Far* (New York: Random House, 1977), pp. 163–9 (p. 165).

26   In a recent essay, novelist Alice Walker wrote: '. . . I submit that any sexual intercourse between a free man and a human being he owns or controls is rape.' (See 'Embracing the Dark and the Light', *Essence*, July 1982, p. 117.) This definition has the advantage of articulating the power that is the context for as well as the substance of the act.

27   William Makepeace Thackeray, *Vanity Fair* (New York: New American Library, 1962), p. 168.

28   De Jesus, *Child of the Dark*, p. 50.

29   Kate Millett, *The Prostitution Papers* (New York: Avon, 1973), pp. 78–9.

30   Linda Lovelace and Mike McGrady, *Ordeal* (Secaucus, NJ: Citadel Press, 1980), p. 66.

31   Maryse Holder, *Give Sorrow Words* (New York: Avon, 1980), p. 3.
32   Millett, *Prostitution Papers*, p. 95.
33   Jenny P. D'Hericourt, *A Woman's Philosophy of Woman; or Woman Affranchised* (New York: Carleton, Publisher, 1864), p. 41.
34   Joseph Proudhon, in D'Hericourt, *Woman's Philosophy*, p. 36.
35   Woolf, *Pargiters*, p. 120.
36   Ellen Glasgow, *The Woman Within* (New York: Hill and Wang, 1980), p. 108.

7

Rosalind Coward
b.1952

'NAUGHTY BUT NICE: FOOD PORNOGRAPHY' from
FEMALE DESIRE (1984)

*In the collection from which this essay is taken, Rosalind Coward brings
the insights of semiological theory to bear on the representation of femininity
in British culture (though her findings certainly have a wider relevance).
The collection as a whole provides a disturbing overview of the 'regime of
pleasure' which constitutes (normal) female sexuality in this culture –
disturbing not only in its concreteness but in the emphasis placed, as here,
on the way familiar patterns of pleasure-seeking tend to reinforce male
power and female powerlessness.*

*The metaphorical concept of 'food pornography' illustrates how critical
analysis can bring out a formal resemblance between outwardly dissimilar
phenomena. On the one hand, suggests Coward, we have an industry
supplying sexual imagery to men for the purposes of a supposedly illicit
(though in fact socially conformist) enjoyment; on the other, an industry
supplying women with an equally obsessional genre of imagery in which
conformity and transgression are again held in balance. Both alike contribute to the positioning of their respective consumers within the sexual
power structure. But whereas men are positioned by sexual pornography
as the dominant gender, women are positioned by food pornography as the
subordinate one.*

*Food pornography speaks to us of our subordination in a double sense:
firstly through the cultural link between cookery and domestic servitude,*

and secondly by playing on our ambivalence – our blend of defiance and submission – towards the social norms which regulate female food intake. Hence the potential in women's imagination not only for a 'virtuous' but also for a 'naughty' or orgiastic variety of food reverie. And hence in turn the prominence in this essay of the idea of guilt *– a condition which consists (on its subjective side) in the feeling of having violated rules or principles that one has nevertheless, at some level, acknowledged as valid. (In this case: be beautiful; be slim; and above all, control your appetites!) The topic of guilt is relatively recessive in current ethical theory, but the reality (in this subjective sense) is probably as central as ever to the moral experience of women. Coward's discussion explores just one of the ideological structures which make feminine self-esteem so inherently elusive.*

There's a full-page spread in a woman's magazine. It's captioned 'Breakfast Special', and shows a picture of every delicious breakfast imaginable.[1] The hungry eye can delight in croissants with butter, exquisitely prepared bacon and eggs, toasted waffles with maple syrup. But over the top of the pictures there's a sinister message: 430 calories for the croissants; 300 for the waffles. The English breakfast takes the biscuit with a top score of 665 calories. It must be a galling sight for the readers of this particular magazine. Because it's *Slimmer* magazine. And one presumes the reader looks on these pleasures in the full knowledge that they had better not be indulged.

This pleasure in looking at the supposedly forbidden is reminiscent of another form of guilty-but-indulgent looking, that of sexual pornography. Sexual pornography as a separate realm of imagery exists because our society defines some explicit pictures of sexual activity or sexual parts as 'naughty', 'illicit'. These images are then made widely available through a massive and massively profitable industry.

The glossy pictures in slimming magazines show in glorious Technicolor all the illicit desires which make us fat. Many of the articles show almost life-size pictures of the real baddies of the dieting world – bags of crisps, peanuts, bars of chocolate, cream puddings. Diet foods are advertised as sensuously as possible. The food is made as appetizing as possible, often with explicit sexual references: 'Tip Top. For Girls who used to say No'; 'Grapefruits. The Least Forbidden Fruit'.

Pictures in slimming magazines and those circulated around the slimming culture are only the hard core of food pictures which are in general circulation in women's magazines. Most women's magazines carry articles about food, recipes or advertising. All are accompanied by larger-than-life, elaborate pictures of food, cross-sections through a cream and strawberry sponge, or close-ups of succulent Orange and Walnut Roast Beef. Recipe books often dwell on the visual impact of food. Robert Carrier has glossy cards showing the dish in question and carrying the recipe on the back – just the right size for the pocket. In the street, billboards confront us with gargantuan cream cakes.

But it is only the unfortunate readers of the slimming magazines who are supposed to use the pictures as a substitute for the real thing. While other forms of food photography are meant to stimulate the desire to prepare and eat the food, for the slimmers it is a matter of feasting the eyes only.

Like sexual pornography, pictures of food provide a photographic genre geared towards one sex. And like sexual pornography, it is a regime of 'pleasure' which is incomprehensible to the opposite sex. This is because these pornographies are creating and indulging 'pleasures' which confirm or trap men and women in their respective positions of power and subordination.

Sexual pornography is an industry dealing in images geared towards men. Sexual pornography is dominated by pictures of women. It shows bits of women's bodies, women engaged in sex acts, women masturbating, women supposedly having orgasms. When the women look at the camera, it is with an expression of sexual arousal, interest and availability. The way in which women are posed for these images presupposes a male viewer, behind the camera, as it were, about to move in on the act.

Pornography is only the extreme end of how images of women are circulated in general in this society. Pornography is defined as being illicit, naughty, unacceptable for public display (though definitions of what is acceptable vary from one epoch to the next). It shows things which generally available images don't – penetration, masturbation, women's genitals. The porn industry then thrives on marketing and circulating these 'illicit' images. But if pornography is meant to be illicit, and hidden, the kinds of images it shows differ little from the more routinely available images of women. Page three nudes in daily papers, advertisements showing women, the representation of sex in non-pornographic films, all draw on the conventions by which women are represented in pornography. Women are made to look into the camera in the same way, their bodies are arranged in the same way, the same glossy photographic techniques are used, there is the same fragmentation of women's bodies, and a concomitant fetishistic concentration on bits of the body.

Many women now think that the way male arousal is catered for in these images is a problem. These images feed a belief that men have depersonalized sexual needs, like sleeping or going to the lavatory. Pornography as it is currently practised suggests that women's bodies are available to meet those needs. Men often say that porn is just fantasy, a harmless way of having pleasure as a substitute for the real thing. But women have begun to question this use of the term 'pleasure'. After all, the pleasure seems conditional on feeling power to use women's bodies. And maybe there's only a thin line between the fantasy and the lived experience of sexuality where men do sometimes force their sexual attentions on women.

If sexual pornography is a display of images which confirm men's sense of themselves as having power over women, food pornography is a regime of pleasurable images which has the opposite effect on its viewers – women. It indulges a pleasure which is linked to servitude and therefore confirms the subordinate position of women. Unlike sexual pornography, however, food porn cannot even be used without guilt. Because of pressures to diet, women have been made to feel guilty about enjoying food.

The use of food pornography is surprisingly widespread. All the women I have talked to about food have confessed to enjoying it. Few activities it seems rival relaxing in bed with a good recipe book. Some indulged in full-colour pictures of gleaming bodies of Cold Mackerel Basquaise lying invitingly on a bed of peppers, or perfectly formed chocolate mousse topped with mounds of cream. The intellectuals expressed a preference for erotica, Elizabeth David's historical and literary titillation. All of us used the recipe books as aids to oral gratification, stimulants to imagine new combinations of food, ideas for producing a lovely meal.

Cooking food and presenting it beautifully is an act of servitude. It is a way of expressing affection through a gift. In fact, the preparation of a meal involves intensive domestic labour, the most devalued labour in this society. That we should aspire to produce perfectly finished and presented food is a symbol of a willing and enjoyable participation in servicing other people.

Food pornography exactly sustains these meanings relating to the preparation of food. The kinds of pictures used always repress the process of production of a meal. They are always beautifully lit, often touched up. The settings are invariably exquisite – a conservatory in the background, fresh flowers on the table. The dishes are expensive and look barely used.

There's a whole professional ideology connected with food photography. The *Focal Encyclopaedia of Photography* tells us that in a 'good food picture', 'the food must be both perfectly cooked and perfectly displayed' if it is to appeal to the magazine reader. The photographer 'must decide in advance on the correct style and arrangement of table linen, silver, china, flowers. Close attention to such details is vital because the final pictures must survive the critical inspection of housewives and cooks.' Food photographers are supposed to be at the service of the expert chef, but sometimes 'the photographer learns by experience that certain foodstuffs do not photograph well.' And in such circumstances, 'he must be able to suggest reasonable substitutes.' Glycerine-covered green paper is a well-known substitute for lettuce, which wilts under the bright lights of a studio. And fast-melting foods like ice-cream pose interesting technical problems for the food photographer. Occasionally, they do get caught out – I recently saw a picture of a sausage dinner where a nail was clearly visible, holding the sausage to its surroundings! Virtually all meals shown in these photos are actually inedible. If not actually made of plaster, most are sprayed or treated for photographing. How ironic to think of the perfect meal destined for the dustbin.

Food photographs are the culinary equivalent of the removal of unsightly hairs. Not only do hours of work go into the preparation of the settings and the dishes, but the finished photos are touched up and imperfections removed to make the food look succulent and glistening. The aim of these photos is the display of the perfect meal in isolation from the kitchen context and the process of its production. There are no traces of the hours of shopping, cleaning, cutting up, preparing, tidying up, arranging the table and the room which in fact go into the production of a meal. Just as we know that glamorous models in the adverts don't really look as they appear, so we know perfectly well about the hours of untidy chaos involved in the preparation of a meal. We know that photos of glamour models are touched up, skin blemishes removed, excess fat literally cut out of the picture. And – subconsciously at least – we probably realize the same process has been at work on the Black Forest Gateau. But the ideal images still linger in our minds as a lure. A meal should really look like the pictures. And that's how the images produce complicity in our subordination. We aim at giving others pleasure by obliterating the traces of our labour.

But it is not as if, even if we could produce this perfect meal, we could wholeheartedly enjoy it. Because at the same time as food is presented as the one legitimate sensual pleasure for women we are simultaneously told that women shouldn't eat too much. Food is Naughty but Nice, as the current Real Dairy Cream advertisement announces.

This guilt connected with eating has become severe over the last few decades. It's a result of the growing pressure over these years towards the ideal shape of women. This shape is more like an adolescent than a woman, a silhouette rather than a soft body. There's a current dictum in slimming circles: 'If you can pinch an inch, you may need to lose weight.' This seems a particularly vicious control of female contours in a society obsessed with eating and uninterested in physical exertion. Dieting is the forcible imposition of an ideal shape on a woman's body.

The presentation of food sets up a particular trap for women. The glossy, sensual photography legitimates oral desires and pleasures for women in a way that sexual interest for women is never legitimated. At the same time, however, much of the food photography constructs a direct equation between food and fat, an equation which can only generate guilt about oral pleasures. Look at the way advertising presents food, drawing a direct equation between what women eat and what shape they will be. Tab is the low-calorie drink from Coca-Cola. Its advertising campaign shows a glass of the stuff which is in the shape of a woman's body! Beside the glass are the statistics 35" 22" 35". A Sweetex advertisement shows two slender women and exhorts 'Take the lumps out of your life. Take Sweetex'! Heinz promotes its 'Slimway Mayonnaise' with a picture of a very lurid lobster and the caption 'Mayonnaise without guilt'. Tea even 'adds a little weight to the slimming argument'. Another soft-drink company exhorts: 'Spoil yourself, not your figure', which is a common promise for slimming foods. Nor is this phenomenon confined to slimming foods. Women's magazines have articles about whether 'your taste buds are ruining your figure', and creamy foods are offered as wicked but worth it.

An equation is set up in this kind of writing and these pictures between what goes into the mouth and the shape your body will be. It is as if we swallow a mouthful and it goes immediately, without digestion, to join the 'cellulite'. If we give this a moment's thought, we realize it is nonsense. There's no direct correlation between food into the mouth and fat; that's about the *only* thing on which all the diet experts agree. People have different metabolisms, use food differently. Different things in different people's lives affect what they eat and what effect that eating has on overall health. But the simplistic ideologies behind food and dieting cultures reinforce the guilt associated with food for women. Oral pleasures are only really permissible when tied to the servicing of others in the production of a meal. Women are controlled and punished if they indulge themselves.

The way images of food are made and circulated is not just an innocent catering for pleasures. They also meddle in people's sense of themselves and their self-worth. In a sexually divided and hierarchical society, these pleasures are tied to positions of power and subordination.

NOTES

1 The editors and publishers gratefully acknowledge permission of Grafton Books, © Paladin 1984, to reproduce Rosalind Coward's 'Naughty but Nice: Food Pornography' from her *Female Desire*.

8

Nickie Roberts
b.1949

'SEX, CLASS AND MORALITY' from
THE FRONT LINE (1986)

Nickie Roberts worked for eight years in Soho as a stripper. The Front
Line *tells the story of how she got into the business, how she got out of it,
and her own experiences there. And it tells the stories of eight of her coworkers – peep-show girls, dancers, prostitutes. Her concluding chapter,
which we reprint here, presents her reflections on the industry, and on
public attitudes to it.*

*There are two conditions for sex trade: the existence of people who have
money and are willing to spend it on sex or its visual surrogates, and the
existence of people who lack money and are willing to perform sexual
services in exchange for it. The social fact that there are people in either of
these categories is deplored by feminist opponents of the institutions of the
trade. They criticize arrangements which produce in men an aggressive
sexuality and in women a conception of self-worth tied to the service of
others, and arrangements which endow men with economic power and
deny such power to women. But they do not condemn those who have
made the sex trade their work: opposition to capitalism does not imply
contempt for the working class; those who campaigned for the abolition of
slavery never asked slaves to reform. This is Nickie Roberts's starting
point: one can attack the industry without any moralistic onslaught on its
workers.*

*'Morality' nevertheless is Roberts's concern. In the sex trade, the public
arena of the capitalist marketplace becomes the home of relations that our*

culture deems most private. Conventional morality incorporates a 'double standard' permitting promiscuous sexuality to men and forbidding it to women. The workings of the double standard, and some of its hidden rationale, are nowhere more apparent than in attitudes to participants in the trade. A Royal Commission Report in the 1860s held that 'there is no comparison to be made between prostitutes and the men who consort with them. With the one sex the offence is committed as a matter of gain; with the other it is an irregular indulgence of natural impulse.'* Prostitution as such is no longer a criminal offence in this country, as Roberts points out. But we may still be brought up to believe that the evil of sex trade resides in its workers.

Roberts presents a view of what is immoral which is thoroughly socially situated. She draws attention to the conditions that make women become prostitutes and strippers.** And she exposes the hypocrisy of a male-dominated society that blames women for crimes against women.

> What makes a prostitute is the nature of sexual relationships as they are viewed, created and practised by men. And the other thing that makes a prostitute is that this same society provides the 'goods' needed to fill this demand, through unemployment, poverty, low pay or bad working conditions – the list is endless. In the end, what makes a prostitute is an ideology of commodity and consumption. Once the body is transformed into an object, metamorphosed by a mutilated, handicapped, repressed sexuality, the next thing is to consume it.
>
> Claude Jaget, *Prostitutes – Our Life*

The reaction*** I got from straights was nothing but cruel abuse; a real slagging-off from all quarters.[1] From the political Left, the Right; from some 'feminist' puritans, and other moralists . . . the whole caboodle. I was shocked by the response to my writings! How naïve of me.

I was accused of attacking the sex industry. I was accused of defending the sex industry. One particularly bilious man accused me of simultaneously attacking *and* defending the sex industry. It seemed that some people couldn't get it through their thick skulls that I was in fact – and still am – *attacking* the sex industry and *defending* its workers.

A 'feminist' informed me that the sex industry doesn't exist; it isn't an industry and what we do isn't work. Maybe she thinks it's a hobby . . .

More than anything else, I was accused of being immoral. Nothing new there, I suppose. Except to ask whose 'morality' were my accusers referring to? Why, their own, of course. These paragons tend to forget that we strippers and prostitutes are all too familiar with what lurks beneath the surface of straight society's 'morality'; we have been on the receiving end of it for too long. We *know* that the notion of 'respectability' is nothing but a sham, and that underneath the sham, the facts are pretty slimy. And when we refuse to keep our traps shut, the knowledge we possess then represents a real threat to society's attitudes and beliefs. That's when the moralists start screaming. Too bad. The cover-up job has been going on for too long; all the myths and lies about women like us being 'whores' who just love what we do, or can't help ourselves, or both.

Think of it – all those Lulus and Nanas and Camilles: sluts who couldn't stop even if they wanted to. Figments of male literary imagination. *That's* where all the 'It must really turn you on being a stripper' crap we all get at some point originates. Men's nudge-nudge-wink-wink fantasy that women who work in the sex industry are little more than raging nymphomaniacs.

It's also why to this day male writers, critics, and journalists persist in referring to prostitute women as 'whores'. They use that word with lip-smacking relish, almost with glee. Men love the fantasy of the 'whore'. They prefer that word, with all its connotations of greedy rampant female sexuality. Writing 'prostitute woman' would spoil all the fun, because that brings economics into the picture, raising some very uncomfortable questions about men and women, and power and sex . . . questions that have to be answered.

Female writers, I've noticed, appear to be more at ease with 'tart'. It's a much more genteel way of putting it; a way of metaphorically handling the subject with a pair of tongs, so that the 'good' female can dissociate herself from us baddies. She's not 'immoral', like us.

Back to that again! The question of 'morality'. But in any case, it's high time the whole concept of what is moral and what isn't was redefined: broadened a bit, to include the views of others who might not subscribe to the middle-class Christian version. For instance, there are those of us who would argue that a society which uses the services of women in the sex industry, yet at the same time condemns us for providing those services, is immoral and hypocritical. And is it not immoral that the source of the supply for these services should be working-class women whose only other 'choice' would be a lifetime of drudgery and poverty? Unpaid drudgery in the home, or low-paid drudgery in the factory. Both, more often than not.

Working-class women are expected to accept the life of a drudge without a murmur of complaint. What I and others like me left behind us when we ran away from our home towns was the grey life. Many of us found some *freedom* when we landed in the sex industry. To this day I do not regret what I did; and neither do any of my friends. All the labels we've been given – degraded, exploited, victims – those are the labels I've left behind on the path that was laid down for me originally. As far as I'm concerned, working in crummy factories for disgusting pay was the most degrading and exploitative work I ever did in my life. I'm aware that, in a sense, it was a Hobson's choice for me. I see that now, but I still maintain that I had more control over my life as a worker in the sex factory than as one in an ordinary factory. When I left Lancashire, I was rejecting the whole ethos of living to work and working to live, that had been the lot of my predecessors. I think there should be another word for the kind of work that working-class people do; something to differentiate it from the work middle-class people do; the ones who have careers. All I can think of is *drudgery*. It's rotten and hopeless; not even half a life. It's *immoral*. Yet as I say, it's *expected* of working-class women that they deny themselves everything. Above all, a sense of your own worth as an individual; an awareness of yourself as being a person in your own right, which is something that middle-class people take for granted practically from the moment they learn to speak. *Nowhere* are working-class women allowed the space in which to develop as human beings. We are trained from birth *not* to have any real sense of ourselves as anything other than the work we do: the servers and servicers of our 'betters', whether they be from a 'higher' class or simply our husbands: men. We are not supposed to feel; we are supposed to function. We are not supposed to have any notions about whatever potential we might have. At school, at work, through the media, we get the message loud and clear:

This is what you're worth.

This is all you're going to get . . .

So make the most of it; don't question it; this is the way it's always been. Don't rock the boat. And as for having any aspirations of your own – forget it! Don't bother . . .

So when some of us rebel against our life's 'prospects', why should we be labelled *immoral*? Why should I have to put up with a middle-class feminist asking me why I didn't 'do anything – scrub toilets, even?' rather than become a stripper? What's so liberating about cleaning up other people's shit?

But that's what I keep hearing; time and time again. It drives me round the bend. It seems it's okay to do shitwork and stay poor: that's not immoral – but being a stripper or a prostitute and earning good money *is*. Sometimes it seems that one of society's biggest preoccupations is with the relatively high income women who work in the sex industry make, especially prostitutes. Nowhere is this more clearly evident than in the gutter press's obsession with 'the wages of sin'. It's one of their favourite subjects – 'exposing' prostitute women who are making high wages from their male clients. It seems it's fine that those men should have all that surplus loot in the first place, but it somehow becomes *immoral* when 'Vice Girls' get their greedy mitts on it . . . Never mind the fact that the journalistic pimps are making big salaries out of their 'exposés'; pretending to be prostitutes' clients, acting as *agents provocateurs*. But they're cleaning up society; doing the public a big favour! To my mind, those creatures are the *real* sleaze.

Women's prisons in this country are full of working-class women who have fought back against poverty in one way or another; by shoplifting, DHSS 'fraud' – or by turning to prostitution. Their crime is being poor and being female. But it is prostitutes in particular who receive that most vicious treatment at the hands of the law since they can be convicted on the word of *one* police officer.[2] And since custodial sentences for soliciting and loitering were officially abolished, in January 1983, the number of prostitute women who have been sent to prison has actually *increased*. To get round the law, magistrates simply upped the fines to two, three and four hundred pounds for every court appearance. So the girls are now being sent down for non-payment of fines, which is a particularly vindictive move on the part of the courts, in view of the fact that it is poverty that drives women on to the game in the first place.

'It's all so hypocritical, because the judge can sit there and fine a girl £400, then if she comes up another time, he'll fine her a few thousands. And how's she gonna pay those fines? He's sending her out, on to the streets, because you've got to go and earn it that way to pay the fines. So that makes the government a pimp.' (Yasmin)

It's important to remember in all this that prostitution itself is *not* illegal in this country – although just about everything surrounding it is. 'Loitering' or 'soliciting' in a public place is illegal, and once a woman has been cautioned twice – even if she has not been convicted – she is labelled a 'common prostitute' for life.

The law prohibits women from working together from a flat or a house for safety's sake. Two prostitutes or more constitute a brothel; *that's* why women work from the streets in the first place. It's because of their very illegality that prostitutes are so much more vulnerable to men's violence than are straight women. It's no coincidence that, of the prostitute friends I interviewed for this book, the only one who had *never* experienced violence at the hands of clients was the male prostitute. All the women had experienced rape and/or other abuse. That gives some food for thought. I believe it reflects this society's attitudes about violence towards women generally: that it is not unacceptable. All men may not be rapists, but they do appear to have *carte blanche* in the eyes of the law and the rest of society, as far as beating, robbing, raping – even murdering – prostitutes is concerned.

When I sat and listened to my friends' tales of rape and violence, their total lack of protection from abuse, I was chilled. Anita, describing how her friend got into the 'Yorkshire Ripper's' car because she desperately needed the money *to pay off her court fines*: 'She just wanted to get off the Square, away from the police . . .'

Away from the police – into the car of a murderer. It made my blood run cold; it also made me wonder how many of Peter Sutcliffe's dead prostitute victims got into his car because they had the *legal* pimps to pay off . . .

But so what – they're only 'whores', seems to be society's attitude. In January 1980, the English Collective of Prostitutes issued a statement to the Metropolitan Police Commissioner:

To the Ripper *and* to the police, prostitutes are not decent, we are not 'innocent victims'. What are we guilty of to deserve such a death? 70 per cent of prostitute women in this country are mothers fighting to make ends meet and feed their children. But because we refuse poverty for ourselves and our children, we are treated as criminals. In the eyes of the police we deserve what we get, even death.

Yet even during the Ripper's trial the Attorney General saw fit to declare that in his view, the fact that some of Sutcliffe's victims were not prostitutes was 'perhaps the saddest part of this case' (a remark which in turn prompted some of us to observe that even 'sadder' was the fact that some were not attorney generals).

That Sir Michael Havers could make such a crass statement with apparent impunity, *and* be quoted uncritically in the press, speaks volumes about attitudes towards prostitute women. They somehow *deserve* to die, because they are 'wicked' women. Now that's an immoral attitude.

And what about the clients? The men who use the sex industry, in all its guises. Punters. Where would we be without them? Out of work, for one thing.

There would be no sex industry if there were no customers (*men*, with their higher wages and greater spending power). And the fact that we women can make good money as strippers or prostitutes *only* because of that basic inequality is somewhat ironic and definitely immoral.

It's also immoral that men want to use women's bodies without relating to us as human beings, without considering our feelings – I'm not just talking about within the sex industry, now. It happens throughout society, at home and at work. Everywhere, men expect to be serviced by women – to be looked after, cleaned up after, by wives and girlfriends, and to be sexually serviced by them too. And the sex industry is part of that system; it's yet another service for men that's provided by women. It's exactly as Chloe puts it:

All races, all classes of male just use women throughout, anyway; for working in the house, being a housewife, to the office with the secretaries, to coming to us for their sexual relief. Nice world, isn't it?

The fact is, men run the whole works. It's men who use the sex industry; men who nick the girls on the streets or raid the clubs and saunas; men who make the laws and then carry them through, by fining us or putting us away. Those are the real scandals, yet where is the outcry from straight society? I don't hear a whimper.

Money, sex, power . . . that's what it's all about. In this society, where everything is bought and sold, it stands to reason that those of us who are at the bottom of the pile are going to sell our one remaining 'asset': ourselves. But make no mistake about the fact that *everyone* sells and manipulates in this culture; that is how you survive. And sometimes you don't.

When I first began to write 'My Story', I thought I was out on my own, that nobody from the sex industry had spoken up before me. I was glad to find I was wrong. Many have. I discovered that in the last decade a new movement had blossomed; there were organizations and support groups composed of women who work in the sex industry and women and men who do not throughout the world. Making connections. Now there's a network that links us as far afield as the USA, Canada, Australia, New Zealand, the West Indies, as well as most European countries. A whole chorus of voices who have for so long been silenced, denied human status, denounced as immoral sluts . . . But now we are getting our chance to speak up, *tell what we know*.

The work of those who had begun to fight before me – the French prostitutes who went on strike in 1975,[3] and the English prostitutes who took over the church at King's Cross in 1982[4] – inspired me and gave me the courage to start speaking for myself. Then came the voices of those women and men I had worked with and respected, and loved. Strong voices; the voices of real human beings, not stereotypes, 'victims', or figments of men's imagination. And, when I listened to them speak, that's when I realized what a *true* morality is – the network of courage, support, and caring that all of us recalled in our accounts. As Chloe so eloquently described it:

> To other people we might be all strippers, all prostitutes, but this is where the real respect lies – feelings, loving. We carry a community in our hearts, really.

Every time another of us speaks out about our lives, another connection is forged between us, sex industry workers everywhere.

And we hope also to reach and make connections with straight women, too; so that they can know that we are not the evil 'Vice Girls' beloved of the media, but ordinary women like themselves . . . mothers, daughters, sisters. And we hope to one day touch men's consciences . . .

Working in the sex industry is one of the myriad ways in which women struggle to survive all over the world; we are not outside of society; we are a part of it. As more of us gain the courage and confidence we are finding from each other, we need no longer hang our heads and feel shame for the lives we have been forced into; just as society can no longer deny us our humanity and dismiss us as 'immoral' creatures who do not deserve to be listened to. We have voices, we can speak up, and we *will* be heard. And with our life's story, each of us refutes the concept of 'whore'; the 'whore' of men's fantasies. Now it is their turn to feel ashamed. One day men will change; they'll have to because women are changing. Becoming visible is part of that change, and that is what women who work in the sex industry are doing – becoming visible as human beings.

As for the male sexual dinosaurs, the stupid buggers who persist in clinging to their tired old myths and illusions; they will die out eventually, taking with them their warped ideas about what they think is 'sexuality' – using women as commodities.

In the meantime, Victorian Values prevail, and poor working-class women continue in ever-increasing numbers to sexually service the affluent middle-class men who call them 'whores', and condemn them to the rest of society. But that is *their* 'morality', not ours.

Now, having written this, I can look back on my own life and see my 'escape' from the harsh Lancashire life into the 'freedom' of the Soho sex industry as the blind alley it was. Yet I have no regrets about the choices I made, and I am not ashamed; not any more. I know that the sex and class wars have not abated in this society. Women are still the poorest, and men still expect to be serviced by us in every respect. Until that changes, there can be no true armistice between us.

NOTES

*   Report on the Contagious Diseases Acts (1864, 1866, 1869), cited in M. Trustram, 'Distasteful and Derogatory? Examining Victorian Soldiers for Venereal Disease', in The London Feminist History

Group (eds), *The Sexual Dynamics of History* (London: Pluto Press, 1983).

** She talks about conditions in Britain; others have talked about conditions elsewhere; see, e.g., Laurie Bell (ed.), *Good Girls/Bad Girls: Sex Trade Workers and Feminists Face to Face*, (Toronto: Women's Press, 1987).

*** Roberts is speaking here of the reaction to articles about the sex industry she had published and to the project of the book from which this chapter is taken.

1 'Sex, Class and Morality' from Nickie Roberts' *The Front Line* is reproduced by kind permission of Grafton Books, a division of Harper Collins Publishers Ltd., and Nickie Roberts, © 1986.

2 Information from the English Collective of Prostitutes' Fact-sheet, 'Rules of the Game'.

3 Claude Jaget (ed.), *Prostitutes – Our Life* (Falling Wall Press).

4 Selma James, *Hookers in The House of the Lord*.

II

Ethics and Gender Difference

9

Emma Goldman
1869–1940

'THE TRAGEDY OF WOMEN'S EMANCIPATION' (1911) from
RED EMMA SPEAKS

*Emma Goldman was born in Czarist Russia. In 1886 she emigrated with
her family to the United States of America. As she moved into adulthood
and into socialist and anarchist political circles in New York, Goldman
came to recognize America, 'the land of the free', as in its own way every
bit as exploitative and oppressive as the Russia she had left behind.*

*Goldman's energy for writing, lecturing and campaigning made her a
famous woman, lauded by her audiences, feared and suspected by the
authorities. In 1919 she was deported from the United States, and
returned to the Soviet Union, where to her dismay she immediately found
herself opposing the Bolshevik revolution and the developing Leninist
regime. Lenin told her that 'the revolution was facing too many counter-
revolutionary threats to allow the luxury of free speech.'* In 1921 she
moved to London where she lived the rest of her life.*

*In this piece Emma Goldman laments the limited and unsatisfactory
outcome of the nineteenth- and early twentieth-century moves towards
women's emancipation, in Britain and the United States. The stress on
political and economic emancipation with the implication that freedom,
equality, citizenship and economic independence can be achieved by mere
political reform had in many ways constrained women the more. Women's
lives are equally cramped and distorted whether they slave behind a
typewriter or in a kitchen. Freedom is pictured as a condition of detachment, coolness, seriousness; the experience is one of loneliness. Goldman*

scorns the icy heroines of contemporary fiction and political writing; their negative brand of independence is a far cry from the anarchist ideal of full sexual expression, purged of exploitativeness, and set in a context of co-operative endeavour and warm, comradely human relations.

I begin with an admission: regardless of all political and economic theories, treating of the fundamental differences between various groups within the human race, regardless of class and race distinctions, regardless of all artificial boundary lines between woman's rights and man's rights, I hold that there is a point where these differentiations may meet and grow into one perfect whole.[1]

With this I do not mean to propose a peace treaty. The general social antagonism which has taken hold of our entire public life today, brought about through the force of opposing and contradictory interests, will crumble to pieces when the reorganization of our social life, based upon the principles of economic justice, shall have become a reality.

Peace or harmony between the sexes and individuals does not necessarily depend on a superficial equalization of human beings; nor does it call for the elimination of individual traits and peculiarities. The problem that confronts us today, and which the nearest future is to solve, is how to be one's self and yet in oneness with others, to feel deeply with all human beings and still retain one's own characteristic qualities. This seems to me to be the basis upon which the mass and the individual, the true democrat and the true individuality, man and woman, can meet without antagonism and opposition. The motto should not be: Forgive one another; rather, Understand one another. The oft-quoted sentence of Madame de Staël: 'To understand everything means to forgive everything', has never particularly appealed to me; it has the odour of the confessional; to forgive one's fellow-being conveys the idea of pharisaical superiority. To understand one's fellow-being suffices. The admission partly represents the fundamental aspect of my views on the emancipation of woman and its effect upon the entire sex.

Emancipation should make it possible for woman to be human in the truest sense. Everything within her that craves assertion and activity should reach its fullest expression: all artificial barriers should be broken, and the road towards greater freedom cleared of every trace of centuries of submission and slavery.

This was the original aim of the movement for woman's emancipation. But the results so far achieved have isolated woman and have robbed her of the fountain springs of that happiness which is so essential to her. Merely external emancipation has made of the modern woman an artificial being, who reminds one of the products of French arboriculture with its arabesque trees and shrubs, pyramids, wheels and wreaths; anything, except the forms which would be reached by the expression of her own inner qualities. Such artificially grown plants of the female sex are to be found in large numbers, especially in the so-called intellectual sphere of our life.

Liberty and equality for woman! What hopes and aspirations these words awakened when they were first uttered by some of the noblest and bravest souls of those days. The sun in all his light and glory was to rise upon a new world; in this world woman was to be free to direct her own destiny – an aim certainly worthy of the great enthusiasm, courage, perseverance and ceaseless effort of the tremendous host of pioneer men and women, who staked everything against a world of prejudice and ignorance.

My hopes also move towards that goal, but I hold that the emancipation of woman, as interpreted and practically applied today, has failed to reach that great end. Now, woman is confronted with the necessity of emancipating herself from emancipation, if she really desires to be free. This may sound paradoxical, but is, nevertheless, only too true.

What has she achieved through her emancipation? Equal suffrage in a few states. Has that purified our political life, as many well-meaning advocates predicted? Certainly not. Incidentally, it is really time that persons with plain, sound judgement should cease to talk about corruption in politics in a boarding-school tone. Corruption of politics has nothing to do with the morals, or the laxity of morals, of various political personalities. Its cause is altogether a material one. Politics is the reflex of the business and industrial world, the mottos of which are: 'To take is more blessed than to give'; 'buy cheap and sell dear'; 'one soiled hand washes the other.' There is no hope even that woman, with her right to vote, will ever purify politics.

Emancipation has brought woman economic equality with man; that is, she can choose her own profession and trade; but as her past and present physical training has not equipped her with the necessary strength to compete with man, she is often compelled to exhaust all her energy, use up her vitality, and strain every nerve in order to reach the market value. Very few ever succeed, for it is a fact that women teachers, doctors, lawyers, architects and engineers are neither met with the same confidence as their male colleagues, nor receive equal remuneration. And those that do reach that enticing equality generally do so at the expense of their physical and psychical well-being. As to the great mass of working girls and women, how much independence is gained if the narrowness and lack of freedom of the home is exchanged for the narrowness and lack of freedom of the factory, sweat-shop, department store or office? In addition is the burden which is laid on many women of looking after a 'home, sweet home' – cold, dreary, disorderly, uninviting – after a day's hard work. Glorious independence! No wonder that hundreds of girls are so willing to accept the first offer of marriage, sick and tired of their 'independence' behind the counter, at the sewing or typewriting machine. They are just as ready to marry as girls of the middle class, who long to throw off the yoke of parental supremacy. A so-called independence which leads only to earning the merest subsistence is not so enticing, not so ideal, that one could expect woman to sacrifice everything for it. Our highly praised independence is, after all, but a slow process of dulling and stifling woman's nature, her love instinct and her mother instinct.

Nevertheless, the position of the working girl is far more natural and human than that of her seemingly more fortunate sister in the more cultured professional walks of life – teachers, physicians, lawyers, engineers, etc., who have to make a dignified, proper appearance, while the inner life is growing empty and dead.

The narrowness of the existing conception of woman's independence and emancipation; the dread of love for a man who is not her social equal; the fear that love will rob her of her freedom and independence; the horror that love or the joy of motherhood will only hinder her in the full exercise of her profession – all these together make of the emancipated modern woman a compulsory vestal, before whom life, with its great clarifying sorrows and its deep, entrancing joys, rolls on without touching or gripping her soul.

Emancipation, as understood by the majority of its adherents and exponents, is of too narrow a scope to permit the boundless love and ecstasy contained in the deep emotion of the true woman, sweetheart, mother, in freedom.

The tragedy of the self-supporting or economically free woman does not lie in too many, but in too few experiences. True, she surpasses her sister of past generations in knowledge of the world and human nature; it is just because of this that she feels deeply the lack of life's essence, which alone can enrich the human soul, and without which the majority of women have become mere professional automatons.

That such a state of affairs was bound to come was foreseen by those who realized that, in the domain of ethics, there still remained many decaying ruins of the time of the undisputed superiority of man; ruins that are still considered useful. And, what is more important, a goodly number of the emancipated are unable to get along without them. Every movement that aims at the destruction of existing institutions and the replacement thereof with something more advanced, more perfect, has followers who in theory stand for the most radical ideas, but who, nevertheless, in their everyday practice, are like the average Philistine, feigning respectability and clamouring for the good opinion of their opponents. There are, for example, Socialists, and even Anarchists, who stand for the idea that property is robbery, yet who will grow indignant if anyone owe them the value of a half-dozen pins.

The same Philistine can be found in the movement for woman's emancipation. Yellow journalists and milk-and-water *littérateurs* have painted pictures of the emancipated woman that make the hair of the good citizen and his dull companion stand up on end. Every member of the woman's rights movement was pictured as a George Sand in her absolute disregard of morality. Nothing was sacred to her. She had no respect for the ideal relation between man and woman. In short, emancipation stood only for a reckless life of lust and sin, regardless of society, religion and morality. The exponents of woman's rights were highly indignant at such misrepresentation, and, lacking humor, they exerted all their energy to prove that they were not at all as bad as they were painted, but the very reverse. Of course, as long as woman was the slave of man, she could not be good and pure, but now that she was free and independent she would prove how good she could be and that her influence would have a purifying effect on all institutions in society. True, the movement for woman's rights has broken many old fetters, but it has also forged new ones. The great movement of *true* emancipation has not met with a great race of women who could look liberty in the face. Their narrow, puritanical vision banished man, as a disturber and doubtful character, out of their emotional life. Man was not to be tolerated at any price, except perhaps as the father of a child, since a child cound not very well come to life without a father. Fortunately, the most rigid Puritans never will be strong enough to kill the innate craving for motherhood. But woman's freedom is closely allied with man's freedom, and many of my so-called emancipated sisters seem to overlook the fact that a child born in freedom needs the love and devotion of each human being about him, man as well as woman. Unfortunately, it is this narrow conception of human relations that has brought about a great tragedy in the lives of the modern man and woman.

About fifteen years ago appeared a work from the pen of the brilliant Norwegian Laura Marholm, called *Woman, a Character Study*. She was one of the first to call attention to the emptiness and narrowness of the existing conception of woman's emancipation, and its tragic effect upon the inner life of woman. In her work Laura Marholm speaks of the fate of several gifted women of international fame: the genius Eleonora Duse; the great mathematician and writer Sonya Kovalevskaia; the artist and poet-nature Marie Bashkirtzeff, who died so young. Through each description of the lives of these women of such extraordinary mentality runs a marked trail of unsatisfied craving for a full, rounded, complete and beautiful life, and the unrest and loneliness resulting from the lack of it. Through these masterly psychological sketches one cannot help but see that the higher the mental development of woman, the less possible it is for her to meet a congenial mate who will see in her, not only sex, but also the human being, the friend, the comrade and strong individuality, who cannot and ought not lose a single trait of her character.

The average man with his self-sufficiency, his ridiculously superior airs of patronage towards the female sex, is an impossibility for woman as depicted in the *Character Study* by Laura Marholm. Equally impossible for her is the man who can see in her nothing more than her mentality and her genius, and who fails to awaken her woman nature.

A rich intellect and a fine soul are usually considered necessary attributes of a deep and beautiful personality. In the case of the modern woman, these attributes serve as a hindrance to the complete assertion of her being. For over a hundred years the old form of marriage, based on the Bible, 'Till death doth part', has been denounced as an institution that stands for the sovereignty of the man over the woman, of her complete submission to his whims and commands, and absolute dependence on his name and support. Time and again it has been conclusively proved that the old matrimonial relation restricted woman to the function of man's servant and the bearer of his children. And yet we find many emancipated women who prefer marriage, with all its deficiencies, to the narrowness of an unmarried life; narrow and unendurable because of the chains of moral and social prejudice that cramp and bind her nature.

The explanation of such inconsistency on the part of many advanced women is to be found in the fact that they never truly understood the meaning of emancipation. They thought that all that was needed was independence from external tyrannies; the internal tyrants, far more harmful to life and growth – ethical and social conventions – were left to take care of themselves; and they have taken care of themselves. They seem to get along as beautifully in the heads and hearts of the most active exponents of woman's emancipation, as in the heads and hearts of our grandmothers.

These internal tyrants, whether they be in the form of public opinion or what will mother say, or brother, father, aunt, or relative of any sort; what will Mrs Grundy, Mr Comstock, the employer, the Board of Education say? All these busybodies, moral detectives, jailers of the human spirit, what will they say? Until woman has learned to defy them all, to stand firmly on her own ground and to insist upon her own unrestricted freedom, to listen to the voice of her nature, whether it call for life's greatest treasure, love for a man, or her most glorious privilege, the right to give birth to a child, she cannot call herself emancipated. How many emancipated women are brave enough to acknowledge that the voice of love is calling, wildly beating against their breasts, demanding to be heard, to be satisfied.

The French writer Jean Reibrach, in one of his novels, *New Beauty*, attempts to picture the ideal, beautiful, emancipated woman. This ideal is embodied in a young girl, a physician. She talks very cleverly and wisely of how to feed infants; she is kind, and administers medicines free to poor mothers. She converses with a young man of her acquaintance about the sanitary conditions of the future, and how various bacilli and germs shall be exterminated by the use of stone walls and floors, and by the doing away with rugs and hangings. She is, of course, very plainly and practically dressed, mostly in black. The young man, who, at their first meeting, was overawed by the wisdom of his emancipated friend, gradually learns to understand her, and recognizes one fine day that he loves her. They are young, and she is kind and beautiful, and though always in rigid attire, her appearance is softened by a spotlessly clean white collar and cuffs. One would expect that he would tell her of his love, but he is not one to commit romantic absurdities. Poetry and the enthusiasm of love cover their blushing faces before the pure beauty of the lady. He silences the voice of his nature, and remains correct. She, too, is always exact, always rational, always well behaved. I fear if they had formed a union, the young man would have risked freezing to death. I must confess that I can see nothing beautiful in this new beauty, who is as cold as the stone walls and floors she dreams of. Rather would I have the love songs of romantic ages, rather Don Juan and Madame Venus, rather an elopement by ladder and rope on a moonlight night, followed by the father's curse, mother's moans and the moral comments of neighbours, than correctness and propriety measured by yardsticks. If love does not know how to give and take without restrictions, it is not love, but a transaction that never fails to lay stress on a plus and a minus.

The greatest shortcoming of the emancipation of the present day lies in its artificial stiffness and its narrow respectabilities, which produce an emptiness in woman's soul that will not let her drink from the fountain of life. I once remarked that there seemed to be a deeper relationship between the old-fashioned mother and hostess, ever on the alert for the happiness of her little ones and the comfort of those she loves, and the truly new woman, than between the latter and her average emancipated sister. The disciples of emancipation pure and simple declared me a heathen, fit only for the stake. Their blind zeal did not let them see that my comparison between the old and the new was merely to prove that a goodly number of our grandmothers had more blood in their veins, far more humour and wit, and certainly a greater amount of naturalness, kind-heartedness and simplicity, than the majority of our emancipated professional women who fill the colleges, halls of learning and various offices. This does not mean a wish to return to the past, nor does it condemn woman to her old sphere, the kitchen and the nursery.

Salvation lies in an energetic march onward towards a brighter and clearer future. We are in need of unhampered growth out of old traditions and habits. The movement for woman's emancipation has so far made but the first step in that direction. It is to be hoped that it will gather strength to make another. The right to vote, or equal civil rights, may be good demands, but true emancipation begins neither at the polls nor in courts. It begins in woman's soul. History tells us that every oppressed class gained true liberation from its masters through its own efforts. It is necessary that woman learn that lesson, that she realize that her freedom will reach as far as her power to achieve her freedom reaches. It is, therefore, far more important for her to begin with her inner regeneration, to cut loose from the weight of prejudices, traditions and customs. The demand for equal rights in every vocation of life is just and fair; but, after all, the most vital right is the right to love and be loved. Indeed, if partial emancipation is to become a complete and true emancipation of woman, it will have to do away with the ridiculous notion that to be loved, to be sweetheart and mother, is synonymous with being a slave or subordinate. It will have to do away with the absurd notion of the dualism of the sexes, or that man and woman represent two antagonistic worlds.

Pettiness separates; breadth unites. Let us be broad and big. Let us not overlook vital things because of the bulk of trifles confronting us. A true conception of the relation of the sexes will not admit of conqueror and conquered; it knows of but one great thing; to give of one's self boundlessly, in order to find one's self richer, deeper, better. That alone can fill the emptiness, and transform the tragedy of woman's emancipation into joy, limitless joy.

NOTES

* Emma Goldman, *Red Emma Speaks: Selected Writings and Speeches by Emma Goldman*, ed. Alix Kates Shulman (New York: Random House, 1972), p. 17. Reprinted as *Dancing in the Revolution: Selected Writings and Speeches of Emma Goldman* (Virago: London, 1982).

10

Virginia Woolf
1882–1941

Extracts from *THREE GUINEAS* (1938)

Virginia Woolf owes her fame primarily to her novels, but she was also a prolific literary critic and journalist. Her main works on sexual politics are A Room of One's Own *(1929) and* Three Guineas *(1938). Although in* Three Guineas *Woolf condemns the word 'feminist' as already obsolete, the essay itself – a wide-ranging meditation on how women can help to prevent war – foreshadows much feminist writing of the 1970s and 1980s in warning women of the dangers of uncritical assimilation into male culture, and in insisting on the significance of gender difference for progressive politics.*

Woolf makes brilliant use of a defamiliarizing descriptive technique to capture the absurd and terrifying pretensions of the male sex in its various public capacities. The robes and wigs of judges, the gowns of academics, the medals and plumes of the military all symbolize men's status as representatives of social order and, by contrast, women's exclusion. At the same time, however, Woolf's understanding of gender is thoroughly materialist: women have from time immemorial been expropriated by men, and the two sexes constitute two 'classes' whose economic conditions of existence still 'differ enormously' despite recent improvements in women's civic status. This point emerges all the more forcefully as a result of Woolf's narrow focus on her own social world – the world of those 'whose fathers have been educated at public schools and universities' and who 'expect maids to cook dinner and wash up after dinner'. (In her emphasis on the relative poverty, as well as on the formal disadvantages, of women within this privileged milieu, *Woolf anticipates the thesis of Christine Delphy* that the convention whereby a woman is deemed to belong to the same social class as her husband or father is an ideological device serving to mask the reality of female subordination.)*

There is perhaps a touch of Socratic irony in Woolf's claim that women like herself 'cannot understand . . . what glory, what interest, what manly satisfaction fighting provides' for their brothers – that they are debarred from such understanding by the differences of education and tradition which separate the sexes. But there is no mistaking the seriousness of her invitation to women to think of themselves, with pride, as forming an 'Outsiders Society'. If women are to join in promoting the ideals of justice, liberty and equality, and thus in the struggle for international peace, they must do so in full consciousness of the way their relation to these ideals is mediated by their sexual class membership: '[A]s a woman, I have no country . . . As a woman my country is the whole world.' This consciousness, Woolf argues, will not weaken but empower us in our resistance to militarism. But it will empower us not merely to act as stronger supporters of the male liberal intelligentsia, but – more radically – to break down the structure of male domination which makes militarism possible. It is by insisting on the (political) facts of sexual difference, not by acquiescing in the liberal fiction of actual sexual equality, that women can best work towards the humanitarian goals which rational human beings hold in common.

Three years is a long time to leave a letter unanswered, and your letter has been lying without an answer even longer than that.[1] I had hoped that it would answer itself, or that other people would answer it for me. But there it is with its question – How in your opinion are we to prevent war? – still unanswered.

It is true that many answers have suggested themselves, but none that would not need explanation, and explanations take time. In this case, too, there are reasons why it is particularly difficult to avoid misunderstanding. A whole page could be filled with excuses and apologies; declarations of unfitness, incompetence, lack of knowledge and experience: and they would be true. But even when they were said there would still remain some difficulties so fundamental that it may well prove impossible for you to understand or for us to explain. But one does not like to leave so remarkable a letter as yours – a letter perhaps unique in the history of human correspondence, since when before has an educated man asked a woman how in her opinion war can be prevented? – unanswered. Therefore let us make the attempt; even if it is doomed to failure.

In the first place let us draw what all letter-writers instinctively draw, a sketch of the person to whom the letter is addressed. Without someone warm and breathing on the other side of the page, letters are worthless. You, then, who ask the question, are a little grey on the temples; the hair is no longer thick on the top of your head. You have reached the middle years of life not without effort, at the Bar; but on the whole your journey has been prosperous. There is nothing parched, mean or dissatisfied in your expression. And without wishing to flatter you, your prosperity – wife, children, house – has been deserved. You have never sunk into the contented apathy of middle life, for, as your letter from an office in the heart of London shows, instead of turning on your pillow and prodding your pigs, pruning your pear trees – you have a few acres in Norfolk – you are writing letters, attending meetings, presiding over this and that, asking questions, with the sound of the guns in your ears. For the rest, you began your education at one of the great public schools and finished it at the university.

It is now that the first difficulty of communication between us appears. Let us rapidly indicate the reason. We both come of what, in this hybrid age when, though birth is mixed, classes still remain fixed, it is convenient to call the educated class. When we meet in the flesh we speak with the same accent; use knives and forks in the same way; expect maids to cook dinner and wash up after dinner; and can talk during dinner without much difficulty about politics and people; war and peace; barbarism and civilization – all the questions indeed suggested by your letter. Moreover, we both earn our livings. But . . . those three dots mark a precipice, a gulf so deeply cut between us that for three years and more I have been sitting on my side of it wondering whether it is any use to try to speak across it. Let us then ask someone else – it is Mary Kingsley – to speak for us. 'I don't know if I ever revealed to you the fact that being allowed to learn German was *all* the paid-for education I ever had. Two thousand pounds was spent on my brother's, I still hope not in vain.'[2] Mary Kingsley is not speaking for herself alone; she is speaking, still, for many of the daughters of educated men. And she is not merely speaking for them; she is also pointing to a very important fact about them, a fact that must profoundly influence all that follows: the fact of Arthur's Education Fund. You, who have read *Pendennis*, will remember how the mysterious letters A.E.F. figured in the household ledgers. Ever since the thirteenth century English families have been paying money into that account. From the Pastons to the Pendennises, all educated families from the thirteenth century to the present moment have paid money into that account. It is a voracious receptacle. Where there were many sons to educate it required a great effort on the part of the family to keep it full. For your education was not merely in book-learning; games educated your body; friends taught you more than books or games. Talk with them broadened your outlook and enriched your mind. In the holidays you travelled; acquired a taste for art; a knowledge of foreign politics; and then, before you could earn your own living, your father made you an allowance upon which it was possible for you to live while you learnt the profession which now entitles you to add the letters K.C. to your name. All this came out of Arthur's Education Fund. And to this your sisters, as Mary Kingsley indicates, made their contribution. Not only did their own education, save for such small sums as paid the German teacher, go into it; but many of those luxuries and trimmings which are, after all, an essential part of education – travel, society, solitude, a lodging apart from the family house – they were paid into it too. It was a voracious receptacle, a solid fact – Arthur's Education Fund – a fact so solid indeed that it cast a shadow over the entire landscape. And the result is that though we look at the same things, we see them differently. What is that congregation of buildings there, with a semi-monastic look, with chapels and halls and green playing-fields? To you it is your old school; Eton or Harrow; your old university, Oxford or Cambridge; the source of memories and of traditions innumerable. But to us, who see it through the shadow of Arthur's Education Fund, it is a schoolroom table; an omnibus going to a class; a little woman with a red nose who is not well educated herself but has an invalid mother to support; an allowance of £50 a year with which to buy clothes, give presents and take journeys on coming to maturity. Such is the effect that Arthur's Education Fund has had upon us: So magically does it change the landscape that the noble courts and quadrangles of Oxford and Cambridge often appear to educated men's daughters[3] like petticoats with holes in them, cold legs of mutton, and the boat train starting for abroad while the guard slams the door in their faces.

The fact that Arthur's Education Fund changes the landscape – the halls, the playing grounds, the sacred edifices – is an important one; but that aspect must be left for future discussion. Here we are only concerned with the obvious fact, when it comes to considering this important question – how we are to help you prevent war – that education makes a difference. Some knowledge of politics, of international relations, of economics, is obviously necessary in order to understand the causes which lead to war. Philosophy, theology even, might come in usefully. Now you the uneducated, you with an untrained mind, could not possibly deal with such questions satisfactorily. War, as the result of impersonal forces, is you will agree beyond the grasp of the untrained mind. But war as the result of human nature is another thing. Had you not believed that human nature, the reasons, the emotions of the ordinary man and woman, lead to war, you would not have written asking for our help. You must have argued, men and women, here and now, are able to exert their wills; they are not pawns and puppets dancing on a string held by invisible hands. They can act, and think for themselves. Perhaps even they can influence other people's thoughts and actions. Some such reasoning must have led you to apply to us; and with justification. For happily there is one branch of education which comes under the heading 'unpaid-for education' – that understanding of human beings and their motives which, if the word is rid of its scientific associations, might be called psychology. Marriage, the one great profession open to our class since the dawn of time until the year 1919; marriage, the art of choosing the human being with whom to live life successfully, should have taught us some skill in that. But here again another difficulty confronts us. For though many instincts are held more or less in common by both sexes, to fight has always been the man's habit, not the woman's. Law and practice have developed that difference, whether innate or accidental. Scarcely a human being in the course of history has fallen to a woman's rifle; the vast majority of birds and beasts have been killed by you, not by us; and it is difficult to judge what we do not share.[4]

How then are we to understand your problem, and if we cannot, how can we answer your question, how to prevent war? The answer based upon our experience and our psychology – Why fight? – is not an answer of any value. Obviously there is for you some glory, some necessity, some satisfaction in fighting which we have never felt or enjoyed. Complete understanding could only be achieved by blood transfusion and memory transfusion – a miracle still beyond the reach of science. But we who live now have a substitute for blood transfusion and memory transfusion which must serve at a pinch. There is that marvellous, perpetually renewed, and as yet largely untapped aid to the understanding of human motives which is provided in our age by biography and autobiography. Also there is the daily paper, history in the raw. There is thus no longer any reason to be confined to the minute span of actual experience which is still, for us, so narrow, so circumscribed. We can supplement it by looking at the picture of the lives of others. It is of course only a picture at present, but as such it must serve. It is to biography then that we will turn first, quickly and briefly, in order to attempt to understand what war means to you. Let us extract a few sentences from a biography.

First, this from a soldier's life:

I have had the happiest possible life, and have always been working for war, and have now got into the biggest in the prime of life for a soldier . . . Thank God, we are off in an hour. Such a magnificent regiment! Such men, such horses! Within ten days I hope Francis and I will be riding side by side straight at the Germans.[5]

To which the biographer adds: 'From the first hour he had been supremely happy, for he had found his true calling.' To that let us add this from an airman's life:

We talked of the League of Nations and the prospects of peace and disarmament. On this subject he was not so much militarist as martial. The difficulty to which he could find no answer was that if permanent peace were ever achieved, and armies and navies ceased to exist, there would be no outlet for the manly qualities which fighting developed, and that human physique and human character would deteriorate.[6]

Here, immediately, are three reasons which lead your sex to fight; war is a profession; a source of happiness and excitement; and it is also an outlet for manly qualities, without which men would deteriorate. But that these feelings and opinions are by no means universally held by your sex is proved by the following extract from another biography, the life of a poet who was killed in the European war: Wilfred Owen.

> Already I have comprehended a light which never will filter into the dogma of any national church: namely, that one of Christ's essential commands was: Passivity at any price! Suffer dishonour and disgrace, but never resort to arms. Be bullied, be outraged, be killed; but do not kill... Thus you see how pure Christianity will not fit in with pure patriotism.

And among some notes for poems that he did not live to write are these:

> The unnaturalness of weapons ... Inhumanity of war ... The insupportability of war ... Horrible beastliness of war ... Foolishness of war.[7]

From these quotations it is obvious that the same sex holds very different opinions about the same thing. But also it is obvious, from today's newspaper, that however many dissentients there are, the great majority of your sex are today in favour of war. The Scarborough Conference of educated men, the Bournemouth Conference of working men are both agreed that to spend £300,000,000 annually upon arms is a necessity. They are of opinion that Wilfred Owen was wrong; that it is better to kill than to be killed. Yet since biography shows that differences of opinion are many, it is plain that there must be some one reason which prevails in order to bring about this overpowering unanimity. Shall we call it, for the sake of brevity, 'patriotism'? What then, we must ask next, is this 'patriotism' which leads you to go to war? Let the Lord Chief Justice of England interpret it for us:

> Englishmen are proud of England. For those who have been trained in English schools and universities, and who have done the work of their lives in England, there are few loves stronger than the love we have for our country. When we consider other nations, when we judge the merits of the policy of this country

or of that, it is the standard of our own country that we apply . . . Liberty has made her abode in England. England is the home of democratic institutions . . . It is true that in our midst there are many enemies of liberty – some of them, perhaps, in rather unexpected quarters. But we are standing firm. It has been said that an Englishman's Home is his Castle. The home of Liberty is in England. And it is a castle indeed – a castle that will be defended to the last . . . Yes, we are greatly blessed, we Englishmen.[8]

That is a fair general statement of what patriotism means to an educated man and what duties it imposes upon him. But the educated man's sister – what does 'patriotism' mean to her? Has she the same reasons for being proud of England, for loving England, for defending England? Has she been 'greatly blessed' in England? History and biography when questioned would seem to show that her position in the home of freedom has been different from her brother's; and psychology would seem to hint that history is not without its effect upon mind and body. Therefore her interpretation of the word 'patriotism' may well differ from his. And that difference may make it extremely difficult for her to understand his definition of patriotism and the duties it imposes. If then our answer to your question, 'How in your opinion are we to prevent war?' depends upon understanding the reasons, the emotions, the loyalties which lead men to go to war, this letter had better be torn across and thrown into the waste-paper basket. For it seems plain that we cannot understand each other because of these differences. It seems plain that we think differently according as we are born differently; there is a Grenfell point of view; a Knebworth point of view; a Wilfred Owen point of view; a Lord Chief Justice's point of view and the point of view of an educated man's daughter. All differ. But is there no absolute point of view? Can we not find somewhere written up in letters of fire or gold, 'This is right. This wrong'? – a moral judgement which we must all, whatever our differences, accept? Let us then refer the question of the rightness or wrongness of war to those who make morality their profession – the clergy. Surely if we ask the clergy the simple question: 'Is war right or is war wrong?' they will give us a plain answer which we cannot deny. But no – the Church of England, which might be supposed able to abstract the question from its worldly confusions, is of two minds also. The bishops themselves are at loggerheads. The Bishop of London maintained that 'the real danger to the peace of the world today were the pacifists. Bad as war was dishonour was far worse.' On the other hand, the Bishop of Birmingham[9] described himself as an 'extreme pacifist . . . I cannot see myself that war can be regarded as consonant with the spirit of Christ.' So the Church itself gives us divided counsel – in some circumstances it is right to fight; in no circumstances is it right to fight. It is distressing, baffling, confusing, but the fact must be faced; there is no certainty in heaven above or on earth below. Indeed the more lives we read, the more speeches we listen to, the more opinions we consult, the greater the confusion becomes and the less possible it seems, since we cannot understand the impulses, the motives, or the morality which lead you to go to war, to make any suggestion that will help you to prevent war.

But besides these pictures of other people's lives and minds – these biographies and histories – there are also other pictures – pictures of actual facts; photographs. Photographs, of course, are not arguments addressed to the reason; they are simply statements of fact addressed to the eye. But in that very simplicity there may be some help. Let us see then whether when we look at the same photographs we feel the same things. Here then on the table before us are photographs. The Spanish Government sends them with patient pertinacity about twice a week.[10] They are not pleasant photographs to look upon. They are photographs of dead bodies for the most part. This morning's collection contains the photograph of what might be a man's body, or a woman's; it is so mutilated that it might, on the other hand, be the body of a pig. But those certainly are dead children, and that undoubtedly is the section of a house. A bomb has torn open the side; there is still a birdcage hanging in what was presumably the sitting-room, but the rest of the house looks like nothing so much as a bunch of spillikins suspended in mid air.

Those photographs are not an argument; they are simply a crude statement of fact addressed to the eye. But the eye is connected with the brain; the brain with the nervous system. That system sends its messages in a flash through every past memory and present feeling. When we look at those photographs some fusion takes place within us; however different the education, the traditions behind us, our sensations are the same; and they are violent. You, Sir, call them 'horror and disgust'. We also call them horror and disgust. And the same words rise to our lips. War, you say, is an abomination; a barbarity; war must be stopped at whatever cost. And we echo your words. War is an abomination; a barbarity; war must be stopped. For now at last we are looking at the same picture; we are seeing with you the same dead bodies, the same ruined houses.

Let us then give up, for the moment, the effort to answer your question, how we can help you to prevent war, by discussing the political, the patriotic or the psychological reasons which lead you to go to war. The emotion is too positive to suffer patient analysis. Let us concentrate upon the practical suggestions which you bring forward for our consideration. There are three of them. The first is to sign a letter to the newspapers; the second is to join a certain society; the third is to subscribe to its funds. Nothing on the face of it could sound simpler. To scribble a name on a sheet of paper is easy; to attend a meeting where pacific opinions are more or less rhetorically reiterated to people who already believe in them is also easy; and to write a cheque in support of those vaguely acceptable opinions, though not so easy, is a cheap way of quieting what may conveniently be called one's conscience. Yet there are reasons which make us hesitate; reasons into which we must enter, less superficially, later on. Here it is enough to say that though the three measures you suggest seem plausible, yet it also seems that, if we did what you ask, the emotion caused by the photographs would still remain unappeased. That emotion, that very positive emotion, demands something more positive than a name written on a sheet of paper; an hour spent listening to speeches; a cheque written for whatever sum we can afford – say one guinea. Some more energetic, some more active method of expressing our belief that war is barbarous, that war is inhuman, that war, as Wilfred Owen put it, is insupportable, horrible and beastly seems to be required. But, rhetoric apart, what active method is open to us? Let us consider and compare. You, of course, could once more take up arms – in Spain, as before in France – in defence of peace. But that presumably is a method that having tried you have rejected. At any rate that method is not open to us; both the Army and the Navy are closed to our sex. We are not allowed to fight. Nor again are we allowed to be members of the Stock Exchange. Thus we can use neither the pressure of force nor the pressure of money. The less direct but still effective weapons which our brothers, as educated men, possess in the diplomatic service, in the Church, are also denied to us. We cannot preach sermons or negotiate treaties. Then again although it is true that we can write articles or send letters to the Press, the control of the Press – the decision what to print, what not to print – is entirely in the hands of your sex. It is true that for the past twenty years we have been admitted to the Civil Service and to the Bar; but our position there is still very precarious and our authority of the slightest. Thus all the weapons with which an educated man can enforce his opinion are either beyond our grasp or so nearly beyond it that even if we used them we could scarcely inflict one scratch. If the men in your profession were to unite in any demand and were to say: 'If it is not granted we will stop work', the laws of England would cease to be administered. If the women in your profession said the same thing it would make no difference to the laws of England whatever. Not only are we incomparably weaker than the men of our own class; we are weaker than the women of the working class. If the working women of the country were to say: 'If you go to war, we will refuse to make munitions or to help in the production of goods,' the difficulty of war-making would be seriously increased. But if all the daughters of educated men were to down tools tomorrow, nothing essential either to the life or to the war-making of the community would be embarrassed. Our class is the weakest of all the classes in the state. We have no weapon with which to enforce our will.[11]

The answer to that is so familiar that we can easily anticipate it. The daughters of educated men have no direct influence, it is true; but they possess the greatest power of all; that is, the influence that they can exert upon educated men. If this is true, if, that is, influence is still the strongest of our weapons and the only one that can be effective in helping you to prevent war, let us, before we sign your manifesto or join your society, consider what that influence amounts to. Clearly it is of such immense importance that it deserves profound and prolonged scrutiny. Ours cannot be profound; nor can it be prolonged; it must be rapid and imperfect – still, let us attempt it.

What influence then have we had in the past upon the profession that is most closely connected with war – upon politics? There again are the innumerable, the invaluable biographies, but it would puzzle an alchemist to extract from the massed lives of politicians that particular strain which is the influence upon them of women. Our analysis can only be slight and superficial; still if we narrow our inquiry to manageable limits, and run over the memoirs of a century and a half we can hardly deny that there have been women who have influenced politics. The famous Duchess of Devonshire, Lady Palmerston, Lady Melbourne, Madame de Lieven, Lady Holland, Lady Ashburton – to skip from one famous name to another – were all undoubtedly possessed of great political influence. Their famous houses and the parties that met in them play so large a part in the political memoirs of the time that we can hardly deny that English politics, even perhaps English wars, would have been different had those houses and those parties never existed. But there is one characteristic that all those memoirs possess in common; the names of the great political leaders – Pitt, Fox, Burke, Sheridan, Peel, Canning, Palmerston, Disraeli, Gladstone – are sprinkled on every page; but you will not find either at the head of the stairs receiving the guests, or in the more private apartments of the house, any daughter of an educated man. It may be that they were deficient in charm, in wit, in rank, or in clothing. Whatever the reason, you may turn page after page, volume after volume, and though you will find their brothers and husbands – Sheridan at Devonshire House, Macaulay at Holland House, Matthew Arnold at Lansdowne House, Carlyle even at Bath House, the names of Jane Austen, Charlotte Brontë, and George Eliot do not occur; and though Mrs Carlyle went, Mrs Carlyle seems on her own showing to have found herself ill at ease.

But, as you will point out, the daughters of educated men may have possessed another kind of influence – one that was independent of wealth and rank, of wine, food, dress and all the other amenities that make the great houses of the great ladies so seductive. Here indeed we are on firmer ground, for there was of course one political cause which the daughters of educated men had much at heart during the past 150 years: the franchise. But when we consider how long it took them to win that cause, and what labour, we can only conclude that influence has to be combined with wealth in order to be effective as a political weapon, and that influence of the kind that can be exerted by the daughters of educated men is very low in power, very slow in action, and very painful in use.[12] Certainly the one great political achievement of the educated man's daughter cost her over a century of the most exhausting and menial labour; kept her trudging in processions, working in offices, speaking at street corners; finally, because she used force, sent her to prison, and would very likely still keep her there, had it not been, paradoxically enough, that the help she gave her brothers when they used force at last gave her the right to call herself, if not a full daughter, still a stepdaughter of England.[13]

Influence then when put to the test would seem to be only fully effective when combined with rank, wealth and great houses. The influential are the daughters of noblemen, not the daughters of educated men. And that influence is of the kind described by a distinguished member of your own profession, the late Sir Ernest Wild.

> He claimed that the great influence which women exerted over men always had been, and always ought to be, an indirect influence. Man liked to think he was doing his job himself when, in fact, he was doing just what the woman wanted, but the wise woman always let him think he was running the show when he was not. Any woman who chose to take an interest in politics had an immensely greater power without the vote than with it, because she could influence many voters. His feeling was that it was not right to bring women down to the level of men. He looked up to women, and wanted to continue to do so. He desired that the age of chivalry should not pass, because every man who had a woman to care about him liked to shine in her eyes.[14]

And so on.

If such is the real nature of our influence, and we all recognize the description and have noted the effects, it is either beyond our reach, for many of us are plain, poor and old; or beneath our contempt, for many of us would prefer to call ourselves prostitutes simply and to take our stand openly under the lamps of Piccadilly Circus rather than use it. If such is the real nature, the indirect nature, of this celebrated weapon, we must do without it; add our pigmy impetus to your more substantial forces, and have recourse, as you suggest, to letter signing, society joining and the drawing of an occasional exiguous cheque. Such would seem to be the inevitable, though depressing, conclusion of our inquiry into the nature of influence, were it not that for some reason, never satisfactorily explained, the right to vote,[15] in itself by no means negligible, was mysteriously connected with another right of such immense value to the daughters of educated men that almost every word in the dictionary has been changed by it, including the word 'influence'. You will not think these words exaggerated if we explain that they refer to the right to earn one's living.

That, Sir, was the right that was conferred upon us less than twenty years ago, in the year 1919, by an Act which unbarred the professions. The door of the private house was thrown open. In every purse there was, or might be, one bright new sixpence in whose light every thought, every sight, every action looked different. Twenty years is not, as time goes, a long time; nor is a sixpenny bit a very important coin; nor can we yet draw upon biography to supply us with a picture of the lives and minds of the new-sixpenny owners. But in imagination perhaps we can see the educated man's daughter, as she issues from the shadow of the private house, and stands on the bridge which lies between the old world and the new, and asks, as she twirls the sacred coin in her hand, 'What shall I do with it? What do I see with it? Through that light we may guess everything she saw looked different – men and women, cars and churches. The moon even, scarred as it is in fact with forgotten craters, seemed to her a white sixpence, a chaste sixpence, an altar upon which she vowed never to side with the servile, the signers-on, since it was hers to do what she liked with – the sacred sixpence that she had earned with her own hands herself. And if checking imagination with prosaic good sense, you object that to depend upon a profession is only another form of slavery, you will admit from your own experience that to depend upon a profession is a less odious form of slavery than to depend upon a father. Recall the joy with which you received your first guinea for your first brief, and the deep breath of freedom that you drew when you realized that your days of dependence upon Arthur's Education Fund were over. From that guinea, as from one of the magic pellets to which children set fire and a tree rises, all that you most value – wife, children, home – and above all that influence which now enables you to influence other men, have sprung. What would that influence be if you were still drawing £40 a year from the family purse, and for any addition to that income were dependent even upon the most benevolent of fathers? But it is needless to expatiate. Whatever the reason, whether pride, or love of freedom, or hatred of hypocrisy, you will understand the excitement with which in 1919 your sisters began to earn not a guinea but a sixpenny bit, and will not scorn that pride, or deny that it was justly based, since it meant that they need no longer use the influence described by Sir Ernest Wild.

The word 'influence' then has changed. The educated man's daughter has now at her disposal an influence which is different from any influence that she has possessed before. It is not the influence which the great lady, the Siren, possesses; nor is it the influence which the educated man's daughter possessed when she had no vote; nor is it the influence which she possessed when she had a vote but was debarred from the right to earn her living. It differs, because it is an influence from which the charm element has been removed; it is an influence from which the money element has been removed. She need no longer use her charm to procure money from her father or brother. Since it is beyond the power of her family to punish her financially she can express her own opinions. In place of the admirations and antipathies which were often unconsciously dictated by the need of money she can declare her genuine likes and dislikes. In short, she need not acquiesce; she can criticize. At last she is in possession of an influence that is disinterested.

Such in rough and rapid outlines is the nature of our new weapon, the influence which the educated man's daughter can exert now that she is able to earn her own living. The question that has next to be discussed, therefore, is how can she use this new weapon to help you to prevent war? And it is immediately plain that if there is no difference between men who earn their livings in the professions and women who earn their livings, then this letter can end; for if our point of view is the same as yours then we must add our sixpence to your guinea; follow your methods and repeat your words. But, whether fortunately or unfortunately, that is not true. The two classes still differ enormously. And to prove this, we need not have recourse to the dangerous and uncertain theories of psychologists and biologists; we can appeal to facts. Take the fact of education. Your class has been educated at public schools and universities for five or six hundred years, ours for sixty. Take the fact of property.[16] Your class possesses in its own right and not through marriage practically all the capital, all the land, all the valuables, and all the patronage in

England. Our class possesses in its own right and not through marriage practically none of the capital, none of the land, none of the valuables, and none of the patronage in England. That such differences make for very considerable differences in mind and body, no psychologist or biologist would deny. It would seem to follow then as an indisputable fact that 'we' – meaning by 'we' a whole made [what it is by this distinctive]¹⁷ tradition – must still differ in some essential respects from 'you', whose body, brain and spirit have been so differently trained and are so differently influenced by memory and tradition. Though we see the same world, we see it through different eyes. Any help we can give you must be different from that you can give yourselves, and perhaps the value of that help may lie in the fact of that difference. Therefore before we agree to sign your manifesto or join your society, it might be well to discover where the difference lies, because then we may discover where the help lies also. Let us then by way of a very elementary beginning lay before you a photograph – a crudely coloured photograph – of your world as it appears to us who see it from the threshold of the private house; through the shadow of the veil that St Paul still lays upon our eyes; from the bridge which connects the private house with the world of public life.

Your world, then, the world of professional, of public life, seen from this angle undoubtedly looks queer. At first sight it is enormously impressive. Within quite a small space are crowded together St Paul's, the Bank of England, the Mansion House, the massive if funereal battlements of the Law Courts; and on the other side, Westminster Abbey and the Houses of Parliament. There, we say to ourselves, pausing, in this moment of transition on the bridge, our fathers and brothers have spent their lives. All these hundreds of years they have been mounting those steps, passing in and out of those doors, ascending those pulpits, preaching, money-making, administering justice. It is from this world that the private house (somewhere, roughly speaking, in the West End) has derived its creeds, its laws, its clothes and carpets, its beef and mutton. And then, as is now permissible, cautiously pushing aside the swing doors of one of these temples, we enter on tiptoe and survey the scene in greater detail. The first sensation of colossal size, of majestic masonry is broken up into a myriad points of amazement mixed with interrogation. Your clothes in the first place make us gape with astonishment.[18] How many, how splendid, how extremely ornate they are – the clothes worn by the educated man in his public capacity! Now you dress in violet; a jewelled crucifix swings on your breast; now your shoulders are covered with lace; now furred with ermine; now slung with many linked chains set with precious stones. Now you wear wigs on your heads; rows of graduated curls descend to your necks. Now your hats are boat-shaped, or cocked; now they mount in cones of black fur; now they are made of brass and scuttle shaped; now plumes of red, now of blue hair surmount them. Sometimes gowns cover your legs; sometimes gaiters. Tabards embroidered with lions and unicorns swing from your shoulders; metal objects cut in star shapes or in circles glitter and twinkle upon your breasts. Ribbons of all colours – blue, purple, crimson – cross from shoulder to shoulder. After the comparative simplicity of your dress at home, the splendour of your public attire is dazzling.

But far stranger are two other facts that gradually reveal themselves when our eyes have recovered from their first amazement. Not only are whole bodies of men dressed alike summer and winter – a strange characteristic to a sex which changes its clothes according to the season, and for reasons of private taste and comfort – but every button, rosette and stripe seems to have some symbolical meaning. Some have the right to wear plain buttons only; others rosettes; some may wear a single stripe; others three, four, five or six. And each curl or stripe is sewn on at precisely the right distance apart; it may be one inch for one man, one inch and a quarter for another. Rules again regulate the gold wire on the shoulders, the braid on the trousers, the cockades on the hats – but no single pair of eyes can observe all these distinctions, let alone account for them accurately.

Even stranger, however, than the symbolic splendour of your clothes are the ceremonies that take place when you wear them. Here you kneel; there you bow; here you advance in procession behind a man carrying a silver poker; here you mount a carved chair; here you appear to do homage to a piece of painted wood; here you abase yourselves before tables covered with richly worked tapestry. And whatever these ceremonies may mean you perform them always together, always in step, always in the uniform proper to the man and the occasion.

Apart from the ceremonies such decorative apparel appears to us at first sight strange in the extreme. For dress, as we use it, is comparatively simple. Besides the prime function of covering the body, it has two other offices – that it creates beauty for the eye, and that it attracts the admiration of your sex. Since marriage until the year 1919 – less than twenty years ago – was the only profession open to us, the enormous importance of dress to a woman can hardly be exaggerated. It was to her what clients are to you – dress was her chief, perhaps her only, method of becoming Lord Chancellor. But your dress in its immense elaboration has obviously another function. It not only covers nakedness, gratifies vanity, and creates pleasure for the eye, but it serves to advertise the social, professional or intellectual standing of the wearer. If you will excuse the humble illustration, your dress fulfils the same function as the tickets in a grocer's shop. But, here, instead of saying 'This is margarine; this pure butter; this is the finest butter in the market,' it says, 'This man is a clever man – he is Master of Arts; this man is a very clever man – he is Doctor of Letters; this man is a most clever man – he is a Member of the Order of Merit.' It is this function – the advertisement function – of your dress that seems to us most singular. In the opinion of St Paul, such advertisement, at any rate for our sex, was unbecoming and immodest; until a very few years ago we were denied the use of it. And still the tradition, or belief, lingers among us that to express worth of any kind, whether intellectual or moral, by wearing pieces of metal, or ribbon, coloured hoods or gowns, is a barbarity which deserves the ridicule which we bestow upon the rites of savages. A woman who advertised her motherhood by a tuft of horsehair on the left shoulder would scarcely, you will agree, be a venerable object.

But what light does our difference here throw upon the problem before us? What connection is there between the sartorial splendours of the educated man and the photograph of ruined houses and dead bodies? Obviously the connection between dress and war is not far to seek; your finest clothes are those that you wear as soldiers. Since the red and the gold, the brass and the feathers are discarded upon active service, it is plain that their expensive and not, one might suppose, hygienic splendour is invented partly in order to impress the beholder with the majesty of the military office, partly in order through their vanity to induce young men to become soldiers. Here, then, our influence and our difference might have some effect; we, who are forbidden to wear such clothes ourselves, can express the opinion that the wearer is not to us a pleasing or an impressive spectacle. He is on the contrary a ridiculous, a barbarous, a displeasing spectacle. But as the daughters of educated men we can use our influence more effectively in another direction, upon our own class – the class of educated men. For there, in courts and universities, we find the same love of dress. There, too, are velvet and silk, fur and ermine. We can say that for educated men to emphasize their superiority over other people, either in birth or intellect, by dressing differently, or by adding titles before or letters after their names are acts that rouse competition and jealousy – emotions which, as we need scarcely draw upon biography to prove, nor ask psychology to show, have their share in encouraging a disposition towards war. If then we express the opinion that such distinctions make those who possess them ridiculous and learning contemptible we should do something, indirectly, to discourage the feelings that lead to war. Happily we can now do more than express an opinion; we can refuse all such distinctions and all such uniforms for ourselves. This would be a slight but definite contribution to the problem before us – how to prevent war; and one that a different training and a different tradition puts more easily within our reach than within yours.[19]

That request then for a guinea answered, and the cheque signed, only one further request of yours remains to be considered – it is that we should fill up a form and become members of your society. On the face of it that seems a simple request, easily granted. For what can be simpler than to join the society to which this guinea has just been contributed? On the face of it, how easy, how simple; but in the depths, how difficult, how complicated . . . What possible doubts, what possible hesitations can those dots stand for? What reason or what emotion can make us hesitate to become members of a society whose aims we approve, to whose funds we have contributed? It may be neither reason nor emotion, but something more profound and fundamental than either. It may be difference. Different we are, as facts have proved, both in sex and in education. And it is from that difference, as we have already said, that our help can come, if help we can, to protect liberty, to prevent war. But if we sign this form which implies a promise to become active members of your society, it would seem that we must lose that difference and therefore sacrifice that help. To explain why this is so is not easy, even though the gift of a guinea has made it possible (so we have boasted), to speak freely without fear or flattery. Let us then keep the form unsigned on the table before us while we discuss, so far as we are able, the reasons and the emotions which make us hesitate to sign it. For those reasons and emotions have their origin deep in the darkness of ancestral memory; they have grown together in some confusion; it is very difficult to untwist them in the light.

To begin with an elementary distinction: a society is a conglomeration of people joined together for certain aims; while you, who write in your own person with your own hand are single. You the individual are a man whom we have reason to respect; a man of the brotherhood, to which, as biography proves, many brothers have belonged. Thus Anne Clough, describing her brother, says: 'Arthur is my best friend and adviser . . . Arthur is the comfort and joy of my life; it is for him, and from him, that I am incited to seek after all that is lovely and of good report.' To which William Wordsworth, speaking of his sister but answering the other as if one nightingale called to another in the forests of the past, replies:

> The Blessing of my later years
> Was with me when a Boy:
> She gave me eyes, she gave me ears;
> And humble cares, and delicate fears;
> A heart, the fountain of sweet tears;
> And love, and thought, and joy.[20]

Such was, such perhaps still is, the relationship of many brothers and sisters in private, as individuals. They respect each other and help each other and have aims in common. Why then, if such can be their private relationship, as biography and poetry prove, should their public relationship, as law and history prove, be so very different? And here, since you are a lawyer, with a lawyer's memory, it is not necessary to remind you of certain decrees of English law from its first records to the year 1919 by way of proving that the public, the society relationship of brother and sister has been very different from the private. The very word 'society' sets tolling in memory the dismal bells of a harsh music: shall not, shall not. You shall not learn; you shall not earn; you shall not own; you shall not – such was the society relationship of brother to sister for many centuries. And though it is possible, and to the optimistic credible, that in time a new society may ring a carillon of splendid harmony, and your letter heralds it, that day is far distant. Inevitably we ask ourselves, is there not something in the conglomeration of people into societies that releases what is most selfish and violent, least rational and humane in the individuals themselves? Inevitably we look upon society, so kind to you, so harsh to us, as an ill-fitting form that distorts the truth; deforms the mind; fetters the will. Inevitably we look upon societies as conspiracies that sink the private brother, whom many of us have reason to respect, and inflate in his stead a monstrous male, loud of voice, hard of fist, childishly intent upon scoring the floor of the earth with chalk marks, within whose mystic boundaries human beings are penned, rigidly, separately, artificially; where, daubed red and gold, decorated like a savage with feathers, he goes through mystic rites and enjoys the dubious pleasures of power and dominion while we, 'his' women, are locked in the private house without share in the many societies of which his society is composed. For such reasons, compact as they are of many memories and emotions – for who shall analyse the complexity of a mind that holds so deep a reservoir of time past within it? – it seems both wrong for us rationally and impossible for us emotionally to fill up your form and join your society. For by so doing we should merge our identity in yours; follow and repeat and score still deeper the old worn ruts in which society, like a gramophone whose needle has stuck, is grinding out with intolerable unanimity 'Three hundred millions spent upon arms'. We should not give effect to a view which our own experience of 'society' should have helped us to envisage. Thus, Sir, while we respect you as a private person and prove it by giving you a guinea to spend as you choose, we believe that we can help you most effectively by refusing to join your society; by working for our common ends – justice and equality and liberty for all men and women – outside your society, not within.

But this, you will say, if it means anything, can only mean that you, the daughters of educated men, who have promised us your positive help, refuse to join our society in order that you may make another of your own. And what sort of society do you propose to found outside ours, but in co-operation with it, so that we may both work together for our common ends? That is a question which you have every right to ask, and which we must try to answer in order to justify our refusal to sign the form you send. Let us then draw rapidly in outline the kind of society which the daughters of educated men might found and join outside your society but in co-operation with its ends. In the first place, this new society, you will be relieved to learn, would have no honorary treasurer, for it would need no funds. It would have no office, no committee, no secretary; it would call no meetings; it would hold no conferences. If name it must have, it could be called the Outsiders Society. That is not a resonant name, but it has the advantage that it squares with facts – the facts of history, of law, of biography; even, it may be, with the still hidden facts of our still unknown psychology. It would consist of educated men's daughters working in their own class – how indeed can they work in any other?[21] – and by their own methods for liberty, equality and peace. Their first duty, to which they would bind themselves not by oath, for oaths and ceremonies have no part in a society which must be anonymous and elastic before everything, would be not to fight with arms. This is easy for them to observe, for in fact, as the papers inform us, 'the Army Council have no intention of opening recruiting for any women's corps'.[22] The country ensures it. Next they would refuse in the event of war to make munitions or nurse the wounded. Since in the last war both these activities were mainly discharged by the daughters of working men, the pressure upon them here too would be slight, though probably disagreeable. On the other hand the next duty to which they would pledge themselves is one of considerable difficulty, and calls not only for courage and initiative, but for the special knowledge of the educated man's daughter. It is, briefly, not to incite their brothers to fight, or to dissuade them, but to maintain an attitude of complete indifference. But the attitude expressed by the word 'indifference' is so complex and of such importance that it needs even here further definition. Indifference in the first place must be given a firm footing upon fact. As it is a fact that she cannot understand what instinct compels him, what glory, what interest, what manly satisfaction fighting provides for him – 'without war there would be no outlet for the manly qualities which fighting develops' – as fighting thus is a sex characteristic which she cannot share, the counterpart some claim of the maternal instinct which he cannot share, so is it an instinct which she cannot judge. The outsider therefore must leave him free to deal with this instinct by himself, because liberty of opinion must be respected, especially when it is based upon an instinct which is as foreign to her as centuries of tradition and education can make it.[23] This is a fundamental and instinctive distinction upon which indifference may be based. But the outsider will make it her duty not merely to base her indifference upon instinct, but upon reason. When he says, as history proves that he has said, and may say again, 'I am fighting to protect our country' and thus seeks to rouse her patriotic emotion, she will ask herself, 'What does "our country" mean to me an outsider?' To decide this she will analyse the meaning of patriotism in her own case. She will inform herself on the position of her sex and her class in the past. She will inform herself of the amount of land, wealth and property in the possession of her own sex and class in the present – how much of 'England' in fact belongs to her. From the same sources she will inform herself of the legal protection which the law has given her in the past and now gives her. And if he adds that he is fighting to protect her body, she will reflect upon the degree of physical protection that she now enjoys when the words 'Air Raid Precaution' are written on blank walls. And if he says that he is fighting to protect England from foreign rule, she will reflect that for her there are no 'foreigners', since by law she becomes a foreigner if she marries a foreigner. And she will do her best to make this a fact, not by forced fraternity, but by human sympathy. All these facts will convince her reason (to put it in a nutshell) that her sex and class has very little to thank England for in the past; not much to thank England for in the present; while the security of her person in the future is highly dubious. But probably she will have imbibed, even from the governess, some romantic notion that Englishmen, those fathers and grandfathers whom she sees marching in the picture of history, are 'superior' to the men of other countries. This she will consider it her duty to check by comparing French historians with English; German with French; the testimony of the ruled – the Indians or the Irish, say – with the claims made by their rulers. Still some 'patriotic' emotion, some ingrained belief in the intellectual superiority of her own country over other countries may remain. Then she will compare English painting with French painting; English music with German music; English literature with Greek literature, for translations abound. When all these comparisons have been faithfully made by the use of reason, the outsider will find herself in possession of very good reasons for her indifference. She will find that she has no good reason to ask her brother to fight on her behalf to protect 'our' country. ' "Our country," ' she will say, 'throughout the greater part of its history has treated me as a slave; it has denied me education or any share in its possessions. "Our" country still ceases to be mine if I marry a foreigner. "Our" country denies me the means of protecting myself, forces me to pay others a very large sum annually to protect me, and is so little able, even so, to protect me that Air Raid precautions are written on the wall. Therefore if you insist upon fighting to protect me, or "our" country, let it be understood, soberly and rationally between us, that you are fighting to gratify a sex instinct which I cannot share; to procure benefits which I have not shared and probably will not share; but not to gratify my instincts, or to protect either myself or my country. For,' the outsider will say, 'in fact, as a woman, I have no country. As a woman I want no country. As a woman my country is the whole world.' And if, when reason has said its say, still some obstinate emotion remains, some love of England dropped into a child's ears by the cawing of rooks in an elm tree, by the splash of waves on a beach, or by English voices murmuring nursery rhymes, this drop of pure, if irrational, emotion she will make serve her to give to England first what she desires of peace and freedom for the whole world.

Such then is the conclusion to which our inquiry into the nature of fear has brought us – the fear which forbids freedom in the private house. That fear, small, insignificant and private as it is, is connected with the other fear, the public fear, which is neither small nor insignificant, the fear which has led you to ask us to help you to prevent war. Otherwise we should not be looking at the picture again. But it is not the same picture that caused us at the beginning of this letter to feel the same emotions – you called them 'horror and disgust'; we called them horror and disgust. For as this letter has gone on, adding fact to fact, another picture has imposed itself upon the foreground. It is the figure of a man; some say, others deny, that he is Man himself,[24] the quintessence of virility, the perfect type of which all the others are imperfect adumbrations. He is a man certainly. His eyes are glazed; his eyes glare. His body, which is braced in an unnatural position, is tightly cased in a uniform. Upon the breast of that uniform are sewn several medals and other mystic symbols. His hand is upon a sword. He is called in German and Italian *Führer* or *Duce*; in our own language Tyrant or Dictator. And behind him lie ruined houses and dead bodies – men, women and children. But we have not laid that picture before you in order to excite once more the sterile emotion of hate. On the contrary it is in order to release other emotions such as the human figure, even thus crudely in a coloured photograph, arouses in us who are human beings. For it suggests a connection and for us a very important connection. It suggests that the public and the private worlds are inseparably connected; that the tyrannies and servilities of the one are the tyrannies and servilities of the other. But the human figure even in a photograph suggests other and more complex emotions. It suggests that we cannot dissociate ourselves from that figure but are ourselves that figure. It suggests that we are not passive spectators doomed to unresisting obedience but by our thoughts and actions can ourselves change that figure. A common interest unites us; it is one world, one life. How essential it is that we should realize that unity the dead bodies, the ruined houses prove. For such will be our ruin if you, in the immensity of your public abstractions forget the private figure, or if we in the intensity of our private emotions forget the public world. Both houses will be ruined, the public and the private, the material and the spiritual, for they are inseparably connected. But with your letter before us we have reason to hope. For by asking our help you recognize that connection; and by reading your words we are reminded of other connections that lie far deeper than the facts on the surface. Even here, even now your letter tempts us to shut our ears to these little facts, these trivial details, to listen not to the bark of the guns and the bray of the gramophones but to the voices of the poets, answering each other, assuring us of a unity that rubs out divisions as if they were chalk marks only; to discuss with you the capacity of the human spirit to overflow boundaries and make unity out of multiplicity. But that would be to dream – to dream the recurring dream that has haunted the human mind since the beginning of time; the dream of peace, the dream of freedom. But, with the sound of the guns in your ears you have not asked us to dream. You have not asked us what peace is; you have asked us how to prevent war. Let us then leave it to the poets to tell us what the dream is; and fix our eyes upon the photograph again: the fact.

Whatever the verdict of others may be upon the man in uniform – and opinions differ – there is your letter to prove that to you the picture is the picture of evil. And though we look upon that picture from different angles our conclusion is the same as yours – it is evil. We are both determined to do what we can to destroy the evil which that picture represents, you by your methods, we by ours. And since we are different, our help must be different. What ours can be we have tried to show – how imperfectly, how superficially there is no need to say.[25] But as a result the answer to your question must be that we can best help you to prevent war not by repeating your words and following your methods but by finding new words and creating new methods. We can best help you to prevent war not by joining your society but by remaining outside your society but in co-operation with its aim. That aim is the same for us both. It is to assert 'the rights of all – all men and women – to the respect in their persons of the great principles of Justice and Equality and Liberty.' To elaborate further is unnecessary, for we have every confidence that you interpret those words as we do. And excuses are unnecessary, for we can trust you to make allowances for those deficiencies which we foretold and which this letter has abundantly displayed.

To return then to the form that you have sent and ask us to fill up: for the reasons given we will leave it unsigned. But in order to prove as substantially as possible that our aims are the same as yours, here is the guinea, a free gift, given freely, without any other conditions than you choose to impose upon yourself. It is the third of three guineas; but the three guineas, you will observe, though given to three different treasurers are all given to the same cause, for the causes are the same and inseparable.

Now, since you are pressed for time, let me make an end; apologizing three times over to the three of you, first for the length of this letter, second for the smallness of the contribution, and thirdly for writing at all. The blame for that however rests upon you, for this letter would never have been written had you not asked for an answer to your own.

NOTES

* 'Women in Stratification Studies' in *Close to Home: A Materialist Analysis of Women's Oppression*, trans. and ed. Diana Leonard (London: Hutchinson, 1984).

1 Excerpts from *Three Guineas* by Virginia Woolf, copyright 1938 by Harcourt Brace Jovanovich, Inc. and renewed 1966 by Leonard Woolf, reprinted by permission of the publisher.

2 Stephen Gwynn, *The Life of Mary Kingsley*, p. 15. It is difficult to get exact figures of the sums spent on the education of educated men's daughters. About £20 or £30 presumably covered the entire cost of Mary Kingsley's education (*b.*1862; *d.*1900). A sum of £100 may be taken as about the average in the nineteenth century and even later. The women thus educated often felt the lack of education very keenly. 'I always feel the defects of my education most painfully when I go out,' wrote Anne J. Clough, the first Principal of Newnham. (B. A. Clough, *Life of Anne J. Clough*, p. 60.) Elizabeth Haldane, who came, like Miss Clough, of a highly literate family, but was educated in much the same way, says that when she grew up, 'My first conviction was that I was not educated, and I thought of how this could be put right. I should have loved going to college, but college in those days was unusual for girls, and the idea was not encouraged. It was also expensive. For an only daughter to leave a widowed mother was indeed considered to be out of the question, and no one made the plan seem feasible. There was in those days a new movement for carrying on correspondence classes . . .' (Elizabeth Haldane, *From One Century to Another*, p. 73.) The efforts of such uneducated women to conceal their ignorance were often valiant, but not always successful. 'They talked agreeably on current topics, carefully avoiding controversial subjects. What impressed me was their ignorance and indifference concerning anything outside their own circle . . . no less a personage than the mother of the Speaker of the House of Commons believed that California belonged to us, part of our Empire!' (H. A. Vachell, *Distant Fields*, p. 109.) That ignorance was often simulated in the nineteenth century owing to the current belief that educated men enjoyed it is shown by the energy with which Thomas Gisborne, in his instructive work *On the Duties of Women* (p. 278), rebuked those who recommend women 'studiously to refrain from discovering to their partners in marriage the full extent of their abilities and attainments'. 'This is not discretion but art. It is dissimulation, it is deliberate imposition . . . It could scarcely be practised long without detection.'

But the educated man's daughter in the nineteenth century was even more ignorant of life than of books. One reason for that ignorance is suggested by the following quotation: 'It was supposed that most men were not "virtuous", that is, that nearly all would be capable of accosting and annoying – or worse – any unaccompanied young woman whom they met.' (Mary, Countess of Lovelace, 'Society and the Season' in *Fifty Years, 1882–1932*, p. 37.) She was therefore confined to a very narrow circle; and her 'ignorance and indifference' to anything outside it was excusable. The connection between that ignorance and the nineteenth-century conception of manhood, which – witness the Victorian hero – made 'virtue' and virility incompatible is obvious. In a well-known passage Thackeray complains of the limitations which virtue and virility between them imposed upon his art.

3 Our ideology is still so inveterately anthropocentric that it has been necessary to coin this clumsy term – educated man's daughter – to describe the class whose fathers have been educated at public schools and universities. Obviously, if the term 'bourgeois' fits her brother, it is grossly incorrect to use it of one who differs so profoundly in the two prime characteristics of the bourgeoisie – capital and environment.

4 The number of animals killed in England for sport during the past century must be beyond computation. 1,212 head of game is given as the average for a day's shooting at Chatsworth in 1909. (The Duke of Portland, *Men, Women and Things*, p. 251.) Little mention is made in sporting memoirs of women guns; and their appearance in the hunting field was the cause of much caustic comment. 'Skittles', the famous nineteenth-century horsewoman, was a lady of easy morals. It is highly probable that there was held to be some connection between sport and unchastity in women in the nineteenth century.

5 John Buchan, *Francis and Riversdale Grenfell*, pp. 189, 205.

6 The Earl of Lytton, *Antony (Viscount Knebworth)*, p. 355.

7 *The Poems of Wilfred Owen*, edited by Edmund Blunden, pp. 25, 41.

8 Lord Hewart, proposing the toast of 'England' at the banquet of the Society of St George at Cardiff.

9 Both in the *Daily Telegraph*, 5 February 1937.

10 Written in the winter of 1936–7.

11 There is of course one essential that the educated woman can supply: children. And one method by which she can help to prevent war is to refuse to bear children. Thus Mrs Helena Normanton is of opinion that 'The only thing that women in any country can do to prevent war is to stop the supply of "cannon fodder". ' (Report of the Annual Council for Equal Citizenship, *Daily Telegraph*, 5 March 1937.) Letters in the newspapers frequently support this view. 'I can tell Mr Harry Campbell why women refuse to have children in these times. When men have learnt how to run the lands they govern so that wars shall hit only those who make the quarrels, instead of mowing down those who do not, then women may again feel like having large families. Why should women bring children into such a world as this one is today?' (Edith Maturin-Porch, in the *Daily Telegraph*, 6 September 1937.) The fact that the birth rate in the educated class is falling would seem to show that educated women are taking Mrs Normanton's advice. It was

offered them in very similar circumstances over two thousand years ago by Lysistrata.

12 There are of course innumerable kinds of influence besides those specified in the text. It varies from the simple kind described in the following passage: 'Three years later . . . we find her writing to him as Cabinet Minister to solicit his interest on behalf of a favourite parson for a Crown living . . .' (Lady Londonderry, *Henry Chaplin, a Memoir*, p. 57) to the very subtle kind exerted by Lady Macbeth upon her husband. Somewhere between the two lies the influence described by D. H. Lawrence: 'It is hopeless for me to try to do anything without I have a woman at the back of me . . . I daren't sit in the world without I have a woman behind me . . . But a woman that I love sort of keeps me in direct communication with the unknown, in which otherwise I am a bit lost' (*Letters of D. H. Lawrence*, pp. 93–4), with which we may compare, though the collocation is strange, the famous and very similar definition given by the ex-King Edward VIII upon his abdication. Present political conditions abroad seem to favour a return to the use of interested influence. For example: 'A story serves to illustrate the present degree of women's influence in Vienna. During the past autumn a measure was planned to further diminish women's professional opportunities. Protests, pleas, letters, all were of no avail. Finally, in desperation, a group of well-known ladies of the city . . . got together and planned. For the next fortnight, for a certain number of hours per day, several of these ladies got on to the telephone to the Ministers they knew personally, ostensibly to ask them to dinner at their homes. With all the charm of which the Viennese are capable, they kept the Ministers talking, asking about this and that, and finally mentioning the matter that distressed them so much. When the Ministers had been rung up by several ladies, all of whom they did not wish to offend, and kept from urgent State affairs by this manoeuvre, they decided on compromise – and so the measure was postponed.' (Hilary Newitt, *Women Must Choose*, p. 129.) Similar use of influence was often deliberately made during the battle for the franchise. But women's influence is said to be impaired by the possession of a vote. Thus Marshal von Bieberstein was of opinion that 'Women led men always . . . but he did not wish them to vote.' (Elizabeth Haldane, *From One Century to Another*, p. 258.)

13 English women were much criticized for using force in the battle for the franchise. When in 1910 Mr Birrell had his hat 'reduced to pulp' and his shins kicked by suffragettes, Sir Almeric Fitzroy commented, 'an attack of this character upon a defenceless old man by an organized band of "janissaries" will, it is hoped, convince many people of the insane and anarchical spirit actuating the movement.' (*Memoirs of*

Sir Almeric Fitzroy, Vol. II, p. 425.) These remarks did not apply apparently to the force in the European war. The vote indeed was given to English women largely because of the help they gave to Englishmen in using force in that war. 'On 14 August [1916], Mr Asquith himself gave up his opposition [to the franchise]. "It is true," he said, "[that women] cannot fight in the sense of going out with rifles and so forth, but . . . they have aided in the most effective way in the prosecution of the war."' (Ray Strachey, *The Cause*, p. 354.) This raises the difficult question whether those who did not aid in the prosecution of the war, but did what they could to hinder the prosecution of the war, ought to use the vote to which they are entitled chiefly because others 'aided in the prosecution of the war'? That they are stepdaughters, not full daughters, of England is shown by the fact that they change nationality on marriage. A woman, whether or not she helped to beat the Germans, becomes a German if she marries a German. Her political views must then be entirely reversed, and her filial piety transferred.

14 Robert J. Blackburn, *Sir Ernest Wild, K. C.*, pp. 174–5.

15 That the right to vote has not proved negligible is shown by the facts published from time to time by the National Union of Societies for Equal Citizenship. 'This publication (*What the Vote Has Done*) was originally a single-page leaflet; it has now (1927) grown to a six-page pamphlet, and has to be constantly enlarged.' (M. A. Fawcett and E. M. Turner, *Josephine Butler*, note, p. 101).

16 There are no figures available with which to check facts that must have a very important bearing upon the biology and psychology of the sexes. A beginning might be made in this essential but strangely neglected preliminary by chalking on a large-scale map of England property owned by men, red; by women, blue. Then the number of sheep and cattle consumed by each sex must be compared; the hogsheads of wine and beer; the barrels of tobacco; after which we must examine carefully their physical exercises; domestic employments; facilities of sexual intercourse, etc. Historians are of course mainly concerned with war and politics; but sometimes throw light upon human nature. Thus Macaulay dealing with the English country gentleman in the seventeenth century, says: 'His wife and daughter were in tastes and acquirements below a housekeeper or still-room maid of the present day. They stitched and spun, brewed gooseberry wine, cured marigolds, and made the crust for the venison pasty.'

Again, 'The ladies of the house, whose business it had commonly been to cook the repast, retired as soon as the dishes had been devoured, and left the gentlemen to their ale and tobacco.' (Macaulay, *History of England*, ch. 3.) But the gentlemen were still drinking and the ladies were still withdrawing a great deal later. 'In my mother's young days before her marriage, the old hard-drinking habits of the Regency and of the eighteenth century still persisted. At Woburn Abbey it was the custom for the trusted old family butler to make his nightly report to my grandmother in the drawing-room. "The gentlemen have had a good deal tonight; it might be as well for the young ladies to retire," or, "The gentlemen have had very little tonight," was announced according to circumstances by this faithful family retainer. Should the young girls be packed off upstairs, they liked standing on an upper gallery of the staircase "to watch the shouting, riotous crowd issuing from the dining-room."' (Lord F. Hamilton, *The Days Before Yesterday*, p. 322.) It must be left to the scientist of the future to tell us what effect drink and property have had upon chromosomes.

17   Editors' emendation; original text defective.

18   The fact that both sexes have a very marked though dissimilar love of dress seems to have escaped the notice of the dominant sex owing largely it must be supposed to the hypnotic power of dominance. Thus the late Mr Justice MacCardie, in summing up the case of Mrs Frankau, remarked: 'Women cannot be expected to renounce an essential feature of femininity or to abandon one of nature's solaces for a constant and insuperable physical handicap . . . Dress, after all, is one of the chief methods of women's self-expression . . . In matters of dress women often remain children to the end. The psychology of the matter must not be overlooked. But whilst bearing the above matters in mind the law has rightly laid it down that the rule of prudence and proportion must be observed.' The Judge who thus dictated was wearing a scarlet robe, an ermine cape and a vast wig of artificial curls. Whether he was enjoying 'one of nature's solaces for a constant and insuperable physical handicap', whether again he was himself observing 'the rule of prudence and proportion' must be doubtful. But 'the psychology of the matter must not be overlooked'; and the fact that the singularity of his own appearance together with that of Admirals, Generals, Heralds, Life Guards, Peers, Beefeaters, etc., was completely invisible to him so that he was able to lecture the lady without any consciousness of sharing her weakness, raises two questions: how often must an act be performed before it becomes tradition, and therefore venerable; and what degree of social prestige causes blindness to the remarkable nature of one's own clothes? Singularity of dress, when not associated with office, seldom escapes ridicule.

19   In the New Year's Honours List for 1937, 147 men accepted honours as against 7 women. For obvious reasons this cannot be taken as a measure of their comparative desire for such advertisement. But that it

should be easier, psychologically, for a woman to reject honours than for a man seems to be indisputable. For the fact that intellect (roughly speaking) is man's chief professional asset, and that stars and ribbons are his chief means of advertising intellect, suggests that stars and ribbons are identical with powder and paint, a woman's chief method of advertising her chief professional asset: beauty. It would therefore be as unreasonable to ask him to refuse a Knighthood as to ask her to refuse a dress. The sum paid for a Knighthood in 1901 would seem to provide a very tolerable dress allowance; '21 April (Sunday) – To see Meynell, who was as usual full of gossip. It appears that the King's debts have been paid off privately by his friends, one of whom is said to have lent £100,000, and satisfies himself with £25,000 in repayment plus a Knighthood (Wilfrid Scawen Blunt, *My Diaries*, Part II, p. 8).

20 B. A. Clough, *Memoir of Anne J. Clough*, pp. 38, 67. 'The Sparrow's Nest', by William Wordsworth.

21 In the nineteenth century much valuable work was done for the working class by educated men's daughters in the only way that was then open to them. But now that some of them at least have received an expensive education, it is arguable that they can work much more effectively by remaining in their own class and using the methods of that class to improve a class which stands much in need of improvement. If on the other hand the educated (as so often happens) renounce the very qualities which education should have bought – reason, tolerance, knowledge – and play at belonging to the working class and adopting its cause, they merely expose that cause to the ridicule of the educated class, and do nothing to improve their own. But the number of books written by the educated about the working class would seem to show that the glamour of the working class and the emotional relief afforded by adopting its cause, are today as irresistible to the middle class as the glamour of the aristocracy was twenty years ago (see *A La Recherche du Temps Perdu*.) Meanwhile it would be interesting to know what the true-born working man or woman thinks of the playboys and playgirls of the educated class who adopt the working-class cause without sacrificing middle-class capital, or sharing working-class experience. 'The average housewife', according to Mrs Murphy, Home Service Director of the British Commercial Gas Association, 'washed an acre of dirty dishes, a mile of glass and three miles of clothes and scrubbed five miles of floor yearly.' (*Daily Telegraph*, 29 September 1937.) For a more detailed account of working-class life, see *Life as We Have Known It*, by Co-operative working women, edited by Margaret Llewelyn Davies. The *Life of Joseph Wright* also gives a remarkable account of working-class life at first hand and not through pro-proletarian spectacles.

22 'It was stated yesterday at the War Office that the Army Council have
no intention of opening recruiting for any women's corps.' (*The Times,*
22 October 1937.) This marks a prime distinction between the sexes.
Pacifism is enforced upon women. Men are still allowed liberty of
choice.

23 The following quotation shows, however, that if sanctioned the fighting
instinct easily develops. 'The eyes deeply sunk into the sockets, the
features acute, the amazon keeps herself very straight on the stirrups at
the head of her squadron . . . Five English parlementaries look at this
woman with the respectful and a bit restless admiration one feels for a
"fauve" of an unknown species . . .

   – Come nearer Amalia – orders the commandant. She pushes her
horse towards us and salutes her chief with the sword.

   – Sergeant Amalia Bonilla – continues the chief of the squadron –
how old are you? – Thirty-six – Where were you born? – In Granada –
Why have you joined the army? – My two daughters were militia-
women. The younger has been killed in the Alto de Leon. I thought I
had to supersede her and avenge her. – And how many enemies have
you killed to avenge her? – You know it, commandant, five. The sixth
is not sure. – No, but you have taken his horse. The amazon Amalia
rides in fact a magnificent dapple-grey horse, with glossy hair, which
flatters like a parade horse . . . This woman who has killed five men –
but who feels not sure about the sixth – was for the envoys of the
House of Commons an excellent introducer to the Spanish war.' (Louis
Delaprée, *The Martyrdom of Madrid*, Inedited Witnesses (Madrid,
1937) pp. 34, 5, 6.

24 The nature of manhood and the nature of womanhood are frequently
defined both by Italian and German dictators. Both repeatedly insist
that it is the nature of man and indeed the essence of manhood to fight.
Hitler, for example, draws a distinction between 'a nation of pacifists
and a nation of men'. Both repeatedly insist that it is the nature of
womanhood to heal the wounds of the fighter. Nevertheless a very
strong movement is on foot towards emancipating man from the old
'natural and eternal law' that man is essentially a fighter; witness the
growth of pacifism among the male sex today. Compare further Lord
Knebworth's statement 'that if permanent peace were ever achieved,
and armies and navies ceased to exist, there would be no outlet for the
manly qualities which fighting developed,' with the following statement
by another young man of the same social caste a few months ago:
'. . . it is not true to say that every boy at heart longs for war. It is only
other people who teach it us by giving us swords and guns, soldiers and
uniforms to play with.' (Prince Hubertus Loewenstein, *Conquest of the
Past*, p. 215.) It is possible that the Fascist States by revealing to the

younger generation at least the need for emancipation from the old conception of virility are doing for the male sex what the Crimean and the European wars did for their sisters. Professor Huxley, however, warns us that 'any considerable alteration of the hereditary constitution is an affair of millennia, not of decades.' On the other hand, as science also assures us that our life on earth is 'an affair of millennia, not of decades', some alteration in the hereditary constitution may be worth attempting.

25 Coleridge however expresses the views and aims of the outsiders with some accuracy in the following passage: 'Man must be *free* or to what purpose was he made a Spirit of Reason, and not a Machine of Instinct? Man must *obey*; or wherefore has he a conscience? The powers, which create this difficulty, contain its solution likewise; for *their* service is perfect freedom. And whatever law or system of law compels any other service, disennobles our nature, leagues itself with the animal against the godlike, kills in us the very principle of joyous well-doing, and fights against humanity . . . If therefore society is to be under a *rightful* constitution of government, and one that can impose on rational Beings a true and moral obligation to obey it, it must be framed on such principles that every individual follows his own Reason, while he obeys the laws of the constitution, and performs the will of the state while he follows the dictates of his own Reason. This is expressly asserted by Rousseau, who states the problem of a perfect constitution of government in the following words: *Trouver une forme d'Association – par laquelle chacun s'unisant à tous, n'obeisse pourtant qu'à lui même, et reste aussi libre qu'auparavant,* i.e. To find a form of society according to which each one uniting with the whole shall yet obey himself only and remain as free as before.' (S. T. Coleridge, *The Friend,* Vol. I, pp. 333, 334, 335, 1818 edition.) To which may be added a quotation from Walt Whitman:

'Of Equality – as if it harm'd me, giving others the same chances and rights as myself – as if it were not indispensable to my own rights that others possess the same.'

And finally the words of a half-forgotten novelist, George Sand, are worth considering:

'*Toutes les existences sont solidaires les unes des autres, et tout être humain qui présenterait la sienne isolément, sans la rattacher à celle de ses semblables, n'offrirait qu'une énigme à débrouiller . . . Cette individualité n'a par elle seule ni signification ni importance aucune. Elle ne prend un sens quelconque qu'en devenant une parcelle de la vie générale, en se fondant avec l'individualité de chacun de mes semblables, et c'est par là qu'elle devient de l'histoire.*' (George Sand, *Histoire de ma Vie,* pp. 240–1.)

11

Simone de Beauvoir
1908–1986

'CONCLUSION' from *THE SECOND SEX*
(1949, ENGLISH TRANSLATION 1953)

'One is not born, but rather becomes, a woman. No biological, psycho-logical, or economic fate determines the figure that the human female presents in society; it is civilization as a whole that produces this creature, intermediate between male and eunuch, which is described as feminine.' *The famous opening sentences of* The Second Sex *encapsulate the thesis, central to recent feminist scholarship and politics, that femininity is socially constructed. Simone de Beauvoir's life as an independent and intellectual woman has provided an important role model for feminists, and has also been viewed with scepticism (notably the nature of her relationship with Sartre). Beauvoir fought shy of the label 'feminist' for herself, but never-theless played an active role in French feminist culture until her death in 1986.*

The social construction of femininity is the foundation for feminist inquiry into the sexual division of labour, women's health, kinship re-lations, popular culture and much else. But Beauvoir's conception of femininity as deformed masculinity, a deviation from the norm, distances her from many contemporary feminists. This conception owes much to her commitment to existentialism.

Existentialism takes to an extreme the liberal aspiration to an untram-melled autonomy and self-willed choice. Beauvoir and her existentialist colleagues acknowledged that a completely autonomous life is impossible, because as individuals we are constrained by social and moral norms and bodily needs: this is the human condition. They held nonetheless that we can constantly and deliberately take responsibility for our obedience or disobedience to authority, and even for our response to the imperatives of our bodies. To be truly ethical subjects, exercising our powers of authentic choice, we must, as far as possible, transcend *both the social and the physical.*

Feminist readers are likely to have difficulty with the idea of a way of life that achieves this kind of transcendence. Insofar as men approach this state, it is typically thanks to the labour of women who have relieved them of the burdens of their own physical needs. Should women, whose relation to their body is so different from men's, really aspire to this? In the passage here Beauvoir is clearly saying 'yes'. There are, however, places where she seems to argue that the biological difference between the sexes has a moral or 'existential' significance which is not determined by contingent, historically changeable cultural conditions, but is metaphysical and timeless. On this view women would be destined to represent, and live in, immanence (that is, within the horizon of repetitious physical existence.)

Here Beauvoir discusses the current state and possible outcome of the 'sex war': women must change fundamentally if this is ever to end. In the past women's strategy has been to attempt to imprison men in the feminine world of domestic and bodily relationships. Now, however, women are also fighting the battle on new terrain; they are moving out of their traditional sphere and demanding respect, equality and freedom. Yet they still cling stubbornly to their objecthood, trying to trap men into domesticity, dissatisfied with a sexual relationship unless it is accompanied by 'hours of conversation, and "going out" into the bargain' (p. 202). Austerely contemptuous of this kind of ambivalence, Simone de Beauvoir insists that women, like men, must henceforth learn to walk on the world stage, bravely and alone.

Beauvoir does not think that the emotional autonomy she advocates for women will eradicate difference between the sexes. And for her, a political project of liberation requires men and women to work together in solidarity.

'No, woman is not our brother; through indolence and deceit we have made of her a being apart, unknown, having no weapon other than her sex, which not only means constant warfare but unfair warfare – adoring or hating, but never a straight friend, a being in a legion with *esprit de corps* and freemasonry – the defiant gestures of the eternal little slave.'[1]

Many men would still subscribe to these words of Laforgue; many think that there will always be 'strife and dispute', as Montaigne put it, and that fraternity will never be possible. The fact is that today neither men nor women are satisfied with each other. But the question is to know whether there is an original curse that condemns them to rend each other or whether the conflicts in which they are opposed merely mark a transitional moment in human history.

Legends notwithstanding, no physiological destiny imposes an eternal hostility upon Male and Female as such; even the famous praying mantis devours her male only for want of other food and for the good of the species: it is to this, the species, that all individuals are subordinated, from the top to the bottom of the scale of animal life. Moreover, humanity is something more than a mere species: it is a historical development; it is to be defined by the manner in which it deals with its natural, fixed characteristics, its *facticité*. Indeed, even with the most extreme bad faith, it is impossible to demonstrate the existence of a rivalry between the human male and female of a truly physiological nature. Further, their hostility may be allocated rather to that intermediate terrain between biology and psychology: psychoanalysis. Woman, we are told, envies man his penis and wishes to castrate him; but the childish desire for the penis is important in the life of the adult woman only if she feels her femininity as a mutilation; and then it is as a symbol of all the privileges of manhood that she wishes to appropriate the male organ. We may readily agree that her dream of castration has this symbolic significance: she wishes, it is thought, to deprive the male of his transcendence.

But her desire, as we have seen, is much more ambiguous: she wishes, in a contradictory fashion, *to have* this transcendence, which is to suppose that she at once respects it and denies it, that she intends at once to throw herself into it and keep it within herself. This is to say that the drama does not unfold on a sexual level; further, sexuality has never seemed to us to define a destiny, to furnish in itself the key to human behaviour, but to express the totality of a situation that it only helps to define. The battle of the sexes is not implicit in the anatomy of man and woman. The truth is that when one evokes it, one takes for granted that in the timeless realm of Ideas a battle is being waged between those vague essences the Eternal Feminine and the Eternal Masculine; and one neglects the fact that this titanic combat assumes on earth two totally different forms, corresponding with two different moments of history.

The woman who is shut up in immanence endeavours to hold man in that prison also; thus the prison will become interchangeable with the world, and woman will no longer suffer from being confined there: mother, wife, sweetheart are the jailers. Society, being codified by man, decrees that woman is inferior: she can do away with this inferiority only by destroying the male's superiority. She sets about mutilating, dominating man, she contradicts him, she denies his truth and his values. But in doing this she is only defending herself; it was neither a changeless essence nor a mistaken choice that doomed her to immanence, to inferiority. They were imposed upon her. All oppression creates a state of war. And this is no exception. The existent who is regarded as inessential cannot fail to demand the re-establishment of her sovereignty.

Today the combat takes a different shape; instead of wishing to put man in a prison, woman endeavours to escape from one: she no longer seeks to drag him into the realms of immanence but to emerge, herself, into the light of transcendence. Now the attitude of the males creates a new conflict: it is with a bad grace that the man lets her go. He is very well pleased to remain the sovereign subject, the absolute superior, the essential being; he refuses to accept his companion as an equal in any concrete way. She replies to his lack of confidence in her by assuming an aggressive attitude. It is no longer a question of a war between individuals each shut up in his or her sphere: a caste claiming its rights attacks and is resisted by the privileged caste. Here two transcendences are face to face; instead of displaying mutual recognition, each free being wishes to dominate the other.

This difference of attitude is manifest on the sexual plane as on the spiritual plane. The 'feminine' woman in making herself prey tries to reduce man, also, to her carnal passivity; she occupies herself in catching him in her trap, in enchaining him by means of the desire she arouses in him in submissively making herself a thing. The emancipated woman, on the contrary, wants to be active, a taker, and refuses the passivity man means to impose on her. The 'modern' woman accepts masculine values: she prides herself on thinking, taking action, working, creating, on the same terms as men; instead of seeking to disparage them, she declares herself their equal.

In so far as she expresses herself in definite action, this claim is legitimate, and male insolence must then bear the blame. But in men's defence it must be said that women are wont to confuse the issue. Many women, in order to show by their successes their equivalence to men, try to secure male support by sexual means; they play on both sides, demanding old-fashioned respect and modern esteem, banking on their old magic and their new rights. It is understandable that a man becomes irritated and puts himself on the defensive; but he is also double-dealing when he requires woman to play the game fairly while he denies her the indispensable trump cards through distrust and hostility. Indeed, the struggle cannot be clearly drawn between them, since woman is opaque in her very being; she stands before man not as a subject but as an object paradoxically endued with subjectivity; she takes herself simultaneously as *self* and as *other*, a contradiction that entails baffling consequences. When she makes weapons at once of her weakness and of her strength, it is not a matter of designing calculation: she seeks salvation spontaneously in the way that has been imposed on her, that of passivity, at the same time when she is actively demanding her sovereignty; and no doubt this procedure is unfair tactics, but it is dictated by the ambiguous situation assigned her. Man, however, becomes indignant when he treats her as a free and independent being and then realizes that she is still a trap for him; if he gratifies and satisfies her in her posture as prey, he finds her claims to autonomy irritating; whatever he does, he feels tricked and she feels wronged.

The quarrel will go on as long as men and women fail to recognize each other as equals; that is to say, as long as femininity is perpetuated as such. Which sex is the more eager to maintain it? Woman, who is being emancipated from it, wishes none the less to retain its privileges; and man, in that case, wants her to assume its limitations. 'It is easier to accuse one sex than to excuse the other,' says Montaigne. It is vain to apportion praise and blame. The truth is that if the vicious circle is so hard to break, it is because the two sexes are each the victim at once of the other and of itself. Between two adversaries confronting each other in their pure liberty, an agreement could be easily reached: the more so as the war profits neither. But the complexity of the whole affair derives from the fact that each camp is giving aid and comfort to the enemy; woman is pursuing a dream of submission, man a dream of identification. Want of authenticity does not pay: each blames the other for the unhappiness he or she has incurred in yielding to the temptations of the easy way; what man and woman loathe in each other is the shattering frustration of each one's own bad faith and baseness.

We have seen why men enslaved women in the first place: the devaluation of femininity has been a necessary step in human evolution, but it might have led to collaboration between the two sexes; oppression is to be explained by the tendency of the existent to flee from himself by means of identification with the other, whom he oppresses to that end. In each individual man that tendency exists today; and the vast majority yield to it. The husband wants to find himself in his wife, the lover in his mistress, in the form of a stone image; he is seeking in her the myth of his virility, of his sovereignty, of his immediate reality. But he is himself the slave of his double: what an effort to build up an image in which he is always in danger! In spite of everything his success in this depends upon the capricious freedom of women: he must constantly try to keep this propitious to him. Man is concerned with the effort to appear male, important, superior; he pretends so as to get pretence in return; he, too, is aggressive, uneasy; he feels hostility for women because he is afraid of them, he is afraid of them because he is afraid of the personage, the image, with which he identifies himself. What time and strength he squanders in liquidating, sublimating, transferring complexes, in talking about women, in seducing them, in fearing them! He would be liberated himself in their liberation. But this is precisely what he dreads. And so he obstinately persists in the mystifications intended to keep woman in her chains.

That she is being tricked, many men have realized. 'What a misfortune to be a woman! And yet the misfortune, when one is a woman, is at bottom not to comprehend that it is one,' says Kierkegaard.[2] For a long time there have been efforts to disguise this misfortune. For example, guardianship has been done away with: women have been given 'protectors', and if they are invested with the rights of the old-time guardians, it is in woman's own interest. To forbid her working, to keep her at home, is to defend her against herself and to assure her happiness. We have seen what poetic veils are thrown over her monotonous burdens of housekeeping and maternity: in exchange for her liberty she has received the false treasures of her 'femininity'. Balzac illustrates this manoeuvre very well in counselling man to treat her as a slave while persuading her that she is a queen. Less cynical, many men try to convince themselves that she is really privileged. There are American sociologists who seriously teach today the theory of 'low-class gain', that is to say, the benefits enjoyed by the lower orders. In France, also, it has often been proclaimed – although in a less scientific manner – that the workers are very fortunate in not being obliged to 'keep up appearances'. Like the carefree wretches gaily scratching at their vermin, like the merry Negroes laughing under the lash, and those joyous Tunisian Arabs burying their starved children with a smile, woman enjoys that incomparable privilege: irresponsibility. Free from troublesome burdens and cares, she obviously has 'the better part'. But it is disturbing that with an obstinate perversity – connected no doubt with original sin – down through the centuries and in all countries, the people who have the better part are always crying to their benefactors: 'It is too much! I will be satisfied with yours!' But the munificent capitalists, the generous colonists, the superb males, stick to their guns: 'Keep the better part, hold on to it!'

It must be admitted that the males find in woman more complicity that the oppressor usually finds in the oppressed. And in bad faith they take authorization from this to declare that she has *desired* the destiny they have imposed on her. We have seen that all the main features of her training combine to bar her from the roads of revolt and adventure. Society in general – beginning with her respected parents – lies to her by praising the lofty values of love, devotion, the gift of herself, and then concealing from her the fact that neither lover nor husband nor yet her children will be inclined to accept the burdensome charge of all that. She cheerfully believes these lies because they invite her to follow the easy slope: in this others commit their worst crime against her; throughout her life from childhood on, they damage and corrupt her by designating as her true vocation this submission, which is the temptation of every existent in the anxiety of liberty. If a child is taught idleness by being amused all day long and never being led to study, or shown its usefulness, it will hardly be said, when he grows up, that he chose to be incapable and ignorant; yet this is how woman is brought up, without ever being impressed with the necessity of taking charge of her own existence.

So she readily lets herself come to count on the protection, love, assistance and supervision of others, she lets herself be fascinated with the hope of self-realization without *doing* anything. She does wrong in yielding to the temptation; but man is in no position to blame her, since he has led her into the temptation. When conflict arises between them, each will hold the other responsible for the situation; she will reproach him with having made her what she is: 'No one taught me to reason or to earn my own living'; he will reproach her with having accepted the consequences: 'You don't know anything, you are an incompetent,' and so on. Each sex thinks it can justify itself by taking the offensive; but the wrongs done by one do not make the other innocent.

The innumerable conflicts that set men and women against one another come from the fact that neither is prepared to assume all the consequences of this situation which the one has offered and the other accepted. The doubtful concept of 'equality in inequality', which the one uses to mask his despotism and the other to mask her cowardice, does not stand the test of experience: in their exchanges, woman appeals to the theoretical equality she has been guaranteed, and man the concrete inequality that exists. The result is that in every association an endless debate goes on concerning the ambiguous meaning of the words *give* and *take*: she complains of giving her all, he protests that she takes his all. Woman has to learn that exchanges – it is a fundamental law of political economy – are based on the value the merchandise offered has for the buyer, and not for the seller: she has been deceived in being persuaded that her worth is priceless. The truth is that for man she is an amusement, a pleasure, company, an inessential boon; he is for her the meaning, the justification of her existence. The exchange, therefore, is not of two items of equal value.

This inequality will be especially brought out in the fact that the time they spend together – which fallaciously seems to be the same time – does not have the same value for both partners. During the evening the lover spends with his mistress he could be doing something of advantage to his career, seeing friends, cultivating business relationships, seeking recreation; for a man normally integrated in society, time is a positive value: money, reputation, pleasure. For the idle, bored woman, on the contrary, it is a burden she wishes to get rid of; when she succeeds in killing time, it is a benefit to her:

the man's presence is pure profit. In a liaison what most clearly interests the man, in many cases, is the sexual benefit he gets from it: if need be, he can be content to spend no more time with his mistress than is required for the sexual act; but – with exceptions – what she, on her part, wants is to kill all the excess time she has on her hands; and – like the greengrocer who will not sell potatoes unless the customer will take turnips also – she will not yield her body unless her lover will take hours of conversation and 'going out' into the bargain. A balance is reached if, on the whole, the cost does not seem too high to the man, and this depends, of course, on the strength of his desire and the importance he gives to what is to be sacrificed. But if the woman demands – offers – too much time, she becomes wholly intrusive, like the river overflowing its banks, and the man will prefer to have nothing rather than too much. Then she reduces her demands; but very often the balance is reached at the cost of a double tension: she feels that the man has 'had' her at a bargain, and he thinks her price is too high. This analysis, of course, is put in somewhat humorous terms; but – except for those affairs of jealous and exclusive passion in which the man wants total possession of the woman – this conflict constantly appears in cases of affection, desire and even love. He always has 'other things to do' with his time; whereas she has time to kill; and he considers much of the time she gives him not as a gift but as a burden.

As a rule he consents to assume the burden because he knows very well that he is on the privileged side, he has a bad conscience; and if he is of reasonable good will he tries to compensate for the inequality by being generous. He prides himself on his compassion, however, and at the first clash he treats the woman as ungrateful and thinks, with some irritation: 'I'm too good to her.' She feels she is behaving like a beggar when she is convinced of the high value of her gifts, and that humiliates her.

Here we find the explanation of the cruelty that woman often shows she is capable of practising; she has a good conscience because she is on the unprivileged side; she feels she is under no obligation to deal gently with the favoured caste, and her only thought is to defend herself. She will even be very happy if she has occasion to show her resentment to a lover who has not been able to satisfy all her demands: since he does not give her enough, she takes savage delight in taking back everything from him. At this point the wounded lover suddenly discovers the value *in toto* of a liaison each moment of which he held more or less in contempt: he is ready to promise her everything, even though he will feel exploited again when he has to make good. He accuses his mistress of blackmailing him: she calls him stingy; both feel wronged.

Once again it is useless to apportion blame and excuses: justice can never be done in the midst of injustice. A colonial administrator has no possibility of acting rightly towards the natives, nor a general towards his soldiers; the only solution is to be neither colonist nor military chief; but a man could not prevent himself from being a man. So there he is, culpable in spite of himself and labouring under the effects of a fault he did not himself commit; and here she is, victim and shrew in spite of herself. Sometimes he rebels and becomes cruel, but then he makes himself an accomplice of the injustice, and the fault becomes really his. Sometimes he lets himself be annihilated, devoured, by his demanding victim; but in that case he feels duped. Often he stops at a compromise that at once belittles him and leaves him ill at ease. A well-disposed man will be more tortured by the situation than the woman herself: in a sense it is always better to be on the side of the vanquished; but if she is well-disposed also, incapable of self-sufficiency, reluctant to crush the man with the weight of her destiny, she struggles in hopeless confusion.

In daily life we meet with an abundance of these cases which are incapable of satisfactory solution because they are determined by unsatisfactory conditions. A man who is compelled to go on materially and morally supporting a woman whom he no longer loves feels he is victimized; but if he abandons without resources the woman who has pledged her whole life to him, she will be quite as unjustly victimized. The evil originates not in the perversity of individuals – and bad faith first appears when each blames the other – it originates rather in a situation against which all individual action is powerless. Women are 'clinging', they are a dead weight, and they suffer for it; the point is that their situation is like that of a parasite sucking out the living strength of another organism. Let them be provided with living strength of their own, let them have the means to attack the world and wrest from it their own subsistence, and their dependence will be abolished – that of man also. There is no doubt that both men and women will profit greatly from the new situation.

A world where men and women would be equal is easy to visualize, for that precisely is what the Soviet Revolution *promised*: women reared and trained exactly like men were to work under the same conditions[3] and for the same wages. Erotic liberty was to be recognized by custom, but the sexual act was not to be considered a 'service' to be paid for; woman was to be *obliged* to provide herself with other ways of earning a living; marriage was to be based on a free agreement that the contracting parties could break at will; maternity was to be voluntary, which meant that contraception and abortion were to be authorized and that, on the other hand, all mothers and their children were to have exactly the same rights, in or out of marriage; pregnancy leaves were to be paid for by the State, which would assume charge of the children, signifying not that they would be *taken away* from their parents, but that they would not be *abandoned to* them.

But is it enough to change laws, institutions, customs, public opinion, and the whole social context, for men and women to become truly equal? 'Women will always be women,' say the sceptics. Other seers prophesy that in casting off their femininity they will not succeed in changing themselves into men and they will become monsters. This would be to admit that the woman of today is a creation of nature; it must be repeated once more that in human society nothing is natural and that woman, like much else, is a product elaborated by civilization. The intervention of others in her destiny is fundamental: if this action took a different direction, it would produce a quite different result. Woman is determined not by her hormones or by mysterious instincts, but by the manner in which her body and her relation to the world are modified through the action of others than herself. The abyss that separates the adolescent boy and girl has been deliberately widened between them since earliest childhood; later on, woman could not be other than what she *was made*, and that past was bound to shadow her for life. If we appreciate its influence, we see clearly that her destiny is not predetermined for all eternity.

We must not believe, certainly, that a change in woman's economic condition alone is enough to transform her, though this factor has been and remains the basic factor in her evolution; but until it has brought about the moral, social, cultural and other consequences that it promises and requires, the new woman cannot appear. At this moment they have been realized nowhere, in Russia no more than in

France or the United States; and this explains why the woman of today is torn between the past and the future. She appears most often as a 'true woman' disguised as a man, and she feels herself as ill at ease in her flesh as in her masculine garb. She must shed her old skin and cut her own new clothes. This she could do only through a social evolution. No single educator could fashion a *female human being* today who would be the exact homologue of the *male human being*; if she is brought up like a boy, the young girl feels she is an oddity and thereby she is given a new kind of sex specification. Stendhal understood this when he said: 'The forest must be planted all at once.' But if we imagine, on the contrary, a society in which the equality of the sexes would be concretely realized, this equality would find new expression in each individual.

If the little girl were brought up from the first with the same demands and rewards, the same severity and the same freedom, as her brothers, taking part in the same studies, the same games, promised the same future, surrounded with women and men who seemed to her undoubted equals, the meaning of the castration complex and of the Oedipus complex would be profoundly modified. Assuming on the same basis as the father the material and moral responsibility of the couple, the mother would enjoy the same lasting prestige; the child would perceive around her an androgynous world and not a masculine world. Were she emotionally more attracted to her father – which is not even sure – her love for him would be tinged with a will to emulation and not a feeling of powerlessness; she would not be oriented towards passivity. Authorized to test her powers in work and sports, competing actively with the boys, she would not find the absence of the penis – compensated by the promise of a child – enough to give rise to an inferiority complex; correlatively the boy would not have a superiority complex if it were not instilled into him and if he looked up to women with as much respect as to men.[4] The little girl would not seek sterile compensation in narcissism and dreaming, she would not take her fate for granted; she would be interested in what she was *doing*, she would throw herself without reserve into undertakings.

I have already pointed out how much easier the transformation of puberty would be if she looked beyond it, like the boys, towards a free adult future: menstruation horrifies her only because it is an abrupt descent into femininity. She would also take her young eroticism in much more tranquil fashion if she did not feel a frightened disgust for her destiny as a whole; coherent sexual information would do much to help her over this crisis. And thanks to co-educational schooling, the august mystery of Man would have no occasion to enter her mind: it would be eliminated by everyday familiarity and open rivalry.

Objections raised against this system always imply respect for sexual taboos; but the effort to inhibit all sex curiosity and pleasure in the child is quite useless; one succeeds only in creating repressions, obsessions, neuroses. The excessive sentimentality, homosexual fervours and platonic crushes of adolescent girls, with all their train of silliness and frivolity, are much more injurious than a little childish sex play and a few definite sex experiences. It would be beneficial above all for the young girl not to be influenced against taking charge herself of her own existence, for then she would not seek a demigod in the male – merely a comrade, a friend, a partner. Eroticism and love would take on the nature of free transcendence and not that of resignation; she could experience them as a relation between equals. There is no intention, of course, to remove by a stroke of the pen all the difficulties that the child has to overcome in changing into an adult; the most intelligent, the most tolerant education could not relieve the child of experiencing things for herself; what could be asked is that obstacles should not be piled gratuitously in her path. Progress is already shown by the fact that 'vicious' little girls are no longer cauterized with a red-hot iron. Psychoanalysis has given parents some instruction, but the conditions under which, at the present time, the sexual training and intitiation of woman are accomplished are so deplorable that none of the objections advanced against the idea of a radical change could be considered valid. It is not a question of abolishing in woman the contingencies and miseries of the human condition, but of giving her the means for transcending them.

Woman is the victim of no mysterious fatality; the peculiarities that identify her as specifically a woman get their importance from the significance placed upon them. They can be surmounted, in the future, when they are regarded in new perspectives. Thus, as we have seen, through her erotic experience woman feels – and often detests – the domination of the male, but this is no reason to conclude that her ovaries condemn her to live for ever on her knees.

Virile aggressiveness seems like a lordly privilege only within a system that in its entirety conspires to affirm masculine sovereignty; and woman *feels* herself profoundly passive in the sexual act only because she already *thinks* of herself as such. Many modern women who lay claim to their dignity as human beings still envisage their erotic life from the standpoint of a tradition of slavery: since it seems to them humiliating to lie beneath the man, to be penetrated by him, they grow tense in frigidity. But if the reality were different, the meaning expressed symbolically in amorous gestures and postures would be different, too: a woman who pays and dominates her lover can, for example, take pride in her superb idleness and consider that she is enslaving the male who is actively exerting himself. And here and now there are many sexually well-balanced couples whose notions of victory and defeat are giving place to the idea of an exchange.

As a matter of fact, man, like woman, is flesh, therefore passive, the plaything of his hormones and of the species, the restless prey of his desires. And she, like him, in the midst of the carnal fever, is a consenting, a voluntary gift, an activity; they live out in their several fashions the strange ambiguity of existence made body. In those combats where they think they confront one another, it is really against the self that each one struggles, projecting into the partner that part of the self which is repudiated; instead of living out the ambiguities of their situation, each tries to make the other bear the abjection and tries to reserve the honour for the self. If, however, both should assume the ambiguity with a clear-sighted modesty, correlative of an authentic pride, they would see each other as equals and would live out their erotic drama in amity. The fact that we are human beings is infinitely more important than all the peculiarities that distinguish human beings from one another; it is never the given that confers superiorities: 'virtue', as the ancients called it, is defined at the level of 'that which depends on us'. In both sexes is played out the same drama of the flesh and the spirit, of finitude and transcendence; both are gnawed away by time and laid in wait for by death, they have the same essential need for one another; and they can gain from their liberty the same glory. If they were to taste it, they would no longer be tempted to dispute fallacious privileges, and fraternity between them could then come into existence.

I shall be told that all this is utopian fancy, because woman cannot be transformed unless society has first made her really the equal of man. Conservatives have never failed in such circumstances to refer to that vicious circle; history, however, does not revolve. If a caste is kept in a state of inferiority, no doubt it remains inferior; but liberty can break the circle. Let the Negroes vote and they become worthy of having the vote; let woman be given responsibilities and she is able to assume them. The fact is that oppressors cannot be expected to make a move of gratuitous generosity; but at one time the revolt of the oppressed, at another time even the very evolution of the privileged caste itself, creates new situations; thus men have been led, in their own interest, to give partial emancipation to women: it remains only for women to continue their ascent, and the successes they are obtaining are an encouragement for them to do so. It seems almost certain that sooner or later they will arrive at complete economic and social equality, which will bring about an inner metamorphosis.

However this may be, there will be some to object that if such a world is possible it is not desirable. When woman is 'the same' as her male, life will lose its salt and spice. This argument, also, has lost its novelty: those interested in perpetuating present conditions are always in tears about the marvellous past that is about to disappear, without having so much as a smile for the young future. It is quite true that doing away with the slave trade meant death to the great plantations magnificent with azaleas and camellias, it meant ruin to the whole refined Southern civilization. In the attics of time rare old laces have joined the clear pure voices of the Sistine *castrati*,[5] and there is a certain 'feminine charm' that is also on the way to the same dusty repository. I agree that he would be a barbarian indeed who failed to appreciate exquisite flowers, rare lace, the crystal-clear voice of the eunuch, and feminine charm.

When the 'charming woman' shows herself in all her splendour, she is a much more exalting object than the 'idiotic paintings, over-doors, scenery, showman's garish signs, popular reproductions', that excited Rimbaud; adorned with the most modern artifices, beautified according to the newest techniques, she comes down from the remoteness of the ages, from Thebes, from Crete, from Chichén-Itzá; and she is also the totem set up deep in the African jungle; she is a helicopter and she is a bird; and there is this, the greatest wonder of all: under her tinted hair the forest murmur becomes a thought, and words issue from her breasts. Men stretch forth avid hands towards the marvel, but when they grasp it, it is gone: the wife, the mistress, speak like everybody else through their mouths: their words are worth just what they are worth: their breasts also. Does such a fugitive miracle – and one so rare – justify us in perpetuating a situation that is baneful for both sexes? One can appreciate the beauty of flowers, the charm of women, and appreciate them at their true value; if these treasures cost blood or misery, they must be sacrificed.

But in truth this sacrifice seems to men a peculiarly heavy one; few of them really wish in their hearts for woman to succeed in making it; those among them who hold woman in contempt see in the sacrifice nothing for them to gain, those who cherish her see too much that they would lose. And it is true that the evolution now in progress threatens more than feminine charm alone: in beginning to exist for herself, woman will relinquish the function as double and mediator to which she owes her privileged place in the masculine universe; to man, caught between the silence of nature and the demanding presence of other free beings, a creature who is at once his like and a passive thing seems a great treasure. The guise in which he conceives his companion may be mythical, but the experiences for which she is the source or the pretext are none the less real: there are hardly any more precious, more intimate, more ardent. There is no denying that feminine dependence, inferiority, woe, give women their special character; assuredly woman's autonomy, if it spares men many troubles, will also deny them many conveniences; assuredly there are certain forms of the sexual adventure which will be lost in the world of tomorrow. But this does not mean that love, happiness, poetry, dream, will be banished from it.

Let us not forget that our lack of imagination always depopulates the future; for us it is only an abstraction; each one of us secretly deplores the absence there of the one who was himself. But the humanity of tomorrow will be living in its flesh and in its conscious liberty; that time will be its present and it will in turn prefer it. New relations of flesh and sentiment of which we have no conception will arise between the sexes; already, indeed, there have appeared between men and women friendships, rivalries, complicities, comradeships – chaste or sensual – which past centuries could not have conceived. To mention one point, nothing could seem more debatable than the opinion that dooms the new world to uniformity and hence to boredom. I fail to see that this present world is free from boredom or that liberty ever creates uniformity.

To begin with, there will always be certain differences between man and woman; her eroticism, and therefore her sexual world, have a special form of their own and therefore cannot fail to engender a sensuality, a sensitivity, of a special nature. This means that her relations to her own body, to that of the male, to the child, will never be identical with those the male bears to his own body, to that of the female, and to the child; those who make much of 'equality in difference' could not with good grace refuse to grant me the possible existence of differences in equality. Then again, it is institutions that create uniformity. Young and pretty, the slaves of the harem are always the same in the sultan's embrace; Christianity gave eroticism its savour of sin and legend when it endowed the human female with a soul; if society restores her sovereign individuality to woman, it will not thereby destroy the power of love's embrace to move the heart.

It is nonsense to assert that revelry, vice, ecstasy, passion, would become impossible if man and woman were equal in concrete matters; the contradictions that put the flesh in opposition to the spirit, the instant to time, the swoon of immanence to the challenge of transcendence, the absolute of pleasure to the nothingness of forgetting, will never be resolved; in sexuality will always be materialized the tension, the anguish, the joy, the frustration and the triumph of existence. To emancipate woman is to refuse to confine her to the relations she bears to man, not to deny them to her; let her have her independent existence and she will continue none the less to exist for him *also*: mutually recognizing each other as subject, each will yet remain for the other an *other*. The reciprocity of their relations will not do away with the miracles – desire, possession, love, dream, adventure – worked by the division of human beings into two separate categories; and the words that move us – giving, conquering, uniting – will not lose their meaning. On the contrary, when we abolish the slavery of half of humanity, together with the whole system of hypocrisy that it implies, then the 'division' of humanity will reveal its genuine significance and the human couple will find its true form. 'The direct, natural, necessary relation of human creatures is the *relation of man to woman*,'[6] Marx has said. 'The nature of this relation determines to what point man himself is to be considered as a *generic being*, as mankind; the relation of man to woman is the most natural relation of human being to human being. By it is shown, therefore, to what point the *natural* behaviour of man has become *human* or to what point the *human* being has become his *natural* being, to what point his *human nature* has become his *nature*.'

The case could not be better stated. It is for man to establish the reign of liberty in the midst of the world of the given. To gain the supreme victory, it is necessary, for one thing, that by and through their natural differentiation men and women unequivocally affirm their brotherhood.

NOTES

1 Permission to reproduce Simone de Beauvoir's 'Conclusion' from *The Second Sex* © 1953 English translation granted by Jonathan Cape.

2 *In Vino Veritas*. He says further: 'Politeness is pleasing – essentially – to woman, and the fact that she accepts it without hesitation is explained by nature's care for the weaker, for the unfavoured being, and for one to whom an illusion means more than a material compensation. But this illusion, precisely, is fatal to her ... To feel oneself freed from distress thanks to something imaginary, is that not a still deeper mockery? ... Woman is very far from being *verwahrlost* (neglected), but in another sense she is, since she can never free herself from the illusion that nature has used to console her.'

3 That certain too laborious occupations were to be closed to women is not in contradiction to this project. Even among men there is an increasing effort to obtain adaptation to profession; their varying physical and mental capacities limit their possibilities of choice; what is asked is that, in any case, no line of sex or caste be drawn.

4 I knew a little boy of 8 who lived with his mother, aunt and grandmother, all independent and active women, and his weak old half-crippled grandfather. He had a crushing inferiority complex in regard to the feminine sex, although he made efforts to combat it. At school he scorned comrades and teachers because they were miserable males.

5 Eunuchs were long used in the male choirs of the Sistine Chapel in Rome, until the practice was forbidden by Pope Leo XIII in 1880. Castration caused the boy's soprano voice to be retained into adulthood, and the operation was performed for this purpose. [Translator's note]

6 *Philosophical Works*, Vol. VI (Marx's italics).

12

Audre Lorde
b.1934

*As well as volumes of poetry and essays, Audre Lorde has published
extracts from her diaries which offer insights into the painful and inspiring
aspects of living with cancer. Her life's struggles have been both against
the destructive forces within her body, and against the external forces of
racism, sexism and homophobia. In the United States, in Europe and
in Australia, she has played key roles in campaigns aimed at bridging
political and cultural divisions of class and race.*

*Some subordinated groups are formed by and in the very institutions
that provide for their subordination: work brings working people together,
for instance. But women are not brought together through their subordination to men; institutionalized heterosexuality keeps women apart from
one another. Women have to make their own communities. Where they
unite and organize as women, they unite with others whose specific social
experience may differ widely from their own.*

*The essay reprinted below is concerned with the need for women to face
up to the differences between them which arise from systems of oppression
other than the gender system. Of course there can be difference without
inferiority or superiority. But for us to recognize this is not enough –
not in a world in which difference has everywhere been constructed as
inferiority/superiority. Lorde's essay is concerned with the difficulties,
dangers and possibilities that such a world presents. We have to take
positive action not to acquiesce in those systems in which we ourselves are*

not cast as inferior. We must respond sensitively to the idea that there may be ideological distortions in our own thought. And we must resist the idea that unity among women might require homogeneity – that it is difference as such that we have to eradicate.

Much of western European history conditions us to see human differences in simplistic opposition to each other: dominant/subordinate, good/bad, up/down, superior/inferior.[1,2] In a society where the good is defined in terms of profit rather than in terms of human need, there must always be some group of people who, through systematized oppression, can be made to feel surplus, to occupy the place of the dehumanized inferior. Within this society, that group is made up of Black and Third World people, working-class people, older people and women.

As a 49-year-old Black lesbian feminist socialist mother of two, including one boy, and a member of an inter-racial couple, I usually find myself a part of some group defined as other, deviant, inferior or just plain wrong. Traditionally, in american society, it is the members of oppressed, objectified groups who are expected to stretch out and bridge the gap between the actualities of our lives and the consciousness of our oppressor. For in order to survive, those of us for whom oppression is as american as apple pie have always had to be watchers, to become familiar with the language and manners of the oppressor, even sometimes adopting them for some illusion of protection. Whenever the need for some pretence of communication arises, those who profit from our oppression call upon us to share our knowledge with them. In other words, it is the responsibility of the oppressed to teach the oppressors their mistakes. I am responsible for educating teachers who dismiss my children's culture in school. Black and Third World people are expected to educate white people as to our humanity. Women are expected to educate men. Lesbians and gay men are expected to educate the heterosexual world. The oppressors maintain their position and evade responsibility for their own actions. There is a constant drain of energy which might be better used in redefining ourselves and devising realistic scenarios for altering the present and constructing the future.

Institutionalized rejection of difference is an absolute necessity in a profit economy which needs outsiders as surplus people. As members of such an economy, we have *all* been programmed to respond to the human differences between us with fear and loathing and to handle that difference in one of three ways: ignore it, and if that it not possible, copy it if we think it is dominant, or destroy it if we think it is subordinate. But we have no patterns for relating across our human differences as equals. As a result, those differences have been misnamed and misused in the service of separation and confusion.

Certainly there are very real differences between us of race, age, and sex. But it is not those differences between us that are separating us. It is rather our refusal to recognize those differences, and to examine the distortions which result from our misnaming them and their effects upon human behavior and expectation.

Racism, the belief in the inherent superiority of one race over all others and thereby the right to dominance. Sexism, the belief in the inherent superiority of one sex over the other and thereby the right to dominance. Ageism. Heterosexism. Elitism. Classism.

It is a lifetime pursuit for each one of us to extract these distortions from our living at the same time as we recognize, reclaim and define those differences upon which they are imposed. For we have all been raised in a society where those distortions were endemic within our living. Too often, we pour the energy needed for recognizing and exploring difference into pretending those differences are insurmountable barriers, or that they do not exist at all. This results in a voluntary isolation, or false and treacherous connections. Either way, we do not develop tools for using human difference as a springboard for creative change within our lives. We speak not of human difference, but of human deviance.

Somewhere, on the edge of consciousness, there is what I call a *mythical norm*, which each one of us within our hearts knows 'that is not me.' In america, this norm is usually defined as white, thin, male, young, heterosexual, christian and financially secure. It is with this mythical norm that the trappings of power reside within this society. Those of us who stand outside that power often identify one way in which we are different, and we assume that to be the primary cause of all oppression, forgetting other distortions around difference, some of which we ourselves may be practising. By and large within the women's movement today, white women focus upon their oppression as women and ignore differences of race, sexual preference, class and age. There is a pretence to a homogeneity of experience covered by the word *sisterhood* that does not in fact exist.

Unacknowledged class differences rob women of each other's energy and creative insight. Recently a women's magazine collective made the decision for one issue to print only prose, saying poetry was a less 'rigorous' or 'serious' art form. Yet even the form our creativity takes is often a class issue. Of all the art forms, poetry is the most economical. It is the one which is the most secret, which requires the least physical labour, the least material, and the one which can be done between shifts, in the hospital pantry, on the subway, and on scraps of surplus paper. Over the last few years, writing a novel on tight finances, I came to appreciate the enormous differences in the material demands between poetry and prose. As we reclaim our literature, poetry has been the major voice of poor, working class and Coloured women. A room of one's own may be a necessity for writing prose, but so are reams of paper, a typewriter and plenty of time. The actual requirements to produce the visual arts also help determine, along class lines, whose art is whose. In this day of inflated prices for material, who are our sculptors, our painters, our photographers? When we speak of a broadly based women's culture, we need to be aware of the effect of class and economic differences on the supplies available for producing art.

As we move toward creating a society within which we can each flourish, ageism is another distortion of relationship which interferes with our vision. By ignoring the past, we are encouraged to repeat its mistakes. The 'generation gap' is an important social tool for any repressive society. If the younger members of a community view the older members as contemptible or suspect or excess, they will never be able to join hands and examine the living memories of the community, nor ask the all important question, 'Why?' This gives rise to a historical amnesia that keeps us working to invent the wheel every time we have to go to the store for bread.

We find ourselves having to repeat and relearn the same old lessons over and over that our mothers did because we do not pass on what we have learned, or because we are unable to listen. For instance, how many times has this all been said before? For another, who would have believed that once again our daughters are allowing their bodies to be hampered and purgatoried by girdles and high heels and hobble skirts?

Ignoring the differences of race between women and the implications of those differences presents the most serious threat to the mobilization of women's joint power.

As white women ignore their built-in privilege of whiteness and define *woman* in terms of their own experience alone, then women of Colour become 'other,' the outsider whose experience and tradition is too 'alien' to comprehend. An example of this is the signal absence of the experience of women of Colour as a resource for women's studies courses. The literature of women of Colour is seldom included in women's literature courses and almost never in other literature courses, nor in women's studies as a whole. All too often, the excuse given is that the literatures of women of Colour can only be taught by Coloured women, or that they are too difficult to understand, or that classes cannot 'get into' them because they come out of experiences that are 'too different'. I have heard this argument presented by white women of otherwise quite clear intelligence, women who seem to have no trouble at all teaching and reviewing work that comes out of the vastly different experiences of Shakespeare, Molière, Dostoyefsky and Aristophanes. Surely there must be some other explanation.

This is a very complex question, but I believe one of the reasons white women have such difficulty reading Black women's work is because of their reluctance to see Black women as women and different from themselves. To examine Black women's literature effectively requires that we be seen as whole people in our actual complexities – as individuals, as women, as human – rather than as one of those problematic but familiar stereotypes provided in this society in place of genuine images of Black women. And I believe this holds true for the literatures of other women of Colour who are not Black.

The literatures of all women of Colour recreate the textures of our lives, and many white women are heavily invested in ignoring the real differences. For as long as any difference between us means one of us must be inferior, then the recognition of any difference must be fraught with guilt. To allow women of Colour to step out of stereotypes is too guilt provoking, for it threatens the complacency of those women who view oppression only in terms of sex.

Refusing to recognize difference makes it impossible to see the different problems and pitfalls facing us as women.

Thus, in a patriarchal power system where whiteskin privilege is a major prop, the entrapments used to neutralize Black women and white women are not the same. For example, it is easy for Black women to be used by the power structure against Black men, not because they are men, but because they are Black. Therefore, for Black women, it is necessary at all times to separate the needs of the oppressor from our own legitimate conflicts within our communities. This same problem does not exist for white women. Black women and men have shared racist oppression and still share it, although in different ways. Out of that shared oppression we have developed joint defenses and joint vulnerabilities to each other that are not duplicated in the white community, with the exception of the relationship between Jewish women and Jewish men.

On the other hand, white women face the pitfall of being seduced into joining the oppressor under the pretense of sharing power. This possibility does not exist in the same way for women of Colour. The tokenism that is sometimes extended to us is not an invitation to join power; our racial 'otherness' is a visible reality that makes that quite clear. For white women there is a wider range of pretended choices and rewards for identifying with patriarchal power and its tools.

Today, with the defeat of ERA, the tightening economy and increased conservatism, it is easier once again for white women to believe the dangerous fantasy that if you are good enough, pretty enough, sweet enough, quiet enough, teach the children to behave, hate the right people, and marry the right men, then you will be allowed to co-exist with patriarchy in relative peace, at least until a man needs your job or the neighbourhood rapist happens along. And true, unless one lives and loves in the trenches it is difficult to remember that the war against dehumanization is ceaseless.

But Black women and our children know the fabric of our lives is stitched with violence and with hatred, that there is no rest. We do not deal with it only on the picket lines, or in dark midnight alleys, or in the places where we dare to verbalize our resistance. For us, increasingly, violence weaves through the daily tissues of our living – in the supermarket, in the classroom, in the elevator, in the clinic and the schoolyard, from the plumber, the baker, the saleswoman, the bus driver, the bank teller, the waitress who does not serve us.

Some problems we share as women, some we do not. You fear your children will grow up to join the patriarchy and testify against you, we fear our children will be dragged from a car and shot down in the street, and you will turn your backs upon the reasons they are dying.

The threat of difference has been no less blinding to people of Colour. Those of us who are Black must see that the reality of our lives and our struggle does not make us immune to the errors of ignoring and misnaming difference. Within Black communities where racism is a living reality, differences among us often seem dangerous and suspect. The need for unity is often misnamed as a need for homogeneity, and a Black feminist vision mistaken for betrayal of our common interests as a people. Because of the continuous battle against racial erasure that Black women and Black men share, some Black women still refuse to recognize that we are also oppressed as women, and that sexual hostility against Black women is practised not only by the white racist society, but implemented within our Black communities as well. It is a disease striking the heart of Black nationhood, and silence will not make it disappear. Exacerbated by racism and the pressures of powerlessness, violence against Black women and children often becomes a standard within our communities, one by which manliness can be measured. But these women-hating acts are rarely discussed as crimes against Black women.

As a group, women of Colour are the lowest-paid wage earners in america. We are the primary targets of abortion and sterilization abuse, here and abroad. In certain parts of Africa, small girls are still being sewed shut between their legs to keep them docile and for men's pleasure. This is known as female circumcision, and it is not a cultural affair as the late Jomo Kenyatta insisted, it is a crime against Black women.

Black women's literature is full of the pain of frequent assault, not only by a racist patriarchy, but also by Black men. Yet the necessity for and history of shared battle have made us, Black women, particularly vulnerable to the false accusation that anti-sexist is anti-Black. Meanwhile, womanhating as a recourse of the powerless is sapping strength from Black communities, and our very lives. Rape is on the increase, reported and unreported, and rape is not aggressive sexuality, it is sexualized aggression. As Kalamu ya Salaam, a Black male writer, points out, 'As long as male domination exists, rape will exist. Only women revolting and men made conscious of their responsibility to fight sexism can collectively stop rape.'[3]

Differences between ourselves as Black women are also being misnamed and used to separate us from one another. As a Black lesbian feminist comfortable with the many different ingredients of my identity, and a woman committed to racial and sexual freedom from oppression, I find I am constantly being encouraged to pluck out some one aspect of myself and present this as the meaningful whole, eclipsing or denying the other parts of self. But this is a destructive and fragmenting way to live. My fullest concentration of energy is available to me only when I integrate all the parts of who I am, openly, allowing power from particular sources of my living to flow back and forth freely through all my different selves, without the restrictions of externally imposed definition. Only then can I bring myself and my energies as a whole to the service of those struggles which I embrace as part of my living.

A fear of lesbians, or of being accused of being a lesbian, has led many Black women into testifying against themselves. It has led some of us into destructive alliances, and others into despair and isolation. In the white women's communities, heterosexism is some-times a result of identifying with the white patriarchy, a rejection of that interdependence between women-identified women which allows the self to be, rather than to be used in the service of men. Some-times it reflects a die-hard belief in the protective colouration of heterosexual relationships, sometimes a self-hate which all women have to fight against, taught us from birth.

Although elements of these attitudes exist for all women, there are particular resonances of heterosexism and homophobia among Black women. Despite the fact that woman-bonding has a long and honourable history in the African and African-american commu-nities, and despite the knowledge and accomplishments of many strong and creative women-identified Black women in the political, social and cultural fields, heterosexual Black women often tend to ignore or discount the existence and work of Black lesbians. Part of this attitude has come from an understandable terror of Black male attack within the close confines of Black society, where the punish-ment for any female self-assertion is still to be accused of being a lesbian and therefore unworthy of the attention or support of the scarce Black male. But part of this need to misname and ignore Black lesbians comes from a very real fear that openly women-identified Black women who are no longer dependent upon men for their self-definition may well reorder our whole concept of social relationships.

Black women who once insisted that lesbianism was a white woman's problem now insist that Black lesbians are a threat to Black nationhood, are consorting with the enemy, are basically un-Black. These accusations, coming from the very women to whom we look for deep and real understanding, have served to keep many Black lesbians in hiding, caught between the racism of white women and the homophobia of their sisters. Often, their work has been ignored, trivialized or misnamed, as with the work of Angelina Grimke, Alice Dunbar-Nelson, Lorraine Hansberry. Yet women-bonded women have always been some part of the power of Black communities, from our unmarried aunts to the amazons of Dahomey.

And it is certainly not Black lesbians who are assaulting women and raping children and grandmothers on the streets of our communities.

Across this country, as in Boston during the spring of 1979 following the unsolved murders of twelve Black women, Black lesbians are spearheading movements against violence against Black women.

What are the particular details within each of our lives that can be scrutinized and altered to help bring about change? How do we redefine difference for all women? It is not our differences which separate women, but our reluctance to recognize those differences and to deal effectively with the distortions which have resulted from the ignoring and misnaming of those differences.

As a tool of social control, women have been encouraged to recognize only one area of human difference as legitimate, those differences which exist between women and men. And we have learned to deal across those differences with the urgency of all oppressed subordinates. All of us have had to learn to live or work or co-exist with men, from our fathers on. We have recognized and negotiated these differences, even when this recognition only continued the old dominant/subordinate mode of human relationship, where the oppressed must recognize the masters' difference in order to survive.

But our future survival is predicated upon our ability to relate within equality. As women, we must root out internalized patterns of oppression within ourselves if we are to move beyond the most superficial aspects of social change. Now we must recognize differences among women who are our equals, neither inferior nor superior, and devise ways to use each other's difference to enrich our visions and our joint struggles.

The future of our earth may depend upon the ability of all women to identify and develop new definitions of power and new patterns of relating across difference. The old definitions have not served us, nor the earth that supports us. The old patterns, no matter how cleverly rearranged to imitate progress, still condemn us to cosmetically altered repetitions of the same old exchanges, the same old guilt, hatred, recrimination, lamentation and suspicion.

For we have, built into all of us, old blueprints of expectation and response, old structures of oppression, and these must be altered at the same time as we alter the living conditions which are a result of those structures. For the master's tools will never dismantle the master's house.

As Paulo Freire shows so well in *The Pedagogy of the Oppressed*,[4] the true focus of revolutionary change is never merely the oppressive situations which we seek to escape, but that piece of the oppressor which is planted deep within each of us, and which knows only the oppressors' tactics, the oppressors' relationships.

Change means growth, and growth can be painful. But we sharpen self-definition by exposing the self in work and struggle together with those whom we define as different from ourselves, although sharing the same goals. For Black and white, old and young, lesbian and heterosexual women alike, this can mean new paths to our survival.

> We have chosen each other
> and the edge of each others battles
> the war is the same
> if we lose
> someday women's blood will congeal
> upon a dead planet
> if we win
> there is no telling
> we seek beyond history
> for a new and more possible meeting.[5]

NOTES

1 The editors and publishers gratefully acknowledge permission of Crossing Press © 1984 and Audre Lorde to reproduce 'Age, Race, Class, and

Sex: Women Redefining Difference' from *Sister Outsider*.

2 This paper was delivered at the Copeland Colloquium, Amherst College, April 1980.

3 From 'Rape: A Radical Analysis, An African-American Perspective' by Kalamu.

4 Seabury Press: New York, 1970.

5 From 'Outlines', unpublished poem.

13

June Jordan
b.1936

'REPORT FROM THE BAHAMAS' from
MOVING TOWARDS HOME (1989)

June Jordan* is a black American poet and essayist with a record of political activism reaching back into the 1960s ('All my life I've been studying revolution', she tells us elsewhere**). This moving meditation on the theme of difference and connectedness relies above all on Jordan's keen perception of the way in which economic reality delimits individual experience.

Radical political theory suffers from a standing temptation to believe that agencies of social change must arise spontaneously on the basis of shared 'identities' – being working class, being a woman, etc. But such groupings are in themselves no more certain to be causally effective than the divisions which cut across them: the fact that, say, A and B are both black women tells us nothing a priori *about the prospects for real-life political solidarity between them. Solidarity results not from the bare fact that two or more individuals share a position in some structure of domination, but from the self-conscious, self-defining activity of those individuals in the furtherance of common goals: 'It is not only who you are . . . but what we can do for each other that will determine the connection' (compare Lorde, reading 12).*

Theoretically sophisticated yet entirely free from technicality, Jordan's essay insists at once on the material origins of political action and on its intelligent, purposive character. It is the latter, voluntarist, strand in her argument – the conviction that moral bonds can be created *– which saves this essay from pessimism despite its emphasis on mutual estrangement.*

I am staying in a hotel that calls itself The Sheraton British Colonial.[1] One of the photographs advertising the place displays a middle-aged Black man in a waiter's tuxedo, smiling. What intrigues me most about the picture is just this: while the Black man bears a tray full of 'colourful' drinks above his left shoulder, both of his feet, shoes and trouserlegs, up to 10 inches above his ankles, stand in the also 'colourful' Caribbean salt water. He is so delighted to serve you he will wade into the water to bring you Banana Daquiris while you float! More precisely, he will wade into the water, fully clothed, oblivious to the ruin of his shoes, his trousers, his health, and he will do it with a smile.

I am in the Bahamas. On the phone in my room, a spinning complement of plastic pages offers handy index clues such as CAR RENTAL and CASINOS. A message from the Ministry of Tourism appears among these travellers' tips. Opening with a paragraph of 'WELCOME', the message then proceeds to 'A PAGE OF HISTORY', which reads as follows:

> New World History begins on the same day that modern Bahamian history begins – October 12, 1492. That's when Columbus stepped ashore – British influence came first with the Eleutherian Adventurers of 1647 – After the Revolutions, American Loyalists fled from the newly independent states and settled in the Bahamas. Confederate blockade-runners used the island as a haven during the War between the States, and after the War, a number of Southerners moved to the Bahamas . . .

There it is again. Something proclaims itself a legitimate history and all it does is track white Mr Columbus to the British Eleutherians through the Confederate Southerners as they barge into New World surf, land on New World turf, and nobody saying one word about the Bahamian people, the Black peoples, to whom the only thing new in their island world was this weird succession of crude intruders and its colonial consequences.

This is my consciousness of race as I unpack my bathing suit in the Sheraton British Colonial. Neither this hotel nor the British nor the long-ago Italians nor the white Delta airline pilots belong here, of course. And every time I look at the photograph of that fool standing in the water with his shoes on I'm about to have a West Indian fit, even though I know he's no fool; he's a middle-aged Black man who needs a job and this is his job – pretending himself a servile ancillary to the pleasures of the rich. (Compared to his options in life, I am a rich woman. Compared to most of the Black Americans arriving for this Easter weekend on a three nights four days' deal of bargain rates, the middle-aged waiter is a poor Black man.)

We will jostle along with the other (white) visitors and join them in the tee-shirt shops or, laughing together, learn ruthless rules of negotiation as we, Black Americans as well as white, argue down the price of handwoven goods at the nearby straw market while the merchants, frequently toothless Black women seated on the concrete in their only presentable dress, humble themselves to our careless games:

'Yes? You like it? Eight dollar.'

'Five.'

'I give it to you. Seven.'

And so it continues, this weird succession of crude intruders that, now, includes me and my brothers and my sisters from the North.

This is my consciousness of class as I try to decide how much money I can spend on Bahamian gifts for my family back in Brooklyn. No matter that these other Black women incessantly weave words and flowers into the straw hats and bags piled beside them on the burning dusty street. No matter that these other Black women must work their sense of beauty into these things that we will take away as cheaply as we dare, or they will do without food.

We are not white, after all. The budget is limited. And we are harmlessly killing time between the poolside rum punch and 'The Native Show on the Patio' that will play tonight outside the hotel restaurant.

This is my consciousness of race and class and gender identity as I notice the fixed relations between these other Black women and myself. They sell and I buy or I don't. They risk not eating. I risk going broke on my first vacation afternoon.

We are not particularly women anymore; we are parties to a transaction designed to set us against each other.

'Olive' is the name of the Black woman who cleans my hotel room. On my way to the beach I am wondering what 'Olive' would say if I told her why I chose The Sheraton British Colonial; if I told her I wanted to swim. I wanted to sleep. I did not want to be harassed by the middle-aged waiter or his nephew. I did not want to be raped by anybody (white or Black) at all and I calculated that my safety as a Black woman alone would best be assured by a multi-national hotel corporation. In my experience, the big guys take customer complaints more seriously than the little ones. I would suppose that's one reason why they're big; they don't like to lose money anymore than I like to be bothered when I'm trying to read a goddamned book underneath a palm tree I paid $264 to get next to. A Black woman seeking refuge in a multinational corporation may seem like a contradiction to some, but there you are. In this case it's a coincidence of entirely different self-interests: Sheraton/cash = June Jordan's short run safety.

Anyway, I'm pretty sure 'Olive' would look at me as though I came from someplace as far away as Brooklyn. Then she'd probably allow herself one indignant query before righteously removing her vacuum cleaner from my room; 'and why in the first place you come down you without your husband?'

I cannot imagine how I would begin to answer her.

My 'rights' and my 'freedom' and my 'desire' and a slew of other New World values; what would they sound like to this Black woman described on the card atop my hotel bureau as 'Olive the Maid'? 'Olive' is older than I am and I may smoke a cigarette while she changes the sheets on my bed. Whose rights? Whose freedom? Whose desire?

And why should she give a shit about mine unless I do something, for real, about hers?

It happens that the book that I finished reading under a palm tree earlier today was the novel *The Bread Givers*, by Anzia Yezierska. Definitely autobiographical, Yezierska lays out the difficulties of being both female and 'a person' inside a traditional Jewish family at the start of the twentieth century. That any Jewish woman became anything more than the abused servant of her father or her husband is really an improbable piece of news. Yet Yezierska managed such an unlikely outcome for her own life. In *The Bread Givers*, the heroine also manages an important, although partial, escape from traditional Jewish female destiny. And in the unpardonable, despotic father, the Talmudic scholar of that Jewish family, did I not see my own and hate him twice, again? When the heroine, the young Jewish

child, wanders the streets with a filthy pail she borrows to sell herring in order to raise the ghetto rent and when she cries, 'Nothing
was before me but the hunger in our house, and no bread for the
next meal if I didn't sell the herring. No longer like a fire engine,
but like a houseful of hungry mouths my heart cried, "herring –
herring! Two cents apiece!"' Who would doubt the ease, the sisterhood of conversation possible between that white girl and the Black
women selling straw bags on the streets of paradise because they do
not want to die? And is it not obvious that the wife of that Talmudic
scholar and 'Olive', who cleans my room here at the hotel, have
more in common than I can claim with either one of them?

This is my consciousness of race and class and gender identity as
I collect wet towels, sunglasses, wristwatch, and head towards
a shower.

I am thinking about the boy who loaned this novel to me. He's
white and he's Jewish and he's pursuing an independent study project with me, at the State University where I teach whether or not
I feel like it, where I teach without stint because, like the waiter,
I am no fool. It's my job and either I work or I do without everything you need money to buy. The boy loaned me the novel because
he thought I'd be interested to know how a Jewish-American writer
used English so that the syntax, and therefore the cultural habits of
mind expressed by the Yiddish language, could survive translation.
He did this because he wanted to create another connection between
us on the basis of language, between his knowledge/his love of
Yiddish and my knowledge/my love of Black English.

He had been right about the forceful survival of the Yiddish. And
I had become excited by this further evidence of the written voice
of spoken language protected from the monodrone of 'standard'
English, and so we had grown closer on this account. But then our
talk shifted to student affairs more generally, and I had learned that
this student does not care one way or another about currently jeopardized Federal Student Loan Programmes because, as he explained
it to me, they do not affect him. He does not need financial help
outside his family. My own son, however, is Black. And I am the
only family help available to him and that means, if Reagan succeeds
in eliminating Federal programmes to aid minority students, he will
have to forget about furthering his studies, or he or I or both of us

will have to hit the numbers pretty big. For these reasons of difference, the student and I had moved away from each other, even
while we continued to talk.

My consciousness turned to race, again, and class.

Sitting in the same chair as the boy, several weeks ago, a graduate
student came to discuss her grade. I praised the excellence of her
final paper; indeed it had seemed to me an extraordinary pulling
together of recent left brain/right brain research with the themes of
transcendental poetry.

She told me that, for her part, she'd completed her reading of my
political essays. 'You are so lucky!' she exclaimed.

'What do you mean by that?'

'You have a cause. You have a purpose to your life.'

I looked carefully at this white woman; what was she really saying
to me?

'What do you mean?' I repeated.

'Poverty. Police violence. Discrimination in general.'

(Jesus Christ, I thought: Is that her idea of lucky?)

'And how about you?' I asked.

'Me?'

'Yeah, you. Don't you have a cause?'

'Me? I'm just a middle-aged woman: a housewife and a mother.
I'm a nobody.'

For a while, I made no response.

First of all, speaking of race and class and gender in one breath,
what she said meant that those lucky preoccupations of mine, from
police violence to nuclear wipe-out, were not shared. They were
mine and not hers. But here she sat, friendly as an old stuffed
animal, beaming good will or more 'luck' in my direction.

In the second place, what this white woman said to me meant that
she did not believe she was 'a person' precisely because she had
fulfilled the traditional female functions revered by the father of that
Jewish immigrant, Anzia Yezierska. And the woman in front of me
was not a Jew. That was not the connection. The link was strictly
female. Nevertheless, how should that woman and I, another female,
connect, beyond this bizarre exchange?

If she believed me lucky to have regular hurdles of discrimination
then why shouldn't I insist that she's lucky to be a middle-class
white Wasp female who lives in such well-sanctioned normative

comfort that she even has the luxury to deny the power of the privileges that paralyse her life?

If she deserts me and 'my cause' where we differ, if, for example, she abandons me to 'my' problems of race, then why should I support her in 'her' problems of housewifely oblivion?

Recollection of this peculiar moment brings me to the shower in the bathroom cleaned by 'Olive'. She reminds me of the usual Women's Studies curriculum because it has nothing to do with her or her job: you won't find 'Olive' listed anywhere on the reading list. You will likewise seldom hear of Anzia Yezierska. But yes, you will find, from Florence Nightingale to Adrienne Rich, a white procession of independently well-to-do women writers. (Gertrude Stein/ Virginia Woolf/Hilda Doolittle are standard names among the 'essential' women writers.)

In other words, most of the women of the world – Black and First World and white who work because we must – most of the women of the world persist far from the heart of the usual Women's Studies syllabus.

Similarly, the typical Black History course will slide by the majority experience it pretends to represent. For example, Mary McLeod Bethune will scarcely receive as much attention as Nat Turner, even though Black women who bravely and efficiently provided for the education of Black people hugely outnumber those few Black men who led successful or doomed rebellions against slavery. In fact, Mary McLeod Bethune may not receive even honourable mention because Black History too often apes those ridiculous white history courses which produce such dangerous gibberish as The Sheraton British Colonial 'history' of the Bahamas. Both Black and white history courses exclude from their central consideration those people who neither killed nor conquered anyone as the means to new identity, those people who took care of every one of the people who wanted to become 'a person', those people who still take care of the life at issue: the ones who wash and who feed and who teach and who diligently decorate straw hats and bags with all of their historically unrequired gentle love: the women.

> Oh the old rugged cross
> on a hill far away
> Well I cherish the old rugged cross.

It's Good Friday in the Bahamas. 78 degrees in the shade. Except for Sheraton territory, everything's closed.

It so happens that for truly secular reasons I've been fasting for three days. My hunger has now reached nearly violent proportions. In the hotel sandwich shop, the Black woman handling the counter complains about the tourists; why isn't the shop closed and why don't the tourists stop eating for once in their lives. I'm famished and I order chicken salad and cottage cheese and lettuce and tomato and a hard-boiled egg and a hot-cross bun and apple juice.

She eyes me with disgust.

To be sure, the timing of my stomach offends her serious religious practices. Neither one of us apologizes to the other. She seasons the chicken salad to the peppery max while I listen to the loud radio gospel she plays to console herself. It's a country Black version of 'The Old Rugged Cross'.

As I heave much chicken into my mouth tears start. It's not the pepper. I am, after all, a West Indian daughter. It's the Good Friday music that dominates the humid atmosphere.

Well I cherish the old rugged cross

And I am back, faster than a 747, in Brooklyn, in the home of my parents where we are wondering, as we do every year, if the sky will darken until Christ has been buried in the tomb. The sky should darken if God is in His heavens. And then, around 3 p.m., at the conclusion of our mournful church sevice at the neighbourhood St Phillips, and even while we dumbly stare at the black cloth covering the gold altar and the slender unlit candles, the sun should return through the high gothic windows and vindicate our waiting faith that the Lord will rise again, on Easter.

How I used to bow my head at the very name of Jesus: ecstatic to abase myself in deference to His majesty.

My mouth is full of salad. I can't seem to eat quickly enough. I can't think how I should lessen the offence of my appetite. The other Black woman on the premises, the one who disapprovingly prepared this very tasty break from my fast, makes no remark. She is no fool. This is a job she needs. I suppose she notices that at least I included a hot-cross bun among my edibles. That's something in my favour. I decide that's enough.

I am suddenly eager to walk off the food. Up a fairly steep hill I walk without hurrying. Through the pastel desolation of the little town, the road brings me to a confectionery pink and white plantation house. At the gates, an unnecessarily large statue of Christopher Columbus faces me down, or tries to. His hand is fisted to one hip. I look back at him, laugh without deference, and turn left.

It's time to pack it up. Catch my plane. I scan the hotel room for things not to forget. There's that white report card on the bureau.

'Dear Guests:' it says, under the name 'Olive'. 'I am your maid for the day. Please rate me: Excellent. Good. Average. Poor. Thank you.'

I tuck this memento from the Sheraton British Colonial into my notebook. How would 'Olive' rate *me*? What would it mean for us to seem 'good' to each other? What would that rating require?

But I am hastening to leave. Neither turtle soup nor kidney pie nor any conch shell delight shall delay my departure. I have rested, here, in the Bahamas, and I'm ready to return to my usual job, my usual work. But the skin on my body has changed and so has my mind. On the Delta flight home I realize I am burning up, indeed.

So far as I can see, the usual race and class concepts of connection, or gender assumptions of unity, do not apply very well. I doubt that they ever did. Otherwise why would Black folks forever bemoan our lack of solidarity when the deal turns real. And if unity on the basis of sexual oppression is something natural, then why do we women, the majority people on the planet, still have a problem?

The plane's ready for takeoff. I fasten my seatbelt and let the tumult inside my head run free. Yes: race and class and gender remain as real as the weather. But what they must mean about the contact between two individuals is less obvious and, like the weather, not predictable.

And when these factors of race and class and gender absolutely collapse is whenever you try to use them as automatic concepts of connection. They may serve well as indicators of commonly felt conflict, but as elements of connection they seem about as reliable as precipitation probability for the day after the night before the day.

It occurs to me that much organizational grief could be avoided if people understood that partnership in misery does not necessarily provide for partnership for change: *When we get the monsters off our backs all of us may want to run in very different directions.*

And not only that: even though both 'Olive' and 'I' live inside a conflict neither one of us created, and even though both of us therefore hurt inside that conflict, I may be one of the monsters she needs to eliminate from her universe and, in a sense, she may be one of the monsters in mine.

I am reaching for the words to describe the difference between a common identity that has been imposed and the individual identity any one of us will choose, once she gains that chance.

That difference is the one that keeps us stupid in the face of new, specific information about somebody else with whom we are supposed to have a connection because a third party, hostile to both of us, has worked it so that the two of us, like it or not, share a common enemy. *What happens beyond the idea of that enemy and beyond the consequences of that enemy?*

I am saying that the ultimate connection cannot be the enemy. The ultimate connection must be the need that we find between us. It is not only who you are, in other words, but what we can do for each other that will determine the connection.

I am flying back to my job. I have been teaching contemporary women's poetry this semester. One quandary I have set myself to explore with my students is the one of taking responsibility without power. We had been wrestling ideas to the floor for several sessions when a young Black woman, a South African, asked me for help, after class.

Sokutu told me she was 'in a trance' and that she'd been unable to eat for two weeks.

'What's going on?' I asked her, even as my eyes startled at her trembling and emaciated appearance.

'My husband. He drinks all the time. He beats me up. I go to the hospital. I can't eat. I don't know what/anything.'

In my office, she described her situation. I did not dare to let her sense my fear and horror. She was dragging about, hour by hour, in dread. Her husband, a young Black South African, was drinking himself into more and more deadly violence against her.

Sokutu told me how she could keep nothing down. She weighed 90 lbs at the outside, as she spoke to me. She'd already been hospitalized as a result of her husband's battering rage.

I knew both of them because I had organized a campus group to aid the liberation struggles of Southern Africa.

Nausea rose in my throat. What about this presumable connection: this husband and this wife fled from that homeland of hatred against them, and now what? He was destroying himself. If not stopped, he would certainly murder his wife.

She needed a doctor, right away. It was a medical emergency. She needed protection. It was a security crisis. She needed refuge for battered wives and personal therapy and legal counsel. She needed a friend.

I got on the phone and called every number in the campus directory that I could imagine might prove helpful. Nothing worked. There were no institutional resources designed to meet her enormous, multifaceted and ordinary woman's need.

I called various students. I asked the Chairperson of the English Department for advice. I asked everyone for help.

Finally, another one of my students, Cathy, a young Irish woman active in campus IRA activities, responded. She asked for further details. I gave them to her.

'Her husband', Cathy told me, 'is an alcoholic. You have to understand about alcoholics. It's not the same as anything else. And it's a disease you can't treat any old way.'

I listened, fearfully. Did this mean there was nothing we could do?

'That's not what I'm saying,' she said. 'But you have to keep the alcoholic part of the thing central in everybody's mind, otherwise her husband will kill her. Or he'll kill himself.'

She spoke calmly, I felt there was nothing to do but to assume she knew what she was talking about.

'Will you come with me?' I asked her, after a silence. 'Will you come with me and help us figure out what to do next?'

Cathy said she would but that she felt shy: Sokutu comes from South Africa. What would she think about Cathy?

'I don't know,' I said. 'But let's go.'

We left to find a dormitory room for the young battered wife.

It was late, now, and dark outside.

On Cathy's VW that I followed behind with my own car, was the sticker that reads BOBBY SANDS FREE AT LAST. My eyes blurred as I read and reread the words. This was another connection: Bobby Sands and Martin Luther King Jr and who would believe it? I would not have believed it; I grew up terrorized by Irish kids who introduced me to the word 'nigga'.

And here I was following an Irish woman to the room of a Black

South African. We were going to the room to try to save a life together.

When we reached the little room, we found ourselves awkward and large. Sokutu attempted to treat us with utmost courtesy, as though we were honoured guests. She seemed surprised by Cathy, but mostly Sokutu was flushed with relief and joy because we were there, with her.

I did not know how we should ever terminate her heartfelt courtesies and address, directly, the reason for our visit: her starvation and her extreme physical danger.

Finally, Cathy sat on the floor and reached out her hands to Sokutu.

'I'm here', she said quietly, 'because June has told me what has happened to you. And I know what it is. Your husband is an alcoholic. He has a disease. I know what it is. My father was an alcoholic. He killed himself. He almost killed my mother. I want to be your friend.'

'Oh,' was the only small sound that escaped from Sokutu's mouth. And then she embraced the other student. And then everything changed and I watched all of this happen so I know that this happened: this connection.

And after we called the police and exchanged phone numbers and plans were made for the night and for the next morning, the young South African woman walked down the dormitory hallway, saying goodbye and saying thank you to us.

I walked behind them, the young Irish woman and the young South African, and I saw them walking as sisters walk, hugging each other and whispering and sure of each other and I felt how it was not who they were but what they both know and what they were both preparing to do about what they know that was going to make them both free at last.

And I look out the windows of the plane and I see clouds that will not kill me and I know that someday soon other clouds may erupt to kill us all.

And I tell the stewardess No thanks to the cocktails she offers me. But I look about the cabin at the hundred strangers drinking as they fly and I think even here and even now I must make the connection real between me and these strangers everywhere before those other clouds unify this ragged bunch of us, too late.

NOTES

*   The editors are grateful to Marie Lovibond for drawing their attention
    to this essay.
** 'Nicaragua: Why I had to go there' in *Moving Towards Home:
    Political Essays* (London: Virago, 1989), p. 151.
1   'Report from the Bahamas' from *Moving Towards Home* by June Jordan
    is reproduced by kind permission of Virago Press © UK 1989 and
    June Jordan © US 1989.

14

Jaqueline Rose
b.1949

'FEMININITY AND ITS DISCONTENTS' (1983)

The place, within feminism, of psychoanalysis and of the unconscious mind, has always been controversial. Feminists have accused psychoanalysis both of authoritarianism in its clinical practice, and of collusion with the idea of male sexuality as an untameable force (see Jeffreys, reading 26). They have also charged it with conservative functionalism, that is, defending traditional gender identities and 'normal sexuality' as indispensable to the social order. On the other hand, some feminists have maintained that psychoanalysis provides a powerful critique of patriarchal and sexist society, and locates the roots of sexual oppression in particular social relations, such as mothering. Psychoanalysis then would signpost a possible route to social change.

In this important contribution to the debate Jaqueline Rose argues that both sides in this argument neglect consideration of what is truly revolutionary in Freud's thought. According to Freud our unconscious wishes, desires and drives – inimical to the demands of a bourgeois social order – cannot be completely repressed. The unconscious erupts and manifests itself in physical and psychological pain and disturbance. The importance of this for feminist social thought and ethics is that it negates the bourgeois picture of the rational individual. In the modern tradition of Descartes and Kant the essence of man is a non-bodily, rational self. Psychoanalysis insists that the unconscious interacts with the conscious, that the body and the unconscious can connect, by-passing and thwarting our conscious selves. Like Marxism and feminism, psychoanalytic method goes behind the superficial appearances of social reality and uncovers their structuration. Gender identity is not 'simply achieved' (p. 244); rather, stability of identity (and therefore the current social order) is imperfectly achieved at the cost of massive pain. (This is quite apart from the problems which go with femininity in a sexist society which denigrates and punishes it.)

Jaqueline Rose's paper addresses a fundamental disagreement within feminist discourses of gender. On the one hand, there is a normative model of a feminine psychic, political and physical wholeness, which contrasts with the alienated and emotionally absent condition of masculinity. On the other hand, there is a contrary move to place at the service of feminism the idea of the psyche as split and indeterminate – an idea which challenges the ideological myth of the masculine autonomous and unified subject. Rose herself is critical of the conservative implications of the idea of wholeness. She argues that feminist aspirations to a unified and harmonious psychic and political cohesion are mistaken; feminist politics should not attempt to impose a false coherence on the subject (see Wilson, reading 22). Patriarchy will only be undermined by the subjectivity which refuses to, and cannot, cohere; and the unconscious which will not be still.

Is psychoanalysis a 'new orthodoxy' for feminism?[1] Or does it rather represent the surfacing of something difficult and exceptional but important for feminism, which is on the verge (once again) of being lost? I will argue that the second is the case, and that the present discarding of psychoanalysis in favour of forms of analysis felt as more material in their substance and immediately political in their effects is a *return* to positions whose sensed inadequacy for feminism produced a gap in which psychoanalysis could – fleetingly – find a place.[2] What psychoanalysis offered up in that moment was by no means wholly satisfactory and it left many problems unanswered or inadequately addressed, but the questions which it raised for feminism are crucial and cannot, I believe, be approached in the same way, or even posed, from anywhere else. To ask what are the political implications of psychoanalysis for feminism seems to me, therefore, to pose the problem the wrong way round. Psychoanalysis is already political for feminism – political in the more obvious sense that it came into the arena of discussion in response to the internal needs of feminist debate, and political again in the wider sense that the repudiation of psychoanalysis by feminism can be seen as linking up with the repeated marginalization of psychoanalysis within our general culture, a culture whose oppressiveness for women is recognized by us all.

Before going into this in more detail, a separate but related point needs to be made, and that is the peculiarity of the psychoanalytic object with which feminism engages. Thus to ask for effects from psychoanalysis in the arena of political practice is already to assume that psychoanalytic practice is a-political.[3] Recent feminist debate has tended to concentrate on theory (Freud's theory of femininity, whether or not psychoanalysis can provide an account of women's subordination). This was as true of Juliet Mitchell's defense of Freud[4] as it has been of many of the more recent replies. The result has been that psychoanalysis has been pulled away from its own practice. Here the challenge to psychoanalysis by feminists has come from alternative forms of therapy (feminist therapy and co-counselling). But it is worth noting that the way psychoanalysis is engaged with in much recent criticism already divests it of its practical effects at this level, or rather takes this question as settled in advance (the passing reference to the chauvinism of the psychoanalytic institution, the assumption that psychoanalysis depoliticizes the woman analysand). In this context, therefore, the common theory/practice dichotomy has a very specific meaning in that psychoanalysis can only be held accountable to 'practice' if it is assumed not to be one, or if the form of its practice is taken to have no purchase on political life. This assumes, for example, that there is no politics of the psychoanalytic institution itself, something to which I will return.

Both these points – the wider history of how psychoanalysis has been placed or discarded by our dominant culture, and the detaching of psychoanalysis from its practical and institutional base – are related, in as much as they bring into focus the decisions and selections which have already been made about psychoanalysis before the debate even begins. Some of these decisions, I would want to argue, are simply wrong – such as the broad accusation of chauvinism levelled against the psychoanalytic institution as a whole. In this country at least, the significant impetus after Freud passed to two women – Anna Freud and Melanie Klein. Psychoanalysis in fact continues to be one of the few of our cultural institutions which does not professionally discriminate against women, and in which they could even be said to predominate. This is not of course to imply that the presence of women inside an institution is necessarily feminist, but women have historically held positions of influence inside psychoanalysis which they have been mostly denied in other institutions where their perceived role as 'carers' has relegated them to a subordinate position (e.g. nursing); and it is the case that the first criticisms of Freud made by Melanie Klein can be seen to have strong affinities with later feminist repudiation of his theories.

For those who are hesitating over what appears as the present 'impasse' between feminism and psychoanalysis, the more important point, however, is to stress the way that psychoanalysis is being presented for debate – that is, the decisions which have already been made before we are asked to decide. Much will depend, I suspect, on whether one sees psychoanalysis as a new form of hegemony on the part of the feminist intelligentsia, or whether it is seen as a theory and practice which has constantly been relegated to the outside of dominant institutions and mainstream radical debate alike – an 'outside' with which feminism, in its challenge to both these traditions, has its own important forms of allegiance.

Components of the Culture

In England, the relationship between the institution of psychoanalysis and its more general reception has always been complex, if not fraught. Thus in 1968, Perry Anderson could argue that major therapeutic and theoretical advances inside the psychoanalytic institution (chiefly in the work of Melanie Klein) had gone hand in hand with, and possibly even been the cause of, the isolation of psychoanalysis from the general culture, the slowness of its dissemination (until the Pelican Freud started to appear in 1974, you effectively had to join a club to read *The Standard Edition* of Freud's work), and the failure of psychoanalysis to effect a decisive break with traditions of empiricist philosophy, reactionary ethics, and an elevation of literary 'values', which he saw as the predominant features of our cultural life.[5] Whether or not one accepts the general 'sweep' of his argument, two points from that earlier polemic seem relevant here.

Firstly, the link between empiricist traditions of thought and the resistance to the psychoanalytic concept of the unconscious. Thus psychoanalysis, through its attention to symptoms, slips of the tongue and dreams (that is, to what *insists* on being spoken against what is *allowed* to be said) appears above all as a challenge to the self-evidence and banality of everyday life and language, which have also, importantly, constituted the specific targets of feminism. If we use the (fairly loose) definition which Anderson provided for empiricism as the unsystematic registration of things as they are and the refusal of forms of analysis which penetrate beneath the surface of observable social phenomena, the link to feminism can be made. For feminism has always challenged the observable 'givens' of women's presumed natural qualities and their present social position alike (expecially when the second is justified in terms of the first). How often has the 'cult of common sense', the notion of what is obviously the case or in the nature of things, been used in reactionary arguments against feminist attempts to demand social change? For Anderson in his article of 1968, this espousal of empiricist thinking provided one of the chief forms of resistance to Freud, so deeply committed is psychoanalysis to penetrating behind the surface and conscious manifestations of everyday experience.

Secondly, the relationship between this rejection of psychoanalysis and a *dearth* within British intellectual culture of a Marxism which could both theorize and criticize capitalism as a social totality. This second point received the strongest criticism from within British Marxism itself, but what matters here is the fact that both Marxism *and* psychoanalysis were identified as forms of radical enquiry which were unassimilable to bourgeois norms. In the recent feminist discussion, however – notably in the pages of *Feminist Review* – Marxism and psychoanalysis tend to be posited as antagonistic; Marxism arrogating to itself the concept of political practice and social change, psychoanalysis being accused of inherent conservatism which rationalizes and perpetuates the subordination of women under capitalism, or else fails to engage with that subordination at the level of material life.

In order to understand this, I think we have to go back to the earlier moment. For while the argument that Marxism was marginal or even alien to British thought was strongly repudiated, the equivalent observation about psychoanalysis seems to have been accepted and was more or less allowed to stand. This was perhaps largely because no one on the Left rushed forward to claim a radicalism committed to psychoanalytic thought. *New Left Review* had itself been involved in psychoanalysis in the early 1960s, publishing a number of articles by Cooper and Laing,[6] and there is also a strong tradition, which goes back through Christopher Caudwell in the 1930s, of Marxist discussion of Freud. But the main controversy unleashed by Anderson's remarks centred around Marxism; in an earlier article Anderson himself had restricted his critique to the lack of Marxism and classical sociology in British culture, making no reference to psychoanalysis at all.[7] After 1968 *New Left Review* published Althusser's famous article on Lacan and one article by Lacan,[8] but for the most part the commitment to psychoanalysis was not sustained even by that section of the British Left which had orginally argued for its importance.

Paradoxically, therefore, the idea that psychoanalysis was isolated or cut off from the general culture could be accepted to the extent that this very marginalization was being *reproduced* in the response to the diagnosis itself. Thus the link between Marxism and Freudian psychoanalysis, as the twin poles of a failed radicalism at the heart of British culture, was broken. Freud was cast aside at the very moment when resistance to his thought had been identified as symptomatic of the restrictiveness of bourgeois culture. Juliet Mitchell was the exception. Her defence of Freud[9] needs to be seen as a redress of this omission, but also as a critique of the loss of the concept of the unconscious in the very forms of psychoanalysis (for example, Laing) sponsored by the British Left (the second problem as the cause of the first). In this context the case for psychoanalysis was part of a claim for the fundamentally anti-empiricist and radical nature of Freudian thought. That this claim was made via feminism (could perhaps *only* be made via feminism) says something about the ability of feminism to challenge the orthodoxies of both Left and Right.

Thus the now familiar duo of 'psychoanalysis and feminism' has an additional and crucial political meaning. Not just psychoanalysis *for* feminism or feminism *against* psychoanalysis, but Freudian psychoanalysis and feminism *together* as two forms of thought which relentlessly undermine the turgid resistance of common-sense language to all forms of conflict and political change. For me this specific sequence has been ironically or negatively confirmed (that is, it has been gone over again backwards) by the recent attempt by Michael Rustin to relate psychoanalysis to socialism through a combination of F.R. Leavis and Melanie Klein – the very figures whose standing had been taken as symptomatic of that earlier resistance to the most radical aspects of Freudian thought (Klein because of the confinement of her often challenging ideas to the psychoanalytic institution itself; Leavis because of the inappropriate centrality which he claimed for the ethics of literary form and taste).[10] I cannot go into the details of Rustin's argument here, but its ultimate conservatism for feminism is at least clear; the advancement of 'mothering', and by implication of the role of women as mothers, as the psychic basis on which socialism can be built (the idea that psychoanalysis can *engender* socialism seems to be merely the flip side of the argument which accuses psychoanalysis of producing social conformity).

This history may appear obscure to many feminists who have not necessarily followed the different stages of these debates. But the diversion through this cultural map is, I think, important in so far as it can illustrate the ramifications of feminist discussion over a wider political spectrum, and also show how this discussion – the terms of the argument, the specific oppositions proposed – have in turn been determined by that wider spectrum itself.

Thus it will have crucial effects, for instance, whether psychoanalysis is discussed as an addition or supplement to Marxism (in relation to which it is then found *wanting*), or whether emphasis is laid on the concept of the unconscious. For while it is indeed correct that psychoanalysis was introduced into feminism as a theory which could rectify the inability of Marxism to address questions of sexuality, and that this move was complementary to the demand within certain areas of Marxism for increasing attention to the ideological determinants of our social being, it is also true that undue concentration on this aspect of the theory has served to cut off the concept of the unconscious, or at least to displace it from the centre of the debate. (This is graphically illustrated in Michèle Barrett's book, *Women's Oppression Today*, in which the main discussion of psychoanalysis revolves around the concept of ideology, and that of the unconscious is left to a note appended at the end of the chapter).[11]

Femininity and its Discontents

One result of this emphasis is that psychoanalysis is accused of 'functionalism', that is, it is accepted as a theory of how women are psychically 'induced' into femininity by a patriarchal culture, and is then accused of perpetuating that process, either through a practice assumed to be *prescriptive* about women's role (this is what women *should* do), or because the very effectiveness of the account as a *description* (this is what is demanded of women, what they are *expected* to do) leaves no possibility of change.

It is this aspect of Juliet Mitchell's book which seems to have been taken up most strongly by feminists who have attempted to follow through the political implications of psychoanalysis as a critique of patriarchy.

Thus Gayle Rubin, following Mitchell, uses psychoanalysis for a general critique of a patriarchal culture which is predicated on the exchange of women by men.[12] Nancy Chodorow shifts from Freud to later object relations theory to explain how women's childcaring role is perpetuated through the earliest relationship between a mother and her child, which leads in her case to a demand for a fundamental change in how childcare is organized between women and men in our culture.[13] Although there are obvious differences between these two readings of psychoanalysis, they nonetheless share an emphasis on the social exchange of women, or the distribution of roles for women, across cultures: 'Women's mothering is one of the few universal and enduring elements of the sexual division of labour.'[14]

The force of psychoanalysis is therefore (as Janet Sayers points out)[15] precisely that it gives an account of patriarchal culture as a trans-historical and cross-cultural force. It therefore conforms to the feminist demand for a theory which can explain women's subordination across specific cultures and different historical moments. Summing this up crudely, we could say that psychoanalysis adds sexuality to Marxism, where sexuality is felt to be lacking, and extends beyond Marxism where the attention to specific historical instances, changes in modes of production etc., is felt to leave something unexplained.

But all this happens at a cost, and that cost is the concept of the unconscious. What distinguishes psychoanalysis from sociological accounts of gender (hence for me the fundamental impasse of Nancy Chodorow's work) is that whereas for the latter, the internalization of norms is assumed roughly to work, the basic premise and indeed starting-point of psychoanalysis is that it does not. The unconscious constantly reveals the 'failure' of identity. Because there is no continuity of psychic life, so there is no stability of sexual identity, no position for women (or for men) which is ever simply achieved. Nor does psychoanalysis see such 'failure' as a special-case inability or an individual deviancy from the norm. 'Failure' is not a moment to be regretted in a process of adaptation, or development into normality, which ideally takes its course (some of the earliest critics of Freud, such as Ernest Jones, did, however, give an account of development in just these terms). Instead 'failure' is something endlessly repeated and relived moment by moment throughout our individual histories. It appears not only in the symptom, but also in dreams, in slips of the tongue and in forms of sexual pleasure which are pushed to the sidelines of the norm. Feminism's affinity with psychoanalysis rests above all, I would argue, with this recognition that there is a resistance to identity at the very heart of psychic life. Viewed in this way, psychoanalysis is no longer best understood as an account of how women are fitted into place (even this, note, is the charitable reading of Freud). Instead psychoanalysis becomes one of the few places in our culture where it is recognized as more than a fact of individual pathology that most women do not painlessly slip into their roles as women, if indeed they do at all. Freud himself recognized this increasingly in his work. In the articles which run from 1924 to 1931,[16] he moves from that famous, or rather infamous, description of the little girl struck with her 'inferiority' or 'injury' in the face of the anatomy of the little boy and wisely accepting her fate ('injury' as the *fact* of being feminine), to an account which quite explicitly describes the process of becoming 'feminine' as an 'injury' or 'catastrophe' for the complexity of her earlier psychic and sexual life ('injury' as its *price*).

Elizabeth Wilson and Janet Sayers are, therefore, in a sense correct to criticize psychoanalysis when it is taken as a general theory of patriarchy or of gender identity, that is, as a theory which explains how women wholly internalize the very mode of being which is feminism's specific target of attack; but they have missed out half the (psychonanalytic) story. In fact the argument seems to be circular. Psychoanalysis is drawn in the direction of a general theory of culture or a sociological account of gender because these seem to lay greater emphasis on the pressures of the 'outside' world, but it is this very pulling away from the psychoanalytic stress on the 'internal' complexity and difficulty of psychic life which produces the functionalism which is then criticized.

The argument about whether Freud is being 'prescriptive' or 'descriptive' about women (with its associated stress on the motives and morals of Freud himself) is fated to the extent that it is locked into this model. Many of us will be familiar with Freud's famous pronouncement that a women who does not succeed in transforming activity to passivity, clitoris to vagina, mother for father, will fall ill. Yet psychoanalysis testifies to the fact that psychic illness or distress is in no sense the prerogative of women who 'fail' in this task. One of my students recently made the obvious but important point that we would be foolish to deduce from the external trappings of normality or conformity in a woman that all is in fact well. And Freud himself always stressed the psychic cost of the civilizing process for all (we can presumably include women in that 'all' even if at times he did not seem to do so).

All these aspects of Freud's work are subject to varying interpretation by analysts themselves. The first criticism of Freud's 'phallocentrism' came from inside psychoanalysis, from analysts such as Melanie Klein, Ernest Jones and Karen Horney who felt, contrary to Freud, that 'femininity' was a quality with its own impetus, subject to checks and internal conflict, but tending ultimately to fulfilment. For Jones, the little girl was 'typically receptive and acquisitive' from the outset; for Horney, there was from the beginning a 'wholly womanly' attachment to the father.[17] For these analysts, this development might come to grief, but for the most part a gradual strengthening of the child's ego and her increasing adaptation to reality, should guarantee its course. Aspects of the little girl's psychic life which were resistant to this process (the famous 'active' or 'masculine' drives) were defensive. The importance of concepts such as the 'phallic phase' in Freud's description of infantile sexuality is not, therefore, that such concepts can be taken as the point of insertion of patriarchy (assimilation to the norm). Rather their importance lies in the way that they indicate, through their very artificiality, that something was being *forced*, and in the concept of psychic life with which they were accompanied. In Freud's work they went hand in hand with an increasing awareness of the difficulty, not to say impossibility, of the path to normality for the girl, and an increasing stress on the fundamental divisions, or splitting, of psychic life. It was those who challenged these concepts in the 1920s and 1930s who introduced the more normative stress on a sequence of develoment, and coherent ego, back into the account.

I think we go wrong again, therefore, if we conduct the debate about whether Freud's account was developmental or not entirely in terms of his own writing. Certainly the idea of development is present at moments in his work. But it was not present *enough* for many of his contemporaries, who took up the issue and reinstated the idea of development precisely in relation to the sexual progress of the girl (her passage into womanhood).

'Psychoanalysis' is not, therefore, a single entity. Institutional divisions within psychoanalysis have turned on the very questions about the phallocentrism of analysis, the meaning of femininity, the sequence of psychic development and its norms, which have been the concern of feminists. The accusations came from analysts themselves. In the earlier debates, however, the reproach against Freud produced an account of femininity which was more, rather than less, normative than his own.

The politics of Lacanian psychoanalysis begin here. From the 1930s, Lacan saw his intervention as a return to the concepts of psychic division, splitting of the ego, and an endless (he called it 'insistent') pressure of the unconscious against any individual's pretension to a smooth and coherent psychic and sexual identity. Lacan's specific target was 'ego-psychology' in America, and what he saw as the dilution of psychoanalysis into a tool of social adaptation and control (hence the central emphasis on the concepts of the ego and identification which are often overlooked in discussions of his ideas). For Lacan, psychoanalysis does not offer an account of a developing ego which is 'not *necessarily* coherent',[18] but of an ego which is 'necessarily *not* coherent', that is, which is always and persistently divided against itself.

Lacan could therefore be picked up by a Marxist like Althusser not because he offered a theory of adaptation to reality or of the individual's insertion into culture (Althusser added a note to the English translation of his paper on Lacan criticizing it for having implied such a reading),[19] but because the force of the unconscious in Lacan's interpretation of Freud was felt to undermine the mystifications of a bourgeois culture proclaiming its identity, and that of its subjects, to the world. The political use of Lacan's theory therefore stemmed from its assault on what English Marxists would call bourgeois 'individualism'. What the theory offered was a divided subject out of 'synch' with bourgeois myth. Feminists could legitimately object that the notion of psychic fragmentation was of little immediate political advantage to women struggling for the first time to find a voice, and trying to bring together the dissociated components of their life into a political programme. But this is a very different criticism of the political implications of psychoanalysis than the one which accuses it of forcing women into bland conformity with their expected role.

Psychoanalysis and History: The History of Psychoanalysis

What, therefore, is the political purchase of the concept of the unconscious on women's lived experience? And what can it say to the specific histories of which we form a part?

One of the objections which is often made against psychoanalysis is that it has no sense of history, and an inadequate grasp of its relationship to the concrete institutions which frame and determine our lives. For even if we allow for a moment the radical force of the psychoanalytic insight, the exclusiveness or limited availability of that insight tends to be turned, not against the culture or state which mostly resists its general (and publicly funded) dissemination,[20] but against psychoanalysis itself. The 'privatization' of psychoanalysis comes to mean that it only refers to the individual as private, and the concentration on the individual as private is then seen as reinforcing a theory which places itself above history and change.

Again I think that this question is posed back to front, and that we need to ask, not what psychoanalysis has to say about history, but rather what is the history of psychoanalysis, that is, what was the intervention of psychoanalysis into the institutions which, at the time of its emergence, were controlling women's lives? And what was the place of the unconscious, historically, in that? Paradoxically, the claim that psychoanalysis is a-historical dehistoricizes it. If we go back to the beginnings of psychoanalysis, it is clear that the concept of the unconscious was radical at exactly that level of social 'reality' with which it is so often assumed to have nothing whatsoever to do.

Recent work by feminist historians is of particular importance in this context. Judith Walkowitz, in her study of the Contagious Diseases Acts of the 1860s, shows how state policy on public hygiene and the state's increasing control over casual labour, relied on a category of women as diseased (the suspected prostitute stubjected to forcible examination and internment in response to the spread of venereal disease in the port towns).[21] Carol Dyhouse has described how debates about educational opportunity for women constantly returned to the evidence of the female body (either the energy expended in their development towards sexual reproduction meant that women could not be educated, or education and the overtaxing of the brain would damage their reproductive capacity).[22] In the birth control controversy, the Malthusian idea of controlling the reproduction, and by implication the sexuality, of the working class served to counter the idea that poverty could be reduced by the redistribution of wealth.[23] Recurrently in the second half of the nineteenth century, in the period immediately prior to Freud, female sexuality became the focus of a panic about the effects of industrialization on the cohesion of the social body and its ability to reproduce itself comfortably. The importance of all this work (Judith Walkowitz makes this quite explicit) is that 'attitudes' towards women cannot be consigned to the sphere of ideology, assumed to have no purchase on material life, so deeply implicated was the concept of female sexuality in the legislative advancement of the state.[24]

Central to all of this was the idea that the women was wholly responsible for the social well-being of the nation (questions of social division transmuted directly into the moral and sexual responsibility of subjects), or where she failed in this task, that she was disordered or diseased. The hysteric was either the overeducated woman, or else the women indulging in non-procreative or uncontrolled sexuality (conjugal onanism), or again the woman in the lock hospitals which, since the eighteenth century, had been receiving categories refused by the general hospitals ('infectious diseases, "fever", children, maternity cases, mental disorders, as well as venereal diseases').[25] It was these hospitals which, at the time of the Contagious Diseases Acts, became the place of confinement for the diseased prostitute in a new form of collaborative relationship with the state.

This is where psychoanalysis begins. Although the situation was not identical in France, there are important links. Freud's earliest work was under Charcot at the Salpêtrière Clinic in Paris, a hospital for women: 'five thousand neurotic indigents, epileptics, and insane patients, many of whom were deemed incurable'.[26] The 'dregs' of society comprised the inmates of the Salpêtrière (psychoanalysis does not start in the Viennese palour). Freud was working under Charcot whose first contribution to the study of hysteria was to move it out of the category of sexual malingering and into that of a specific and accredited neurological disease. The problem with Charcot's work is that while he was constructing the symptomatology of the disease (turning it into a respected object of the medical institution), he was reinforcing it as a special category of behaviour, visible to the eye, and the result of a degenerate hereditary disposition.

Freud's intervention here was two-fold. Firstly, he questioned the visible evidence of the disease – the idea that you could know a hysteric by looking at her body, that is, by reading off the symptoms of nervous disability or susceptibility to trauma. Secondly (and this second move depended on the first), he rejected the idea that hysteria was an 'independent' clinical entity, by using what he uncovered in the treatment of the hysterical patient as the basis of his account of the unconscious and its universal presence in adult life.

The 'universalism' of Freud was not, therefore, an attempt to remove the subject from history; it stemmed from his challenge to the category of hysteria as a principle of classification for certain socially isolated and confined individuals, and his shifting of this category into the centre of everybody's psychic experience: 'Her hysteria can therefore be described as an acquired one, and it pre-supposed nothing more than the possession of what is probably a very wide-spread proclivity – the proclivity to acquire hysteria.'[27] The reason why the two moves are interdependent is because it was only by penetrating behind the visible symptoms of disorder and asking what it was that the symptom was trying to *say*, that Freud could uncover those unconscious desires and motives which he went on to expose in the slips, dreams and jokes of individuals paraded as normal. Thus the challenge to the entity 'hysteria', that is, to hysteria *as* an entity available for quite specific forms of social control, relied on the concept of the unconscious. 'I have attempted', wrote Freud, 'to meet the problem of hysterical attacks along a line other than *descriptive*'.[28] Hence Freud's challenge to the visible, to the empirically self-evident, to the 'blindness of the seeing eye'.[29] . . . It is perhaps this early and now mostly forgotten moment which can give us the strongest sense of the force of the unconscious as a concept against a fully social classification relying on empirical evidence as its rationale.

The challenge of psychoanalysis to empiricist forms of reasoning was therefore the very axis on which the fully historical intervention of psychoanalysis into late nineteenth-century medicine turned. The theories of sexuality came after this first intervention (in *Studies on Hysteria*, Freud's remarks on sexuality are mostly given in awkward footnotes suggesting the importance of sexual abstinence for women as a causal factor in the etiology of hysteria). But when Freud did start to investigate the complexity of sexual life in response to what he uncovered in hysterical patients, his first step was a similar questioning of social definitions, this time of sexual perversion as 'innate' or 'degenerate', that is, as the special property of a malfunctioning type.[30] In fact, if we take dreams and slips of the tongue (both considered before Freud to result from lowered mental capacity), sexuality and hysteria, the same movement operates each time. A discredited, pathological or irrational form of behaviour is given its psychic value by psychoanalysis. What this meant for the hysterical woman is that instead of just being looked at or examined, she was allowed to *speak*.

Some of the criticisms which are made by feminists of Freudian psychoanalysis, especially when it is filtered through the work of Lacan, can perhaps be answered with reference to this moment. Most often the emphasis is laid either on Lacan's statement that 'the unconscious is structured like a language', or on his concentration on mental representation and the ideational contents of the mind. The feeling seems to be that the stress on ideas and language cuts psychoanalysis off from the materiality of being, whether that materiality is defined as the biological aspects of our subjectivity, or as the economic factors determining our lives (one or the other and at times both).

Once it is put like this, the argument becomes a version of the debate within Marxism over the different instances of social determination and their hierarchy ('ideology' versus the 'economic') or else it becomes an accusation of idealism (Lacan) against materialism (Marx). I think this argument completely misses the importance of the emphasis on language in Lacan and of mental representation in Freud. The statement that 'the unconscious is structured like a language' was above all part of Lacan's attempt to establish a continuity between the seeming disorder of the symptom or dream and the normal language through which we recognize each other and speak. And the importance of the linguistic sign (Saussure's distinction between the signifier and the signified)[31] was that it provided a model internal to language itself of that form of indirect representation (the body speaking because there is something which cannot be said) which psychoanalysis uncovered in the symptomatology of its patients. Only if one thing can stand for another is the hysterical symptom something more than the logical and direct manifestation of physical or psychic (and social) degeneracy.

This is why the concept of the unconscious – as indicating an irreducible discontinuity of psychic life – is so important. Recognition of that discontinuity in us all is in a sense the price we have to pay for that earlier historical displacement.

Feminism and the Unconscious

It is, however, this concept which seems to be lost whenever Freud has been challenged on those ideas which have been most problematic for feminism, in so far as the critique of Freudian phallocentrism so often relies on a return to empiricism, on an appeal to 'what actually happens' or what can be *seen* to be the case. Much of Ernest Jones's criticism of Freud, for example, stemmed from his conviction that girls and boys could not conceivably be ignorant of so elementary a fact as that of sexual difference and procreation.[32] And Karen Horney, in her similar but distinct critique, referred to 'the manifestations of so elementary a principle of nature as that of the mutual attraction of the sexes'.[33] We can compare this with Freud: 'from the point of view of psycho-analysis the exclusive sexual interest felt by men for women is also a problem that needs elucidating and is not a self-evident fact based upon an attraction that is ultimately of a chemical nature'.[34] The point is not that one side is appealing to 'biology' (or 'nature') and the other to 'ideas', but that Freud's opening premise is to challenge the self-evidence of both.

The feminist criticism of Freud has of course been very different since it has specifically involved a rejection of the evidence of this particular norm: the normal femininity which, in the earlier quarrel, Freud himself was considered to have questioned. But at this one crucial level – the idea of an unconscious which points to a fundamental division of psychic life and which therefore challenges any form of empiricism based on what is there to be observed (even when scientifically tested and tried) – the very different critiques are related. In *Psychoanalysis and Feminism*, Juliet Mitchell based at least half her argument on this point but it has been lost. Thus Shulamith Firestone, arguing in *The Dialectic of Sex* that the girl's alleged sense of inferiority in relation to the boy was the logical outcome of the observable facts of the child's experience, had to assume an unproblematic and one-to-one causality between psychic life and social reality with no possibility of dislocation or error.[35] The result is that the concept of the unconscious is lost (the little girl rationally recognizes and decides her fate) and mothering is deprived of its active components (the mother is seen to be only subordinate and in no sense powerful for the child).[36] For all its more obvious political appeal, the idea that psychic life is the unmediated reflection of social relations locks the mother and child into a closed subordination which can then only be broken by the advances of empiricism itself:

> Full mastery of the reproductive process is in sight, and there has been significant advance in understanding the basic life and death process. The nature of ageing and growth, sleep and hibernation, the chemical functioning of the brain and the development of consciousness and memory are all beginning to be understood in their entirety. This acceleration promises to continue for another century, or however long it takes to achieve the goal of Empiricism: total understanding of the laws of nature.[37]

Shulamith Firestone's argument has been criticized by feminists who would not wish to question, any more than I would, the importance of her intervention for feminism.[38] But I think it is important that the part of her programme which is now criticized (the idea that women must rely on scientific progress to achieve any change) is so directly related to the empiricist concept of social reality (what can be *seen* to happen) which she offers. The empiricism of the goal is the outcome of the empiricism at the level of social reality and psychic life. I have gone back to this moment because, even though it is posed in different terms, something similar seems to be going on in the recent Marxist repudiation of Freud. Janet Sayers's critique of Juliet Mitchell, for example, is quite explicitly based on the concept

of 'what actually and specifically happens' ('in the child's environment' and 'in the child's physical and biological development').[39]

Utopianism of the Psyche

Something else happens in all of this which is probably the most
central issue for me: the discarding of the concept of the unconscious
seems to leave us with a type of utopianism of psychic life. In this
context it is interesting to note just how close the appeal to biology
and the appeal to culture as the determinants of psychic experience
can be. Karen Horney switched from one to the other, moving from
the idea that femininity was a natural quality, subject to checks, but
tending on its course, to the idea that these same checks, and indeed
most forms of psychic conflict, were the outcome of an oppressive
social world. The second position is closer to that of feminism, but
something is nonetheless missing from both sides of the divide. For
what has happened to the unconscious, to that divided and disordered subjectivity which, I have argued, had to be recognized in us
all if the category of hysteria as a peculiar property of one class of
women was to be disbanded? Do not both of these movements make
psychic conflict either an accident or an obstacle on the path to
psychic and sexual continuity – a continuity which, as feminists, we
recognize as a myth of our culture only to reinscribe it in a different
form on the agenda for a future (post-revolutionary) date?

Every time Freud is challenged, this concept of psychic cohesion
as the ultimate object of our political desires seems to return. Thus
the French feminist and analyst, Luce Irigaray, challenges Lacan
not just for the phallocentrism of his arguments, but because the
Freudian account is seen to cut women off from an early and un-
troubled psychic unity (the primordial state of fusion with the mother)
which feminists should seek to restore. Irigaray calls this the 'imaginary' of women (a reference to Lacan's idea of a primitive narcissism which was for him only ever a fantasy). In a world felt to be
especially alienating for women, this idea of psychic oneness or
primary narcissism has its own peculiar force. It appears in a different form in Michèle Barrett's and Mary McIntosh's excellent
reply to Christopher Lasch's thesis that we are witnessing a regret-
table decline in the patriarchal family.[40] Responding to his accusation that culture is losing its super-ego edge and descending into

narcissism, they offer the particularly female qualities of mothering (Chodorow) and a defence of this very 'primary narcissism' in the name of women against Lasch's undoubtedly reactionary lament. The problem remains, however, that whenever the 'feminine' comes into the argument as a quality in this way we seem to lose the basic insight of psychoanalysis – the failure or difficulty of femininity for women, and that fundamental psychic division which in Freud's work was its accompanying and increasingly insistent discovery. If I question the idea that psychoanalysis is the 'new orthodoxy' for feminists, it is at least partly because of the strong political counter-weight of this idea of femininity which appears to repudiate both these Freudian insights together.

To return to the relationship between Marxism and psychoanalysis with which I started, I think it is relevant that the most systematic attack we have had on the hierarchies and organization of the male Left[41] gives to women the privilege of the personal in a way which divests it (*has* to divest it) of complexity at exactly this level of the conflicts and discontinuities of psychic life. Like many feminists, the slogan 'the personal is political' has been central to my own political development; just as I see the question of sexuality, as a political issue which *exceeds* the province of Marxism ('economic', 'ideological' or whatever), as one of the most important defining character-istics of feminism itself. But the dialogue between feminism and psychoanalysis, which is for me the arena in which the full complexity of that 'personal' and that 'sexuality' can be grasped, constantly seems to fail.

In this article, I have not answered all the criticisms of psycho-analysis. It is certainly the case that psychoanalysis does not give us a blueprint for political action, or allow us to deduce political con-servatism or radicalism directly from the vicissitudes of psychic experience. Nor does the concept of the unconscious sit comfortably with the necessary attempt by feminism to claim a new sureness of identity for women, or with the idea of always conscious and deli-berate political decision-making and control (psychoanalysis is *not* a voluntarism).[42] But its challenge to the concept of psychic identity is important for feminism in that it allows into the political arena problems of subjectivity (subjectivity *as* a problem) which tend to be suppressed from other forms of political debate. It may also help us to open up the space between different notions of political identity –

between the idea of a political identity for feminism (what women require) and that of a feminine identity for women (what women are or should be), especially given the problems constantly encountered by the latter and by the sometimes too easy celebration of an identity amongst women which glosses over the differences between us.

Psychoanalysis finally remains one of the few places in our culture where our experience of femininity can be spoken as a problem that is something other than the problem which the protests of women are posing for an increasingly conservative political world. I would argue that this is one of the reasons why it has not been released into the public domain. The fact that psychoanalysis cannot be assimilated directly into a political programme as such does not mean, therefore, that it should be discarded, and thrown back into the outer reaches of a culture which has never yet been fully able to heed its voice.

NOTES

1 The editors and publishers gratefully acknowledge the permission of Jaqueline Rose Copyright © 1983 and *Feminist Review* to reproduce 'Femininity and its Discontents'.

2 First published in *Feminist Review*, 14, Summer 1983, pp. 5–21, this essay was originally requested by the editors of *Feminist Review* to counter the largely negative representation of psychoanalysis which had appeared in the journal, and as a specific response to Elizabeth Wilson's 'Psychoanalysis: Psychic Law and Order', *Feminist Review*, 8, Summer 1981. (See also Janet Sayers, 'Psychoanalysis and Personal Politics: A Response to Elizabeth Wilson', *Feminist Review*, 10, 1982.) As I was writing the piece, however, it soon became clear that Elizabeth Wilson's article and the question of *Feminist Review*'s own relationship to psychoanalysis could not be understood independently of what has been – outside the work of Juliet Mitchell for feminism – a fairly consistent repudiation of Freud within the British Left. In this context, the feminist debate over Freud becomes part of a larger question about the importance of subjectivity to our understanding of political and social life. That this was in fact the issue became even clearer when Elizabeth Wilson and Angie Weir published an article 'The British Women's Movement' in *New Left Review*, 148, November–December 1984, which dismissed the whole area of subjectivity and psychoanalysis from feminist politics together with any work by feminists (historians

and writers on contemporary politics) who, while defining themselves as socialist feminists, nonetheless query the traditional terms of an exclusively class-based analysis of power.

3 Wilson, 'Psychoanalysis', p. 63.

4 *Psychoanalysis and Feminism* (London: Allen Lane, 1974).

5 Perry Anderson, 'Components of the National Culture', *New Left Review*, 50, July–August 1968.

6 David Cooper, 'Freud Revisited' and 'Two Types of Rationality', *New Left Review*, 20, May–June 1963, and 29, January–February 1965; R. D. Laing 'Series and Nexus in the Family' and 'What is Schizophrenia?', *New Left Review*, 15, May–June 1962, 28, November–December 1964.

7 Anderson, 'Origins of the Present Crisis', *New Left Review*, 23, January–February 1964; see also E. P. Thompson, 'The Peculiarities of the English', *Socialist Register*, 1965.

8 Louis Althusser, 'Freud and Lacan', tr. Ben Brewster, *New Left Review*, 55, March–April 1969; Jacques Lacan, 'The Mirror Phase', tr. Jan Meil, *New Left Review*, 51, September–October 1968.

9 Juliet Mitchell, 'Why Freud?', *Shrew*, November–December 1970, and *Psychoanalysis and Feminism*.

10 Michael Rustin, 'A Socialist Consideration of Kleinian Psychoanalysis', *New Left Review*, 131, January–February 1982.

11 Michèle Barrett, *Women's Oppression Today: Problems in Marxist Feminist Analysis* (London: Verso, 1980), ch. 2, pp. 80–3.

12 See Gayle Rubin, 'The Traffic in Women' in *Towards an Anthropology of Women*, ed. Rayner Reiter (New York: Monthly Review Press, 1975) and for a critique of the use of Lévi-Strauss on which this reading is based, Elizabeth Cowie, 'Woman as Sign', *m/f*, 1, 1978.

13 Nancy Chodorow, *The Reproduction of Mothering: Psychoanalysis and the Sociology of Gender* (Berkeley: University of California Press, 1978).

14 Ibid., p. 3.

15 Sayers, 'Psychoanalysis and Personal Politics', 92.

16 Sigmund Freud, 'The Dissolution of the Oedipus Complex' (1924); 'Some Psychical Consequences of the Anatomical Distinction Between the Sexes' (1925), *The Standard Edition of the Complete Psychological Works* (hereafter SE; London: Hogarth, 1955–74), XIX; *Pelican Freud Library* (hereafter PF; Harmondsworth: Penguin, 1976–85), 7; 'Female Sexuality', SE XXI, PF 7.

17 Ernest Jones, 'The Phallic Phase', *IJPA*, 14, Part 1, 1933, 265; Karen Horney, 'On the Genesis of the Castration Complex in Women' (1924), *Feminine Psychology*, (London: RKP, 1967), p. 53.

18 Wilson, 'Reopening the Case – Feminism and Psychoanalysis', opening

seminar presentation in discussion with Jacqueline Rose, London 1982. This was the first of a series of seminars on the subject of feminism and psychoanalysis which ran into 1983; see articles by Parveen Adams, Nancy Wood and Claire Buck, *m/f*, 8, 1983.

19 Althusser, 'Freud and Lacan'; see publisher's note in *Lenin and Philosophy and Other Essays* (London: New Left Books, 1971), pp. 189–90.

20 For a more detailed discussion of the relative assimilation of Kleinianism through social work in relation to children in this country, especially through the Tavistock Clinic in London, see Rustin, 'A Socialist Consideration', p. 85 and note. As Rustin points out, the state is willing to fund psychoanalysis when it is a question of helping children to adapt, but less so when it is a case of helping adults to remember.

21 Judith Walkowitz, *Prostitution and Victorian Society: Women, Class and the State* (London and New York: Cambridge University Press, 1980).

22 Carol Dyhouse, *Girls Growing Up in Late Victorian and Edwardian England* (London: Routledge and Kegan Paul, 1981).

23 Angus McLaren, *Birth Control in Nineteenth-Century England* (London: Croom Helm, 1978).

24 Walkowitz, *Prostitution and Victorian Society*, p. 69.

25 Ibid., p. 59.

26 Ilza Veith, *Hysteria: the History of a Disease* (London: University of Chicago Press, 1975), p. 229.

27 Freud, *Studies on Hysteria*, SE II, PF 3, p. 122; p. 187.

28 Freud, 'Preface and Footnotes to Charcot's Tuesday Lectures' (1892–94), SE I, p. 137.

29 *Studies on Hysteria*, SE II, PF 3, p. 117; p. 181.

30 Freud, *Three Essays on the Theory of Sexuality*, SE VII, PF 7, Part 1.

31 Ferdinand de Saussure, *Cours de linguistique générale* (1915) (Paris: Payot, 1972); tr. Roy Harris, *Course in General Linguistics* (London: Duckworth, 1983), pp. 65–70.

32 Jones, 'The Phallic Phase', 15.

33 Horney, 'The Flight from Womanhood' (1926), in *Feminine Psychology*, p. 68.

34 *Three Essays*, SE VII, PF 7, p. 146n; p. 57n.

35 Shulamith Firestone, *The Dialectic of Sex* (London: The Women's Press, 1979).

36 See Mitchell, 'Shulamith Firestone: Freud Feminized', *Psychoanalysis and Feminism*, Part 2, Section 2, ch. 5.

37 Firestone, *Dialectic of Sex*, p. 170.

38 Ibid., introduction by Rosalind Delmar.

39 Sayers quoted by Wilson in 'Reopening the Case'.

40 Michèle Barrett and Mary McIntosh, 'Narcissism and the Family: A Critique of Lasch', *New Left Review*, 135, September–October 1982.
41 Sheila Rowbotham, Lynne Segal and Hilary Wainwright, *Beyond the Fragments: Feminism and the Making of Socialism* (London: Merlin, 1979).
42 Sayers, 'Psychoanalysis and Personal Politics', 92–3.

15

Judith Williamson
b.1954

'NUCLEAR FAMILY? NO THANKS' from
CONSUMING PASSIONS (1986)

*In its edifying, Victorian guise, the view that women are innately 'more
moral' than men would be rejected out of hand by contemporary feminists.
Yet the thought itself is by no means extinct. The question remains open
within feminism: are women natural leaders in the morality of conservation?*

*This essay is, on one level, a commentary on current political events.
But its immediate topic, the Greenham movement, introduces a discussion
of the more abstract question just outlined. Identifying herself both as a
feminist and as a supporter of anti-nuclear activism, Judith Williamson
draws a distinction between (i) the* tactical *appeal to naturalistic assumptions about women as nurturers, and (ii) 'believing our own propaganda',
i.e. actually endorsing those assumptions.*

The essay is a polemic against the idea that anything *in our political
identity comes to us 'naturally' – unmediated by social relations and social
consciousness. It is a plea for the retention of the classical conception of
politics as a domain of thought and choice. The argument against confronting the military-industrial complex with maternalist pathos is not just
that it is ineffective in practice (symbolic acts of protest can be valuable as
long as we recognize them for what they are), but that it is ultimately
infantilizing; this approach threatens to reduce the woman who opposes
nuclear weapons to the same status as a badge-wearing 'Baby Against the
Bomb'. For Williamson, a biologically determined protective drive can
never be a substitute for informed understanding of the socio-economic*

formations that threaten us. (Not that she would be debarred from think-
ing, with Woolf, reading 10, and Soper, reading 20, that women's actual
socio-economic position may make certain moral insights more accessible to
them than to men.)

It is tempting to sum up Williamson's argument in the language of the
Enlightenment – to say that she defends the idea of politics as a domain of
reason, not sentiment. This opposition is, of course, misleading in that
disciplined thought often results in discoveries to which strong emotion –
anger, horror, fear – is the only appropriate response. But still, if we
dismiss analysis in favour of the purely expressive gesture of resistance, we
stand to lose the best thing rationalist politics has to offer: the promise of a
fundamental *transformation of the social order. And that would include a*
transformation of the social processes by which women come to perceive
themselves as naturally 'motherly'.

There is a familiar car sticker which pictures a smiling sun wreathed
by the words 'Nuclear Power? No thanks'.[1] From the tone of the
answer, one might think the question posed had been 'More sherry?'
rather than 'Destruction of life on earth?' But the multinational
commercial interests and the governments that serve them are unlikely to listen to this genteel reply because they never asked a
question in the first place. The persistent faith of the middle class in
politeness is perversely inappropriate in a world which it governs
largely through the ruthless pursuit of political and economic power.
The car sticker, with its cheerily inane smile, makes the mistake of
suggesting that a choice has been offered. It hasn't.

I should say at the outset that I am totally opposed to nuclear
power and nuclear weapons – their danger is not in question. What I
do want to query are some of the ideological strategies of the anti-
nuclear movement. The campaigns against nuclear fuels and nuclear
missiles are extremely important, and are impressive in a great many
ways. Yet in a few aspects they involve assumptions that are in direct
conflict with either a feminist or a socialist understanding. There is
an emphasis on motherhood, the family, woman as nature and as
provider – exactly the myths about femininity that the women's
movement has tried to question. There is also an emphasis on the
individual and personal – related, as always, to the family/parent-
hood domain – rather than on the social, which is perhaps why this
particular political arena is especially appealing to the middle classes.

In the same way that it is difficult to criticize one's mother, because she is always right, so it is very difficult for feminists to criticize the Greenham Common campaign, because it seems haloed with that Women's Righteousness which has traditionally gone hand in hand with our oppression. Motherhood is always good, whether in Nazi propaganda or Persil ads; it lends a 'natural goodness' to the notion of 'Women Against the Bomb'. In the patriarchal values of modern capitalism, Woman is the great provider of nature and nurture: 'There are two men in my life, to one I am a mother, to the other I'm a wife. And I give them both the best. With Natural Shredded Wheat.' Is that ideology really so different from this:'I think that most women are really in touch with what life is about. You can't even contemplate having a child without considering the value of that life and the struggle people have bringing up children, putting in all those hours and hours of caring. A lot of women do that not even with children, but with the home, making a wonderful place for people to get by day-to-day living [sic]. You just can't contemplate that being destroyed . . .'[2]

As if it is simply the *home*, with all the 'hours and hours' of caring (and dusting and polishing) one has put into it, that women can't bear to see destroyed! What about our society, cities, hospitals, libraries, histories, cultures, all the human achievements of thousands of years of social life? A social life that is women's work, as much as men's. We have been *taught* to think of our own families, homes and children as the extent of our political concern and the sole focus for our 'caring'. On 12 December 1982 a demonstration took place in which the perimeter fence of the Greenham airbase was hung with symbols of whatever people most valued; it ended up covered in family snaps, wedding photos, anniversary cards (even some pictures of the Pope!) plus nappies, teddy bears and other symbols of childhood. Although the decoration of the fence was a powerful symbolic act in itself, the most persistent image was that of the nuclear family; and in a sense *what* the fence came to symbolize was the potential destruction of bourgeois family life by the bomb.

For women to identify with this image of the family seems like a giant step back from the politics of the women's liberation movement. Of course, the great irony about this notion of women as *inherently* more 'caring' than men (rather than as *conditioned* to be so) is that the most right-wing and militaristic Prime Minister we have had since the last war is a woman. But it can be argued that, like Lady Macbeth, she is going against her 'nature'. Women are supposedly the same the world over: 'Women can identify with women of Russia and Eastern bloc countries. We're just the same. A woman in Russia is the same as myself – the same emotions, leading the same sort of life. In no way will I be a part of anything that will murder her.' While one can admire the internationalist sentiment of this, the idea of women being fundamentally the same throughout the world can act as a cover for real differences in and between societies. The idea that women's 'Nature' can be mobilized against the nuclear threat also tends to naturalize that threat; as if men naturally created nuclear weapons and women naturally opposed them. This glosses over the actual system of political and economic power which profits from the production of nuclear weapons. But many of those who oppose nuclear weapons do not, in other ways, oppose that system. Nuclear war is undiscriminating: it is fatal for oppressor and oppressed alike. Yet it is the relations of social oppression already in existence which have produced nuclear weapons, and which must therefore be attacked by any opponent of those weapons. The basic fear of destruction for oneself and one's children has no more political meaning in itself than the fear of being run over. Not that this is by any means the prerogative of women: in his book *The Dialectics of Disaster – a Preface to Hope*, Ronald Aronson says, with wounded pride: 'As a father, I cannot be a father, because my girls are not safe and I cannot make them safe.' This ideology *limits* the notion of caring to parenthood; conveniently, since if the values of 'caring' were taken beyond the family they would involve fighting for far more radical changes in society.

There is one sense in which the idea of 'caring' *is* taken beyond the individual. But it is taken not into the realm of the *social*, but of the *natural*. Women apparently have more concern for the planet than men; and a more symbiotic relation to nature. 'You are a spring and if you copy this letter and send it to ten other women, who then do the same, we will become rivers that will flow together on December 12th and become an ocean of women's energy' (leaflet). There is a semi-mystical relation between women and ecology which again hinges upon the role of women as mothers – 'As women we wish to protect all life on this planet' (another leaflet) – and suggests some primeval state of unity between women and the earth – 'men have taken our property rights in the earth'. The ecology movement is very important, but where it combines with this particular kind of 'feminism', the result is a set of ideas uncomfortably close to the ideology of patriarchy itself. 'Babies Against the Bomb', for example, draws on a sentimentality and notion of 'human nature' which are on the same level as 'human interest' items in the popular press. It turns a political movement into a natural one, in the same way that taking action 'because' one is a woman undermines the political deliberation of that action. Individual babies even have their own slogans: 'Amy Against the Bomb' proclaimed the placard on the pram of a few-weeks-old baby on one demonstration. If babies, who do not make decisions, are against the bomb, what does this imply about the movement as a whole? Surely we should claim social consciousness, not natural instincts, as the basis of concerted action – especially since women have traditionally been regarded as instinctive bundles of emotion rather than as thinking, arguing people.

Unfortunately this traditional image has been the one most courted by some women in the peace movement, not only as the basis for their action but in its method as well. There is the wool weaving: 'We spin and thread ourselves together as women for this day . . .' reads one leaflet, and another: 'How will you do the action? Weave wool, link arms, sing . . .'. This can provide a powerful image – the whole point of such action is that woven wool *cannot* stop bombs, it is a symbol of *peace*. Yet sometimes it is treated as if it really had a mystical effect. One leaflet describes a 'full moon festival' at Greenham where 'a rainbow dragon will be *born* by joining the creative work of thousands of women . . . after the dragon is *born* at Greenham *she* will be taken by women from another country, to another celebration for life. This is the start of *her* journey around the earth, spreading and joining women's creativity and strength' (my italics). The whole ideology of 'women's creativity' as limited to traditional 'domestic' forms and to birth – both metaphoric and literal – has become reinforced by these so-called feminist activities. Most revealing of all is this description of 'keening' (a sort of high-pitched whine): 'Keening is something traditionally done by women and is now confined to mourning. It's a means of expression without words, without having to get tied up in various arguments, facts and figures, whys and wherefores. You can just show how you feel.'

But is 'just showing how you feel' always the best way to convince others of your cause? The notion of self-expression has taken on a major role in women's anti-nuclear activities, and while there is clearly a positive value in this for the women concerned, sometimes the means to an end becomes an end in itself. 'Every now and then we'd link arms in a big circle and dance around the top of the silo. We were all ecstatic, overtaken by the brilliant feeling that we'd actually done it!' The *experience* of the action becomes almost a substitute for the *purpose* of the action:

> We leapt up. I can only say we had a sort of celebration. We hugged and kissed each other and felt wonderful. It was extra-ordinary. We felt as if we'd won a victory in a way – a moral victory. Somehow we found ourselves in this enormous circle. I don't know how many of us there were. There were enough to make a really big circle that took up the whole of the road, right from the base fence across to the other side of the road. We took up the whole of the space, dancing and singing for a while. It was lovely. Then one woman suggested that we should stand in silence to calm ourselves down. So we all stood in this enormous circle, smiling in silence for a few minutes. It seemed quite a long time. It was very restful and calming and we felt very close to each other.

Direct action has been a powerful form of publicity for the anti-nuclear campaign, but it can also be seen as a therapeutic outlet for the feelings of powerlessness which are engendered by the very existence of nuclear weapons. Of course it is crucial for people to feel solidarity and strength or there is no emotional fuel for the move-ment. But as with all political campaigns, many other feelings and values are channelled into the nuclear issue, so that both the weapons and the actions against them come to function in the realm of the *symbolic*:

> The silos . . . are a focal point of all the negative things that are going on in the world – paranoia, greed, misuse of power, violence, a lack of imagination for alternatives. In my mind I saw them as revolting man-made boils on the earth's surface, full of evil. I wanted to let out all the feelings I have about the threat of nuclear war, the fear and the dread. And I wanted to

concentrate on the future, to feel optimistic . . . I kept thinking about celebrating life. What actually happened was that I did that. When we got to the silos, even though we were so excited, I stood quietly for a few minutes, with my eyes closed, and let it all drain out of me.

Many of these descriptions give the impression that symbolic acts are not seen as such, but *feel* to the participants as if they have a direct effect. Dancing on silos does not get rid of them.

But it does attract media and public attention to them. The women at Greenham have forced the media to focus on the nuclear issue and have mobilized public opinion all over the country. It is here that the emphasis on the family, parenthood and people's individual responsibilities becomes so effective: turning society's own values against itself, showing how the Government's policies undermine and threaten those very institutions and relations it claims to cherish – the family unit and parental control. When Mrs Thatcher announces that parents should take more responsibility for their children, and a mother can reply that she is doing just that by fighting against nuclear weapons, there is a publicity score for the anti-nuclear movement that Saatchi and Saatchi would be glad to have thought up. As one woman says: 'I've got two young children, and I've taken responsibility for their passage into adulthood. Everyone tells me they are my responsibility. The Government tells me this. It is my responsibility to create a world fit for them to grow up in. I can't say I'm responsible for my children not catching whooping cough and *not* responsible for doing anything about the threat of annihilation which hangs over them . . .'. Babies with badges, women holding hands in non-violent (and essentially non-effective) protest – all these are the perfect media images to catch the sympathy of any 'feeling person' and to illustrate the essential righteousness of the anti-nuclear cause. Such an important and broad-based campaign has to tap whatever popular sentiments it can to gain support; and the nuclear family is a highly efficient propaganda weapon. But do we really need to believe our own propaganda? The Government constructs its defence of missile policies (cf. party political broadcasts and 'The Peace Game') in the form of advertisements, complete with persuasive male voice-over selling us the nuclear detergent to protect our homes and children.

If we are to meet them on their own ground, let us at least do it with our eyes wide open.

NOTES

1 The editors and publishers gratefully acknowledge the permission of Marion Boyars Publishers (London, New York) © 1986 to reproduce J. Williamson's 'Nuclear Family? No Thanks' from *Consuming Passions: The Dynamics of Popular Culture*.
2 Quoted in Alice Cook and Gwyn Kirk *Greenham Women Everywhere*. All further quotes below are taken from different women's accounts collected in this book. They are not quotations from the authors.

16

Seyla Benhabib
b.1950

'THE GENERALIZED AND THE CONCRETE OTHER' from
SEYLA BENHABIB AND DRUCILLA CORNELL (EDS),
FEMINISM AS CRITIQUE (1987)

The context for this essay was created by the contribution of psychologist Carol Gilligan to the theory of cognitive moral development associated with Jean Piaget and Lawrence Kohlberg. (Piaget's The Moral Judgement of the Child, *1932, postulated a fixed sequence of developmental stages through which we move towards an ever-greater reliance on abstract concepts such as those of justice, right and duty.) Empirical research based on this theory has revealed women's habits of moral reasoning as on the whole more 'primitive' than men's: women emerge as less concerned with principle, less fully emancipated from the tendency to respond intuitively to particular moral situations. Gilligan's findings, recorded in her book* In a Different Voice *(1982), conformed to this pattern; but her interpretation was novel in that she rejected the usual negative evaluation of feminine difference, arguing instead that the privileging of abstract, legalistic reasoning within the developmental model was a reflection of male gender privilege. The overall effect of her work, therefore, is to recommend a revision of our conception of maturity in moral judgement – an acknowledgement that sensitivity to the particular situation is a mark of cognitive strength, not weakness. And this is a feminist intervention in the sense that it represents women's strong suit in moral judgement no longer as incidental, but as essential to the matter in hand.*

Seyla Benhabib teaches political science and philosophy at the New School for Social Research, New York. This example of her work is an exercise in feminist ideological critique, directed at once against the bourgeois and patriarchal assumptions of liberal political theory and against the Piaget-Kohlberg model of moral development. Benhabib interprets the latter tradition in terms of the former, noting the survival in Kohlberg of the privilege assigned by liberalism to abstract universality, i.e. to the attempt to mediate between conflicting private interests by recourse to principles which can be grasped without reference to concrete individual differences.

Benhabib's 'generalized other' is a fellow-citizen pictured simply as a bearer of rights, duties and moral dignity: the historical process which has produced just these human beings with their own peculiar needs and desires, these 'concrete others', is systematically ignored by the tradition which has given us such epistemological devices as the social contract, the general will, the categorical imperative and the 'veil of ignorance'. This neglect, Benhabib suggests, is non-accidentally related to the way in which the Kohlberg doctrine undervalues the appreciation of contextual detail: each body of theory orders its subject-matter in terms of a conceptual hierarchy which subordinates 'feminine' matter (the concrete) to 'masculine' form (the abstract).

But in addition to these informal accusations of gender bias, the liberal tradition of abstract universalism is open to a more technical charge of incoherence. How can the idea of merely numerical distinctness – of a plurality of human units stripped of everything which constitutes our actual *moral difference from one another – do justice to the process of securing harmony between individual wills? Benhabib's constructive proposal is that we should develop a moral epistemology regulated, as in liberalism, by the ideal of universality, but responsible also to the concrete reality of all the individual lives which a different (and better) social order would have to bind together. If we want to know what sort of social order might qualify as 'acceptable to any rational being', the way to find out is not by purely* a priori *methods but by consenting to learn, discursively or 'dialogically', what the 'otherness' of other people consists in. Women, like all socially subordinate groups, have an interest in the success of this argument, for the refusal of consideration to our 'concrete otherness' lies at the heart of patriarchal ideology.*

Can there be a feminist contribution to moral philosophy?[1] That is to say, can those men and women who view the gender–sex system of our societies as oppressive, and who regard women's emancipation as essential to human liberation, criticize, analyse and when necessary replace the traditional categories of moral philosophy in order to contribute to women's emancipation and human liberation? By focusing on the controversy generated by Carol Gilligan's work, this chapter seeks to outline such a feminist contribution to moral philosophy.[2]

1   The Kohlberg–Gilligan Controversy

Carol Gilligan's research in cognitive, developmental moral psychology recapitulates a pattern made familiar to us by Thomas Kuhn.[3] Noting a discrepancy between the claims of the original research paradigm and the data, Gilligan and her coworkers first extend this paradigm to accommodate anomalous results. This extension then allows them to see some other problems in a new light; subsequently, the basic paradigm, namely, the study of the development of moral judgement, according to Lawrence Kohlberg's model, is fundamentally revised. Gilligan and her coworkers now maintain that Kohlbergian theory is valid only for measuring the development of one aspect of moral orientation, which focuses on the ethics of justice and rights.

In a 1980 article on 'Moral Development in Late Adolescence and Adulthood: A Critique and Reconstruction of Kohlberg's Theory', Murphy and Gilligan note that moral-judgement data from a longitudinal study of 26 undergraduates scored by Kohlberg's revised manual replicate his original findings that a significant percentage of subjects appear to regress from adolescence to adulthood.[4] The persistence of this relativistic regression suggests a need to revise the theory. In this article they propose a distinction between 'postconventional formalism' and 'postconventional contextualism'. While the [first][5] postconventional type of reasoning solves the problem of relativism by constructing a system that derives a solution to all moral problems from concepts like social contract or natural rights, the second approach finds the solution in that 'while no answer may be objectively right in the sense of being context-free, some answers and some ways of thinking are better than others.'[6] The extension of the original paradigm from postconventional formalist to postconventional contextual then leads Gilligan to see some other discrepancies in the theory in a new light, and most notably among these, women's persistently low score when compared with their male peers. Distinguishing between the ethics of justice and rights and the ethics of care and responsibility allows her to account for women's moral development and the cognitive skills they show in a new way. Women's moral judgement is more contextual, more immersed in the details of relationships and narratives. It shows a greater propensity to take the standpoint of the 'particular other', and women appear more adept at revealing feelings of empathy and sympathy required by this. Once these cognitive characteristics are seen not as deficiencies, but as essential components of adult moral reasoning at the postconventional stage, then women's apparent moral confusion of judgement becomes a sign of their strength. Agreeing with Piaget that a developmental theory hangs from its vertex of maturity, 'the point towards which progress is traced', a change in 'the definition of maturity', writes Gilligan, 'does not simply alter the description of the highest stage but recasts the understanding of development, changing the entire account.'[7] The contextuality, narrativity and specificity of women's moral judgement is not a sign of weakness or deficiency, but a manifestation of a vision of moral maturity that views the self as a being immersed in a network of relationships with others. According to this vision, the respect for each other's needs and the mutuality of effort to satisfy them sustain moral growth and development.

When confronted with such a challenge, it is common that adherents of an old research paradigm respond by arguing

(a) that the data base does not support the conclusions drawn by revisionists;
(b) that some of the new conclusions can be accommodated by the old theory; and
(c) that the new and old paradigms have different object domains and are not concerned with explaining the same phenomena after all.

In his response to Gilligan, Kohlberg has followed all three alternatives.

(a) The data base In his 1984 'Synopses and Detailed Replies to Critics', Kohlberg argues that available data on cognitive moral

development does not report differences among children and adolescents of both sexes with respect to justice reasoning.[8] 'The only studies', he writes, 'showing fairly frequent sex differences are those of adults, usually of spouse housewives. Many of the studies comparing adult males and females without controlling for education and job differences... do report sex differences in favor of males'.[9] Kohlberg maintains that these latter findings are not incompatible with his theory.[10] For, according to this theory, the attainment of stages four and five depends upon experiences of participation, responsibility and role taking in the secondary institutions of society such as the workplace and government, from which women have been and still are to a large extent excluded. The data, he concludes, does not damage the validity of his theory but shows the necessity for controlling for such factors as education and employment when assessing sex differences in adult moral reasoning.

(b) Accommodation within the old theory Kohlberg now agrees with Gilligan that 'the acknowledgement of an orientation of care and response usefully enlarges the moral domain.'[11] In his view, though, justice and rights, care and responsibility, are not two *tracks* of moral development, but two moral *orientations*. The rights orientation and the care orientation are not bipolar or dichotomous. Rather, the care-and-response orientation is directed primarily to relations of special obligation to family, friends and group members, 'relations which often include or presuppose general obligations of respect, fairness and contract'.[12] Kohlberg resists the conclusion that these differences are strongly 'sex related'; instead, he views the choice of orientation 'to be primarily a function of setting and dilemma, not sex'.[13]

(c) Object domain of the two theories In an earlier response to Gilligan, Kohlberg had argued as follows:

Carol Gilligan's ideas, while interesting, were not really welcome to us, for two reasons... The latter, we thought, was grist for Jane Loewinger's mill in studying stages of ego development, but not for studying the specifically moral dimension in reasoning... Following Piaget, my colleagues and I have had the greatest confidence that reasoning about justice would

lend itself to a formal structuralist or rationalist analysis . . .
whereas questions about the nature of the 'good life' have not
been as amenable to this type of statement.[14]

In his 1984 reply to his critics, this distinction between moral and
ego development is refined further. Kohlberg divides the ego domain
into the cognitive, interpersonal and moral functions.[15] Since, however, ego development is a necessary but not sufficient condition for
moral development, in his view the latter can be studied independently of the former. In light of this clarification, Kohlberg regards
Murphy's and Gilligan's stage of 'postconventional contextualism' as
one more concerned with questions of ego as opposed to moral
development. While not wanting to maintain that the acquisition
of moral competencies ends with reaching adulthood, Kohlberg
nevertheless insists that adult moral and ego development studies
only reveal the presence of 'soft' as opposed to 'hard' stages. The
latter are irreversible in sequence and integrally related to one another
in the sense that a subsequent stage grows out of, and presents a
better solution to problems confronted at, an earlier stage.[16]

It will be up to latter-day historians of science to decide whether,
with these admissions and qualifications, Kohlbergian theory has
entered the phase of 'ad-hocism', in Imre Lakatos's words,[17] or
whether Gilligan's challenge, as well as that of other critics, has
moved this research paradigm to a new phase, in which new problems and conceptualizations will lead to more fruitful results.

What concerns me in this chapter is the question: what can feminist theory contribute to this debate? Since Kohlberg himself regards an interaction between normative philosophy and the empirical
study of moral development as essential to his theory, the insights of
contemporary feminist theory and philosophy can be brought to bear
upon some aspects of his theory. I want to define two premises as
constituents of feminist theorizing. First, for feminist theory the
gender–sex system is not a contingent but an essential way in which
social reality is organized, symbolically divided and lived through
experientially. By the 'gender–sex' system I understand the social–
historical, symbolic constitution, and interpretation of the anatomical
differences of the sexes. The gender–sex system is the grid through
which the self develops an *embodied* identity, a certain mode of being
in one's body and of living the body. The self becomes an I in that

it appropriates from the human community a mode of psychically, socially and symbolically experiencing its bodily identity. The gender–sex system is the grid through which societies and cultures reproduce embodied individuals.[18]

Second, the historically known gender–sex systems have contributed to the oppression and exploitation of women. The task of feminist critical theory is to uncover this fact, and to develop a theory that is emancipatory and reflective, and which can aid women in their struggles to overcome oppression and exploitation. Feminist theory can contribute to this task in two ways: by developing an *explanatory–diagnostic analysis* of women's oppression across history, culture and societies, and by articulating an *anticipatory–utopian critique* of the norms and values of our current society and culture, such as to project new modes of togetherness, of relating to ourselves and to nature in the future. Whereas the first aspect of feminist theory requires critical, social-scientific research, the second is primarily normative and philosophical: it involves the clarification of moral and political principles, both at the meta-ethical level with respect to their *logic of justification* and at the substantive, normative level with reference to their concrete content.[19]

In this chapter I shall be concerned with articulating such an anticipatory-utopian critique of universalistic moral theories from a feminist perspective. I want to argue that the *definition* of the moral domain, as well as the ideal of *moral autonomy*, not only in Kohlberg's theory but in universalistic, contractarian theories from Hobbes to Rawls, lead to a *privatization* of women's experience and to the exclusion of its consideration from a moral point of view (part 2). In this tradition, the moral self is viewed as a *disembedded* and *disembodied* being. This conception of the self reflects aspects of male experience; the 'relevant other' in this theory is never the sister but always the brother. This vision of the self, I want to claim, is incompatible with the very criteria of reversibility and universalizability advocated by defenders of universalism. A universalistic moral theory restricted to the standpoint of the 'generalized other' falls into epistemic incoherencies that jeopardize its claim to adequately fulfil reversibility and universalizability (part 3).

Universalistic moral theories in the Western tradition from Hobbes to Rawls are *substitutionalist*, in the sense that the universalism they defend is defined surreptitiously by identifying the experiences of a specific group of subjects as the paradigmatic case of the human as such. These subjects are invariably white, male adults who are propertied or at least professional. I want to distinguish *substitutionalist* from *interactive* universalism. Interactive universalism acknowledges the plurality of modes of being human, and differences among humans, without endorsing all these pluralities and differences as morally and politically valid. While agreeing that normative disputes can be settled rationally, and that fairness, reciprocity and some procedure of universalizability are constituents, that is, necessary conditions of the moral standpoint, interactive universalism regards difference as a starting-point for reflection and action. In this sense 'universality' is a regulative ideal that does not deny our embodied and embedded identity, but aims at developing moral attitudes and encouraging political transformations that can yield a point of view acceptable to all. Universality is not the ideal consensus of fictitiously defined selves, but the concrete process in politics and morals of the struggle of concrete, embodied selves, striving for autonomy.

2 *Justice and the Autonomous Self in Social Contract Theories*

Kohlberg defines the privileged object domain of moral philosophy and psychology as follows:

> We say that *moral* judgements or principles have the central function of resolving interpersonal or social conflicts, that is, conflicts of claims or rights . . . Thus moral judgements and principles imply a notion of equilibrium, or reversibility of claims. In this sense they ultimately involve some reference to justice, at least insofar as they define 'hard' structural stages.[20]

Kohlberg's conception of the moral domain is based upon a strong differentiation between justice and the good life.[21] This is also one of the cornerstones of his critique of Gilligan. Although acknowledging that Gilligan's elucidation of a care-and-responsibility orientation 'usefully enlarges the moral domain',[22] Kohlberg defines the domain of *special relationships of obligation* to which care and responsibility are oriented as follows: 'the spheres of kinship, love, friendship, and sex that elicit considerations of care are usually understood to be spheres of personal decision-making, as are, for instance, the problems of marriage and divorce.'[23] The care orientation is said thus to concern domains that are more 'personal' than 'moral in the sense of the formal point of view'.[24] Questions of the good life, pertaining to the nature of our relationships of kinship, love, friendship and sex, on the one hand, are included in the moral domain but, on the other hand, are named 'personal' as opposed to 'moral' issues.

Kohlberg proceeds from a definition of morality that begins with Hobbes, in the wake of the dissolution of the Aristotelian–Christian world-view. Ancient and medieval moral systems, by contrast, show the following structure: a definition of man-as-he-ought-to-be, a definition of man-as-he-is, and the articulation of a set of rules or precepts that can lead man as he is into what he ought to be.[25] In such moral systems, the rules which govern just relations among the human community are embedded in a more encompassing conception of the good life. This good life, the *telos* of man, is defined ontologically with reference to man's place in the cosmos.

The destruction of the ancient and medieval teleological conception of nature through the attack of medieval nominalism and modern science, the emergence of capitalist exchange relations and the subsequent division of the social structure into the economy, the polity, civil associations and the domestic-intimate sphere, radically alters moral theory. Modern theorists claim that the ultimate purposes of nature are unknown. Morality is thus emancipated from cosmology and from an all-encompassing world-view that normatively limits man's relation to nature. The distinction between justice and the good life, as it is formulated by early contract theorists, aims at defending this privacy and autonomy of the self, first in the religious sphere and then in the scientific and philosophical spheres of 'free thought' as well.

Justice alone becomes the centre of moral theory when bourgeois individuals in a disenchanted universe face the task of creating the legitimate basis of the social order for themselves. What 'ought' to be is now defined as what all would have rationally to agree to in order to ensure civil peace and prosperity (Hobbes, Locke), or the 'ought' is derived from the rational form of the moral law alone (Rousseau, Kant). As long as the social bases of co-operation and the rights claims of individuals are respected, the autonomous bourgeois subject can define the good life as his mind and conscience dictate.

The transition to modernity does not only privatize the self's relation to the cosmos and to ultimate questions of religion and being. First with Western modernity the conception of privacy is so enlarged that an intimate domestic-familial sphere is subsumed under it. Relations of 'kinship, friendship, love, and sex', indeed, as Kohlberg takes them to be, come to be viewed as spheres of 'personal decision-making'. At the beginning of modern moral and political theory, however, the 'personal' nature of the spheres does not mean the recognition of equal, female autonomy, but rather the removal of gender relations from the sphere of justice. While the bourgeois male celebrates his transition from conventional to post-conventional morality, from socially accepted rules of justice to their generation in light of the principles of a social contract, the domestic sphere remains at the conventional level. The sphere of justice from Hobbes through Locke and Kant is regarded as the domain where independent, male heads of household transact with one another, while the domestic-intimate sphere is put beyond the pale of justice and restricted to the reproductive and affective needs of the bourgeois paterfamilias. Agnes Heller has named this domain the 'household of the emotions'.[26] An entire domain of human activity, namely, nurture, reproduction, love and care, which becomes the woman's lot in the course of the development of modern, bourgeois society, is excluded from moral and political considerations, and relegated to the realm of 'nature'.

Through a brief historical genealogy of social contract theories, I want to examine the distinction between justice and the good life as it is translated into the split between the public and the domestic. This analysis will also allow us to see the implicit ideal of autonomy cherished by this tradition.

At the beginning of modern moral and political philosophy stands a powerful metaphor: the 'state of nature'. This metaphor is at times said to be fact. Thus, in his *Second Treatise of Civil Government*, John Locke reminds us of 'the two men in the desert island, mentioned by Garcilasso de la Vega . . . or a Swiss and an Indian, in the woods of America'.[27] At other times it is acknowledged as fiction. Thus, Kant dismisses the colourful reveries of his predecessors and transforms the 'state of nature' from an empirical fact into a transcendental concept. The state of nature comes to represent the idea of *Privatrecht*, under which are subsumed the right of property and 'thinglike rights of a personal nature' (*'auf dingliche Natur persönliche Rechte'*), which the male head of a household exercises over his wife, children and servants.[28] Only Thomas Hobbes compounds fact and fiction, and against those who consider it strange 'that Nature should thus dissociate, and render men apt to invade, and destroy one another',[29] he asks each man who does not trust 'this Inference, made from the passions', to reflect why 'when taking a journey, he arms himself, and seeks to go well accompanied; when going to sleep, he lockes his dores; when even in his house he lockes his chests . . . Does he not there as much accuse mankind by his actions, as I do by my words?'[30] The state of nature is the looking-glass of these early bourgeois thinkers in which they and their societies are magnified, purified and reflected in their original, naked verity. The state of nature is both nightmare (Hobbes) and utopia (Rousseau). In it the bourgeois male recognizes his flaws, fears and anxieties, as well as dreams.

The varying content of this metaphor is less significant than its simple and profound message: in the beginning man was alone. Again it is Hobbes who gives this thought its clearest formulation. 'Let us consider men . . . as if but even now sprung out of the earth, and suddenly, like mushrooms, come to full maturity, without all kind of engagement to each other.'[31] This vision of men as mushrooms is an ultimate picture of autonomy. The female, the mother of whom every individual is born, is now replaced by the earth. The denial of being born of woman frees the male ego from the most natural and basic bond of dependence. Nor is the picture very different for Rousseau's noble savage who, wandering wantonly through the woods, occasionally mates with a female and then seeks rest.[32]

The state-of-nature metaphor provides a vision of the autonomous self: this is a narcissist who sees the world in his own image; who has no awareness of the limits of his own desires and passions; and who cannot see himself through the eyes of another. The narcissism of this sovereign self is destroyed by the presence of the other. As Hegel expresses it:

Self-consciousness is faced by another self-consciousness; it has come *out of itself*. This has a twofold significance: first, it has *lost* itself, for it finds itself as an *other* being; secondly, in doing so it has superseded the other, for it does not see the other as an essential being, but in the other sees its own self.[33]

The story of the autonomous male ego is the saga of this initial sense of *loss* in confrontation with the other, and the gradual recovery from this original narcissistic wound through the sobering experience of war, fear, domination, anxiety and death. The last instalment in this drama is the social contract: the establishment of the law to govern all. Having been thrust out of their narcissistic universe into a world of insecurity by their sibling brothers, these individuals have to reestablish the authority of the father in the image of the law. The early bourgeois individual not only has no mother but no father as well; rather, he strives to reconstitute the father in his own self-image. What is usually celebrated in the annals of modern moral and political theory as the dawn of liberty is precisely this destruction of political patriarchy in bourgeois society.

The constitution of political authority civilizes sibling rivalry by turning their attention from war to property, from vanity to science, from conquest to luxury. The original narcissism is not transformed; only now ego boundaries are clearly defined. The law reduces insecurity, the fear of being engulfed by the other, by defining mine and thine. Jealousy is not eliminated but tamed; as long as each can keep what is his and attain more by fair rules of the game, he is entitled to it. Competition is domesticized and channeled towards acquisition. The law contains anxiety by defining rigidly the boundaries between self and other, but the law does not cure anxiety. The anxiety that the other is always on the lookout to interfere in your space and appropriate what is yours; the anxiety that you will be subordinated to his will; the anxiety that a group of brothers will usurp the law in the name of the 'will of all' and destroy 'the general will', the will of the absent father, remains. The law teaches how to repress anxiety and to sober narcissism, but the constitution of the self is not altered. The establishment of private rights and duties does not overcome the inner wounds of the self; it only forces them to become less destructive.

This imaginary of early moral and political theory has had an amazing hold upon the modern consciousness. From Freud to Piaget, the relationship to the brother is viewed as the humanizing experience that teaches us to become social, responsible adults.[34] As a result of the hold of this metaphor upon our imagination, we have also come to inherit a number of philosophical prejudices. For Rawls and Kohlberg, as well, the autonomous self is disembedded and disembodied; moral impartiality is learning to recognize the claims of the other who is just like oneself; fairness is public justice; a public system of rights and duties is the best way to arbitrate conflict, to distribute rewards and to establish claims.

Yet this is a strange world; it is one in which individuals are grown up before they have been born; in which boys are men before they have been children; a world where neither mother, nor sister, nor wife exist. The question is less what Hobbes says about men and women, or what Rousseau sees the role of Sophie to be in Emile's education. The point is that in this universe, the experience of the early modern female has no place. Woman is simply what men are not; namely, they are not autonomous, independent, but by the same token, nonaggressive but nurturant, not competitive but giving, not public but private. The world of the female is constituted by a series of negations. She is simply what he happens not to be. Her identity becomes defined by a lack – the lack of autonomy, the lack of independence, the lack of the phallus. The narcissistic male takes her to be just like himself, only his opposite.

It is not the misogynist prejudices of early modern moral and political theory alone that lead to women's exclusion. It is the very constitution of a sphere of discourse which bans the female from history to the realm of nature, from the light of the public to the interior of the household, from the civilizing effect of culture to the repetitious burden of nurture and reproduction. The public sphere, the sphere of justice, moves into historicity, whereas the private sphere, the sphere of care and intimacy, is unchanging and timeless. It pulls us toward the earth even when we, as Hobbesian mush-rooms, strive to pull away from it. The dehistoricization of the private realm signifies that, as the male ego celebrates his passage from nature to culture, from conflict to consensus, women remain in a timeless universe, condemned to repeat the cycles of life.

This split between the public sphere of justice, in which history is made, and the atemporal realm of the household, in which life is reproduced, is internalized by the male ego. The dichotomies are not only without but within. He himself is divided into the public person and the private individual. Within his chest clash the law of reason and the inclination of nature, the brilliance of cognition and the obscurity of emotion. Caught between the moral law and the starry heaven above and the earthly body below,[35] the autonomous self

strives for unity. But the antagonism – between autonomy and nurturance, independence and bonding, sovereignty of the self and
relations to others – remains. In the discourse of modern moral and
political theory, these dichotomies are reified as being essential to the
constitution of the self. While men humanize outer nature through
labour, inner nature remains ahistorical, dark and obscure. I want to
suggest that contemporary universalist moral theory has inherited
this dichotomy between autonomy and nurturance, independence
and bonding, the sphere of justice and the domestic, personal realm.
This becomes most visible in its attempt to restrict the moral point of
view to the perspective of the 'generalized other'.

3   The Generalized vs the Concrete Order

Let me describe two conceptions of self–other relations that delin-
eate both moral perspectives and interactional structures. I shall
name the first the standpoint of the 'generalized'[36] and the second
that of the 'concrete' other. In contemporary moral theory these
conceptions are viewed as incompatible, even as antagonistic. These
two perspectives reflect the dichotomies and splits of early modern
moral and political theory between autonomy and nurturance, independence and bonding, the public and the domestic, and more
broadly, between justice and the good life. The content of the
generalized as well as the concrete other is shaped by this dichotomous characterization, which we have inherited from the modern
tradition.

The standpoint of the generalized other requires us to view each
and every individual as a rational being entitled to the same rights
and duties we would want to ascribe to ourselves. In assuming the
standpoint, we abstract from the individuality and concrete identity
of the other. We assume that the other, like ourselves, is a being who
has concrete needs, desires and affects, but that what constitutes his
or her moral dignity is not what differentiates us from each other,
but rather what we, as speaking and acting rational agents, have
in common. Our relation to the other is governed by the norms
of *formal equality* and *reciprocity*: each is entitled to expect and to
assume from us what we can expect and assume from him or her.
The norms of our interactions are primarily public and institutional

ones. If I have a right to X, then you have the duty not to hinder me from enjoying X and conversely. In treating you in accordance with these norms, I confirm in your person the rights of humanity and I have a legitimate claim to expect that you will do the same in relation to me. The moral categories that accompany such interactions are those of right, obligation and entitlement, and the corresponding moral feelings are those of respect, duty, worthiness and dignity.

The standpoint of the concrete other, by contrast, requires us to view each and every rational being as an individual with a concrete history, identity and affective-emotional constitution. In assuming this standpoint, we abstract from what constitutes our commonality. We seek to comprehend the needs of the other, his or her motivations, what s/he searches for, and what s/he desires. Our relation to the other is governed by the norms of *equity* and *complementary reciprocity*: each is entitled to expect and to assume from the other forms of behaviour through which the other feels recognized and confirmed as a concrete, individual being with specific needs, talents and capacities. Our differences in this case complement rather than exclude one another. The norms of our interaction are usually private, noninstitutional ones. They are norms of friendship, love and care. These norms require in various ways that I exhibit more than the simple assertion of my rights and duties in the face of your needs. In treating you in accordance with the norms of friendship, love and care, I confirm not only your *humanity* but your human *individuality*. The moral categories that accompany such interactions are those of responsibility, bonding and sharing. The corresponding moral feelings are those of love, care and sympathy and solidarity.

In contemporary universalist moral psychology and moral theory, it is the viewpoint of the 'generalized other' that predominates. In his article on 'Justice as Reversibility: The Claim to Moral Adequacy of a Highest Stage of Moral Development', for example, Kohlberg argues that:

> [M]oral judgements involve role-taking, taking the viewpoint of the others conceived as *subjects* and coordinating these viewpoints . . . Second, equilibriated moral judgements involve principles of justice or fairness. A moral situation in disequilibrium is one in which there are unresolved, conflicting claims.

A resolution of the situation is one in which each is 'given his due' according to some principle of justice that can be recognized as fair by all the conflicting parties involved.[37]

Kohlberg regards Rawls's concept of 'reflective equilibrium' as a parallel formulation of the basic idea of reciprocity, equality and fairness intrinsic to all moral judgements. The Rawlsian 'veil of ignorance', in Kohlberg's judgement, not only exemplifies the formalist idea of universalizability but that of perfect *reversibility* as well.[38] The idea behind the veil of ignorance is described as follows: 'The decider is to initially decide from a point of view *that ignores his identity* (veil of ignorance) under the assumption that decisions are governed by maximizing values from a viewpoint of rational egoism in considering each party's interest.'[39]

What I would like to question is the assumption that 'taking the viewpoint of others' is truly compatible with this notion of fairness as reasoning behind a 'veil of ignorance'.[40] The problem is that the defensible kernel of the ideas of reciprocity and fairness are thereby identified with the perspective of the disembedded and disembodied generalized other. Now since Kohlberg presents his research subjects with hypothetically constructed moral dilemmas, it may be thought that his conception of 'taking the standpoint of the other' is not subject to the epistemic restrictions that apply to the Rawlsian original position. Subjects in Kohlbergian interviews do not stand behind a veil of ignorance. However, the very *language* in which Kohlbergian dilemmas are presented incorporates these epistemic restrictions. For example, in the famous Heinz dilemma, as in others, the motivations of the druggist as a concrete individual, as well as the history of the individuals involved, are excluded as irrelevant to the definition of the moral problem at hand. In these dilemmas, individuals and their moral positions are represented by abstracting from the narrative history of the self and its motivations. Gilligan also notes that the implicit moral epistemology of Kohlbergian dilemmas frustrates women, who want to phrase these hypothetical dilemmas in a more contextual voice, attuned to the standpoint of the concrete other. The result is that

> though several of the women in the abortion study clearly articulate a postconventional metaethical position, none of them

are considered principled in their normative moral judgements of Kohlberg's hypothetical dilemmas. Instead, the women's judgements point toward an identification of the violence inherent in the dilemma itself, which is seen to compromise the justice of any of its possible resolutions.[41]

Through an immanent critique of the theories of Kohlberg and Rawls, I want to show that ignoring the standpoint of the concrete other leads to epistemic incoherence in universalistic moral theories. The problem can be stated as follows: according to Kohlberg and Rawls, moral reciprocity involves the capacity to take the standpoint of the other, to put oneself imaginatively in the place of the other, but under conditions of the 'veil of ignorance', the *other as different from the self* disappears. Unlike in previous contract theories, in this case the other is not constituted through projection, but as a consequence of total abstraction from his or her identity. Differences are not denied; they become irrelevant. The Rawlsian self does not know

> his place in society, his class position or status; nor does he know his fortune in the distribution of natural assets and abilities, his intelligence and strength, and the like. Nor, again, does anyone know his conception of the good, the particulars of his rational plan of life, or even the special features of his psychology such as his aversion to risk or liability to optimism or pessimism.[42]

Let us ignore for a moment whether such selves who also do not know 'the particular circumstances of their own society' can know anything at all that is relevant to the human condition, and ask instead, are these individuals *human selves* at all? In his attempt to do justice to Kant's conception of noumenal agency, Rawls recapitulates a basic problem with the Kantian conception of the self, namely, that noumenal selves cannot be *individuated*. If all that belongs to them as embodied, affective, suffering creatures, their memory and history, their ties and relations to others, are to be subsumed under the phenomenal realm, then what we are left with is an empty mask that is everyone and no one. Michael Sandel points out that the difficulty in Rawls's conception derives from his attempt to be consistent with the Kantian concept of the autonomous self, as a being freely choosing his or her own ends in life.[43] However, this moral and political concept of autonomy slips into a metaphysics according to which it is meaningful to define a self independently of *all* the ends it may choose and all and any conceptions of the good it may hold.[44] At this point we must ask whether the *identity* of any human self can be defined with reference to its capacity for agency alone. Identity does not refer to my potential for choice alone, but to the actuality of my choices, namely, to how I as a finite, concrete, embodied individual, shape and fashion the circumstances of my birth and family, linguistic, cultural and gender identity into a coherent narrative that stands as my life's story. Indeed, if we recall that every autonomous being is one born of others and not, as Rawls, following Hobbes, assumes, a being 'not bound by prior moral ties to another',[45] the question becomes: how does this finite, embodied creature constitute into a coherent narrative those episodes of choice and limit, agency and suffering, initiative and dependence? The self is not a thing, a substrate, but the protagonist of a life's tale. The conception of selves who can be individuated prior to their moral ends is incoherent. We could not know if such a being was a human self, an angel or the Holy Spirit.

If this concept of the self as mushroom, behind a veil of ignorance, is incoherent, then it follows that there is no real *plurality* of perspectives in the Rawlsian original position, but only a *definitional identity*. For Rawls, as Sandel observes, 'our individuating characteristics are given empirically, by the distinctive concatenation of wants and desires, aims and attributes, purposes and ends that come to characterize human beings in their particularity'.[46] But how are we supposed to know what these wants and desires are independently of knowing something about the person who holds these wants, desires, aims and attributes? Is there perhaps an 'essence' of anger that is the same for each angry individual; an essence of ambition that is distinct from ambitious selves? I fail to see how individuating characteristics can be ascribed to a transcendental self who can have any and none of these, who can be all or none of them.

If selves who are epistemologically and metaphysically prior to their individuating characteristics, as Rawls takes them to be, cannot be human selves at all; if, therefore, there is no human *plurality* behind the veil of ignorance but only *definitional identity*, then this has consequences for criteria of reversibility and universalizability said to be constituents of the moral point of view. Definitional identity leads to *incomplete reversibility*, for the primary requisite of reversibility, namely, a coherent distinction between me and you, the self and the other, cannot be sustained under these circumstances. Under conditions of the veil of ignorance, the other disappears.

It is no longer plausible to maintain that such a standpoint can universalize adequately. Kohlberg views the veil of ignorance not only as exemplifying reversibility but universalizability as well. This is the idea that 'we must be willing to live with our judgement or decision when we trade places with others in the situation being judged'.[47] But the question is, *which* situation? Can moral situations be individuated independently of our knowledge of the agents involved in these situations, of their histories, attitudes, characters and desires? Can I describe a situation as one of arrogance or hurt pride without knowing something about you as a concrete other? Can I know how to distinguish between a breach of confidence and a harmless slip of the tongue, without knowing your history and your character? Moral situations, like moral emotions and attitudes, can only be individuated if they are evaluated in light of our knowledge of the history of the agents involved in them.

While every procedure of universalizability presupposes that 'like cases ought to be treated alike' or that I should act in such a way I should also be willing that all others in a like situation act like me, the most difficult aspect of any such procedure is to know what constitutes a 'like' situation or what it would mean for another to be exactly in a situation like mine. Such a process of reasoning, to be at all viable, must involve the viewpoint of the concrete other, for situations, to paraphrase Stanley Cavell, do not come like 'envelopes and golden finches', ready for definition and description, 'nor like apples ripe for grading'.[48] When we morally disagree, for example, we do not only disagree about the principles involved; very often we disagree because what I see as a lack of generosity on your part you construe as your legitimate right not to do something; we disagree because what you see as jealousy on my part I view as my desire to have more of your attention. Universalistic moral theory neglects such everyday, interactional morality and assumes that the public standpoint of justice, and our quasi-public personalities as right-bearing individuals, are the center of moral theory.[49]

Kohlberg emphasizes the dimension of ideal role-taking or taking the viewpoint of the other in moral judgement. Because he defines the other as the generalized other, however, he perpetuates one of the fundamental errors of Kantian moral theory. Kant's error was to assume that I, as a pure rational agent reasoning for myself, could reach a conclusion that would be acceptable for all at all times and places.[50] In Kantian moral theory, moral agents are like geometricians in different rooms who, reasoning alone for themselves, all arrive at the same solution to a problem. Following Habermas, I want to name this the 'monological' model of moral reasoning. In so far as he interprets ideal role-taking in the light of Rawls's concept of a 'veil of ignorance', Kohlberg as well sees the silent thought process of a single self who imaginatively puts himself in the position of the other as the most adequate form of moral judgement.

I conclude that a definition of the self that is restricted to the standpoint of the generalized other becomes incoherent and cannot individuate among selves. Without assuming the standpoint of the concrete other, no coherent universalizability test can be carried out, for we lack the necessary epistemic information to judge my moral situation to be 'like' or 'unlike' yours.

4   A Communicative Ethic of Need Interpretations and the Relational Self

In the preceding parts of this chapter I have argued that the distinction between justice and the good life, the restriction of the moral domain to questions of justice, as well as the ideal of moral autonomy in these theories, result in the privatization of women's experience and lead to epistemological blindness toward the concrete other. The consequence of such epistemological blindness is an internal inconsistency in universalistic moral theories, in so far as these define 'taking the standpoint of the other' as essential to the moral point of view. My aim has been to take universalistic moral theories at their word and to show through an immanent critique, first of the 'state of nature' metaphor and then of the 'original position', that the conception of the autonomous self implied by these thought experiments is restricted to the 'generalized other'.

This distinction between the generalized and the concrete other raises questions in moral and political theory. It may be asked whether, without the standpoint of the generalized other, it would be possible to define a moral point of view at all. Since our identities as concrete others are what distinguis us from each other according to gender, race, class, cultural differentials, as well as psychic and natural abilities, would a moral theory restricted to the standpoint of the concrete other not be a racist, sexist, cultural relativist, discriminatory one? Furthermore, without the standpoint of the generalized other, it may be argued, a political theory of justice suited for modern, complex societies is unthinkable. Certainly rights must be an essential component in any such theory. Finally, the perspective of the 'concrete other' defines our relations as private, noninstitutional ones, concerned with love, care, friendship and intimacy. Are these activities so gender-specific? Are we not all 'concrete others'?

The distinction between the 'generalized' and the 'concrete other', as drawn in this chapter so far, is not a *prescriptive* but a *critical* one.[51] My goal is not to prescribe a moral and political theory consonant with the concept of the 'concrete other'. For, indeed, the recognition of the dignity and worthiness of the generalized other is a *necessary*, albeit not *sufficient*, condition to define the moral standpoint in modern societies. In this sense, the concrete other is a critical concept that designates the *ideological* limits of universalistic discourse. It signifies the *unthought*, the *unseen*, and the *unheard* in such theories. This is evidenced by Kohlberg's effort, on the one hand, to enlarge the domain of moral theory such as to include in it relations to the concrete other and, on the other hand, to characterize such special relations of obligation as 'private, personal' matters of evaluative life-choices alone. Urging an examination of this unthought is necessary to prevent the preemption of the discourse of universality by an unexamined particularity. Substitutionalist universalism dismisses the concrete other, while interactive universalism acknowledges that every generalized other is also a concrete other.

From a meta-ethical and normative standpoint, I would argue, therefore, for the validity of a moral theory that allows us to recognize the dignity of the generalized other through an acknowledgement of the moral identity of the concrete other. The point is not to juxtapose the generalized to the concrete other or to see normative validity in one or another standpoint. The point is to think through the ideological limitations and biases that arise in the discourse of universalist morality through this unexamined opposition. I doubt that an easy integration of both points of view, of justice and of care, is possible, without first clarifying the moral framework that would allow us to question both standpoints and their implicit gender presuppositions.

For this task a model of communicative need interpretations suggests itself. Not only is such an ethic, as I interpret it, compatible with the dialogic, interactive generation of universality, but most significant, such an ethic provides the suitable framework within which moral and political agents can define their own concrete identities on the basis of recognizing each other's dignity as generalized others. Questions of the most desirable and just political organization, as well as the distinction between justice and the good life, the public and the domestic, can be analysed, renegotiated and redefined in such a process. Since, however, all those affected are participants in this process, the presumption is that these distinctions cannot be drawn in such a way as to privatize, hide and repress the experiences of those who have suffered under them, for only what all could consensually agree to be in the best interest of each could be accepted as the outcome of this dialogic process.

One consequence of this communicative ethic of need interpretations is that the object domain of moral theory is so enlarged that not only rights but needs, not only justice but possible modes of the good life, are moved into an anticipatory–utopian perspective. What such discourses can generate are not only universalistically prescribable norms, but also intimations of otherness in the present that can lead to the future.

In his current formulation of his theory, Kohlberg accepts this extension of his stage six perspective into an ethic of need interpretations, as suggested first by Habermas.[52] However, he does not see the incompatibility between the communicative ethics model and the Rawlsian 'original position'.[53] In defining reversibility of perspectives, he still considers the Rawlsian position to be paradigmatic.[54] Despite certain shared assumptions, the communicative model of need interpretations and the justice model of the original position need to be distinguished from each other.

First, the condition of ideal role-taking is not to be construed as a *hypothetical* thought process, carried out singly by the moral agent or the moral philosopher, but as an *actual* dialogue situation in which moral agents communicate with one another. Second, it is not necessary to place any epistemic constraints upon such an actual process of moral reasoning and disputation, for the more knowledge is available to moral agents about each other, their history, the particulars of their society, its structure and future, the more rational will be the outcome of their deliberations. Practical rationality entails epistemic rationality as well, and more knowledge rather than less contributes to a more rational and informed judgement. To judge rationally is not to judge as if one did not know what one could know, but to judge in light of all available and relevant information. Third, if there are no knowledge restrictions upon such a discursive situation, then it also follows that there is no privileged subject matter of moral disputation. Moral agents are not only limited to reasoning about primary goods which they are assumed to want whatever else they want. Instead, both the *goods* they desire and their *desires* themselves become legitimate topics of moral disputation. Finally, in such moral discourses agents can also change levels of reflexivity, that is, they can introduce metaconsiderations about the very conditions and constraints under which such dialogue takes place and evaluate their fairness. There is no closure of reflexivity in this model as there is, for example, in the Rawlsian one, which enjoins agents to accept certain rules of the bargaining game prior to the very choice of principles of justice.[55] With regard to the Kohlbergian paradigm, this would mean that moral agents can challenge the relevant *definition* of a moral situation, and urge that this very definition itself become the subject matter of moral reasoning and dispute.

A consequence of this model of communicative ethics would be that the language of rights and duties can now be challenged in light of our need interpretations. Following the tradition of modern social contract theories, Rawls and Kohlberg assume that our affective-emotional constitution, the needs and desires in light of which we formulate our rights and claims, are private matters alone. Their theory of the self, and in particular the Rawlsian metaphysics of the moral agent, do not allow them to view the constitution of our inner nature in *relational* terms.

A relational-interactive theory of identity assumes that inner nature, while being unique, is not an immutable given.[56] Individual need-interpretations and motives carry within them the traces of those early childhood experiences, phantasies, wishes and desires as well as the self-conscious goals of the person. The grammatical logic of the word 'I' reveals the unique structure of ego identity: every subject who uses this concept in relation to herself knows that all other subjects are likewise 'I's. In this respect the self only becomes an I in a community of other selves who are also I's. Every act of self-reference expresses simultaneously the uniqueness and difference of the self as well as the commonality among selves. Discourses about needs and motives unfold in this space created by commonality and uniqueness, generally shared socialization, and the contingency of individual life-histories.

The nonrelational theory of the self, which is privileged in contemporary universalist moral theory, by contrast, removes such need interpretations from the domain of moral discourse. They become 'private', nonformalizable, nonanalyzable and amorphous aspects of our conceptions of the good life. I am not suggesting that such conceptions of the good life either *can* or *should* be universalized, but only that our affective-emotional constitution, as well as our concrete history as moral agents, ought to be considered accessible to moral communication, reflection and transformation. Inner nature, no less than the public sphere of justice, has a historical dimension. In it are intertwined the history of the self and the history of the collective. To condemn it to silence is, as Gilligan has suggested, not to hear that other voice in moral theory. I would say more strongly that such discourse continues women's oppression by privatizing their lot and by excluding from moral theory a central sphere of their activities.

As the Second Wave of the Women's Movement both in Europe and the US has argued, to understand and to combat woman's oppression it is no longer sufficient to demand woman's political and economic emancipation alone; it is also necessary to question those psychosexual relations in the domestic and private spheres within which women's lives unfold, and through which gender identity is reproduced. To explicate woman's oppression it is necessary to uncover the power of those symbols, myths and fantasies that entrap both sexes in the unquestioned world of gender roles. Perhaps one of the most fundamental of these myths and symbols has been the ideal of autonomy conceived in the image of a disembedded and disembodied male ego. This vision of autonomy was and continues to be based upon an implicit politics which defines the domestic, intimate sphere as ahistorical, unchanging and immutable, thereby removing it from reflection and discussion.[57] Needs, as well as emotions and affects, become merely given properties of individuals, which moral philosophy recoils from examining, on the grounds that it may interfere with the autonomy of the sovereign self. Women, because they have been made the 'housekeeper of the emotions' in the modern, bourgeois world, and because they have suffered from the uncomprehended needs and fantasies of the male imagination, which has made them at once into Mother Earth and nagging bitch, the Virgin Mary and the whore, cannot condemn this sphere to silence. What Carol Gilligan has heard are those mutterings, protestations and objections that women, confronted with ways of posing moral dilemmas that seemed alien to them, have voiced. Only if we can understand why their voice has been silenced, and how the dominant ideals of moral autonomy in our culture, as well as the privileged definition of the moral sphere, continue to silence women's voices, do we have a hope of moving to a more integrated vision of ourselves and of our fellow humans as generalized as well as 'concrete' others.

NOTES

1 'The Generalized and the Concrete Other: The Kohlberg-Gilligan Controversy and Feminist Theory' by Seyla Benhabib from *Feminism as Critique* (Eds. Benhabib, S. and Cornell, D.), © Basil Blackwell 1987, is reprinted by kind permission of the author.

2 Earlier versions of this chapter were read at the Conference on 'Women and Morality', SUNY at Stony Brook, 22–4 March 1985, and at the 'Philosophy and Social Science' Course at the Inter-University Center in Dubrovnik, Yugoslavia, 2–4 April 1985. I would like to thank participants at both conferences for their criticisms and suggestions. Larry Blum and Eva Feder Kittay have made valuable suggestions for corrections. Nancy Fraser's commentary on this work, 'Toward a Discourse Ethic of Solidarity', *Praxis International*, 5, 4 (January 1986), 425–30, as well as her paper, 'Feminism and the Social State', *Salmagundi* (forthcoming), have been crucial in helping me articulate the political implications of the position developed here. A slightly altered version of this chapter has appeared in the Proceedings of the Women and Moral Theory Conference, edited by E. F. Kittay and Diana T. Meyers, *Women and Moral Theory* (New Jersey: Rowman and Littlefeld, 1987), pp. 154–78.

3 Thomas Kuhn, *The Structure of Scientific Revolutions*, 2nd edn (Chicago: University of Chicago Press, 1970), pp. 52ff.

4 John Michael Murphy and Carol Gilligan, 'Moral Development in Late Adolescence and Adulthood: A Critique and Reconstruction of Kohlberg's Theory', *Human Development*, 23 (1980), 77–104.

5 Editors' emendation.

6 Murphy and Gilligan, 'Moral Development', p. 83.

7 Carol Gilligan, *In a Different Voice: Psychological Theory and Women's Development* (Cambridge, MA: Harvard University Press, 1982), pp. 18–19.

8 Lawrence Kohlberg, 'Synopses and Detailed Replies to Critics', with Charles Levine and Alexandra Hewer, in L. Kohlberg, *Essays on Moral Development* (San Francisco: Harper and Row, 1984), Vol. II; The Psychology of Moral Development, p. 341.

9 Ibid., p. 347.

10 There still seems to be some question as to how the data on women's moral development is to be interpreted. Studies which focus on late adolescents and adult males and which show sex differences, include J. Fishkin, K. Keniston and C. MacKinnon, 'Moral Reasoning and Political Ideology', *Journal of Personality and Social Psychology*, 27 (1983), 109–19; N. Haan, J. Block and M. B. Smith, 'Moral Reasoning of Young Adults: Political-Social Behavior, Family Background, and Personality Correlates', *Journal of Personality and Social Psychology*, 10 (1968), 184–201; C. Holstein, 'Irreversible, Stepwise Sequence in the Development of Moral Judgment: A Longitudinal Study of Males and Females', *Child Development*, 47 (1976), 51–61. While it is clear that the available evidence does not throw the model of stage-sequence development as such into question, the prevalent presence of sex differences in moral reasoning does raise questions about *what* exactly this model might be measuring. Norma Haan sums up this objection to the Kohlbergian paradigm as follows: 'Thus the moral reasoning of males who live in technical, rationalized societies, who reason at the level of formal operations and who *defensively intellectualize and deny interpersonal and situational detail*, is especially favoured in the Kohlbergian scoring system,' in 'Two Moralities in Action Contexts: Relationships to Thought, Ego Regulation, and Development', *Journal of Personality and Social Psychology*, 36 (1978), 287; emphasis mine. I think Gilligan's studies also support the finding that inappropriate 'intellectualization and denial of interpersonal, situational detail' constitutes one of the major differences in male and female approaches to moral problems. This is why, as I argue in the text, the neat separation between ego and moral development, as drawn by Kohlberg and others, seems inadequate to deal with this problem, since certain ego attitudes – defensiveness, rigidity, inability to empathize, lack of flexibility – do seem to be favoured over others –

nonrepressive attitude towards emotions, flexibility, presence of empathy.

11 Kohlberg, 'Synopses', p. 340.

12 Ibid., p. 350.

13 Ibid., p. 350.

14 L. Kohlberg, 'A Reply to Owen Flanagan and Some Comments on the Puka–Goodpaster Exchange', *Ethics*, 92 (April 1982), 316. Cf. also Gertrud Nunner-Winkler, 'Two Moralities? A Critical Discussion of an Ethic of Care and Responsibility Versus an Ethics of Rights and Justice', in Kurtines and J. L. Gewirtz (eds), *Morality, Moral Behavior and Moral Development* (New York: John Wiley and Sons, 1984), p. 355. It is unclear whether the issue is, as Kohlberg and Nunner-Winkler suggest, one of distinguishing between 'moral' and 'ego' development or whether cognitive-development moral theory does not presuppose a model of ego development which clashes with more psychoanalytically oriented variants. In fact, to combat the charge of 'maturationism' or 'nativism' in his theory, which would imply that moral stages are *a priori* givens of the mind unfolding according to their own logic, regardless of the influence of society or environment upon them Kohlberg argues as follows: 'Stages', he writes, 'are equilibrations arising from interaction between the organism (with its structuring tendencies) and the structure of the environment (physical or social). Universal moral stages are as much a function of universal features of social structure (such as institutions of law, family, property) and social interactions in various cultures, as they are products of the general structuring tendencies of the knowing organism' (Kohlberg, 'A Reply to Owen Flanagan', 521). If this is so, then cognitive-developmental moral theory must also presuppose that there is a *dynamic* between self and social structure whereby the individual learns, acquires or internalizes the perspectives and sanctions of the social world. But the mechanism of this dynamic may involve learning as well as resistance, internalization as well as projection and fantasy. The issue is less whether moral development and ego development are distinct – they may be distinguished conceptually and yet in the history of the self they are related – but whether the model of ego development presupposed by Kohlberg's theory is not distortingly *cognitivistic* in that it ignores the role of affects, resistance, projection, phantasy and defense mechanisms in socialization processes.

15 Kohlberg, 'Synopses', p. 398.

16 For this formulation, see J. Habermas, 'Interpretive Social Science vs. Hermeneuticism', in N. Haan, R. Bellah, P. Rabinow and W. Sullivan (eds), *Social Science as Moral Inquiry* (New York: Columbia University Press, 1983), p. 262.

17 Imre Lakatos, 'Falsification and the Methodology of Scientific Research Programs', in Lakatos and A. Musgrave (eds), *Criticism and the Growth of Knowledge* (Cambridge, UK: Cambridge University Press, 1970), pp. 117ff.

18 Let me explain the status of this premise. I would characterize it as a 'second-order research hypothesis' that both guides concrete research in the social sciences and that can, in turn, be falsified by them. It is not a statement of faith about the way the world is: the cross-cultural and transhistorical universality of the sex–gender system is an empirical fact. It is also most definitely not a normative proposition about the way the world *ought* to be. To the contrary, feminism radically challenges the validity of the sex–gender system in organizing societies and cultures, and advocates the emancipation of men and women from the unexamined and oppressive grids of this framework. The historian Kelly-Gadol succinctly captures the meaning of this premise for empirical research:

> Once we look to history for an understanding of woman's situation, we are, of course, already assuming that woman's situation is a social matter. But history, as we first come to it, did not seem to confirm this awareness . . . The moment this is done – the moment that one assumes that women are part of humanity in the fullest sense – the period or set of events with which we deal takes on a wholly different character or meaning from the normally accepted one. Indeed what emerges is a fairly regular pattern of relative loss of status for women precisely in those periods of so-called progressive change . . . Our notions of so-called progressive developments, such as classical Athenian civilization, the Renaissance and the French Revolution, undergo a startling reevaluation . . . Suddenly we see these ages *with a new, double vision– and each eye sees a different picture.* ('The Social Relations of the Sexes: Methodological Implications of Women's History', *Signs*, 1, 4 (1976); emphasis mine.)

19 For further clarification of these two aspects of critical theory, see Part 2, 'The Transformation of Critique', in my *Critique, Norm, and Utopia: A Study of the Foundations of Critical Theory* (New York: Columbia University Press, 1986).

20 Kohlberg, 'Synopses', p. 216.

21 Although frequently invoked by Kohlberg, Nunner-Winkler and also Habermas, it is still unclear *how* this distinction is drawn and how it is justified. For example, does the justice/good life distinction correspond to sociological definitions of the public vs the private? If so, what is meant by the 'private'? Is women-battering a 'private' or a 'public' matter? The relevant sociological definitions of the private and the public are shifting in our societies, as they have shifted historically. I

therefore find little justification for an [un]examined reliance upon changing juridical and social definitions in moral theory. [Editors' emendation.] Another way of drawing this distinction is to separate what is universalizable from what is culturally contingent, dependent upon the species of concrete life-forms, individual histories and the like. Habermas, in particular, relegates questions of the good life to the aesthetic-expressive sphere, cf. 'A Reply to My Critics', in John B. Thompson and David Held (eds), *Habermas: Critical Debates* (Cambridge, MA: MIT Press, 1982), p. 262; 'Moralbewusstsein und kommunikatives Handeln', in *Moralbewusstsein und kommunikatives Handeln* (Frankfurt: Suhrkamp, 1983), pp. 190ff. Again, if privacy in the sense of intimacy is included in the 'aesthetic-expressive' sphere, we are forced to silence and privatize most of the issues raised by the Women's Movement, which concern precisely the quality and nature of our 'intimate' relations, fantasies and hopes. A traditional response to this is to argue that in wanting to draw this aspect of our lives into the light of the public, the Women's Movement runs the risk of authoritarianism because it questions the limits of individual 'liberty'. In response to this legitimate political concern, I would argue that there is a distinction between questioning life-forms and values that have been oppressive for women, and making them 'public' in the sense of making them accessible to reflection, action and transformation, and in the sense of revealing their *socially constituted* character, on the one hand, and making them 'public' in the sense that these areas be subject to legislative and administrative state action. The second may, but need not, follow from the first. Because feminists focus on pornography as an 'aesthetic-expressive' mode of denigrating women, it does not thereby follow that their critique should result in public legislation against pornography. Whether there ought to be this kind of legislation needs to be examined in the light of relevant legal, political, constitutional, etc., arguments. Questions of political authoritarianism arise at this level, but not at the level of a critical-philosophical examination of traditional distinctions that have privatized and silenced women's concerns.

22 Kohlberg, 'Synopses', p. 340.
23 Ibid., pp. 229–30.
24 Ibid., p. 360.
25 Alasdair MacIntyre, *After Virtue* (Notre Dame: University of Notre Dame Press, 1981), pp. 50–1.
26 Agnes Heller, *A Theory of Feelings* (Holland: Van Gorcum, 1979), pp. 184ff.
27 John Locke, 'The Second Treatise of Civil Government' in *Two Treatises of Government*, ed. and with an introduction by Thomas I.

Cook (New York: Haffner Press, 1947), p. 128.

28   Immanuel Kant, *The Metaphysical Elements of Justice*, tr. John Ladd (New York: Liberal Arts Press, 1965), p. 55.

29   Thomas Hobbes, *Leviathan* (1651), ed. and with an introduction by C. B. Macpherson (Harmondsworth: Penguin Books, 1980), p. 186. All future citations are to this edition.

30   Hobbes, *Leviathan*, p. 187.

31   Thomas Hobbes, 'Philosophical Rudiments Concerning Government and Society', in Sir W. Molesworth (ed.), *The English Works of Thomas Hobbes*, Vol. II (Darmstadt: Wissenschaftliche Buchgesellschaft, 1966), p. 109.

32   J-J. Rousseau, 'On The Origin and Foundations of Inequality Among Men', in J-J. Rousseau, *The First and Second Discourse*, ed. R. D. Masters, tr. Roger D. and Judith R. Masters (New York: St Martin's Press, 1964), p. 116.

33   G. W. F. Hegel, *Phänomenologie des Geistes*, 6th edn, ed. Johannes Hoffmeister (Hamburg: Felix Meiner, 1952), Philosophische Bibliothek 114, p. 141; translation used here *Phenomenology of Spirit*, tr. A. V. Miller (Oxford: Clarendon Press, 1977), p. 111.

34   Sigmund Freud, *Moses and Monotheism*, tr. Katharine Jones (New York: Vintage, Random House, 1967), pp. 103ff.; Jean Piaget, *The Moral Judgment of the Child*, tr. Marjorie Gabain (New York: Free Press, 1965), pp. 65ff. Cf. the following comment on boys' and girls' games: 'The most superficial observation is sufficient to show that in the main the legal sense is far less developed in little girls than in boys. We did not succeed in finding a single collective game played by girls in which there were as many rules and, above all, as fine and consistent an organization and codification of these rules as in the game of marbles examined above' (p. 77).

35   Kant, 'Critique of Practical Reason' in *Critique of Practical Reason and Other Writings in Moral Philosophy*, tr. and ed. and with an introduction by Louis White Beck (Chicago: University of Chicago Press, 1949), p. 258.

36   Although the term 'generalized other' is borrowed from George Herbert Mead, my definition of it differs from this. Mead defines the 'generalized other' as follows: 'The organized community or social group which gives the individual his unity of self may be called the "generalized other". The attitude of the generalized other is the attitude of the whole community.' George Herbert Mead, *Mind, Self and Society. From the Standpoint of a Social Behaviorist*, ed. and with introduction by Charles W. Morris (Chicago: University of Chicago Press, 1955), p. 154. Among such communities Mead includes a ball team as well as political clubs, corporations and other more abstract

social classes or subgroups such as the class of debtors and the class of creditors (ibid., p. 157). Mead himself does not limit the concept of the 'generalized other' to what is described in the text. In identifying the 'generalized other' with the abstractly defined, legal and juridical subject, contract theorists and Kohlberg depart from Mead. Mead criticizes the social contract tradition precisely for distorting the psychosocial genesis of the individual subject, cf. ibid., p. 233.

37 Kohlberg, 'Justice as Reversibility: The Claim to Moral Adequacy of a Highest Stage of Moral Judgment', in *Essays on Moral Development* (San Francisco. Harper and Row, 1981), Vol. I: *The Philosophy of Moral Development*, p. 194.

38 Whereas all forms of reciprocity involve some conceptions of reversibility these vary in degree: reciprocity can be restricted to the reversibility of actions but not of moral perspectives, to behavioral role models but not to the principles which underlie the generation of such behavioural expectations. For Kohlberg, the 'veil of ignorance' is a model of perfect reversibility, for it elaborates the procedure of 'ideal role-taking' or 'moral musical chairs' where the decider 'is to successively put himself imaginatively in the place of each other actor and consider the claims each would make from his point of view' (Kohlberg, 'Justice as Reversibility', p. 199). My question is: are there any real 'others' behind the 'veil of ignorance' or are they indistinguishable from the self?

39 Kohlberg, 'Justice as Reversibility', p. 200; my emphasis.

40 I find Kohlberg's general claim that the moral point of view entails reciprocity, equality and fairness unproblematic. Reciprocity is not only a fundamental *moral* principle, but defines, as Alvin Gouldner has argued, a fundamental *social norm*, perhaps in fact the very concept of a social norm: 'The Norm of Reciprocity: A Preliminary Statement', *American Sociological Review*, 25 (April 1960), 161–78. The existence of ongoing social relations in a human community entails some definition of reciprocity in the actions, expectations and claims of the group. The fulfilment of such reciprocity, according to whatever interpretation is given to it, would then be considered fairness by members of the group. Likewise, members of a group bound by relations of reciprocity and fairness are considered equal. What changes through history and culture are not these formal structures implicit in the very logic of social relations (we can even call them social universals), but the criteria of inclusion and exclusion. Who constitutes the *relevant* human groups: masters vs slaves, men vs women, Gentiles vs Jews? Similarly, *which* aspects of human behaviour and objects of the world are to be regulated by norms of reciprocity: in the societies studied by Lévi-Strauss, some tribes exchange sea shells for women. Finally, *in terms of*

what is the equality among members of a group established: would this be gender, race, merit, virtue or entitlement? Clearly Kohlberg presupposes a *universalist–egalitarian* interpretation of reciprocity, fairness and equality, according to which all humans, in virtue of their mere humanity, are to be considered beings entitled to reciprocal rights and duties.

41 Gilligan, *In a Different Voice*, p. 101.

42 John Rawls, *A Theory of Justice*, 2nd edn (Cambridge, MA: Harvard University Press, 1971), p. 137.

43 Michael J. Sandel, *Liberalism and the Limits of Justice* (Cambridge, MA: Harvard University Press, 1982), p. 9.

44 Sandel, *Liberalism and the Limits of Justice*, pp. 47ff.

45 Rawls, *A Theory of Justice*, p. 128.

46 Sandel, *Liberalism and the Limits of Justice*, p. 51.

47 Kohlberg, 'Justice as Reversibility', p. 197.

48 Stanley Cavell, *The Claim of Reason* (Oxford: Oxford University Press, 1982), p. 265.

49 A most suggestive critique of Kohlberg's neglect of interpersonal morality has been developed by Norma Haan in 'Two Moralities in Action Contexts', 286–305. Haan reports that 'the formulation of formal morality appears to apply best to special kinds of hypothetical, rule-governed dilemmas, the paradigmatic situation in the minds of philosophers over the centuries' (302). Interpersonal reasoning, by contrast, 'arises within the context of moral dialogues between agents who strive to achieve balanced agreement, based on compromises they reach or on their joint discovery of interests they hold in common' (303). For a more extensive statement see also Norma Haan, 'An Interactional Morality of Everyday Life', in *Social Science as Moral Inquiry*, 218–51. The conception of 'communicative need interpretations', which I argue for below, is also such a model of interactional morality which, nonetheless, has implications for *institutionalized* relations of justice or for public morality as well.

50 Cf. E. Tugendhat, 'Zur Entwicklung von moralischen Begründungsstrukturen im modernen Recht', *Archiv für Recht und Sozialphilosophie*, Vol. LXVIII (1980), 1–20.

51 Although I follow the general outline of Habermas's conception of communicative ethics, I differ from him in so far as he distinguishes sharply between questions of justice and the good life (see note 21 above) and in so far as in his description of the 'seventh stage', he equivocated between concepts of the 'generalized' and the 'concrete other'; cf. J. Habermas, 'Moral Development and Ego Identity', in *Communication and the Evolution of Society*, tr. T. McCarthy (Boston: Beacon Press, 1979), pp. 69–95. The 'concrete other' is introduced in

his theory through the back door, as an aspect of ego autonomy, and as an aspect of our relation to inner nature. I find this implausible for reasons discussed above.

52 See Habermas, ibid., p. 90, and Kohlberg's discussion in 'Synopses', pp. 35–86.

53 In an earlier piece, I have dealt with the strong parallelisms between the two conceptions of the 'veil of ignorance' and the 'ideal speech situation'; see my 'The Methodological Illusions of Modern Political Theory: The Case of Rawls and Habermas', *Neue Hefte für Philosophie*, 21 (Spring 1982), 47–74. With the publication of the *Theory of Communicative Action*, Habermas himself has substantially modified the various assumptions in his original formulation of communicative ethics, and the rendition given here follows these modifications; for further discussion see my 'Toward a Communicative Ethics', in *Critique, Norm, and Utopia*, ch. 8.

54 Kohlberg, 'Synopses', pp. 272, 310.

55 Cf. Rawls, *A Theory of Justice*, pp. 118ff.

56 For recent feminist perspectives on the development of the self, cf. Dorothy Dinnerstein, *The Mermaid and the Minotaur: Sexual Arrangements and Human Malaise* (New York: Harper and Row, 1976); Jean Baker Miller, 'The Development of Women's Sense of Self', work-in-progress paper published by the Stone Center for Developmental Services and Studies at Wellesley College, 1984; Nancy Chodorow, *The Reproduction of Mothering: Psychoanalysis and the Sociology of Gender* (Berkeley: University of California Press, 1978); Jessica Benjamin, 'Authority and the Family Revisited: Or, a World Without Fathers?' *New German Critique*, 13 (1978), 35–58; Jane Flax, 'The Conflict Between Nurturance and Autonomy in Mother–Daughter Relationships and within Feminism', *Feminist Studies*, 4, 2 (June 1981), 171–92; and I. Balbus, *Marxism and Domination* (Princeton: Princeton University Press, 1982).

57 The distinction between the public and the private spheres is undergoing a tremendous realignment in late capitalist societies as a result of a complicated series of factors, the chief of which may be the changing role of the state in such societies in assuming more and more tasks that were previously more or less restricted to the family and reproductive spheres, e.g. education, early child care, health care, care for the elderly, and the like. Also, recent legislation concerning abortion, wife battering, and child abuse, to name a few areas, suggests that the accepted legal definitions of these spheres have begun to shift as well. These new sociological and legislative developments point to the need to fundamentally rethink our concepts of moral, psychological and legal autonomy, a task hitherto neglected by formal-universalist moral

theory. I do not want by any means to imply that the philosophical critique voiced in this paper leads to a blue-eyed adumbration [sic] of these developments or to the neglect of their contradictory and ambivalent character for women. My analysis would need to be complemented by a critical social theory of the changing definition and function of the private sphere in late-capitalist societies. As I have argued elsewhere, these social and legal developments not only lead to an extension of the perspective of the 'generalized other', by subjecting more and more spheres of life to legal norm, but create the potential for the growth of the perspective of the 'concrete other', that is, an association of friendship and solidarity in which need interpretations are discussed and new needs created. I see these associations as being created by new social movements like ecology and feminism, in the interstices of our societies, partly in response to and partly as a consequence of, the activism of the welfare state in late-capitalist societies; cf. *Critique, Norm, and Utopia*, pp. 343–53. I am much indebted to Nancy Fraser for her elaboration of the political consequences of my distinction between the 'generalized' and the 'concrete' other in the context of the paradoxes of the modern welfare state in her 'Feminism and the Social State' (*Salmagundi*, April 1986). An extensive historical and philosophical analysis of the changing relation between the private and the public is provided by Linda Nicholson in her book, *Gender and History: The Limits of Social Theory in The Age of the Family* (New York: Columbia University Press, 1986).

III

Towards a Feminist Ethics

17

Alexandra Kollontai
1872–1952

'SEXUAL RELATIONS AND THE CLASS STRUGGLE' (1911)
from *SELECTED WRITINGS*

Alexandra Kollontai was a leading figure in the Russian Revolution of 1917 and in the post-revolutionary government headed by Lenin. She was the most important writer of her time on the relation between socialism and women's liberation, arguing in particular for the abolition of the private family and for the reconstruction of (hetero)sexual relationships on a basis of love, trust and understanding.

Kollontai was in many ways an orthodox communist. During the 1920s and 1930s she served as Soviet ambassador first to Norway and then to Sweden, maintaining throughout an attitude of loyalty to the Stalin regime, although it is likely that only her comparatively obscure position saved her from the purges in which many of her fellow-revolutionaries perished. Again, she always rejected the supposedly 'bourgeois' feminism which identified men as the main oppressors of women, insisting on the political priority of class over gender (of which she had in any case no rigorous theory).* Yet her vision of the transformation of sex roles under communism, including as it did the collectivization of domestic work and childcare, was too subversive to be left in circulation during the Stalinist period, and on her death her part in the Revolution went almost uncommemorated. (Kollontai has been officially 'rehabilitated' in the USSR since the 1960s, though her negative attitude to the family has been suppressed.)

The present essay confirms that for Kollontai socialism took precedence over feminism. It is clear from this piece that the question uppermost in her mind is the nature of an ideal proletarian morality – a way of life appropriate to the class which is to take the 'fortress of the future' – and that the ultimate goal of a communist society informs all her thinking about sexual questions. Kollontai does, however, issue a recognizably feminist challenge to the socialist movement when she refuses to postpone consideration of such questions until 'after the revolution'. To devote energy to them is not an indulgence but an integral part of the class struggle, which can be waged successfully 'only with the help of new spiritual values, created within and answering the needs of the [working] class'.

Kollontai does not attempt to apply the historical-materialist method directly to the understanding of female subordination. For her the current 'sexual crisis' comprises, on one hand, psychological distortions traceable to the capitalist form of production (the loneliness of modern industrial society, the bourgeois obsession with private property); on the other, a 'belief' or 'traditional idea' that the two sexes are of unequal worth. She argues, following Engels, that this mistaken 'idea' will be eradicated by 'a change in the economic role of woman, and her independent involvement in production'. But she also looks forward here, in a more personal vein, to a time when the principle of wifely submission will be replaced by that of 'comradely solidarity' between the sexes. And she is confident that the egalitarian impulse of communism will find expression in a tendency towards non-hierarchical, mutually respectful sexual partnerships. In this sense her views foreshadow those of contemporary feminists who have advocated the 'eroticization of equality' (see Jeffreys, reading 26) – though the faith of women like Kollontai that such a development would result spontaneously from communist revolution is a thing of the past.

Among the many problems that demand the consideration and attention of contemporary mankind, sexual problems are undoubtedly some of the most crucial.[1] There isn't a country or a nation, apart from the legendary 'islands', where the question of sexual relationships isn't becoming an urgent and burning issue. Mankind today is living through an acute sexual crisis which is far more unhealthy and harmful for being long and drawn-out. Throughout the long journey of human history, you probably won't find a time when the problems of sex have occupied such a central place in the life of society; when the question of relationships between the sexes has been like a conjuror, attracting the attention of millions of troubled people; when sexual dramas have served as such a never-ending source of inspiration for every sort of art.

As the crisis continues and grows more serious, people are getting themselves into an increasingly hopeless situation, and are trying desperately by every available means to settle the 'insoluble question'. But with every new attempt to solve the problem, the confused knot of personal relationships gets more tangled. It's as if we couldn't see the one and only thread that could finally lead us to success in controlling the stubborn tangle. The sexual problem is like a vicious circle, and however frightened people are and however much they run this way and that, they are unable to break out.

The conservatively inclined part of mankind argue that we should return to the happy times of the past, we should re-establish the old foundations of the family and strengthen the well-tried norms of sexual morality. The champions of bourgeois individualism say that we ought to destroy all the hypocritical restrictions of the obsolete code of sexual behaviour. These unnecessary and repressive 'rags' ought to be relegated to the archives – only the individual conscience, the individual will of each person can decide such intimate questions. Socialists, on the other hand, assure us that sexual problems will only be settled when the basic reorganization of the social and economic structure of society has been tackled. Doesn't this 'putting off the problem until tomorrow' suggest that we still haven't found that one and only 'magic thread'? Shouldn't we find or at least locate this 'magic thread' that promises to unravel the tangle? Shouldn't we find it now, at this very moment?

This history of human society, the history of the continual battle between various social groups and classes of opposing aims and interests, gives us the clue to finding this 'thread'. It isn't the first time that mankind has gone through a sexual crisis. This isn't the first time that the pressure of a rushing tide of new values and ideals has blurred the clear and definite meaning of moral commandments about sexual relationships. The 'sexual crisis' was particularly acute at the time of the Renaissance and the Reformation, when a great social advance pushed the proud and patriarchal feudal nobility who were used to absolute command into the background, and cleared the way for the development and establishment of a new social force

– the bourgeoisie. The sexual morality of the feudal world had developed out of the depths of the 'tribal way of life' – the collective economy and the tribal authoritarian leadership that stifles the individual will of the individual member. This clashed with the new and strange moral code of the rising bourgeoisie. The sexual morality of the bourgeoisie is founded on principles that are in sharp contradiction to the basic morality of feudalism. Strict individualism and the exclusiveness and isolation of the 'nuclear family' replace the emphasis on 'collective work' that was characteristic of both the local and regional economic structure of patrimonial life. Under capitalism the ethic of competition, the triumphant principles of individualism and exclusive private property, grew and destroyed whatever remained of the idea of the community, which was to some extent common to all types of tribal life. For a whole century, while the complex laboratory of life was turning the old norms into a new formula and achieving the outward harmony of moral ideas, men wandered confusedly between two very different sexual codes and attempted to accommodate themselves to both.

But in those bright and colourful days of change, the sexual crisis, although profound, did not have the threatening character that it has assumed in our time. The main reason for this is that in 'the great days' of the Renaissance, in the 'new age' when the bright light of a new spiritual culture flooded the dying world with its clear colours, flooded the bare monotonous life of the Middle Ages, the sexual crisis affected only a relatively small part of the population. By far the largest section of the population, the peasantry, was affected only in the most indirect way and only as, slowly, over the course of centuries, a change in the economic base, in the economic relations of the countryside, took place. At the top of the social ladder a bitter battle between two opposing social worlds was fought out. This involved also a struggle between their different ideals and values and ways of looking at things. It was these people who experienced and were threatened by the sexual crisis that developed. The peasants, wary of new things, continued to cling firmly to the well-tried tribal tradition handed down from their forefathers, and only under the pressure of extreme necessity modified and adapted this tradition to the changing conditions of their economic environment. Even at the height of the struggle between the bourgeois and the feudal world the sexual crisis by-passed the 'class of tax-payers'. As the upper strata of society went about breaking up the old ways, the peasants in fact seemed to be more intent on clinging firmly to their traditions. In spite of the continuous whirlwinds that threatened overhead and shook the very soil under their feet, the peasants, especially our Russian peasantry, managed to preserve the basis of their sexual code untouched and unshaken for many centuries.

The story today is very different. The 'sexual crisis' does not spare even the peasantry. Like an infectious disease it 'knows neither rank nor status'. It spreads from the palaces and mansions to the crowded quarters of the working class, looks in on the peaceful dwelling places of the petty bourgeoisie, and makes its way into the heart of the countryside. It claims victims in the villas of the European bourgeoisie, in the fusty basement of the worker's family, and in the smoky hut of the peasant. There is 'no defence, no bolt' against sexual conflict. To imagine that only the members of the well-off sections of society are floundering and are in the throes of these problems would be to make a grave mistake. The waves of the sexual crisis are sweeping over the threshold of workers' homes, and creating situations of conflict that are as acute and heartfelt as the psychological sufferings of the 'refined bourgeois world'. The sexual crisis no longer interests only the 'propertied'. The problems of sex concern the largest section of society – they concern the working class in its daily life. It is therefore hard to understand why this vital and urgent subject is treated with such indifference. This indifference is unforgivable. One of the tasks that confronts the working class in its attack on the 'beleaguered fortress of the future' is undoubtedly the task of establishing more healthy and more joyful relationships between the sexes.

What are the roots of this unforgivable indifference to one of the essential tasks of the working class? How can we explain to ourselves the hypocritical way in which 'sexual problems' are relegated to the realm of 'private matters' that are not worth the effort and attention of the collective? Why has the fact been ignored that throughout history one of the constant features of social struggle has been the attempt to change relationships between the sexes, and the type of moral codes that determine these relationships; and that the way personal relationships are organized in a certain social group has had a vital influence on the outcome of the struggle between hostile social classes?

The tragedy of our society is not just that the usual forms of behaviour and the principles regulating this behaviour are breaking down, but that a spontaneous wave of new attempts at living is developing from within the social fabric, giving man hopes and ideals that cannot yet be realized. We are people living in the world of property relationships, a world of sharp class contradictions and of an individualistic morality. We still live and think under the heavy hand of an unavoidable loneliness of spirit. Man experiences this 'loneliness' even in towns full of shouting, noise and people, even in a crowd of close friends and work-mates. Because of their loneliness men are apt to cling in a predatory and unhealthy way to illusions about finding a 'soul mate' from among the members of the opposite sex. They see sly Eros as the only means of charming away, if only for a time, the gloom of inescapable loneliness.

People have perhaps never in any age felt spiritual loneliness as deeply and persistently as at the present time. People have probably never become so depressed and fallen so fully under the numbing influence of this loneliness. It could hardly be otherwise. The darkness never seems so black as when there's a light shining just ahead.

The 'individualists', who are only loosely organized into a collective with other individuals, now have the chance to change their sexual relationships so that they are based on the creative principle of friendship and togetherness rather than on something blindly physiological. The individualistic property morality of the present day is beginning to seem very obviously paralysing and oppressive. In criticizing the quality of sexual relationships modern man is doing far more than rejecting the outdated forms of behaviour of the current moral code. His lonely soul is seeking the regeneration of the very essence of these relationships. He moans and pines for 'great love', for a situation of warmth and creativity which alone has the power to disperse the cold spirit of loneliness from which present day 'individualists' suffer.

If the sexual crisis is three-quarters the result of external socio-economic relationships, the other quarter hinges on our 'refined individualistic psyche', fostered by the ruling bourgeois ideology. The 'potential for loving' of people today is, as the German writer Meisel-Hess puts it, at a low ebb. Men and women seek each other in the hope of finding for themselves, through another person, a means to a larger share of spiritual and physical pleasure. It makes no difference whether they are married to the partner or not, they give little thought to what's going on in the other person, to what's happening to their emotions and psychological processes.

The 'crude individualism' that adorns our era is perhaps nowhere as blatant as in the organization of sexual relationships. A person wants to escape from his loneliness and naïvely imagines that being 'in love' gives him the right to the soul of the other person – the right to warm himself in the rays of that rare blessing of emotional closeness and understanding. We individualists have had our emotions spoiled in the persistent cult of the 'ego'. We imagine that we can reach the happiness of being in a state of 'great love' with those near to us, without having to 'give' up anything of ourselves.

The claims we make on our 'contracted partner' are absolute and undivided. We are unable to follow the simplest rule of love – that another person should be treated with great consideration. New concepts of the relationships between the sexes are already being outlined. They will teach us to achieve relationships based on the unfamiliar ideas of complete freedom, equality and genuine friendship. But in the meantime mankind has to sit in the cold with its spiritual loneliness and can only dream about the 'better age' when all relationships between people will be warmed by the rays of 'the sun god', will experience a sense of togetherness, and will be educated in the new conditions of living. The sexual crisis cannot be solved unless there is a radical reform of the human psyche, and unless man's potential for loving is increased. And a basic transformation of the socio-economic relationships along communist lines is essential if the psyche is to be re-formed. This is an 'old truth' but there is no other way out. The sexual crisis will in no way be reduced, whatever kind of marriage or personal relationships people care to try.

History has never seen such a variety of personal relationships – indissoluble marriage with its 'stable family', 'free unions', secret adultery; a girl living quite openly with her lover in so-called 'wild marriage'; pair marriage, marriage in threes and even the complicated marriage of four people – not to talk of the various forms of commercial prostitution. You get the same two moral codes existing side by side in the peasantry as well – a mixture of the old tribal way of life and the developing bourgeois family. Thus you get the permissiveness of the girls' house[2] side by side with the attitude that fornication, or men sleeping with their daughters-in-law, is a disgrace. It's surprising that, in the face of the contradictory and tangled forms of present-day personal relationships, people are able to preserve a faith in moral authority, and are able to make sense of these contradictions and thread their way through these mutually destructive and incompatible moral codes. Even the usual justification – 'I live by the new morality' – doesn't help anyone, since the new morality is still only in the process of being formed. Our task is to draw out from the chaos of present-day contradictory sexual norms the shape, and make clear the principles, of a morality that answers the spirit of the progressive and revolutionary class.

Besides the already mentioned inadequacies of the contemporary psyche – extreme individuality, egoism that has become a cult – the 'sexual crisis' is made worse by two characteristics of the psychology of modern man: (i) the idea of 'possessing' the married partner; (ii) the belief that the two sexes are unequal, that they are of unequal worth in every way, in every sphere, including the sexual sphere.

Bourgeois morality, with its introverted individualistic family based entirely on private property, has carefully cultivated the idea that one partner should completely 'possess' the other. It has been very successful. The idea of 'possession' is more pervasive now than under the patrimonial system of marriage relationships. During the long historical period that developed under the aegis of the 'tribe', the idea of a man possessing his wife (there has never been any thought of a wife having undisputed possession of her husband) did not go further than a purely physical possession. The wife was obliged to be faithful physically – her soul was her own. Even the knights recognized the right of their wives to have *chichesbi* (platonic friends and admirers) and to receive the 'devotion' of other knights and minnesingers. It is the bourgeoisie who have carefully tended and fostered the ideal of absolute possession of the 'contracted partner's' emotional as well as physical 'I', thus extending the concept of property rights to include the right to the other person's whole spiritual and emotional world. Thus the family structure was strengthened and stability guaranteed in the period when the bourgeoisie were struggling for domination. This is the ideal that we have accepted as our heritage and have been prepared to see as an unchangeable moral absolute! The idea of 'property' goes far beyond the boundaries of 'lawful marriage'. It makes itself felt as an inevitable ingredient of the most 'free' union of love. Contemporary lovers with all their respect for freedom are not satisfied by the knowledge of the physical faithfulness alone of the person they love. To be rid of the eternally present threat of loneliness, we 'launch an attack' on the emotions of the person we love with a cruelty and lack of delicacy that will not be understood by future generations. We demand the right to know every secret of this person's being. The modern lover would forgive physical unfaithfulness sooner than 'spiritual' unfaithfulness. He sees any emotion experienced outside the boundaries of the 'free' relationship as the loss of his own personal treasure.

People 'in love' are unbelievably insensitive in their relations to a third person. We have all no doubt observed this strange situation – two people who love each other are in a hurry, before they have got to know each other properly, to exercise their rights over all the relationships that the other person has formed up till that time, to look into the innermost corners of their partner's life. Two people who yesterday were unknown to each other, and who come together in a single moment of mutual erotic feeling, rush to get at the heart of the other person's being. They want to feel that this strange and incomprehensible psyche, with its past experience that can never be suppressed, is an extension of their own self. The idea that the married pair are each other's property is so accepted that when a young couple who were yesterday each living their own separate lives are today opening each other's correspondence without a blush, and making common property of the words of a third person who is a friend of only one of them, this hardly strikes us as something unnatural. But this kind of 'intimacy' is only really possible when people have been working out their lives together for a long period of time. Usually a dishonest kind of closeness is substituted for this genuine feeling, the deception being fostered by the mistaken idea that a physical relationship between two people is a sufficient basis for extending the rights of possession to each other's emotional being.

The 'inequality' of the sexes – the inequality of their rights, the unequal value of their physical and emotional experience – is the other significant circumstance that distorts the psyche of contemporary man and is a reason for the deepening of the 'sexual crisis'. The 'double morality' inherent in both patrimonial and bourgeois society has, over the course of centuries, poisoned the psyche of men and women. These attitudes are so much a part of us that they are more difficult to get rid of than the ideas about possessing people that we have inherited only from bourgeois ideology. The idea that the sexes are unequal, even in the sphere of physical and emotional experience, means that the same action will be regarded differently according to whether it was the action of a man or a woman. Even the most 'progressive' member of the bourgeoisie, who has long ago rejected the whole code of current morality, easily catches himself out at this point since he too in judging a man and a woman for the same behaviour will pass different sentences. One simple example is enough. Imagine that a member of the middle-class intelligensia who is learned, involved in politics and social affairs – who is in short a 'personality', even a 'public figure' – starts sleeping with his cook (a not uncommon thing to happen) and even becomes legally married to her. Does bourgeois society change its attitude to this man, does the event throw even the tiniest shadow of doubt as to his moral worth? Of course not.

Now imagine another situation. A respected woman of bourgeois society – a social figure, a research student, a doctor or a writer, it's all the same – becomes friendly with her footman, and to complete the scandal marries him. How does bourgeois society react to the behaviour of the hitherto 'respected' woman? They cover her with 'scorn', of course! And remember, it's so much the worse for her if her husband, the footman, is good-looking or possesses other 'physical qualities'. 'It's obvious what she's fallen for', will be the sneer of the hypocritical bourgeoisie.

If a woman's choice has anything of an 'individual character' about it she won't be forgiven by bourgeois society. This attitude is a kind of throwback to the traditions of tribal times. Society still wants a woman to take into account, when she is making her choice, rank and status and the instructions and interests of her family. Bourgeois society cannot see a woman as an independent person separate from her family unit and outside the isolated circle of domestic obligations and virtues. Contemporary society goes even further than the ancient tribal society in acting as woman's trustee, instructing her not only to marry but to fall in love only with those people who are 'worthy' of her.

We are continually meeting men of considerable spiritual and intellectual qualities who have chosen as their friend-for-life a worthless and empty woman, who in no way matches the spiritual worth of the husband. We accept this as something normal and we don't think twice about it. At the most friends might pity Ivan Ivanovich for having landed himself with such an unbearable wife. But if it happens the other way round, we flap our hands and exclaim with concern, 'How could such an outstanding woman as Maria Petrovna fall for such a nonentity? I begin to doubt the worth of Maria Petrovna.' Where do we get this double criterion from? What is the reason for it? The reason is undoubtedly that the idea of the sexes being of 'different value' has become, over the centuries, a part of man's psychological make-up. We are used to evaluating a woman not as a personality with individual qualities and failings irrespective of her physical and emotional experience, but only as an appendage of a man. This man, the husband or the lover, throws the light of his personality over the woman, and it is this reflection and not the woman herself that we consider to be the true definition of her emotional and moral make-up. In the eyes of society the personality of a man can be more easily separated from his actions in the sexual sphere. The personality of a woman is judged almost exclusively in terms of her sexual life. This type of attitude stems from the role that women have played in society over the centuries, and it is only now that a re-evaluation of these attitudes is slowly being achieved, at least in outline. Only a change in the economic role of woman, and her independent involvement in production, can and will bring about the weakening of these mistaken and hypocritical ideas.

The three basic circumstances distorting the modern psyche – extreme egoism, the idea that married partners possess each other, and the acceptance of the inequality of the sexes in terms of physical and emotional experience – must be faced if the sexual problem is to be settled. People will find the 'magic key' with which they can break out of their situation only when their psyche has a sufficient store of 'feelings of consideration', when their ability to love is greater, when the idea of freedom in personal relationships becomes fact, and when the principle of 'comradeship' triumphs over the traditional idea of 'inequality' and submission. The sexual problems cannot be solved without this radical re-education of our psyche.

But isn't this asking too much? Isn't the suggestion utopian, without foundation, the naive notion of a dreaming idealist? How are you honestly going to raise mankind's 'potential for loving'? Haven't

wise men of all nations since time immemorial, beginning with
Buddha and Confucius and ending with Christ, been busying themselves over this? And who can say if the 'potential for loving' has
been raised? Isn't this kind of well-meaning daydream about the
solution of the sexual crisis simply a confession of weakness and a
refusal to go on with the search for the 'magic key'?

Is that the case? Is the radical re-education of our psyche and our
approach to sexual relationships something so unlikely, so removed
from reality? Couldn't one say that, on the contrary, while great
social and economic changes are in progress, the conditions are being
created that demand and give rise to a new basis for psychological
experience that is in line with what we have been talking about?
Another class, a new social group, is coming forward to replace the
bourgeoisie, with its bourgeois ideology, and its individualistic code
of sexual morality. The progressive class, as it develops in strength,
cannot fail to reveal new ideas about relationships between the sexes
that form in close connection with the problems of its social class.

The complicated evolution of socio-economic relations taking
place before our eyes, which changes all our ideas about the role of
women in social life and undermines the sexual morality of the
bourgeoisie, has two contradictory results. On the one hand we
see mankind's tireless efforts to adapt to the new, changing socio-
economic conditions. This is manifest either in an attempt to preserve the 'old forms' while providing them with a new content
(the observance of the external form of the indissoluble, strictly
monogamous marriage with an acceptance, in practice, of the freedom of the partners) or in the acceptance of new forms which
contain however all the elements of the moral code of bourgeois
marriage (the 'free' union where the compulsive possessiveness of the
partners is greater than within legal marriage). On the other hand we
see the slow but steady appearance of new forms of relationships
between the sexes that differ from the old norms in outward form
and in spirit.

Mankind is not groping its way toward these new ideas with much
confidence, but we need to look at its attempt, however vague it is at
the moment, since it is an attempt closely linked with the tasks of the
proletariat as the class which is to capture the 'beleaguered fortress'
of the future. If, amongst the complicated labyrinth of contradictory
and tangled sexual norms, you want to find the beginnings of more

healthy relationships between the sexes – relationships that promise to lead humanity out of the sexual crisis – you have to leave the 'cultured quarters' of the bourgeoisie with their refined individualistic psyche, and take a look at the huddled dwelling-places of the working class. There, amidst the horror and squalor of capitalism, amidst tears and curses, the springs of life are welling up.

You can see the double process which we have just mentioned working itself out in the lives of the proletariat, who have to exist under the pressure of harsh economic conditions, cruelly exploited by capitalism. You can see both the process of 'passive adjustment' and that of active opposition to the existing reality. The destructive influence of capitalism destroys the basis of the worker's family and forces him unconsciously to 'adapt' to the existing conditions. This gives rise to a whole series of situations with regard to relationships between the sexes which are similar to those in other social classes. Under the pressure of low wages the worker inevitably tends to get married at a later age. If twenty years ago a worker usually got married between the ages of 20 and 25, he now shoulders the cares of a family only towards his 30th year. The higher the cultural demands of the worker – the more he values the opportunity of being in contact with cultural life, of visiting theatres and lectures, of reading papers and magazines, of giving his spare time to struggle and politics or to some favourite pursuit such as art or reading etc. – the later he tends to get married. But physical needs won't take a financial situation into consideration: they insist on making themselves felt. The working-class bachelor, in the same way as the middle-class bachelor, looks to prostitution for an outlet. This is an example of the passive adjustment of the working class to the unfavourable conditions of their existence. Take another example. When the worker marries, the low level of pay forces the worker's family to 'regulate' childbirth just as the bourgeois family does. The frequent cases of infanticide, the growth of prostitution – these are all expressions of the same process. These are all examples of adjustment by the working class to the surrounding reality. But this is not a process characteristic of the proletariat alone. All the other classes and sections of the population caught up in the world process of capitalist development react in this way.

We see a difference only when we begin to talk about the active, creative forces at work that oppose rather than adapt to the repressive reality, and about the new ideals and attempts at new relationships between the sexes. It is only within the working class that this active opposition is taking shape. This doesn't mean that the other classes and sections of the population (particularly the middle-class intelligentsia who, by the circumstances of their social existence, stand closest to the working class) don't adopt the 'new' forms that are being worked out by the progressive working class. The bourgeoisie, motivated by an instinctive desire to breathe new life into their dead and feeble forms of marriage, seize upon the 'new' ideas of the working class. But the ideals and code of sexual morality that the working class develops do not answer the class needs of the bourgeoisie. They reflect the demands of the working class and therefore serve as a new weapon in its social struggle. They help shatter the foundations of the social domination of the bourgeoisie. Let us make this point clear by an example.

The attempt by the middle-class intelligentsia to replace in-dissoluble marriage by the freer, more easily broken ties of civil marriage destroys the essential basis of the social stability of the bourgeoisie. It destroys the monogamous, property-orientated family. On the other hand, a greater fluidity in relationships between the sexes coincides with and is even the indirect result of one of the basic tasks of the working class. The rejection of the element of 'submission' in marriage is going to destroy the last artificial ties of the bourgeois family. This act of 'submission' on the part of one member of the working class to another, in the same way as the sense of possessiveness in relationships, has a harmful effect on the pro-letarian psyche. It is not in the interests of that revolutionary class to elect only certain members as its independent representatives, whose duty it is to serve the class interests before the interests of the individual, isolated family. Conflicts between the interests of the family and the interests of the class which occur at the time of a strike or during an active struggle, and the moral yardstick with which the proletariat views such events, are sufficiently clear evidence of the basis of the new proletarian ideology.

Suppose family affairs require a businessman to take his capital out of a firm at a time when the enterprise is in financial difficulties. Bourgeois morality is clear-cut in its estimate of his action: 'The interests of the family come first.' We can compare with this the attitude of workers to a strikebreaker who defies his comrades and goes to work during a strike to save his family from being hungry. 'The interests of the class come first.' Here's another example. The love and loyalty of the middle-class husband to his family are sufficient to divert his wife from all interests outside the home and end up by tying her to the nursery and the kitchen. 'The ideal husband can support the ideal family' is the way the bourgeoisie looks at it. But how do workers look upon a 'conscious' member of their class who shuts the eyes of his wife or girlfriend to the social struggle? For the sake of individual happiness, for the sake of the family, the morality of the working class will demand that women take part in the life that is unfolding beyond the doorsteps. The 'captivity' of women in the home, the way family interests are placed before all else, the widespread exercise of absolute property rights by the husband over the wife – all these things are being broken down by the basic principle of the working-class ideology of 'comradely solidarity'. The idea that some members are unequal and must submit to other members of one and the same class is in contradiction with the basic proletarian principle of comradeship. This principle of comradeship is basic to the ideology of the working class. It colours and determines the whole developing proletarian morality, a morality which helps to re-educate the personality of man, allowing him to be capable of positive feeling, capable of freedom instead of being bound by a sense of property, capable of comradeship rather than inequality and submission.

It is an old truth that every new class that develops as a result of an advance in economic growth and material culture offers mankind an appropriately new ideology. The code of sexual behaviour is a part of this ideology. However it is worth saying something about 'proletarian ethics' or 'proletarian sexual morality', in order to criticize the wellworn idea that proletarian sexual morality is no more than 'superstructure', and that there is no place for any change in this sphere until the economic base of society has been changed. As if the ideology of a certain class is formed only when the breakdown in socio-economic relationships, guaranteeing the dominance of that class, has been completed! All the experience of history teaches us that a social group works out its ideology, and consequently its sexual morality, in the process of its struggle with hostile social forces.

Only with the help of new spiritual values, created within and answering the needs of the class, will that class manage to strengthen its social position. It can only successfully win power from those groups in society that are hostile to it by holding to these new norms and ideals. To search for the basic criteria for a morality that can reflect the specific interests of the working class, and to see that the developing sexual norms are in accordance with these criteria – this is the task that must be tackled by the ideologists of the working class. We have to understand that it is only by becoming aware of the creative process that is going on within society, and of the new demands, new ideals and new norms that are being formed, only by becoming clear about the basis of the sexual morality of the progressive class, that we can possibly make sense of the chaos and contradictions of sexual relationships and find the thread that will make it possible to undo the tightly rolled up tangle of sexual problems.

We must remember that only a code of sexual morality that is in harmony with the problems of the working class can serve as an important weapon in strengthening the working class's fighting position. The experience of history teaches us that much. What can stop us using this weapon in the interests of the working class, who are fighting for a communist system and for new relationships between the sexes that are deeper and more joyful?

NOTES

* See Mary Buckley, *Women and Ideology in the Soviet Union* (Harvester Press: Brighton, 1989), ch. 1.

1 The editors and publishers gratefully acknowledge permission of Allison and Busby Ltd © 1977 to reproduce 'Sexual Relations and the Class Struggle' from *Selected Writings*, translated by Alix Holt.

2 In the traditional Russian villages, the young girls would often get together to rent an old hut or a room in someone's house. They would gather there in the evenings to tell stories, do needlework and sing. The young men would come to join in the merrymaking. Sometimes it seems that the merrymaking would become an orgy, though there are conflicting ideas about this.

18

Emma Goldman
1869–1940

'JEALOUSY: CAUSES AND A POSSIBLE CURE' (*C*.1912)
from *RED EMMA SPEAKS*

For biographical details of Emma Goldman see chapter 9.

At the heart of all anarchist thought is an emphasis on the value of individual autonomy – a belief that all relations between individuals should be voluntary, and that relations of authority and domination are inherently damaging and immoral. This principle is incompatible with the existence of the 'state' in the modern sense, just as it is incompatible with feudalism or dictatorship. Anarchists argue for the limitation of state action, and in the long term, the destruction of the state altogether.

The last few decades have seen the emergence of a 'right-wing' variety of anarchist thought centring on personal and private property relations, and on the principle that an individual's property (that is, goods acquired through a formally legitimate transaction) is sacrosanct: the property right is the most fundamental right of man. This principle, and the workings of an unregulated market economy, are held to be crucial to an ethical society.*

For Emma Goldman, by contrast, property relations as much as relations of authority are inherently unethical, *and their centrality in bourgeois society creates a tendency for all human relations to be lived as if they were property relations. House owners must protect their houses, and prevent others using or taking possession of them. They are then likely to extend this attitude into other spheres of life – to family, friendship and sexuality. Jealousy proceeds from proprietariness, which disfigures human relationships and debases love. Love can flourish only with freedom.*

In Goldman's analysis, then, the structure of our feelings conforms to that of our social institutions. Only when we outgrow our present authoritarian institutions – above all, that of private property – will our emotions begin to reflect our own individual being. No longer able to accuse others of responsibility for our pain (as the jealous lover does), we shall then have to accept this pain for what it is: ours alone. But we shall find our compensation in the experience – exceptional today – of genuinely voluntary sexual union.

No one at all capable of an intense conscious inner life need ever hope to escape mental anguish and suffering.[1] Sorrow and often despair over the so-called eternal fitness of things are the most persistent companions of our life. But they do not come upon us from the outside, through the evil deeds of particularly evil people. They are conditioned in our very being; indeed, they are interwoven through a thousand tender and coarse threads with our existence.

It is absolutely necessary that we realize this fact, because people who never get away from the notion that their misfortune is due to the wickedness of their fellows never can outgrow the petty hatred and malice which constantly blames, condemns, and hounds others for something that is inevitable as part of themselves. Such people will not rise to the lofty heights of the true humanitarian to whom good and evil, moral and immoral, are but limited terms for the inner play of human emotions upon the human sea of life.

The 'beyond good and evil' philosopher, Nietzsche, is at present denounced as the perpetrator of national hatred and machine gun destruction; but only bad readers and bad pupils interpret him so. 'Beyond good and evil' means beyond prosecution, beyond judging, beyond killing, etc. *Beyond Good and Evil* opens before our eyes a vista the background of which is individual assertion combined with the understanding of all others who are unlike ourselves, who are different.

By that I do not mean the clumsy attempt of democracy to regulate the complexities of human character by means of external equality. The vision of 'beyond good and evil' points to the right to oneself, to one's personality. Such possibilities do not exclude pain over the chaos of life, but they do exclude the puritanic righteousness that sits in judgement on all others except oneself.

It is self-evident that the thoroughgoing radical – there are many half-baked ones, you know – must apply this deep, humane recognition to the sex and love relation. Sex emotions and love are among the most intimate, the most intense and sensitive, expressions of our being. They are so deeply related to individual physical and psychic traits as to stamp each love affair an independent affair, unlike any other love affair. In other words, each love is the result of the impressions and characteristics the two people involved give to it. Every love relation should by its very nature remain an absolutely private affair. Neither the State, the Church, morality, or people should meddle with it.

Unfortunately this is not the case. The most intimate relation is subject to proscriptions, regulations, and coercions, yet these external factors are absolutely alien to love, and as such lead to everlasting contradictions and conflict between love and law.

The result of it is that our love life is merged into corruption and degradation. 'Pure love', so much hailed by the poets, is in the present matrimonial, divorce and alienation wrangles, a rare specimen indeed. With money, social standing and position as the criteria of love, prostitution is quite inevitable, even if it be covered with the mantle of legitimacy and morality.

The most prevalent evil of our mutilated love-life is jealousy, often described as the 'green-eyed monster' who lies, cheats, betrays, and kills. The popular notion is that jealousy is inborn and therefore can never be eradicated from the human heart. This idea is a convenient excuse for those who lack ability and willingness to delve into cause and effect.

Anguish over a lost love, over the broken thread of love's continuity, is indeed inherent in our very beings. Emotional sorrow has inspired many sublime lyrics, much profound insight and poetic exultation of a Byron, Shelley, Heine, and their kind. But will anyone compare this grief with what commonly passes as jealousy? They are as unlike as wisdom and stupidity. As refinement and coarseness. As dignity and brutal coercion. Jealousy is the very reverse of understanding, of sympathy and of generous feeling. Never has jealousy added to character, never does it make the individual big and fine. What it really does is to make him blind with fury, petty with suspicion, and harsh with envy.

Jealousy, the contortions of which we see in the matrimonial tragedies and comedies, is invariably a one-sided, bigoted accuser, convinced of his own righteousness and the meanness, cruelty and guilt of his victim. Jealousy does not even attempt to understand. Its one desire is to punish, and to punish as severely as possible. This notion is embodied in the code of honour, as represented in duelling or the unwritten law. A code which will have it that the seduction of a woman must be atoned with the death of the seducer. Even where seduction has not taken place, where both have voluntarily yielded to the innermost urge, honour is restored only when blood has been shed, either that of the man or the woman.

Jealousy is obsessed by the sense of possession and vengeance. It is quite in accord with all other punitive laws upon the statutes which still adhere to the barbarous notion that an offence, often merely the result of social wrongs, must be adequately punished or revenged.

A very strong argument against jealousy is to be found in the data of historians like Morgan, Reclus and others, as to the sex relations among primitive people. Anyone at all conversant with their works knows that monogamy is a much later sex form which came into being as a result of the domestication and ownership of women, and which created sex monopoly and the inevitable feeling of jealousy.

In the past, when men and women intermingled freely without interference of law and morality, there could be no jealousy, because the latter rests upon the assumption that a certain man has an exclusive sex monopoly over a certain woman and vice versa. The moment anyone dares to trespass this sacred precept, jealousy is up in arms. Under such circumstances it is ridiculous to say that jealousy is perfectly natural. As a matter of fact, it is the artificial result of an artificial cause, nothing else.

Unfortunately, it is not only conservative marriages which are saturated with the notion of sex monopoly; the so-called free unions are also victims of it. The argument may be raised that this is one more proof that jealousy is an inborn trait. But it must be borne in mind that sex monopoly has been handed down from generation to generation as a sacred right and the basis of purity of the family and the home. And just as the Church and the State accepted sex monopoly as the only security to the marriage tie, so have both justified jealousy as the legitimate weapon of defense for the protection of the property right.

Now, while it is true that a great many people have outgrown the legality of sex monopoly, they have not outgrown its traditions and habits. Therefore they become as blinded by the 'green-eyed monster' as their conservative neighbours the moment their possessions are at stake.

A man or woman free and big enough not to interfere or fuss over the outside attractions of the loved one is sure to be despised by his conservative, and ridiculed by his radical, friends. He will either be decried as a degenerate or a coward; often enough some petty material motives will be imputed to him. In any event, such men and women will be the target of coarse gossip or filthy jokes for no other reason than that they concede to wife, husband or lovers the right to their own bodies and their emotional expression, without making jealous scenes or wild threats to kill the intruder.

There are other factors in jealousy: the conceit of the male and the envy of the female. The male in matters sexual is an impostor, a braggart, who forever boasts of his exploits and success with women. He insists on playing the part of a conqueror, since he has been told that women want to be conquered, that they love to be seduced. Feeling himself the only cock in the barnyard, or the bull who must clash horns in order to win the cow, he feels mortally wounded in his conceit and arrogance the moment a rival appears on the scene – the scene, even among so-called refined men, continues to be woman's sex love, which must belong to only one master.

In other words, the endangered sex monopoly together with man's outraged vanity in ninety-nine cases out of a hundred are the antecedents of jealousy.

In the case of woman, economic fear for herself and children and her petty envy of every other woman who gains grace in the eyes of her supporter invariably create jealousy. In justice to woman be it said that for centuries past, physical attraction was her only stock in trade, therefore she must needs become envious of the charm and value of other women as threatening her hold upon her precious property.

The grotesque aspect of the whole matter is that men and women often grow violently jealous of those they really do not care much about. It is therefore not their outraged love, but their outraged conceit and envy which cry out against this 'terrible wrong'. Likely as not the woman never loved the man whom she now suspects and spies upon. Likely as not she never made an effort to keep his love.

But the moment a competitor arrives, she begins to value her sex property for the defense of which no means are too despicable or cruel.

Obviously, then, jealousy is not the result of love. In fact, if it were possible to investigate most cases of jealousy, it would likely be found that the less people are imbued with a great love the more violent and contemptible is their jealousy. Two people bound by inner harmony and oneness are not afraid to impair their mutual confidence and security if one or the other has outside attractions, nor will their relations end in vile enmity, as is too often the case with many people. They may not be able, nor ought they to be expected, to receive the choice of the loved one into the intimacy of their lives, but that does not give either one the right to deny the necessity of the attraction.

As I shall discuss variety and monogamy two weeks from tonight, I will not dwell upon either here, except to say that to look upon people who can love more than one person as perverse or abnormal is to be very ignorant indeed. I have already discussed a number of causes for jealousy to which I must add the institution of marriage which the State and Church proclaim as 'the bond until death doth part'. This is accepted as the ethical mode of right living and right doing.

With love, in all its variability and changeability, fettered and cramped, it is small wonder if jealousy arises out of it. What else but pettiness, meanness, suspicion and rancour can come when man and wife are officially held together with the formula 'from now on you are one in body and spirit.' Just take any couple tied in such a manner, dependent upon each other for every thought and feeling, without an outside interest or desire, and ask yourself whether such a relation must not become hateful and unbearable in time.

In some form or other the fetters are broken, and as the circumstances which bring this about are usually low and degrading, it is hardly surprising that they bring into play the shabbiest and meanest human traits and motives.

In other words, legal, religious and moral interference are the parents of our present unnatural love and sex life, and out of it jealousy has grown. It is the lash which whips and tortures poor mortals because of their stupidity, ignorance and prejudice.

But no one need attempt to justify himself on the ground of being a victim of these conditions. It is only too true that we all smart under the burdens of iniquitous social arrangements, under coercion and moral blindness. But are we not conscious individuals, whose aim it is to bring truth and justice into human affairs? The theory that man is a product of conditions has led only to indifference and to a sluggish acquiescence in these conditions. Yet everyone knows that adaptation to an unhealthy and unjust mode of life only strengthens both, while man, the so-called crown of all creation, equipped with a capacity to think and see and above all to employ his powers of initiative, grows ever weaker, more passive, more fatalistic.

In this sense I speak of a possible cure of jealousy, after I have attempted to prove that its cause lies in our coerced, crippled love-life. I hold that every man and woman can help to cure jealousy. The first step towards this is a recognition that they are neither the owners nor controllers nor dictators over the sex functions of the wife or the husband. The second step is that they both grow too proud to accept love or affection which is not gladly or voluntarily given. Anything offered out of duty, because of the marriage licence, isn't the genuine thing. It is counterfeit. Whatever we attempt to hold by force, by jealous threats or scenes, through spying and snooping, through mean tricks and soul tortures, is not worth keeping. It only leaves a bad taste behind, and the mind and heart-destroying doubt whether or not we have succeeded in bringing back the wayward lamb.

There is nothing more terrible and fatal than to dig into the vitals of one's loved ones and oneself. It can only help to tear whatever slender threads of affection still inhere in the relation and finally bring us to the last ditch, which jealousy attempts to prevent, namely, the annihilation of love, friendship and respect.

Jealousy is indeed a poor medium to secure love, but it is a secure medium to destroy one's self-respect. For jealous people, like dope-fiends, stoop to the lowest level and in the end inspire only disgust and loathing.

Anguish over the loss of love or a nonreciprocated love among people who are capable of high and fine thoughts will never make a person coarse. Those who are sensitive and fine have only to ask themselves whether they can tolerate any obligatory relation, and an emphatic *no* would be the reply. But most people continue to live near each other although they have long ceased to live with each other – a life fertile enough for the operation of jealousy, whose methods go all the way from opening private correspondence to murder. Compared with such horrors, open adultery seems an act of courage and liberation.

A strong shield against the vulgarity of jealousy is that man and wife are not of one body and one spirit. They are two human beings, of different temperament, feelings and emotions. Each is a small cosmos in himself, engrossed in his own thoughts and ideas. It is glorious and poetic if these two worlds meet in freedom and equality. Even if this lasts but a short time it is already worthwhile. But, the moment the two worlds are forced together all the beauty and fragrance ceases and nothing but dead leaves remain. Whoever grasps this truism will consider jealousy beneath him and will not permit it to hang as a sword of Damocles over him.

All lovers do well to leave the doors of their love wide open. When love can go and come without fear of meeting a watch-dog, jealousy will rarely take root because it will soon learn that where there are no locks and keys there is no place for suspicion and distrust, two elements upon which jealousy thrives and prospers.

NOTES

* See for example Robert Nozick, *Anarchy, State, and Utopia* (Basil Blackwell: Oxford, 1974).
1 Emma Goldman, *Red Emma Speaks*, ed. Alix Kates Shulman.

19

Adrienne Rich
b.1929

'WOMEN AND HONOR: SOME NOTES ON LYING' (1975)
from *ON LIES, SECRETS AND SILENCE*

Adrienne Rich is a writer, teacher and activist. She has published ten collections of poetry, a collection of essays (from which the 'Notes' below are taken) and a book on the experience and institution of motherhood. She 'became a mother in the family-centred, consumer-oriented Freudian-American world of the 1950s'. She was already a poet.

Rich has been called a 'separatist'. But she rejects all those simple categorizations of women that would be involved in a general prescription of lesbian separatism. She regards lesbianism as 'a continuum', a 'range – through each woman's life and throughout history – of woman-identified experience', including experiences of 'primary intensity between and among women'.* What she advocates is women's finding contexts in which they are free of men and happy to be so.

Rich writes here for women-identified women. And we may be struck by the fact that these 'Notes' are not only meant for such women but have nothing to say to anyone else. Her choice of the term 'honor' may remind us of the spurious loyalties of male institutions; if it does, its appropriation by Rich may illustrate the subversiveness of writing about a world un-mediated by men. We have an instance of 'disloyalty to civilization'. Yet the value of these 'Notes' is as a piece of first-order ethics, concerned with the enormous difficulty and supreme importance of achieving truthfulness and transparency in our relations with one another.**

(These notes are concerned with relationships between and among women. When 'personal relationship' is referred to, I mean a relationship between two women. It will be clear in what follows when I am talking about women's relationships with men.)

The old, male idea of honor. A man's 'word' sufficed – to other men – without guarantee.

'Our Land Free, Our Men Honest, Our Women Fruitful' – a popular colonial toast in America.

Male honor also having something to do with killing: *I could not love thee, Dear, so much/Lov'd I not Honour more* ('To Lucasta, On Going to the Wars'). Male honor as something needing to be avenged: hence, the duel.

Women's honor, something altogether else: virginity, chastity, fidelity to a husband. Honesty in women has not been considered important. We have been depicted as generically whimsical, deceitful, subtle, vacillating. And we have been rewarded for lying.

Men have been expected to tell the truth about facts, not about feelings. They have not been expected to talk about feelings at all.

Yet even about facts they have continually lied.

We assume that politicians are without honor. We read their statements trying to crack the code. The scandals of their politics: not that men in high places lie, only that they do so with such indifference, so endlessly, still expecting to be believed. We are accustomed to the contempt inherent in the political lie.

. . .

To discover that one has been lied to in a personal relationship, however, leads one to feel a little crazy.

. . .

Lying is done with words, and also with silence.

The woman who tells lies in her personal relationships may or may not plan or invent her lying. She may not even think of what she is doing in a calculated way.

A subject is raised which the liar wishes buried. She has to go downstairs, her parking meter will have run out. Or, there is a telephone call she ought to have made an hour ago.

She is asked, point-blank, a question which may lead into painful talk: 'How do you feel about what is happening between us?' Instead of trying to describe her feelings in their ambiguity and confusion, she asks, 'How do *you* feel?' The other, because she is trying to establish a ground of openness and trust, begins describing her own feelings. Thus the liar learns more than she tells.

And she may also tell herself a lie: that she is concerned with the other's feelings, not with her own.

But the liar is concerned with her own feelings.

The liar lives in fear of losing control. She cannot even desire a relationship without manipulation, since to be vulnerable to another person means for her the loss of control.

The liar has many friends, and leads an existence of great loneliness.

. . .

The liar often suffers from amnesia. Amnesia is the silence of the unconscious.

To lie habitually, as a way of life, is to lose contact with the unconscious. It is like taking sleeping pills, which confer sleep but blot out dreaming. The unconscious wants truth. It ceases to speak to those who want something else more than truth.

In speaking of lies, we come inevitably to the subject of truth. There is nothing simple or easy about this idea. There is no 'the truth', 'a truth' – truth is not one thing, or even a system. It is an increasing complexity. The pattern of the carpet is a surface. When we look closely, or when we become weavers, we learn of the tiny multiple threads unseen in the overall pattern, the knots on the underside of the carpet.

This is why the effort to speak honestly is so important. Lies are usually attempts to make everything simpler – for the liar – than it really is, or ought to be.

In lying to others we end up lying to ourselves. We deny the importance of an event, or a person, and thus deprive ourselves of a part of our lives. Or we use one piece of the past or present to screen out another. Thus we lose faith even with our own lives.

The unconscious wants truth, as the body does. The complexity and fecundity of dreams come from the complexity and fecundity of the unconscious struggling to fulfil that desire. The complexity and fecundity of poetry come from the same struggle.

. . .

An honorable human relationship – that is, one in which two people have the right to use the word 'love' – is a process, delicate, violent, often terrifying to both persons involved, a process of refining the truths they can tell each other.

It is important to do this because it breaks down human self-delusion and isolation.

It is important to do this because in so doing we do justice to our own complexity.

It is important to do this because we can count on so few people to go that hard way with us.

. . .

I come back to the questions of women's honor. Truthfulness has not been considered important for women, as long as we have remained physically faithful to a man, or chaste.

We have been expected to lie with our bodies: to bleach, redden, unkink or curl our hair, pluck eyebrows, shave armpits, wear padding in various places or lace ourselves, take little steps, glaze finger and toe nails, wear clothes that emphasized our helplessness.

We have been required to tell different lies at different times, depending on what the men of the time needed to hear. The Victorian wife or the white southern lady, who were expected to have no sensuality, to 'lie still'; the twentieth-century 'free' woman who is expected to fake orgasms.

We have had the truth of our bodies withheld from us or distorted; we have been kept in ignorance of our most intimate places. Our instincts have been punished: clitoridectomies for 'lustful' nuns or for 'difficult' wives. It has been difficult, too, to know the lies of our complicity from the lies we believed.

The lie of the 'happy marriage', of domesticity – we have been complicit, have acted out the fiction of a well-lived life, until the day we testify in court of rapes, beatings, psychic cruelties, public and private humiliations.

Patriarchal lying has manipulated women both through falsehood and through silence. Facts we needed have been withheld from us. False witness has been borne against us.

And so we must take seriously the question of truthfulness between women, truthfulness among women. As we cease to lie with our bodies, as we cease to take on faith what men have said about us, is a truly womanly idea of honor in the making?

. . .

Women have been forced to lie, for survival, to men. How to unlearn this among other women?

'Women have always lied to each other.'
'Women have always whispered the truth to each other.'

Both of these axioms are true.

'Women have always been divided against each other.'
'Women have always been in secret collusion.'

Both of these axioms are true.

In the struggle for survival we tell lies. To bosses, to prison guards, the police, men who have power over us, who legally own us and our children, lovers who need us as proof of their manhood.

There is a danger run by all powerless people that we forget we are lying, or that lying becomes a weapon we carry over into relationships with people who do not have power over us.

. . .

I want to reiterate that when we talk about women and honor or women and lying, we speak within the context of male lying, the lies of the powerful, the lie as false source of power.

Women have to think whether we want, in our relationships with each other, the kind of power that can be obtained through lying.

Women have been driven mad, 'gaslighted', for centuries by the refutation of our experience and our instincts in a culture which validates only male experience. The truth of our bodies and our minds has been mystified to us. We therefore have a primary obligation to each other: not to undermine each others' sense of reality for the sake of expediency; not to gaslight each other.

Women have often felt insane when cleaving to the truth of our experience. Our future depends on the sanity of each of us, and we have a profound stake, beyond the personal, in the project of describing our reality as candidly and fully as we can to each other.

. . .

There are phrases which help us not to admit we are lying: 'my privacy', 'nobody's business but my own'. The choices that underlie these phrases may indeed be justified; but we ought to think about the full meaning and consequences of such language.

Women's love for women has been represented almost entirely through silence and lies. The institution of heterosexuality has forced the lesbian to dissemble, or be labeled a pervert, a criminal, a sick or dangerous woman, etc., etc. The lesbian, then, has often been forced to lie, like the prostitute or the married woman.

Does a life 'in the closet' – lying, perhaps of necessity, about ourselves to bosses, landlords, clients, colleagues, family, because the law and public opinion are founded on a lie – does this, can it, spread into private life, so that lying (described as *discretion*) becomes an easy way to avoid conflict or complication? Can it become a strategy so ingrained that it is used even with close friends and lovers?

Heterosexuality as an institution has also drowned in silence the erotic feelings between women. I myself lived half a lifetime in the lie of that denial. That silence makes us all, to some degree, into liars.

When a woman tells the truth she is creating the possibility for more truth around her.

. . .

The liar leads an existence of unutterable loneliness.

The liar is afraid.

But we are all afraid: without fear we become manic, hubristic, self-destructive. What is this particular fear that possesses the liar?

She is afraid that her own truths are not good enough.

She is afraid, not so much of prison guards or bosses, but of something unnamed within her.

The liar fears the void.

The void is not something created by patriarchy, or racism, or capitalism. It will not fade away with any of them. It is part of every woman.

'The dark core', Virginia Woolf named it, writing of her mother. The dark core. It is beyond personality; beyond who loves us or hates us.

We begin out of the void, out of darkness and emptiness. It is part of the cycle understood by the old pagan religions, that materialism denies. Out of death, rebirth; out of nothing, something.

The void is the creatrix, the matrix. It is not mere hollowness and anarchy. But in women it has been identified with lovelessness, barrenness, sterility. We have been urged to fill our 'emptiness' with children. We are not supposed to go down into the darkness of the core.

Yet, if we can risk it, the something born of that nothing is the beginning of our truth.

The liar in her terror wants to fill up the void, with anything. Her lies are a denial of her fear; a way of maintaining control.

. . .

Why do we feel slightly crazy when we realize we have been lied to in a relationship?

We take so much of the universe on trust. You tell me: 'In 1950 I lived on the north side of Beacon Street in Somerville.' You tell me: 'She and I were lovers, but for months now we have only been good friends.' You tell me: 'It is 70 degrees outside and the sun is shining.' Because I love you, because there is not even a question of lying between us, I take these accounts of the universe on trust: your address twenty-five years ago, your relationship with someone I know only by sight, this morning's weather. I fling unconscious tendrils of belief, like slender green threads, across statements such as these, statements made so unequivocally, which have no tone or shadow of tentativeness. I build them into the mosaic of my world. I allow my universe to change in minute, significant ways, on the basis of things you have said to me, of my trust in you.

I also have faith that you are telling me things it is important I should know; that you do not conceal facts from me in an effort to spare me, or yourself, pain.

Or, at the very least, that you will say, 'There are things I am not telling you.'

When we discover that someone we trusted can be trusted no longer, it forces us to re-examine the universe, to question the whole instinct and concept of trust. For awhile, we are thrust back onto some bleak, jutting ledge, in a dark pierced by sheets of fire, swept by sheets of rain, in a world before kinship, or naming, or tenderness exist; we are brought close to formlessness.

. . .

The liar may resist confrontation, denying that she lied. Or she may use other language: forgetfulness, privacy, the protection of someone else. Or, she may bravely declare herself a coward. This allows her to go on lying, since that is what cowards do. She does not say, *I was afraid*, since this would open the question of other ways of handling her fear. It would open the question of what is actually feared.

She may say, *I didn't want to cause pain.* What she really did not want is to have to deal with the other's pain. The lie is a short-cut through another's personality.

. . .

Truthfulness, honor, is not something which springs ablaze of itself; it has to be created between people.

This is true in political situations. The quality and depth of the politics evolving from a group depends in very large part on their understanding of honor.

Much of what is narrowly termed 'politics' seems to rest on a longing for certainty even at the cost of honesty, for an analysis which, once given, need not be re-examined. Such is the deadendedness – for women – of Marxism in our time.

Truthfulness anywhere means a heightened complexity. But it is a movement into evolution. Women are only beginning to uncover our own truths; many of us would be grateful for some rest in that struggle, would be glad just to lie down with the sherds we have painfully unearthed, and be satisfied with those. Often I feel this like an exhaustion in my own body.

The politics worth having, the relationships worth having, demand that we delve still deeper.

. . .

The possibilities that exist between two people, or among a group of people, are a kind of alchemy. They are the most interesting thing in life. The liar is someone who keeps losing sight of these possibilities.

When relationships are determined by manipulation, by the need for control, they may possess a dreary, bickering kind of drama, but they cease to be interesting. They are repetitive; the shock of human possibilities has ceased to reverberate through them.

When someone tells me a piece of the truth which has been withheld from me, and which I needed in order to see my life more clearly, it may bring acute pain, but it can also flood me with a cold, sea-sharp wash of relief. Often such truths come by accident, or from strangers.

It isn't that to have an honorable relationship with you, I have to understand everything, or tell you everything at once, or that I can know, beforehand, everything I need to tell you.

It means that most of the time I am eager, longing for the possibility of telling you. That these possibilities may seem frightening, but not destructive, to me. That I feel strong enough to hear your tentative and groping words. That we both know we are trying, all the time, to extend the possibilities of truth between us.

The possibility of life between us.

NOTES

* 'Compulsory Heterosexuality and Lesbian Existence', *Signs*, 5 (1980) 648. (This article is reprinted in Ann Snitow, Christine Stansell and Sharon Thompson (eds), *Desire: The Politics of Sexuality* (London: Virago, 1984).)

** The bracketed italicized sentences which start the piece, and the ellipsis marks within it, are Rich's own. Rich wrote the following preface to the 'Notes' for the *Lies, Secrets and Silence* collection (*On Lies, Secrets and Silence: Selected Prose 1966–78* (London: Virago, 1977)):

These notes were first read at the Hartwick Women Writers' Workshop, founded and directed by Beverly Tanenhaus, at Hartwick College, Oneonta, New York, in June 1975. They were published as a pamphlet by Motheroot Press in Pittsburgh, 1977; in *Heresies: A Feminist Magazine of Art and Politics*, Vol. 1, No. 1; and in a French translation by the Québecois feminist press, Les Editions du Remue-Ménage, 1979.

It is clear that among women we need a new ethics; as women, a new morality. The problem of speech, of language, continues to be primary. For if in our speaking we are breaking silences long established, 'liberating ourselves from our secrets' in the words of Beverly Tanenhaus, this is in itself a first kind of action. I wrote *Women and Honor* in an effort to make myself more honest, and to understand the terrible negative power of the lie in relationships between women. Since it was published, other women have spoken and written of things I did not include: Michelle Cliff's 'Notes on Speechlessness' in *Sinister Wisdom*, No. 5, led Catherine Nicolson (in the same issue) to write of the power of 'deafness', the frustration of our speech by those who do not want to hear what we have to say. Nelle Morton has written of the act of 'hearing each other into speech'. (Her paper, 'Beloved Image!', was delivered at the National Conference of the American Academy of Religion, San Francisco, California, December 28, 1977.) How do we listen? How do we make it possible for another to break her silence? These are some of the questions which follow on the ones I have raised here.

1 'Women and Honor: Some Notes on Lying' is reprinted from *On Lies, Secrets and Silence: Selected Prose 1966–1978*, by Adrienne Rich, by permission of © 1979, W. W. Norton and Company Inc., USA and Virago Press Ltd, London.

20

Kate Soper
b.1943

'CONTEMPLATING A NUCLEAR FUTURE' from
DOROTHY THOMPSON (ED.),
OVER OUR DEAD BODIES (1983)

In this essay Kate Soper offers some personal reflections on the prospect of nuclear war; her hope is to communicate something of the 'will to live' which, though itself deeper than politics, fuels the political struggle for nuclear disarmament. The essay reflects the passionate urgency, and the accompanying surge of optimism, which characterized that struggle in many European countries in the early 1980s.

Soper comments briefly on the reasons why it is appropriate for women in particular to speak about the nuclear threat: her points here are (i) that women are not handicapped in their thinking about matters of life and death by exemption from the discipline of caring for children; and (ii), perhaps more strikingly, that women's part in reproduction includes experiences whose 'crude biological vitality' lends the greatest possible piquancy to the thought of nuclear destruction. She is anxious, however, to avoid the suggestion that emotive arguments can take the place of technical ones: her real concern is not with motherhood as such but with considerations about the role of connectedness and continuity in endowing day-to-day activity with meaning.

'Connectedness', on the face of it, is as much a synchronic as a diachronic notion. The world of material things, institutions and relationships through which individuals establish and express their individuality is a world which exists around us at any given moment. But as we reflect on

the way our (human) identity is sustained by involvement in the actually existing social world, we see that this involvement is meaningful to us only on the assumption that the common life of which we are a part will extend into an indefinite future. It does not matter that we ourselves will die or that our personal hopes may come to nothing; what matters is that the social totality of hopes and possibilities shall not be closed off.

It is this relational conception of human subjectivity that forms the philosophical core of Soper's argument. In endorsing that conception, she is at one with the tradition of critical theory – both feminist and socialist – which has challenged the idea of an abstract or 'unconditioned' moral personality (compare Benhabib, reading 16). In this essay the contrasting view of our sense of purpose and value – the view that this sense is dependent on a resilient, but not indestructible, network of social relations – is revealed not just as an academic doctrine, but as an idea capable of inspiring the will to resist destruction.

To recognize the truth about the immensity of the peril we face is not necessarily to be moved to do much about it, nor even to feel repelled by it.[1] Many, perhaps most people, are aware in some sense that we may stand only a few years away from the end of human civilization and possibly of the world itself. But few sense this as in contradiction with their being alive now, or feel responsible for its prevention. To speak of a lack of responsibility and not of the impotence of ordinary people may seem divisive and even elitist. I am not suggesting, however, that people are directly to blame, or that if it were not for a general apathy, the situation could change overnight. For the economic and political forces (and their concrete embodiments in the institutions and instruments of war) confront us as implacable givens of existence. They loom like mighty towers against which the assault of the individual will, however determined, seems in vain. The letter one sends to Brezhnev or Reagan or Thatcher telling of the agony of sleepless nights spent in fear, meets with a courteous reply reminding us of the crucial role of nuclear missiles in allowing us to rest sound in our beds. Those who control our lives do indeed appear to be beyond the reach of our control. I am therefore blaming no one for quailing before the combined forces of militarism, neo-imperialism, multinational capital and Soviet bureaucracy, and retreating instead to the more humane business of their private lives. The responsibility of which I am speaking, however, is an awareness and feeling of concern which in a way transcends politics, while at the same time being the source of our power and self-respect as individuals, and thus in the last analysis the support of all conventional authority. I am speaking of an interest in our own humanity, of a care for our own species and the world we inhabit.

This common sense of humanity cannot overcome the divisions of class or gender or race. It cannot alleviate the suffering of the Third World, nor any other form of oppression. But a concern for our own survival as a species must be the implicit assumption of all struggles for emancipation, for these struggles, in their various ways, aim to establish more harmonious forms of coexistence on earth.

In face of the global nuclear threat, we as individuals need to rediscover this common responsibility to ourselves. We have allowed our rulers, operating in the interests of 'capitalism' or 'socialism' or 'global stability' to transfuse this life-blood of political power into the bodies of their cherished institutions, the World Bank, the Pentagon, the Kremlin, NATO, the Warsaw Pact; and these now seem to animate our world and to be the heart upon which we depend for our existence. But if the heart is pumping towards its own destruction, then it is vital that we find ways of reversing this flow of power.

To do this, we must in the first place inform ourselves in as much detail as possible about what is going on in the name of our protection. We must equip ourselves with data about the effects of nuclear weapons and with the arguments used in the political debate surrounding nuclear arms and disarmament. In addition to providing ourselves with factual and political information, we need now, I think, to reflect more on what it is, psychologically, that has made the struggle for disarmament so urgent for us personally. And we need to try to communicate this without too many fears for its 'emotive' nature or its political naivety. We need to inspire others with our will to live.

It is particularly relevant in this connection that women should speak. For by virtue of their role in human reproduction, their statements are given the authority of experiences that men do not have. Some of these experiences match in their crude biological vitality the crude wreck of biology that would be the experience of nuclear war. The starkness of contrast between the event of conception and the event which irradiates the womb, between the act of giving birth and the act which evaporates the child: this is something which women owe it to the world to talk about.

By thinking and speaking of these fundamental issues which the prospect of war brings us back to, but whose communication tends to be submerged beneath the more normal forms of political discourse, I believe that we can begin to regenerate ourselves as individual sources of power. We can begin to restore a sense of our own organic extension in the world, and thereby be shocked into responsibility. It has sometimes struck me that there is an odd paradox about the nuclear threat: for while, on the one hand, it presents itself as the most indomitable force that has ever confronted the individual, it is also a great political leveller. It took nuclear weapons to make me realize the full extent of the paltriness, the impoverished understanding and the sheer irrationality of most of those who govern me. I have not ever deferred readily to politicians, but I can no longer look on now in the same way while they are allowed to fumble around with the entire future of the world. It is almost as if I were a passenger in a storm-rocked boat who has suddenly realized that the captain is drunk. The feeling is: if they are going to behave like this, then I am going to have to do the job for them. After all, we have got to prevent nuclear holocaust.

Two years ago, I rejoined CND and have been active in it since.[2] During that time I have not acquired any official political status I did not enjoy before: by all the formal criteria of power in our society, I am as powerless as I ever was. In reality I have acquired far more control over the destiny of world affairs than I held two years ago. In order to understand this, we have to understand that power of the kind I am talking about is not like natural energy, convertible but always quantitatively constant. It is more like love: we do not love the first child half as much in order to love the second. Likewise, to gain this power you do not have to feel obliged, *in the first instance*, to take power from somewhere else – from the Pentagon or the Kremlin or wherever. You need only to energize it within yourself through some process of realization, of responsibility. This process will be different for different individuals. I want to describe the form it took for me.

Imagine human civilization being blown apart within a few moments of your finishing reading this sentence. It seems an absurd suggestion. What spurred me into working for nuclear disarmament was a kind of conversion in my thoughts about war that made me realize that ideas of that kind were not nearly as absurd as they ought to be. I ceased viewing nuclear war as an indefinitely receding future possibility, moving away from us as we moved forward in time, and confronted it as an imminency. For the first time, I felt its menace as part of the fabric of our current existence.

What followed was a very frightening and depressing period in which I found myself placed imaginatively in various scenarios: I thought of myself going to work in a situation of mounting international tension; I thought of myself eating breakfast as the news came through that the country was on war alert; I thought of myself in bed with the children asleep as the sirens started wailing; I thought of myself huddled in some makeshift shelter whose corners had caught fire. I tried to think of myself coping with such moments, and could not: there were no psychological resources to draw upon.

I sensed also something of the shock of what it would be like for life in full swing to be suddenly arrested; and I began to think more fully about what it meant for us to live out our lives in the context of the possible total blackout of human civilization. I was struck by the tension that the prospect of nuclear obliteration introduced between the importance of our lives and their possible vacuity. In thinking about my everyday activities, in the context of a possible abrupt ending to everything, I came to regard them in a fresh light: when I thought of each act as possibly the last of its kind that I was ever to undertake, the most mundane task seemed weighted down with an unnatural importance. At the same time, in that I was thinking of my activities as possibly cut off from the future into which they would otherwise have flowed, even the most major undertakings seemed utterly pointless. Because I was reflecting in this way upon the status of each present act and its relations with the future, I ceased for a time to act habitually. My life went on in all its activities just as before, but I was no longer immersed in it in the same way. The daily round of action temporarily lost its fluidity. Each moment in it seemed preceded by another moment of suspended action in which I questioned the purpose of what was being done if, in the next moment, I and the world I knew could cease to exist.

This was a period, then, in which the fear of nuclear war moved out of the background it had occupied throughout most of my life. I became aware in a way I had not been before of the horror that nuclear war would bring about. Above all, perhaps, what was new was a sense of contradiction; a sense of there being an impossibility about our current existence. It is a simple truth that we cannot live our lives as if the end of the world could occur. It is equally true that it is part of the reality of our lives that they have to be lived in the context of that possible occurrence. These truths are incompatible, but they come together now and will continue to do so, unless existing nuclear policies are reversed, for all the time of human history yet to come.

We have managed to place our lives within a dimension that is both so objectively real, and yet so inhuman, that it can only be thought about at the risk of a breakdown in normal living. Either we take on the prospect of possible global annihilation in all seriousness – and feel our hold on ordinary living slip; or, in the interests of remaining true to ourselves as authentic human beings possessed of our ordinary concerns, we deny the reality of that possible outcome. To live in minute-by-minute awareness that apocalypse is not the fabrication of a visionary but something that can be engineered concretely at the touch of a button – that, I suggest, is in fundamental conflict with what we mean by living.

It is this fact, I believe, which explains why even those who do confront the reality of our situation today, cannot dwell on it for long; and it is this which perhaps explains why so many people, possibly the majority, do not 'live' with the threat of nuclear war at all. What is important is not an analysis of this 'repression' but the attempt to lift it a little, however disturbing it may be to do so. Many people do seem to be doing that. There is no doubt that they are 'waking up', sometimes quite suddenly, to the horror of total death in nuclear war. And they are finding, as I did, that the only way out of the overriding sense of incapacity is to work for nuclear disarmament, often with consuming energy.

The threat to which we are subjected by the possible use of nuclear weapons has no exact parallel in earlier human experience. The fear it inspires is likewise without precedent, first because it is scientifically warranted, and secondly because it afflicts us all in some form. There have been isolated religious sects who have anticipated the end of the world, no doubt with absolute conviction that it would come on the appointed date. There has been superstitious dread of apocalypse. There has been the real fear of those who lived through the years of plague that human life was terminating. But never, I think, have people collectively, in the midst of life and health, been subject to the threat of sudden extinction we now face. The primitive watchers of the eclipse may have genuinely believed that the world *might* end at the point of total eclipse; and the victims of the plague may have felt that they were indeed experiencing its ending. But there is a great deal of difference between either the *uncertain* expectations of the former or the actual suffering of the latter, and our definite knowledge in anticipation that the world *will* end (at least in any form in which we currently know it as our world) if nuclear weapons are ever used on a large scale. Our experience differs from that of previous generations, in that we knowingly, but in a sense painlessly, live in history at a point where history could end tomorrow.

This sounds dramatic, but it is scarcely much of an exaggeration. The risk of nuclear war is increasing, and it is very unlikely to be limited. Even if nuclear war could be limited, the threat of its being total remains with us now and will do so as long as current arsenals are retained. It is this which I am claiming to be a unique form of terror – so terrifying that if we dwell on it seriously it is with paralysing consequences for our attempt to 'live'.

I have already linked our denial of the threat of war to our dependency on the prospect of the future to give content and meaning to the present. Our reliance in this respect goes beyond the span of time of our individual lives. To appreciate this we have only to look at our attitude to dying. This may seem a morbid theme to pursue, but in a climate where people are being daily conditioned into acceptance of the viability of conducting nuclear war, then any discussion, however disconcerting, that serves to alert us to what is being jeopardized by reliance on the fragile mechanism of deterrence, seems justified.

Now it may be said, in criticism of my points so far, that with or without the prospect of nuclear war, the fact remains (given the proverbial bus that each of us might at any moment walk under) that the end is always nigh for everyone. While this is true, it misses the point, for there is a crucial difference between living with the threat of the end of history and living with the threat of individual death. If it is only in the light of the future that we are able to go on living while we are alive, it is also only in the light of a future in which we, as individuals, will not be alive, that we can come to terms with dying. It is against the background of ongoing life that the prospect of death becomes tolerable and we can accept its possible imminency at any point. But to be faced with the prospect of collective death is to be disarmed of all the usual resources which allow us to come to terms with our individual mortality.

Should anyone doubt the contrast here, I ask her to consider those resources: the memories in which we are conserved by those who have known and loved us; our tangible bequests in the form of the things we made, the children we raised, the garden we planted, the poem we wrote . . . I ask her to consider dying in the context of all that, and then to consider a death without a heritage of that kind, a death coincident with the destruction of all memories and material embodiments of ourselves. It is not a prospect from which we can draw much solace.[3]

To know our attitudes now to the prospect of collective death is not, of course, to know anything of what it would be like to go through it. Yet it is perhaps worth reflecting on the actual experience recorded by the victims of the Hiroshima and Nagasaki bombs. If we cannot now think 'realistically' about some future ending of the world, it is because we have glimpsed the truth that if we *were* to experience it, the experience would not be one to which we could react with any normal human sensibility. It could not be undergone as a *human* experience, eliciting feelings of despair, grief or compassion:

> In Hiroshima, survivors not only expected that they too would soon die, they had a sense that *everyone* was dying, that 'the world is ending'. Rather than panic, the scene was one of slow motion – of people moving away from the centre of destruction, but dully and almost without purpose. They were, as some among them put it, 'so broken and confused that they moved and behaved like automatons . . . a people who walked in the realm of dreams'. Some tried to do something to help others, but most felt themselves to be so much a part of the dead world that, as another remembered, they were 'not really alive'.

This numbing, or closing off of the mind by the victims of Hiroshima, 'so that no more horror could enter it', this was the reality then which seems to find a kind of reflection in our present repression of the prospect of collective death.[4]

Now let me turn from death to life. Let me dwell instead on the role of the future in making our lives as we live them rich, meaningful and worth cherishing. Let me dwell on the role of a continuing history, and what it contributes in the way of language and culture and institutions of all kinds, to making us who we are – to giving us an 'objective' and non-biological dimension to existence without which we would simply not exist as human personalities. If we do not take account of this, we do not take account of the complexity of human life and of what distinguishes it from that of other species. Unlike other animals, our transmission of ourselves, the substance and continuity of our existence, is not confined to what we *in*herit genetically, but exists outside of ourselves, not being part of our biology at all. All of us, whether we like it or not, are born into an already existing world of material things (houses, parks, schools, churches), institutions (the family, government, the educational system) and modes of relating to each other (through language, forms of authority, behavioural conventions). This objectively existing world that we encounter at the moment of birth and have to live in thereafter, and to mould our personality within, is not something redundant to the person we become – as if, in its absence, we could remain as before in our true and singular existence. For while it is certainly true that we are *not* our language, or culture or our works of various kinds, it is equally true that we are not who we are without them. And it is largely through the differentiation that is allowed to us by the richness of this social world that we become as individual and unique as we do. All sparrows are much the same, give or take some minor differences in behaviour, health or feathering, precisely because they are confined to the limited individuation that is permitted by genetics. We, by contrast, acquire our individuality through what might be called a continuous 'extension' of ourselves in an objective realm – for example, in our children, friends, lovers, work, hobbies, pets and so on. Nothing, it seems to me, is more natural for human beings than to pursue this kind of 'self-extension' in various modes of loving, reproducing, creating and working; and it is this which gives human existence its specificity.

Nuclear war will destroy most, if not all, of the social bases that allow us to acquire an objective dimension of personality, even if it leaves a number of bodies unscathed. Even now the threat of war is eroding this dimension to the extent that it is curbing a spontaneous process of self-extension. I am thinking here of all those who have felt, in contemplating nuclear war, something of the pain expressed in Shakespeare's sonnet:

> That time will come and take my love away,
> This thought is as a death, which cannot choose,
> But weep to have that which it fears to lose

I am thinking, for example, of those who have been deterred from having children (or at least felt more pangs about doing so) by the horror of what may lie in store for them. I am thinking of the way in which the prospect of an absolute 'coming to dust' of all our projects can make us doubt the ultimate value of any long-term undertaking. For in these ways, creation of all kinds can seem blighted in the bud by the question that puts its future in question.

At the same time, the threat of nuclear war can lead to a simple refusal to look towards the future at all. The 'live for the day' attitude has, of course, always been a component (and by no means a wholly negative one) in our attitudes to the transience of human life and its unpredictability. If it is pervasive now, however, it reflects not so much a joyous irresponsibility as a rather sombre and reasoned estimation of the chances of having a normal life span. If young people tend to nihilism today, who is to blame them? It is, in fact, the height of hypocrisy for them to be condemned for improvidence and instability by 'elders and betters' who have never raised a voice in criticism of the nuclear policies that have made providence seem pointless and allowed stability to be identified with a balance of terror. In any case, against the disdain for permanence must be set the fact that many young people *are* planning for the future with CND if not with the Prudential.

There is hope, too, in the fact that not all reactions to the nuclear threat tend to solipsism or nihilism. In many people it seems to inspire an almost defiant kind of forward-lookingness. Instead of the cautious retreat from life or unconcern for its future, there is a sense that we must show confidence in its continuity in order, precisely, to secure it, and that by placing some 'stake' in the human race (most obviously and materially by having children) you help to guarantee its survival.

There is no doubt, however, that we invest in the future in this way only at the cost of complicating and intensifying our fear of nuclear war. This, at any rate, is my experience, for it is when I think about children – my own and children in general – that I feel most despairing. The despair is not so much to do with some possible future holocaust which they might have to suffer and die in. It is more to do with a society that can allow such a total contradiction between the tender, patient, day-to-day care that parents and nurses and teachers bestow on children, and the callousness of nuclear decision-making. Perhaps it is here, if anywhere, that there are connections to be made between militarism and a sexual division of labour. Why, on the one hand, should I be able to see in nuclear weapons things that melt eyeballs, blast bodies to bloody fragments and burn the flesh to the bone of living people, while military strategists see in them only counters in a game? Why is it that while I flinch at every euphemism they produce, these experts continue to computate their equations of terror and to offer their dispassionate appraisals of 'lethality factors' and 'collateral damage'? Some part of the answer, I suspect, must lie in the fact that this largely masculine body of personnel has never had to attend to children, intimately, day after day, ministering to their simplest physical needs.

These, of couse, will be dismissed as emotive and feminine arguments. Or it will be said, perhaps, that *everyone* agrees that nuclear war would be more hellish than any other hell unleashed by war; the point is how to prevent it. I will argue through the irrationality of deterrence and current nuclear policy with anyone who cares to take me on: I will do so in detail, coldly and even clinically. But in a final moment of feminine intuition, I might well want to add that much of the 'rationality' of those who offer their 'realistic' scenarios is utterly and completely out of touch with the reality of what nuclear weapons can do – and thus in turn with a significant part of the reason for not wanting to have them.

If our lives as human beings owe so much to what is not a mere matter of biology, then we cannot identify survival simply with the salvaging of the physical body. Too often this truth is forgotten in the dispute over the viability of civil defence measures against nuclear war. The opponents of civil defence are quite right to highlight the inadequacy of such measures, but what also needs to be emphasized is that the whole discussion is conducted in the light of a very restricted, and even degenerate, concept of 'survival'. Thus, to those who assure me that shelters can provide a measure of physical protection, I am inclined to say: 'So what?' – for the fact that a significant proportion of people might survive a nuclear war physically unscathed seems to me largely irrelevant to the question of human survival.

We should be clear that if we are going to allow ourselves to talk about 'surviving' nuclear war, then we are not talking about survival in any recognizable form. The life that any physical survivors of nuclear war would be condemned to live out cannot be compared, as some have suggested, to the life of the Middle Ages, nor even to that of the Stone Age. Those who lived in those periods were not reproducing themselves in the knowledge that their entire familiar world had but latterly, and by human agency, been blown apart – the world of their production and consumption *was* their familiar world. Nor were they 'struggling' for existence with a nature contaminated, possibly beyond repair, by the effects of radiation. To survive nuclear war would not be to regress to some earlier stage of civilization; it would be to live *after* the development of civilization had come to an end. It would in that sense be to live outside history. Even if a minority of survivors were to scratch together enough to satisfy their physical needs, their life would be one without the distinction between work and leisure, without any sense of community and without any culture. It would be the most physically tortuous life imaginable, and either emotionally barren or wracked by grief, remorse and longing. I do not believe that there would be many who could see their lives in such circumstances as anything but a waiting period before death, as a failure of *human* survival.

We have somehow to summon up within ourselves the will to confront this possible death of human existence. We have also continually to remind ourselves of *how* possible it is: some thousands of missiles are waiting in their silos to make it come true; whole military establishments exist to put them into operation; there are scores of people who are ready and willing to execute whatever orders they receive. I do not think one can dwell on this impending disaster very long without awakening the need to rescue humanity from it. This at any rate is my 'optimism of the will'. Nuclear disarmament can be achieved. The numbers demanding it are already massive. Provided they continue to multiply at the current rate, then the balance of history can be tipped in favour of the forces of sanity. We must stop thinking of a world without nuclear weapons as a kind of impossible Golden Age. Either we make it come true in our epoch, or we are living in the last epoch.

NOTES

1   'Contemplating a Nuclear Future' by Kate Soper from *Over Our Dead Bodies: Women Against the Bomb*, ed. D. Thompson is reproduced with permission from Virago Press Ltd., © 1983.
2   The catalyst for this 'conversion' was reading E.P. Thompson's pamphlet, *Protest and Survive*, a document that has had historic import in the resurgence of the peace movement in Britain.
3   It is true that some individuals (e.g. complete hermits) deny themselves such resources. Others may 'perversely' want to 'take everyone else with them' when they go. But the point is that these cases are exceptional and arguably therefore to be understood as pathological.
4   Perhaps it will be said that there will be consolation in religion. Not being a religious person, I would not want to pronounce on this. I have sometimes wondered, however, to what extent religious people are able to reconcile the hell that would be nuclear war with the inheritance of the Kingdom of Heaven which they presumably believe would be its sequel.

See also:
Jonathan Schell, *The Fate of the Earth* (Picador, 1982).
R. Lifton and K. Erikson, 'Nuclear War's Effect on the Mind', *New York Times*, 15 March, 1982.

21

Catharine A. MacKinnon
b.1946

'PRIVACY V. EQUALITY: BEYOND ROE V. WADE' (1983)
from *FEMINISM UNMODIFIED*

Catharine MacKinnon is a US professor (and sometimes practitioner) of law, and a feminist theorist and activist. A summary of her position is given in her dictum 'sexuality is to feminism what work is to Marxism.' Marxism and MacKinnon's feminism are both theories about how a set of social arrangements provide for the unequal distribution of power. Social relations are definitive of social class for Marxists, and of sexual class (gender) for MacKinnon. But in MacKinnon the theoretically important social relations are not conceived economically, as they are by Marx and by Delphy (reading 5). Whereas both Marx and Delphy see the expropriation of work as constitutive of oppression (of labour by capital in Marx, of women by men in Delphy), MacKinnon sees the expropriation of women's sexuality as fundamental.

We do not have to adopt MacKinnon's theory wholesale in order to share her perspective on abortion. Hers is a political perspective: the question to be answered is where the power to decide should be placed. (As in Petchesky, reading 24, the answer to this question will determine who faces the moral question about the rightness of abortion in any particular case.) From this perspective, abortion is located in its actual social context, in which men have more power than women in determining what acts of sexual intercourse take place. Conception, although it is an event in a woman's body, results from something over which the woman cannot be assumed to have had full control.

MacKinnon here expresses her opposition to the view, enshrined in a piece of US case law, that a woman has a right to choose whether to have an abortion which derives from her right to privacy – to freedom from undue state intrusion. On this view, the woman's right is founded in the liberal distinction between the public and private spheres; it is a right she has qua *individual; and it is a right she will only be able to exercise if she has sufficient material resources. MacKinnon argues that this conception of the relevant right is incorrect. Women do not in fact belong to the class (that is, of male individuals) that liberal theory has historically been designed to protect, but to a complementary class which collectively lacks power in the very sphere in which individual autonomy is supposedly being upheld. And a woman's right of control over her body should not be seen as a conditional right, to spend money in a particular way if one is lucky enough to have it.*

MacKinnon's arguments about abortion law demonstrate, quite generally, why a gender-neutral conception of the legal subject must be rejected: it is not only false to the facts but also inimical to women's interests.

> In a society where women entered sexual intercourse willingly, where adequate contraception was a genuine social priority, there would be no 'abortion issue' . . . Abortion is violence . . . It is the offspring, and will continue to be the accuser of a more pervasive and prevalent violence, the violence of rapism.
>
> Adrienne Rich, *Of Woman Born* (1976)

Roe v. Wade[1,2] guaranteed the right to choose abortion, subject to some countervailing considerations, by conceiving it as a private choice, included in the constitutional right to privacy. In this critique of that decision, I first situate abortion and the abortion right in the experience of women. The argument is that abortion is inextricable from sexuality, assuming that the feminist analysis of sexuality is our analysis of gender inequality. I then criticize the doctrinal choice to pursue the abortion right under the law of privacy. The argument is that privacy doctrine reaffirms and reinforces what the feminist critique of sexuality criticizes: the public/private split. The political and ideological meaning of privacy as a legal doctrine is connected with the concrete consequences of the public/private split for the lives of women. This analysis makes *Harris v. McRae*,[3] in which public funding for abortions was held not to be required, appear consistent with the larger meaning of *Roe*.

I will neglect two important explorations, which I bracket now. The first is: what are babies to men? On one level, men respond to women's rights to abort as if confronting the possibility of their own potential nonexistence – at *women's* hands, no less. On another level, men's issues of potency, of continuity as a compensation for mortality, of the thrust to embody themselves or their own image in the world, underlie their relation to babies (as well as to most else). To overlook these meanings of abortion to men as men is to overlook political and strategic as well as fundamental theoretical issues and to misassess where much of the opposition to abortion is coming from. The second issue I bracket is one that, unlike the first, has been discussed extensively in the abortion debate: the moral rightness of abortion itself. My stance is that the abortion choice must be legally available and must be *women's*, but not because the fetus is not a form of life. In the usual argument, the abortion decision is made contingent on whether the fetus is a form of life. I cannot follow that. Why should women not make life or death decisions? This returns us to the first bracketed issue.

The issues I will explore have largely not been discussed in the terms I will use. Instead, I think, women's embattled need to survive in a world hostile to our survival has precluded our exploring these issues as I am about to. That is, the perspective from which we have addressed abortion has been shaped and constrained by the very situation that the abortion issue puts us in and requires us to address. We have not been able to risk thinking about these issues on our own terms because the terms have not been ours. The attempt to grasp women's situation on our own terms, from our own point of view, defines the feminist impulse. If doing that is risky, our situation also makes it risky not to. So, first feminism, then law.

Most women who seek abortions became pregnant while having sexual intercourse with men. Most did not mean or wish to conceive. In contrast to this fact of women's experience, which converges sexuality with reproduction with gender, the abortion debate has centred on separating control over sexuality from control over reproduction, and on separating both from gender and the life options of the sexes. Liberals have supported the availability of the abortion choice as if the woman just happened on the fetus.[4] The political right, imagining that the intercourse preceding conception is usually voluntary, urges abstinence, as if sex were up to women, while defending male authority, specifically including a wife's duty to submit to sex. Continuing with this logic, many opponents of state funding of abortions, such as supporters of some versions of the Hyde Amendment, would permit funding of abortions when pregnancy results from rape or incest.[5] They make *exceptions* for those special occasions during which they presume women did *not* control sex. From all this I deduce that abortion's proponents and opponents share a tacit assumption that women significantly do control sex.

Feminist investigations suggest otherwise. Sexual intercourse, still the most common cause of pregnancy, cannot simply be presumed coequally determined. Feminism has found that women feel compelled to preserve the appearance – which, acted upon, becomes the reality – of male direction of sexual expression, as if male initiative itself were what we want, as if it were that which turns us on. Men enforce this. It is much of what men want in a woman. It is what pornography eroticizes and prostitutes provide. Rape – that is, intercourse with force that is recognized as force – is adjudicated not according to the power or force that the man wields, but according to indices of intimacy between the parties. The more intimate you are with your accused rapist, the less likely a court is to find that what happened to you was rape. Often indices of intimacy include intercourse itself. If 'no' can be taken as 'yes', how free can 'yes' be?

Under these conditions, women often do not use birth control because of its social meaning, a meaning we did not create. Using contraception means acknowledging and planning the possibility of intercourse, accepting one's sexual availability, and appearing nonspontaneous. It means appearing available to male incursions. A good user of contraception can be presumed sexually available and, among other consequences, raped with relative impunity. (If you think this isn't true, you should consider rape cases in which the fact that a woman had a diaphragm in is taken as an indication that what happened to her was intercourse, not rape. 'Why did you have your diaphragm in?') From studies of abortion clinics, women who repeatedly seek abortions (and now I'm looking at the repeat offenders high on the list of the Right's villains, their best case for opposing abortion as female irresponsibility), when asked why, say something like, 'The sex just happened.' Like every night for two and a half years.[6] I wonder if a woman can be presumed to control access to her sexuality if she feels unable to interrupt intercourse to insert a diaphragm; or worse, cannot even want to, aware that she risks a pregnancy she knows she does not want. Do you think she would stop the man for any other reason, such as, for instance, the real taboo – lack of desire? If she would not, how is sex, hence its consequences, meaningfully voluntary for women? Norms of sexual rhythm and romance that are felt interrupted by women's needs are constructed against women's interests. Sex doesn't look a whole lot like freedom when it appears normatively less costly for women to risk an undesired, often painful, traumatic, dangerous, sometimes illegal, and potentially life-threatening procedure than to protect themselves in advance. Yet abortion policy has never been explicitly approached in the context of how women get pregnant, that is, as a consequence of intercourse under conditions of gender inequality; that is, as an issue of forced sex.

Now, law. In 1973 *Roe v. Wade* found that a statute that made criminal all abortions except those to save the life of the mother violated the constitutional right to privacy.[7] The privacy right had been previously created as a constitutional principle in a case that decriminalized the prescription and use of contraceptives.[8] Note that courts use the privacy rubric to connect contraception with abortion through privacy in the same way that I just did through sexuality. In *Roe* that right to privacy was found 'broad enough to encompass a woman's decision whether or not to terminate her pregnancy'. In 1977 three justices observed, 'In the abortion context, we have held that the right to privacy shields the woman from undue state intrusion in and external scrutiny of her very personal choice.'[9]

In 1981 the Supreme Court in *Harris v. McRae* decided that this right to privacy did not mean that federal Medicaid programmes had to fund medically necessary abortions. Privacy, the Court had said, was guaranteed for 'a woman's *decision* whether or not to terminate her pregnancy'. The Court then permitted the government to support one decision and not another: to fund continuing conceptions and not to fund discontinuing them. Asserting that decisional privacy was nevertheless constitutionally intact, the Court stated that 'although the government may not place obstacles in the path of a woman's exercise of her freedom of choice, it need not remove those not of its own creation.'[10] It is apparently a very short step from that which the government has a duty *not* to intervene in to that which it has *no* duty to intervene in.

The idea of privacy, if regarded as the outer edge of the limitations on government, embodies, I think, a tension between the preclusion of public exposure or governmental intrusion, on the one hand, and autonomy in the sense of protecting personal self-action on the other. This is a tension, not just two facets of one whole right. In the liberal state this tension is resolved by demarking the threshold of the state at its permissible extent of penetration into a domain that is considered free by definition: the private sphere. It is by this move that the state secures to individuals what has been termed 'an inviolable personality' by ensuring what has been called 'autonomy or control over the intimacies of personal identity'.[11] The state does this by centring its self-restraint on body and home especially bedroom. By staying out of marriage and the family, prominently meaning sexuality – that is to say, heterosexuality – from contraception through pornography to the abortion decision, the law of privacy proposes to guarantee individual bodily integrity, personal exercise of moral intelligence, and freedom of intimacy.[12] But if one asks whether *women's* rights to these values have been guaranteed, it appears that the law of privacy works to translate traditional social values into the rhetoric of individual rights as a means of subordinating those rights to specific social imperatives.[13] In feminist terms, I am arguing that the logic of *Roe* consummated in *Harris* translates the ideology of the private sphere into the individual woman's legal right to privacy as a means of subordinating women's collective needs to the imperatives of male supremacy.

This is my retrospective on *Roe v. Wade.* Reproduction is sexual, men control sexuality, and the state supports the interest of men as a group. *Roe* does not contradict this. So why was abortion legalized? Why were women even imagined to have such a right as privacy? It is not an accusation of bad faith to answer that the interests of men as a social group converged with the definition of justice embodied in law in what I call the male point of view. The way the male point of view constructs a social event or legal need will be the way that social event or legal need is framed by state policy. For example, to the extent that possession is the point of sex, illegal rape will be sex with a woman who is not yours unless the act makes her yours. If part of the kick of pornography involves eroticizing the putatively prohibited, illegal pornography – obscenity – will be prohibited enough to keep pornography desirable without ever making it truly illegitimate or unavailable. If, from the male standpoint, male is the implicit definition of human, maleness will be the implicit standard by which sex equality is measured in discrimination law. In parallel terms, abortion's availability frames, and is framed by, the conditions men work out among themselves to grant legitimacy to women to control the reproductive consequences of intercourse.

Since Freud, the social problem posed by sexuality has been perceived as the problem of the innate desire for sexual pleasure being repressed by the constraints of civilization. In this context, the inequality of the sexes arises as an issue only in women's repressive socialization to passivity and coolness (so-called frigidity), in women's so-called desexualization, and in the disparate consequences of biology, that is, pregnancy. Who defines what is sexual, what sexuality therefore is, to whom what stimuli are erotic and why, and who defines the conditions under which sexuality is expressed – these issues are not even available to be considered. 'Civilization's' answer to these questions fuse women's reproductivity with our attributed sexuality in its definition of what a woman is. We are defined as women by the uses to which men put us. In this context it becomes clear why the struggle for reproductive freedom has never included a woman's right to refuse sex. In this notion of sexual liberation, the equality issue has been framed as a struggle for women to have sex with men on the same terms as men: 'without consequences'. In this sense the abortion right has been sought as freedom from the reproductive consequences of sexual expression, with sexuality defined as centred on heterosexual genital intercourse. It is as if biological organisms, rather than social relations, reproduced the species. But if your concern is not how more people can get more sex, but who defines sexuality – pleasure and violation both – then the abortion right is situated within a very different problematic: the social and political problematic of the inequality of the sexes. As Susan Sontag said, 'Sex itself is not liberating for women. Neither is more sex . . . The question is, what sexuality shall women be liberated to enjoy?'[14] To address this requires reformulating the problem of sexuality from the repression of drives by civilization to the oppression of women by men.

Arguments for abortion under the rubric of feminism have rested upon the right to control one's own body – gender neutral. I think that argument has been appealing for the same reasons it is inadequate: socially, women's bodies have not been ours; we have not controlled their meanings and destinies. Feminists tried to assert that control without risking pursuit of the idea that something more might be at stake than our bodies, something closer to a net of relations in which we are (at present unescapably) gendered.[15] Some feminists have noticed that our right to decide has become merged with the right of an overwhelmingly male profession's right not to have its professional judgement second-guessed by the government.[16] But most abortion advocates argue in rigidly and rigorously gender-neutral terms.

Thus, for instance, Judith Jarvis Thomson's argument that an abducted woman had no obligation to be a celebrated violinist's life support system meant that women have no obligation to support a fetus.[17] The parallel seems misframed. No woman who needs an abortion – no woman, period – is valued, no potential a woman's life might hold is cherished, like a gender-neutral famous violinist's unencumbered possibilities. The problems of gender are thus underlined here rather than solved, or even addressed. Too, the underlying recognition in the parallel of the origin of the problem in rape – the origin in force, in abduction, that gives the hypothetical much of its moral weight – would confine abortions to instances in which force is recognized as force, like rape or incest. The applicability of this to the normal case of abortion is neither embraced nor disavowed, although the parallel was meant to apply to the normal case, as is abortion policy, usually. This parable is constructed precisely to begin the debate after sex occurred, yet even it requires discussion of intercourse in relation to rape in relation to conception, in order to make sense. Because this issue has been studiously avoided in the abortion context, the unequal basis on which woman's personhood is being constructed is obscured.

In the context of a sexual critique of gender inequality, abortion promises to women sex with men on the same reproductive terms as men have sex with women. So long as women do not control access to our sexuality, abortion facilitates women's heterosexual availability. In other words, under conditions of gender inequality, sexual liberation in this sense does not free women; it frees male sexual aggression. The availability of abortion removes the one remaining legitimized reason that women have had for refusing sex besides the headache. As Andrea Dworkin put it analysing male ideology on abortion, 'Getting laid was at stake.'[18] The Playboy Foundation has supported abortion rights from day one; it continues to, even with shrinking disposable funds, on a level of priority comparable to that of its opposition to censorship.

Privacy doctrine is an ideal vehicle for this process. The liberal ideal of the private – and privacy as an ideal has been formulated in liberal terms – holds that, so long as the public does not interfere, autonomous individuals interact freely and equally. Conceptually, this private is hermetic. It *means* that which is inaccessible to, unaccountable to, unconstructed by anything beyond itself. By definition, it is not part of or conditioned by anything systematic or outside of it. It is personal, intimate, autonomous, particular, individual, the original source and final outpost of the self, gender neutral. It is, in short, defined by everything that feminism reveals women have never been allowed to be or to have, and everything that women have been equated with and defined in terms of *men's* ability to have. To complain in public of inequality within it contradicts the liberal definition of the private. In this view, no act of the state contributes to – hence should properly participate in – shaping the internal alignments of the private or distributing its internal forces. Its inviolability by the state, framed as an individual right, presupposes that the private is not already an arm of the state. In this scheme, intimacy is implicitly thought to guarantee symmetry of power. Injuries arise in violating the private sphere, not within and by and because of it.

In private, consent tends to be presumed. It is true that a showing of coercion voids this presumption. But the problem is getting anything private to be perceived as coercive. Why one would allow force in private – the 'why doesn't she leave' question asked of battered women – is a question given its urgency by the social meaning of the private as a sphere of choice. But for women the measure of the intimacy has been the measure of the oppression. This is why feminism has had to explode the private. This is why feminism has seen the personal as the political. The private is the public for those for whom the personal is the political. In this sense, there is no private, either normatively or empirically. Feminism confronts the fact that women have no privacy to lose or to guarantee. We are not inviolable. Our sexuality is not only violable, it is – hence, we are – seen *in* and *as* our violation. To confront the fact that we have no privacy is to confront the intimate degradation of women as the public order.

In this light, a right to privacy looks like an injury got up as a gift. Freedom from public intervention coexists uneasily with any right that requires social preconditions to be meaningfully delivered. For example, if inequality is socially pervasive and enforced, equality will require intervention, not abdication, to be meaningful. But the right to privacy is not thought to require social change. It is not even thought to require any social preconditions, other than nonintervention by the public. The point of this for the abortion cases is not that indigency – which was the specific barrier to effective choice in *Harris* – is well within the public power to remedy, nor that the state is exempt in issues of the distribution of wealth. The point is rather that *Roe v. Wade* presumes that government nonintervention into the private sphere promotes a woman's freedom of choice. When the alternative is jail, there is much to be said for this argument. But the *Harris* result sustains the ultimate meaning of privacy in *Roe*: women are guaranteed by the public no more than what we can get in private – that is, what we can extract through our intimate associations with men. Women with privileges get rights.

So women got abortion as a private privilege, not as a public right. We got control over reproduction that is controlled by 'a man or The Man', an individual man or the doctors or the government. Abortion was not decriminalized; it was legalized. In *Roe* the government set the stage for the conditions under which women gain access to this right. Virtually every ounce of control that women won out of this legalization has gone directly into the hands of men – husbands, doctors, or fathers – or is now in the process of attempts to reclaim it through regulation.[19] This, surely, must be what is meant by reform.

It is not inconsistent, then, that framed as a privacy right, a woman's decision to abort would have no claim on public support and would genuinely not be seen as burdened by that deprivation. Privacy conceived as a right against public intervention and disclosure is the opposite of the relief that *Harris* sought for welfare women. State intervention would have provided a choice women did *not* have in private. The women in *Harris*, women whose sexual refusal has counted for particularly little, needed something to make their privacy effective.[20] The logic of the Court's response resembles the logic by which women are supposed to consent to sex. Preclude the alternatives, then call the sole remaining option 'her choice'. The point is that the alternatives are precluded *prior* to the reach of the chosen legal doctrine. They are precluded by conditions of sex, race and class – the very conditions the privacy frame not only leaves tacit but exists to *guarantee*.

When the law of privacy restricts intrusions into intimacy, it bars change in control over that intimacy. The existing distribution of power and resources within the private sphere will be precisely what the law of privacy exists to protect. It is probably not coincidence that the very things feminism regards as central to the subjection of women – the very place, the body; the very relations, heterosexual; the very activities, intercourse and reproduction; and the very feelings, intimate – form the core of what is covered by privacy doctrine. From this perspective, the legal concept of privacy can and has shielded the place of battery, marital rape, and women's exploited labour; has preserved the central institutions whereby women are *deprived* of identity, autonomy, control and self-definition; and has protected the primary activity through which male supremacy is expressed and enforced. Just as pornography is legally protected as individual freedom of expression – without questioning whose freedom and whose expression and at whose expense – abstract privacy protects abstract autonomy, without inquiring into whose freedom of action is being sanctioned at whose expense.

To fail to recognize the meaning of the private in the ideology and reality of women's subordination by seeking protection behind a right *to* that privacy is to cut women off from collective verification and state support in the same act. I think this has a lot to do with why we can't organize women on the abortion issue. When women are segregated in private, separated from each other, one at a time, a right to that privacy isolates us at once from each other and from public recourse. This right to privacy is a right of men 'to be let alone'[21] to oppress women one at a time. It embodies and reflects the private sphere's existing definition of womanhood. This is an instance of liberalism called feminism, liberalism applied to women as if we *are* persons, gender neutral. It reinforces the division between public and private that is *not* gender neutral. It is at once an ideological division that lies about women's shared experience and that mystifies the unity among the spheres of women's violation. It is a very material division that keeps the private beyond public redress and depoliticizes women's subjection within it. It keeps some men out of the bedrooms of other men.[22]

NOTES

1 'Privacy v. Equality: Beyond Roe v. Wade' is reprinted by permission of the publishers from *Feminism Unmodified* by Catharine A. MacKinnon, Cambridge, Mass.: Harvard University Press, © 1987 by the President and Fellows of Harvard College.
2 Roe v. Wade, 410 U.S. 113 (1973).
3 Harris v. McRae, 448 U.S. 297 (1980). This is not to support the *Harris* ruling or to propose individual hearings to determine coercion prior to allowing abortions. Nor is it to criticize Justice Blackmun, author of the majority opinion in *Roe*, who undoubtedly saw legalizing abortion as a way to help women out of a desperate situation, which it has done.
4 D. H. Regan, 'Rewriting *Roe v. Wade*', *Michigan Law Review*, 77, 1569 (1979), in which the Good Samaritan happens upon the fetus.
5 As of 1973, ten states that had made abortion a crime had exceptions for rape and incest; at least three had exceptions for rape only. Many of these exceptions were based on Model Penal Code §230.3 (Proposed Official Draft 1962), quoted in Doe v. Bolton, 410 U.S. 179, 205–07, App. B (1973), permitting abortion, inter alia, in cases of 'rape, incest, or other felonious intercourse'. References to states with incest and rape exceptions can be found in Roe v. Wade, 410 U.S. 113 n.37 (1973). Some versions of the Hyde Amendment, which prohibits use of public money to fund abortions, have contained exceptions for cases of rape or incest. All require immediate reporting of the incident.
6 Kristin Luker, *Taking Chances: Abortion and the Decision Not to Contracept* (1976).
7 Roe v. Wade, 410 U.S. 113 (1973).
8 Griswold v. Connecticut, 381 U.S. 479 (1965).
9 Eisenstadt v. Baird, 405 U.S. 438 (1972).
10 Harris v. McRae, 448 U.S. 297 (1980).
11 T. Gerety, 'Redefining Privacy', *Harvard Civil Rights–Civil Liberties Law Review*, 12, 233, 236 (1977).
12 Kenneth I. Karst, 'The Freedom of Intimate Association', *Yale Law Journal*, 89, 624 (1980); 'Developments – The Family', *Harvard Law Review*, 93, 1157 (1980); Doe v. Commonwealth Atty, 403 F. Supp.

1199 (E. D. Va. 1975), *aff'd without opinion*, 425 U.S. 901 (1976), but cf. People v. Onofre, 51 N.Y.2d 476 (1980), *cert. denied* 451 U.S. 987 (1981). The issue was finally decided, for the time, in Bowers v. Hardwick, 106 S. Ct. 2841 (1986) (statute criminalizing consensual sodomy does not violate right to privacy).

13 Tom Grey, 'Eros, Civilization and the Burger Court', *Law and Contemporary Problems*, 43, 83 (1980).

14 Susan Sontag, 'The Third World of Women', *Partisan Review*, 40, 188 (1973).

15 See Adrienne Rich, *Of Woman Born: Motherhood as Experience and Institution* (1977), ch. 3, esp. pp. 47, 48: 'The child that I carry for nine months can be defined *neither* as me or as not-me' (emphasis in the original).

16 Kristin Booth Glen, 'Abortion in the Courts: A Lay Woman's Historical Guide to the New Disaster Area', *Feminist Studies*, 4, 1 (1978).

17 Judith Jarvis Thomson, 'A Defense of Abortion', *Philosophy and Public Affairs*, 1, 47 (1971).

18 Andrea Dworkin, *Right Wing Women: The Politics of Domesticated Females* (1983). You must read this book. See also Friedrich Engels arguing on removing private housekeeping into social industry, *Origin of the Family, Private Property and the Sate* (1884).

19 H. L. v. Matheson, 450 U.S. 398 (1981); Bellotti v. Baird, 443 U.S. 622 (1979); but cf. Planned Parenthood of Central Missouri v. Danforth, 428 U.S. 52 (1976).

20 See Dworkin, *Right Wing Women*, pp. 98–9.

21 S. Warren and L. Brandeis, 'The Right to Privacy', *Harvard Law Review*, 4, 190, 205 (1890); but note that the right of privacy under some *state* constitutions has been held to *include* funding for abortions: Committee to Defend Reproductive Rights v. Meyers, 29 Cal. 3d 252 (1981); Moe v. Secretary of Admin. and Finance, 417 N.E.2d 387 (Mass. 1981).

22 As Andrea Dworkin once said to me, women may identify with the fetus not only because what happens to it, happens to them, but also because, like them, it is powerless and invisible. The vicissitudes of abortion law and policy have vividly expressed that commonality while purporting to relieve it. The discussion in this speech is a beginning attempt to recast the abortion issue toward a new legal approach and political strategy: sex equality.

22

Elizabeth Wilson
b.1936

'UTOPIAN IDENTITIES' (1988) from *HALLUCINATIONS*

Elizabeth Wilson lectures in the Department of Applied Social Studies at the Polytechnic of North London. In books and essays written over the last twenty years, she has articulated a particular view of the development of feminism and Left politics in Britain, and commented extensively on aspects of contemporary culture.

The typical agent of moral philosophy today is portrayed as needing often to raise the question 'What should I do?' For a woman of raised political consciousness, there will seem to be a prior, more fundamental question: 'What should I be?' The utopian feminist heroine is someone who has answered this question and magically reconstructed herself, thereby achieving contentment in a politically active and personally rewarding life. But we aren't heroines, and we don't inhabit utopia. If we have to cast off our old identities, what identities should we, as feminists, assume? Elizabeth Wilson talks about the difficulties of finding our feminist selves in the actual world that we do inhabit. She uses a discussion of some literary forms as a means of reflecting the problems we face in conceiving a contented feminist identity. Her own response to these problems is to explore the instability, the ambiguities and fragmentation, of identity. She suggests that if we think of our identities as fluid, we may become aware that rejection of our old ways does not require affirmation of some new mode of being that is correct, stable and authentic.

For many women 'finding feminism' consists in coming to experience consciously a discontent that relates to being female. One understands one's discontent, perhaps, when one sees that women generally are oppressed, and that femaleness is a part of one's self-definition. In consciousness-raising groups, for example, women's expressions of their personal distress are taken to expose a collective social being of womanhood. But the idea that one has identified all ills by recognizing the oppression of gender may lead one already to a dangerously homogeneous view of women (see, for instance, Rich, reading 19). And there could hardly be a straightforward path from this kind of social diagnosis of what is wrong in one's own life to making things all right there. If a woman decides not to participate in patriarchal institutions, she is not automatically rid of the restrictions and conflicting demands on members of her sex; and the constant small indignities that make up the quotidian existence of most women are the more likely to be felt as irritating. Nor (and this is more immediately Wilson's concern) can the recognition of one's problems as existing in a gendered social structure free one of those problems: on the contrary, it is a recognition that one's own thought and behaviours display patterns that one hopes that thinking about oneself will cure one of.

We might look to the confessional literature and to role models to determine what we are striving to become. But we should be wary, Wilson thinks. Her examination of some likely candidates for role models is intended to create in us a reluctance to suppose that their destination could be our goal. What is presented in literature as exemplary may place emphasis on life's conflicts at the expense of blurring over the real difficulties of removing them. If the resolution of subjective conflict requires the reconstruction of one's self, then the use of memory to recover how things were for one's self in the past cannot be a matter of gaining some simple veridical overview of one's life. We may be lured by the fictional promise that the conflicts of subjectivity can be removed. We may be led to indulge in the fantasy of psychic wholeness. But in any case, we must reject the assumption that there is a single set of ingredients that makes up the good feminist life.

None of this is exactly inspiring for anyone who thought that feminism might teach her how to live correctly. So far as learning is concerned, Wilson sees more hope through a kind of writing which does not tell of rejected identities as those against which the author has eventually triumphed, but in which the author can acknowledge her constant refusal to embrace particular identities: a condition of psychic flux need not be an inherently unsatisfactory transitional moment on the way to a stopping-

place. (In Wilson, diversity of ideals of the good life is associated with a postmodernist scepticism about the idea of improvement. We note that value pluralism as such has not always seemed to be an obstacle to the modern belief in moral progress.)

> I have always prided myself on my ability to let my own life stand as one example of the road women take to feminism.
>
> Cora Kaplan

The identity of 'feminist' was always a problem for me.[1] Not only the world at large, but also other feminists seemed to interpret it as a kind of character armour, unfractured by doubt or vulnerability. No chink in her armour for a feminist; she must be a heroine, a warrior woman, an inspiration to others. Moving between the twin poles of suffering and triumph which constituted the approved feminist path, she made the journey from victim to heroine.

I was neither. And besides, certainty for me had never resided in what I *was*, but in the ability to act. Initially the women's movement had opened up for me the possibility of liberation through action, a release from the introspection of identity. But gradually a new identity was imposed upon me, as alienating and oppressive as the old personas I had cast off. And this just at the same time as old problems, old uncertainties returned: the 'return of the repressed'.

Yet paradoxically in the hollow and alienated space between public feminism and private moodiness a former identity, of writer, was able to live again.

The women's movement erupted as a politics of experience: women burned to testify to what had been lost, silenced or never allowed to emerge into consciousness. Directly experiential and personal writing was seen as political rather than as literary; indeed, there may have been a rejection of the whole conventional artistic enterprise as women seized on confessional writing as a way of giving consciousness-raising a more permanent form.

In the early writings of the women's movement women aimed to express the radical otherness of their experience, in testimonies that still mirrored the world, but which made it strange because their angle of vision was different. These were to be narratives of truth, and women were to bear witness to the authenticity of their lives, a hidden and neglected truth, but all the more subversive for that.

I'm not sure how deliberately the women's liberationists of the late 1960s and early 1970s chose or used genres that seemed to serve the purpose of speaking our oppression. In the beginning I suspect we just plunged in. But, since no beginning is ever completely new, the enterprise drew on and adapted existing forms: the political polemic and theoretical writing as well as experiential literature. Indeed theoretical and experiential writing have been for feminism two sides of the same coin, the one investigating the other. Raw experience is marshalled into intellectual coherence and given a pattern within feminist theory, while confessional writing rebels against the elitism and distance of academic discourse and returns women's experience to its immediacy. But neither would leave the other as it had been. The experience of women would operate to disclose the hollowness of the claims of academic theory to objectivity and neutrality, while theory would elucidate experience. This theoretical insight would then inform political action.

Yet the fact that the purpose was always political could lead to difficulties. Political writing is meant not only to change people's minds but also to change the world. Theory on the other hand may become an end in itself, leading further and further into the convoluted passages of the mind rather than onto the highways of the world, while the political message may flatten the complexity of our lived experience to the one-dimensional caricature I came to feel was imposed upon my own experience and which can reduce dense, contradictory life to a pattern book for right-on women.

These difficulties have to do with the peculiar nature of women's place in society (whether this is defined as oppressive or not). It is clear that women are unequal to men, and not only that but their over-sexualized role can lead to a form of degradation. Yet at the same time the very inequality and degradation can seem to be rooted in what is fundamental to human life: the difference between men and women, a difference that is perceived and experienced as necessary, desirable and indeed pleasurable.

Women's exploration of this contradictory position is therefore bound to be fraught with difficulty and it is bound to open up what Cora Kaplan calls 'the Pandora's box of female subjectivity'.[2] Pandora's box contained all the evils of the world, as well as hope, and women have found that the desire to politicize the personal is not easily fulfilled; to map political solutions onto this knotty, resist-

ant, obdurate female subjectivity has led to a flood of writing and
theorizing that has extended the maze of subjective experience rather
than bringing us out of the wood and into the clear light of day on
open ground. We still glimpse the shining horizons intermittently
through a tangle of branches. The wide plains of non-contradictory
existence seem just as far off however fast we travel. Like Alice
through the Looking Glass.

But: 'It is better to travel hopefully than to arrive.' The journey
itself has become the objective and women's writing has gradually
changed.

An anthropologist, George Devereux, said that all research is
really autobiographical. Certainly mine was. I wrote about the welfare state in order to try to make sense of my own frustrating and
inauthentic experience as a social worker. I wrote about women in
the 1950s, in what I thought of as a form of depersonalized autobiography, in order to dispel what I felt to be a feminist myth of the
1970s – that women were pushed back into the home after World
War Two, that they were once more immured and restricted; when
my memory of the 1950s was at least in part a sense of new possibilities, of the 'modern' as the key to the ideology of the period, my
memory the memory of a period that was forward, not backward
looking.

I turned to explicitly autobiographical writing in order to inter-
rogate what I experienced as a further set of distortions – the un-
truths of that feminist identity I had found forced upon me and
which I found so oppressive; and which I felt was falsely celebrated
in a particular feminist genre: feminist confessional writing. The
feminist confession could almost become a formula: a childhood
characterized by emotional neglect, poverty, often sexual abuse; a
period as a wife and mother struggling with the recalcitrance of men
and the social isolation of the housewife – the 'problem that has
no name'; at length escape to a new world, through education,
divorce or employment, or a combination of these; the discovery of
feminism; finally recognition by the media and worldly success,
together with in all likelihood the fulfilment of lesbian relationships.

This story is not so different from that narrated in the novels of
the 'Angry Young Men' of 1950s Britain, who wrote of escape from
the prison of working-class or lower middle-class life, rejecting the
norms of respectability and deference, and the defeated hopes in

which they saw their parents suffocated. Those writers, however, displayed a certain cynicism about the affluent bourgeois freedoms to which they nevertheless continued to aspire. Feminist confessional literature by contrast expressed utopian impulses; a wholly new consciousness, a transformed way of life is possible within the confines of the old. Or rather we can burst through the barriers of alienated consciousness and material oppression by what is truly a triumph of the will.

I hesitate, wondering if my description is a caricature, whether I am confusing the travesty of feminism produced by the mass media with self-stereotyping. There were many different stories; not all feminist writings had happy endings. Not all were triumphalist. But the Strong Woman – who often became an Iron Maiden – of feminism *was* created within as well as outside the women's movement, too often imposing a particular structure of experience and response, consigning other feelings, other lives, to the dustbin of the 'politically incorrect.' New silences replaced the old. What appeared at first as a revolutionary 'speaking out', 'finding a voice' or 'breaking silence' could prove to be something rather different.

In addition the confession usually remained, in a literary sense, a conservative or at least a traditional form, its realism barely questioned. Readers and writers alike appeared to assume that the testimony reflected 'truth' in a straightforward way. These were photographs of reality. At first there seemed no recognition that, like all representations, they were artfully constructed. And too many of the writers of the feminist confessional work understood their alienation and confusion as part of the false consciousness of the pre-feminist period, feminism then being offered as a solution to these oppressive states of being.

For example, two of the most successful pieces of confessional writing to come out of the European women's movement were Anja Meulenbelt's *The Shame is Over*, originally published in Holland in 1975, and Verena Stefan's *Shedding*, published in the same year in Germany (and described on the cover of the American edition as 'the bible of the German women's movement'). Both were best-sellers. Each charts the progress of a young woman against the background of the 'sexual liberation' of the early 1960s and the students' and women's movements of the late 1960s and early 1970s: a journey from a false self to a new feminist self. But I read *Shedding* in 1985 and by then it seemed an outdated text which revealed the ideologies of the women's movement as crude and unsatisfactory. The heroine-narrator moves through a series of relationships which correspond to her development as a feminist, from sexual subjection to autonomy. She has a black, then a white radical lover, sexual relations with both being depicted as heavy and humourless. Neither man even begins to understand the heroine's desire for self-determination. She in turn grants neither of them any authenticity. Women's oppression is for her the only 'truth', even racism being judged as insignificant by comparison, while Left politics is a mere male masquerade.

The heroine moves forward to a lesbian relationship, but this also fails. The two women seem to feel no spontaneous sexual attraction for each other, and soon take refuge in the idea that their relationship is essentially maternal. However the ideology of motherhood is not explored, nor does there seem to be any awareness that the equation of lesbian with maternal feelings is a cliché of conservative psychoanalytic thought. There is a gap between the relationship described and the rhetoric of the period about 'women loving women', and the resulting effect is of dishonesty and equivocation. Ultimately the protagonist's acceptance of herself as an autonomous woman comes to imply a view of *all* relationships as constraining and restrictive; at the end of the book she is alone. Celibate solitude is implicitly advanced as the journey's end of the search for selfhood, an ending which is surprisingly similar to that of another best-seller about a young girl who comes to self-knowledge through the failures of her sexual relationships: Rosamund Lehmann's *Dusty Answer*, published in 1927:

> She was going home again to be alone. She smiled, thinking suddenly that she might be considered an object for pity, so complete was her loneliness.
>
> One by one they had all gone from her. . . . She was rid at last of the weakness, the futile obsession of dependence on other people. She had nobody now except herself; and that was best.[3]

This is a recognizable moment in the life of many young *middle-class* women. They savour that moment of coming to adulthood and freedom from intimate relationships even more than young men, since family intimacy *is* often restrictive for women, and the moment of freedom usually brief. (Most young women from the working class never experience it at all, even today.) Solitude, however, can hardly be a *political* solution, or indeed a solution of any kind. This is to elevate a mood or a phase to a significance whose weight it cannot bear.

In Anja Meulenbelt's autobiography the heroine's development is again charted through sexual relationships, from traditional marriage, through 'sexual liberation', to lesbianism. But Rosalind Coward has rightly pointed out that 'the centrality attributed to sexual consciousness has always been a potential problem in feminist novels for it seems to reproduce the dominant ways in which women are defined in this society – through their sexual relationships.'[4] Since, however, contemporary feminism has carried over from the culture at large the belief that our sexual being *is* the core of ourselves, that in which our identity most essentially resides, it would be difficult to avoid placing it at the centre of the feminist confession.

It must be that many women read *The Shame Is Over* and *Shedding* with an instant recognition of their own pain. Yet that very identification with the *problem* makes it difficult to draw back from the conclusion, or to take issue with the analysis, even if it is less satisfactory. Although these were counter-cultural works, they tended to substitute, for dominant ideologies about women, feminist truisms which acted in terms of closure rather than opening out and encouraging exploration of that which we cannot yet wholly understand.

Rosalind Coward argues that as the feminist novel/autobiography has become more predictable it has lost all political edge, and that 'transparent' writing (realism) 'where the heroine just moves unanalytically through experiences, is much more likely to end up endorsing dominant ideologies than questioning them'. For her, both Rosie Boycott's *A Nice Girl Like Me* and Alison Fell's more serious autobiographical novel, *Every Move You Make*, both published in 1984, are little more, at times, than counter-cultural Mills and Boon romances in which men 'find the heroine compellingly attractive', while she gains neither affirmation nor insight from these relationships, but simply heads towards breakdown for reasons neither she nor the reader understands. This can then be interpreted, Rosalind Coward argues, as a moral tale against the dangers of the 1970s

counter-culture, with its half-baked notions of sexual experimenta-
tion and drug abuse. Yet Alison Fell's novel could alternatively be
read as an attempt to get beyond the dimension of confessional
writing that so offended me in my desire to explore ambiguity,
vulnerability and 'wrong emotions': the imperative of affirmation,
the ideological pressure to 'celebrate' womanhood and women's
triumphs, the longing for the strong woman.

These women become 'role models', women on whom we should
model ourselves. This is very dubious. The 'exemplary' life inevitably embodies values and assumptions that shouldn't and can't be
made universal, as Margaret Walters and Mary Evans have pointed
out in relation to Simone de Beauvoir:

> It would seem that in its search for universal explanations, and
> definitions, of women's subordination, feminism is . . . deeply
> attracted by the idea of a universal, trans-historical feminist: a
> feminist for all cultures and all political systems . . .
>
> To mythologize de Beauvoir is . . . to diminish her. As a life-
> long champion of the Left, and of civil rights and liberties for
> women and minorities, she is one of the most eminent and
> courageous figures of the twentieth century; as a champion of
> 'freedom' or 'choice' for women, she becomes a manipulable
> symbol for many of those beliefs and ideologies within the West
> that diminish human freedom.[5]

At the worst the promotion of women writers as role models becomes
confused with mere publicity and may turn into what Helen Taylor
calls 'the most suspect kind of heroine worship', at which point we
are in danger of forgetting that 'the problem for radical readers and
critics is that the obsession with the author rather than the text has
been rightly identified as a bourgeois preoccupation which has worked
against women's interests.'[6]

In so far as the feminist confession-writer puts herself forward as
the exceptional woman who paradoxically typifies the problems faced
by a whole generation of women, she creates herself – even if unintentionally – as a star. The role of the star, according to Richard
Dyer, is to represent in a condensed form certain of the irresolvable
social conflicts in a society and to provide a 'solution' to them in

ideology. S/he and audience together create a magical solution to insoluble difficulties, and 'these star-audience relationships are only an intensification of the conflicts and exclusions experienced by everyone.'[7] That is to say, the conflicts may be *simultaneously* highlighted and smoothed over by the 'star' representation and this may also be the effect of some confessional writings: both to express and magically to solve dilemmas. This makes their challenge to the status quo at best partial.

The role model is a highly selective representation, and almost inevitably she will turn out to have feet of clay. Heroic qualities may be undercut by the heroine's further evolution. In 1985 Dutch lesbians were telling me: 'Oh – Anja Meulenbelt's relating to men again – she's "come out" as a heterosexual.' I heard these words spoken on separate occasions by different lesbians, but always with the same wry irony, as the new 'truth' appeared to annul the inspirational confession of a past decade. In fact, to elevate women to the status of heroine is to do both them and ourselves a serious, even a mutilating injustice. To demand of other women that they be wonderful on our behalf is to see them as abstractions, and is to deny something that Anja Meulenbelt herself identified as important: the right to try new identities, new ways of living and new politics – and to *fail*. The certainties of affirmation are always only half-truths.

It has been pointed out[8] that the need to 'affirm' and the 'realism' of confessional texts at times combined to create the feminist equivalent of 'socialist realism'. In the Soviet Union the question of the relevance of art to the vast majority of the population and its role in revolutionary struggle was of great importance, and socialist realism was intended to ensure its progressive role. However, it was liable to self-caricature, and at times under Stalin was very narrowly defined. Artists and writers were required to use traditional, non-experimental forms to express the triumphant truths of the Revolution. Nothing was to be shown that was 'negative' or 'decadent', and it had to be stated in the simplest possible way because 'the masses' were not capable of understanding anything more difficult.

There is something equally patronizing or else rather self-indulgent about the feminist equivalent. Theory is too difficult for us, failure and conflict are too painful; we must have utopia, that is, a non-existent place where everything is perfect. 'News from Nowhere' must always be good news. This is like Soviet defensiveness, which felt that to admit to any failure was to be defeatist, to betray weakness. So, for a woman, it can come to be defined as counter-revolutionary to admit to wrong thoughts or desires, to be anything less than a heroine.

Yet if the feminist confessional assumes transparent realism, feminist theory by contrast has made no such assumption; on the contrary, the feminist theoretical investigation of subjective experience has sometimes courted obscurity, and readers (usually other women) have sometimes felt alienated by an abstraction deemed to be unnecessarily obscure. The accusation of a wilful obscurantism has in particular frequently been levelled – paradoxically – at psychoanalytic feminist writing; paradoxically, because psychoanalysis more than any other theory explicitly incorporates autobiography and memory within its theoretical discourse, while its object is the exploration of identity.

Psychoanalysis introduced a whole new dimension to the concept of confession. It did much more than simply unveil the past, uncovering the 'truth'. It explored the way in which the recollection of the past involves a constant reworking of the notion of 'self'. The recall of the past, its dredging up from the unconscious and into memory is not a simple process of recall, but is rather the creation of something new.[9] It is rather as when jewellery or silver is dredged from some treasure trove at the bottom of the sea after centuries; eroded, encrusted with barnacles, the precious objects have undergone a 'sea change'.

Autobiography then becomes simultaneously an interrogation of and the construction of identity. It can no longer be the telling of a straightforward story, the revealing of a pre-existent self, a person who was there from the beginning, a recall of the past 'as it was'. Realism ceases to be the presentation of 'the truth', and turns out to be just another style, another way of creating an effect. And Freud's work coincided with the abandonment of realism in many branches of art (although also with the beginnings of film, most dream-like, yet most 'real' of all art forms). Art in a new, 'modernist' guise questioned its own construction, questioned its own representations of reality, and the deconstruction of appearances raised questions, as did also Freud's work, about the coherence of author, hero, self. Once autobiography had been seen as a source of truth, and the autobiographical author as an example to be followed; now, autobiography has come to be seen as another literary genre.

Although, therefore, the Strong Woman or heroic role model has always been seductive to contemporary feminism, there are other feminist writings which challenge it. At the same time, experiential writing has been used to challenge the abstract norms of academic discourse. Feminists have questioned the language, the form and the content of writing. In the early 1970s Sheila Rowbotham, in *Woman's Consciousness, Man's World,* tried to connect her own experience as a girl growing up in the 1950s to her Marxist-feminist analysis of women's lives under capitalism. A new language is needed:

> Our oppression is . . . internalized. . . . It is not just a question of being outside existing language. We can never hope to enter and change it from inside. We can't just occupy existing words. We have to change the meanings of words before we take them over. . . . The exclusion of women from all existing language demonstrates our profound alienation from any culture which can generalize itself.[10]

After writing *Sexual Politics,* one of the earliest and most widely read theoretical texts of the women's movement, Kate Millett rejected academic discourse. In the introduction to her next book, *The Prostitution Papers,* she contrasted academic writing with the new style she had developed:

> I no longer clung to that bleak pretence of objectivity routinely required of PhD candidates. . . . My language had to reflect the experience itself; colloquial, excited, immediate . . . I was writing at last out of direct emotional involvement. I began to write the way I talk and feel.[11]

Kate Millett was also one of the first of the contemporary feminists to look to confessional writing as a way of getting at troublesome female subjectivity, although she rejected the idea of confession for its suggestion of 'owning up' to something shameful. She believed that 'the shame is over' (the title of Anja Meulenbelt's book is in fact this quotation from Kate Millett). As Linda Anderson puts it:

> What Kate Millett experienced as published author was an inability to reconcile inner and outer experience. The publicity not only destroyed her privacy but . . . seemed to negate her own inner experience . . . Both [*Flying* and *Sita*] seem to

chart a process of near breakdown and also to defend Millett
against it.[12]

Kate Millett acknowledged a debt to Doris Lessing's autobiographical novel, *The Golden Notebook*, which had been published in 1962,
and which became an influential text for the American women's
movement. Doris Lessing and Simone de Beauvior are perhaps the
great mothers (heroines in the most ambivalent sense) of white
feminist writing. Both sustain a belief in the form of writing they
have chosen as a form whereby they can bear witness to the truth.
What lurks, for them, at the edge of this truth, as its Other, is madness, although each responds differently to it. Doris Lessing is prepared to endure the disintegration of identity it appears to involve;
Simone de Beauvoir locates madness in other women – women who
in her novel *The Mandarins* especially, are likely to attack the heroine
(her alter ego) – while she maintains what seems like a fairly rigid
persona as a shield against fragmentation and insanity. Both of these
writers also engage with, yet finally reject psychoanalysis.

Today, madness as a threat to female identity seems, in literature
at least, to have receded, although (as Carolyn Steedman pointed out
in a review of Elaine Showalter's history of women and madness, *The
Female Malady*) the latest chapter in this history is the phenomenon
of many feminists undergoing therapy and analysis. Nor is it that
there are fewer women psychiatric patients than there used to be. As
a literary preoccupation, however, madness looms less large in a
literature that has accepted fragmentation and which constantly
questions its own boundaries and the boundaries of the self. The
dichotomy of sanity and madness dissolves in this negation of literary
and psychic divisions, just as it is no longer a question of false
consciousness opposed to truth.

Today it increasingly also seems as if feminist writers are likely to
reject outright the traditional division between 'academic' or 'critical'
and 'creative' writing, writing novels and autobiographies as well as
theory; they also construct texts that do not conform to one genre or
another. Carolyn Steedman, for example, in *Landscape for a Good
Woman*, uses fragments of autobiography and reminiscences of her
mother as a kind of oral history and analytic recall by means of
which she mounts a theoretical critique of a certain tradition of
working-class history. The mother in her narrative rejects the identity of the warm, and indeed matriarchal, working-class 'Mum'

celebrated in the British sociology of the 1950s. Instead she yearns for a New Look outfit, which becomes a symbolic representation of women's desire, as against the heroic imperatives of a sentimentalized working class. Laura Marcus[13] has perceptively pointed out that Carolyn Steedman does not question the concept of 'identity' in so many words, yet her book asserts individuality by means of a series of refusals of *identification*: the coldness between mother and daughter; the refusal to share an identity with middle-class feminists ('I . . . feel the painful familiar sense of exclusion from these stories of middle-class little-girlhood and womanhood, envy of those who belong'); the refusal to affirm.

Even here, though, there remains a bedrock of authenticity. She questions the stereotypes of feminism and class-belonging in which a one-dimensional awareness of oppression both creates an identity – at once individual and collective – and absolves the subject from the guilt of alienated consciousness. Yet this refusal in turn absolves *her* from false consciousness; may in its turn become a 'correct' self-positioning.

In my own books, *Mirror Writing* and *Prisons of Glass*, I too implicitly questioned the authenticity that has been taken as the hallmark of feminist writing. These books were simultaneously autobiographical and fictional. They aimed *not* to have a heroine with whom the reader would identify. Both aimed to prioritize the inconsistent and fragmentary over the coherent. (Whether they were successful or not is another matter.) In them I attempted to investigate the clichés of oppression I wished to escape.

This involved a distancing from confessional material, and, since the hallmark of confessional writing is immediacy, sincerity, this distancing may seem too artificed, irony may seem to ill suit the material, or may coarsen into caricature or camp. There was something that jarred about all this – although caricature and camp are meant to jar and can be powerful expressions of refusal. Yet irony, mockery, refusal can undercut every position. And it may be that in my very rejection of a transparent authenticity I covertly claimed the higher truth of the postmodern flux of identity and the disintegration of reality. As much as the compulsion to affirm, this too could become a modish and apolitical substitute for the holding in tension of incompatible intuitions.

By which I mean: not only as individuals, but collectively and socially we feel a sense of cultural disintegration; like Stephen

Spender's parents as he describes them in his autobiography, *Worlds Within Worlds*: an Edwardian couple circling in a waltz – even though the ballroom floor had fallen away they still carried on as if it were still there. 'Things can't go on like this,' we say, 'but stable conditions need by no means be pleasant conditions . . . to decline is no less stable, no more surprising, than to rise . . . there is only one limit beyond which things cannot go: annihilation.'[14] Walter Benjamin wrote these words in the period of the Weimar Republic. Today, once again, misery and euphoria dance wildly together. What the British spent on Christmas in 1987 would have wiped out the IMF debts of three 'Third World' countries, yet there are seventeen million Britons living in poverty.

Jeering, jarring, camp irony; a Weimar response. The hysteria can fuse enjoyment, horror, disavowal. To write may aestheticize our sense of fragmentation or confusion. Yet, we women who write, why do we do it, we hardly know. Is it our privilege, our refuge? Perhaps by writing, especially in the experiential vein, we aestheticize our lives. We 'give style to our character',[15] live life as art. Perhaps we are experimenting with 'that most terrible drug – ourselves – which we take in solitude'.[16]

Perhaps, though, the drug, taken not in solitude but collectively, alters its properties. Or perhaps we are like the Surrealists, who also experimented with the drug of subjectivity, but who did so because they 'sought to win the energies of intoxication for the revolution.'[17] The retrieval of the past, or its reworking, then becomes a way out of its thrall (as in the psychoanalytic cure), a renewal of the self, as the painful manufacture of memories becomes an acceptance of the self or selves those memories then become. From these we can then perhaps fashion an identity that is fluid rather than fragmented. Change becomes a part of identity rather than its fracturing. We are then not forced to choose between an inauthentic past and trans-cendent future heroine, but may inhabit less exaggerated, less self-conscious, non-utopian identities.

NOTES

1   E. Wilson's 'Utopian Identities', No. 21 from *Hallucinations: Life in a Postmodern City* is reproduced by permission of Radius Publishers, © 1988.

2 Cora Kaplan, 'Pandora's Box: Subjectivity, Class and Sexuality in Socialist Feminist Criticism', in *Sea Changes: Culture and Feminism* (London: Verso, 1986).

3 Rosamund Lehmann, *Dusty Answer* (Harmondsworth: Penguin 1982), p. 302. (Originally published in 1927.)

4 Rosalind Coward, 'Cautionary Tales', *New Socialist*, July/August 1984, 47.

5 Mary Evans, 'A Postscript on de Beauvoir', *New Left Review*, No. 159, September/October 1986, 127. See also Margaret Walters, 'The Rights and Wrongs of Women: Mary Wollstonecraft, Harriet Martineau, Simone de Beauvoir', in Juliet Mitchell, and Ann Oakley (eds), *The Rights and Wrongs of Women* (Harmondsworth: Penguin, 1976).

6 Helen Taylor, 'The Cult of the Woman Author', *Women's Review*, No. 5, March 1986, 40.

7 Richard Dyer, *Stars* (London: British Film Institute, 1979), p. 37.

8 I am unable to trace the source of this insight.

9 See Linda Anderson, 'At the Threshold of the Self: Women and Autobiography', in Moira Monteith (ed.), *Women's Writing: A Challenge to Theory* (Brighton: The Harvester Press, 1986).

10 Sheila Rowbotham, *Woman's Consciousness, Man's World* (Harmondsworth: Penguin, 1973), p. 33.

11 Kate Millett, *The Prostitution Papers* (London: Paladin, 1973), p. 10.

12 Anderson, 'At the Threshold of the Self', p. 64.

13 Laura Marcus, ' "Enough About You, Let's Talk About Me": Recent Autobiographical Writing', *New Formations*, No. 1, Spring 1987.

14 Walter Benjamin, 'Surrealism', p. 54.

15 See Richard Bellamy, 'Postmodernism and the End of History', *Theory Culture and Society*, Vol. 4, No. 4, 1987.

16 Benjamin, 'Surrealism', p. 237.

17 Ibid.

23

Susan F. Parsons
b.1954

'FEMINISM AND THE LOGIC OF MORALITY:
A CONSIDERATION OF ALTERNATIVES' (1987)

As a result of the experience of teaching in a variety of settings, Susan Parsons is committed to adult education and to the practice of philosophy in an interdisciplinary context. The essay we reprint here is an exploration of where feminist concerns fit into moral epistemology as we know it. To the extent that feminism fails to fit, there are questions about how we (feminists) should conceive morality. At the end of her essay, Parsons suggests how we might start to answer them.

The three positions that Parsons distinguishes are constituted by styles of thinking about and within ethics. The divisions between them are not standard 'text-book' ones: they correspond to different views about how thinking is circumscribed, to different places at which the claims of reason may be held to impinge – outside a gendered reality (liberalism), within human nature (naturalism), within a set of actual historic circumstances (social constructionism). Certain familiar positions may seem to be excluded by these divisions, most notably twentieth-century versions of non-cognitivism. But it would be wrong to think that non-cognitivism is simply unaccounted for in Parsons's scheme. Some of the attractions of non-cognitivism might be explained by seeing it as a recoil from the liberal myth of transcendence. Or, again, it might be thought of as a position that could be classified with liberalism for Parsons's purposes. (Reason determines the correctness of cognition; and if you conceive the operation of reason in abstraction from particular human practices, then when you come to scrutinize what goes on in the ethical domain, you are quite likely to think that it has no place there. In short, you arrive at non-cognitivism, which, from this point of view, looks like an extreme of liberalism.)

Parsons see some difficulty about accommodating feminism whichever way we turn. Her argument, very roughly, is this. Feminists have gender in view. But if reason is supposed to be transcendent, then the gender system will not be open to rational view; and if reason is supposed to be humanly situated (naturalism), or socially situated (constructionism), then a particular gender system will be perceived as springing from certain fundamental facts, about our nature, or about our socio-historical situation. The problem we face is that of gaining a perspective on gendered reality as a changeable reality.

Liberal feminists, Parsons argues, are bound to underestimate the amount of social reconstruction that a feminist outlook demands. And feminists who are influenced by naturalism in Parsons's sense will lack any conception of the task of reconstruction except for a separatist, and ultimately pessimistic, one. The naturalists have put a new essentialism of gender in place of liberal rationalism, Parsons suggests: in celebrating some features of actual women, and criticizing some features of actual men, phenomena which are in fact specifically patriarchal have been presented as timeless and inevitable.

The social constructionist must view the phenomena of gender as changeable elements of reality. But this is no easy task. For one may ask: if values are immanent in social practices, how could anyone be in a position to make a value judgement condemning an accepted practice? Or, again: if my gendered subjectivity is socially constituted, how can I achieve a critical perspective on that subjectivity? Must I forfeit the very sense of self that allows me to engage in intellectual activity in the first place?

Parsons's suggestion for finding answers to these questions requires us to see ourselves both as sensitive to the social order and as developing within it. An imaginative moral subject who participates in a pre-existing tradition of critical theory – such as the (admittedly newish) tradition of feminism – may extend her insight into social reality and thus be able to intervene creatively in it.

As a feminist and a moral philosopher, I have for some time been interested in the understanding of morality which emerges from the great variety of feminist writing.[1] It has, first of all, been intriguing that the shift from liberal to radical and socialist feminisms has been paralleled by developments within moral philosophy generally and this process reveals many of the same concerns and disillusionments with liberal morality in particular. Part of what I want to do here is to outline the reasoning which lies behind this move away from the prevailing tradition of thinking regarding morality, so that it is more clear to us exactly what difficulties the question of gender raises in the process. However, it seems to me that the alternative approaches also are not without their problems. The moral arguments of some feminists raise again the spectre of naturalism in which critical distance is sacrificed and the point of being particularly 'moral' seems to be lost. Likewise the arguments of others suggest such a thorough-going social determinism that the person who decides or is responsible for her behaviour and values is lost. Thus the other purpose of this piece is to try to understand the problems inherent within these non-liberal approaches to feminist morality.

I think I am probably a 'sceptical feminist' but of a different variety to Janet Radcliffe Richards.[2] My scepticism is not based on the belief that an unbiased examination of the 'facts of life' will yield the obvious solution to our problem, if we only would choose to view them rationally. Rather, mine is based on a concern that feminist issues are challenging moral philosophy in such radical ways that we need to tread with care over the ground in front of us. We should be more clear than I think we now are about what new beliefs regarding morality will be required of us, and ought really I think to be questioning quite seriously whether and in what sense we are ready to adopt a much-altered view of what morality is, how it works within the individual's own decision-making, and what moral imperatives might finally mean. It would be ironic indeed if the moral enthusiasm with which feminists have, throughout the years, pleaded their case were to result in such a total revamping of the moral enterprise that the possibility for future changes of this kind became more remote. I would finally like to argue, therefore, for an understanding of morality in which the elements of attachment and imagination are balanced, a view which I think is a more constructive way forward for moral philosophy, and which also illuminates feminist concerns more sensitively.

Liberalism

In moral philosophy, liberalism is characterized by a particular approach to moral issues which has provided the rhetoric for political thinking about social and legal policies, and its influence in this regard is so widespread as to pass almost unnoticed in our society. Its history reveals its central concern with rational behaviour. Thus the belief that we can by the reasonable acceptance of principles control our actions to conform to what we know is good or right is the keystone of its construction of morality. What is required of the moral person is the choice, in a moment of freedom and detachment, of the principles for behaviour which one is prepared to live by, and a corresponding commitment to some ideal or value which is believed, felt or held to be important. Nothing necessarily limits this chosen commitment, and it is viewed as an entirely personal matter in which the mature individual engages in reflection upon those abstract directives which could form the basis for responsible choices. One's principles then become general, universalizable statements which serve as the first premise in a practical syllogism and it is up to each moral agent to guide future decisions in accordance with these. Rational behaviour is understood to be the control of choices, that is, reaching practical conclusions by calculating the best means to one's chosen end, or the best way of carrying out one's general principles. Living with other agents within a liberal society should present no difficulties for the majority of evaluative decisions, since we are free to choose how we wish to live, but this freedom can become the rallying cry of liberation movements which seek to extend social and political tolerance of personal choice. Problems emerge when it becomes clear that there is no limit, on this account, to what can be chosen as a first principle, since the description of these is formal and empty of particular evaluative content.[3]

This argument would be incomplete, therefore, without some suggestion that there are bounds to the kinds of things which may be chosen and that these limits are a feature of the nature of rationality. From the writings of Kant to those of Rawls, Gewirth or Nagel, the argument is that the structure of our moral thinking in itself furnishes the necessary criteria for values, which those who are rational recognize and conform to. Those who seek for the autonomous self-legislation which this view of morality supports, discover the implicit demand for consistency and non-contradiction, at the very least, in their moral reasoning or, more than this, may realize the basis for altruism inherent within our capacity for generalized, universal thinking.[4] The hope here is to discover the basis for an absolute morality, which is universally applicable and relevant, and which can serve as the basis for a sense of justice beyond the particular interests or backgrounds of any group of individuals. This absolutism is predicated on the assumption that such universal standards will not be found as part of the world, that moral values are not part of the ordinary furniture of our social or physical environment, but rather are uniquely discovered as rational necessities which require our obedience. On this view, rationality is more than a method for solving problems but yields substantive moral principles which are self-justifying and authoritative. These cluster around the notion of the equal worth of persons. The judgement of equality is founded on the capacity for reasoning about what is good (Kant), or an innate sense of justice (Rawls), or the fact that persons are prospective agents with intentions to fulfil (Gewirth and Singer). In this way, a kind of common denominator is indicated to which social and practical problems can be referred for solution and the basis for a liberal society is laid.

The liberal understanding of morality relies on the belief that each of us is capable of transcendent consciousness, that we can withdraw from the impulses of the body, the conditioning of our social milieu, and the limits of the natural environment in order to reflect upon what is the case and what ought to be done. This faculty for self-knowledge and criticism is central to liberalism, the only question being whether the principles for behaviour upon which morality relies are chosen or discovered by the free rationality of the moral agent. Morality is understood to be a special human activity both because its objects are epistemologically unique and ontologically autonomous, and because its activity of practical reasoning epitomizes the control which knowledge can have over behaviour. Liberal moralists are concerned to provide a description of moral reasoning which best represents these distinctive elements and thus retains the peculiar character of human consciousness in its relation to the world.[5]

In the early work of Simone de Beauvoir, the emphasis on this type of freedom of choice is applied to feminist concerns. Like the Sartrean ontology upon which it is built, de Beauvoir's understanding of the life and consciousness of woman is divided between a concern for the material embodiment of her self, and for the nihilating capacity of her human consciousness. Insofar as the body is concerned, 'the data of biology' demonstrate that certain physical facts 'cannot be denied – but in themselves they have no significance'.[6] The human body may be 'the instrument of our grasp upon the world', by means of which we develop a peculiar perspective upon our environment, but it does not 'establish for [woman] a fixed and inevitable destiny'.[7] Thus, the 'body is not enough to define her as a woman',[8] but furnishes only the material stuff of existence upon which the transcendent consciousness works. The activity of this nothingness, *pour-soi*, is to distinguish itself from being, *en-soi*, and it does so by refusing to abandon its unique identity as freedom and by constantly determining the meaning or value of whatever comes its way. The risk of choice which this constant freedom entails brings dizziness, but women can accept, in the same way as men, a resolve to avoid all forms of bad faith, *mauvaise foi*, in order to lead an authentic life.

> Woman is the victim of no mysterious fatality, the peculiarities that identify her as specifically a woman get their importance from the significance *placed upon* them. They can be surmounted, in the future, when they are *regarded* in new perspectives.[9]

To remain fully human demands the constant tension of being and nothingness in which the individual projects herself into being by means of her intentions and schemes for living, and it is in this process that values are created by human agency. The 'enormous burden' of such creative responsibility has, so far, only been bearable to men, but it is her belief that women will come one day 'to regard the universe as [their] own . . . to justify the universe by changing it, by thinking about it, by revealing it'.[10] It is thus consistent with the understanding of humanness which this type of existentialism represents that women are understood to have fundamentally the same requirements of rational moral behaviour as men.

Janet Radcliffe Richards, in *The Sceptical Feminist*, searches for the rational principles by which such feminist moral thinking could be guided. Like de Beauvoir, she argues that women have the same capacity for judgement and valuation as men, and that, to be consistent with this, women must discover independently of their biological nature what principles best encapsulate and protect the worth of persons. After a careful and detached scrutiny of 'the proper place of nature', Radcliffe Richards believes that reason alone can reveal the necessary precepts for use in solving the practical issues of women's lives. She suggests: 'The first of these principles is that *the most important purpose of society is to improve the well-being of sentient things, which should all be as well off as possible.*' With this rational guide, we are saved the problem of the utterly free choice which continually plagued Sartre's attempt at moral philosophy, and find the missing link between the insistence upon personal decision and the recognition that we live with other persons in society.[11] In addition to this statement of the end which moral judgements should be seeking to fulfil, there is also a principle regarding means, namely: '*everyone's well-being is to be considered equally; when social structures are planned no individual or group is to be given more consideration than any other.*'[12] Radcliffe Richards argues that these principles are 'intuitively acceptable' to rational persons and their consistent working out is the project of the critical feminist as she seeks for the distribution of equal rights in her society.

Thus, the history of feminist thinking in the modern world reveals some very close links with this type of moral reasoning. From the early days during the Enlightenment through to the development of utilitarian thinking in the nineteenth century, feminists have made use of this understanding of rational moral behaviour in order to plead the case for women's rights. It has been a strong point of their arguments that the liberation of women is not merely consistent with liberal views of morality but that opposition to such extensions of justice is self-defeating in that it contradicts its own presumptions. Liberal feminists thus persevere in their application of universal principles and assume that biological facts can get no purchase here. The insistence upon the special character of moral values means a rejection of naturalism of any kind. If values are not part of 'the fabric of the world',[13] if good is a non-natural property, then morality relies upon the human acts of willing, choosing, valuing, practically reasoning. And the logical extension of this, as feminists saw, was that descriptions of their physical or psychological natures could in no way entail evaluations of the meaning or importance of these facts. Valuing is personal and, accepting the abstract definition of what constitutes such personhood, feminists find no grounds for the exclusion of women from this special human activity, nor from its natural outcome in the revision of society.[14]

However, such a view of reason may prove to be itself the victim of the genderedness which it seeks to overcome by its transcendence; its very abstractions may be implicitly formulated in a gendered way. Instead of presenting an understanding of reason which is in fact available to both men and women, Western thinkers have predicated their descriptions of this human faculty on two assumptions: firstly, that nature is understood to be feminine and it is nature which reason transcends in order to function at all, and, secondly, that women are understood to be more bound by their embodiment while reason is capable of thinking itself beyond this prison. 'Rationality has been conceived as transcendence of the feminine; and the "feminine" itself has been partly constituted by its occurrence within this structure.'[15] The irony is, as Lloyd suggests, that 'Gender, after all, is one of the things from which truly rational thought is supposed to prescind',[16] so the discovery of 'the maleness of the Man of Reason' will not come as a welcome insight to those who believe that reason is beyond such relativities and determinations. If woman is the being who is formed as one of the terms in the dualism, if she is 'the Other' which it is the project of free rationality to elude, then participation in moral reasoning, understood in this way, becomes an implicit recognition of the superiority of the male, and particularly inappropriate for a feminist project.

> This genderedness of our concepts is embodied by liberal societies in the division of public from private areas of life. The presumption that human beings are rational, metaphysically free, prudential calculators of marginal utility – and all think alike in this regard in the public sphere of politics and understanding – is used as a contrast model for the qualities and activities in a private world from which the public sphere is bifurcated theoretically.[17]

The difficulty is not just that the moral principles appropriate to the public realm may not fit the needs and realities of the private;[18] but, more than this, that they may no longer be workable at all, once the separation upon which they are founded has been exposed. Liberal feminism works so long as its devaluation of the private sphere is acceptable to women, so long as women view their problem as restriction or confinement which can be overcome by transcendence, by entering the public realm on the same terms as men. But when the private realm is itself asserted to have important insights into the nature of good and to provide a fund of moral values unavailable in the public, then the method of reasoning founded upon such contradictions breaks down. It is thus dishonest at that point to claim the irrelevance of gender in the formulation of these principles in the first place. Many current moral debates conducted in liberal terms, like those involving abortion or new fertilization techniques or even our treatment of animals, suffer, I think, from exactly this kind of difficulty in applying rational principles. It becomes clear in the course of these arguments both that abstract principles, like equal worth or respect for agency, may not be full enough for all our moral needs and thus distort to some extent our understanding of the issues, but also that to use them at all relies upon an acceptance of a dualistic framework which may no longer be tenable.

As liberal feminists try to make use of this approach to moral decision, they may find that the transcendence of reason around which it revolves turns out to be illusory. Is it really possible for us to discover a 'decontextualized and ahistorical' definition of justice which all '"right-minded people" would accept'?[19] The claim that such abstractions are self-verifying may be merely disguised prejudice, for they only seem convincing within the socio-historical context out of which they emerge. The moral and political recommendations of liberal feminists could, therefore, be viewed as culturally relative, not universally sound as they believe, and to be unaware of this determination of our moral ideas and values is to promote the illusion that the rational person can utter and believe timeless truths. The case becomes 'enfeebled' because it recognizes no perspective from which its own can be challenged. The attempt at complete objectivity results in isolation and estrangement from the real lived conditions which feed the moral consciousness in the first place and it is an awareness and sensitivity to these which may provide us with the grounds for social and political change.

Liberal thinking is thus characterized by a longing for objectivity, but it does not escape the suspicion that its construction of rational moral precepts is context-dependent. The intention of providing such a picture of rationality is to assure us of a kind of aloof perspective from which to comprehend and judge particular cases, so that values come to reside in the world and attach themselves to facts wherever we consider them appropriate. However, the adopting of moral onlooks [sic] may not really take place in such a neatly segregated way.[20] Our acceptance of particular values may have a great deal to do with our sensitivity to certain facts which take on importance as we reflect on our situation, and our attempt to encapsulate these values into condensed generalizations may only disguise their attachment to the facts from which they emerged. The proponents of this model may be attempting to escape the inevitable vertigo of moral reasoning by promoting a 'consoling myth' of transcendence which is unsuitable and illusory.

> It is only an illusion that our paradigm of reason, deductive argument, has its rationality discernible from a standpoint not necessarily located within the practice itself . . . The cure for the vertigo, then, is to give up the idea that philosophical thought, about the sorts of practice in question, should be undertaken at some external standpoint, outside our immersion in our familiar forms of life.[21]

Abandoning the myth may help us to avoid the simplistic moral psychology which divides desires or commitments from beliefs and struggles to reattach them in some way.[22] And it may also encourage us to appreciate the presence of moral realities within our world, in and amongst the ordinary facts we perceive.

Naturalism

An alternative style of thinking about morality is available in naturalism and, while in many ways its proponents' values overlap with those of liberalism, nevertheless its view of decision-making is distinctive and it presents another interpretation of rationality. The structure of naturalistic morality is built up around human nature; some description of this nature forms the central core from which the motives for moral behaviour spring and to which moral actions are directed. Under the influence of Aristotelian thinking, naturalism views the moral project as teleological, its *raison d'être* being to bring to fulfilment those features of our humanness which are present as potentialities within us and which constitute our uniqueness as human.[23] To act rationally is to train oneself in the choices which will allow the realization of one's nature. Thus rationality is not transcendent in the same way as in the previous model, for human nature is not considered something confining or restricting which must be overcome in order to discover what is good. Rather, rationality works within the boundaries set by what we are. In general, because this nature of ours is multi-faceted and multi-layered, there is plenty of space within it for self-transcendence to occur, in moments of thoughtfulness or self-reflection. Butler considered this to be the primary function of the conscience, knowledge shared with oneself about one's attitudes or behaviour, and it requires no metaphysical detachment in order to function as a critical yet sympathetic judge of our selves.[24] What is needed, therefore, is some understanding of our nature, since this furnishes the entire context of moral thinking, and as we develop and deepen this knowledge of ourselves, so our moral reasoning becomes more relevant and fortunate.

Naturalism thus warrants the grasping of moral issues 'from the inside out'.[25] Moral decisions are related ultimately, not to the first premise of a syllogism which sets out some universal imperative or principle of action, but rather to some characterization of our selves, our problems, our possibilities. This characterization is both evaluative and descriptive; it is formulated both as a set of beliefs about our basic human needs, interests and distinctive properties, and as an implicit appraisal of the relative importance and desirability of these features. Some hierarchical ordering of these makes the act of choosing what to do more clear, for decisions become a matter of discerning, considering, discriminating within the context of these priorities what is to be done in given circumstances. The understanding of human nature provides a more or less elaborate and detailed specification of the kinds of things which are held to *be* true of oneself and which one ought also to *make* true by one's choices. Thus, morality is as much a matter of being a certain kind of person as it is of doing certain kinds of things. It requires the development of those qualities of character by which moral discernment also improves, and reciprocally, the ability to distinguish the important features of a situation is what the attainment of a virtue consists in.

> In moral upbringing what one learns is not to behave in conformity with rules of conduct but to see situations in a special light, as constituting reasons for acting; this perceptual capacity, once acquired, can be exercised in complex novel circumstances, not necessarily capable of being foreseen or legislated for by a codifier of the conduct required by virtue, however wise or thoughtful he (sic) might be.[26]

The circularity of this process is unavoidable since naturalism claims no standpoint outside our natures from which we could view the progress of morality or make any sense of its activities. It represents therefore an alternative moral epistemology.

Feminists have also used this model in order to express the special nature of women's lives. Radical feminists, in particular, have asserted the uniqueness of woman, the positive qualities of her character, the important insights which she brings to moral considerations. Rather than appealing to some abstract understanding of what constitutes personhood, radical feminists assert the necessary link between biology and personal identity, so that, in particular, men and women are understood to be two different kinds of person. The biological make-up of each is claimed to be more than a mere factual description of external properties, since any such description is, at the same time, an assessment of relevant features which have moral import. What has been mistaken in the past, according to this view, is not what the liberal feminists argue – namely that woman's value has been tied to her embodiment, a tie which rational thought and judgement can finally detach – but rather that the understanding of the meaning or value of that embodiment has been wrong. And this reassessment can only take place from within gender, not from outside, from within the onlook regarding one's embodiment, not from without. The inappropriateness of the evaluative descriptions of women's nature from our tradition is increasingly *felt* by women who now, on the basis of their own lived experience, call for other features of their natures to be given credit, to be considered 'salient', to be rendered meaningful within a new onlook. It is the point of radical feminist writings to offer this new vision of woman and, through their utopian fictions, to provide some happier prospect for the renewal of society in which women's morality predominates.

In the work of Carol Gilligan on the moral development of women, a subject which had always remained hidden within studies of the purported moral development of human beings, she illustrates the pervasive maleness of the model of moral maturity which had so far been used in work of this kind. Men have described morality in terms familiar to them and have thereby considered boys, in their development, and men, in their later life, as the ones who develop most fully, while girls never reach the final crowning stages and are thus classified as 'morally immature'. Freud already had proclaimed this in his observation that women refuse 'blind impartiality' in decisions and thus have an inadequate sense of 'justice',[27] an observation which Gilligan's discussions with women confirm. The result has been a lived contradiction, expressed by Virginia Woolf as 'a mind which was slightly pulled from the straight and made to alter its clear vision in deference to external authority'.[28] Women experience this in self-doubts, and in a divided conscience, when their 'public assessment and private assessment . . . are fundamentally at odds',[29] and the resulting confusion constitutes the major hurdle in women's moral development. What emerges from Gilligan's study is that women consider moral issues in quite a different way to men, that indeed the liberal model of morality, which is so widely assumed to belong to humanity in general, is alien to women, fitting uncomfortably to their lives and misrepresenting their ideas and interests. Thus, 'a morality of rights and noninterference may appear frightening to women in its potential justification of indifference and unconcern'.[30] Women seem much more concerned, in *their* definition of what constitutes morality, with relationships, interdependence, intimacy. To question the belief that this latter is a deformed or immature morality is to begin to undermine some fundamental assumptions about what the logic of morality is. Gilligan herself begins to interpret this in terms of rejecting 'the Greek ideal of knowledge as a correspondence between mind and form', in favour of 'the Biblical conception of knowing as a process of human relationship'.[31] Her challenge is that the essence of morality may, in fact, be its perspective-bound, relational quality.

This point is pressed home most vehemently in the writings of Mary Daly, and her work reveals the extreme implications of taking such an 'inside' view of morality. The critical part of her analysis is a methodical investigation of man's creation of woman, a vivid and gruesome study of the way in which man makes woman into 'the Other'. Man's understanding of woman as less human, as imperfect or deficient in relation to himself, as incapable of transcending nature, as an object or possession requiring his moulding and direction, reveals the fundamental link between his moral ideas and his own embodiment. He is revealed as the one who seeks domination, who attempts to control nature, who makes and produces things, who creates culture and its images, and he does these things as the natural expression of his physiological makeup. His morality is bound up with his interpretation of his own biology, and is thus labelled 'phallic morality' and its social outcome, 'patriarchy'. Daly's critique is intended to be sweeping and general, for she wants to expose the entire world-view which has been built up around male nature as it expresses itself in every place and time.

As her positive suggestion, she urges the expression of woman's own embodiment, by means of reclaiming the language of misogyny. All words are to be rewritten with feminist meanings foremost and, by means of this simple trick, the domination by the alien body-mind of man will be broken.[32] These new insights come, not from some external perspective, but from looking hard at the words which women have, up until now, been willing to utilize for their own self-understanding, until the penny drops and they see their own oppression. Likewise, this freedom is gained by a reinterpretation of actions, which once again does not rely upon women's abandoning what comes naturally to her. Those activities which have been kept in their place within patriarchal societies, which have been mistrusted and labelled 'sin' – most importantly women's spirituality and communion with nature – these are to be freed from determination by male priorities and fears, and allowed full freedom of expression and realization as woman's superiority. Woman's own self-image is restored to her by means of finding within her place and her own nature those qualities by which she can experience the joy of living and the world, hopefully, can be freed from its devastation by man. She then can see the various features of her life which have been distorted and misjudged, and, viewing them in a new light, come to evaluate herself positively. Daly's feminist recreation of woman is naturalistic reasoning about moral values; the meaning of the moral

imperatives in her scheme is to be discovered within her reinterpretation of the meaning of gender. Her portrayal of the situation as
a struggle between female and male, life and death is separatist,
dualistic and uncompromising, for there is no possibility of one
seeing the other point of view by leaving their own nature behind.[33]
What is called for here is the reconsideration of our view of gender
'from the inside out', and it reveals just how deeply these issues may
cut into our moral epistemology. To reconsider moral concerns in
this area is to look more closely at what exists within the terms of our
available moral vocabulary until we recognize something new and
discern a different reality. The issue which radical feminism finds at
the heart of morality is the need for such renewed vision.

However, it is the logic of this moral vision which constitutes the
central problem facing a naturalistic account. This is the root of the
challenge, by liberal thinkers, that such moral reasoning is guilty of
committing the naturalistic fallacy.[34] Women who identify goodness
with whatever a woman does, and assume evil to be *by definition* what
is of male origin or intention, are committing this fallacy and the
problem with engaging in this fallacious reasoning is that moral
language becomes either contradictory or redundant. Since, according to the liberal model, it is by means of our rational distance from
embodiment that we are capable of evaluation at all, 'naturalistic'
feminists seem to depend upon an objective principle of judgement
which their description of good, as 'equivalent to what is female',
cannot accommodate. If good is defined as a natural property, then
the use of the word 'good' becomes unnecessary; if it has some
special meaning, then it is contradictory to define it in purely naturalistic terms. Naturalism therefore seems self-defeating. Morality
which prides itself upon being intrinsically partisan leaves no room
for getting outside by means of increasing generalities or abstractions. The notion of a transcendent rationality has been one way of
avoiding the narrowness, and ultimate circularity, of this concern by
indicating to us the rational necessity for discovering independent
criteria by which to assess particular actions or policies, criteria
which can be applied to any circumstance at any time.

Naturalism runs the risk of being so deterministic in its description of the basis for moral evaluation, that the force of 'ought' is lost
in its moral prescriptions. Many radical feminist arguments seem to
reiterate what has previously been said of women in a new guise,

namely that 'biology determines destiny.' The response of radical feminists to the history of male determination of biology is to urge a reversal of values, but within the same overall confines of physical determination. The landscape is still dominated by sexual differences; biology is both the problem and the solution.[35] What is in danger of being lost from such an account is the fact that *how* biological realities shape our thinking and acting is partly, at least, up to us. This argument does not demonstrate well enough how our interpretations of biology interact with physical realities in the first place. Is the force of one point of view overcome by the force of another? Does the change from one view to another occur without language and thought? If the vocabulary of our oppression is utterly alien to the new one of liberation, then how do we recognize its presence or appreciate its importance to life? If the process of this re-evaluation of biological facts does not occur on the basis of some detached criterion, which radical feminists seem intent upon debunking, then how it does take place needs more careful examination. Otherwise we are left with the need for some conversion to a new point of view, a conversion shaped by realities more powerful than our consciousness of them.

While naturalism makes it easier to understand the attachment of an onlook to its natural grounding and context, which is essential to its construction of morality, it makes more difficult the prospect of coming to find a common ground by means of each individual leaving behind the particular aspects of her perspective. If rational considerations are bounded in the way that naturalism suggests, then this affects relations between women and men very deeply. The notion of two separate moralities can result in a distortion of our full understanding of what morality is. There are instances of imperatives for men's lives which require of them also a concern for relationships, for sacrifice of their personal interests to benefit the group and these suggest that morality is one, though it may be bisexual.[36] There are increasing numbers of men who believe themselves to be genuinely in sympathy with the values and qualities of life which radical feminists admire. Thus, they also decry the elimination from public life of the values traditionally consigned to the private realm, and it seems particularly inappropriate to call their concern self-centred, or deviously power-seeking, merely because they are biological males.[37] Male writers have been just as damning of phallic morality, seeing in it all the fears and insecurities which plague the psyche of man and encourage his pretentious destruction of nature.[38] How are we to *understand* these moral arguments if the gulf between men and women is so wide? Surely we do find ourselves in sympathy with some of what is said; we can at least make sense of it and appreciate its impulses. Naturalism makes plain to us the discreteness and particularity of vision which is characteristic of both moral and aesthetic values, but it also requires some description of the hinges which remain for the door between two points of view to be opened successfully.

The emphasis in naturalism on the particularity of moral onlooks can mask the presupposition which nevertheless seems to be essential to morality of any kind – namely, that its impulse is towards the general and inclusive. Without such transcendent appeal, moral language may become superfluous and the claim of feminists no more or less important than those of anyone else looking after their own interests. Naturalism furnishes this by means of a conception of shared human nature, thus confining the spaces in which moral thinking takes place. Its description of this, however, can become just as decontextualized and ahistorical as the liberal emphasis on universal rationality. Unless we recognize our participation in the creation of this context, we will be left with a preconditioning of life too heavy to be shifted by creative thought. Particularities of embodiment may shape our evaluations, but these are, in the end, what we make of them. How such generalizations regarding the essence of human nature actually work in our moral reasoning becomes an important matter, therefore, and one which we should handle with care.

Social Constructionism

Yet another way of understanding morality is available from those who would claim that moral ideas and values are a construct of various social conditions, including both material and ideological elements. Rather than emphasizing the autonomous person who freely decides how to act as in the liberal approach, and rather than assuming that human nature by itself can form a sufficient background for choices, this approach presumes the priority, both historically and epistemologically, of the social over the individual. The distinctive features of this approach are, firstly, the moral significance which is given to roles and relationships within a certain social order, and, secondly, an observation that our language and therefore our thought are confined to the parameters of the socially defined. The first aspect is expressed by the claim that the general moral principles and particular practical guidelines which we use for decision-making are the products of the needs and interests of the social group. They are already established as possibilities when we reflect upon a given situation or problem. We learn our behaviour and our self-identity in the first place as members of a group and in the process of this practical education, a way of life in which we also share is imposing itself upon us. Once again, Aristotle is the seminal figure here in demonstrating the link between value and social function, and, according to this case, in suggesting that practical decisions can be related non-syllogistically to statements of one's role, rather than to general principles or universal imperatives.[39] Our understanding of ourselves as moral beings is fundamentally shaped by networks of relationship and institutional customs, and we are therefore acting out these pre-existing patterns in our personal choices.[40] Values are thus part of the fabric of society into which we are woven; they embody social concerns and they confirm the social ordering necessary for a way of life to continue. Without such foundation, they lose their attachment to the very realities to which they are intended to bring meaning.[41]

The second aspect of this approach is expressed in the Wittgensteinian notion of language games, which suggests the limits of our rational transcendence and the concurrent determination of consciousness and behaviour. We are always thinking within one strand of language or another, and there is no place altogether outside these which can provide us with a pivotal point. Thus, once again, the supposed objectivity of liberal principles collapses into particular context-dependent concerns of particular groups or individuals.[42] Morality cannot therefore be a matter of leaving or transcending some world in order to discover what one ought to do, nor does it require us to return to impose this advice upon ourselves. Rather it is a matter of learning how to play the game and discovering within the rules what one is expected to do in order to qualify as a player. How we see ourselves and how we learn to act within various social contexts are parts of the same process, and their interdependence makes the link between thought and behaviour real.[43] What is creative about our moral reasoning must then be the construction of new variations which are possible within these bounds, and they are tested by whether or not they work successfully in these terms.

There are feminist writings which rely upon this social constructionist model of morality, and its distinctiveness becomes more clear when we consider the way in which gender issues cut across its field. These feminists have tried to demonstrate the determination of women's lives by the various role models and opportunities for expression which society makes available, and have shown how women's consciousness and morality is an internalization of such outward social necessities. When young, women are taught their self-identity in terms of certain expectations and possibilities, and learn to relate moral decisions about behaviour to these directly, from statement of role to evaluative conclusion. Thus, de Beauvoir is again used, this time for her belief that women are made, not born; it is the intention of this view to disclaim 'biological essentialism' of any kind which would materially and physically determine what woman is. Social roles and relationships not only define women's lives and become deeply carved into their self-understanding, but they are learned as behaviour patterns which have moral importance and which express, in a social way, what women understand themselves to be personally. It is the task of the critical feminist to become aware of these determinations by using available language and thought, and by means of this description of the nature of women's lives, to test the fit between any particular set of social institutions and some notion of what would be more fulfilling for women. There is no attempt here to discover universal principles which apply to all persons regardless of gender, nor to find some ahistorical understanding of women's nature that can be used as a permanent foundation for revision. Rather, these feminists believe that within present realities lie the seeds of change, which the women who understand the morality of the present order can nourish, by their critical insights, into a healthier new society grown out of the past.

Juliet Mitchell is a good example of this type of feminist thinking, particularly in her early book, *Woman's Estate*. It is important for women to be precisely aware of the economic functions which their lives are meant to perform, to see how the four social structures of Production, Reproduction, Sexuality and Socialization oppress their lives and build upon their supposed biological weaknesses and proclivities. The second step is to understand the ideological covering of these functions, since it is this which women take into their consciousness and are thereby produced as women. Ideology provides the sense of historical continuity and gives the illusion of a permanent, autonomous source of value. In each of these areas, women are exploited by cultural necessities and made to believe that these functions are essential to her nature. To understand this is to become critically aware of the imperfections, or contradictions, of the present social order, and it is in the gap between these and her own self-awareness that women's new understanding is to make its impact.[44] Thus we begin with the factual questions: 'What is the situation of the different structures today? What is the concrete situation of the women in each of the positions in which they are inserted?' and we discover there the sources of change. 'A revolutionary movement must base its analysis on the uneven development of each structure, and attack the weakest link in the combination. This may then become the point of departure for a general transformation.'[45] Mitchell understands this change as the breakup of 'an oppressive monolithic fusion',[46] after which each of these functions can begin to discover a new identity and express themselves as 'life-giving', rather than as institutionalized death. It is her hope that a new social order can be devised out of the antipathies and alienation of the old, which will more adequately express the 'bio-social universal' of human existence, and it is this which furnishes the basis for the moral consciousness to pry open the oppression of any given order.

Rosalind Coward, on the other hand, rejects the 'base/superstructure' model of Mitchell's analysis, in which revolutionary morality can get a grip, and offers instead a description of the tightly-knit relation of consciousness to culture. Like radical feminists, she claims that women's consciousness is produced and structured by an ideology which expresses the biological and psychological needs of men. The interest of men in promoting their particular perception of sexuality and in developing a culture which expresses this phallic superiority, has so far dominated human history. This universality of cultural production demonstrates the way in which biological realities are mediated via social constructions and discourses. Therefore, unlike radical feminists, she claims that there is no way to get back through all of this to a pure or unstructured conception of what the reality underlying it all might be. As a result, she is more pessimistic about changes within the terms so far established. Her book is an attempt to demonstrate,

> that various accounts of the family or the history of the family rely on a notion of the sexual drive as a given, which has as its aim sexual reproduction. Concomitantly, men and women are theorized as having radically different aims and pleasures; sexual relations and sexuality are seen as the same thing, both deriving from absolute sexual difference in the service of reproduction.[47]

This determination of our categories of thought is so profound that Coward believes all of the discourses so far used to understand ourselves have relied, with the exception of psychoanalysis, 'on a notion of sexual identity (and therefore sexual regulation) as pre-given'.[48] It thus becomes 'virtually impossible' for us to break out of this circle and understand ourselves in any other way.

Discourse-analysis, however, does provide for Coward a critical basis, for it helps us to find what is invisible or hidden within what exists.

> In the fullness of the discourse, there are oversights, lacunae, the 'blanks on the crowded text'. To see these blanks, something more than close attention is needed. What is required is a new gaze, an informed gaze, itself not the product of any one individual, but made possible by changes on (sic) the exercise of vision, changes in social and political conditions.[49]

The unique challenge of feminism is to ask unasked questions and, in so doing, to make the gaps in present structures more obvious. In this task of deconstructing what is given, new possibilities can emerge, but these are understood, not as somehow more adequate to an underlying humanness which might lie outside our discourse, but rather as more adequate to the particular *discourse* of feminism itself. Having untied the link between our language and some foundational reality, there is left only our language, in one form or another, and its relative values and moral expressions. Freudian analysis at least provides a critique of sexual constructions from the standpoint of an 'initial bisexuality', but Coward herself goes further into eradicating 'the individual', who is supposed to go through such sexual developments, from discourse altogether. The result of her version of social constructionism is that the idea of a coherent subject who is either the outcome or the origin of social roles is seen as 'a fantasy'. Thus, 'not only is identity a construct, but it is also continuously and precariously reconstructed'.[50] In the end, male and female are constructions of social identities relying upon this notion of a centred self which has instincts, dispositions, anatomical characteristics and behavioural patterns, and it is only in finally coming to terms with, and rejecting, this, that feminism can carry through its radical argument for getting beyond dualism.

This view of morality understands values, therefore, to be fundamentally expressive both of social requirements in themselves and of the human exigencies around which the society is formed. Values are created out of material conditions; they constitute the meaning that has been constructed out of the lives and circumstances of the participants in society.[51] Their authority is thus understood by those within the system, as it were, and cannot be grasped independently of this. What becomes more problematic here is to explain, without reference to a transcendent rationality, how a society could ever imperfectly express its required values, or vice versa, how any values could ever be used as critical of the society from which they emerged in the first place. Without reducing itself to a blind tautological statement that what a society values is what it values, this view must both maintain that values are intelligible within a way of life, and that social and historical changes occur on account of the imperfect fit of values to the realities which they supposedly serve. The dialectical method of resolving this problem suggests that, due to the historical (i.e. non-static) character of human social life, it is always conceivable for the individual or group awareness to stretch beyond its horizons into future possibilities. However, either these must rely on some unrealized potential which exists now within the order of things, and that requires some 'base' which the 'superstructure' imperfectly mirrors, that is, a non-linguistic reality against which the language of values can be measured. Or this method needs some view of the outer reaches of imagination or thought which would have to be, to some extent, free of being fixed by social realities, and indeed be capable of judging or criticizing them; and this thought might then be considered 'unreal' and lose its character of immanence because we could not get a handle on its meanings.

Part of the case which is made here is the same as the one the liberals hoped to make, namely that biology and value are not necessarily linked in any authoritative way. Women who realize this can thus be freed to reconsider the meaning of their biological existence in ways that may be felt as more authentic, and this view seems to suggest that it is possible for us to do this. Indeed, it is the responsibility of the reflective woman to do so. On the other hand, its description of the social character of language and values makes it plain that whatever those links have been thought to be, however the ties between biology and value have been knitted, has served and continues to serve as an expression of some underlying need or reality. While we would like therefore to fly as birds into imaginative new principles of judgement, we discover our feet of clay which fix us in an even more rigidly determined reality. In turning to Freud, both Mitchell and Coward find evidence for this universalism of patriarchy. While the former believes that Freud is describing women in a particular society – namely under the conditions of advanced capitalism – which might ultimately be overthrown so that their 'true' natures could be realized, the latter considers such optimism to be naive, since the base in human nature upon which the revolution could be constructed is believed to be deterministic.[52] The freedom which is supposed to be produced by this realization of our social determination seems therefore to be elusive. We are still not the makers of ideology, no matter how unattached *it* may be from natural realities, and thus the totality of women's oppression seems more unassailable than ever.[53] One wonders why we are thinking about it.

Ultimately, social constructionism can become too concerned to debunk our notion of what is 'real' by claiming that our handle on reality is linguistically shaped. Thus, 'the categories through which we appropriate "the real" in thought are discursively constructed rather than given by the real.' At one level, this insight is 'tautological to the point of banality', since it only serves to indicate that 'our *knowledge* of the real cannot exist outside discourse.' Admitting that this is the case, however, does not require us to sever the bonds of knowledge and reality altogether, so that all becomes discourse or varieties of language use.[54] We can avoid the dogmatism of distinctive viewpoints, and the determination of moral values by non-moral realities, not by doing away with these distinctions altogether, but by making wiser and more careful use of them. Indeed Barrett, quoting Timpanaro, calls this a kind of 'extraordinary arrogance' which conjures away external reality by claiming the only valid object of study to be *our knowledge of* objects of study.[55] Giving us the perspective of the divine but without any of its power seems of little point. To focus so exclusively on how our thought understands itself is to lose the initial attachment to natural human activities which language must have in order to be learned, and to overlook the discernment of 'salient' features of reality which it is the concern of morality to represent in some overall pattern of meaning.

What is challenged by these issues is the nature of the moral agent. While the initial enthusiasm for this approach was surely fired by personal experience and concern, it ends by threatening the existence of a person at all who might have lived this or could alter it. On the one hand, this is a way of describing our complicity in the structures that shape our lives such that no individual guilt is incurred. Since we are utterly the products, mind and body alike, of material or ideological conditions, it is more easily understandable that so many women live out their lives in perfect conformity to their situation, without question or even unhappiness. If we are what we have been made to be, then no disruption can or need occur, and personal responsibility is absolved. Here is the passivity of the consciousness which only receives from its surroundings the material it requires for moral reflection. On the other hand, the extent of this impersonal determination makes us feel the hopelessness of our circumstances even more keenly, but without giving us the necessary grasp of some reality by which to shift the present one. No longer may a revolution be effected by a poem,[56] since even this will be shaped by prevalent meanings and existing possibilities. This viewpoint encourages us to look back upon ourselves, our language and our values in a way which might be consoling, but which leaves us with no way to grasp the future that is not yet determined because it has not yet happened. How that future is to come about may not be predestined, and it is certainly part of our moral experience to sense some risk, some responsibility, some decision by which it may be realized. The phenomenology of the moral consciousness reveals the active attempt of individuals to grasp or make sense of their situations in ways that are novel, and indeed it may be this very activity upon which future hopes inevitably must be founded.

What this suggests is that we need to find some balance in this perspective between the inner and the outer points of view. One of the things we can do is to examine the windscreen of the car we are driving so that we can notice its cracks, see where it is smudged, observe the way in which the particular material of which it is made distorts our vision of what is around us, or find the clear spaces by which we can get a good view of what lies ahead. In this way, we become aware of our finitude, our limitations, our unique perspective which constitutes our identity as persons with a point of view. But it is quite another thing actually to drive the car, an activity in which *staring at* the windscreen would be a serious liability since it is what we need to *use* in order to be able to get anywhere at all. Unless we desist from the activity for which windscreens were originally devised and found practicable, we must sometimes merely use them to go forward without noticing them. So with our moral concepts and language. It is the human activity of making sense of life which gave rise to these in the first instance, albeit in a social environment, and they retain what meaning they have in the context of human purposes and pursuits, interests and intentions. Examining them to see just how limited and proscribed they are, finding the bits of dirt that blur our moral vision, criticizing the criteria which are used for judgement, is necessary for moral clarity, but is not the end in itself. The point of such refinement of moral vision is to move forward towards a closer approximation of language and reality, or of social mores with the human activities from which they spring. Feminist challenges in this area may turn out to be an instance of Williams's claim that 'reflection may destroy knowledge', since what we find here is, ultimately, the inability to provide moral knowledge or guidelines when one is so heavily sedated by an overdose of self-reflection.[57]

Conclusion

Feminist writings, by contributing to the present criticisms of moral epistemology, have left in their wake a great number of issues which now call for some imaginative and sensitive handling if we are to develop in our understanding of the moral enterprise. We need to consider an account which is not only more satisfactory in its understanding of feminist concerns, but also more adequate as a rendering of the logic of moral reasoning, for these two are inextricably bound up with one another.

From the liberal perspective on morality, feminism seems to provide no unusual or disturbing challenge, since its requirements are believed to fit comfortably with the general principles for just treatment and considerations of equal rights which are central to its moral prescriptions. Continuing dissatisfaction from feminists in this area seems inappropriate since their needs are so easily accommodated. Feminist issues are either treated as trivial because their resolution seems, on liberal grounds, so patently obvious; or they seem to be irrelevant to liberal principles, because any attention paid to the uniqueness of the women's issue, as opposed to any other, is an unnecessary fuss for such abstractions as justice and equality; or they are considered to be uninteresting for any 'real' concern of morality since feminist demands are personal or partisan. There are presumably many who believe that the theoretical moral issues raised by feminism have therefore been resolved and nothing further remains to be *said*, though there may be a lot more to *do* to clear away the remnants of injustice. The way in which liberalism expresses its concern for women's issues is to emphasize what it takes to be the obvious need of any morality, namely, some general principles regarding what ought to be done. These are understood to have a rational necessity which enhances the human freedom by means of which they are discovered and, thus, they are believed to be the best hope for retaining distinctively human qualities. Having distilled this essence of morality, liberalism need only pursue the practical business of applying its principles in an even-handed way. This is what moral reasoning requires and, in its exercise, there are no gender distinctions.

The trouble with both the naturalistic and social constructionist accounts is that the temptation to generalization is once again present, although the lines are drawn in slightly different ways. In the first case, the move towards finding a common denominator in human nature leads to a tension within its account of morality. Beginning with an analysis of the way in which decisions are tied up with our understanding of ourselves, it helpfully illuminates the particularity of moral choices. Yet it increasingly presses for the description of the foundation for morality and in so doing conjures up abstractions of another kind to liberalism, but which are nonetheless ahistorical and essentialist.[58] The recognition of this natural grounding becomes a statement of such overall patterns that it lends itself to an endless search for counter-examples. In this case, what begins as a genuine reconstructive task using feminist insights ends as either hopelessly separatist or too vague for the derivation of any helpful guidelines. Indeed, unless analysis of the logic of onlooks regarding our human-ness is handled with more care, there will be nothing to prevent the traditional, long-lasting descriptions of the male–female relationship from being trotted out once again, with a reactionary sneer of disdain.

Likewise, in social constructionism, the effect of feminism has been to make us aware of the very deep consciousness and symbolic value of gender as it seems to express itself over and over again in the construction of social organizations, roles, and relationships. As a critique of the way in which value is expressed and ordered in social groups, this perspective challenges us to be more self-aware of the determination of thought and language by these gender categories, but its conclusions seem morally self-stultifying. Feminist questions arose in the first instance, presumably because of some gaps or imperfections in the fit between moral injunctions, with all their underlying assumptions, and lived experience. To raise questions about the confinement of women's lives by social definitions was to discuss something about which women cared and which was there-fore understood to be more than a bland factual analysis of what does and does not exist. However, not only the original morality, but now also one's concern about it are viewed as instances of the uninten-tional construction of meanings; for the spaces which we think we have 'chosen' to occupy as social revolutionaries are in fact the ones laid out for us by the available options. What reality there was to begin with, against which the present order of things seemed to measure up so badly, now turns out itself to be fabricated, as a projection of present meanings. Once we understand this, there is nothing available to us for moral awareness, and moral sensitivity becomes reduced to the one-dimensional phenomenon of thought thinking about itself. Such generalities require detachment to be grasped but there is nothing further to be done with them; morality can be abandoned as 'humanistic' or 'essentialist'.

My concern with these tendencies in naturalism and social constructionism is for the loss of the person, which becomes either a particular instance of general human essence or a decentred self. It seems to me that this is not only too high a price to pay for the feminist insights which may be derived from these accounts, but also an unnecessary abstraction for any development of practicable feminist morality. And this is the task which really now should face us. Perhaps I could just begin to sketch out such an account. Morality is a matter of personal development in sensitivity towards ourselves and the others with whom we share life, a sensitivity which is practised by deepening one's insights into present social realities, by learning to discern the nuances of meaning in the language and thought which confront us, and by committing ourselves to realizing some possibilities as more fulfilling than others. As in artistic creation, we can hear more harmonies or visualize more arrangements, the more attuned we become to what is already there; our innovative contribution comes as we make those real, and they are fortunate when they do in fact work. Human nature provides the overall context in which the reasoning mind searches for its possible courses of action, and it does so within the confines of social structures. Moral thinking comes up against social and natural realities that are not entirely of our own making and these are subject to continuous historical changes. This can be seen, not as a limitation to our moral questioning, but rather as a source of its purpose and significance, since ultimately there are choices which will or will not succeed, in the here and now, in creating human fulfilment. We understand what these might be as our sensitivity to particular instances and realities develops. The active dialogue between the changing aspects of our humanness amidst various social interactions and our enquiring imagination is what shapes moral questions and their answers. Reality and imagination are bound together. We can form our new self-understanding imaginatively out of the materials given to us by taking advantage of the spaces within what is there. In this process, new meanings will emerge as the dimensions of our insight are opened out, and we will discover the sources of moral inspiration for use in the future.[59]

NOTES

1 'Feminism and the Logic of Morality' by S. F. Parsons is reprinted from *Radical Philosophy*, 47, Autumn 1987, with permission of the Radical Philosophy editorial collective.

2 Janet Radcliffe Richards, *The Sceptical Feminist* (Harmondsworth: Penguin, 1982).

3 See the discussion of this problem in Sartrean ethics by Mary Warnock, *Existentialist Ethics* (London: Macmillan, 1967), pp. 18–52. For the issues raised by the prescriptivist account see J. L. Mackie, *Ethics: Inventing Right and Wrong* (Harmondsworth: Penguin, 1981), esp. part 4 on 'Universalization'. Mackie states: 'On this view there are only formal, but no material, constraints on what can count as moral. The form, universal prescriptivity, is determined by the logic of moral terms, but the content is entirely a matter for decision by the person – or of course it may be a group of persons – who makes the moral judgements or subscribes to and adopts the moral system' (pp. 85–6).

4 H. J. Paton, *The Moral Law* (London: Hutchinson University Library, 1969), pp. 67–8 [The categorical imperative]. See also Thomas Nagel, *The Possibility of Altruism* (Oxford: Clarendon Press, 1970).

5 See Bernard Williams, *Ethics and the Limits of Philosophy* (London: Fontana, 1985) for a discussion of the impasse between two aspects of moral thinking: on the one hand the risk of free choice which morality implies and, on the other, the attempt to ground this choice in some limiting facts about rationality.

6 Simone de Beauvoir, *The Second Sex* (New York: Bantam Books, 1974), p. 31.

7 Ibid., p. 29.

8 Ibid., p. 33.

9 Ibid., p. 685, my italics.

10 Ibid., p. 671.

11 See de Beauvoir's recognition of the insufficiency of freedom alone to resolve the problems of women, 'It is not to be supposed, however, that the mere combination of the right to vote and a job constitutes complete emancipation . . .' (*The Second Sex*, p. 639). Her thinking in response to this, however, creates problems for the liberal model; see Ann Foreman, *Femininity as Alienation* (London: Pluto Press, 1978), ch. 8.

12 Radcliffe Richards, *The Sceptical Feminist*, p. 121.

13 Mackie, *Ethics*, p. 15.

14 Mary Wollstonecraft, *A Vindication of the Rights of Women* (Dublin, 1793): 'Let woman share the rights and she will emulate the virtues of

man; for she must grow more perfect when emancipated, or justify the authority that chains such a being to her duty – if the latter, it will be expedient to open a fresh trade with Russia for whips' (p. 256).

15 Genevieve Lloyd, *The Man of Reason* (London: Methuen, 1984), p. 104.

16 Ibid., p. ix.

17 Jean Bethke Elshtain, *Public Man, Private Woman* (Oxford: Martin Robertson, 1981), p. 118.

18 See Marjorie Weinzweig, 'Philosophy, Femininity and Feminism', *Philosophical Books*, Vol. 24, No. 3, July 1983, for a discussion of the inappropriateness of the notion of freedom as 'self-control' which is possessed by both men and women, particularly in the areas of sexual relations and of pregnancy and childbirth. See also Radcliffe Richards's reply.

19 Jean Grimshaw, 'Feminism: History and Morality', *Radical Philosophy*, 30, Spring 1982, p. 3.

20 Donald Evans, *The Logic of Self-Involvement* (London: SCM Press, 1963): '. . . if I *do* deliberate concerning the formulation or acceptance of a typical onlook, it is misleading to depict the logical structure of this deliberation either in terms of a decision-*that* and a decision-*to* which are completely independent, or in terms of a decision-*that* which is totally dependent on a decision-*to*' (p. 137).

21 John McDowell, 'Virtue and Reason', *The Monist*, Vol. 62, No. 3, July 1979, pp. 346 and 341.

22 John McDowell, 'Are Moral Requirements Hypothetical Imperatives?', *The Aristotelian Society*, Suppl. Vol. LII, 1978, p. 18.

23 See G. J. Warnock, *Contemporary Moral Philosophy*, 20 (London: Macmillan, 1967): '. . . if it were not the case that there existed a certain range of considerations, having to do in general with the welfare of human beings, about which most people cared very much some of the time, and cared to some extent much of the time, then not only would moral argument, however conclusive, be pointless and ineffective; moral discourse would simply not occur' (p. 71).

24 Bishop Joseph Butler, *Sermons* (1726), edited by W. R. Matthews (London: Bell, 1969). See the very clear discussion of this matter in Mary Midgley, *Beast and Man* (London: Methuen, 1980), pp. 266–74.

25 McDowell, 'Virtue and Reason', p. 331.

26 McDowell, 'Are Moral Requirements Hypothetical Imperatives?', p. 21. See also his description of 'salience' in 'Virtue and Reason', pp. 344–5.

27 Carol Gilligan, *In a Different Voice* (Cambridge, MA: Harvard University Press, 1982), p. 18. See Sigmund Freud, 'Femininity', in *New*

Introductory Lectures on Psychoanalysis (New York: W. W. Norton & Co, 1933): 'Women have but little sense of justice . . . We also say of women that their social instincts are weaker than those of men, and that their capacity for the sublimation of their instincts is less' (p. 184).

28 Quoted by Gilligan, *In a Different Voice*, p. 16, from Virginia Woolf, *A Room of One's Own* (New York: Harcourt, Brace and World, 1929), p. 76.

29 Gilligan, *In a Different Voice*, p. 16.

30 Ibid., p. 22.

31 Ibid., p. 173.

32 Mary Daly, *Pure Lust* (London: The Women's Press, 1984); see the entries in 'Websters' First New Intergalactic Wickedary of the English Language'.

33 Thus Daly abandons hope for a Tillichian overcoming of dualism by means of increasing abstraction, in favour of a more gnostic, and Jungian opposition of forces. Compare Mary Daly, *Beyond God the Father* (Boston: Beacon Press, 1973) in which there is a 'beyond' described in chs 3, 4 and 7, with *Gyn/Ecology: The Metaethics of Radical Feminism* (London: The Women's Press, 1979) and *Pure Lust*, in which no such 'place' exists.

34 See especially Radcliffe Richards, *The Sceptical Feminist*, pp. 25–9 passim.

35 Alison Jaggar, *Feminist Politics and Human Nature* (Brighton: Harvester Press, 1983); see pp. 98, 107. Cf. Janet Sayers, *Biological Politics* (London: Tavistock, 1982), p. 188. This problem also seems to be characteristic of the feminist writings of Luce Irigaray, as discussed by Margaret Whitford, 'Luce Irigaray and the Female Imaginary: Speaking as a Woman', *Radical Philosophy*, 43, Summer 1986.

36 Frigga Haug, 'Morals also have Two Genders', *New Literary Review*, Vol. 143, Jan/Feb 1984.

37 For a good example, see Robert Paul Wolff, 'There's Nobody Here But Us Persons', in C. Gould and M. Wartofsky (eds.), *Women and Philosophy* (New York: G. P. Putnam's Sons, 1976), pp. 128–44.

38 See particularly Brian Easlea, *Science and Sexual Oppression* (London: Weidenfeld and Nicolson, 1981), and *Fathering the Unthinkable* (London: Pluto Press, 1983).

39 Aristotle, *Nicomachean Ethics* (Indianapolis: Bobbs-Merrill, 1962), translated by Martin Ostwald. See Book One, section 7 in which goodness is related to function. See also Dorothy Emmet, *Rules, Roles and Relations* (London: Macmillan, 1966); Philippa Foot, 'Goodness and Choice', *The Aristotelian Society*, Suppl. Vol. XXXV, 1961; and G. E. M. Anscombe, 'Modern Moral Philosophy' and 'On Brute Facts', in *Analysis*, Vol. 18, 1958.

40 F. H. Bradley, 'My Station and Its Duties', in *Ethical Studies*, 2nd edn. (Oxford: Oxford University Press, 1927).

41 See A. C. MacIntyre, *A Short History of Ethics* (London: Routledge and Kegan Paul, 1976) for a description of the history of ethics from this viewpoint. See also his argument that unless such community is restored in the modern world, morality will have lost its meaning for us. The confusion of moral perspectives in our day leaves us with no way of choosing between available alternatives without a meaningful social context. *After Virtue* (London: Duckworth, 1982).

42 See Williams, *Ethics*, ch. 2 on 'The Archimedean Point'. See also McDowell, 'Aesthetic Value, Objectivity, and the Fabric of the World', in Eva Schaper (ed.), *Pleasure, Preference and Value* (Cambridge: Cambridge University Press, 1983) for a critique of this possibility.

43 Ludwig Wittgenstein, *On Certainty* (Oxford: Basil Blackwell, 1969) translated by G. E. M. Anscombe and Denis Paul: 'It is our *acting* which lies at the bottom of the language-game' (para. 204). See also Gilbert Ryle, *The Concept of Mind* (London: Hutchinson, 1949).

44 Juliet Mitchell, *Woman's Estate* (New York: Vintage Books, 1973). See particularly chs. 5 and 6 which illustrate these conditions of women's lives and consciousness.

45 Ibid., p. 122.

46 Ibid., p. 150.

47 Rosalind Coward, *Patriarchal Precedents: Sexuality and Social Relations* (London: Routledge and Kegan Paul, 1983), p. 188.

48 Ibid., p. 259. See also her article on 'Psychoanalysis and Patriarchal Structures' co-authored with E. Cowie and S. Lipshitz in *Papers on Patriarchy* (Lewes: Women's Publishing Collective, 1976) in which she describes more fully the acquisition of gender consciousness in children. For an anthropologist's analysis of this universal gender construction, see Sherry B. Ortner, 'Is Female to Male as Nature is to Culture?' in M. Z. Rosaldo and L. Lamphere (eds.), *Woman, Culture and Society* (California: Stanford University Press, 1974).

49 Coward, *Patriarchal Precedents*, p. 1, quoting from Althusser.

50 Ibid., p. 265. See also her book, co-authored with John Ellis, *Language and Materialism* (London: Routledge and Kegan Paul, 1977), especially chs. 1 and 5 which offer a critique of humanistic reification.

51 Karl Marx, *The German Ideology* (London: Lawrence and Wishart, 1974): '. . . language, like consciousness, only arises from the need, the necessity, of intercourse with other men . . . Consciousness is, therefore, from the very beginning a social product . . .' (pp. 50–1).

52 Coward, 'Re-reading Freud', *Spare Rib*, May 1978. She also criticizes the limitations of Marxism for its economic determinism, which tends to yield a universalist thesis regarding the necessary ideology of

women's oppression. See 'Re-thinking Marxism', *m/f*, 2, 1978.

53 See the critiques of both Mitchell and Coward in Sayers, *Biological Politics*, pp. 134–45 and Foreman, *Femininity as Alienation*, pp. 48–51.

54 Michèle Barrett, *Women's Oppression Today: Problems in Marxist Feminist Analysis* (London: Verso, 1984), pp. 34–5.

55 Ibid., pp. 35–6. See also the review by Howard Feather, 'Reconstructing Structural Marxism', *Radical Philosophy*, 43, Summer 1986, in which similar epistemological problems are discussed with reference to Althusser, particularly p. 35.

56 Attributed to Virginia Woolf. See how this problem is described by Joseph McCarney, 'What Makes Critical Theory "Critical"?', *Radical Philosophy*, 42, Winter/Spring 1986.

57 Williams, *Ethics*, especially ch. 9, 'Relativism and Reflection'.

58 See my initial attempt to formulate this in 'Feminism and Moral Reasoning', *Australasian Journal of Philosophy*, special issue on Women and Philosophy, June 1986.

59 My thinking throughout this piece has been greatly stimulated by Sabina Lovibond, *Realism and Imagination in Ethics* (Oxford: Basil Blackwell, 1983). While I have not quoted directly from this work, I want to acknowledge her provocative analysis of moral epistemology and to express a hope that one day I can investigate her suggestions in a more full and direct way. My thanks also to the members of the Radical Philosophy Group for very helpful comments on the first draft of this paper, which has benefitted from their careful attention.

24

Rosalind Pollack Petchesky
b.1942

'MORALITY AND PERSONHOOD: A FEMINIST PERSPECTIVE'
extract from *ABORTION AND WOMAN'S CHOICE* (1988)

In this spirited defence of the pro-choice position on abortion, Rosalind Petchesky uses the idea of historicity *on two levels: firstly in order to situate the present debate and to shed light on the terms in which it is conducted, and secondly in order to support her own 'feminist-humanist' account of the moral standing of the fetus.*

Petchesky's discussion draws a sense of urgency from her perception of anti-abortion activism in the 1980s as part of the 'battle for moral hegemony . . . accompanying a right-wing economic and political resurgence'. The special animus of the New Right towards feminism has led US conservatives to attempt an ambitious revision of the dominant, rationalist, conception of personhood and to seek to confer on fetuses a 'right to life' under the 14th Amendment to the Constitution. The prospect that women might win for themselves the same measure of moral autonomy promised to men by bourgeois liberalism has thus brought out into the open the conservative conviction that where liberal ideals run counter to the requirements of male supremacy, it is liberalism that must give way.

The three strands identified by Petchesky in contemporary anti-abortion rhetoric are 'religious symbolism', 'biological reductionism' and 'maternal revivalism'. (Her discussion under the last heading sounds an implicit note of warning with respect to the emerging feminist discourse of maternalism: see, contrastingly, Williamson, reading 15, and Ruddick, reading 25.) All three, she argues, are obliged to suppress the social dimension of personality and so to 'demean human life and the moral value of consciousness'. Whatever makes the fetus into a person, be it the receipt of a 'soul' from God or the possession of a 'genetic package' inscribed in the individual's DNA, is held by anti-abortionists to date from the moment of conception, so that the human status of the fetus owes nothing to the gradual emergence of subjectivity through interaction with a world of pre-existing human subjects. In particular, the individuality and moral competence of the pregnant woman is eclipsed (on this view) by her role as 'mother', a condition pictured as one of absolute dedication to the welfare of one's offspring. (This is a reassertion of the functionalist idea, inherited from antiquity, that the female sex exists specifically for the purposes of reproduction.)

Petchesky's response, issuing from a moral standpoint which is 'feminist, socialist and humanist', rests on a distinction between the biological concept of life and the more complex, because distinctively ethical, concept of personality. The reason why (human) life can exist without personality is that the latter develops over time and in a context of multiple social relationships; its presence, then, is not an all-or-nothing matter but one of degree. In an intriguing bid to do justice to the significance intuitively attached to the moment of 'quickening', Petchesky is willing to posit a social, *or incipiently social, relation between pregnant woman and fetus – a relation which, as it were, sets the scene for the appearance of an as yet non-existent 'self'. In this way she builds into her discussion the familiar thought that the fetus is a* potential *person, and uses this idea to explain how feminists, too, can think of the fetus as capable in principle of making moral claims on the pregnant woman. But Petchesky insists throughout on the* actual *personality of the woman and on the authority of her judgement for or against the continuation of a particular pregnancy. The assertion of women's right to make this (moral) decision for themselves defines a position which is itself not moral, but political.*

Biological Reductionism

Increasingly, in response to accusations of religious bias and violations of church–state separation, the evidence marshaled by anti-abortionists to affirm the personhood of the fetus is not its alleged possession of a soul but its possession of a human body and genotype.[1] In addition, by relying on biological, or genetic, determinism, the 'right-to-life' movement asserts a claim to scientific objectivity.

Biological determinism grows out of the social Darwinism and eugenics of the nineteenth and early twentieth centuries, which were applied in the service of racism, class domination and population control. Its essential core is an attempt to explain the meaning and direction of human society, behaviour and values in terms of bio-chemistry and what we can observe about heredity: 'For sociobio-logists and believers in natural aristocracies of class and sex, the properties of society are determined by the intrinsic properties of individual human beings, individuals are the expression of their genes, and genes are nothing but self-replicating molecules.'[2] All human life is reduced to its chemical bits. It is no accident, of course, that the 'right-to-life' movement draws on mechanistic bio-logical explanation as well as religion to legitimate its moral and social philosophy. For it does so in a general ideological climate that has seen the revival of genetic 'theories' of race and reductionist theories of genetics; the rise of sociobiology in the social sciences; and, as part of the backlash against feminism, the renewed respect-ability of biological arguments supporting gender distinctions.[3]

'Fetal personhood' doctrine draws upon biological determinism in several ways. Its crudest expression is the profusion of antiabortion imagery presenting the fetus as 'baby'. It is a propagandistic *tour de force* to have taken the notion of 'personhood' (a metaphysical, moral idea) and translated it into a series of arresting visual images that are utterly physiological and often just plain morbid. Various techniques are used to convey the idea that the fetus is literally a baby from the moment of conception: (1) photographs of fetuses at different stages of development, revealing recognizable physiological features; (2) photographs of aborted (bloody, gory) fetuses, particularly those aborted late; (3) clinical descriptions of fetal development, with special emphasis on the formation of heartbeat, fingerprints, fingers and toes; (4) juxtaposition or alternation of pictures of fetuses with pictures of live babies, reinforcing the idea of their identity; and (5) the constant use of language referring to fetuses as 'babies', 'children' or 'unborn children'.[4]

The fetus as an image of the small, the helpless and the mortal is made to *embody* one's desire for protection, for the safety of the womb; hence its power as a symbol to manipulate emotions. Through an erroneous attempt to portray the fetus as a miniature replica of you or me, this imagery not only denies the subtle processes of biological development but also seeks to arouse one's sense of identity with the fetus. Indeed, continually stressing the 'small fingers and toes' or the capacity of the fetus to 'feel pain' excites this kind of identification, through a psychological mechanism that reduces the sense of 'humanity' to its most primitive biological and sentimental manifestations. The purpose of shocking, scaring and eliciting morbid fears is connected to the biologistic reduction of the meaning of 'human life'. 'Right-to-life' rhetoric communicates the worst horrors of our age; abortion is 'killing babies', clinics are 'death camps' and 'abortion chambers', clinicians who perform abortions are 'death peddlers' and 'Nazi murderers'. Their emphasis on fetuses 'hacked to pieces' or 'burned' in saline solution is polemical, since it refers to only 5 per cent of all abortions.[5] For people who claim to uphold 'life', as critics have frequently noted, 'right-to-lifers' are enormously preoccupied, even obsessed, with death and the remnants of aborted fetuses, apotheosizing and even displaying them in public rituals.

This symbolic representation of fetal 'personhood' in the guise of human embodiment (in contrast, note, to 'ensoulment') is reinforced on a more sophisticated level through an appeal by anti-abortionists to biological science. Thus Jesse Helms, in introducing the 'human life statute' (S. 158) in the Senate, cited, not moral and religious authorities, but sources on human embryology; and Noonan takes for granted that the argument for fetal personhood is established in 'biological knowledge common to all Americans'.[6] Using biological and theological language almost interchangeably, 'pro-life' spokesmen, in supporting the Helms statute in the Senate, argued that science is now able to determine 'when human life begins' and that this settles the matter of the moral and legal status of the fetus.[7] Because it can be shown that every fertilized human egg is genetically unique, possessing a distinct human genotype, they claim, it can be inferred that the zygote is a human person in a moral sense. The Protestant theologian and opponent of abortion Paul Ramsey expounded this argument, which Peter Steinfels calls the 'genetic package' argument, back in the 1960s:

> microgenetics seems to have demonstrated what religion never could, and biological science to have resolved an ancient theological dispute. The human individual comes into existence first

as a minute informational speck, drawn at random from many other minute informational specks his parents possessed out of the common gene pool. This took place at the moment of impregnation. There were, of course, an unimaginable number of combinations of specks on his paternal and maternal chromosomes that did not come to be *when they were refused and he began to be*. Still (with the exception of identical twins), no one else in the entire history of the human race has ever had or will ever have exactly the same genotype. Thus, it can be said that the individual *is whoever he is going to become from the moment of impregnation*. Thereafter, his subsequent development may be described as a process of becoming the one he already is.[8]

Ramsey's statement is a wondrous example of theological opinion masquerading as biological fact. Into the randomness of human fertilization and genetic pairing he conveniently reads the Calvinist doctrine of predestination: We are all that we can ever be from the moment of conception. Indeed, there is even the suggestion, in the image of millions of possible combinations 'refused' and only one selected, of a divine and inscrutable will. Such an interpretation is peculiarly alien to the stance of modern science, including molecular biology, which is one of rigorous *indeterminacy*:

the traditional opinion, which most of us are still unconsciously guided by, is that the child conceived on any one occasion is the unique and necessary product of that occasion: *that* child would have been conceived, we tend to think, or no child at all. This interpretation is quite false. . . . Only over the past one hundred years has it come to be realized that the child conceived on any one occasion belongs to a vast cohort of Possible Children, any one of whom might have been conceived and born if a different spermatozoon had chanced to fertilize the mother's egg cell – and the egg cell itself is only one of very many. *It is a matter of luck then, a sort of genetic lottery.* And sometimes it is cruelly bad luck – some terrible genetic conjunction, perhaps which once in ten or twenty thousand times will bring together a matching pair of damaging recessive genes. Such a misfortune, *being the outcome of a random process*, is, *considered in isolation, completely and essentially pointless*. It is not even strictly true to say that a particular inborn abnormality must have lain within the genetic potentiality of the parents, for the malignant gene may have arisen *de novo* by mutation. The whole process is *unhallowed* – is, in the older sense of that word, *profane*.[9]

Abortions occur continually in nature, and we do not experience them as sacred events – quite the contrary. Even in a narrowly biological sense, it is impossible to say with certainty that a particular embryo will develop into a particular human being, since it may be spontaneously aborted or may turn out to be a decidedly unhumanlike mutation.[10]

If molecular biology cannot be relied on to ascertain the sanctity of genetic uniqueness, how much less can it tell us about the relationship between the *genotype* and the *person*. The most striking fallacy in the genetic arguments of anti-abortionists is their leap from the *fact* of genetic individuality – a characteristic not only of humans but of all living things, including cows and chameleons – to the *value* of human personhood. This is a problem, in part, of confusing the self, the person, with her or his genetic basis, ignoring the enormously complex interaction between genes, environment, and development that ultimately determines who or what an actual person becomes. To say that who I am is codified from the moment of my conception is to deny most people's common-sense assumptions about who they are, their selfhood, and its roots in conscious experience. But it also contradicts the caveats of well-known geneticists (those of a humanist persuasion) against confusing genetic *potentiality* with *actual* human personality and character, which are highly influenced by culture.[11] Manier sums up this genetic fallacy with great elegance:

Since our general concept of humanity is more than a biological concept, no amount of biological evidence can provide adequate warrant for any claim concerning the starting point of individual life. . . . Further, it is misleading to assert that 'a being with a human genetic code is a man,' as if there were specific evidence from molecular biology warranting that assertion. In fact, it has no more empirical significance than 'a rose is a rose,' since the only means of identifying genetic material as human is by direct comparison with DNA already identified as human.[12]

Thus the broader problem with the idea that the fetus is a 'person' from conception is its concept of personhood, or even humanity, for it either rests on a theological premise – 'ensoulment' – or it reduces to a crude, mechanistic biologism. In legal and moral terms, this means that the concept of 'person' (moral) is totally collapsed into the concept of 'human life' (biological, or generic).[13] In fact, as Dr Leon Rosenberg testified in the Senate hearings on S. 158, there is *not* agreement among scientists about the question of 'when human life begins', nor any way to determine the answer definitively.[14] But I submit that *the beginning of human life is not the issue*, for it can be argued that fetuses, even if they are 'human life', are still not human *persons*. It might be conceded that the fetus is a *form* of life insofar as it is alive (as established by EEG readings, heartbeat and other biological responses) and it is human (in the narrow and morally insignificant sense that it is composed of authentically human genes or DNA, derived from genetically human parents). Yet, agreeing on this reduction of the fetus's identity to its genetic material does not move us one step toward knowing what *value* to give the fetus, what *rights* it has (either as a class or in a particular case), or whether to regard it as a person in the moral and legal sense (which is the only sense there is).[15]

That the fetus is human and may even have a 'right to life' does not prove that abortion is 'morally (im)permissible', because being 'human in a genetic sense' is distinct from being 'human in a moral sense' – that is, from being a person. The fetus is not a human person in this latter sense; therefore, whatever rights it may have 'could not possibly outweigh the right of a woman to obtain an abortion, since the rights of actual persons invariably outweigh those of any potential person whenever the two conflict'.[16] This position suggests that we may acknowledge the fetus's 'potentiality' and its 'sanctity of life' while rejecting its 'personhood'. To deny that the fetus is a 'full human person' does not necessarily mean denying that the fetus, as a *potentially* human and presently sentient being, is morally deserving of consideration, or even that it can make moral or emotional claims on those in charge of its care – mainly pregnant women. The problem is that whatever those claims may be, they frequently come into conflict with the rights and needs of women and others with whom they are connected who *are* (in the opinion of feminists and humanists) full human persons. But the 'right-to-life' position either denies such conflict or dissolves it into a definition of 'motherhood' that makes the fetus's life determinant of the woman's.

Maternal Revivalism

Like its view of the fetus, the 'right-to-life' view of motherhood is a remarkably Victorian mixture of religious and biological-determinist elements. On the one hand, there is the Augustinian image of woman as ordained by God to procreate; the passive receptacle of the male seed, 'selfish' and 'sinful' if she evades that destiny and directs her sexuality to nonprocreative ends. Abortion, from this view, is a sin against God in defiance of woman's nature, for which she is morally culpable. Hence the message communicated in 'right-to-life' literature, demonstrations and harassment of women at abortion clinics. Women who get abortions are 'murdering their own children', putting their 'selfish desires' before their 'own children's lives', and will suffer terrible guilt. But what if the woman does not feel agony or guilt but, like many women after an abortion, feels mainly relief that a difficult problem has been put behind her? One anti-humanist, 'pro-life' writer insists that the woman's feelings have nothing to do with whether or not she *is* guilty, which is determined by her objective relation to the 'moral law' and not by 'subjective experience'. She '*ought* to feel guilty' because she has in fact committed 'an evil of incomprehensible dimensions'.[17] The fundamentalist doctrine that 'man's nature is wholly corrupt' is opposed here to 'the humanist tenet that man is basically good'. The very idea of human progress and social or moral development or 'enrichment' in history is anathema to this doctrine, which asserts 'the wickedness of man' (and, assuredly, of woman) as the source of every human (i.e., social) problem. Hence, 'why have mothers, in the name of the liberation of womanhood, demanded the death of their own children?' For the anti-humanist 'pro-lifer', the answer is quite simple: 'human wickedness'.[18]

The 'right-to-life' doctrine of the fetus's 'personhood' and the aborting woman's 'selfishness' is akin to the anti-humanist philosophy of the New Right. Anti-humanism, as professed by the 'right-to-life' and 'pro-family' movements, pits itself squarely against every intellectual and philosophical tradition that grew out of the Enlightenment and secularism. Marxism and feminism are of course denounced by the Right, but so are all philosophies, including radical Christian movements such as liberation theology, whose central focus is social change on this earth or even human, as opposed to divine or scriptural, ends. When Weyrich describes the Moral Majority as 'a Christian democratic movement rooted in the authentic Gospel, not the social gospel', he is attacking and distinguishing his politics from those Christian movements in the United States and Latin America that ally with the poor to change oppressive social conditions.[19] All social movements, including labour movements, peasant uprisings, anti-colonial struggles, civil rights, and anti-nuclear protests, would thus be categorized by the New Right under 'materialistic, atheistic humanism', charged with the sin of making human life and human pleasure on earth the measure of all value. But a particular condemnation is reserved for feminism and the movement for sexual liberation. The New Right associates this branch of humanism most closely with hedonism, equated with 'doing whatever feels good', with 'moral perversity and total corruption'.

By the end of the 1970s, some 'right-to-lifers' began to promote the view that women who get abortions are themselves victims – of profiteering doctors or coercion by Planned Parenthood – and should be offered protection and Christian compassion.[20] In this view, abortion is depicted as contrary to woman's true desires and interests as mothers, invariably a source of anguish and 'ambivalence'. Yet this profession of 'compassion' and support for pregnant women is simply a more paternalistic version of the idea of an innate maternalism, which abortion violates. In a major 'right-to-life' propaganda piece, Francis A. Schaeffer, a fundamentalist minister, and C. Everett Koop, US surgeon general and head of the National Institutes of Health under Reagan, refer to women who have had abortions as 'aborted mothers' and 'bereft mothers' filled with bitterness and 'sorrow':

> With many of the women who have had abortions, their 'motherliness' is very much present even though the child is gone . . . One of the facts of being a human being is that in spite of the abnormality of human beings and the cruelty of their actions, there still exist the hopes and fears, the longings and aspirations, that can be bundled together in the word *mother-*

liness. To stamp out these feelings is to insure that many women will turn into the kind of hard people they may not want to be.[21]

Like the fundamentalist fire-and-brimstone view, the implication of the 'Christian compassionate' view of abortion is the basic precept of all patriarchal ideology: Motherhood – and indeed 'motherliness', a *state of being* and not just a social role or relationship – is the primary purpose of a woman's life. Abortion is thus 'abnormal', 'unnatural'; a woman who undergoes an abortion is subverting her own nature and will surely suffer or become 'hardened' (read, un-motherly, *unwomanly*). Whether the 'pro-life Christian' confronts her 'suffering' with pity or hatred, the point is that suffer she must, for procreation and child-rearing are woman's 'privileged position and purpose in human history' and to renounce them – whether once or for good – is to place herself outside female nature and 'human history'.

More ancient than the idea of the fetus as person, the primacy and necessity of woman as Mother has been a continuous ideological thread in anti-abortion pronouncements since the nineteenth century. Callahan quotes the Catholic theologian Bernard Häring, writing in 1966 in terms that lay bare the deeper passions underlying 'right-to-life' sentiments:

> If it were to become an accepted principle of moral teaching on motherhood to permit a mother whose life was endangered simply to 'sacrifice' the life of her child in order to save her own, motherhood would no longer mean absolute dedication to each and every child.[22]

Because the pregnant woman is Mother, she must be ready to die for the fetus. More than the survival of the individual fetus, what is ultimately at stake in the abortion struggle, in this view, is the 'moral teaching' of motherhood as 'absolute dedication'. It is the *idea* of woman as Mother, and of the fetus as the tie that binds her to marital chastity and selflessness, that takes precedence over anything else. The woman who has an abortion makes a clear statement about her life and her understanding of her moral and social commitments relative to a potential maternal relationship; she renounces, defies the concept of motherhood as total self-sacrifice for the sake of others. On some level, perhaps, she even asserts her capacity to exercise control over life and death – and this makes her particularly, ineffably dangerous.[23] Thus does anti-abortion ideology reveal its association, not only with anti-feminism, but with the most primitive traditions of misogyny.

Contemporary opponents of abortion reflect these elements of misogynist thinking in their perpetuation of the myth that women who get abortions do so mostly for reasons of 'convenience' and to repudiate motherhood.[24] We have seen that the social reality behind this perception is complex; motherhood has assumed a *different* place in many women's lives during the past decade, interwoven with work and study, deferred but hardly abandoned. What is important here is the tremendous emotionalism and hostility toward women that the perception of change has apparently generated. The cry that women are 'killing their children' (you too, it seems to say, might have been an abortion) signals a new wave of 'momism' and 'motherhood revivalism', a fundamental current of the New Right's moral offensive. This cry touches deep nerves – fears of maternal abandonment, fears that women will no longer mother. The assumption behind it, that woman's purpose is to exemplify 'unselfishness' through motherhood, is not often challenged even by those who claim to favour 'choice'.[25] Recently, a rash of disclaimers and apologies by liberals, leftists and even some feminists in the popular media, confessing 'ambivalence' about abortion,[26] reveal the extent to which 'right-to-life' ideology has penetrated the dominant culture and fostered guilt, even without a change in the law. More than ever, we need a feminist morality of abortion, one that addresses the issues that 'right-to-lifers' raise in human, social terms and moves well beyond them.

Toward a Feminist-Humanist Concept of Personhood

The doctrine of fetal personhood is morally offensive from a feminist, socialist and humanist standpoint because what makes human life distinct is its capacity for consciousness and sociability. To reduce it to genetics, to equate Holocaust victims with aborted fetuses, is to demean human life and the moral value of consciousness. It is, moreover, to demean pregnant women, who are treated in this perspective as the physical vessels for genetic messages rather than responsible moral agents. Motherhood in this sense becomes, not a socially determined relationship, but a physiological function, a 'fact of life'. At the same time, 'right-to-life' ideology equates pregnancy with motherhood as it has been defined in modern Western patriarchal culture – as a moral and social duty. Although pregnant nulliparous women do not usually regard themselves as 'mothers', since in their experience there is no 'child' with whom they have a relationship, this doctrine tells them they should become instantaneously 'motherly' from the moment of conception.

Reducing motherhood to a passive biological state is a way of dehumanizing it, stripping it of dependence on women's consciousness. Oddly enough, however, imposing an absolute maternal duty on pregnant women induces the same deadening passivity. Biological determinism and moral absolutism arrive at the same end. The anti-abortionists' charge that women who get abortions are invariably 'selfish' and 'irresponsible' insults not only women as moral agents but motherhood as a human practice and a conscious, demanding activity. By insisting that the abortion question has only one answer, the 'right-to-life' position denies the role of human will and judgement in moral decision-making, particularly in decision-making about childbirth and sex. It thus denies the full human personhood of women.

What is necessary to personhood, it would seem, is *personality* – the existence of a self, which implies a psychological and a social component beyond mere biological integrity or vitalism, involving some degree of self-awareness in relation to others. What it means to be human involves an irreducible social or relational basis without which the very concept of humanity, or persons as actual or developing moral beings, makes no sense. Now, a difficulty we run into here is the tendency of liberal moral philosophers, following in the classical and particularly Kantian tradition, to associate personhood with attributes of developed human beings – not only 'consciousness' but 'reasoning', 'self-motivated activity', even the ability to 'judge between right and wrong'.[27] One problem with this rationalist-individualist concept of personhood, as I suggested earlier, was always its use in the interests of a ruling elite to exclude those considered insufficiently 'rational' or 'motivated' or 'civilized' from the civic or even the moral community: slaves, women, children, the colonized. In this respect, the concerns of some of those who oppose abortion contain a decent, though I believe mistaken, moral impulse. They are concerns shared by many liberals, especially Catholics, who disapprove of abortion, although they do not identify with the conservative politics of the organized 'pro-life' movement. That impulse is (1) to affirm the Kantian principle of a 'person' as one who is a being in and for herself, an end rather than a means; and (2) to deny that this involves a set of intellectual or cognitive prerequisites that would exclude or disqualify a whole range of human beings considered 'inferior' or 'unfit'. These are concerns meant to appeal, not unreasonably, to leftists and especially feminists, sensitive to the political consequences (for women, for blacks) of a 'moral' tradition that elevates mind and reason and denigrates the body.[28] Antiabortionists frequently raise the prospect of a 'slippery slope' (always a polemical device) that leads from fetuses to 'euthanasia' among the mentally disabled, the physically disabled, the elderly, and so on. More persuasive perhaps is their argument that the classical definition of personhood leaves no way to distinguish between infants and fetuses and therefore would allow infanticide:

If to be human *means* to be a person, to be a self-conscious subject of experience, or if it means to be rational, this state of affairs does not come to pass until a long while after the birth of a baby. A human infant acquires its personhood and self-conscious subjective identity through 'Thou–I' encounters with other selves; and a child acquires essential rationality even more laboriously. If life must be human in these senses before it has any sanctity and respect or rights due it, infanticide would seem to be justified under any number of conditions.[29]

What concept of personhood would avoid biological reductionism yet include newborn babies, as well as allowing for the developmental variations in the fetus at different stages; that is, would accord with the common-sense notions about who has a 'right to life' and who does not that most people in fact apply in everyday life? While there are practical historical reasons why infanticide has mostly fallen into disuse (not the least of which is access to legal birth control and abortion!), there is a coherent philosophical explanation for why most people treat babies differently from fetuses, and late

fetuses differently from early ones. This explanation lies in a theory
of personhood whose elements are humanist, socialist and feminist.

The Kantian principle of treating persons as ends in themselves,
with intrinsic value, is an elegant version of the bourgeois myth of
atomized individuals; it disregards that the necessary premise for
such persons to exist is the prior human world of interrelationships,
interdependence – in short, of social life. Philosophers of diverse
persuasions have understood that the preformed, self-sufficient
monad – of which the fetus as person is a vulgarization – is not
only philosophically but socially (*and biologically*) implausible. The
Catholic humanist Jacques Maritain presents a concept of the person
that is insistent in its emphasis on not only spirituality but sociability: 'The person is a whole, but it is not a closed whole, it is an
open whole . . . It tends by its very nature to social life and to communion . . . demands an entrance into relationship with other persons. To state it rigorously, the person cannot be alone.'[30] The
Marxist humanist Agnes Heller clarifies the necessary interrelation-
ship or 'synthesis' between 'self-consciousness', or 'I-consciousness',
and consciousness of being part of a larger whole, a 'species-being' in
Marx's sense: 'The Individual is a person who "synthesizes" in
himself the chance uniqueness of his individuality with the universal
generality of the species,' who has a *consciousness* not only of himself/
herself as an end but of 'his (her) world. Every person forms his
world and thus himself too.'[31] 'Personhood' or 'humanism' in this
view is not static, not a set of physical or even intellectual 'properties'; rather, it is a *process*, a continual *coming to consciousness*. We
become humanized, in a never-ending development that involves, as
consciousness, rational and 'moral' faculties but, more primally,
feelings, sensations, the body – and always in a context of *relationship* with others. It is this relationship, this interdependence, that
humanizes us; the particular physical, verbal or intellectual mode of
relating is secondary. Seen from this perspective of humanization as
a continual process of 'movement toward liberation'[32] or greater
consciousness, personhood must inevitably involve some differences
of degree. Moral philosophy cannot avoid distinguishing 'between
the human and the "truly human"',[33] as for example when we speak
of the 'inhumanity of man'. More important, this theoretical perspective on personhood may help us to formulate a more precise
philosophical approach to the meaning of fetuses and infants at

different stages of development than either the 'right-to-life' or the rationalist-individualist position allows.

We begin to see, then, why anti-abortionists jump so easily between two apparently contradictory positions – the 'ensoulment' argument (that the fetus has a perfectly independent soul from the moment of conception) and the 'genetic package' argument (that all we are and can be is perfectly contained in our DNA). Both arguments rest on the false premise of totally isolated, self-sufficient individuals connected only to God or their own biochemical structure. Both explicitly reject any *social* conception of human beings or humanness; any other person, including the biological mother, becomes inconsequential. But the idea of 'persons' as self-contained atoms is a fallacy at any stage of human development and certainly at its inception. Without consciousness, awareness of others, or ability to communicate its needs, the fetus cannot be a being 'in and for itself' (a person); it is less so even than a mature animal. Its identity as a 'human life' is thus all the more inevitably endowed or bound up with contextual meanings; it *is* the social context and the value placed on the fetus by those immediately concerned in its care that determine to a large extent its value in the world and even its rights.

Nothing could illustrate more clearly the fallacy in 'right-to-life' thinking about personhood than the frequently voiced claim that the fetus exhibits 'sensitivity to pain' and therefore should be recognized as human. This is equivalent to saying that the fetus 'feels bad' when we abort it, which is absurd, since we do not know, nor can we know, what the fetus 'feels'. Pain as a concept refers only to subjective feelings, not to biological responses that can be measured; sensitivity to touch and reflex actions, on the other hand, can be found in plants and have little to do with pain. It is precisely because the fetus is not a subjectivity and therefore cannot take cognizance of or communicate its 'bad' feelings that we cannot recognize it as a person. We can only recognize its value in a context of relationships with others, defined by *their* subjectivity. For loving 'expectant parents', an unwanted abortion is an event occasioning mourning and a deep sense of loss because of the social context of longings, care and expectations that envelop the pregnancy. The scarcity of children available for adoption to infertile couples, or the desires of a potential father or grandparent for a child, may be other circumstances that endow the fetus with value. But those are as extrinsic and utilitarian (i.e., bound to particular interests) as are the pregnant woman's wants and needs, and cannot be used to argue that the fetus has value in and of itself.

If, however, a relational concept of personhood requires an existent self-awareness, then it becomes difficult indeed to include the newborn infant. Where can we derive any moral principle against killing small babies other than from the subjective reality that babies are nice and responsive and we like them better than fetuses? The problem here results from assumptions about consciousness and the humanization process, shared by Marxists as well as liberals (and all who have not broken fully from the Enlightenment tradition), that focus exclusively on verbal and 'rational' modes of communication. To correct these outmoded assumptions, we can look at theories of developmental and object relations that psychologists have proposed about the formation of the 'self' in the infant; we can even look at the lived experience of pregnant women, which supports those theories.[34] They tell us that the emergence of a 'self' – the psychological process of individuation in which the child begins to acquire a consciousness of itself in relation to, and separate from, others, and thus a consciousness *of* others – occurs, and *can only occur*, in an interactive and social context.

The relationship with others constructs the self in a complex and sometimes protracted process of reciprocal perceptual and later emotional cues, so that the 'self' could not possibly be a genetic or inborn property. Thus, the anti-abortion argument that 'I cannot will that my mother should have had an abortion when she was pregnant with me', so I cannot 'consistently deny to others the right to life that I claim for myself', is illogical. There was no self, no 'me', during my mother's pregnancy with me, with whom my present self is continuous.[35] The fetus has no interest in preserving its body because it has no 'self', no consciousness: '. . . while you have interests regarding your body, your body and its parts have no interest of their own, and in its earliest stages a fetus is only a body and not a self at all. . . .'[36] While the self, the *person*, cannot exist separately from its body and its sensory apparatus, which is the biological precondition for its consciousness, the body predates the self and may survive its extinction (as consciousness).

What, then, of the 'preindividuated' infant prior to its development of self-awareness, and of the fetus in its later stages? A social, relational concept of personhood, because it is focused on process rather than some illusory substance or property, allows us the possibility, the only humanist possibility, of encompassing such beings within our moral framework. It gives human content to the otherwise mystical, abstract notion of 'potentiality'. Human pregnancy, like any other human experience, is never raw biology; its biological dimensions are mediated by the social process of coming into relationship, in this case the earliest, most elemental relationship, which is what humanizes it. 'Relationship' means, first, that there is *interdependence*; and, second, that there is *consciousness* of this, even if that consciousness is one-sided for a time. Willis captures the human reality of pregnancy when she says: 'There is no way a pregnant woman can passively let the fetus live; she must create and nurture it with her own body, a symbiosis that is often difficult, sometimes dangerous, uniquely intimate.'[37] The idea of a 'symbiosis', however, can only refer to a social or cultural construct, a learned response. On the level of 'biology alone', the dependence is one-way – the fetus is a parasite.[38] Not only is it not a part of the woman's body, but it contributes nothing to her sustenance. It only draws from her: nutrients, immunological defenses, hormonal secretions, blood, digestive functions, energy. Even the concept of 'viability', *whenever* it may occur, is meaningless – a device to protect doctors against lawsuits and to denigrate the role of the pregnant woman in prenatal nurturing. What does it mean to speak of viability in a society that has no intention of providing care for the children of working mothers, much less aborted fetuses? More important, the fetus is never viable insofar as it remains utterly dependent for its survival on the mother or another human caretaker until long after birth.

Yet pregnancy, like all relationships, is characterized by mutual dependency in a social and moral sense. For the pregnant woman, whether she wants the fetus or not, is caught up irrevocably in a condition of intimacy with and perhaps longing for it as well. The experience of going through a full-term pregnancy, bearing a child, and giving it up for adoption is punitive and traumatic for a woman because the relationship by then is real; it exists. No woman who has ever borne a child needs to be told that its 'personality' and certainly its relationship to her begin to emerge well before its birth. It is not surprising that until relatively recently (and perhaps still) the moment of 'quickening' was considered by most women the dividing line between the nonexistence and existence of a 'child'. The movements of the fetus are signs, communications, that denote to the pregnant woman its life and its dependence on and relationship to herself. Certainly up until that time a pregnant woman is in no sense a 'mother', for the simple reason that motherhood is a *socially* constructed relationship, not a biological condition alone (the situation of adoption is an obvious example). She is not yet a mother any more than the man who has inseminated a fertile ovum with his sperm becomes from that moment a 'father'. With the onset of movement in the uterus, the woman begins to develop her consciousness of interrelatedness. That consciousness, emerging out of reciprocal sensory activity, marks the beginning of the social relationships that are the necessary and sole basis through which the fetus's development of a 'self', its *humanization*, is possible.

The point is not that the fetus now has a 'subjective' relationship with this particular 'mother' but that it has objectively entered the community of human beings through its social interaction with (and not only its physical dependency on) *an* other. Its earliest 'socialization' occurs through its body and the interdependence of its body with a conscious human being. The fact that the (post-'quickening') fetus or the early infant is not yet a 'self' does not negate this reciprocal quality. Piaget, for example, discovered that the 3-month-old infant, in the process of 'assimilating' visual images (a hand) to motor activity and sucking, engages in imitation of the caretaker's movements, even before there is any recognition 'of another's body and his own body'.[39] But of course, the existence of the other and its (her/his) *attentive consciousness* is the necessary precondition for the imitative activity to occur. What is irreducible and indispensable in this humanization process (the formation of the 'person') is *the subjectivity of the pregnant woman*, her consciousness of existing in a relationship with the fetus. Short of artificial wombs and Brave New World laboratories (which may be the 'final solution' 'right-to-lifers' have in mind), there is no getting around this, no eliminating the pregnant woman as active agent of the fetus's 'personhood'. For it is *her* consciousness that is the condition of its humanization, of its consciousness evolving from the potential to the actual.

In the everyday practices of abortion and childbearing, more clearly than in opinion polls or surveys of attitudes, we can read the social

record of a moral sense about abortion that comes close to the one
I have just presented. If 1.5 million abortions a year indicate a compelling need and desire for abortion among women, we may also
notice that between 92 and 96 per cent of those abortions occur
within the first trimester, and over half within the first 8 weeks.[40]
These data are significant in understanding popular values about
'fetal life'. They confirm the sense that most women have, in term
pregnancies, of developmental differences that correspond to differences, changes, in their relationship/obligation/bond to the fetus.
This sense determines, too, that a miscarriage often has a different
meaning when it occurs in the first or second month of a pregnancy,
when it may not even be noticed, than when it occurs in the fifth or
sixth month, when it becomes the occasion of mourning – the *loss* of
'someone'. Even our ordinary language expresses this. We say, 'She
had a miscarriage', in the earlier case, and after some hard-to-define
but real point later on, 'She lost her baby.'

Peter Steinfels, editor of *Commonweal* and a forceful spokesperson
for liberal Catholic opposition to abortion, urges liberal Catholics to
admit 'quite frankly that the moral status of the fetus in its early
development is a genuinely difficult problem'. Steinfels acknowledges that to equate 'a disc the size of a period or an embryo one-
sixth of an inch long and with barely rudimentary features' with
'Albert Einstein and Anne Frank as human beings' is 'based on bad
biology'. He thereby opens up the possibility of different degrees
of 'life' or 'personhood', for such acknowledgement implies that
humanization is a developmental process rather than a distinct
moment or quality.[41]

Looking again at the data for 1978–9 regarding the gestational
period in which abortions occur, the impression of a kind of implicit
moral code among women is strengthened if we break down who are
the small number of women who get 'late' abortions (after 12 weeks)
and why. As we might expect, the 5 to 8 per cent of abortions in
those years that occurred after the first trimester tended to be among
teenagers.[42] Delayed abortions among teenagers are mainly the result
not of personal attitudes so much as of public policies that (1) create
legal and administrative obstacles for teenagers who seek abortions,
(2) restrict Medicaid funding for abortion, and (3) support a dominant culture and 'morality' that punish the sexuality of unmarried
young women. In a different sexual culture with unrestricted avail-

ability of legal, publicly funded abortion services, nearly all abortions (except in a small number of health-related cases) would occur early in a pregnancy. This would be desirable from the standpoint of women's health and well-being as well as sensibility to the fetus and its development.

Given this developmental view of pregnancy and its moral implications, what would be a feminist-humanist position on amniocentesis and other forms of prenatal diagnosis? For amniocentesis usually implies an intention to abort if the fetus does not meet certain specifications, and to abort at a relatively late stage of fetal development. (The procedure cannot be performed earlier than at 16 weeks of gestation.) 'Right-to-lifers' have opposed these techniques almost as strongly as abortion, citing them as support of the 'slippery slope' argument and inevitable contributing factors to the escalation of abortion. But this has little basis in fact. In the gestational data cited earlier, pregnant women aged 30–39 had lower percentages of abortions after 9 weeks than other age groups, indicating that abortion following amniocentesis is not a frequent occurrence among them.[43] In short, amniocentesis would seem to have had a negligible impact on abortion rates. This is not to say that abortion following amniocentesis in the second trimester raises no moral questions or poses no hard dilemmas for women (or prospective parents). It does not follow from the feminist position that holds that only a pregnant woman can decide about abortion that abortion raises no moral issues, or that the fetus makes no moral claims on the pregnant woman.

Here we need to distinguish between the *political question* – who should decide – and the *moral question* – whether abortion is right or wrong in a given instance – and begin to enunciate feminist principles for the latter as well as the former. The situation of prenatal diagnosis followed by a decision to abort is a specific one because it nearly always involves a context in which pregnancy is desired but a *particular* fetus is rejected for its characteristics. That such choices may be morally ambiguous or even immoral in certain cases seems unquestionable. Choosing to abort solely on the basis of gender preference, whether for male or female, would be grossly sexist and therefore anti-feminist and immoral. A different case is that of Down's syndrome, one of the most common concerns of women undergoing amniocentesis. Down's syndrome represents a wide-ranging disorder in terms of its symptoms, although the chromosomal abnormality detected through amniocentesis is always the same, and one can never know with certainty that one is rejecting a 'nonfunctional' individual. Similarly, with neural tube defects such as spina bifida, it *may* turn out that one chooses abortion when surgical correction is possible. And, of course, the question of what is 'humanly' functional is a morally laden one.[44] A decision to undergo abortion in such cases is probably always made in terms of competing moral claims to those of the fetus: limited family or community resources; obligations to other children; or the pregnant couple's sense of the limits on their capacity for, and vision of, parenting. It could hardly be otherwise, since pregnancies always exist in a context of social relations and moral commitments, not in isolation.[45]

The other side of the matter is the immeasurable human benefit of a social and medical context in which such a choice exists. For the 5 per cent of tested women who receive a positive amniocentesis result, the prospect of ending the pregnancy and undergoing a second-trimester abortion is undoubtedly painful and anguished; some prefer to go through with the pregnancy. But for most, it seems nothing short of miraculous that what used to be a question of ill fate – the responsibility for a child born with severe, incapacitating handicaps – is now subject to human intervention and choice. Like safe, legal abortion, amniocentesis may be an occasion of sorrow *at the same time* as it is a condition of expanded human freedom and consciousness.[46]

The point here, then, is not the particular outcome of the decision one way or the other so much as it is that such moral decisions are *inevitably hard*; they must be approached with the fullest attention and care given toward all their consequences on the part of those immediately involved. This might be called the 'ethic of people being allowed to work out their own ethic', to take their own moral judgements seriously.[47] In this regard, a feminist morality of abortion cannot totally separate the political question of who decides from the moral question of what decision to make, any more than it can prejudge what is 'right' in a particular case by reference to some holy writ. For it is women whom the culture trains in 'maternal thinking', to exercise care in regard to questions about life; it is pregnant women themselves whose consciousness is closest to the reality of the fetus and the total circumstances in which it exists. In the last analysis, their decisions are most likely to be morally informed. What the anti-abortion movement is about is the discrediting of women's moral judgement.

NOTES

1 'Toward a Feminist–Humanist Concept of Personhood', from R. Petchesky's *Abortion and Woman's Choice*, 1988, is reproduced by kind permission of Verso.

2 R. C. Lewontin, 'The Corpse in the Elevator', *New York Review of Books*, 29 (20 January 1983), 34.

3 One nasty example is Michael Levin, 'The Feminist Mystique', *Commentary*, 70 (December 1980), 25–30.

4 This synopsis is based on examination of dozens of pieces of anti-abortion propaganda material produced between 1975 and 1980 by 'pro-life' groups and widely available through churches and National Right-to-Life Committee chapters.

5 Drusilla Burnham, 'Induced Terminations of Pregnancy: Reporting States, 1979', US Department of Health and Human Services, National Center for Health Statistics, *Monthly Vital Statistics Report*, 31 (Oct. 25, 1982), Table 9.

6 See *Congressional Record*, 19 January 1981, p. S287; and John T. Noonan, Jr, *A Private Choice: Abortion in America in the Seventies* (New York: Free Press, 1979), p. 59.

7 The text of the 'human life statute' reads: '1. The Congress finds that present day scientific evidence indicates a significant likelihood that actual human life exists from conception.

'The Congress further finds that the 14th Amendment to the Constitution of the United States was intended to protect all human beings.

'Upon the basis of these findings, . . . the Congress hereby declares that for the purpose of enforcing the obligation of the States under the 14th Amendment not to deprive persons of life without due process of law, human life shall be deemed to exist from conception, without regard to race, sex, age, health, defect, or condition of dependency; and for this purpose "person" shall include all human life as defined herein.' In addition, the bill would deny to federal courts jurisdiction over abortion. It was this aspect, so blatantly in violation of the Constitution, that lost the bill the support of even many conservatives.

8 Paul Ramsey, 'The Morality of Abortion', in *Life or Death: Ethics and*

Options, ed. Edward Shils et al. (Portland, Ore.: Reed College, 1968), pp. 61–2. The same mystification of molecular biology is contained in C. Everett Koop, 'A Physician Looks at Abortion', in Ganz: 'That one cell with its 46 chromosomes contains the whole genetic code, written in molecules of DNA, that will, if not interrupted, make a human being just like you or me, with the potential for God-consciousness' (p. 9).

9 P. B. Medawar, 'Genetic Options: An Examination of Current Fallacies', in Shils et al., *Life or Death*, pp. 99–100.

10 Callahan, *Abortion: Law, Choice and Morality*, pp. 377–82, makes this point with great cogency.

11 For example, Theodosius Dobzhansky writes: 'human behaviour is in the main genetically unfixed; it shows a remarkably high degree of phenotypic plasticity. It is acquired in the process of socialization, of training received from other individuals. Its base is set by the genes, but the direction and extent of its development are, for the most part, culturally, rather than biologically, determined' (*The Biological Basis of Human Freedom* (New York: Columbia University Press, 1956), p. 130). Similarly, C. H. Waddington: 'The first step in the under-standing of heredity is to realize that what a pair of parents donate to their offspring is a set of potentialities, not a set of already formed characteristics. . . . Any one genotype may give rise to many somewhat different phenotypes, corresponding to the different environments in which development occurs' (*The Nature of Life* (Chicago: University of Chicago Press, 1961), p. 29).

12 Edward Manier, 'Abortion and Public Policy in the U.S.: A Dialectical Examination of Expert Opinion', in Edward Manier, William Liu and David Solomon (eds), *Abortion: New Directions for Policy Studies* (Notre Dame: University of Notre Dame Press, 1977), p. 170.

13 Thus the legal memorandum that provided the theoretical ammunition for 'pro-life' sponsors of S. 158 justifies Congress's authority to over-ride the Supreme Court in *Roe v. Wade* on the unexamined assumption that 'if Congress decides that unborn children are human life for the purpose of the fourteenth amendment's protection of life, it follows logically that for this purpose they are persons as well. By common usage of language, any human being must be recognized as a person' (Stephen H. Galebach, 'A Human Life Statute', *Congressional Record*, 19 January 1981, p. S289). It by no means 'follows logically' nor is it a matter of 'common usage' to equate fetuses with persons in this way.

14 Bernard Weinraub, 'Senator Agrees to Extend Hearings on Abortion Bill', *New York Times*, 25 April 1981, p. A7. See also Walter Sullivan, 'Onset of Human Life: Answer on Crucial Moment Elusive', *New York*

Times, 4 May 1981, p. B12; and Harriet S. Meyer, 'Science and the "Human Life Bill"', Commentary, *Journal of the American Medical Association*, 246 (21 August 1981), 837–9.

15 Callahan, *Abortion*, pp. 377–8, 388–9.

16 Mary Anne Warren, 'On the Moral and Legal Status of Abortion', in *Today's Moral Problems*, ed. Richard A. Wasserstrom (New York: Macmillan, 1979), pp. 37–9, 48.

17 Richard L. Ganz, 'Psychology and Abortion: The Deception Exposed', in Ganz, pp. 30, 33.

18 Ibid., pp. 35–6.

19 *Conservative Digest*, 5 (August 1979), 18. Typical of fundamentalist right-wing attacks on 'secular humanism' in relation to abortion are Ganz, in Ganz, pp. 26–42; and Francis A. Schaeffer and C. Everett Koop, *Whatever Happened to the Human Race?* (Old Tappan, NJ: Fleming H. Revell, 1978). In a like-spirited address before the Institute on Religious Life's Conference in St Louis, 22 April 1978, Rep. Henry Hyde expressed concern over the rise of left-wing and feminist dissidents within the church who are critical of the church's social policies – a trend he sees as posing 'serious problems for the church'. The text of this speech is available from Rep. Hyde's office.

20 One practical manifestation of this view has been the attempt to expose abortion clinics as 'exploiters' of women. Another is the effort to provide 'positive alternatives' to abortion through such vehicles as the counseling group Birthright and the 'pregnancy hotline'.

21 Schaeffer and Koop, *Whatever Happened to the Human Race?*, p. 52.

22 Callahan, *Abortion*, p. 421.

23 On the ancient origins and continuities of myths embodying men's fear of women's power over mortality, see Simone de Beauvoir, *The Second Sex* (New York: Bantam, 1961), ch. 9; Rich, *Of Woman Born* (London: Virago, 1977), chs. 3 and 4; and Philip E. Slater, *The Glory of Hera* (Boston: Beacon, 1968), chs. 8 and 9.

24 Thus, for example, one social scientist refers to abortion as 'an easy alternative for women who perceived that having children was no longer one of the attractive feminine roles'. William T. Liu, 'Abortion and the Social System', in Manier, Liu, and Solomon, *Abortion*, p. 147.

25 Callahan, a liberal supporter of women's 'right to decide', expresses diffidence toward women who get abortions for what he considers to be 'selfish' or not 'serious reasons', which turn out to be any reasons not grounded in maternal duty, either to other children or to 'the good of mankind' (*Abortion*, pp. 429–31). This contradicts the strong

arguments he makes later on about women's right to define the abortion situation as they see fit.

26 See, for example, Betty Friedan, 'Feminism's Next Step', *New York Times Magazine*, 15 July 1981, 14–15; Mary Meehan, 'Abortion: The Left Has Betrayed the Sanctity of Life', *Progressive*, 44 (September 1980), 32–34; Leslie Savan, 'Abortion Chic: The Attraction of Wanted-Unwanted Pregnancies', *Village Voice*, 4–10 February 1981, 32; and Elizabeth Moore and Karen Mulhauser, 'Pro and Con: Does Free Abortion Hurt the Poor and Minorities?' *In These Times*, 28 February 1979, 18. (This 'debate' stirred an angry exchange of feminist criticisms and editorial rejoinders in subsequent issues of *In These Times*, considered a leading left-wing newspaper.) For a trenchant critique of this trend on the left, see Stacey Oliker, 'Abortion and the Left: The Limits of "Pro-Family" Politics', *Socialist Review*, 56 (March–April 1981), 71–95.

27 See Warren, 'On the Moral and Legal Status of Abortion', pp. 45–7; Callahan, *Abortion*, pp. 497–8; and Steinfels, 'The Search for an Alternative', *Commonweal*, 108 (30 November 1981), quoting Charles Hartshorne, p. 661, for this sort of thinking.

28 See Spelman for an excellent feminist critique of this dualist tradition; and O'Brien, ch. 1.

29 Ramsey, 'The Morality of Abortion', p. 60.

30 Jacques Maritain, *The Rights of Man and Natural Law* (London: Geoffrey Bles, 1958), pp. 6–7, 10, 27, 37.

31 Agnes Heller, 'Marx's Theory of Revolution and the Revolution in Everyday Life', in Hegedus, Heller, Markus, and Vajda, *The Humanisation of Socialism*, pp. 46–7.

32 Maritain, *Rights of Man*, p. 27.

33 Steinfels, 'The Search for an Alternative', p. 661.

34 See, for example, Jacques Lacan, 'Le Stade du Miroir comme Formateur de la Fonction du Je', in *Ecrits I* (Paris: Editions de Seuil, 1966); Nancy Chodorow, *The Reproduction of Mothering* (Palo Alto, Calif: Stanford University Press, 1978), pp. 46–51; W. R. D. Fairbairn, *An Object-Relations Theory of the Personality* (New York: Basic Books, 1952); Alice Balint, 'Love for the Mother and Mother-Love', in *Primary Love and Psycho-Analytic Technique*, ed. Michael Balint (New York: Liveright, 1965), pp. 91–108; idem, *The Early Years of Life: A Psychoanalytic Study* (New York: Basic Books, 1954); and Jean Piaget, *The Origins of Intelligence in Children*, trans. Margaret Cook (New York: Norton, 1952).

35 Quoted from Alasdair MacIntyre, in Manier, 'Abortion', p. 20.

36 Roger Wertheimer, 'Philosophy on Humanity', in Manier, Liu, and Solomon, *Abortion*, p. 130.
37 Ellen Willis, 'Abortion: Is a Woman a Person?' in *Beginning to See the Light: Pieces of a Decade* (New York: Knopf, 1981), p. 208.
38 My thanks to Randy Reiter for helping me to clarify this point.
39 Piaget, *The Origins of Intelligence*, pp. 108–9.
40 Burnham, 'Induced Terminations of Pregnancy', Table 4; and US Department of Health and Human Services, Centers for Disease Control, *Abortion Surveillance*, Annual Summary 1978 (Atlanta, Ga., 1980), Table 15. It is for this reason that the 'viability' issue would seem blown out of proportion by both feminists and anti-abortionists. New technology that 'pushes forward' the so-called point of 'viability' will not affect the vast majority of abortions.
41 Steinfels, 'The Search for an Alternative', p. 663. See also Callahan's interesting discussion of the 'developmental school's' approach to understanding the fetus, *Abortion*, pp. 384–90.
42 *Abortion Surveillance*, p. 4 and Table 15.
43 Around 95 per cent of women undergoing amniocentesis have negative results, and among those who test positively for any of the one hundred defects currently diagnosable with this procedure, not all elect to undergo abortion. Robert F. Murray, Jr, 'Technical Issues and Problems Related to Amniocentesis' (lecture given at Symposium on the Dilemmas and Decisions of Prenatal Diagnosis, New York City Community College, Division of Continuing Education, 26 April 1980). Much of my thinking about amniocentesis and prenatal diagnosis is based on having attended this excellent conference. My thanks to Dean Fannie Eisenstein for inviting me to attend.
44 Ruth Hubbard, 'Prenatal Diagnosis and the Problematic Quest for Certainty' (keynote address, New York City Community College Symposium on Prenatal Diagnosis); and Wendy Carlton, ' "Wrongful Life", "Wrongful Birth", Antenatal Testing: The Silent Revolution in Children's Rights' (paper presented at the American Sociological Association meeting, Toronto, 24–28 August 1981), pp. 8–9.
45 A different perspective from the one presented here is that of parents of a fetus diagnosed to be severely hydrocephalic (brain damaged and enlarged by build-up of fluid, causing retardation or death), who gladly consented to every heroic pyrotechnic the medical profession can offer. After a marathon of brain shunts, catheters, needles, etc., the infant was born with compounded anomalies and malformations and died at the age of 5 weeks. The father observed: 'We're sad that Mark's gone. . . . But I can't feel guilty about anything we did or didn't do. Mark suffered a lot, both before his birth and afterward. But I felt that

if I had asked him, "Do you want to go through with this?" if he had been able to answer he always would have said yes' (Robin Marantz Henig, 'Saving Babies Before Birth', *New York Times Magazine*, 28 February 1982, p. 46). This is an expression of 'fetal personhood' ideology: the apotheosis of life under any conditions, the more suffering the holier; the projection of the parent's moral illusions on to the unconscious, unknowing fetus. Whether parents *should* have this 'choice', whether society's already inequitably distributed medical resources should be deflected into 'saving' such fetuses, is another question.

46 I do not subscribe to the view that the existence of a technique limits choice because it compels its use. This is an anti-technological form of technological determinism, attributing to the technique magical power over people's relation to it. My sense is that in this case the technique potentially widens the framework for moral praxis and a more conscious life; there is nothing wrong with individuals wanting 'certainty'. The very real potential for *abuse*, on the other hand (e.g., pressure on women to undergo the procedure when it may be unnecessary or risky), is a function not of the technique but of the organization and politics of existing medical care.

47 My thanks to Marty Fleisher for this observation.

25

Sara Ruddick
b.1935

Extract from *MATERNAL THINKING* (1990)

Sara Ruddick teaches philosophy and women's studies at the New School for Social Research in New York. In Maternal Thinking *she sets out to define for herself a critical, yet not wholly negative relation to the intellectualist ideals in which she has been educated: 'not [to] reject Reason, [but to] honour Reason differently'.* Her work thus forms part of a larger effort to make good the incompleteness of philosophy by endowing it with a 'different', female, voice.*

Ruddick builds on the 'practicalist' assumption, common to twentieth-century thinkers as dissimilar in other respects as Wittgenstein and Habermas, that standards of rationality are immanent in collective human activity. Her project is to give an account of the specific rationality which characterizes the activity of 'mothering', but we are not to understand this in a narrowly biological way: although Ruddick defers to current social reality to the extent of writing about mothers in the feminine gender, she points out in a preliminary note that in principle 'mothering work is as suitable to men as to women.'

Maternal Thinking *is an exercise in ideal description – a method which is as old as European ethical theory, but which has been out of fashion during the present century thanks to the widely held belief in a radical 'fact – value distinction'. In the present case the descriptive task is to make explicit what mothers* qua *mothers are trying to do, and what they are actually doing in so far as they are realizing the aims internal to their own practice. This kind of exercise, argues Ruddick, should not be confused with moralizing about the beauty of motherhood. Yet the connection between ideal and actuality cannot be purely contingent: 'to say that an ideal governs is to say . . . that in an ordinary way, much of the time, the ideal is nearly fulfilled', and in this sense Ruddick's discussion is after all a celebration of the resilience and effectiveness of real-life mothers.*

The three objectives or 'demands' which Maternal Thinking *identifies as constitutive of the work of mothering are* preservation, growth *and* social acceptability.** The extract reprinted here concerns all three, but perhaps especially the first. It deals with the discipline of sustaining daily routines or emerging from difficult situations with the minimum of damage to children – a policy which is not simply instrumental to the future good of adulthood, but which defines a 'non-violence of daily life that is itself a goal to which longer-range aims must be adapted'.*

The pragmatism of Ruddick's conception of mothering, and her emphasis on surviving crises as opposed to applying abstract principles, link her with that tendency in recent feminist theory which exalts sensitivity to the particular situation above 'masculine' theoreticism. (For discussion of this tendency, see Benhabib, reading 16.) But it would be misleading to suggest that Ruddick wants to dispense with abstract moral concepts altogether, for in her view one of the central tasks of motherhood is to bring children to prefer justice *to the 'temporary pleasures of tyranny and exploitation'. Hence the underlying rationalist commitment suggested by her decision to write about maternal* thinking; *and hence, too, the appropriateness of her appeal to the classic texts of Gandhi and Martin Luther King on non-violent resistance.*

Although mothers might wish it otherwise, conflict is a part of maternal life.[1] A mother finds herself embattled with her children, with an 'outside' world at odds with her or their interests, with a man or other adults in her home, with her children's enemies. She is spectator and arbiter of her children's battles with each other and their companions. If there were a job description for mothers, it might read in part:

> Teaches her children – and herself – when to fight and when to make peace. When battles occur, she prevents her children – and herself – from deliberately or predictably perpetrating or submitting to techniques of struggle that are damaging. Learns

to distinguish serious harm from permissible hurt and teaches her children this. Names violence when it occurs and teaches her children to take responsibility for their violent assaults. Maintains conditions of peacefulness so that her children may grow in safety. Is available, when called on, to help her communities develop policies for minimizing and strategies for resolving conflict.

This description of a 'good enough' mother is also a description of a person whose work is governed by ideals of nonviolence.

The defining activity of nonviolent activism is peacemaking, that sustained effort to create conditions of 'peace' in which people can self-respectfully pursue their individual and collective projects free of the structural violences of poverty, tyranny and bigotry. Nonviolent peacemaking is governed by four ideals: renunciation, resistance, reconciliation and peacekeeping. Nonviolent activists renounce violent strategies and weapons. They resist, nonviolently, the violence of others, including their policies of bigotry, greed and exploitation. The aim of nonviolent battle is responsible reconciliation in which crimes are named and responsibility for them is assigned. Peacekeepers find ways to avoid battles whenever possible and to halt necessary nonviolent battles as soon as aggression is turned back and the aims of justice are secured.

In examining maternal practice through the lens of nonviolence, I look for evidence of an ongoing attempt to renounce and resist violence, to reconcile opponents, and to keep a peace that is as free as possible from assaultive injustice. That is, I ask if there are principles in the practices of mothering that coincide with the four ideals of nonviolence. In attributing ideals of nonviolence to peacemaking mothers, I speak about what they *aim* to teach children, but I say nothing about their pedagogical success. Mothers have little control over the decisions their draft-age children make about when or how to fight. Children are provoked to, encouraged in, and sometimes conscripted for violence by friends, public officials and counselors, as well as by the frustrations and injustices of their lives. I do not intend to blame mothers once again for others' policies or their children's actions. In saying that mothers are governed by ideals of nonviolence, I am not talking primarily about mothers' effects on children but about the ideals that determine how mothers themselves think about anger, injury, conflict and battle.

Those governed by an ideal can be identified by the efforts they make, by their shame, guilt and determination to change when they fail to follow the ideal, and by their pleasure in their own and others' success. Mothers who beat and tyrannize their children or passively watch others do so and who show no signs of remorse or attempts to get help cannot be said to be governed by ideals of nonviolence. Nor is remorse sufficient to show such governance; indifferently abusive people can apologize many times over without seeking help or determining to change their violent ways. To say that an ideal governs is to say, at the least, that in an ordinary way, much of the time, the ideal is nearly fulfilled. Otherwise, ideals only mystify, as a sentimental mother-speech generally mystifies the realities of maternal life. In the peacemaking practices I describe, nonviolence is honored not in the exception but as the rule.

In speaking of those maternal practices that are governed by ideals of nonviolence, I am not attributing success to mothers. Almost all mothers remember actions of theirs that were violent, that is, actions which if repeated often would have damaged their children. As in maternal thinking as a whole, to say that an ideal governs is to identify a kind of struggle, not to record an achievement. The question is whether mothers count failure as a nonviolent activist would count it, not whether they fail. In speaking of mothers' failure to be nonviolent, I do not refer to pathological abuse or neglect but to the failures of 'good enough' mothers who only imperfectly fulfil the ideals that govern them. When I speak of temptations to assault and abandon and of the passivity, timidity, vengeance and battle lust that are liabilities of maternal work, I am talking about temptations and liabilities that are part of maternal nonviolence, not exceptions to it.

My description of maternal practices governed by ideals of nonviolence does not include all mothers everywhere. Considerable maternal violence, collective and individual, exists. In most cultures certain accepted maternal practices elicit from outsiders surprised disapproval if not outright horror – for example, tightly swaddling infants, circumcising female children, or denying teenagers the information about sexuality that is necessary to their safety. Many individual mothers are pathologically violent – they abuse their children deliberately and regularly, apparently indifferent to damage. It is difficult even for trained investigators to assess the extent of maternal nonviolence. If a mother is violent ten minutes out of ten waking hours or one day out of seven, it is the violent act rather than the nonviolent practice that is remembered. Given the vulnerability of children, this is as it should be. On the other hand, children accept abuses done to them if they become routine, especially if an abusive mother claims to be acting for the good of the child.

In my discussion, I put these socially critical questions to one side. I aim to identify principles of maternal nonviolence that I believe could contribute to collective, public understandings of peacemaking. For my purpose, it is sufficient that there are *some* maternal practices actually governed by the ideals I articulate. Because I am not measuring statistical extent but rather articulating governing ideals, I refer only to those peacemaking maternal practices – atypical as they may be – that I have seen. When for stylistic ease I revert to the idiom of achievement – 'mothers do . . . mothers say . . . mothers believe . . .' – I always mean only that what *some* mothers do, say, and believe is evidence of a maternal effort and that this effort is characteristic of at least some maternal practices of nonviolence.

I am aware, however, that my epistemological restraint is often betrayed by my rhetoric. In the past years I have watched mothers intensively in a variety of circumstances and neighbourhoods. I have seen slaps and pulling and heard shrieking abuse – especially when children endanger themselves or others by sticking their heads out a closing subway door, running into the street, or sending a skateboard skidding into a passer-by. I know that children suffer from their caretakers far worse violence than anything I have seen and that the epidemic of drug addiction makes abuse increasingly likely. Yet I have found myself repeatedly struck not by maternal violence but by resilient, nonviolent mothering under considerable provocation in difficult circumstances. While poverty and isolation make nonviolence a miracle, the miracle seems to occur. After several years of thinking about these issues, I believe that there are many voices of maternal nonviolence, with different mothers and cultures of mothers pursuing nonviolence in their own flawed and imperfect ways. Hence it is out of respect as much as stylistic laziness that I revert to the idiom of achievement: 'Mothers do . . . mothers say . . . mothers try.'[2]

Ideals of Nonviolence

The most controversial and distinguishing ideal of nonviolent action is the renunciation of 'violent' strategies and weapons. Simone Weil defined 'force' – roughly her term for 'violence' – as whatever 'turned a person into a thing', treating that person as if he counted for nothing.[3] Gandhi spoke of 'ahimsa', noninjury, a refusal to harm.[4] More prosaically, I take a violent act or policy as one that is either intended to damage or can predictably be expected to damage a person against whom it is wielded and for which there is no compensatory benefit for the person damaged. By damage, I mean serious and apparently long-lasting harm or injury. By compensatory benefit, I mean some good that the damaged person may expect from her injuries, as, for example, a patient hopes to benefit from assaultive chemotherapy.

Although damage is painful and harmful, not all pain and harm are violent. If I fall and break my arm I have not suffered violence. Violence is almost always coercive, inflicted without a person's consent, but people also inflict violence on themselves. The drug addict and anorexic are not, typically, coerced into the behaviour that damages them. Someone violent to herself or cooperating in her own violence treats herself as a 'thing' of no value; says to herself 'I do not count.' Damage can be psychological as well as physical and can be indirectly as well as directly visited on the violated person. A person whose loved one is killed or tortured is an indirect victim of violence. However, the clearest case of damage is physical injury or harm to the violated person. Other kinds of damage are understood by analogy to this central case, in which the human body becomes the place of pain and domination.

Whether in the midst of action or in moments of calm reflection, it is often very difficult to identify violence. The most elaborate definitions cannot substitute for judgement and indeed must be altered in its light. Who is to say whether damage could have been predicted? How serious is 'serious', how long 'long-lasting'? Who is to determine compensatory benefit? Although I worry over these questions in other discussions of nonviolence, for my purposes here I have clear enough cases of violence to anchor a definition. Torturing a person, burning her with napalm, destroying her home and provisions, killing her loved ones – all these routine acts of tyranny and war are clearly violent. So are painful and extensive beatings, sexual assault on vulnerable young people, and humiliating practices of shaming – the routine acts of domestic tyranny and violence.

In the renunciation of violent weapons and strategies, it is customary to distinguish those who are relatively weaponless and powerless from those who believe they could, if they chose, use violence effectively. Mothers, as we have seen, often feel powerless in respect to their children and, typically, are actually powerless in respect to men in their home and social group. Minority or poor mothers are also powerless in respect to men and women of governing classes and races.

Like other powerless people, mothers resort to nonviolent strategies because they do not have weapons – guns, legal clout, money or any other tools with which to work one's will on others. Like the powerless everywhere, mothers are often enraged. Officials callously neglect or deliberately injure their children. Mothers feel as if they relinquish pleasures and ambitions to do important human work only to find that their work is taken for granted and their word for naught. Fantasies of revenge must thrive among mothers. Yet they are rarely capable of violent revenge on their own or their children's behalf. Officials – teachers, welfare workers, landlords, doctors and the like – can retaliate against the children as well as the mothers themselves at the hint of maternal violence. Even maternal anger is apt to be punished or trivialized (the 'hysteria' of an 'overinvolved' or 'embittered' woman). Nor, ideally, can mothers turn against their children whom they are pledged to protect. To get their way, mothers engage in nonviolent techniques that are familiar from more public struggles: prayer, persuasion, appeasement, self-suffering, negotiation, bribery, invocation of authority, ridicule and many other sorts of psychological manipulation. These techniques may go to the edge of violence – of real damage – without endangering either a mother, her children, or the people they fight against.

From the perspective of nonviolent activism, what is striking about mothers is their commitment to nonviolent action in precisely those situations where they are undeniably powerful, however powerless they may feel – namely, in their battles with children. Children are vulnerable creatures and as such elicit either aggression or care. Recalcitrance and anger tend to provoke aggression, and children can be angrily recalcitrant. Typically, the mother who confronts her children is herself young, hassled if not harassed by officials in an outside world, usually by her own employers, and often by adults she lives with. She brings to confrontations with her children psychological and physical strengths which are potentially lethal. Her ability to damage her children increases the more alone she is with them, the less others are available to go to the children's aid. Yet it is these same circumstances of frustration and loneliness that will tempt her to violence when faced with her children's recalcitrance. I can think of no other situation in which someone subject to resentments at her social powerlessness, under enormous pressures of time and anger, faces a recalcitrant but helpless combatant with so much restraint. This is the nonviolence of the powerful.

It might be thought that, like other powerful people, mothers only appear to renounce violence while actually maintaining control by the fear they inspire. It does not follow, however, that because mothers are fearsome, their control is typically and primarily a function of fear. Control by fear and threat is always fragile. Threats must be sufficiently frightening to deter but not so frightening as to have undesired effects. When adults are frightened, they may react by deceiving those who frighten them, resenting and abandoning them, resisting them courageously out of self-respect, or becoming so terrified that they no longer can play or work. Young children, only barely able to distinguish the illusory from the legitimate fear, are still more likely to respond unpredictably and destructively when frightened. Although many mothers threaten, often ritualistically, their threats are often limited not only in number but, more important, by the context of protectiveness in which they occur. Those mothers who are governed by ideals of nonviolence know this and ensure that their threats occur amid effective, trustworthy means of nonviolent control.

Because they are powerful, mothers can also discipline a child by deliberately inflicting pain through measures that do not risk damaging a child, such as controlled 'spanking', a deliberate use of pain quite distinct from damaging beatings or angry blows. Frequently, mothers who threaten or resort to the infliction of pain draw their children into the discipline, requiring them to pick a switch from the yard or to agree on and then count the number of strokes. I have heard such mothers defend their discipline as a measured expression of justice that prevents less worthy, capricious expressions of anger. Mothers (like me) who criticize the infliction of pain point out the danger that controlled violence will escalate into uncontrolled abuse, especially if a child becomes actively resistant. Moreover, both mothers and children can become sexually excited by the conjunction of pain, domination and submission. Most generally, the social construction of a child's body as a vulnerable locus of pain seems a preparation for later public domination and submission, even if it does not humiliate or sexually confuse the young child.

Although I believe that the deliberate infliction of pain is predictably, though not invariably, damaging to a child, my point here is that it is within practices governed by ideals of nonviolence that mothers argue about pain in the ways I report. In my experience of maternal arguments, mothers do not advocate bullying, capriciousness, or any sort of physically damaging violence. Despite deeply felt generational, cultural, or temperamental differences among mothers, they seem to agree that a practice, *if damaging*, should be renounced and then go on to argue about damage. If my experience is at all typical, these maternal debates about the benefits and dangers of inflicting pain do not contradict but rather actually reflect an ongoing maternal effort to be governed by the ideal of renunciation, however differently the ideal is interpreted.

As their discussions about pain make clear, mothers who renounce violence must find some acceptable ways to train and control. This requires recognizing violence in its many forms. Beyond certain clear and visible acts of physical damage, the distinction of what actions seriously harm and injure varies from family to family and from culture to culture. There is a tendency among pacifist theorists to escalate the requirements for 'ahimsa', or noninjury, considering even thoughts and wishes as damaging acts. Gandhi's description of ahimsa provides a striking example of such an inclusive definition:

> Not to hurt any living thing is no doubt a part of ahimsa. But it is its least expression. The principle of ahimsa is hurt by every evil thought, by undue haste, by lying, by hatred, by wishing ill to anybody.[5]

> Ahimsa really means that you may not offend anybody, you may not harbour an uncharitable thought even in connection with one who may consider himself to be your enemy.[6]

Impatience is a phase of violence.[7]

Mothers who embrace the Gandhian ideal will be in for sleepless nights. It would be nearly impossible for mothers to renounce uncharitable thoughts and angers, let alone impatience. Rather, their task is to determine which hurts, hates, impatience and lying are damaging and which strategies are effective and consonant with safety, development, and conscientiousness. Maternal conversations, heard in a certain spirit, are as filled with controversy about the morality and effectiveness of strategies as are the meetings of war cabinets. By my definition, any strategy of fighting or resisting that does not actually damage an opponent is nonviolent. The trick is to distinguish permissible hurt from damaging harm, nonviolent coercion from damaging force. 'Forcing' a child to go to bed or grabbing a knife from his hand is, in almost all contexts, nonviolent though coercive. An inoculation is a permissible hurt. But many bribes, threats, lures, reprimands and other manipulative nonviolent techniques become questionable when development and conscientiousness are at stake.

Of the many controversial techniques of nonviolent manipulation, the uses of 'self-suffering' – shame and guilt – are especially prominent because of the role they played in the public nonviolence associated with Gandhi and Martin Luther King, Jr. A self-sufferer takes upon herself the pain involved in fighting. Willingness to suffer is considered a condition of endurance and a testament to seriousness and courage. To assume rather than to inflict suffering is also, for both King and Gandhi, an expression of love. In the midst of the brutal violence of the civil rights movement, King promised: 'Send your hooded perpetrators of violence into our community at the midnight hour and best us and leave us half dead, and we shall still love you.'[8] This echoes his mentor Gandhi: 'Love ever suffers, never resents, never revenges itself . . . The test of love is *tapasya* and *tapasya* means self-suffering.'[9] Self-suffering is also a weapon that induces guilt and shame in the conscientious opponent and sympathy in the 'whole world [that] watches'. The famous nonviolent, unarmed assault on the salt mines in India, where Satyagrahi marched in unbroken ranks against soldiers who beat them, was an instance of self-suffering and, proleptically, a fulfilment of King's promise: 'Be ye assured we will wear you down by our capacity to suffer.'[10]

Whatever its public uses, in maternal nonviolence self-suffering is morally and practically limited. Self-suffering is sometimes a prominent maternal strategy. Mothers may manipulatively display the pain their children cause them, adeptly employing the tears and tones of suffering. Yet mothers often realize that children are not and cannot afford to be too long and deeply affected by maternal tears. The limits of self-suffering are part of a general limitation on provoking children's guilt and shame. A child's conscientiousness develops slowly and unpredictably. While the capacity for shame and guilt may be necessary for conscientiousness, excessive guilt leads to anger, indifference or inhibition while humiliating shame damages a precariously developing self.

Like any other nonviolent strategy, techniques of self-suffering may be evaluated in terms of an insistence, central to pacifism, on the inseparability of means and end. Although Gandhi spoke of ahimsa as the means to truth, saying that 'without Ahimsa it is not possible to seek and find Truth,' he undermined this distinction conceptually and practically:

> Ahimsa and Truth are so intertwined that it is practically impossible to disentangle and separate them. They are like two sides of a coin, or rather a smooth, unstamped metallic disc. Who can say which is the obverse and which is the reverse.[11]

To paraphrase Gandhi, if the preservation and growth of children is truth, then a criterion of its realization is that it be achieved nonviolently. However closely an outcome resembles an original goal – a child asleep or in school – a method that damages a child has failed. Drugging a child to sleep or dragging her into a school room is not a means to but a perversion of the end they allegedly achieve.

Although the ends of mothering cannot be achieved violently and still remain maternal ends, nonviolence is not a mother's only goal. Mothers aim to nurture and train an adult capable of work and love. They also typically have aims for their children that are related to their religious, political or intellectual groups. These long-range goals inform some intermediate choices and help a mother to make sense of her work as a whole. Nonetheless, they must be pursued flexibly, with attention to particular challenges and circumstances.

Gandhi held on to the distant aim of home rule through years of actions, compromises and settlement. Yet in the course of struggle, the long-range goal was too general to dictate strategy. Rather it was the nonviolence of ongoing struggle that gradually, over time, gave meaning to the goal. Similarly, a mother cannot decide what to do with a bullying or frightened child by appealing to models of adulthood. It is the nonviolence of daily life that is itself a goal to which longer-range aims must be adapted. Gandhi never gave up the goal of home rule. Mothers, by contrast, may be called on to relinquish religious or political aims that are dear to them. All the more important for mothers to learn to interpret long-range goals flexibly as they attend to the specific tasks at hand. As Gandhi would say, 'The way is the truth'; or as feminists put it, 'The process is the project.'

There is nothing simple about a commitment to nonviolence. A mother often finds herself confronted with seemingly untenable choices. Either she gives her child sleeping pills or he will go sleepless and become increasingly unable to sleep; either she locks a child in her room or she continues to beat on her brother, all other means of prevention having failed; either she drags him sobbing into the classroom or reinforces his fear that school is indeed a dangerous place. Mothers have to do *something* – nighttimes and school days arrive, siblings must live together. Relief comes when a difficult day or phase has passed. The issue again is what counts as success. To the extent that a child is damaged, i.e., controlled violently, the ends of preservation and growth are compromised.

Partly because nonviolent fighting is exhausting and peace and quiet are such a relief, most mothers avoid battles when they can and end unavoidable battles quickly. To be sure, some mothers seem to thrive on battle with or among their children. The perception of a child's separateness, central to fostering growth and conscientiousness, is needed to prevent mothers from taking their children's part in battles with an inappropriate enthusiasm. Although she may be tempted to fight more often and with more fervour than children require, it is in a mother's self-interest to limit battles. Most of her children's 'enemies' are members of her neighbourhood and school community, often indeed children of close friends. Typically a mother will be held and will hold herself responsible for any damage her children cause or suffer if nonviolence turns to violence. In children's battles, as in adults', escalation can be swift – a shouting child stomps on the baby's stomach, an insulting taunt is met with a brick to the head. Moreover, even nonviolent battle has its cost. Hurting and being hurt are part of fighting. Scraped knees and feelings usually mend with astonishing speed, but they can also be stubbornly immune to aid; even the most nonviolent strategy can go awry and leave its scars.

Peace is the more secure, the fewer weapons at hand. In domestic as in public life, there is no substitute for disarmament. Ideally, a mother keeps her house and yard as weapon-free as possible, despite the advertising of toys far more lethal than play pistols and the increasing popularity in the United States of keeping real, dangerous guns at home. She also tries to disarm her neighbours' children. It would be unrealistic to leave weapons about, let alone to pile them up deliberately, and then to expect children not to use them when provoked. But as in public life, disarmament can never be complete. Even if real guns are banned, there are always weapons available to the weak as well as the strong – blocks, rocks, play trucks and sewing needles, for example. Moreover, bigger children are often as physically capable of seriously injuring a smaller child as is a mother herself. Although weapons should be eliminated wherever possible, there is no substitute for the renunciation of violence. By example and precept a mother has to train children not to stamp on the baby, throw a rock at the head, push a toddler in the river, or squirt insecticide in an enemy's face.

To keep the peace, a peacemaking mother, as best she can, creates ways for children and adults to live together that both appear to be and are fair. She distributes goods and privileges, listens carefully to complaints, and respectfully explains the unavoidable differences in powers and rewards that are inevitable among adults and children of different ages. Faced with rivalry, tyranny or greed, nonviolent mothers do not sit passively by, letting a stronger or older child annex the possessions or exploit the smaller or more vulnerable one. Arbitrating and restraining, mothers appeal to interests the children share – or invent them. In reinforcing the fragile affections that survive rivalry and inevitable inequality, mothers who are guided by ideals of nonviolence work for the day that their children will come to prefer justice to the temporary pleasures of tyranny and exploitation.

A mother who aspires to nonviolence makes a peace worth keeping. But the best peace should not entirely prevent battle. Premature appeasement or totalitarian techniques of controlling conflict, though comforting, prevent children from learning how to recognize what they want, articulate their desire, and set out to achieve it. Such evasive techniques leave them unpractised in victory or defeat and therefore unmindful of the necessity for and ways to achieve reconciliation. They encourage those who are treated unjustly to despair of change and allow those who dominate, either through strength or oppression, to remain oblivious to the cost their dominance exacts on themselves and others. To put the matter starkly, children whose conflict is always managed for them are trained both to submit to power and to exercise abusive power over others.

Mothers are often accused of appeasement and totalitarian control. They walk away from the scene, lie to make a child feel better, insist on the appearance of affection where there is none, bribe or threaten children into denying their anger and hurt, or create small rituals of disorder – shouts, slaps and tears – that appear to express conflict while burying it in noise. Most mothers have sometimes done these things. The belief dies hard that children will be so good, or an order so artful, that fighting will disappear. Yet for the most part, mothers appreciative of nonviolence know that 'peace and quiet' can mask many kinds of violence; some battles with and between children should and must take place.

Even more important than her attitude toward children's battles is a nonviolent mother's commitment to resist authorities and policies that are unjust or harmful. Like anyone else, in the face of superior power, mothers often succumb to fearfulness and despair. But they also often name and encourage, in themselves and their children, the duty to resist, and they recognize their lack of resistance as failure. Most striking is the courageous resistance, in the face of danger, against enormous odds, by mothers who live in poverty, tyranny and slavery. In quieter times, more fortunate mothers exhibit their own barely visible courage as they get for their children what they need and learn to say no to those who hurt them. When they identify resistance as a virtue, mothers try to teach children to stand up for themselves and others, knowing that mothers themselves may be the first authority a child resists and that those around them, including other mothers, may criticize the spiritedness they have fostered. An unusually spunky mother, Grace Paley's Faith, the same character who took it to be part of her work to raise children 'righteously up', faces the consequences of another mother's disapproval:

> How can you answer that boy?
> 'You don't,' says Mrs Julius Finn. . . . 'You answer too much, Faith Asbury, and it shows. Nobody fresher than Richard.'
> 'Mrs Finn,' I scream in order to be heard, for she's some distance away and doesn't pay attention the way I do. 'What's so terrible about fresh. EVIL is bad, WICKED is bad. ROBBING, MURDER, and PUTTING HEROIN IN YOUR BLOOD is bad.'
> 'Blah, blah,' she says, deaf to passion. 'Blah to you.'[12]

Peacekeeping is the art of avoiding battle; the challenge is to recognize when peacekeeping should end and battle begin. Resistance is the art of discerning, and then having the courage to fight, violences. The challenge is to recognize when fighting is no longer justified but is motivated by vengeance, battle pleasure or inertia. In peace campaigns there is often a tension between those gifted in nonviolent fighting and those adept at peacekeeping. A peace politics must co-ordinate and reward the efforts of both kinds of work. Similarly, some mothers will be more adept at peacekeeping, others at resisting. In maternal conversations, mothers often help each other develop both gifts while using their special talents on behalf of each other's children.

Nonviolent battles are meant to end quickly, but not any end will do. People who have fought must be reconciled; harder, once non-violent battle is won, people who have been abused must forgive. King's views are not atypical:

> Forgiveness does not mean ignoring what has been done or putting a false label on an evil act. It means rather that the evil act is no longer a barrier to the relationship. . . . The evil deed of the enemy-neighbour, the thing that hurts, never quite expresses all that he is. . . . We must not seek to hate or humiliate the enemy but to seek his understanding. . . . Hate multiplies hate, violence multiplies violence. . . . Hate scars the soul. . . .

Like an unchecked cancer, hate corrodes the personality and
eats away its vital unity.[13]

In public battles, where peoples and nations are hatefully and
violently abused, to forgive is as intellectually confusing and morally
controversial as is renunciation of violence at the outset. For mothers,
by contrast, the ideal of responsible reconciliation is a routine aspect
of training and education. Mothers name the evils that are done to or
by their children. It is wrong (usually) to lie, bully or humiliate,
although children – and mothers – do these things. It is also wrong
to suffer such insults in silence or to forgive perpetrators before the
deed is named and the agent held responsible. Mothers, like children, are tempted to patch up prematurely, make do and forget.
After all, many 'crimes' by and against children are trivial, and some
cheerful forgetting is necessary to get through the day. But nonviolence is not simple. There is no rule for distinguishing the trivial
'childish' escapade from more serious hurt. While moralism has its
clear limits, cheery forgetfulness is no morality at all. Truthful,
responsible reconciliation protects children from their own or others'
hatred, which 'scars the soul', and also from forgetful indifference to
pain that they have inflicted or suffered and that, like hate, 'corrodes
the personality and eats away its vital unity'.[14]

Assigning and taking responsibility comes fairly easily to mothers,
even when they themselves have become violent. Maternal 'forgive-
ness' is a more complicated phenomenon. Mothers often forgive their
children even for serious crimes of violence and bigotry despite their
clear harm. If a passionate loyalty overcomes her ability to name her
child's crime and to urge upon him responsibility for it, then a
mother has failed to live up to the ideal of responsible reconciliation.
While mothers may forgive their children too easily, many find it
difficult to forgive themselves. A responsible reconciliation would
require of mothers a clear-sighted, resiliently cheerful appreciation of
their own imperfections as well as their children's. It is probably
most difficult for mothers to forgive people they perceive as their
children's enemies – hard enough when opponents are children,
almost impossible if the enemies are adults. Often children's 'enemies'
are also a mother's – Father, mate, grandparent or friend who have
treated both mother and child badly. In their harshness, mothers are
not wrong. If mothers can name and take reponsibility, it is much

more likely that the peace that follows battle will be sturdy. Yet hatred does 'scar the soul', frequently also imposing on the injured children a vengeance they no longer need. Often mothers realize this. After the bitterest divorce or most divisive neighbourhood or school battle, there are mothers who let combatants and even outright offenders make amends and resume relationships in the interest of the active connectedness that is 'peace'.

The four ideals of nonviolence – renunciation, resistance, reconciliation and peacekeeping – govern only some maternal practices of some mothers. Yet it is also true that to elucidate these ideals is to describe, from a particular perspective, maternal practice itself. Peacemaking mothers create arrangements that enable their children to live safely, develop happily and act conscientiously; that is, they preserve, nurture and train, exemplifying the commitments of maternal work.

NOTES

*　　*Maternal Thinking: Towards a Politics of Peace* (London: The Women's Press, 1990), p. 9.

**　　Ibid. p. 17.

1　　S. Ruddick's 'Maternal Nonviolence: A Truth in the Making' from her *Maternal Thinking*, 1990, is reproduced by permission of © The Women's Press (UK) and Beacon Press (US).

2　　Whatever the statistical extent of violence among mothers, maternal violence makes up only a small fraction of individual and group violence. Morever, most mothers are women. It seems that the vast majority of violent acts – from incest to child abuse to domestic and public beatings, personal and imperialist armed robbery, and saturation bombing – are performed by men and are often deliberately planned and officially sanctioned by men. While acknowledging statistical association of violence with men – though not of the majority of men with violence – I am here concerned with *mothers'* violence, which is primarily *women's* violence just because most mothers are women. I am also concerned with mothers', and therefore with women's, attraction to or complicity in the violence of others, including violence of lovers, public officials, Fathers and teachers – often, but by no means always, men.

　　A cursory glance at Linda Gordon's *Heroes of Their Own Lives: The Politics and History of Family Violence, Boston 1880–1960* (New

York: Viking, 1988) reveals that in the records Gordon studied, fathers counted for 54 per cent, mothers for 46 per cent of child abusers. Gordon also says that women are more often violent with a spouse, less violent on their own. Not surprisingly, men's abusive behaviour is correlated with their unemployment and with the time they spend with their children. My cursory reading has not yet revealed whether men became abusive because, as a result of unemployment, they take up mothering work (for which they were ill prepared) or whether children were targets of despair and anger (these men couldn't be Fathers) or, presumably, both.

3 Simone Weil, *Iliad, Poem of Force,* Pendle Hill Pamphlet no. 91 (Wallingford, PA), p. 3 and passim.

4 Gandhi's principal writings on nonviolence are collected in *Non-Violent Resistance* (New York: Schocken Books, 1981). A very useful book for understanding Gandhi's theory of nonviolence is Joan Bondurant, *The Conquest of Violence* (Berkeley: University of California Press, 1971). An excellent, brief, and secular discussion of nonviolence is Barbara Deming, 'Revolution and Equilibrium', published, along with other essays on nonviolence, in *We Are All Part of One Another* (Philadelphia: New Society Publishers, 1984). The essay is also printed in pamphlet form published by the A. J. Muste Essay Series (New York: A. J. Muste Institute). The pamphlet is available from the War Resisters' League, 339 Lafayette St, New York, NY 10012. The political theorist Gene Sharp has written extensively on nonviolence, developing a strong tactical defence of its usefulness. See, for example. *Making Europe Unconquerable: The Potential of Civilian Based Deterrence and Defense* (New York: Ballinger Books, 1985). The War Resisters' League is a very helpful guide to the literature of nonviolence, and essays, journals and books can be found in their small bookstore.

Throughout this chapter I invoke the words of Gandhi and King as an aid of identifying maternal nonviolence. I do not, however, believe that there is any simple translation of domestic to public nonviolence.

5 Gandhi, cited in Bondurant, *The Conquest of Violence*, p. 24.

6 Gandhi, cited in Bondurant, *The Conquest of Violence*, p. 26.

7 Gandhi, *Non-Violent Resistance*, p. 73.

8 Martin Luther King, Jr, 'Loving Your Enemies,' sermon delivered Christmas 1957, Montgomery, Alabama, p. 11. King's writings have been collected in *A Testament of Hope: The Essential Writings of Martin Luther King, Jr*, ed. James Melvin Washington (San Francisco: Harper & Row, 1986). Here I use pamphlet number 1 in the A. J. Muste Essay Series (New York: A. J. Muste Institute). This pamphlet, available from the War Resisters' League, includes 'Loving Your Enemies',

'Letter from the Birmingham Jail', and 'Why We Are in Vietnam?'

9   Gandhi, cited in Bondurant, *The Conquest of Violence*, p. 26.

10 King, 'Loving Your Enemies', p. 11.

11 Gandhi, *Non-Violent Resistance*, p. 42. The march against the salt mines was led by Gandhi's followers and took place after Gandhi was arrested during his march to the sea to procure salt – a witty and effective protest against the salt tax. The event is depicted in the movie *Gandhi* and described in most accounts of Gandhi's campaigns. See, for example, Erik Erikson, *Gandhi's Truth* (New York: Norton, 1969).

12 Grace Paley, 'Faith in a Tree', in *Enormous Changes at the Last Minute* (New York: Farrar Straus and Giroux, 1987), p. 85. This passage was pointed out by Jane Lazarre, a mother of black sons who, along with her husband, was determined to raise her children to resist but also feared for their safety in a hostile world. She then had to steel herself to remain calm – though she was in fact both proud and frightened – when her adolescent sons were 'fresh' not only to her but, more worrisome, to authorities on whose goodwill they depended.

13 King, 'Loving Your Enemies', pp. 4–8 and passim.

14 King, 'Loving Your Enemies', p. 8.

26

Sheila Jeffreys
b.1952

'PORNOGRAPHY' and 'CREATING THE SEXUAL FUTURE'
extracts from *ANTICLIMAX* (1990)

Sheila Jeffreys is a historian who has previously written about the politics of sexuality in the age of 'first-wave' feminism (The Spinster and her Enemies, *1985*). *In* Anticlimax, *another work combining history with polemic, she seeks to recall feminism to its original aim of ending sexual oppression and abuse. Turning a sceptical eye on the 'sexual revolution' of the 1950s and 1960s, she rejects the standard Left-liberal view that since sex means pleasure and pleasure is a good thing, any development which makes this good thing more generally accessible is necessarily progressive. Her own view of 'sex', by contrast, is relentlessly critical: she argues that what the revolutionaries have been talking about under this label is in fact the specific practice of* heterosexuality, *which Jeffreys equates with 'eroticized dominance and submission'. (For her, then, 'heterosexual' is a semi-technical term held in place by an act of 'persuasive definition'.)*

In the first chapter of Anticlimax *Jeffreys urges us to take seriously the conviction of the pre-1960s 'sexologists' that 'normal' (i.e. male-dominant, penetrative) heterosexual activity was not just a matter of what people did in bed, but was essential to the maintenance of male authority in society at large. In fact, she suggests, the twentieth-century insistence that women should not just submit to sexual intercourse out of 'marital duty' but should be, as it were, spiritually converted to the practice by being made to have orgasms – this war on so-called 'frigidity' and 'prudery' was a* political *response to the challenge of feminism.*

Analogously, but more savagely, the decensorship of pornography in the second half of the century should be seen as a further escalation of the sex war – an unleashing of overt male aggression against women. (For Jeffreys as for other radical feminists, 'all pornography teaches the inferiority of women as a class' in that it represents women not as persons but as objects for sexual use by men.) The older marriage guidance manuals taught how to use sex to secure an appropriate (i.e. patriarchal) power-relation between husband and wife; now pornography 'educates the male public' in cruder, more desperate methods of sexual domination.

These two moments of anti-feminist reaction have a common feature in that each seeks to enlist the support of women themselves for practices which actually strengthen the sexual power-structure: in one case 'normal' sex with the (preferably vaginal) orgasm as the symbol of female sub-mission; in the other a range of more or less sado-masochistic variants in which women are once again being invited – though now more daringly or paradoxically – to find fulfilment through 'surrender' to their own desires. (For those with a background of feminist struggle, this invitation is the more seductive in that it can exploit very real feelings of exhaustion or defeat.)

Anticlimax *is inspired by the belief that feminism is in crisis and that its survival as a radical political movement is under threat. The threat comes not simply from the prevalence of pornography, which in itself has a consciousness-raising as well as an intimidatory effect, but from the acceptance by many self-professed feminists of heterosexual values – that is, of an eroticism based on sexual difference, which in practice means sexual inequality. In order to overcome this failure of nerve, Jeffreys argues, we need to question the common-sense of the sexual libertarian tradition. That tradition 'has no word or category for sexual response that is not positive'; feminism, by contrast, needs such words because without them it is impossible to gain any critical perspective on our present emotional tendencies. If there is no hope that critical reflection can alter, however gradually, the pattern of response which takes our own sub-ordination as a route to orgasm, then there can be no such thing as feminism – for there can be no prospect of healing the psychological damage which makes us desire to be dominated by men.*

Jeffreys, however, defends the politically optimistic view that such healing is possible and that, through sensitive attention to our own sexual feelings, we can distinguish between those which do and those which do not stem from an eroticized power difference. 'However important heterosexual desire has been in our lives we will all have some experience of its opposite . . . of sexual desire and practice which does not leave us feeling betrayed . . . which eroticizes mutuality and equality.' By building on this basis of positive experience we can work towards the 'egalitarian eroticism' which Jeffreys labels 'homosexual desire' and which she considers indispensable to women's liberation. (Although for her 'heterosexual' and 'homosexual' are ethical rather than empirical categories, Jeffreys does in fact hold that in the existing state of society a truly feminist sexuality will be homosexual in the ordinary sense, i.e. lesbian.)

Jeffreys thus rehabilitates in the name of feminism an idea which can be traced back to the rationalist moral philosophies of Plato and Aristotle – that of a contrast between 'true' and 'false' pleasures, i.e. between (i) those phenomena which genuinely deserve to be called 'pleasures', and (ii) those which we initially think of as pleasures but which, in the light of moral or political enquiry, we should no longer want to describe as such. The suggestion that pleasure might not be something we could recognize infallibly by introspection, but might only declare its real nature to us in a theoretically mediated way, is alien to the empiricist tradition to which liberalism (including sexual liberalism) belongs. Jeffreys's discussion helps us see, however, that feminism – in common with other critical social theories – has reason to be receptive to this unfamiliar thought.

PORNOGRAPHY

One result of the 'sexual revolution' was that pornography was 'derepressed'.[1] The pornography industry exploded into growth in the late sixties and early seventies and became a massive, multi-billion-dollar industry. It also became visible in a way that it had not been before. Pornography no longer had to be under the counter, but appeared on news-stands and at supermarket checkouts. The content changed too. Gay Talese's book, *Thy Neighbour's Wife*, describes the transformation that took place in the pornography industry in the late fifties and early sixties. In the 1950s American girlie magazines relied upon drawings of scantily clad women since use of photographs and nakedness could invite wholesale repression. A changing climate towards sexuality was necessary before the pornbrokers felt brave enough to experiment with photographs of women in veils of wispy clothing and then entirely naked. In the

1960s the porn industry made great strides. Decensorship, which was based upon the derepression of sadomasochism and woman-hatred, allowed pornography to come in from the cold. Hiding at first behind the protection of 'great works of art' which differed little in their values from high-street porn, the pornbrokers built their empires.

The sheer visibility of the porn industry had a consequence which the pornbrokers may not have intended. Women were able to look at pornography and for the first time had at their disposal a panoramic view of what constituted male sexuality. During the 1970s pornography became more and more concerned with sadomasochism and much more brutal in its portrayal of women. Where once whole bodies or parts of bodies constituted the staple of pornography, women were now being shown simply as available holes. The first London anti-pornography group was formed in 1977 because we saw double-page spreads of women's genitals, called 'split beaver' or 'salmon sandwich', in shop windows and being perused by young boys in corner newsagents' shops. We decided we needed to study pornography, to see exactly what was in it and understand what it told us about men's attitude to women, about male sexuality and about the construction of heterosexuality. As daughters of the sexual revolution we had to overcome feelings of guilt at not liking pornography. Reprogrammed by our experience in the 1960s to see 'explicit' sex in movies and books as a positive good and naked-ness as desirable, we had to overcome some powerful conditioning through consciousness-raising sessions before we could articulate our rage. Women can only seriously critique any expression of sexuality when they have thrown the junk of psychoanalytic notions of inhibitions and repression out of the window.

Women formed feminist anti-pornography groups in Britain and the US with a sense of horror and rage. Pornography gave the lie to any idea that women were gradually achieving equality. Pornography made it clear that what constituted sex under male supremacy was precisely the eroticized subordination of women. Inequality was sexy and the sexiness of this inequality was the grease that oiled the machinery of male supremacy. The sexiness of inequality, it became clear, was the unacknowledged motor force of male supremacy. Through sexual fantasy men were able to reinforce the sense of their power and of women's inferiority daily and be rewarded for every thought and image of women subordinated with sexual pleasure; a pleasure acknowledged to be the most valuable form of pleasure in male-supremacist culture.

Pornography could not be ignored by feminists who were concerned to end male violence. An examination of pornography revealed that all the varieties of male violence against women were depicted in pornography as pleasurable to men and to women too. Women raped and tortured in pornography claimed to love and seek their abuse. Incest was shown as harmless and good fun for all the family. It became clear that pornography provided a textbook for and justification of such violence. The defenders of pornography have always most consistently denied any link between pornography and male violence. They have claimed that pornography was a privileged exception to other media in that it had no effect on the way its users felt about the world. But feminists could not see pornography as an exception.

The campaigns against pornography were a logical extension of earlier 1970s campaigns against sex stereotyping in school textbooks such as Janet and John readers. Feminists challenged the sexism in the representation of girls as helping Mummy with aprons on while boys helped Daddy to clean the car. This campaign inspired no howls of rage from publishers, civil liberties unions, other feminists, and men in general. Certainly no special organizations of women on the left were formed to protect the sexism of school reading materials. Such organizations are being set up to protect pornography.

Feminists have been forced to use men's research on the effects of pornography to support their argument that pornography could affect attitudes and behaviour. The pornographers and their supporters have demanded proof that sex offenders use porn immediately prior to committing acts of violence. No such evidence is required of the effects of sex stereotyping in textbooks. Indeed, the argument about textbooks has been nearly won. Without any direct evidence that women need to read Janet and John books just before each occasion on which they don an apron, publishers and libraries, schools and education authorities have moved towards using less obviously prejudiced material. Why then is such a different degree of proof required of pornography's consciousness-lowering potential? The sex stereotyping in pornography is blatantly obvious. Indeed it is not contested by its defenders. Pornography is much used by adolescent and teenage boys and now seen by children as never before because of the burgeoning of porn videos which men use on the living-room television. Why is pornography seen as a privileged category of representation?

The big difference between sex stereotyping in children's reading material and sex stereotyping in pornography is that the use of pornography offers positive reinforcement to its users. Girls playing with toy vacuum cleaners do not have the same orgasmic potential as women shown as holes in pornography. Sexual response to pornography is possible for both men and women. The protection of this 'pleasure' makes the defence of pornography more important for male supremacists than the defence of Janet and John books. Another reason for the rush to defend pornography, despite the conflict with logic required for its defence, is that at this stage in the history of western male supremacy the sexualizing of inequality might have taken over from the division of labour as a bastion of male power.

Feminists were outraged at the way pornography justified and promoted sexual violence but the feminist critique has never been limited to violent pornography. Feminists have always asserted that all pornography teaches the inferiority of women as a class. Andrea Dworkin describes the ideology of male sexual domination that pornography revealed:

> The ideology of male sexual domination posits that men are superior to women by virtue of their penises; that physical possession of the female is a natural right of the male; that sex is, in fact, conquest and possession of the female, especially but not exclusively phallic possession; that the use of the female body for sexual or reproductive purposes is a natural right of men; that the sexual will of men properly and naturally defines the parameters of woman's sexual being, which is her whole identity.[2]

New York Women Against Pornography describe the process involved in making women an inferior class in pornography as 'objectification'. They define objectification as:

> [a] process through which a powerful group establishes and maintains dominance over a less powerful group by teaching

that the subordinate group is less than human or like an object. This precludes the powerful group from identifying with or sympathizing with the less powerful group.[3]

They explain that objectification is the 'precondition for violence against oppressed groups' and provide two historical examples of objectification being deliberately used to facilitate such violence, in Hitler's Germany against the Jews and by the American army in Vietnam. The difference between such objectification and the objectification of women is that the latter is sexualized.

Defenders of pornography assert, as Comfort does in *The Joy of Sex*, that men want to be sex objects too. This shows a failure to grasp the politics of the process of objectification. There have been a couple of attempts by the male pornography industry to create analogous magazines for women such as *Playgirl*. The problem with objectifying men for the consumption of women is that it is not sexy. In heterosexuality the attractiveness of men is based upon their power and status. Objectification removes that power and status. Naked beefcake is not a turn-on for women because objectification subordinates the object group. Pornography is not egalitarian and gender-free. It is predicated upon the inequality of women and is the propaganda that makes that inequality sexy. For women to find passive, objectified men sexy in large enough numbers to make a pornography industry based upon such images viable, would require the reconstruction of women's sexuality into a ruling-class sexuality. In an egalitarian society objectification would not exist and therefore the particular buzz provided by pornography, the excitement of eroticized dominance for the ruling class, would be unimaginable.

Pornography and the Abuse of Women

Pornography apologists engage in special pleading and insist that pornographic images, unlike any other kind of images in our culture, have no effect on the way anyone thinks. Evidence provided by feminists, however, shows the connection between pornography and abuse. Rather than concentrating on trying to connect pornography with one-off attacks on women by strangers, it is useful to look at the more common forms of abuse within ongoing relationships. There is evidence that pornography has led to new forms of abuse. The pornographic imagination might have thought of these abuses before, but for the averagely slow learner in the area of sexuality, the less-creative male mind, pornography undoubtedly educates. An example of this is 'throat rape'. Dworkin explains: 'We see an increase since the release of *Deep Throat* in throat rape – where women show up in emergency rooms because men believe they can penetrate, deep-thrust, to the bottom of a woman's throat.'[4] Throat rape can lead to death through suffocation as well as other forms of physical damage. Dworkin provides an example of throat rape from pornography. The woman suffers violence and considerable pain but ends up loving it.

> He could kill me with [his cock], she thought. He didn't need a gun in his hand.
>
> As his hot organ filled her mouth and throat, Sandy felt him beginning to thrust his hips forward. The shiny cockhead crammed into the back of her throat. She tried to take as much of his cock into her mouth as possible, but it filled her throat so full that she couldn't at first get it down. She swallowed and swallowed at each of his forward thrusts, but her throat wouldn't stretch large enough to accommodate him. It wasn't until he grabbed her hair with his left fist and held her head against the force of his tool that she was able to relax her throat muscles enough that his cock raped its way over her tongue and buried itself in the passage to her stomach.
>
> Pain seared through her throat like she had swallowed a hot branding iron as her throat stretched to its maximum capacity . . . She nursed greedily at his body.[5]

Feminists began to amass evidence of the ways in which pornography directly educated men in how to abuse women, for presentation in Minneapolis in support of the anti-pornography ordinance. This ordinance, constructed by Catharine MacKinnon and Andrea Dworkin, would have allowed women to take action against pornographers under civil rights legislation to get recompense for the injuries pornography had caused them. Shelter workers told of cases in which pornography was implicated in the torture of wives. One woman's husband acted out a scene he had discovered in a magazine. 'She was forcibly stripped, bound and gagged. And with help from her husband, she was raped by a German Shepherd.'[6]

One woman, in the Minneapolis evidence, explained that her husband used pornography 'like a textbook' when sexually abusing her.

> In fact, when he asked me to be bound, when he finally convinced me to do it, he read in the magazine how to tie the knots and how to bind me in a way that I couldn't get out. And most of the scenes that we – most of the scenes where I had to dress up or go through different fantasies were the exact scenes that he had read in the magazines.[7]

The Minneapolis evidence contains many examples where pornography has clearly inspired particular instances of sexual abuse. One woman told of being gang raped by hunters in the woods when she was 13 and camping with the girl scouts. She came across three deer hunters reading pornography magazines in the afternoon.

> I turned to walk away and one of the men yelled, 'There is a live one.' And I thought they meant a deer and so I ducked and tried to run away . . . two men held their guns at my head and the first man hit my breast with his rifle and they continued to laugh. And the first man raped me and when he was finished they started making jokes about how I was a virgin and I didn't know how they knew I was a virgin but they did . . . The second man raped me . . . when the second man was finished, the third man was not able to get an erection and they, the other men, told me to give him a blow job and I didn't know what a blow job was. The third man forced his penis into my mouth and told me to do it and I didn't know what I was supposed to be doing.[8]

An Assistant County Attorney gave evidence of the links between pornography and sexual abuse that he had found in hundreds of cases of abuse of adults and children. He explained that the police did not look for pornography but found it 'often' in cases of assault on women and in 'very close to the majority of cases' of sexual abuse of children. The pornography would be found in the home of the abuser.

A native American woman gave evidence of the way in which the pornographic teaching manuals led to the racist targeting of particular women of colour. The two white men who raped her were inspired by the video game 'Custer's Revenge' in which a native American woman is attacked. She explains that they let her know from the beginning that they hated her people and 'they screamed in my face as they threw me to the ground. "This is more fun than Custer's Last Stand."'[9]

Evidence from a group of women who had worked as prostitutes showed how pornography had been used on them in the course of their work, providing the model scenarios for gruesome rapes and assaults. They explained that, 'Women were forced constantly to enact specific scenes that men had witnessed in pornography.'[10] The young women entering prostitution would be trained and accustomed by the use of pornography, ' . . . the man would show either magazines or take you to a movie and then afterwards instruct her to act in the way that the magazines or films depicted.'[11]

Pornography, then, educates the male public. It would be very surprising if it did not.

Pornography as a Practice

The publication of Linda Lovelace's *Ordeal* drew feminist attention to the experience of the women used in the production of pornography. Apologists argue that pornography is simply 'fantasy'. But live women are used and abused in the production of pornography. Their experience is fact and not fantasy. Linda Marciano was the prisoner of a violently abusive pimp who sexually tortured her and used her in prostitution and pornography. She is famous for having been the apparently enthusiastic star of the porn movie *Deep Throat*. Marciano was forced to engage in sex acts with a dog by three men who threatened her with a gun. This was filmed to make a porn movie. When Marciano did eventually escape her pimp she became involved in the anti-pornography struggle and sought ways of achieving legal redress for the fact that such vicious pornography, made while she was a slave, was still being watched all over the world. Out of her search for redress and the efforts of her lawyer, Catharine MacKinnon, the anti-pornography ordinance was born.

Pornography is not just produced for strictly commercial reasons.

Amateur pornography is produced when women are filmed or photo-
graphed as part of abuse they are being subjected to. The attack
upon the woman is turned into pornography, introducing, as Andrea
Dworkin points out, 'a profit motive into rape'.[12] Many witnesses at
Minneapolis gave examples of being filmed during sessions of abuse
either by husbands or, in the case of prostitutes, by pimps and by
clients. Valerie Heller, in a description of how she was sexually
abused routinely in childhood by three male members of her family,
explained how her 28-year-old stepbrother made pornography out of
his abuse of her.

> What I remember most about Carl taking pictures of me is that
> I was not allowed to do 'certain things' while the pictures were
> being taken. I could and in fact had to do those same 'certain
> things' when pictures were not being taken. I recall thinking,
> how come Carl does not want my mouth touching his cock
> while pictures are being taken? Today I know why: because
> actual physical contact was considered hard-core porn and hard-
> core was not as easily sold as soft-core porn was.[13]

The filming of sexual assault, particularly in the case of child sexual
assault, gives the attacker lasting satisfaction as well as offering the
possibility of profit.

There has been a concentration in feminist organizing on opposing
'violent' pornography but it is pornography itself that feminists need
to oppose and not just 'violence'. Catharine MacKinnon provides
an analysis of the relationship between pornography of any kind
and male supremacy. She asserts that what is sexual under male
supremacy is the subordination of women. Therefore there is no
possibility of separating OK porn from porn which is violent.
Pornography, she explains, is necessarily hierarchical, with women
on the bottom, because if it was not it would not be sexy.

> Under male dominance, whatever sexually arouses a man is sex.
> In pornography, the violence *is* the sex. The inequality is sex.
> Pornography does not work, sexually, without hierarchy. If
> there is no inequality, no violation, no dominance, no force,
> there is no sexual arousal.[14]

She explains why it is difficult for those living in male supremacy, in which the values of pornography are the conventional wisdom, to see the harm that pornography does to women.

> If pornography is an act of male supremacy, its harm is the harm of male supremacy made difficult to see because of its pervasiveness, potency and success in making the world a pornographic place. Specifically, the harm cannot be discerned from the objective standpoint because it *is* so much of 'what is'. Women live in the world pornography creates. We live its lie as reality . . . So the issue is not what the harm of pornography is, but how the harm of pornography is to become visible. As compared to what? To the extent pornography succeeds in constructing social reality, it becomes *invisible as harm*.[15]

Pornography's significance to male supremacy, MacKinnon argues, is that it 'institutionalizes the sexuality of male supremacy'. And it is this sexuality, the eroticized inequality of women and power of men, which fuels male supremacy and constructs the gender system.

> With the rape and prostitution in which it participates, pornography institutionalizes the sexuality of male supremacy, which fuses the eroticization of dominance and submission with the social construction of male and female. Gender is sexual.[16]

When the feminist campaign against pornography first got under way it was possible to attack pornography as a male product designed for male consumption. This is not so true in the 1980s. Women are now being won as an audience for pornography. Women are being told – by libertarian theorists – that because 'women are equal now' it is all right for women to enjoy pornography. According to a feminist analysis the conscription of women into the use of pornography is tied to the new opportunities offered to women in the last quarter century, but in order to defeat women's emancipation rather than pander to it. While women may have greater opportunities in work, more money and more independence, they are being pressured by the sex industry, lovers, the therapy profession and doctors to become complicit in their oppression through the use of pornography. The fierceness and brutality of 1970s pornography was a backlash against feminism which reassured men. The selling of the idea of pornography to women in the 1980s is a more sophisticated and effective way of bolstering male power.

. . .

CREATING THE SEXUAL FUTURE

Heterosexual Desire

Heterosexual desire is eroticized power difference.[17] Heterosexual desire originates in the power relationship between men and women, but it can also be experienced in same-sex relationships. Heterosexuality as an institution is founded upon the ideology of 'difference'. Though the difference is seen as natural, it is in fact a difference of power. When men marry women they carry into the relationship considerable social and political power. The organizations of state will back their power through religion, the courts, the social services. Their use of battering and rape within marriage will be condoned through these institutions. The women they marry will generally have less earning power since women's wages are lower than men's. The women will be trained not to use physical strength or be aggressive. They will have been inculcated with social expectations of service, obedience and self-sacrifice. But this is not enough to ensure male power. Means of reinforcing the power differences are employed when men choose partners. They are encouraged to seek in marriage women who are smaller in stature and younger in age. The serious taboos that exist against men marrying women who are taller or older are too well known to need emphasis.

But there are taboos also against men marrying women with the slightest possible advantage in terms of education or earning power. To show the extent to which the ruling male establishment accepts and supports male power in marriage, we need only look at the way that criminologists explain crimes of violence against women. A 1975 study interviewed the wives of rapists and incest offenders to understand why the husbands committed the offences. The authors, Garrett and Wright, found that the wives had, on average, about one year more schooling than their husbands. They suggest that these 'powerful' wives deliberately married men to whom they could feel superior. The men were then driven to their assaults by a feeling of inferiority. The authors conclude that 'for this sample, rape and incest by husbands served as a particularly useful lever by which the wives can further build positions of moral and social dominance.'[18] Male power is so normal to these men that women who happen to be married to less educated men are credited with a power complex and responsibility for their husbands' sexually abusive behaviour. Presumably the fact that men routinely select less educated women to marry is seen as unquestionably appropriate behaviour. In support of their conclusions, Garrett and Wright use a study in which educational advantage in wives is said to explain wife battering. The power that men have in marriage, both that which is given them by the sex-role training of a male-supremacist society and that which they individually seek out, is so much part of the fabric of life that it is invisible to male academics. They only notice and object when such male power is not total.

It would be a matter for some astonishment, surely, if, in this carefully engineered situation of inequality, men's sexual desire for women turned out to be egalitarian. It is not of course. Men need to be able to desire the powerless creatures they marry. So heterosexual desire for men is based upon eroticizing the otherness of women, an otherness which is based upon a difference of power. Similarly, in the twentieth century, when women have been required to show sexual enthusiasm for men, they have been trained to eroticize the otherness of men, i.e. men's power and their own subordination. The avalanche of sexual advice and 'scientific' sexological literature testifies to the efforts required to construct heterosexual desire. Sexologists over the last hundred years have argued that male sexuality is inevitably aggressive, active and delights in inflicting pain. Female sexuality has been seen as its opposite: inevitably submissive, passive and delighting in the receiving of pain. Sexologists have differed in the form of explanation they have offered for this phenomenon. Havelock Ellis used an evolutionary explanation, Freud used childhood influences in the family but resorted to biology in the final analysis. But they have been united in seeing this system as inflexible.

Feminists in both waves of feminism in this century have opposed this sexological prescription. They have demanded that men change their sexual behaviour and they have opposed the sexological version of women's sexuality. Recently, libertarian gay men and lesbians have proclaimed sadomasochism to be a revolutionary sexuality and have stated that 'power' is inherent in sexuality.

Once the eroticizing of otherness and power difference is learned, then in a same-sex relationship, where another gender is absent, otherness can be reintroduced through differences of age, race, class, the practice of sadomasochism or role playing. So it is possible to construct heterosexual desire within lesbianism and heterosexual desire is plentifully evident in the practice of gay men. The opposite of heterosexual desire is the eroticizing of sameness, a sameness of power, equality and mutuality. It is homosexual desire.

Sexual Pleasure

Under male supremacy, sex consists of the eroticizing of women's subordination. Women's subordination is sexy for men and for women too. For years this was a secret within women's liberation. In order to challenge men's pornography which reiterated that women enjoyed pain and humiliation, and to campaign against sexual violence in a culture which asserted that women enjoyed sexual abuse, feminists denied that women were masochists. Feminist theorists of male violence would acknowledge that women had sadomasochistic fantasies but assert that there was a huge difference between the fantasy and the reality. No women, they said, wanted abuse. The existence of s/m fantasies was not really dealt with as an issue because of its explosive potential. This left the women's liberation movement wide open to attack when a sadomasochist lobby developed.

It should not be a surprise to find that s/m fantasy is significant in women's sex lives. Women may be born free but they are born into a system of subordination. We are not born into equality and do not have equality to eroticize. We are not born into power and do not have power to eroticize. We are born into subordination and it is in subordination that we learn our sexual and emotional responses. It would be surprising indeed if any woman reared under male supremacy was able to escape the forces constructing her into a member of an inferior slave class.

From the discriminating behaviour of her mother while she is still in the cradle, through a training in how to sit and move without taking up space or showing her knickers, how to speak when spoken to and avert her gaze from men, a girl learns subordination. She is very likely to experience overt sexual harassment from men. She will experience unwanted overtures from males and will have to learn to respond positively or negatively. Training of this kind is not geared to creating a strong and positive emotional and sexual personality in any woman. Within women's liberation negative self-image, lack of confidence, worries about appearance, negative emotional patterns in relationships, have all received attention from consciousness-raising groups. The burgeoning of feminist therapy in place of consciousness-raising as the movement has lost its radical edge testifies to the urgency with which women are seeking to overcome our conditioning. But the negative effects of this training on our sexual feelings have scarcely been explored.

Sex has been seen as different. Feminists accepted the basic idea of the sexual revolution that sexual response was an ultimate good. According to sexual revolutionary ideology, how sexual response was achieved was of little or no importance so long as it was achieved. Sex, we were led to understand, was somehow disconnected with the rest of life. It was a pleasurable garden of delights which was un-affected by the outside real world and certainly had no effect on the workings of the real world. Therefore, the fact that women might have sexual feelings which mirrored the undesirable emotional responses they were trying to change was seen as no problem. A sexual problem for a feminist was understood to be lack of orgasm or the correct number of orgasms. Masochism was not on the agenda. The fact that for many women orgasm and masochism, especially in masturbation, were apparently inextricably connected was avoided or positively affirmed.

The construction of women's sexual pleasure only became a subject for serious debate with the development of the feminist challenge to pornography. Campaigners who had sexual responses to the mate-rials they were opposing found themselves in a dilemma. There was a pressure to conceal such responses for fear of disapproval. Campaigners who claimed never to have experienced any kind of response to sadomasochistic material appeared scandalized at those who did. How was it possible, after all, to campaign against some-thing which turned you on? Speakers against pornography would receive hostility from women who felt guilty about their response to pornographic material and turned their anger on to the messengers rather than the material. It became necessary to explain that a sexual response to pornography was not at all unusual, was not a reason for guilt or shame and did not preclude our anger at pornography. It was possible to be even more angry at pornography because it revealed the extent to which our subordination had affected those feelings we had been encouraged to feel were most our own.

To deal with the problem of the eroticizing of our subordination we really need a new language, and a new way of categorizing our sexual feelings. There is a cultural assumption in a post-sexual-revolution society that sexual arousal is 'pleasure'. This makes it particularly painful to experience pornography, which clearly shows the humiliation of women, as sexually arousing. We feel guilt at having taken pleasure in or 'enjoyed' the oppression of women. The literature of the libertarians has no word or category for sexual response that is not positive, no word that would allow us to describe the complexity of our feelings in such a situation. This is not an accident. Part of the repertoire of techniques for political control is the control of language. It is hard to 'think' about things for which no word is available. Women are not supposed to think in a way which is not positive about sex. In the absence of a word which could distinguish negative sexual feelings or experience the libertarians are able to label feminists as 'anti-sex'. They have a one-dimensional view of sex as inevitably good. Thus only two positions on sexuality are acknowledged, pro and anti sex. A feminist approach to the question of desire requires the invention of a new language. We need to be able to describe sexual response which is incontrovertibly negative.

Linda Gordon and Ellen Dubois give us an example of the confusion felt by some feminists about women's sexual response. They are libertarians and see sexual response as positive and even revolutionary for women. They include women's capacity for orgasm in their description of how nineteenth-century middle-class women engaged in 'resistance that actually challenged' the 'sexual system', i.e. the supposedly repressive morality of the nineteenth century.[19] These women apparently had orgasms, according to a survey of the time. 40 per cent reported orgasms occasionally, 20 per cent frequently, and 40 per cent never. Since we can assume that these women were in unregenerately oppressive relationships it is difficult to see how their orgasms were 'resistance'. Their orgasms indicate a remarkable ability to accommodate themselves to their oppression so that they can find in it a source of satisfaction, but that is very different from resistance. The absence of orgasm might more appropriately be seen as a form of resistance in such a situation. It is, after all, lack of orgasm which the sexologists have treated as resistance to male power all this century.

The libertarian feminists, as well as the sexologists from whom they take their inspiration, have seen sexual response as inevitably positive and generally revolutionary, but when we look at the situations in which men and women can experience orgasm, this approach has to be questioned. Men experience orgasms whilst killing women. Girls and women can have orgasms during rape and sexual abuse and then spend years in guilt and shame for 'enjoying' what happened to them. In fact the body is capable of physiological responses quite unconnected with an emotional state of 'pleasure'. Similarly the mind can cause a sexual response in situations where words like 'enjoy' or 'pleasure' are entirely inappropriate. Most women probably have experience of waking from sexual dreams involving rape or abuse, feeling uncomfortable or distressed. This is quite different from the feelings of well-being that can be associated with a positive sexual experience. The sexologists and their libertarian heirs have mandated that women distrust their feelings. In *The ABZ of Love* and *The Joy of Sex*, women are required to overcome their 'inhibitions' and rename their discomfort 'pleasure'. But if we listen to our feelings about sex sensitively instead of riding roughshod over them through guilt or anxiety about being prudes, we can work out what is positive and what is negative. The negative feelings are about eroticized subordination or heterosexual desire.

In the early years of this wave of feminism there was criticism of the dominance and submission roles of heterosexuality. As well as a dominant concern with the possibilities for women's sexual pleasure and how these had been limited in relationships with men, there was a real desire for equality. In the 1980s, in a feminist community which has accepted use of the term 'post-feminism', this search for equality in sex is being vigorously challenged both by some heterosexual women and by some lesbians. The British heterosexual feminist theorist Sheila Rowbotham explained in 1984 why she and some other feminists had given up the attempt to 'democratize' desire. She says that 'moral earnestness' came to grief when confronted with 'lust, romantic fantasy, fear of ageing, sado-masochism'. The most serious reason for abandoning the attempt to democratize desire was the fact that such equality was not sexy. She recounts the experience of an American therapist who encouraged her clients to democratize their relationships. The couples kept returning to her with a new problem, they were 'unable to summon up desire. Love yes, but not desire.'[20]

Feminists have always been uncomfortably aware that men's sexual passion was likely to fade if relationships were democratized. Rowbotham tells us that this is a problem for women too. The sociologist Jessie Bernard's 1972 book *The Future of Marriage* dealt at length with the issue of men's difficulties with democratic desire. She explains that research as long ago as the 1950s had suggested that the search for companionate marriage was destroying marital sex life. Companionate marriages were to be based upon equality.

> Veroff and Feld were beginning to raise disturbing questions about the way an ideology oriented toward egalitarian companionship might affect the sexual component of marriage . . . they were speculating that the conception of the 'traditional marital relationship [as] a friendship relationship may play havoc with the potential that the marital role has to permit sexual and interpersonal activity.' In other words, can you mix companionship and sex? The future of marriage rides on the answer.[21]

In tune with the hopefulness of the early 1970s Bernard answers: 'Can you mix companionship and sex? My own answer, is, Yes, you can.'[22] Bernard did not see men's linking of power and aggression with sex as biological or innate. She saw this linkage as being about status and she was optimistic about change. Women's refusal to accept inferior status was bound to cause men to transform their sexual responses in their own interests.

But Rowbotham's answer is very different. She concludes that the feminists like herself who tried to change had:

> too great a confidence that in altering the outward manifestation, the pattern of relationships in which we experienced desire, our inner feelings would fall automatically into place. There was an incongruity between overt democracy and hidden yearnings.[23]

She recommends the abandonment of the task of democratizing desire in favour of recognizing 'its capacity to surprise, to take us unawares'. She then embarks upon a lyrical description of what she sees as the characteristics of 'desire'.

> Desire has the capacity to shift us beyond commonsense. It is our peep at the extraordinary. It is the chink beyond the material world.
>
> The glimpse we still have in common. And in its daftness desire is thus a democrat, not the solemn, public face of democracy, but the inward openness which is prepared like the fool to step over the cliff.
>
> True it can land us down with a bump. Folly, fear, embarrassment, humiliation, violence, tumble about with ecstasy and bliss. Desire is a risk, but so is freedom.[24]

As feminists we might have to ask, as Rowbotham does not, who profits from the undemocratic nature of desire under male supremacy. We might find it worrying that there should be such an asymmetry in the ways that male and female desire are constructed. For all her attempts to provide a metaphysical status for desire, not to be questioned by ordinary mortals, feminists find that desire does not exist beyond the material world but in it, and is formed out of the material inequalities between men and women. What Rowbotham tries to disguise is that the 'risk' of desire lies in the fact that it is based upon the eroticizing of women's subordination. To equate the 'risk' of desire with the 'risk' of freedom is a shoddy and quite prestidigitational trick. It may well be that some women, as well as plenty of men, will choose their ability to experience a particular form of sexual passion over the desire to be free, but they are not the same thing. Indeed a feminist approach to sex would suggest that women's freedom cannot be achieved whilst some people who see themselves as radical and progressive place their right to take pleasure from women's lack of freedom before the task of creating freedom.

The defence of heterosexual desire within feminism is associated with a tendency to promote the validity of heterosexuality as a sexual choice and to attack lesbians for questioning it. A spate of writers in the mid-1980s started to talk about the necessity for heterosexuality to 'come out of the closet' on the grounds that lesbians had forced heterosexual women to feel embarrassed about their preferences. It is an astonishingly insensitive choice of term comparing as it does the real oppression of lesbians with the discomfort some heterosexual women who are aware of the incongruity of their 'desire' might feel within women's liberation. Rowbotham uses the phrase and it seems clear from the rest of the article that she defines heterosexuality as eroticized power difference. The resurgence of heterosexual desire, or eroticized power defference, is seen by such women as emerging bravely from a closet that it was never in. In a sadosociety heterosexual desire is very 'out' indeed.[25]

Eileen Phillips is another heterosexual socialist feminist who validates the conflict and fear involved in heterosexual desire. She describes 'desire' as:

> unnecessary, irrational, an excess – and also compelling. When going to meet the desired one, we can be sweating, our legs trembling, our heart beating fast – in fact behaviourally we can be exhibiting all the symptoms of fear. Yet it feels exciting as well as scary, the very strangeness producing a peculiar sort of clarity which often eludes us in many other activities of daily life.[26]

It looks as if desire is not being very democratic here either. Phillips provides this description of desire in combination with an attack on lesbian feminism as a 'politics of voluntarism and male banishment' and disparages attempts by both lesbians and heterosexual women to challenge the centrality of sexual intercourse. It seems that Phillips, Rowbotham and other such feminists understand very well that the sexual attraction involved in heterosexuality is eroticized power difference. Since they have rejected the lesbian alternative they have no choice but to attack lesbian feminists who offer a cogent critique of their sexual choice. Lesbian feminists are a problem because they question the necessity for any woman to organize her life around the eroticizing of her own subordination.

Rowbotham's retreat from the pursuit of sexual equality is not taking place in a vacuum. Mainstream heterosexual feminism in America gives evidence of a similar phenomenon. In May 1986 *Ms* magazine produced a health issue called 'The Beauty of Health'. The only article on sex in the magazine was an interview with a husband and wife sex advice team called the Mershorers. Entitled 'Going for the Big "O"', the article advised women how to have multiple orgasms through masochism. It might have been expected that a feminist health magazine dealing with sex would touch on some of those problems that really interfere with sexual well-being for women, such as sexual abuse, pornography and sadomasochism. In fact, far from recognizing sadomasochism as a health problem, the sexologists see it as a way to achieve sexual health.

The goal of the Mershorers' advice is how to get not just one orgasm but up to a hundred. The Mershorers' book recounts the ways in which some multi-orgasmic women achieve their success. These ways include various forms of eroticized subordination such as the wearing of gender-fetishized clothing and 'the minister's sister who craves bondage and group sex'.[27] But what they have in common is the ability to 'completely let go'. It turns out that this requires surrender. Here we are back in the 1950s. Marc Mershorer explains:

> The woman is out there, competing with men, used to guarding her vulnerabilities – she has to. But the requirements out there in the world are much different from the requirements for deriving pleasure from making love. And that's a real contradiction today for many women.
>
> But – and this is a very important concept for a woman to understand – when a woman lets go, gives up, she is surrendering herself, not to her partner, but to Nature. She's giving herself to herself.[28]

The Mershorers seem to have been aware that they were being interviewed for a feminist magazine. So though the woman still surrenders in strict conformity with sexological prescriptions she no longer surrenders to the man but to 'Nature' and 'herself'. This slight change does not alter the construction of male and female sexuality though it might disinfect it a little. Men are not being advised to 'surrender'. It is difficult to see how sex as it is constructed under male supremacy could survive if men went in for surrendering. The Mershorers tell us that no matter what changes feminism and changing social realities have wrought in women's role outside the bedroom, inside it she must continue as before.

An article in *Cosmopolitan* magazine in 1985 has the same themes but pays even less lip service to feminism, though *Cosmopolitan* has a reputation for being sexually progressive. The article 'Sexual Surrender' seeks to instruct women how to achieve 'satisfying sexual surrender'. This is defined as 'when we accept – or surrender to – our deep psychological needs for connection, intimacy, and the full expression of our sexuality'.[29] According to the writer men can and should surrender in sex too, but men's and women's sexuality is different, so obviously they won't be doing so as often or in the same way. She explains:

> In their sincere attempts not to be sexist, both men and women risk overlooking the real differences between them. As George Gilder writes in *Sexual Suicide*, 'There are no human beings; there are just men and women, and when they deny their divergent sexuality, they reject the deepest sources of identity and love. They commit sexual suicide.'[30]

The differences that women should acknowledge are the old-fashioned ones of male aggression and female submission. Men's aggression is largely socially constructed, the article tells us, but none the less unchangeable, because 'centuries of biological and cultural reinforcement have taught men to forge ahead, making, doing, conquering and controlling' with the result that men 'feel aggressive during sexual intercourse'.[31] So women must accept traditional gender roles in sexual behaviour although these may be more apparent than real since in sexual intercourse the man 'appears to control' and the woman 'appears to surrender'.

Like the Mershorers the writer of this article shows an awareness that such a prescription might seem incongruous to women reared in a world of feminism and greater opportunities. Woman is assured that she can be liberated in the public sphere as long as she remains a traditional passive woman in the bedroom. Considering that sexologists throughout the twentieth century have been convinced that 'surrender' in the bedroom did not stop at the bedroom door but spilt over into the whole relationship with a man and other areas of life, then the surrender that is being vaunted must actually be the antidote to feminism. Women may have greater opportunities but while they surrender in bed they will become no real threat to male privilege. Accordingly the *Cosmopolitan* article admonishes women that though 'the freedom to earn equal pay and satisfaction through a career' have been a 'tremendous breakthrough' women should not 'throw out the old-fashioned joys of womanhood in the bargain'. The old-fashioned joys turn out to consist of being the object of male sexual attention in the form of being 'pursued, chosen and adored'. The *Cosmopolitan* article concludes with a warning that is clearly anti-feminist. Women must not try to be too equal.

> Part of those old-fashioned joys is being pursued, chosen and adored. It's hard to pursue someone who is already pursuing. Although contemporary women are still developing their ability to take charge, being cast in the role of the one who surrenders is potentially a woman's greatest asset.[32]

The resurgence of heterosexual desire within feminism after a brief period in which it was questioned fits into the increasingly sadistic tenor of male-supremacist society. Women Against Pornography in New York point out that men's pornography has become more and more violent and sadistic in the late 1970s and early 1980s. The androgyny and unisex of the late 1960s and early 1970s has given way to a pronounced gender fetishism in fashion and in the entertainments industry. This new gender fetishism focuses much more obviously than that of the 1950s on violence. The language of fashion in the early 1980s has been heavily reliant on black leather, chains and handcuffs. There is a much more prominent sexual aggression in fashion. The mini skirt of the 1960s looks tame and domesticated compared with the tiny clinging, black, late 1980s variety.

How can the increasingly sadistic tone of male-supremacist culture be explained? It cannot simply reflect the right-wing turn of politics and the move towards nuclear confrontation of Reaganism and Thatcherism. Certainly masculine values dominate the enterprise culture of the 1980s, but the 1950s too were a time of cold war and McCarthyism, and such overt sadism did not infuse the culture then. This new aggressive masculinity can be explained as an answer to the threat of women's liberation, an answer made possible by the sexual revolution which normalized male sexual aggression. It certainly seems effective, particularly inasmuch as it has percolated through into the women's liberation movement itself.

Homosexual Desire

The demolition of heterosexual desire is a necessary step on the route to women's liberation. Freedom is indivisible. It is not possible to keep little bits of unfreedom, such as in the area of sexuality, because they give some people pleasure, if we are serious about wanting women's liberation. Male-supremacist sexuality is constructed from the subordination of women. If women were not subordinate then sex as the eroticized subordination of women would not be thinkable. Those who wish to fight feminists in order to retain dominance and submission sex are standing in the path of a feminist revolution. Feminist revolution is not 'sexy' because it would remove those material power differences between the sexes on which eroticized power difference is based. To retain sadomasochism it is necessary to prevent the progress of women's liberation. It should not surprise us, therefore, to discover the libertarians launching vigorous attacks on feminism, lesbian feminism and lesbian separatism. It should not surprise us that the libertarians have achieved a serious slowing down and in some cases destruction of feminist initiatives against violence against women. The feminist challenge to male violence cannot thrive in harmony with the promotion of sadomasochistic values by women who in some cases call themselves feminists and in others escape challenge through the wearing of a radical veneer.

The feminist fight against male violence requires the reconstruction of male sexuality. The abuse and murder of women and girls cannot be separated from sexual 'fantasy' and pornography. The relationships of power that exist in the world do not exist as a result of nature but as a result of being imagined and created by those who benefit from them. The subordination of women is 'thought' in the fantasy and the practice of sex. The 'thought' of women's sexual subordination delivers powerful reinforcement to men's feelings of dominance and superiority. The liberation of women is unimaginable in this situation since it would disrupt the possibilities of pleasure. But even if men cannot imagine it, it is necessary that we should. If we cannot imagine our liberation then we cannot achieve it.

Male sexuality must be reconstructed to sever the link between power and aggression and sexual pleasure. Only then can women be relieved of the restrictions placed upon their lives and opportunities by male sexual objectification and aggression. Men's pleasure in women's subordination is a powerful bulwark of their resistance to women's liberation. The reconstruction of male sexuality must extend to gay men too. While they vigorously promote eroticized dominance and submission as sex they constitute a serious obstacle to women's liberation. It is not to be expected that men, gay or straight, will voluntarily choose to relinquish the pleasure and privilege they derive from the eroticized subordination of women. Though some are capable of political integrity and of working against their own interests as a class, we cannot expect this to take place on any mass scale.

As women and as lesbians our hope lies only in other women. We must work towards the construction of homosexual desire and practice as a most important part of our struggle for liberation. However important heterosexual desire has been in our lives we will all have some experience of its opposite. We will have experience of sexual desire and practice which does not leave us feeling betrayed, a sexual desire and practice which eroticizes mutuality and equality. It is this avenue that we should seek to open up while gradually shutting down those responses and practices which are not about sexual 'pleasure' but the eroticizing of our subordination. We need to develop sensitive antennae for evaluating our sexual experience. None of this will be easy. It will take some effort, but then nobody said that the journey to our liberation would be an easy ride. The question we have to ask ourselves is whether we want our freedom or whether we want to retain heterosexual desire. Feminists will choose freedom.

The libertarians are trying to turn feminism into a movement for sexual liberation. Ti-Grace Atkinson described the problem clearly as long ago as 1975 in a speech to the Masochists' Liberation Front, a precursor of the s/m lesbians of the 1980s. She explained:

> Feminists are on the fence, at the moment, on the issue of sex.
> But I do not know any feminist worthy of that name who, if
> forced to choose between freedom and sex, would choose sex.
> She'd choose freedom every time.[33]

She contrasts this with the stated choice of a masochist in an s/m publication: 'if an M has to choose between oppression and chastity, the M considers chastity the worse alternative.'[34] She asserts that 'By no stretch of imagination is the Women's Movement a movement for sexual liberation' and explains that 'That used to be an old Left-Establishment joke on feminism: that feminists were just women who needed to get properly laid.'

It is in the interests of the male ruling class that some women are now asserting that sexual liberation and women's liberation are analogous. This should be particularly clear from the fact that the sexual liberation that such women are pursuing replicates the hopes and dreams of our oppressors. It is the liberation not of 'sex' but of sadomasochism. They are seeking to gain more satisfaction from their oppression in a way which a century of sexological literature has confidently predicted would subordinate women. Masochism, the sexologists believed, would disempower women and render us quiescent. It would cause us to embrace our oppression and cease to struggle against it. The last laugh over the sadomasochism of lesbian or pre-lesbian women must go to the male establishment. Women have been lured into accepting a substitute for their liberation which is designed to ensure that they cannot achieve liberation. The aim of the sexological industry over the last century was that women would be trained to eroticize their subordination. The result they hoped for was that women would then have a stake in prolonging their own oppression and resist any attempt to end it. The resurgence of heterosexual desire among some ex-feminists shows how successful the sexologists have been. They have been successful in a period of backlash against feminism but feminism has not yet completely died out. If we are to revive the movement for our liberation then we must start working towards the construction of an egalitarian sexuality.

Our struggle for liberation does not necessarily require chastity, though many women do choose this path and it is an honourable choice. Such a strategy could only cause disbelief in a male-supremacist society in which sex has been made holy. Sex is holy because of its role as a sacred ritual in the dominant/submissive relationship between men and women. The importance attached to sex defies rationality and can only be explained in this political way. But we can also choose, as many of us have done, to work towards homosexual desire if that suits our lives and relationships. We must remember that homosexual desire will not be recognized as 'sex'. We do not even possess suitable words to describe it. The course of eroticizing equality and mutuality has received no prizes from male supremacy or its agents but it is time we shared our wisdom and experience, learned from feminists and lesbians in our history and became proud of what distinguishes lesbian experience from male-supremacist culture.

Psychoanalysts have described lesbianism pejoratively as 'narcissistic regression'.[35] This means that in loving their own sex lesbians are in fact loving themselves and need to mature into loving the other, i.e. men. Narcissism is seen as negative and dangerous. In fact, the psychoanalysts have spotted the basis of homosexual desire. It is heretical in this culture deliberately to avoid the rituals of sadomasochistic sex and to choose to eroticize sameness and equality. Differences of race and class can provide power differences to eroticize even in same-sex relationships. Lesbians committed to the creation of an egalitarian sexuality must be prepared to challenge this too, since same-sex relationships do not automatically ensure a symmetry of power and privilege. It is not surprising that sexologists who have been dedicated to the construction of heterosexual desire and are enthusiastic about lesbian sadomasochism have derided lesbian love. We should value what our enemies find most threatening.

Readers who consider themselves to be heterosexual will probably be wondering whether homosexual desire can fit into an opposite-sex relationship. In a society which was not founded upon the subordination of women there would be no reason why it should not. But we do not live in such a society. We live in a society organized around heterosexual desire, around otherness and power difference. It is difficult to imagine what shape a woman's desire for a man would take in the absence of eroticized power difference since it is precisely this which provides the excitement of heterosexuality today.

Heterosexuality is the institution through which male-supremacist society is organized and as such it must cease to function. It is difficult to imagine at this point what shape any relationship between different sexes would take when such a relationship was a free choice, when it was not privileged in any way over same-sex relationships and when it played no part in organizing women's oppression and male power. In such a situation, when heterosexuality was no longer an institution, we cannot yet be sure what women would choose.

NOTES

1 'Pornography' and 'Creating the Sexual Future' from *Anticlimax* by S. Jeffreys are reproduced by kind permission of The Women's Press, © 1990.

2 Andrea Dworkin, *Pornography: Men Possessing Women* (Perigee: New York, 1981), p. 203.

3 New York Women Against Pornography, Slide Show Script, 1985, p. 9.

4 Andrea Dworkin, *Letters from a War Zone* (Secker and Warburg: London, 1988), p. 278.

5 Ibid., p. 238.

6 Everywoman (eds), *Pornography and Sexual Violence: Evidence of the Links* (Everywoman, London, 1988), p. 104.

7 Ibid., p. 70.

8 Ibid., p. 60.

9 Everywoman, *Pornography*, p. 100.

10 Ibid., p. 72.

11 Ibid., p. 75.

12 Dworkin, *Letters from a War Zone*, p. 279.

13 Women Against Pornography, *Newsreport*, Vol. 7, No. 1, 1985.

14 Catharine MacKinnon, 'Not a Moral Issue', *Yale Law and Policy Review*, Vol. 2, No. 2, Spring 1984, 343.

15 Ibid., 335.

16 Ibid., 326.

17 Copyright © 1990 by The Women's Press.

18 Sheila Jeffreys, 'The Sexual Abuse of Children in the Home', in Scarlet Friedman and Elizabeth Sarah (eds), *On the Problem of Men* (London: The Women's Press, 1982), p. 61.

19 Linda Gordon and Ellen Dubois, 'Seeking Ecstasy on the Battlefield: Danger and Pleasure in Nineteenth-century Feminist Sexual Thought', in Carole S. Vance (ed.), *Pleasure and Danger: Exploring Female Sexuality* (Routledge and Kegan Paul: Boston, 1984), p. 36.

20 Sheila Rowbotham, 'Passion off the Pedestal', *City Limits* magazine, No. 126, 2–8 March 1984, 21.

21 Jessie Bernard, *The Future of Marriage* (Yale University Press: New Haven, Ct., 1982 (first published 1972)), p. 140.

22 Ibid., p. 155.

23 Rowbotham, 'Passion off the Pedestal', 21.

24 Ibid.

25 See Mary Daly and Jane Caputi, *Webster's First New Intergalactic Wickedary* (The Women's Press: London, 1987), p. 94. Daly and Caputi define the 'sadosociety' as: 'society spawned by phallic lust: the sum of places/times where the beliefs and practices of sadomasochism are The Rule'.

26 Eileen Phillips, *The Left and the Erotic* (Lawrence and Wishart: London, 1983), p. 34.

27 Sarah Crichton, 'Going for the Big "O"', *Ms* magazine, New York, May 1986, 86.

28 Ibid.

29 Elizabeth Brenner, 'Sexual Surrender', *Cosmopolitan* magazine, Vol. 19, No. 4, October 1985, 106.

30 Ibid.

31 Ibid.

32 Ibid.

33 Ti-Grace Atkinson, 'Why I'm Against S/M Liberation', in Robin Ruth Linder et al. (eds), *Against Sadomasochism* (Frog in the Well Press: San Francisco, 1982), p. 91.

34 Ibid.

35 See the section on 'Sex and Psychology' in Dolores Klaich, *Woman Plus Woman: Attitudes Toward Lesbianism* (New English Library: London, 1975).

Bibliography

I
ETHICS and FEMINISM

Under 'Journals' below, we have included those we know which sometimes print articles in the area where ethics overlaps with either women's studies or gender studies. Relevant special issues of these and other journals are cited separately and included under 'Edited Collections'. And we have singled out some journal articles under 'Selected Articles'.

Like the readings collected in this volume, the works cited under 'Edited Collections', 'Selected Articles' and 'Books' are confined to works (i) by women, (ii) containing material within the area of ethics, (iii) that make a contribution to feminist debate. (See 'Introduction' for some remarks on our principles of selection.) It should go without saying that this Bibliography is by no means exhaustive.

Many of the works have been published in various editions, or in different places; where we know of several editions, we have included the details only of the most recent British one.

JOURNALS

Atlantis: A Women's Studies Journal
Canadian Journal of Feminist Ethics
Canadian Women's Studies Journal
Ethics
Feminist Issues
Feminist Review
Feminist Studies
Hypatia: A Journal of Feminist Philosophy
M/F

New Left Review
Radical Philosophy
Signs: A Journal of Women in Culture and Society

EDITED COLLECTIONS

Andolsen, Barbara, Hilkert, Gudorf, Christine E. and Pellaver, Mary D. (eds), *Women's Consciousness, Women's Conscience: A Reader in Feminist Ethics* (Minneapolis: Winston, 1985)

Arditti, Rita, Klein, Renate Duelli and Minden, Shelley (eds), *Test-Tube Women: What Future for Motherhood?* (London: Pandora, 1984)

Australasian Journal of Philosophy, Supplementary Issue 64, June 1986

Bell, Laurie (ed.), *Good Girls/Bad Girls: Sex Trade Workers and Feminists Face to Face* (Toronto: Women's Press, 1987)

Benhabib, Seyla and Cornell, Drucilla (eds), *Feminism as Critique* (Oxford: Polity, 1987)

Bishop, Sharon and Weinzweig, Marjorie (eds), *Philosophy and Women* (Belmont, California: Wadsworth Publishing Co. Inc., 1979)

Brennan, Teresa (ed.), *Between Feminism and Psychoanalysis* (London: Routledge, 1989)

Brunt, Rosalind and Rowan, Caroline (eds), *Feminism, Culture and Politics* (London: Lawrence and Wishart, 1982)

Caldecott, Leonie and Leland, Stephanie (eds), *Reclaim the Earth: Women Speak Out for Life on Earth* (London: The Women's Press, 1983)

Canadian Journal of Philosophy, Special Issue, Fall 1987 (*Science, Morality and Feminist Theory*)

Cartledge, Sue and Ryan, Joanna (eds), *Sex and Love: New Thoughts on Old Contradictions* (London: The Women's Press, 1983)

Chester, Gail and Dickey, Julienne (eds), *Feminism and Censorship: The Current Debate* (Dorset: Prism Press, 1988)

Code, Lorraine, Mullett, Sheila and Overall, Christine (eds), *Feminist Perspectives: Women's Essays on Method and Morals* (Toronto: University of Toronto Press, 1987)

Driver, Emily and Droisen, Audrey (eds), *Child Sexual Abuse: Feminist Perspectives* (London: Macmillan, 1989)

Gamman, Lorraine and Marshment, Margaret (eds), *The Female Gaze: Women as Viewers of Popular Culture* (London: The Women's Press, 1988)

Gould, Carol (ed.), *Beyond Domination: New Perspectives on Women and Philosophy* (Totowa, New Jersey: Rowman and Littlefield, 1983)

Griffiths, Morwenna and Whitford, Margaret (eds), *Feminist Perspectives in*

Philosophy (Basingstoke, Hampshire: Macmillan, 1988)

Harding, Sandra and Hintikka, Merrill B. (eds), *Discovering Reality: Feminist Perspectives on Epistemology, Metaphysics, Methodology, and Philosophy of Science* (Dordrecht, Boston and London: D. Reidel Publishing Co., 1983)

Kanter, Hannah, Lefanu, Sarah, Shah, Shaila and Spedding, Carole (eds), *Sweeping Statements: Writings from the Women's Liberation Movement 1981–83* (London: The Women's Press, 1984)

Kennedy, Ellen and Mendus, Susan (eds), *Women in Western Political Philosophy* (Brighton: Wheatsheaf, 1987)

Kishwar, Madhu and Vanita, Ruth (eds), *In Search of Answers: Indian Women's Voices from Manushi* (London: Zed Press, 1984)

Kittay, Eva and Meyers, Diana (eds), *Women and Moral Philosophy* (Totowa, New Jersey: Rowman and Littlefield, 1986)

Lederer, Laura (ed.), *Take Back the Night* (New York: Morrow, 1986)

Marks, Elaine and de Courtivron, Isabelle (eds), *New French Feminisms: An Anthology* (Brighton: Harvester, 1981)

Mitchell, Juliet and Oakley, Ann (eds), *What is Feminism?* (Oxford: Blackwell, 1986)

Moi, Toril (ed.), *The Kristeva Reader* (Oxford: Blackwell, 1986)

Moi, Toril (ed.), *French Feminist Thought: A Reader* (Oxford: Blackwell, 1987)

The Monist, Vol. 57, Issue 1, January 1973 (*Women's Liberation: Ethical, Social and Political Issues*)

Moraga, Cherrie and Anzaldua, Gloria (eds), *This Bridge Called My Back: Writings by Radical Women of Color* (New York: Kitchen Table Press, 1983)

Nicholson, Linda J. (ed.), *Feminism/Postmodernism* (London: Routledge, 1990)

Pateman, Carole and Gross, Elizabeth (eds), *Feminist Challenges: Social and Political Theory* (London: Allen & Unwin, 1986)

Radical Philosophy, Issue 34, Summer 1983 (*Women, Gender and Philosophy*)

Rossi, Alice (ed.), *The Feminist Papers: From Adams to de Beauvoir* (New York: Columbia University Press, 1973)

Sargent, Lydia (ed.), *The Unhappy Marriage of Marxism and Feminism* (London: Pluto, 1986)

Sayers, Janet, Evans, Mary and Redclift, Nanneke (eds), *Engels Revisited* (London: Tavistock, 1987)

Shanley, Mary Lyndon and Pateman, Carole (eds), *Feminist Interpretations and Political Theory* (Oxford: Polity, 1991)

Snitow, Ann, Stansell, Christine and Thompson, Sharon (eds), *Desire: The Politics of Sexuality* (London: Virago, 1984)

Spallone, Patricia (ed.), *Beyond Conception* (London: Macmillan, 1989)

Spender, Dale (ed.), *Feminist Theorists: Three Centuries of Women's Intellectual Traditions* (London: The Women's Press, 1983)

Stern, Madeleine B. (ed.), *The Victoria Woodhull Reader* (Weston, Massachusetts: M & S Press, 1974)

Thompson, Dorothy (ed.), *Over Our Dead Bodies: Women Against the Bomb* (London: Virago, 1983)

Vance, Carol (ed.), *Pleasure and Danger: Exploring Female Sexuality* (London: Routledge and Kegan Paul, 1984)

Vetterling-Braggin, Mary, Elliston, Frederick A. and English, Jane (eds), *Feminism and Philosophy* (Totowa, New Jersey: Littlefield, Adams & Co., 1982)

Whitford, Margaret (ed.), *The Irigaray Reader* (Oxford: Blackwell, 1991)

SELECTED ARTICLES

Annas, Julia, 'Plato's Republic and Feminism', *Philosophy*, 51, 1976

Baier, Annette, 'Hume: the Woman's Moral Theorist', in Eva Kittay and Diane Meyers (eds), *Women and Moral Philosophy* (Rowman and Littlefield, Totowa, NJ, 1986)

Baier, Annette, 'Trust and Antitrust', *Ethics*, Vol. 96, 1986

Baier, Annette, 'The Need for More than Justice', *Canadian Journal of Philosophy*, supplement, 1987

Code, Lorraine, 'Second Persons', *Canadian Journal of Philosophy*, supplement, 1987

Friedman, Marilyn, 'Feminism and Modern Friendship: Dislocating the Community', *Ethics*, Vol. 99, 1989

Gilligan, Carol, 'In a Different Voice: Women's Conceptions of Self and of Morality', *Harvard Education Review*, Vol. 47, 1977

Gould, Carol, 'Freedom and Women', *Journal of Social Philosophy*, Vol. 15, 1984

Grimshaw, Jean, 'Feminism, History and Morality', *Radical Philosophy*, No. 30, 1982

Held, Virginia, 'Non-contractual Society', *Canadian Journal of Philosophy*, supplement, 1987

Held, Virginia, 'Birth and Death', *Ethics*, Vol. 99, 1989

Le Doeuff, Michèle, 'Women and Philosophy' (trans. Debbie Pope), *Radical Philosophy*, No. 17, 1977

Lovibond, Sabina, 'Feminism and Postmodernism', *New Left Review*, No. 178, 1989

Morgan, Kathryn Pauly, 'Amazons, Spinsters and Women: A Career of One's Own', *Proceedings of The Philosophy of Education Society*, Vol. 34

(ed. Gary Fenstemacher), 1978

Morgan, Kathryn Pauly, 'Romantic Love, Altruism and Self-respect', *Hypatia*, Vol. 1, 1986

Morgan, Kathryn Pauly, 'Women and Moral Madness', *Canadian Journal of Philosophy*, supplement, 1987

Okin, Susan Moller, 'Philosopher Queens and Private Wives: Plato on Women and the Family', *Philosophy and Public Affairs*, Vol. 6, 1976

Okin, Susan Moller, 'Justice and Gender', *Philosophy and Public Affairs*, Vol. 16, 1987

Okin, Susan Moller, 'Women and the Making of the Sentimental Family', *Philosophy and Public Affairs*, Vol. 11, 1982

Parsons, Susan F., 'Feminism and the Logic of Morality: A Consideration of Alternatives', *Radical Philosophy*, 54, 1987

Pateman, Carole, 'The Disorder of Women: Women, Love and the Sense of Justice', *Ethics*, Vol. 91, 1980

Pateman, Carole, 'Feminism and Democracy', in G. Duncan (ed.), *Democratic Theory and Practice* (Cambridge: Cambridge University Press, 1983)

Rich, Adrienne, 'Compulsory Heterosexuality and Lesbian Existence', *Signs: Journal of Women in Culture and Society*, Vol. 5, 1980

Spelman, Elizabeth, 'Woman as Body: Ancient and Contemporary Views', *Feminist Studies*, Vol. 8, 1981

Thomson, Judith Jarvis, 'A Defence of Abortion', *Philosophy and Public Affairs*, Vol. I, 1971

Tronto, Joan, 'Woman's Morality: Beyond Gender Difference to a Theory of Care', *Signs*, Vol. 12, 1987

Young, Iris Marion, 'Towards a Critical Theory of Justice', *Social Theory and Practice*, Vol. 7, 1981

Young, Iris Marion, 'The Ideal of Community and the Politics of Difference', *Social Theory and Practice*, Vol. 12, 1986

BOOKS

Barrett, Michèle, *Women's Oppression Today: Problems in Marxist Feminist Analysis* (London: Verso, 1980)

Barrett, Michèle and McIntosh, Mary, *The Anti-Social Family* (London: Verso, 1982)

de Beauvoir, Simone, *The Ethics of Ambiguity*, trans. Bernard Frechtman (New York: Citadel Press, 1948)

de Beauvoir, Simone, *The Second Sex*, trans. H. Parshley (Harmondsworth: Penguin, 1972)

Benjamin, Jessica, *The Bonds of Love: Psychoanalysis, Feminism and the Problem of Domination* (London: Virago, 1990)

Brownmiller, Susan, *Against Our Will: Men, Women and Rape* (New York: Bantam, 1976)

Burton, Clare, *Subordination: Feminism and Social Theory* (Hertfordshire: George Allen & Unwin, 1985)

Cameron, Deborah and Frazer, Elizabeth, *The Lust to Kill: A Feminist Investigation of Sexual Murder* (Oxford: Polity, 1987)

Chodorow, Nancy, *The Reproduction of Mothering: Psychoanalysis and the Sociology of Gender* (Berkeley: University of California Press, 1978)

Code, Lorraine, *Epistemic Responsibility* (Hanover, New Hampshire: University Press of New England, 1987)

Coole, Diana, *Women in Political Theory: From Ancient Misogyny to Contemporary Feminism* (Hemel Hempstead: Harvester Wheatsheaf, 1988)

Corea, Gena, *The Mother Machine: Reproductive Technologies from Artificial Insemination to Artificial Wombs* (New York: Harper and Row, 1985)

Coward, Rosalind, *Female Desire* (London: Paladin, 1984)

Daly, Mary, *Beyond God the Father: Towards a Philosophy of Women's Liberation* (London: Women's Press, 1973)

Daly, Mary, *Gyn/Ecology: The Metaethics of Radical Feminism* (London: Women's Press, 1983)

Davis, Angela, *Women, Race and Class* (London: The Women's Press, 1982)

Davis, Angela, *Women, Culture and Politics* (London: The Women's Press, 1984)

Delphy, Christine, *Close to Home: A Materialist Analysis of Women's Oppression*, trans. and ed. Diana Leonard (London: Hutchinson, 1984)

Dinnerstein, Dorothy, *The Rocking of the Cradle and the Ruling of the World* (London: The Women's Press, 1987); previously published as *The Mermaid and the Minotaur: Sexual Arrangements and Human Malaise* (New York: Harper and Row, 1976)

Dworkin, Andrea, *Pornography: Men Possessing Women* (London, The Women's Press, 1981)

Dworkin, Andrea, *Right Wing Women: The Politics of Domesticated Females* (London: The Women's Press, 1983)

Ehrenreich, Barbara, *The Hearts of Men: American Dreams and the Flight from Commitment* (London: Pluto, 1983)

Eisenstein, Hester, *Contemporary Feminist Thought* (London: Allen and Unwin, 1984)

Eisenstein, Zillah R., *Capitalist Patriarchy and the Case for Socialist Feminism* (New York: Monthly Review Press, 1979)

Eisenstein, Zillah R., *The Radical Future of Liberal Feminism* (New York:

Longman Inc., 1981)

Elshtain, Jean Bethke, *Public Man, Private Woman: Women in Social and Political Thought* (Princeton, New Jersey: Princeton University Press, 1981)

Faderman, Lillian, *Surpassing the Love of Men: Romantic Friendship and Love between Women from the Renaissance to the Present* (London: The Women's Press, 1985)

Figes, Eva, *Patriarchal Attitudes* (London: Panther Books, 1972)

Firestone, Shulamith, *The Dialectic of Sex* (London: The Women's Press, 1979)

Friedan, Betty, *The Feminine Mystique* (Harmondsworth: Penguin, 1963)

Friedan, Betty, *The Second Stage* (London: Michael Joseph, 1982)

Frye, Marilyn, *The Politics of Reality* (Trumansburg, New York: The Crossing Press, 1983)

Gilligan, Carol, *In a Different Voice: Psychological Theory and Women's Development* (Cambridge, Massachusetts: Harvard University Press, 1982)

Goldman, Emma, *Red Emma Speaks*, ed. Alix Kates Shulman (New York: Random House, 1972)

Greer, Germaine, *The Female Eunuch* (London: Paladin, 1971)

Greer, Germaine, *Sex and Destiny: The Politics of Human Fertility* (London: Secker and Warburg, 1984)

Griffin, Susan, *Pornography and Silence: Culture's Revenge Against Nature* (London: The Women's Press, 1981)

Grimshaw, Jean, *Feminist Philosophers: Women's Perspectives on Philosophical Traditions* (Brighton: Wheatsheaf, 1986)

Hamilton, Cicely, *Marriage as a Trade* (London: The Women's Press, 1981)

Hartsock, Nancy, *Money, Sex and Power: Toward a Feminist Historical Materialism* (New York: Longman, 1983)

Hoagland, Sarah Lucia, *Lesbian Ethics: Towards New Value* (Palo Alto, California: Institute of Lesbian Studies, 1988)

Hooks, Bell, *Ain't I a Woman: Black Women and Feminism* (London: Pluto Press, 1982)

Hooks, Bell, *Feminist Theory: From Margin to Centre* (Boston: South End Press, 1984)

Hooks, Bell, *Talking Back: Thinking Feminist, Thinking Black* (Boston, Massachusetts: South End Press, 1989)

Irigaray, Luce, *Ethique de la différence sexuelle* (Paris: Minuit, 1984)

Irigaray, Luce, *Speculum of the Other Woman*, trans. Gillian C. Gill (Ithaca, New York: Cornell University Press, 1985)

Irigaray, Luce, *This Sex Which is Not One*, trans. Catherine Porter and Carolyn Burke (Ithaca: Cornell University Press, 1987)

Le Doeuff, Michèle, *Hipparchia's Choice: An Essay Concerning Women,*

Philosophy, Etc trans. Trista Selous (Oxford: Blackwell, 1991)

Jaggar, Alison M., *Feminist Politics and Human Nature* (Brighton: Harvester, 1983)

Janssen-Jurreit, Marie-Louise, *Sexism: The Male Monopoly on History and Thought* (London: Pluto Press, 1982)

Jeffreys, Sheila, *The Spinster and her Enemies: Feminism and Sexuality 1880–1930* (London: Pandora, 1985)

Jeffreys, Sheila, *Anticlimax: A Feminist Perspective on the Sexual Revolution* (London: The Women's Press, 1990)

Jordan, June, *Moving Towards Home: Political Essays* (London: Virago, 1989)

Kaplan, Cora, *Sea Changes: Culture and Feminism* (London: Verso, 1986)

Kappeler, Susanne, *The Pornography of Representation* (Oxford: Polity, 1986)

Kollontai, Alexandra, *Selected Writings* trans. and ed. Alix Holt (London: Allison and Busby, 1977)

Lloyd, Genevieve, *The Man of Reason: 'Male' and 'Female' in Western Philosophy* (London: Methuen, 1984)

Lorde, Audre, *Sister Outsider* (Trumansberg, New York: The Crossing Press, 1984)

Lorde, Audre, *Uses of the Erotic: The Erotic as Power* (Brooklyn, New York: Out and Out Books, 1978)

MacKinnon, Catharine A., *Feminism Unmodified: Discourses on Life and Law* (Cambridge, Massachusetts: Harvard University Press, 1987)

MacKinnon, Catharine A., *Toward a Feminist Theory of the State* (Cambridge, Massachusetts: Harvard University Press, 1989)

McMillan, Carol, *Woman, Reason and Nature* (Oxford: Blackwell, 1982)

Midgley, Mary and Hughes, Judith, *Women's Choices: Philosophical Problems Facing Feminism* (London: Weidenfeld and Nicholson, 1983)

Millett, Kate, *Sexual Politics* (London: Virago, 1977)

Mitchell, Juliet, *Women's Estate* (Harmondsworth: Penguin, 1971)

Mitchell, Juliet, *Psychoanalysis and Feminism* (London: Allen Lane, 1974)

Noddings, Nel, *Caring: A Feminine Approach to Ethics and Moral Education* (Berkeley: University of California Press, 1984)

Noddings, Nel, *Women and Evil* (Berkeley: University of California Press, 1989)

O'Brien, Mary, *The Politics of Reproduction* (London: Routledge and Kegan Paul, 1981)

Okin, Susan Möller, *Women in Western Political Thought* (London: Virago, 1980)

Okin, Susan Möller, *Justice, Gender and the Family* (New York: Basic Books, 1989)

Pateman, Carole, *The Sexual Contract* (Oxford: Polity, 1988)

Pateman, Carole, *The Disorder of Women* (Oxford: Polity, 1989)

Petchesky, Rosalind Pollack, *Abortion and Woman's Choice: The State, Sexuality and Reproductive Freedom* (London: Verso, 1988)

Raymond, Janice, *A Passion for Friends: Toward a Philosophy of Female Friendship* (London: The Women's Press, 1986)

Rich, Adrienne, *Of Woman Born: Motherhood as Experience and Institution* (London: Virago, 1977)

Rich, Adrienne, *On Lies, Secrets and Silence: Selected Prose 1966–78* (London: Virago, 1977)

Richards, Janet Radcliffe, *The Sceptical Feminist: A Philosophical Enquiry* (Harmondsworth: Penguin, 1982)

Roberts, Nickie, *The Front Line: Women in the Sex Industry Speak* (London: Grafton, 1988)

Rose, Jacqueline, *Sexuality in the Field of Vision* (London: Verso, 1986)

Ruddick, Sara, *Maternal Thinking: Towards a Politics of Peace* (London: The Women's Press, 1990)

Sanger, Margaret, *The New Motherhood* (London: Jonathan Cape, 1922)

Segal, Lynne, *Is the Future Female?: Troubled Thoughts on Contemporary Feminism* (London: Virago, 1987)

Sichtermann, Barbara, *Femininity: The Politics of the Personal*, trans. John Whitlam, ed. Helga Geyer-Ryan (Oxford: Polity, 1986)

Soper, Kate, *Troubled Pleasures: Writings on Politics, Gender and Hedonism* (Oxford: Blackwell, 1990)

Spelman, Elizabeth, *Inessential Woman: Problems of Exclusion in Feminist Thought* (London: The Women's Press, 1990)

Sydie, R.A., *Natural Women, Cultured Men: A Feminist Perspective on Sociological Theory* (Milton Keynes: Open University Press, 1987)

Taylor, Harriet, *The Enfranchisement of Women* (published with J.S. Mill, *The Subjection of Women*, London: Virago, 1983)

Welch, Sharon D., *A Feminist Ethic of Risk* (Minneapolis: Fortress Press, 1990)

Whitford, Margaret, *Luce Irigaray: Philosophy in the Feminine* (London: Routledge, 1991)

Williamson, Judith, *Consuming Passions: The Dynamics of Popular Culture* (London: Marion Boyars, 1986)

Wilson, Elizabeth with Weir, Angela, *Hidden Agendas: Theory, Politics, and Experience in the Women's Movement* (London: Tavistock, 1986)

Wilson, Elizabeth, *Hallucinations: Life in a Postmodern City* (London: Hutchinson Radius, 1988)

Wollstonecraft, Mary, *A Vindication of the Rights of Woman*, ed. Miriam Brody Kramnick (Harmondsworth: Penguin, 1975)

Woolf, Virginia, *Three Guineas* (Harmondsworth: Penguin, 1977)

Woolf, Virginia, *A Room of One's Own* (London: Granada, 1977)

II

THE MALE TRADITION

The other bibliography is confined to works by women who share a feminist commitment. The present one is confined to works by men, and it includes expressions of quite disparate views. Our aim in compiling it has been not only to make reference to men who are known to have advanced the cause of sexual equality in their day, but also to draw attention to a *misogynist* tradition. We think that such a tradition tends to be ignored: passages in which writers of the past make explicit their negative estimation of the worth of women are sometimes treated as if they were merely products of the author's idiosyncracies, or as if they were now 'anachronisms'. Wishing to attract notice to such passages, we had thought of keeping two separate lists. But in fact some male writers resist classification as either friends or foes of women, so that separation proved impossible.

Plato (427–347 BC), *Republic* V, 449a–471e (on female guardians and abolition of private families within the guardian class)
Other relevant passages: *Republic* III, 395de; IV, 439bc; VIII, 557c; X, 605e
Symposium, esp. 180c–185c (discourse of Pausanias); 189c–193d (discourse of Aristophanes); 201d–212d (discourse of Socrates/Diotima).
Timaeus 42bc, 49–51, 90e–91a
Laws VI, 780d–781b
For further references see Julia Annas, 'Plato's *Republic* and Feminism', *Philosophy*, 51 (1976), 307–21; Luce Irigaray, *Speculum of the Other Woman*, trans. Gillian C. Gill, pp. 152–9.
Aristotle (384–322 BC), *Politics* I, esp. chs 12–13
On the Generation of Animals I, chs 19–23; II, chs 1 (732a) and 4 (738b); IV, ch. 1 (766a)